THE ROUTLEDGE HANDBOOK OF POLITICAL EPISTEMOLOGY

As political discourse had been saturated with the ideas of "post-truth", "fake news", "epistemic bubbles", and "truth decay", it was no surprise that in 2017 *The New Scientist* declared: "Philosophers of knowledge, your time has come." Political epistemology has old roots, but is now one of the most rapidly growing and important areas of philosophy.

The Routledge Handbook of Political Epistemology is an outstanding reference source to this exciting field, and the first collection of its kind. Comprising 41 chapters by an international team of contributors, it is divided into seven parts:

- Politics and truth: historical and contemporary perspectives
- Political disagreement and polarization
- Fake news, propaganda, and misinformation
- Ignorance and irrationality in politics
- Epistemic virtues and vices in politics
- Democracy and epistemology
- Trust, expertise, and doubt.

Within these sections crucial issues and debates are examined, including: post-truth, disagreement and relativism, epistemic networks, fake news, echo chambers, propaganda, ignorance, irrationality, political polarization, virtues and vices in public debate, epistocracy, expertise, misinformation, trust, and digital democracy, as well as the views of Plato, Aristotle, Mòzi, medieval Islamic philosophers, Mill, Arendt, and Rawls on truth and politics.

The Routledge Handbook of Political Epistemology is essential reading for those studying political philosophy, applied and social epistemology, and politics. It is also a valuable resource for those in related disciplines such as international relations, law, political psychology, political science, communication studies, and journalism.

Michael Hannon is Assistant Professor of Philosophy at the University of Nottingham, UK. He is author of *What's the Point of Knowledge?* (2019), and is writing the forthcoming Routledge book *Political Epistemology: An Introduction*.

Jeroen de Ridder is Associate Professor of Philosophy at Vrije Universiteit Amsterdam, and Professor (by special appointment) of Christian Philosophy at the University of Groningen, The Netherlands.

ROUTLEDGE HANDBOOKS IN PHILOSOPHY

Routledge Handbooks in Philosophy are state-of-the-art surveys of emerging, newly refreshed, and important fields in philosophy, providing accessible yet thorough assessments of key problems, themes, thinkers, and recent developments in research.

All chapters for each volume are specially commissioned, and written by leading scholars in the field. Carefully edited and organized, *Routledge Handbooks in Philosophy* provide indispensable reference tools for students and researchers seeking a comprehensive overview of new and exciting topics in philosophy. They are also valuable teaching resources as accompaniments to textbooks, anthologies, and research-orientated publications.

Also available:

THE ROUTLEDGE HANDBOOK OF MODALITY
Edited by Otávio Bueno and Scott A. Shalkowski

THE ROUTLEDGE HANDBOOK OF PRACTICAL REASON
Edited by Kurt Sylvan and Ruth Chang

THE ROUTLEDGE HANDBOOK OF PHILOSOPHY OF EUROPE
Edited by Darian Meacham and Nicolas de Warren

THE ROUTLEDGE HANDBOOK OF SOCIAL AND POLITICAL PHILOSOPHY OF LANGUAGE
Edited by Justin Khoo and Rachel Katharine Sterken

THE ROUTLEDGE HANDBOOK OF POLITICAL EPISTEMOLOGY
Edited by Michael Hannon and Jeroen de Ridder

For more information about this series, please visit: https://www.routledge.com/Routledge-Handbooks-in-Philosophy/book-series/RHP

THE ROUTLEDGE HANDBOOK OF POLITICAL EPISTEMOLOGY

Edited by Michael Hannon and Jeroen de Ridder

Routledge
Taylor & Francis Group

LONDON AND NEW YORK

First published 2021
by Routledge
2 Park Square, Milton Park, Abingdon, Oxon OX14 4RN

and by Routledge
52 Vanderbilt Avenue, New York, NY 10017

Routledge is an imprint of the Taylor & Francis Group, an informa business

© 2021 selection and editorial matter Michael Hannon and Jeroen de
Ridder; individual chapters, the contributors

British Library Cataloguing-in-Publication Data
A catalogue record for this book is available from the British Library

Library of Congress Cataloging-in-Publication Data
Names: Hannon, Michael (Michael J.), editor. |
Ridder, Jeroen de, editor.
Title: The Routledge handbook of political epistemology /
Edited by Michael Hannon and Jeroen de Ridder.
Other titles: Handbook of political epistemology
Description: Abingdon, Oxon; New York, NY: Routledge, 2021. |
Series: Routledge handbooks in philosophy | Includes
bibliographical references and index.
Identifiers: LCCN 2020047803 (print) | LCCN 2020047804 (ebook) |
ISBN 9780367345907 (hardback) | ISBN 9780429326769 (ebook)
Subjects: LCSH: Knowledge, Theory of—Political aspects. | Knowledge,
Theory of—Social aspects. | Political science—Philosophy. |
Disinformation—History.
Classification: LCC BD175 .R655 2021 (print) | LCC BD175 (ebook) |
DDC 320.01—dc23
LC record available at https://lccn.loc.gov/2020047803
LC ebook record available at https://lccn.loc.gov/2020047804

ISBN: 978-0-367-34590-7 (hbk)
ISBN: 978-0-367-75468-6 (pbk)
ISBN: 978-0-429-32676-9 (ebk)

Typeset in Bembo
by codeMantra

CONTENTS

List of figures   x
List of tables   xi
Notes on contributors   xii
Acknowledgements   xviii

    General introduction   1
    Michael Hannon and Jeroen de Ridder

PART 1
Politics and truth: historical and contemporary perspectives   **9**

    Introduction to Part 1   11

1 Democracy and knowledge in ancient Greece   13
    Tamer Nawar

2 Identifying upward: political epistemology in an early Chinese
    political theory   24
    Chris Fraser

3 Epistemology and politics in Islamic philosophy   35
    Anthony Booth

4 Mill, liberalism, and epistemic diversity   45
    Paul Kelly

5   Hannah Arendt and the role of truth in politics   55
    Yasemin Sari

6   Politics, truth, post-truth, and postmodernism   65
    Simon Blackburn

7   Tyranny, tribalism, and post-truth politics   74
    Amanda R. Greene

PART 2
Political disagreement and polarization   **85**

    Introduction to Part 2   87

8   The polarization of American politics   90
    Shanto Iyengar

9   Politics, deep disagreement, and relativism   101
    J. Adam Carter

10 Epistemic permissivism and reasonable pluralism   113
    Richard Rowland and Robert Mark Simpson

11 Political disagreement: epistemic or civic peers?   123
    Elizabeth Edenberg

12 Epistemic networks and polarization   133
    Daniel J. Singer, Patrick Grim, Aaron Bramson,
    Bennett Holman, Jiin Jung, and William J. Berger

13 Affective polarization, evidence, and evidentialism   145
    Emily C. McWilliams

14 The point of political belief   156
    Michael Hannon and Jeroen de Ridder

PART 3
Fake news, propaganda, and misinformation   **167**

    Introduction to Part 3   169

15 What is fake news?   171
    Axel Gelfert

16 The cognitive science of fake news   181
    Neil Levy and Robert M. Ross

17 Filter bubbles, echo chambers, online communities   192
    Hanna Kiri Gunn

18 Modeling how false beliefs spread   203
    Cailin O'Connor and James Owen Weatherall

19 Regulating the spread of online misinformation   214
    Étienne Brown

20 Propaganda, irrationality, and group agency   226
    Megan Hyska

PART 4
Ignorance and irrationality in politics   **237**

    Introduction to Part 4   239

21 Is political ignorance rational?   241
    Ilya Somin

22 Pragmatic encroachment and political ignorance   253
    Kenneth Boyd

23 Is political irrationality a myth?   263
    Jeffrey Friedman

24 The irrational attempt to impute irrationality to one's
    political opponents   274
    Keith E. Stanovich

25 Asymmetrical irrationality: are only other people stupid?   285
    Robin McKenna

PART 5
Epistemic virtues and vices in politics   **297**

    Introduction to Part 5   299

26 Epistemic vices, ideologies, and false consciousness   301
    Quassim Cassam

27 Engaging closed-mindedly with your polluted media feed   312
    Heather Battaly

28 Virtues and vices in public and political debates   325
    Alessandra Tanesini

29 Vices of the privileged and virtues of the oppressed in epistemic
    group dynamics   336
    José Medina

30 Epistemic corruption and political institutions   347
    Ian James Kidd

PART 6
Democracy and epistemology   **359**

    Introduction to Part 6   361

31 An epistemic argument for democracy   363
    Hélène Landemore

32 In defense of epistocracy: enlightened preference voting   374
    Jason Brennan

33 A pragmatist epistemic argument for democracy   384
    Robert B. Talisse

34 Epistemic norms of political deliberation   395
    Fabienne Peter

35 The epistemic responsibilities of citizens in a democracy   407
    Cameron Boult

36 The epistemic case for non-electoral forms of democracy   419
    Alexander Guerrero

PART 7
Trust, expertise, and doubt   **431**

    Introduction to Part 7   433

37 The role of scientific expertise in democracy   435
    Heather Douglas

Contents

38 Experts, public policy, and the question of trust   446
    Maria Baghramian and Michel Croce

39 Testimony, deference, and value   458
    Hallvard Lillehammer

40 The skeptic and the climate change skeptic   469
    Alex Worsnip

41 Online trust and distrust   480
    Mark Alfano and Emily Sullivan

Index   *493*

FIGURES

8.1   ANES party feeling thermometers (1976–2016)   91
12.1 Two disconnected epistemic networks   134
12.2 Illustration of a high school gossip epistemic network through time   135
12.3 Pictures of example divided networks   138
12.4 Example beliefs through time with threshold values (ε) of (a) 0.01, (b) 0.15,
      and (c) 0.25 in the Hegselmann and Krause (2002) model   139

TABLES

35.1   On the epistemic responsibilities of citizens in a democracy   409

CONTRIBUTORS

Mark Alfano is Associate Professor of Philosophy at Macquarie University. His work encompasses subfields in philosophy (epistemology, moral psychology, philosophy of science), social science (social psychology, personality psychology), and computer science. He also brings digital humanities methods to bear on both contemporary problems and the history of philosophy (especially Nietzsche). He has experience with R, Tableau, LIWC, and Gephi.

Maria Baghramian is Full Professor of American Philosophy at the School of Philosophy, University College Dublin, and the coordinator of the Horizon 2020 EU project Policy, Expertise and Trust in Action (PEriTiA). She is also a Member of the Royal Irish Academy.

Heather Battaly is Professor of Philosophy at the University of Connecticut. She works on virtues and vices in epistemology and ethics.

William J. Berger is a Fellow in the Philosophy, Politics, and Economics Program at the University of Pennsylvania.

Simon Blackburn is the Bertrand Russell Professor Emeritus at the University of Cambridge, and remains a Fellow of Trinity College. His career included teaching at Oxford, and the University of North Carolina at Chapel Hill, as well as many visiting positions. He has written extensively on the subject of truth, and is especially known for contributions to moral philosophy and the philosophy of decision making. His books include the *Oxford Dictionary of Philosophy*.

Anthony Booth is currently Reader in Philosophy and Head of the Department of Philosophy at the University of Sussex, UK. He specializes primarily on the ethics of belief, both in the 'Western' and Islamic traditions, and is the author of *Islamic Philosophy and the Ethics of Belief* (2016) and *Analytic Islamic Philosophy* (2019).

Cameron Boult is an Assistant Professor of Philosophy at Brandon University, Canada. He works on social epistemology and epistemic normativity, and has been published in, among other places, *Philosophy and Phenomenological Research*, *The Philosophical Quarterly*, and *Synthese*. He is currently working on a book-length study of epistemic blame.

Kenneth Boyd works on a number of issues in epistemology, including what we can and cannot learn from one another, the epistemology of groups, and understanding. He is currently a postdoc at the University of Southern Denmark.

Aaron Bramson is a research scientist at the Riken Center for Biosystems Dynamics Research and the Department of General Economics at Ghent University.

Jason Brennan is the Robert J. Elizabeth Flanagan Family Professor of Strategy, Economics, Ethics, and Public Policy at the McDonough School of Business, Georgetown University. He specializes in politics, philosophy, and economics.

Étienne Brown is Assistant Professor in the Department of Philosophy at San José State University, where he teaches digital ethics to aspiring computer scientists. His current research focuses on misinformation and fake news. He holds a PhD in philosophy from the Sorbonne.

J. Adam Carter is Reader in Philosophy at the University of Glasgow, where he is Deputy Director of the COGITO Epistemology Research Centre. His books include *Metaepistemology and Relativism* (Palgrave Macmillan, 2016), *A Critical Introduction to Knowledge-How* (with Ted Poston, Bloomsbury, 2018), *This is Epistemology* (with Clayton Littlejohn, Wiley-Blackwell, 2020), *The Philosophy of Group Polarization* (with Fernando Broncano-Berrocal, Routledge, 2020), and *Digital Knowledge* (Routledge, forthcoming).

Quassim Cassam is Professor of Philosophy at the University of Warwick. He was previously Knightbridge Professor of Philosophy at Cambridge University, Professor of Philosophy at UCL, and Reader in Philosophy at Oxford University. He is the author of six books, including *Vices of the Mind: From the Intellectual to the Political* (Oxford, 2019), *Conspiracy Theories* (Polity, 2019), and *Self-Knowledge for Humans* (Oxford, 2014). His current research interests include the philosophy of terrorism and extremism, and he is writing a book on extremism.

Michel Croce is postdoctoral fellow at University College Dublin, where he works as part of PEriTiA, a major European funded project on policy, expertise, and trust. His current research focuses on the philosophy of expertise, moral epistemology, and the philosophy of education.

Heather Douglas is a philosopher of science who works on the relationships among science, values, and democratic publics. She is an Associate Professor in the Department of Philosophy at Michigan State University and an AAAS fellow.

Elizabeth Edenberg is an Assistant Professor of Philosophy at The City University of New York, Baruch College (USA). She specializes in political philosophy, political epistemology, and the ethics of emerging technology.

Chris Fraser is Lee Chair in Chinese Thought and Culture in the Departments of Philosophy and of East Asian Studies at the University of Toronto. His most recent book is *Late Classical Chinese Thought* (Oxford).

Jeffrey Friedman, a Visiting Scholar in the Committee on Degrees in Social Studies, Harvard University, is the author of *Power without Knowledge: A Critique of Technocracy* (Oxford University Press, 2019). He is also the editor of *Critical Review* and of *The Rational Choice Controversy: Economic Models of Politics Reconsidered* (Yale University Press).

Axel Gelfert is Professor of Theoretical Philosophy at Technische Universität Berlin. His work focuses on the intersection of social epistemology and philosophy of science and technology. He is the author of *A Critical Introduction to Testimony* (2014) and *How to Do Science with Models* (2016).

Amanda R. Greene is a Lecturer in Philosophy at University College London. Her research focuses on political philosophy, ethics, and ancient philosophy. She has held research fellowships at Princeton, Columbia, and the University of Chicago Law School. Her current book project is entitled *Legitimacy: The Morality of Power in Politics, Business, and Civil Society.*

Patrick Grim is a Distinguished Teaching Professor of Philosophy Emeritus at Stony Brook University and a Philosopher in Residence at the Center for Study of Complex Systems at the University of Michigan.

Alexander Guerrero is Associate Professor of Philosophy at Rutgers University-New Brunswick. His work is in epistemology, political and moral philosophy, and legal philosophy. His book, *The Lottocratic Alternative* (Oxford University Press, 2021), defends the idea that lotteries, not elections, should be used to select political representatives.

Hanna Kiri Gunn is an Assistant Professor in Cognitive and Information Sciences at the University of California, Merced. Her research focuses on themes in social epistemology including agency, community, new media, and the Internet.

Michael Hannon is Assistant Professor of Philosophy at the University of Nottingham. He is author of *What's the Point of Knowledge?* (Oxford University Press, 2019) and is currently writing a book for Routledge titled *Political Epistemology: An Introduction.*

Bennett Holman is an Assistant Professor of History and Philosophy of Science at Underwood International College at Yonsei University and a member of the Faculty of Humanities at the University of Johannesburg.

Megan Hyska is an Assistant Professor in the Philosophy Department at Northwestern University. Her research concerns the way that conversations are organized into topics (i.e. discourse-level information structure) and how an understanding of this phenomenon provides new tools for studying things like partisanship, polarization, and propaganda via linguistic data.

Shanto Iyengar is Professor of Political Science and the William Roberson Coe Professor of American Studies at Stanford University. His areas of expertise include the news media, public opinion, and political campaigns. He is the author of *Media Politics: A Citizen's Guide* (Norton, 2015), *News That Matters* (University of Chicago Press, 1987, 2010), *Is Anyone Responsible?* (University of Chicago Press, 1991), *The Media Game: American Politics in the Television Age* (Macmillan, 1993), *Explorations in Political Psychology* (Duke University Press, 1995), and *Going Negative* (Free Press, 1995). He can be reached at siyengar@stanford.edu.

Jiin Jung is a Visiting Professor of Brain, Behavior, and Quantitative Science at the University of Kansas.

Paul Kelly is Professor of Political Theory at the London School of Economics and Political Science. He is author and editor of 16 books and writes on both the history of political ideas and issues of contemporary political theory. He is currently completing a book on international political theory entitled *Conflict, War and Revolution*.

Ian James Kidd is an Assistant Professor of Philosophy at the University of Nottingham. His research interests include character epistemology, epistemic injustice, and their application to debates in political and educational debates. Some recent publications include *The Routledge Handbook to Epistemic injustice* (with José Medina and Gaile Pohlhaus, Jr.) and *Vice Epistemology* (with Heather Battaly and Quassim Cassam). His website is www.ianjameskidd.weebly.com.

Hélène Landemore is a tenured Associate Professor of Political Science at Yale University. She is the author of *Democratic Reason: Politics, Collective Intelligence, and the Rule of the Many* (Princeton University Press, 2013) and *Open Democracy: Reinventing Popular Rule for the Twenty-First Century* (Princeton University Press, 2020).

Neil Levy is Professor of Philosophy at Macquarie University and a senior research fellow at the Uehiro Centre for Practical Ethics, University of Oxford. He works on many topics, with an emphasis on issues at the intersection of philosophy and psychology.

Hallvard Lillehammer is Professor of Philosophy in the School of Social Sciences, History and Philosophy at Birkbeck College, University of London. He is the author of *Companions in Guilt: Arguments for Ethical Objectivity* (2007).

Robin McKenna is a Lecturer in Philosophy at the University of Liverpool. Before coming to Liverpool he worked in Austria (at the University of Vienna) and Switzerland (at the University of Geneva). He completed his PhD at the University of Edinburgh. Most of his work is in epistemology, but he is also interested in philosophy of language, philosophy of science and ethics. Within epistemology, he works on various topics in applied epistemology, feminist epistemology, and social epistemology more broadly. He is currently writing a book on ideal and non-ideal theory in epistemology.

Emily C. McWilliams is an Assistant Professor of Philosophy, and a member of the founding faculty of the undergraduate liberal arts degree program at Duke Kunshan University in Kunshan, China. She works various on issues at the intersections of epistemology, ethics, and feminist philosophy.

José Medina is Walter Dill Scott Professor of Philosophy at Northwestern University. He works primarily in critical race theory and social and political epistemology. His books include *The Epistemology of Resistance* (2013), recipient of the *North-American Society for Social Philosophy Book Award*. His recent and ongoing scholarship addresses epistemic dysfunctions and pathologies of public discourse and ways of resisting them through collective actions and forms of activism that he terms 'epistemic activism'.

Tamer Nawar is Assistant Professor of Philosophy at the University of Groningen.

Cailin O'Connor is a philosopher of science and applied mathematician specializing in models of social interaction. She is Associate Professor of Logic and Philosophy of Science and a member of the Institute for Mathematical Behavioral Science at the University of California, Irvine. She is currently co-administering the NSF Grant *Consensus, Democracy, and the Public Understanding of Science.* Her book *The Misinformation Age*, co-authored with James Owen Weatherall, was published in 2019 with Yale Press, and her book *The Origins of Unfairness* was also published in 2019 with Oxford University Press.

Fabienne Peter is Professor of Philosophy at the University of Warwick, specializing in political philosophy, moral philosophy, and social epistemology. She has written extensively on political legitimacy and on political epistemology, and she is the author of *Democratic Legitimacy* (Routledge, 2009).

Jeroen de Ridder is Associate Professor of Philosophy at Vrije Universiteit Amsterdam and Professor (by special appointment) of Christian Philosophy at the University of Groningen. His research interests are in social epistemology and political epistemology.

Robert M. Ross is a postdoctoral research fellow in the Department of Philosophy at Macquarie University. His work focuses on the cognitive science of belief formation.

Richard Rowland is a Lecturer in Value Theory at the University of Leeds who works on metaethics and normativity. Much of their work is on epistemic and practical normativity, and moral disagreement.

Yasemin Sari is Assistant Professor of Philosophy in the Department of Philosophy and World Religions at the University of Northern Iowa. Dr. Sari completed her PhD in Philosophy at the University of Alberta. Her current research takes up the global refugee crisis.

Robert Mark Simpson is an Associate Professor of Philosophy at University College London. His research interests are mainly in social and political philosophy, with a focus on free speech.

Daniel J. Singer is an Associate Professor of Philosophy at the University of Pennsylvania and the director of the Computational Social Philosophy Lab, of which the rest of the contributors are members.

Ilya Somin is Professor of Law at George Mason University. He is the author of *Free to Move: Foot Voting, Migration, and Political Freedom* (2020), and *Democracy and Political Ignorance: Why Smaller Government is Smarter* (rev. ed. 2016).

Keith E. Stanovich is Professor Emeritus of Applied Psychology at the University of Toronto. He is the author of *The Bias that Divides Us* (forthcoming with MIT Press). He has received the Thorndike Career Achievement Award from the American Psychological Association.

Emily Sullivan is Assistant Professor of Philosophy at Eindhoven University of Technology. Her research explores the intersection between philosophy and data and computer science. She investigates how explanations and data-driven models can promote and be designed for epistemic values such as accuracy, knowledge, and understanding.

Robert B. Talisse is W. Alton Jones Professor of Philosophy at Vanderbilt University. He specializes in political philosophy, focusing on democratic theory, liberalism, and political epistemology. In addition, he pursues research interests in classical and contemporary pragmatism.

Alessandra Tanesini is Professor of Philosophy at Cardiff University. Her new book *The Mismeasure of the Self: A Study in Vice Epistemology* is forthcoming with Oxford University Press.

James Owen Weatherall is Professor of Logic and Philosophy of Science at the University of California, Irvine, where he is also a member of the Institute for Mathematical Behavioral Science and the Center for Cosmology. The author of three books and approximately 50 peer-reviewed articles and book chapters; his research has concerned a broad range of topics in philosophy of science, social epistemology, and mathematical physics. In addition to his scholarly writing, he has written on topics in physics, economics, and philosophy of science for many newspapers and magazines; he has contributed to several interdisciplinary policy reports and white papers, most recent of which was a report on online political influence commissioned by the Joint Research Centre of the European Commission.

Alex Worsnip is Associate Professor of Philosophy at the University of North Carolina at Chapel Hill. He is currently working primarily on rationality and on political epistemology. He is the author of more than 20 published articles in venues such as the *Journal of Philosophy*, *Ethics*, and *Mind*.

ACKNOWLEDGEMENTS

We'd like to start by thanking our editor, Tony Bruce, for suggesting this project and inviting us to edit this handbook. Without his encouragement and support, this book simply would not exist. We'd also like to thank Adam Johnson at Routledge for guiding us along the way.

We also owe deep thanks to the external referees who kindly agreed to read and provide feedback on draft chapters during the review stage of this process. In particular, we would like to thank Jason Baehr, Ryan Byerly, Matt Duncombe, Michael Fuerstein, Bjørn Gunnar Hallsson, Jon Hoover, Mike Huemer, Maxime Lepoutre, Federica Liveriero, Hui-Chieh Loy, Kevin McCain, Eliot Michaelson, Boaz Miller, Rik Peels, Chris Ranalli, Eric Schliesser, Jon Robson, Lani Watson, and Eric Winsberg. Joris Koch also deserves thanks for helping us out with some last-minute editorial work.

This project was also supported by generous funding provided by the Dutch Research Council (NWO) Vidi grant entitled 'Knowledgeable Democracy: A Social-Epistemological Inquiry', project 276-20-024.

Finally, we'd like to thank all the contributors to this volume, who were somehow able to stick to the timeline even in the midst of a global pandemic.

GENERAL INTRODUCTION

Michael Hannon and Jeroen de Ridder

Political epistemology is a newly thriving field at the intersection of epistemology and political philosophy, but it has old roots. In the *Republic*, Plato attacked the epistemic merits of democracy in favor of rule by the knowers. In *On Liberty*, John Stuart Mill touted the epistemic benefits of deliberation for citizens; in his *Considerations on Representative Government*, he advocated for plural voting for those with more education in order to improve the quality of political decisions. In "Truth and Politics," Hannah Arendt analyzed the relationship between truth and political freedom. In *Political Liberalism*, John Rawls put the question of deep political disagreements at the center of his inquiry, ultimately arguing that cooperation across disagreements requires setting aside debates about the truth of particular views and instead adopting an agnostic epistemological position. Political philosophers reacted to Rawls by further debating the role that truth, epistemic justification, and the epistemic quality of decisions should play in establishing the legitimacy of democracy.

While thinkers have been interested in topics at the intersection of political philosophy and epistemology at least since ancient Greece, the past few years have witnessed an outpouring of new research in this area. For example, new work has been published on propaganda, fake news, belief polarization, political disagreement, conspiracy theories, the epistemic merits of (and challenges to) democracy, voter ignorance, irrationality in politics, intellectual virtues and vices in political thinking, distrust, the role of experts in a democracy, and the epistemic harms of filter bubbles and echo chambers.

This rush of interest was largely sparked by two major events: the UK Brexit vote and the election of Donald Trump. But the themes that motivate this new research are deeper and more epistemological. For instance, it has become increasingly difficult to discern legitimate sources of evidence, misinformation spreads faster and farther than ever, and there is a widely felt sense—rightly or wrongly—that the role of truth in politics has decayed in recent years. It is therefore no coincidence that political discourse is currently saturated with epistemic notions like "post-truth," "fake news," "epistemic bubbles," and "alternative facts." Now more than ever there is a need to bring together foundational discussions of truth, knowledge, democracy, polarization, pluralism, and related issues. This handbook attempts to do just that.

Although scholars have been busy charting new ways in which epistemological considerations can (and should) figure into contemporary discussions about politics, this work has been largely fragmented into individual discussions. For example, while discussions of political disagreement between citizens have taken center stage in political philosophy since Rawls's *Political Liberalism*, discussions of disagreement in epistemology often proceed independently of the literature in political philosophy. Conversely, the political philosophy literature on reasonable disagreement often continues to develop without integrating the large body of recent epistemological work on disagreement. In addition, social epistemologists have been writing about the social dimensions of knowledge, the reliability of testimony, group belief, etc., but these discussions have been largely unconnected to distinctively political concerns.

This handbook explores ways in which the analytic and conceptual tools of epistemology bear on political philosophy, and vice versa. A premise underlying the selection of themes and chapters for this handbook is that, beyond a certain point, progress on certain foundational issues in political philosophy cannot be achieved without attending to the epistemological questions raised by them, nor can epistemology be fully valuable unless it addresses urgent social and political issues. This handbook aims to promote more cross-pollination of ideas, as well as consolidate new work in political epistemology, by bringing political philosophers and epistemologists into direct conversation. As an overview of the landscape, this handbook also aims to provide students and scholars with an up-to-date, accurate, and comprehensive idea of the topics, questions, and problems in political epistemology.

Finally, we also believe that political epistemology offers exciting opportunities for interdisciplinary work at the intersection of philosophy and psychology, economics, political science, communication science, and sociology. This is why this handbook includes a few chapters that summarize empirical research on, for instance, political polarization, voter knowledge, and cognitive bias. When political epistemology aims to contribute to debates in society about the role of truth and knowledge in politics, it cannot do so without paying careful attention to empirical information. At the same time, empirical research can benefit from the conceptual toolbox and rigor of philosophical reflection. This can refine ongoing empirical research projects as well as generate new lines of inquiry.

Overview of the parts

This handbook includes 41 chapters that are organized into the following seven parts:

* Politics and truth: historical and contemporary perspectives
* Political disagreement and polarization
* Fake news, propaganda, misinformation
* Ignorance and irrationality in politics
* Epistemic virtues and vices in politics
* Democracy and epistemology
* Trust, expertise, and doubt.

Political epistemology includes a diverse range of topics, so these categories are not intended to be exhaustive, but they do cover a large amount of work in the emerging field of political epistemology. By carving up the terrain in this way, we hope to give some meaningful shape to this broad and rich area of scholarship. (It is worth noting that we decided not to include a part about epistemic injustice in this handbook. While this is no doubt an important area of political epistemology, we wanted to avoid significant overlap with two other recent handbooks: the *Routledge Handbook of Epistemic Injustice*, edited by José Medina, Ian James Kidd, and Gail Pohlhaus Jr., and the *Routledge Handbook of Feminist Philosophy of Science*, edited by Sharon Crasnow and Kristen Intemann.)

Each part begins with a brief introduction to the relevant area of work, followed by five to seven chapters on more specific themes. Each chapter has been written for a general audience and presupposes no detailed knowledge of the area. Nearly all the chapters have been newly written for this volume, making this book an entirely new contribution to the emerging field of political epistemology.

In the remainder of this introduction, we will briefly map out the terrain of political epistemology by outlining the seven themes around which this handbook centers. While this division of parts is inevitably somewhat artificial (there is much overlap across these parts), we believe these categories broadly capture the dominant topics in contemporary political epistemology. We think this way of dividing up the terrain lends a natural unity to seemingly diverse areas of scholarship, and we expect the chapters in this volume speak to one another across a variety of issues. We anticipate the collection will open up fruitful new avenues of research by ensuring a robust discussion between political philosophers and epistemologists, but also more broadly between philosophers and empirical disciplines studying politics such as political science, communication science, psychology, and sociology.

Part 1: Politics and truth: historical and contemporary perspectives

The handbook starts by exploring the fraught relationship between politics and truth from both historical and contemporary perspectives. The first three chapters, by Tamer Nawar, Chris Fraser, and Anthony Booth, trace several ways in which political philosophy and epistemology have intersected in the philosophical thought of ancient Greece, early Chinese political theory, and medieval Islamic philosophy. For example, ancient Greek philosophers were often critical of the epistemic features of democratic institutions, as revealed by the work of Plato and hellenistic thinkers such as the Stoics. In contrast, ancient Chinese thinkers seemed to ground the legitimacy of political authority in a sophisticated social epistemology. In the medieval era, Islamic philosophers wrestled with issues concerning the role and function of expertise in politics, which is a hotly debated contemporary issue. Jumping forward to the nineteenth and twentieth centuries, Paul Kelly and Yasemin Sari explore the political epistemology of John Stuart Mill and Hannah Arendt, respectively. Mill defends free speech, deliberation, and liberalism on largely epistemic grounds: public debate provides citizens with "the opportunity of exchanging error for truth," and even unpopular opinions can improve and develop our political ideas, without which our "mental development is cramped" (ibid: 39). Yet Arendt worried that truth has a "coercive" or "despotic" power that threatens to stifle political debate. Her anxiety about truth is closely connected to the alleged rise of "post-truth" politics, which is the focus of chapters by Simon Blackburn and Amanda Greene. They explore questions like: What are the defining traits of post-truth politics, if any? What are its underlying causes? And what is the relationship between postmodernism and post-truth?

Part 2: Political disagreement and polarization

Political debates are becoming increasingly polarized in Western democracies. Citizens have highly unfavorable views of each other, often regarding each other as immoral, stupid, lazy, and even threatening to each other's way of life. The chapters in this part explore the causes, consequences, and possible antidotes to political polarization and intractable disagreement in politics.

Several chapters trace the origins of increasing polarization and partisan animosity to the role of social identity in politics. For example, Shanto Iyengar argues that political opponents dislike each other as a consequence of group identity, while Michael Hannon and Jeroen de Ridder claim that the psychological basis for political behavior is often group identity and not individuals' political beliefs. This part also explores the extent to which political disagreements are rational or justified. For instance, Emily McWilliams examines how political beliefs are the result of self-serving biases that make people unwilling to change their beliefs, but she claims that these cognitive biases do not undermine the justification of these beliefs according to an evidentialist theory of epistemic justification.

Several authors in this part (and elsewhere in this handbook) attempt to illustrate how key ideas from epistemology can shed light on foundational issues in political philosophy. For example, Daniel Singer and his colleagues use the tools of formal social epistemology to investigate political polarization, while J. Adam Carter draws on key ideas in epistemology and philosophy of language to deepen our understanding of entrenched political disagreement. However, Elizabeth Edenberg recommends caution about applying the conceptual tools of epistemology to particular debates in political philosophy. She says that recent work in the epistemology of disagreement, for instance, is focused on a different level of analysis than work on disagreement by political philosophers. This makes it difficult to apply ideas from one domain to the other. In broad agreement with Edenberg, Richard Rowland and Robert Simpson claim there are important differences in our epistemic attitudes when we compare the political domain to the non-political domain. Nevertheless, these authors all agree that we can learn important lessons (even about how *not* to do political epistemology) by considering how the methods and concepts of epistemology bear on political philosophy, and vice versa.

Part 3: *Fake news, misinformation, and propaganda*

Concerns about fake news have featured prominently in public discourse over the past few years. Several countries have created task forces to combat it; others have tried to outlaw it or to push for stricter regulations for social media platforms complicit in the rapid spreading of fake news. But it would be a mistake to think fake news is an entirely novel phenomenon. To give just one example, historian Frank Mott's 1950 overview of the history of American journalism, *American Journalism: A History of Newspapers in the United States through 260 Years*, describes the so-called "yellow journalism" from the early twentieth century in eerily familiar terms. According to Mott, this brand of tabloid journalism relied on:

> the familiar aspects of sensationalism—crime news, scandal and gossip, divorces and sex, and stress upon the reporting of disasters and sports; [...] the lavish use of pictures, many of them without significance, inviting the abuses of picture-stealing and 'faked' pictures; [... and] impostures and frauds of various kinds, such as 'faked' interviews and stories (p. 539).

So even though our epistemic environment may seem to be more hostile than ever, we shouldn't fall into the trap of assuming we ever lived in an epistemically pristine paradise.

Some chapters in this part—those by Axel Gelfert and Megan Hyska in particular—therefore put fake news and misinformation in broader perspectives by connecting them to the more familiar philosophical categories of lies, bullshit, and propaganda. When we try to understand fake news and misinformation better, it's helpful to differentiate between its production, its consumption, and its distribution. Neil Levy and Robert Ross address the consumption side by summarizing work from cognitive science about why and to what extent people actually believe fake news. Two chapters, one by Hanna Gunn and one by Cailin O'Connor and James Owen Weatherall, offer a window on the distribution and spread of misinformation. The former discusses the phenomena of echo chambers and filter bubbles, while the latter shows how formal models can shed light on how bad actors can exploit features of social-epistemic networks to manipulate public opinion. Finally, Étienne Brown looks at what can be done to fight misinformation.

Part 4: *Ignorance and irrationality in politics*

One of the most consistent findings in political science over at least the past 60 years is the staggering depth of citizens' ignorance about politics in modern democracies. Another consistent finding from psychology is the extent to which our belief-forming processes are shaped by cognitive bias and perhaps even irrational. The chapters in this part center around two issues: the extent and causes of citizen ignorance, and whether (and in what ways) belief-formation in politics is epistemically irrational, even if it may reflect instrumental rationality on the part of citizens.

A common belief is that democracies require informed voters if they are to function well. But when the price of informing yourself adequately is too high, it makes sense for voters to let their beliefs be guided by desires for comfort, affiliation, and belonging. Does this conflict with the epistemic demands of democracy? If it is true, as some political scientists and psychologists allege, that political belief-formation is primarily driven by social identities and "tribal" allegiances, does this make us irrational? This part explores these questions, in addition to questions like: Are we too quick to describe our political opponents as irrational? Are there genuine partisan differences in rational thinking? The chapters by Jeffrey Friedman, Keith Stanovich, and Robin McKenna all suggest that the desire to impute irrationality to our political opponents is misguided, driven by our own ignorance or biases. They do not deny that citizens often lack political knowledge, but they cast doubt on common narratives about the irrationality of would-be voters. The chapters in this part also reflect on the implications of widespread ignorance and/or irrationality for democratic theory.

Part 5: *Epistemic virtues and vices in politics*

Virtue epistemology has grown into an influential research program in epistemology over the past four decades. And more recently, virtue epistemology's bad cousin, vice epistemology, has leapt onto the scene. Very broadly speaking, virtue and vice epistemology are concerned with what it is to think well or badly. Even though the world of politics and government offers plenty of examples of both excellent and poor thinking, and it hardly needs saying that politics can benefit from well-informed and intellectually virtuous citizens and politicians, it is still somewhat rare for virtue and vice epistemologists to target political belief-formation, reasoning, and discourse directly.

The chapters in this part take steps to remedy this situation. They either employ the potential of virtue- and vice-theoretical notions for making sense of how we think and argue about politics, or they use examples from politics to develop and sharpen virtue and vice epistemology further. The chapters by Heather Battaly, Alessandra Tanesini, and José Medina fall into the former category. Battaly considers whether closed-mindedness, typically considered a vice, is actually permissible or perhaps even a virtue when engaging with politicized (mis)information. Drawing on results from psychology, Alessandra Tanesini pushes back against the idea that deliberation does not change people's minds. There is plenty of evidence it can when people have the right (virtuous) motivations and when they deliberate well. Medina employs intellectual virtue and vice theory to analyze the epistemic behavior of groups. Ian James Kidd's contribution is an example of the latter category—it uses examples from recent politics and an analysis of corrupting processes to develop a robustly collective construal of epistemic vice. Quassim Cassam explores the limits of vice epistemology and is critical of its analytical and explanatory potential. He worries that imputations of vice to others who disagree with us may themselves be manifestations of epistemic vice.

Part 6: *Democracy and epistemology*

What is the relevance of epistemology to discussions of democracy and political legitimacy? A foundational question in democratic theory is how important it is that political decisions are *good* decisions. While it might seem uncontroversial that we want political institutions to promote good decisions, it is also important that these decisions be made by good or appropriate *procedures*. These criteria can conflict. If we suppose, for instance, that the masses are highly ignorant or prejudiced (see Part 4), then a democratic procedure may lead to bad outcomes, at least from an epistemic perspective. In contrast, an utterly elitist or authoritarian procedure could, in principle, produce the best decisions.

If morally bad procedures can produce epistemically good outcomes, and if morally good procedures can produce epistemically bad outcomes, then how much weight should be given to each of these considerations in the best account of political institutions? Is political legitimacy grounded in facts about the *procedure* of how political decisions are made, or does political legitimacy reside in the *epistemic quality* of the outcome (as measured by some procedure-independent standard)? This part explores several important themes in the diverse literature on epistemic approaches to—and problems with—democracy: for instance, the epistemic value of deliberation; the benefits of epistocracy (rule by the knowers); the epistemic foundations of political legitimacy; and the epistemic case for non-electoral forms of democracy.

Hélène Landemore provides an epistemic defense of democracy. She argues that democracy is epistemically superior to oligarchy (including rule by the few best) because it makes maximal use of the cognitive diversity of its citizens. But Jason Brennan doubts that democracy is the best way to achieve our epistemic goals. He argues that democracies incentivize voters to remain ignorant and behave irrationally, so we should reject democracy in favor of epistocracy, which apportions political power on the basis of epistemic competence. Taking a middle path, Alexander Guerrero argues in favor of non-electoral forms of democracy on epistemic grounds.

The chapters by Fabienne Peter and Robert Talisse take up the question of what makes political decision-making legitimate. They both argue, in different ways, that political decisions are legitimate only if they result from well-ordered political deliberation. But what makes for well-ordered deliberation, and what can we reasonably expect from citizens? In the final chapter of this part, Cameron Boult investigates the epistemic responsibilities of citizens in a democracy.

Part 7: Trust, expertise, and doubt

Issues of trust and expertise already came up implicitly in previous parts. Where can we find trustworthy information when our information environment is polluted by misinformation? Whom should we trust in a polarized society, when even experts often disagree? What to do when there is, moreover, meta-disagreement about who the experts are and how they ought to be identified? Isn't there an inherent tension between honoring democratic ideals of equality, freedom of speech, and "one person one vote," on the one hand, and deferring to experts or giving extra weight to their opinions on the other? The chapters in this final part bring these questions to the fore and provide a variety of perspectives for thinking about them, as well as suggested answers and solutions.

Two chapters, one by Heather Douglas and the other by Maria Baghramian and Michel Croce, take on the notion of expertise directly and offer a historical perspective on the role of experts in a democratic society (Douglas) and conceptual analyses of expertise and trust (Baghramian and Croce). Hallvard Lillehammer addresses the concern that deference to expert judgments undermines individual autonomy and democratic equality and suggests that it doesn't. Mark Alfano and Emily Sullivan bring an institutional perspective on trust to the table. A key problem nowadays is deciding what and whom to trust *online*. They argue that we need drastic structural reforms—breaking up tech monopolies—to make online platforms more trustworthy. Alex Worsnip's chapter is another fine example of how theorizing about old philosophical problems, such as the challenge of radical skepticism, can shed new light on a contemporary political and social problem: climate change skepticism.

PART 1

Politics and truth

Historical and contemporary perspectives

INTRODUCTION TO PART 1

Politics and truth have always had a fraught relationship. In the *Republic*, Plato recommends that political elites knowingly propagate a "noble lie" to maintain social harmony. In "Truth and Politics," Hannah Arendt observes that "from the viewpoint of politics, truth has a despotic character." Her anxiety about truth is that it forecloses disagreement and deliberation, which is the very essence of political life. According to John Stuart Mill, deliberating in public about politics is good for a democracy because it affords citizens "the opportunity of exchanging error for truth" (1859: 21). But if politics is essentially a realm of contestation, then truth might not be an appropriate category for political discourse. Indeed, some have rejected the very idea of objective truths in politics. Whatever we think about truth's role in politics, Arendt was certainly right that "no one ever doubted that truth and politics are on rather bad terms with each other."

The first part of this handbook explores the vexed relationship between truth and politics from both historical and contemporary perspectives. In Chapter 1, Tamer Nawar considers the role of knowledge in Athenian democracy. As Nawar points out, ancient philosophers were often critical of the epistemic features of democratic institutions. He examines the principal institutions of Athenian democracy and also clarifies Plato's epistemic argument against democracy. Nawar then examines Aristotle's more optimistic view about democracy and knowledge, which is rooted in the epistemic power of groups. This lays the groundwork for much contemporary work in political epistemology (see, for example, the chapter by Hélène Landemore). Nawar concludes by examining what Hellenistic and post-Hellenistic philosophers had to say about democracy and knowledge.

In Chapter 2, Chris Fraser argues that, according to ancient Chinese Mohists, social epistemology plays a crucial role for the legitimacy of political authority. In particular, the Mohists claim that political stability is achieved when the subjects of a state identify with the norms of judgment and conduct promulgated by its leaders. This doctrine of "identifying upwards" gives social epistemology a vital role in justifying the legitimacy of political authority because the norms that ground legitimacy are both moral and epistemic. Thus, political authority and epistemic authority are deeply intertwined on this conception of politics.

In Chapter 3, Anthony Booth explores the relationship between epistemology and politics in Islamic philosophy. He explains how medieval Islamic philosophers wrestled with the issue of the role and function of expertise in politics, which is a topic we are still grappling with today (see Part 7 of this handbook). Booth argues that medieval Islamic philosophers held an epistemological view that he calls "Islamic Moderate Evidentialism," and Booth finds parallels of this idea in the mid-twentieth-century revolutionary Islamism of Sayyid Qutb and Abul A'la Maududi. Finally, Booth shows how understanding this movement from the perspective of medieval Islamic philosophy can shed light on other schools of political thought.

In Chapter 4, Paul Kelly gives an overview of Mill's argument for liberalism and the conditions of acquiring knowledge. Mill believed that knowledge was ultimately based on inductions from experience that are always open to review and falsification, so the growth of knowledge would require freedom of speech and a rejection of censorship. In fact, Mill says we must not paternalistically attempt to spare people from error because that would under-mine the epistemic basis for testing new beliefs and appreciating existing views. Thus, Mill defends the importance of error and unpopular opinion, as well as freedom from government limitation, because they serve an educative function in the broader process of democratic deliberation. However, Kelly points out that Mill's domestic politics is far more progressive than his views about international politics, where Mill defends imperialism and is less toler-ant of diversity or error.

In Chapter 5, Yasemin Sari reassesses Hannah Arendt's view about the role of truth in politics. In particular, Sari examines the idea that people have a "right to unmanipulated factual information," which Arendt says is crucial for establishing freedom of opinion. This chapter aims not only to demonstrate that factual truths play a key role in politics, but also to bring a new perspective to democratic theory by clarifying the relationship between factual truths and political judgment.

In Chapter 6, Simon Blackburn reflects on whether the very idea of political epistemol-ogy has doubtful application. While politics needs to be informed by knowledge from di-verse fields, he claims there is no special, purely political element in its epistemology. Politics is more directly concerned with deciding what to do, and it is here that knowledge is a rare commodity, according to Blackburn. This is because we seldom know in advance which decisions are best, and we may not even know whether we could have done better with hindsight. This chapter ends by arguing that, contrary to what many writers have claimed, postmodern thought has little to do with the "post-truth" atmosphere.

In Chapter 7, the final chapter of this part, Amanda Greene tells a "tale of two tribes" with different political outlooks: the 'heartlanders', whose concern for truthfulness is anchored in personal and relational integrity, and the 'metropolitans', whose concern for truthfulness is anchored in impartiality and cosmopolitanism. According to Greene, each group exhibits qualities of truthfulness – sincerity and accuracy – in ways that the other group does not recognize. The result is that each group interprets the other group's political participation as an abandonment of truth for the sake of power, thereby undermining political legitimacy. Greene builds on the work of Bernard Williams and John Stuart Mill to argue that finding common ground is necessary if truth is to play a role in the resistance of tyranny.

1

DEMOCRACY AND KNOWLEDGE IN ANCIENT GREECE

Tamer Nawar

1 Introduction

Ancient philosophers were often critical of the epistemic features of democratic institutions. I first offer a critical review of the principal institutions of Athenian democracy. I then clarify what I take to be Plato's central argument against democracy, which turns upon its epistemic failings. I then examine Aristotle's views about democracy and knowledge and his views concerning the epistemic powers of groups. Finally, I conclude by examining what Hellenistic and post-Hellenistic philosophers had to say about democracy and knowledge.

2 Athenian democracy

There is evidence for egalitarianism, collective deliberation, and public discussion in various pre-modern societies (the kings of the *Iliad* engaged in some collective deliberation, e.g. *Iliad* 14.27ff, but there were risks for speakers of lesser status, 2.211ff). However, it seems that *governing* by the citizenry – *dēmokratia*, i.e. rule (*kratos*) by the people (*dēmos*) – originated in ancient Greece in the sixth Century BCE. Athens was not the only ancient Greek democracy in the classical period and – despite what is often claimed (even by eminent authorities) – it may not have been the first (for the evidence concerning archaic city-states, see Robinson 1997; Hansen and Nielsen 2004; for classical democracies other than Athens, cf. Robinson 2011). However, Athens is the best documented ancient democracy and – despite two brief oligarchic interruptions (in 411 and 404 BCE) – it was arguably the most successful on several measures (cf. Morris 2004; Ober 2015).

Ancient democracies, including that of Athens, were not liberal and are typically characterised as *direct*, *participatory*, or *deliberative* (as opposed to *representative*). In the fourth century (c. 340 BCE), Athens' citizenship was made up of perhaps 30,000 or so adult males (the population was significantly larger; Attica probably had over 200,000 inhabitants). Women, foreigners, and slaves were not full citizens and had no direct access to political participation but there was some diversity in terms of wealth and occupation among the (adult male) citizenry and all full citizens had *isonomia* (equality before the law) and *isēgoria* (equal right to public speech). The principal offices and institutions of Athenian democracy included the following:

- The *ekklēsia* (assembly): was responsible for passing decrees (but not laws) in domestic and foreign matters, electing magistrates, and several others matters. Meetings, which were open to all citizens and held 40 times a year, were usually attended by over 6,000 citizens. Votes were often made by show of hands.
- The *dikastai* (jurors): 6,000 citizens (over the age of 30), who served for one year and were selected by lot from those who applied. From this pool, *nomothetai* (legislators) and juries for the *dikastēria* (popular courts) were drawn.
  - Legislators (1,000+ jurors): passed laws. They met infrequently.
  - Popular courts (200+ jurors in private cases, 500+ in public cases; in some cases very much more than 500): passed judgement on court cases (which rarely lasted more than a few hours). They met very frequently.
- The *boulē* (council): 500 citizens (over the age of 30), who served for one year and could only serve twice in their lifetimes. They were chosen by lot from those who applied. They drafted agendas and proposals for the assembly. They met very frequently.

While there has been some disagreement among historians over the precise nature and function of these institutions, it is worth emphasising at least three facts.

First, voting was sometimes done by ballot and sometimes by show of hands but the manner in which votes were counted was often not straightforward (at least by modern lights, cf. Schwartzberg 2010). Despite some famous exceptions, such as the trial of Socrates (where the votes were split *fairly* closely), something like consensus may have been the norm.

Second, the popular courts were fairly 'political' institutions. They acted as checks on leading politicians and were also responsible for much public policy (cf. Aristotle *Politics* 1274a4–5).

Third, significant influence was exerted by a 'political class' with significant wealth who often had rhetorical education, i.e. the kind of people who would have paid very good money to be taught by Protagoras and other sophists (itinerant philosophy, politics, and economics teachers who were much in demand in ancient Greece; several readers of this piece will presumably fall into one of these groups or the other).[1] However, although it was sometimes claimed that Athens was a democracy primarily *in name* (e.g. Thucydides 2.65.9), it is unclear that elites *dominated* Athenian political life (Hansen 1987, 1991). At any time, a significant number of those who served as jurors and who attended the assembly would have previously served in the council and instead of seeking approval in occasional elections, leading political speakers and members of the elite had to continually command or commandeer public approval. As a result, they could expect close scrutiny and ran significant risks (cf. Balot 2014).

It has been argued, most notably by Josiah Ober (1989, 2008), that Athens' success in an unforgiving environment was largely due to the role of its democratic institutions in promoting rational deliberation and efficiently employing the knowledge of its citizens (and even that Athens serves as a case study for the success of direct democracies, Ober 2017). Thus, for instance, while democratic deliberation imposed significant costs, Ober (2006, 2008) argues that knowledge dispersed among the citizenry could be aggregated through social networking (e.g. in demes and in the *boulē*) and social incentives (e.g. honours). Ober also suggests that public rituals, ceremonies, and other practices allowed those who shared the relevant preferences to better coordinate their actions (cf. Chwe 2001) and the nature and settings of meetings (e.g. in the courts) was such that they contributed towards a sense of unity and allowed a large body of citizens to build common knowledge. Athens' direct democracy was thus able to effectively employ the dispersed knowledge of its citizens to a degree other political arrangements (including representative democracy) could not match. The involvement of Athenian citizens led to: more realistic and sustainable policy; non-experts contributing relevant knowledge which would not come to light in deliberations among experts; and increased transparency and accountability (which decreased corruption and partial interests).

Ober's account of Athenian democracy has been highly influential and is attractive in several respects, but faces some potential objections. First, the state of the evidence makes it difficult to measure many of the relevant variables – let alone to attempt to discern a causal relation between them – and the fates of other states (e.g. successful, non-democratic states and unsuccessful, democratic states) seem to constitute counter-evidence to several of Ober's central theses. Even if one were to grant that Athens was most successful when most democratic, it seems that Ober is – at best – offering an *eikos muthos* (likely story) about how ancient Athens *may* have effectively employed the knowledge of its citizens. (One might draw parallels with the kind of optimistic story that Plato's Protagoras offers about democratic elements in *Protagoras* 320c8ff.) Second, one might worry that there is a certain circularity in arguing that Athens was successful because it was distinctively effective in employing its citizens' knowledge while assuming that Athens was distinctively effective in employing its citizens' knowledge effectively at least in part *because* it was successful. Third, and most saliently, while it seems plausible that the relevant democratic institutions and processes may have effectively aggregated the *preferences* and *opinions* of the citizenry, it is far less clear that such processes led to *epistemic* benefits or convergence upon truth or knowledge (rather than mere agreement). It is difficult to identify knowledge as such, and the merest acquaintance with human affairs yields an incredible wealth of examples of 'successful' but profoundly and utterly epistemically incompetent agents. This last point is, I think, best understood as the kernel of recurring criticisms of democratic institutions in Plato's dialogues. It is to this issue that I now turn.

3 Plato's master argument against democracy

While Plato (or Plato's Socrates) should perhaps not be read as an unqualified enemy of democracy,[2] the discussions of the shortcomings of democracy in Plato's dialogues are among the most interesting and influential of the ancient world.[3] Plato is well aware of the difficulties in recognising experts as such, but the case for epistocracy is fairly straightforward. Just as a person who is in need of medical attention should submit themselves to the expertise of a doctor, so too – the thought goes – those in need of governing should submit themselves to someone with expertise in ruling (*Republic* 488a–489c; cf. *Statesman* 293a–b, 297e). Any reader of the *Republic* will be familiar with the fact the imagined city-state of Kallipolis includes few democratic elements and that Plato's Socrates thinks that: democracies unjustly treat unequals as if they were equals; are not conducive to unity; are excessively focused on freedom and thereby libertine; and are unstable and liable to dissolve into tyranny (e.g. *Republic* 555b–561d). However, what I take to be Plato's 'master argument' against democracy turns upon its perceived epistemic failings and is, in its simplest form, best understood as going something like this:

1 If α lacks knowledge of the relevant kind K, then α cannot rule well (advise well, prescribe action well, etc.);
2 The *dēmos* lacks knowledge of the relevant kind K;
3 The *dēmos* cannot rule well.

Thus, (1) claims that possession of the relevant kind of knowledge, understanding, or expertise (*epistēmē, technē*) is a necessary condition of successful rule or various kinds of political action. (For discussion, see Nawar 2018: 379–87; cf. 2017.) That is to say, those who wish to govern (advise, etc.) well must have a certain kind of knowledge (cf. *Statesman* 258b, 259a, 301e–302b; *Republic* 473c–d; *Gorgias* 455b–d).[4] While Plato evidently sets the bar on this sort of knowledge rather high, the precise nature of this knowledge or expertise is not immediately clear and seems to be sketched somewhat differently in different dialogues. For instance, in the *Republic*, it seems to involve an abstruse grasping of the Good *sub specie aeternitatis*, whereas in other works (such as the *Statesman* and perhaps the *Euthydemus*) it seems to be an adaptable managerial expertise whose kernel involves knowing when and where to apply other kinds of expertise (cf. *Statesman* 304bff).[5]

Concerning (2), Plato's Socrates agrees with figures like Thucydides but differs significantly from several of his contemporaries. Protagoras seemingly claimed that *all* citizens have a share of the relevant kind of knowledge (e.g. political expertise [*politikē*], *Protagoras* 322bff) *and that* even the worst and most ignorant of those brought up in a *polis* learn something of the relevant knowledge (*Protagoras* 329dff). In contrast, Plato's Socrates thinks that sophists like Protagoras wrongly assign the term 'wisdom' (*sophia*) to the opinions (*dogmata*) of the majority (*Republic* 493a; cf. *Protagoras* 317a) and that the knowledge required for good political rule is in fact very difficult to achieve and *not at all* widespread (*Statesman* 292d–e). Genuine knowledge or expertise requires resilience in the face of dialectical examination and – the thought goes – it is a necessary condition of having knowledge or expertise of any kind that its possessor must be able to impart it to others (cf. *Meno* 93aff; *Protagoras* 319aff). However, those who are often praised for their political expertise cannot withstand dialectical examination. Moreover, whatever they have they cannot impart to others. Therefore, etc.

Moreover, Plato's Socrates offers several reasons for thinking that the citizenry of any democracy akin to the Athenian *cannot* possess the kind of knowledge required for ruling well (*Statesman* 292e, 297b–c, 300e; cf. *Republic* 493e–494a; *Theaetetus* 201a–c). The relevant reasons are difficult to succinctly state, but two deserve special mention.

First, there are various institutional impediments to attaining knowledge (cf. Nawar 2013). The democratic institutions of Athens do not – the thought goes – allow for substantive 'exchange of reasons' or the favourable epistemic procedures some philosophers and theorists (e.g. Estlund 2007) hope to find in democracies. More concretely, the heckling or clamour [*thorybos*] of the assembly makes it difficult to deliberate well or for opposing voices to be heard (cf. *Apology* 20e, 32b–c; *Rep.* 492b–c); simply producing some number of 'witnesses' in support of some claim is *not* straightforwardly truth conducive (*Gorgias* 471e–472a); there was little opportunity for cross-examination; and there was in any case insufficient time for proper examination of any kind (e.g. *Apology* 37a7–b2; *Gorgias* 455aff). These concerns are nicely summarised at *Theaetetus* 201a–c, where Socrates discusses several reasons why Athenian jurors might be able to arrive at true *doxa* (opinion, belief, or judgement) but cannot attain *epistēmē* (knowledge or understanding) (Burnyeat 1982; Nawar 2013).

Second, not only are there barriers to obtaining knowledge in democratic contexts, but there is frequent convergence upon falsehood and Plato's Socrates often seems to think that there is something *epistemically malignant* about political discourse as it is typically practised in democratic contexts. Plato's concerns turn upon a cluster of features concerning rhetoric, philosophical psychology (cf. *Phaedrus* 271aff), and the relation between pleasure and truth. In the *Protagoras*, Plato notes the 'spell' cast by figures such as Protagoras (e.g. 315a, 328d; cf. *Apology* 17a; *Euthydemus* 289e–290a), and in the *Apology*, Plato's Socrates observes that the prosecution's speeches were so effective that as a defendant he himself was almost carried away by them despite knowing them not to be true (*Apology* 17a). In the *Gorgias*, Gorgias claims that rhetoric allows public speakers to persuade (*peithein*) (rather than *teach* [*didaskein*]) their ignorant listeners in such a way that they end up *enslaving* their listeners (*Gorgias* 452e, 459a; cf. *Theaetetus* 201a–c; *Statesman* 304c–d). While the extent to which Plato's Socrates thinks orators control their audiences is debatable (cf. Yunis 1996; Schofield 2006; Nawar 2013), he does think that existing rhetorical practice is a form of flattery (*kolakeia*, 463b1, 464c5ff) and a pleasure-oriented knack (*empeiria*, 462c3ff). It is dedicated to satisfying the desires of its listeners (in a memorable image, orators are compared to pastry chefs who feed their patrons delicious but unhealthy treats, *Gorgias* 521e–522a; cf. Moss 2007), but the rational faculties of the listeners are largely or entirely bypassed (cf. Nawar 2013). Simply put, wishful thinking is plentiful and critical thinking is in short supply. Moreover, while praise is gratifying to hear, few people take criticism well (cf. *Menexenus* 235d). So why should public speakers tell crowds hard truths and suffer as a result when they can instead get ahead by pandering to popular biases and telling flattering falsehoods? Under such epistemically unfavourable conditions, ill-informed opinion is often enshrined as fact and justified dissent faces punishment (cf. *Statesman* 298aff; *Republic* 516e–517a).

4 Aristotle on democracy and knowledge

Aristotle's discussion of the epistemic virtues and vices of democracies is rich but often difficult to interpret. On the one hand, it is often thought that Aristotle is more optimistic than Plato's Socrates about the accuracy of commonly held beliefs (e.g. *Rhetoric* 1355a14–18; *Nicomachean Ethics* 1172b35–1173a1; cf. *Metaphysics* 993a30–b7; *Eudemian Ethics* 1216b30–1; *Rhetoric* 1395a10–12) and some of Aristotle's remarks concerning his so-called 'endoxic method' (e.g. *Nicomachean Ethics* 1145b2–7; cf. 1098b27–29) might be taken to commit him to preserving *endoxa* ('reputable opinions'), i.e. 'those opinions held by everyone, or by the majority, or the wise' (*Topics* 100b21–23, 101a11–13), where possible. Moreover, Aristotle's account of the citizen as someone who participates in political deliberation, judging, and ruling seems well suited to democratic regimes (as Aristotle himself notes, *Politics* 1275b5–7),[6] and one might think that Aristotle's account of rhetoric offers a sketch of how the emotional effects of rhetoric may be epistemically virtuous rather than vicious (cf. Dow 2015). If Aristotle indeed thinks that the views of the proverbial man on the Clapham omnibus track the truth rather well, then one might think that Aristotle would thereby be inclined to reject the second premise of what I called 'Plato's Master Argument' (see (2) above) and to offer a more positive appraisal of the epistemic features of democracy.

On the other hand, there are reasons to think that Aristotle is no friend of democracy and that he largely agrees with Plato's Socrates on the epistemic defects of direct democracies.[7] For instance, if we return to the claims made in the previous paragraph, it often seems that Aristotle is often merely claiming that commonly held beliefs are accurate *to some extent* (not that they are highly accurate) and the so-called 'endoxic method' is either rather limited in its applicability or else is something that Aristotle frequently disregards. Equally, the degree to which Aristotle finds an epistemically appropriate role for the arousal of emotions in rhetoric is debatable,[8] and insofar as Aristotle countenances democratic elements his reasons seem to be largely pragmatic (e.g. he worries about faction and civil war and thus offers concessions to the wider populace, cf. *Politics* 1330a25–28). Moreover, he seems to think little of farmers, tradesmen, and other common professions which would make up the bulk of the citizenry in an ancient democracy. More concretely, Aristotle thinks those who govern should have sufficient wealth and leisure so as not to have to engage in business or labour (e.g. *Politics* 1328b33–1329a26) and he thinks the ways of life of tradesmen and the like allow for little in the way of practical wisdom and excellence or virtue and do not easily enable people to be good citizens in a good city (e.g. *Politics* 1260a39–b2; 1281b21–28; 1319a19–38).

An important passage in the *Politics* effectively illustrates the interpretative difficulties of discerning Aristotle's views towards the epistemic features of democracy. In *Politics* 3.11, Aristotle discusses the conditions under which the many – although they are not individually excellent – may collectively prove better than the excellent few, but Aristotle's discussion is often extremely elliptical and is also highly dialectical and seemingly aporetic. It begins thus:

> The view that the majority rather than those who are the best people, albeit few, should be in control would seem to be well stated, and to involve some puzzles, though perhaps also some truth. For the many, each of whom individually is not an excellent man, nevertheless may, when they have come together, be better than the few best people, not individually but collectively, just as dinners to which many people contribute are better than dinners provided at one person's expense. (Aristotle *Politics* 1281a40–b3, trans. Reeve)[9]

Here, and in what follows, Aristotle offers a series of considerations, examples, and analogies to illustrate his claims, but precisely what Aristotle hopes to illustrate and his own attitude towards said claims is not entirely clear. The passage just quoted might be taken to anticipate something akin to Condorcet's jury theorem or else to suggest that Aristotle is providing an account of how the *dēmos* may collectively have the kind of knowledge or virtue required for effective political action even though the members of the *dēmos* individually lack such knowledge or virtue (Aristotle would thereby be offering a reason to reject the second premise of the 'Master Argument' I attributed to Plato). Some have indeed read the passage along such lines (e.g. Waldron 1995). Thus construed, Aristotle is illustrating the benefits of epistemic heterogeneity or diversity (in something like the manner made familiar by Hong and Page 2004 and Surowiecki 2004) and how – through reason giving exchanges in *deliberative* democratic contexts – a crowd of persons who are not especially knowledgeable individually may epistemically outperform groups of experts. Others think that Aristotle has in mind a more straightforwardly additive summation procedure or 'sheer aggregation' in *representative* democratic contexts (e.g. Lane 2013). However, it has also been argued that Aristotle is not in fact making an epistemic point at all (Cammack 2013) (or at least not directly).[10] Any satisfactory account of Aristotle's views on the epistemic features of democracy must make some headway in resolving the interpretative difficulties of *Politics* 3.11 and must also address how Aristotle conceives of the virtue and practical wisdom of political and social groups.

5 Democracy and knowledge in Hellenistic and post-Hellenistic philosophy

While the rise of Macedon brought about enormous changes in the Greek world, the Greek *polis* endured and philosophers continued to think about politics. The Stoics in particular seem to have given significant attention to political thought but their views are difficult to reconstruct on the basis of the surviving evidence. Unlike the Epicureans (who are usually understood as quietists, cf. Diogenes Laertius 10.119–120), the Stoics claimed that, provided there is no obstacle, ideal rational agents should engage in politics and do so with an eye to promoting virtue (Diogenes Laertius 7.121).[11] Given the nature of the Hellenistic age, it is understandable that our sources preserve practical advice concerning how Stoics should advise kings (e.g. Plutarch *De Stoicorum Repugnantiis* 1043c), but it has been argued that early Stoics, such as Zeno of Citium (334–262 BCE), the founder of the Stoa, had a 'tendency towards democracy' (Erskine 1990) and that the Stoic preference for a mixed constitution (i.e. one which combined monarchical, aristocratic, and democratic elements, cf. Diogenes Laertius 7.131) was a later development.

However, it is not clear to me that the Stoics had reason to be favourably disposed towards democracy. Whatever role Zeno may have played in third-century Athenian politics (Erskine's case rests primarily upon historical reconstruction of the political context, but one should keep in mind that Zeno was not an Athenian citizen), preference for a mixed constitution *seems* to be attributed to both Zeno and Chrysippus (Diogenes Laertius 7.131). Moreover, and more saliently for those interested in political epistemology, the Stoics claimed that rulers must *know* (*gignōskō*) about good things and bad things and that only those who possess such knowledge are fit for public office or should serve as jurors or speakers (Diogenes Laertius 7.122). They thereby seem to accept the first premise of the 'Master Argument' I attributed to Plato. Moreover, while the Stoics took knowledge or apprehension (*katalēpsis*) to be fairly common and widespread (Nawar 2014a), the kind of knowledge required for ruling well seems to be a form of *wisdom*, i.e. a steadfast and rationally resilient system of such apprehensions or items of knowledge possessed only by the wise (cf. Sextus Empiricus *Adversus Mathematicos* 7.151–53; Stobaeus 2.73.16–74.3 = LS 40H; Nawar 2014a), which the Stoics thought was not at all widespread.[12] It seems that the Stoics would thereby also accept the second premise of the Platonic argument against democracy.

In his history of the rise of republican Rome, the Greek historian Polybius (c. 200–118 BCE) was inclined to view classical Athens as successful *in spite of* its democratic nature and – in Platonic fashion – likened it to a ship without a captain while warning of the dangers posed by political flattery of the populace (Polybius 6.44, 57). Polybius's view of Rome as embodying a mixed constitution was influential (cf. Cicero *De Re Publica* 1.45, 69), but the precise extent and nature of Rome's democratic elements is more controversial.[13] Roman citizens did not have the kind of political equality enjoyed by the citizens of classical Athens, but the *populus* elected magistrates and played an important legislative role in the Roman republic.

Cicero thought democracy wrongly treats unequals as equals and does not allow for distinctions in *dignitas* (*De Re Publica* 1.43, 53). He was inclined to criticise the libertine nature of democracy by offering paraphrases of Plato (*De Re Publica* 1.66–67; cf. Plato *Republic* 562c–563e) while emphasising that aristocratic government by the virtuous avoids the dangers of monarchic rule, on the one hand, and the errors and thoughtlessness (*error et temeritas*) of popular rule, on the other (*De Re Publica* 1.44, 52, 65). Cicero gives significant attention to rhetoric in various works and discusses eloquence, trust (*fides*), and the nature of the ideal political speaker in significant detail. However, although he thinks that good political orators should give pleasure to their listeners and move their emotions (e.g. Cicero *Brutus* 184–88), he seems to give relatively little attention to epistemic issues. While Roman liberty or freedom (*libertas*) (e.g. Cicero *De Re Publica* 1.55, 69) has been much discussed (cf. Pettit 1996, 1997; Skinner 1998), Roman *consilium* and the epistemic features of the democratic elements of the Roman republic have thus far attracted less in the way of attention from political and philosophical scholars and may merit further investigation.

Given that Hellenistic monarchs and Roman emperors were no less susceptible to flattery than democratic populaces, it is unsurprising that the philosophers of later antiquity had much to say about political flattery and frankness of speech (*parrēsia*). However, although later antiquity saw no shortage of practical advice for kings, there seems to have been relatively little interest in philosophically examining the virtues and vices of different forms of government or attending to their epistemic features. Philosophical writers such as Plutarch touched upon the democracies of the past (his biographies of ancient figures – many of them Athenians – frequently repeat the kinds of criticisms of the Athenian *dēmos* one finds in Plato's more sour moments), but it seems that democracy attracted little interest in the Roman empire. Even when commenting on Plato's *Republic*, later Platonists seem to have been inclined to focus their attention on other, 'higher' matters and even Augustine – who gave significant attention to various epistemic matters of significant philosophical interest (cf. Nawar 2019) and offered arguably unprecedented attention to testimony (cf. King and Ballantyne 2009; Nawar 2015), how reasoning can go wrong in group settings (cf. Nawar 2014b), and various features of social epistemology and rhetoric – showed little interest in democracy or the epistemic features of particular political contexts.

Notes

1 On Plato's telling, Protagoras promised to teach men good judgement (*euboulia*) and political expertise (*politikē technē*) and make them into good citizens (*Protagoras* 318e–a). For Protagoras's relativistic views and responses to them, see Nawar (2020).

2 The *Laws* (for which, see Bobonich 2002; Annas 2017) makes the case for a 'mixed constitution' which combines monarchical and democratic elements (e.g. *Laws* 693d–694a). For an influential discussion of (Plato's) Socrates, see Kraut (1984). On the importance of conversation and dialogic elements, see McCabe (2015); Duncombe (2016).

3 Criticism of democracy and admiration of Sparta is fairly widespread in extant classical works, but often seems to be driven primarily by elitist snobbery. On Sparta and its portrayals, see Cartledge (2001); Powell and Hodkinson (2002). For useful overviews of Greek political thought, see Ober (1998); Balot (2006).

4 For discussion of the characterisation of this expertise as *kingly* and discussions of ancient accounts of monarchy, see Atack (2020).

5 The extent to which the relevant sketches are consistent is controversial and has long been so (since at least John Stuart Mill and Benjamin Jowett, see Schofield 2006). Readers of Plato have long wondered how useful the knowledge of the good sketched in the *Republic* might be (e.g. *Nicomachean Ethics* 1096b31–1097a14, but cf. *Republic* 500a–d). For discussion of the relevant expertise in the *Statesman*, see Cooper (1997); Lane (1998); El Murr (2014). On the *Euthydemus*, see Nawar (2017). For Plato's views on expertise, as well as those of Isocrates, the Sophists, Hippocratic writers, and several others, see Nawar (2018, forthcoming). Despite the interpretative difficulties, it seems fairly clear that, in contrast to some other figures, Plato's Socrates thinks the relevant kind of knowledge involves a deep and holistic understanding of things (cf. Schwab 2016) as well as the ability to do various things (cf. Nawar 2017, forthcoming) and that possession of mere opinions or judgements (*doxai*) – even if true or correct – is not enough for good political rule (cf. *Crito* 47aff).

6 Aristotle characterises the citizen *simpliciter* as one who has a share in judging (*krisis*), ruling (*archē*), and deliberation (*bouleusis*) or as someone who shares in ruling and being ruled (*Politics* 1275a22–23, 1275b17–21, 1283b42–1284a3). Cf. Miller (1995); Kraut (2001); Schofield (2011); Inamura (2015); Riesbeck (2016).

7 Aristotle often characterises democracies in terms of their prioritisation of freedom and equality (e.g. *Politics* 1290a40–b1, 1294a10–11; 1317a40ff; *Rhetoric* 1366a4), but he thinks democracies wrongly accord freedom too great a value (cf. *Politics* 1310a28–38; 1317a40ff) and that political equality should exist only between those who are indeed equals in all the relevant respects and not merely equal in one respect (e.g. freedom) (*Politics* 1280a9ff; 1301a25ff).

8 Aristotle's views of the epistemic features of rhetoric are complex and controversial. However, one may note that Aristotle discusses the potential for bias and partiality in those who listen to deliberative oratory (e.g. *Rhetoric* 1354b4–11; cf. *Politics* 1330a20–5) and how arousal of the emotions (or at least certain emotions) impairs the judgements of jurors (cf. *Rhetoric* 1354a16–25). He suggests that enthymemes (i.e. the kinds of arguments which are the principal stock in trade of genuine rhetoric) do not or should not end up leaving an emotional effect upon the listener (*Rhetoric* 1418a6–17; cf. *Rhetoric* 1404a1–5).

9 Note that part of the text is corrupt. I here simply offer Reeve's (2017) translation.
10 For important discussion, see also Bouchard (2011); Schofield (2011); Bobonich (2015). For useful discussion of distinct models of 'institutional epistemology', see Anderson (2006).
11 Zeno may have seen a kind of cosmopolitan community comprised entirely of wise citizens as an ideal, but it has also been argued that this was a later development within Stoic thought (for discussion, cf. Schofield 1991, 1999; Vogt 2008). The few reports that have come down to us about Zeno's *Politeia* (*Republic*) focus principally on scandalous details concerning sexual relations, incest, and cannibalism.
12 According to the Stoics, the wise – who alone were free (*eleutheros*) and *kings* (*basileas*) – were incredibly rare individuals (Plutarch *De Stoicorum Repugnantiis* 1048e; *De Communibus Notitiis adversus Stoicos* 1076b–c; Sextus Empiricus *Adversus Mathematicos* 7.432; Alexander of Aphrodisias *De Fato* 199.14–22 = LS 61N).
13 It has been argued that Rome should be viewed as a democracy (and even a direct or deliberative democracy, e.g. Millar 1998; cf. Lintott 1999; Morstein-Marx 2004). Cicero would have been horrified.

References

Anderson, E. (2006). 'The Epistemology of Democracy', *Episteme* 3, 8–22.
Annas, J. (2017). *Virtue and Law in Plato and Beyond* (Oxford: Oxford University Press).
Atack, C. (2020). *The Discourse of Kingship in Classical Greece* (Routledge: Oxford).
Balot, R. (2006). *Greek Political Thought* (Oxford: Blackwell).
——— (2014). *Courage in the Democratic Polis: Ideology and Critique in Classical Athens* (Oxford: Oxford University Press).
Bobonich, C. (2002). *Plato's Utopia Recast: His Later Ethics and Politics* (Oxford: Clarendon Press).
——— (2015). 'Aristotle, Political Decision Making, and the Many', in T. Lockwood and T. Samaras (eds.), *Aristotle's Politics: A Critical Guide* (Cambridge: Cambridge University Press), 142–62.
Bouchard, E. (2011). 'Analogies du pouvoir partagé: remarques sur Aristote, Politique III.11', *Phronesis* 56, 162–79.
Burnyeat, M. F. (1982). 'Socrates and the Jury: Paradoxes in Plato's Distinction between Knowledge and True Belief', *Proceedings of the Aristotelian Society* 54, 173–91.
Cammack, D. (2013). 'Aristotle on the Virtue of the Multitude', *Political Theory* 41, 175–202.
Cartledge, P. (2001). *Spartan Reflections* (London: Duckworth).
Chwe, M. (2001). *Rational Ritual: Culture, Coordination, and Common Knowledge* (Princeton, NJ: Princeton University Press).
Cooper, J. (1997). 'Plato's *Statesman* and Politics', *Proceedings of the Boston Area Colloquium in Ancient Philosophy* 13, 71–104.
Dow, J. (2015). *Passions & Persuasion in Aristotle's Rhetoric* (Oxford: Oxford University Press).
Duncombe, M. (2016). 'Thought as Internal Speech in Plato and Aristotle', *History of Philosophy and Logical Analysis* 19, 105–25.
El Murr, D. (2014). *Savoir et gouverner: Essai sur la science politique platonicienne* (Paris: Vrin).
Erskine, A. (1990). *The Hellenistic Stoa: Political Thought and Action* (London: Duckworth).
Estlund, D. (2007). *Democratic Authority: A Philosophical Framework* (Princeton, NJ: Princeton University Press).
Hansen, M. H. (1987). *The Athenian Assembly in the Age of Demosthenes* (Oxford: Blackwell).
——— (1991). *The Athenian Democracy in the Age of Demosthenes: Structure, Principles, and Ideology* (Oxford: Blackwell).
Hansen, M. H. and T. H. Nielsen (2004). *An Inventory of Archaic and Classical Poleis* (Oxford: Oxford University Press).
Hong, L. and S. Page (2004). 'Groups of Diverse Problem Solvers can Outperform Groups of High-Ability Problem Solvers', *Proceedings of the National Academy of Sciences* 101, 16385–89.
Inamura, K. (2015). *Justice and Reciprocity in Aristotle's Political Philosophy* (Cambridge: Cambridge University Press).
King, P. and N. Ballantyne (2009). 'Augustine on Testimony', *Canadian Journal of Philosophy* 39, 195–214.
Kraut, R. (1984). *Socrates and the State* (Princeton, NJ: Princeton University Press).

————— (2001). *Aristotle: Political Philosophy* (Oxford: Oxford University Press).

Lane, M. (1998). *Method and Politics in Plato's Statesman* (Cambridge: Cambridge University Press).

————— (2013). 'Claims to Rule: The Case of the Multitude', in M. Deslauriers and P. Destrée (eds.), *The Cambridge Companion to Aristotle's Politics* (Cambridge: Cambridge University Press), 247–74.

Lintott, A. (1999). *The Constitution of the Roman Republic* (Oxford: Clarendon Press).

McCabe, M. M. (2015). *Platonic Conversations* (Oxford: Oxford University Press).

Millar, F. (1998). *The Crowd in Rome in the Late Republic* (Ann Arbor: University of Michigan Press).

Miller, F. D., Jr. (1995). *Nature, Justice, and Rights in Aristotle's Politics* (Oxford: Clarendon Press).

Morris, I. (2004). 'Economic Growth in Ancient Greece', *Journal of Institutional and Theoretical Economics* 160, 709–42.

Morstein-Marx, R. (2004). *Mass Oratory and Political Power in the Late Roman Republic* (Cambridge: Cambridge University Press).

Moss, J. (2007). 'The Doctor and the Pastry Chef: Pleasure and Persuasion in Plato's *Gorgias*', *Ancient Philosophy* 27, 229–49.

Nawar, T. (2013). 'Knowledge and True Belief at *Theaetetus* 201a–c', *British Journal for the History of Philosophy* 21, 1052–70.

————— (2014a). 'The Stoic Account of Apprehension', *Philosophers' Imprint* 14, 1–21.

————— (2014b). '*Adiutrix Virtutum?* Augustine on Friendship and Virtue', in S. Stern-Gillet and G. Gurtler (eds.), *Ancient and Medieval Concepts of Friendship* (Albany: State University of New York Press), 197–225.

————— (2015). 'Augustine on the Varieties of Understanding and Why There Is No Learning from Words', *Oxford Studies in Medieval Philosophy* 3, 1–31.

————— (2017). 'Platonic Know-How and Successful Action', *European Journal of Philosophy* 25, 944–62.

————— (2018). 'Thrasymachus' Unerring Skill and the Arguments of *Republic* I', *Phronesis* 63, 359–91.

————— (2019). 'Augustine's Defence of Knowledge against the Sceptics', *Oxford Studies in Ancient Philosophy* 56, 215–65.

————— (2020). 'Relativism in Ancient Greek Philosophy', in M. Kusch (ed.), *The Routledge Handbook of Philosophy of Relativism* (Oxford: Routledge), 41–49.

————— (forthcoming). 'Dynamic Modalities and Teleological Agency: Plato and Aristotle on Skill and Ability', in T. Johansen (ed.), *Productive Knowledge in Ancient Philosophy: The Concept of Techne* (Cambridge: Cambridge University Press).

Ober, J. (1989). *Mass and Elite in Democratic Athens: Rhetoric, Ideology, and the Power of the People* (Princeton, NJ: Princeton University Press).

————— (1998). *Political Dissent in Democratic Athens: Intellectual Critics of Popular Rule* (Princeton, NJ: Princeton University Press).

————— (2006). 'From Epistemic Diversity to Common Knowledge: Rational Rituals and Cooperation in Democratic Athens', *Episteme* 3, 214–33.

————— (2008). *Democracy and Knowledge: Innovation and Learning in Classical Athens* (Princeton, NJ: Princeton University Press).

————— (2015). *The Rise and Fall of Classical Greece* (Princeton, NJ: Princeton University Press).

————— (2017). *Demopolis: Democracy before Liberalism in Theory and Practice* (Cambridge: Cambridge University Press).

Pettit, P. (1996). 'Freedom as Antipower', *Ethics* 106, 576–604.

————— (1997). *Republicanism: A Theory of Freedom and Government* (Oxford: Clarendon Press).

Powell, A. and S. Hodkinson (2002) (eds.). *Sparta: Beyond the Mirage* (London: Classical Press of Wales).

Reeve, C. D. C. (2017). *Aristotle: Politics, a New Translation* (Indianapolis, IN: Hackett).

Riesbeck, D. J. (2016). *Aristotle on Political Community* (Cambridge: Cambridge University Press).

Robinson, E. W. (1997). *The First Democracies: Early Popular Government outside Athens* (Stuttgart: F. Steiner).

————— (2011). *Democracy Beyond Athens: Popular Government in the Greek Classical Age* (Cambridge: Cambridge University Press).

Schofield, M. (1991). *The Stoic Idea of the City* (Cambridge: Cambridge University Press).

————— (1999). *Saving the City: Philosopher-Kings and Other Classical Paradigms* (London: Routledge).

————— (2006). *Plato: Political Philosophy* (Oxford: Oxford University Press).

————— (2011). 'Aristotle and the Democratization of Politics', in B. Morison and K. Ierodiakonou (eds.), *Episteme, etc.* (Oxford: Oxford University Press), 285–301.

Schwab, W. (2016). 'Understanding *epistēmē* in Plato's *Republic*', *Oxford Studies in Ancient Philosophy* 51, 41–85.

Schwartzberg, M. (2010). 'Shouts, Murmurs, and Votes: Acclamation and Aggregation in Ancient Greece', *The Journal of Political Philosophy* 18, 448–68.

Skinner, Q. (1998). *Liberty before Liberalism* (Cambridge: Cambridge University Press).

Surowiecki, J. (2004). *The Wisdom of Crowds: Why the Many are Smarter than the Few and How Collective Wisdom Shapes Business, Economies, Societies, and Nations* (New York: Double Day).

Vogt, K. (2008). *Law, Reason, and the Cosmic City: Political Philosophy in the Early Stoa* (Oxford: Oxford University Press).

Waldron, J. (1995). 'The Wisdom of the Multitude: Some Reflections on Book 3, Chapter 11 of Aristotle's *Politics*', *Political Theory* 23, 563–84.

Yunis, H. (1996). *Taming Democracy: Models of Political Rhetoric in Classical Athens* (Ithaca, NY: Cornell University Press).

2

IDENTIFYING UPWARD

Political epistemology in an early Chinese political theory

Chris Fraser

> So what do we reckon brings order to the state and the people? If superiors in governing get the facts about subordinates, there is good order; if they fail to get the facts about subordinates, there is disorder. (*Mòzǐ*)

Political epistemology is the study of how epistemic matters interact with political concerns. The political thought of the *Mòzǐ*, a collection of writings by anonymous hands presenting the philosophy of Mò Dí 墨翟 (fl. ca. 430 BC) and his followers, the Mohists, is potentially instructive as to how social epistemology is fundamentally intertwined with political relations.

The Mohists formed one of early China's most prominent social and philosophical movements. Spread geographically across the pre-imperial Chinese world, their school was active for about 300 years, from Mò Dí's lifetime in the middle of the fifth century BC to roughly the middle of the second century BC They presented China's first systematic ethical and political theories, grounded in a distinctive brand of communitarian consequentialism. For the Mohists, "right" or "righteous" (*yì* 義) is what tends to promote the benefit of all, understood as material wealth, a thriving population, and social order. Social order includes, negatively, the absence of crime, deceit, harassment, injury, conflict, and aggression, and, positively, neighborly assistance, charity for the destitute, and fulfillment of the relational virtues associated with the social roles of ruler and subject, father and son, and elder and younger brother. Rulers are to be benevolent, subjects loyal, fathers kind, sons filially devoted, and brothers fraternally loving and respectful.[1]

The Mohists see a stable political society as achieved through a process they call "identifying upward," by which the subjects of a state identify with unified norms of judgment and conduct promulgated by leaders through a pyramidal political hierarchy. These socially shared norms the Mohists regard as instituted through the creation of political authority, which is justified partly by its effectiveness in implementing unified norms by which to organize social life.

The unified norms propagate from the top of the hierarchy downward. At the same time, however, the Mohists hold that upward identification and thus political legitimacy can be maintained only if those at the bottom of the hierarchy endorse how the norms are implemented. Crucially, if those in authority and those they govern do not agree on the facts pertinent to observing and enforcing the norms, people may cease to identify upward, undermining social unity and defeating the justification for political authority. The legitimate, effective exercise of authority rests on shared judgments grounded in unified norms. Hence, as the epigram above puts it, only if those holding political authority grasp the factual situation among their subordinates can there be stable social order—this grasp being based on reports from the people below, employing unified standards of judgment.

The Mohists may be mistaken that consensus on norms can be achieved only through the exercise of political authority. Indeed, their own discussion already hints at an alternative approach to reaching agreement. But I will suggest they are probably on the right track in contending that the legitimacy of political authority can be sustained only if the institutions by which it is exercised embody shared norms and judgments. In this respect, the legitimacy of political authority indeed depends on whether those subject to authority identify upward. And as we will see, people's willingness to identify upward rests, in turn, on social epistemological factors.

The origin of political authority

The Mohists present what is likely history's earliest speculative account of the origin of political authority from a state of nature. Their texts offer three overlapping, slightly different versions of this account, which are probably arranged in chronological order of composition. I will summarize shared features of the first two versions, which run closely parallel, and then later highlight a key development in the third version bearing on political epistemology.

A distinctive feature of the Mohist account is that the state of nature is marked by a radical plurality of norms. People each follow their own, individual conception of what is "right" (*yì*). (Some may think the death of a parent calls for a three-year mourning ritual, for example, while others may think a three-day ritual is enough.) This diversity breeds disagreement, as individuals each assume their conception of right should be universal and so apply it to condemn others' conceptions. The disagreement, in turn, leads to conflict and social chaos. People injure each other, families scatter, social cooperation ceases, and humanity falls into a disorderly state like that among nonhuman animals. An implication is that people can live a properly human life only through participation in an orderly political society.[2]

The people of the world come to understand that disorder arises because there are no political leaders to unify the norms everyone follows concerning what is right. Hence, a virtuous, capable, and wise person is selected and established as the "Son of Heaven," or supreme ruler, subordinate only to Heaven (*tiān* 天, a sky or nature deity). The Son of Heaven is charged with bringing about good order by unifying the norms followed by all the world.

Toward this end, the new ruler establishes a pyramidal structure of political authority with himself at the apex, three dukes below him, lords and high officials of various states below them, then heads of districts, and finally village heads. Officials at each level are chosen for their competence and virtue. Once the officials are in place, the ruler proclaims that everyone must "identify upward" or "conform upward" (*shàng tóng* 上同) with the norms of their superiors, having no heart to "ally together below." People are to identify with the leadership and by so doing join in following and promulgating a unified set of norms. Specifically, they are to report good or bad conduct to their superiors, emulate their superiors' judgments of right or wrong, recommend to them anything they find of value, and remonstrate with them if superiors commit errors. These practices will be rewarded and praised; failure to perform them will be punished and criticized.

All those who hear or see something good must report it to their superiors; all those who hear or see something bad must also report it to their superiors. What superiors deem right, you must also deem right; what superiors deem wrong, you must also deem wrong. If you possess something good, present it; if superiors commit errors, admonish them. Identify upward with your superiors and have no heart to align together below. When superiors get hold of people who do these things, they will reward them, and when the myriad people hear about them, they will praise them. (12/12–17)

Once the Son of Heaven has issued this policy, leaders at each level of the hierarchy implement it by proclaiming that their subjects must report good and bad conduct to the leader the next level up and emulate him in their judgments of right or wrong, their statements, and their actions. The village heads announce these orders:

As to all the myriad people of the village, all will identify upward with the district head and dare not align together below. What the district head deems right, you must also deem right; what the district head deems wrong, you must also deem wrong. Eliminate your bad statements and learn the good statements of the district head; eliminate your bad conduct and learn the good conduct of the district head. (12/19–21)

The district heads repeat a parallel announcement calling on their people to emulate the lord of their state; the lord of each state then similarly calls on his people to emulate the Son of Heaven. Through this society-wide practice of model emulation, leaders at the level of the district, state, and realm unify the norms of everyone under their rule. Society as a whole then looks beyond the Son of Heaven to identify upward with Heaven itself:

Once the world is in order, the Son of Heaven again unites the world's norms of righteousness to identify upward with Heaven. (13/22–42)

Since the Mohists believe Heaven is a perfectly reliable moral exemplar, the requirement to identify upward with Heaven is intended to ensure that the content of the unified norms conforms to the objectively correct ethical *dào* 道, or way.

For the Mohists, then, political authority is justified by its effectiveness in unifying norms of judgment and conduct so as to bring about good order and thereby promote the benefit of all. Political society originates with the emergence of a leader who unifies norms; it is sustained by people's collective acceptance of and cooperation with the unified norms. The status of certain norms as authoritative is instituted through the invention of political authority, and conformity to such norms is the core of obedience to political authority.

In the Mohist origin story, violent conflict in the state of nature arises from normative anarchy—and not, as in the more familiar Hobbesian scenario, from individuals' untrammeled pursuit of self-interest. People cannot live together harmoniously because they cannot determine what norms to take as a basis for doing so. Everyone has their own view of what is right, none of them authoritative or convincing to others. But why do the Mohists think only political authority can resolve this disagreement over norms? Couldn't the community negotiate an agreement among themselves? For example, couldn't people settle on an overlapping consensus between their different conceptions of what is right? The Mohists do not seem to notice this route, perhaps because acting on an overlapping consensus is itself a norm about which, *ex hypothesi*, people disagree. Another suggestion might be that the Mohists could invoke their deity, Heaven, to settle normative disputes. Perhaps Heaven could intervene, commanding people to follow divinely revealed norms. Again, however, the Mohists seem to assume that appealing to Heaven is itself a norm about which people must first agree before they can converge in following Heaven's lead.

A further question is whether the Mohist origin scenario might be incoherent. People in the state of nature are depicted as living in families, alongside others in communities. Any form of community life probably presupposes at least some shared norms, so this depiction may conflict with the hypothesis that people held diverse, incompatible views of what is right. Perhaps, however, the Mohists could allow that the different norms people affirmed might overlap in various ways. The crux of their view is that *if* there were a community without any political hierarchy, conflicts between the norms affirmed by its members would likely arise eventually, and resolving these would require the invention of political authority.

Political authority and epistemic authority

The Mohist stance, then, is that political authority is needed to underwrite the moral epistemological authority by which people can jointly take some one set of norms to be the correct, appropriate, or authoritative basis for interacting with each other and organizing community life. In effect, before the invention of political authority, there is no such thing as intersubjective authority of any kind, and thus, there are no objective, authoritative standards of correct or appropriate judgment or conduct. For the Mohists, the very notion of authoritative status is social and political; epistemic and normative authority and correctness are byproducts of political authority.[3] Hence, the process of establishing unified norms, and so reaching epistemic and normative consensus, inherently involves identifying *upward*. Consensus is intertwined with commitment to a hierarchical structure of authority.

The consensus the Mohists envision primarily concerns norms governing ethical judgment and conduct, or what people deem "right" (*yì*). These norms clearly pertain to moral epistemology. But the unified norms probably also include epistemic norms in a broader sense that covers judgments of empirical fact.[4] For the Mohists, correctness of assertion—and thus knowledge—is determined by the correct use of "names," or words, and the norms that determine the correct use of names are probably among those settled through the process of identifying upward. The terms the texts use for the attitudes of deeming right or wrong that people are to learn from their superiors—*shì* 是 (right, approve, "this") and *fēi* 非 (wrong, condemn, "not-this")—apply to both evaluative and empirical matters, including the issue of what is or is not correctly referred to by various "names." Moreover, the Mohists do not distinguish neatly between ethical or evaluative judgments and descriptive or empirical judgments. They call on political subordinates to model their statements or assertions (*yán* 言) on their leaders', without distinguishing between descriptive reports of fact and prescriptive or ethical teachings. Similarly, their discussion of criteria for evaluating whether to accept or reject assertions seamlessly blends ethical, prudential, and descriptive issues. The descriptive, empirical question of whether something exists is to be settled by the same criteria as the political question of whether some policy is effective or the ethical question of whether some practice is right.[5] It is also clear from the Son of Heaven's initial policy announcement that the aim of identifying upward is not simply to converge on unified norms but to share information relevant to their observance. As the next section will explain, legitimate political authority rests on consensus regarding factual reports as well as ethical norms.

Given the links between political and epistemic authority, the Mohists' description of the origin of political authority raises questions about the exit from the state of nature that bear as well on the conditions for epistemic consensus. If people in the state of nature disagree so radically about what is right, how do they manage to agree in diagnosing and resolving the cause of their predicament? How do they agree on the qualifications of the emergent leader, and how are they persuaded to identify upward with him? How do they bootstrap themselves from normative and epistemic anarchy into a political society organized around shared norms?

The Mohist picture seems to be that people each realize, by their own norms or standards, that life in the state of nature is intolerably chaotic—subhuman, the texts imply—and thus that political authority is needed to secure order through unified norms. Given this shared acknowledgment of the need for leadership, people can converge in following a leader even though they do not yet agree on the content of the norms the leader will promulgate. The texts do not specify exactly how the Son of Heaven is selected, saying only that he is chosen for his virtues, wisdom, and competence. The implication is that, whether the Son of Heaven asserts himself or is put forward by others, he has sufficiently compelling personal qualities that some critical mass of people begin to defer to him, at least tacitly and conditionally. The process could be similar to other scenarios in which a leader spontaneously emerges from an unstructured group, as when children tacitly acknowledge a better or more confident player as captain of a pickup ball team or neighbors look to an experienced local activist to coordinate a community project. Recognizing that their problems can be resolved only by cooperating under the coordination of a leader, people tacitly converge in treating someone who seems experienced, competent, or knowledgeable as their chief, and others fall into line. Once a leader is established among some portion of a population, others are likely to acknowledge his authority as well, particularly if his leadership is perceived as effective. As the Mohists describe the transition to political society, political authority need not rest on people's explicit consent, as expressed in a contract, for example. But clearly it is established by either their choice of or at least their tacit cooperation with a ruler they expect will unify norms and achieve good order. Once the superior-subordinate relation has been established, members of the community share a basis for converging on unified norms: they do so by identifying with and conforming to the leadership.

At the same time, however, the Mohists' hypothetical picture implicitly presents an alternative to their explicit stance that norms can be unified only if people identify upward with political authority. People in the Mohist state of nature ultimately do manage to step back from normative anarchy, recognize the cause of their predicament, and converge in following a charismatic leader. That they can spontaneously cooperate in these ways suggests the Mohists may have misidentified the actual basis for normative and epistemic consensus. The leader's role seems mainly that of a catalyst for agreement, not its source. A more fundamental explanation may be that, reacting to violent chaos induced by stubborn, universal disagreement, people begin to value consensus, and thus cooperation and coordination, more than they value their original conception of right. They come to appreciate community and unity and thus are prepared to identify with the emerging political hierarchy. What they can agree on—and thus justify to each other—begins to take priority over their personal, idiosyncratic convictions. Contrary to the Mohists' own claims, then, arguably their narrative of the exit from the state of nature implies that political authority is not the origin of consensus but its product. As we will see, this point is reinforced by their discussion of how normative and epistemic consensus are needed to sustain authority and how they can persist even in a community that ceases to identify upward. That people identify upward may be a necessary condition for the legitimacy of political authority, but it may not be the fundamental explanation of how consensus and authority emerge.

Epistemic unity and social order

A crucial dimension of the hierarchical political society the Son of Heaven establishes is that conformity to the unified norms is encouraged through a system of incentives and disincentives. Conformity to the norms is rewarded and praised, as is reporting of others' good or bad conduct, recommending valuable resources to superiors, and remonstrating with superiors over their errors. Failure to conform, report, and recommend or remonstrate is punished and criticized. These rewards and punishments are dispensed through the rough equivalent of a civil service system plus a legal system. They may take various forms, including job appointments or dismissals, promotions or demotions, gifts or fines, criminal penalties, and public acclaim or condemnation. They are the leadership's primary levers of power, the means by which to encourage good conduct and sanction wrongdoing. The administration of rewards and punishments thus implements and embodies the shared norms that hold political society together. We can think of rewards and punishments as concrete outcomes of the social institutions that manage government administration, law enforcement, and criminal justice.

For this reason, the Mohists stress the importance of allocating rewards and punishments reliably and consistently in line with the unified norms, such that the common people endorse how they are administered. Failure to maintain the people's approval in dispensing rewards and punishments undermines the project of identifying upward and accordingly may cause political authority to lose legitimacy and social order to break down. The crucial role of rewards and punishments makes social epistemology pivotal to maintaining legitimate political authority. Rewards and punishments can embody unified norms only if members of society largely endorse how the leadership dispenses them, and this endorsement rests on lower and higher ranks of the political hierarchy agreeing in their understanding and assessment of the relevant facts.

This epistemological concern is reflected in the epigram at the head of this chapter, taken from the third version of "Identifying Upward." This version of the doctrine highlights the social epistemological issue of how to ensure that the leadership and the people below converge in judgments about the facts on the basis of which the unified norms are enforced. The text begins by claiming that the "task of the wise" is "to calculate what puts the state and the common people in order and do it" (13/1). What, then, brings order to the state and its people?

> If superiors in governing get the facts about subordinates, there is order; if they don't get the facts about subordinates, there is disorder. How do we know it is so? If superiors in governing get the facts about subordinates, then this is understanding what the people have done good or wrong. If they understand what the people have done good or wrong, they get hold of good people and reward them and get hold of vicious people and punish them. If good people are rewarded and vicious people punished, the state will surely be in order. (13/2–4)

The phrase rendered "the facts about subordinates" is semantically richer than the English translation suggests. *Qíng* 情, the word interpreted as "facts," implies a thorough grasp of the actual circumstances among the people, along with, perhaps, understanding and winning over their sentiments, as *qíng* can also refer to feelings. The reference to what people have done good or wrong is also ambiguous. Besides good or wrong conduct, the phrasing could be interpreted as referring to what people *judge* to be good or wrong.

Either way, the gist is that those in power must genuinely understand circumstances among the people, so that they can ensure rewards and punishments go to those who indeed merit them. In the third version of "Identifying Upward," this is the focal issue by which the need for unified norms is introduced. Only if leaders can govern by getting people to identify upward with unified norms, claims the text, is it possible for them to reliably understand the conditions among those below (13/7). In this version of the doctrine, the concrete practice of identifying upward primarily concerns reporting to superiors at the level of the clan, state, and realm any conduct that displays either care for and benefit to the community or disregard for and harm to them (see, e.g., 13/23–25). Care and benefit are treated as basic values—care being a standing disposition to engage in mutually beneficial interaction with others—and unifying the community's norms lies in encouraging everyone to communicate upward any conduct that manifests care and benefit or their opposites. Through this reporting, those in power "get the facts" about those below and can reward or punish the right people.

The dimension of identifying upward stressed here, then, is epistemic: people not only share the norms of caring about and benefiting society but identify with the political hierarchy such that they report the information leaders need to encourage and enforce conformity to these norms. The result is that lower and higher levels of the hierarchy agree in their grasp of the facts on the basis of which authority is exercised and, accordingly, on the appropriateness of rewards and punishments. Epistemic unity—shared knowledge of the relevant facts—is treated as a condition for political unity, social stability, and the appropriate functioning of the civil service and legal system.[6] Through the political hierarchy, members of society share norms of judgment, cooperate in exchanging information, and accordingly reach consensus about facts relevant to political administration, including the allocation of rewards and punishments. When the system functions effectively, the Mohists claim, leaders' epistemic acuity becomes nearly godlike. They quickly learn of worthy or criminal conduct, problems to solve, and resources to use even at great remove, almost as if they were omniscient, because everyone assists them in passing information up through the hierarchy (12/61–69).[7]

An intriguing consequence of the social epistemological dimension of identifying upward is that the need for epistemic unity constrains the norms that the Son of Heaven can impose on society. The norms cannot be arbitrary or formulated only to serve only his own interests, for they must attract the ongoing endorsement and cooperation of the people—as, the Mohists think, norms such as caring about and benefiting the community will. Rulers must be publicly perceived to act in ways the people below agree are appropriate. For the ruler's norms to function effectively in maintaining political unity and social order, those below must agree with those above concerning their content and implementation, drawing on a shared grasp of the relevant facts.

How political legitimacy can collapse

What happens if those in power fail to maintain the needed normative and epistemic consensus? For example, what if they abuse their position by governing mainly for their own and their cronies' benefit, such that their subjects turn against them?

As we have seen, the Mohists hold that in the state of nature political authority is needed to bestow authoritative status on society's shared norms. Once political society is up and running, however, they seem to think the situation changes. If leaders fail to implement the norms that sustain political society in ways publicly perceived as appropriate, the norms can escape the leadership's grasp and work as a unifying force directly among the people themselves. People may rally together around norms that have become detached from the political hierarchy, answering to each other rather than to their superiors. They "ally together below," as the Mohists put it, rather than identifying upward. Society's unified norms break down, as there are now at least two competing sets of norms, those of the leadership and those of the people. Accordingly, those in power lose legitimacy, as they now fail to achieve the basic end for which they were entrusted with authority, unifying society's norms.

Mohist writings explicitly address such a scenario, claiming that unlike the sage-kings of old, who governed so as to promote benefit and eliminate harm to the people (12/51–52), rulers in their day govern for the sake of their cronies and relatives, appointing them to official positions just to enjoy high rank and salary (12/52–61). If leaders are not perceived to act for the benefit of the people, the Mohists predict, people will ally together in resistance, withhold information, and refuse to identify upward.

> The people know that the superiors don't really install government leaders to bring good order to the people. Hence they all ally together, concealing things, and none are willing to identify upward with their superiors. Thus superiors and subordinates have different norms. If superiors and subordinates have different norms, rewards and praise are not enough to encourage good, while punishments and penalties are not enough to discourage viciousness. (12/52–55)

A pivotal consequence of this breakdown in the unified norms is that the ruler's rewards and punishments lose their leverage over the people, since the community no longer endorses how he allocates them (12/55–61, 13/17–22). The people allied together below may condemn those the ruler praises while praising those he punishes. Ultimately, the Mohists contend, people respect the approval or disapproval of their peers in the community more than rewards or punishments from a ruler whose norms the community rejects. As they see it, people will not obey leaders who are unable to unify the norms of the community.

> If superiors and subordinates have different norms, those the superiors reward are those the community condemns. It's said, people dwell together in communities. If people are condemned in the community, then even supposing they are rewarded by superiors, this isn't enough to encourage them…If people are praised in the community, then even supposing they are punished by superiors, this isn't enough to discourage them. (12/56–59)

If the community comes to reject their superiors' norms in this way, the political system fails, as rewards and punishments—the main levers of power—lose their effectiveness in maintaining social order. Society reverts to a state of nature, without a functioning government.

> If one is established to govern a state and to act as the people's government leader, yet one's rewards and praise are not enough to encourage good, while one's punishments and penalties are not enough to discourage viciousness, then isn't this the same as… when people first arose, before there were government leaders? (12/59–61)

Political authority is justified by its effectiveness in leading people to identify upward with the unifying norms of political society and so achieve good social order. If people cease to do so because they reject the leaders' norms, this justification collapses, and the ruler's claim to legitimate authority disintegrates.

By implication, then, the Mohists take consensus about the appropriateness of political appointments and the allocation of rewards and punishments to be a necessary condition for political legitimacy. Fully understood, identifying upward requires consensus not just about abstract norms but about the concrete application of the norms, which draws, in turn, on consensus concerning the pertinent facts, as communicated through the political hierarchy. If the people below disagree enough with their superiors about the facts that they regularly dispute how rewards and punishments are administered, normative unity is lost. Even supposing rulers pay lip service to norms the people endorse, if they ignore relevant facts or interpret them differently from the community, in practice they are following disparate norms, which the community may reject. A shared understanding of the facts is necessary for shared observance of the unified norms.

Consensus and institutions

The Mohists tie the legitimacy of political authority to consensus in norms and judgments manifested through identification upward with the political hierarchy. The conception of consensus in play relates to political epistemology along two dimensions. One is that the effective, legitimate implementation of political authority requires a shared, society-wide commitment to some body of norms as authoritative—including epistemic norms, or norms of correct judgment and assertion. The other is that to preserve legitimacy, the hierarchical political system must maintain epistemic consensus. If different ranks in the hierarchy do not agree on the facts and how they pertain to the implementation of society's norms, the normative unity needed to sustain social order and justify political authority may collapse.

The two dimensions are interdependent. Without shared norms, epistemic consensus cannot exist. But if epistemic consensus is not sustained and manifested through implementation of the norms—specifically, by allocating rewards and punishments in a manner the community approves—people cease to identify upward, and the unified norms break down.

Mohist texts seem to assume that the scope of the norms with which people are to identify is comprehensive, covering all areas of life. They do not distinguish a sphere of private life, within which disagreement about values might be tolerated, from public life as members of a polity. They appear to have no notion of reasonable disagreement in political life, and accordingly no conception of politics as a field in which distinct parties advocate diverse values or negotiate different positions about the priority or interpretation of shared values. They share a common traditional Chinese view that the very existence of factions or parties in political society reflects moral failure, either in the leadership or in those who form factions. Competent, virtuous leaders inspire unity, not factionalism; worthy people do what is right, about which there should be little debate. Society should be organized around a comprehensive conception of the *dào* (way)—the correct way of personal, social, and political life—about which all right-thinking people should agree.

The assumption that political society should be organized on the basis of norms embodying a comprehensive conception of the good might appear to render the doctrine of identifying upward irrelevant to our concerns today, since reasonable disagreement about the good seems a salient, ineluctable feature of modern political life. But the feature of their position the Mohists themselves especially emphasize is directly relevant to our discursive and political context. As we have seen, they regard consensus as vital particularly because of its role in underwriting the allocation of rewards and punishments. To appreciate the significance of this view, we need to recognize that Mohist references to rewards and punishments amount to shorthand for the functioning of government institutions such as the civil service and the legal system. The point the Mohists highlight, then, is that such institutions can function effectively only if a consensus obtains across society that they operate according to popularly endorsed norms. Without such a consensus, people may withdraw their support for the political system, because its institutions regularly produce outcomes that defy their view of what is right. Importantly, the consensus must cover not only norms but the facts on the basis of which the norms are applied. Widespread disagreement about the facts, especially between the authorities and the people they govern, subverts identification with the system. If people conclude that their government regularly fails to "get the facts" about the community and respond to them appropriately, they will cease to identify upward, causing the political system to lose legitimacy.

Of course, in our ethical and political climate, the consensus that underlies a stable political society is not expected to be comprehensive, and divergence between disparate conceptions of the good is common. But the Mohists nevertheless offer us a crucial lesson: a prerequisite for a flourishing political society—even a liberal, pluralist one—is a broad, stable consensus that core social and political institutions conform to shared norms. A heterogeneous political society that embraces diverse conceptions of the good can do so only against a backdrop of broad public endorsement of the norms embodied by its institutions and approval of how these institutions respond to the facts.[8]

Conclusion

The Mohist doctrine of identifying upward underscores the vital role of social epistemology in justifying or undermining the legitimacy of political authority. The Mohists hold that legitimate authority and a stable social order can be sustained only if members of a political society identify with its leadership, sharing with them a consensus concerning the norms by which to organize social and political life. People will continue to identify upward, the Mohists think, as long as they agree that society's institutions implement shared norms reliably in line with socially acknowledged facts. Conversely, if disagreement arises concerning either the norms or how effectively institutions implement them, the legitimacy of the political system suffers accordingly. If the disagreement is severe, the system may fail entirely.[9]

Notes

1 For an extended discussion of Mohist thought, see Fraser (2016). For briefer overviews, see Fraser (2002), Loy (2007), Lai (2008), or Van Norden (2007). On political theory, see also Hansen (1992) and Van Norden (2007). On epistemology, see Loy (2008). On Mohist ethics, see especially Robins (2012).

2 This summary is based on *Mòzǐ* 11/1–25 and 12/1–41. Citations to *Mòzǐ* give chapter and line numbers in Hung (1956), by which the corresponding passages can be found in Fraser (2020) or on line at the Chinese Text Project, D. Sturgeon, ed. (https://ctext.org/mozi), using the search tool at https://ctext.org/tools/concordance.

3 This conceptual relationship extends to Mohist epistemic standards such as Heaven's intention (27/73) or the "three models" (35/7), I suggest. Heaven's epistemic and moral authority are inseparable from its political authority (Fraser 2016, pp. 84, 120), and the "three models" rest on the political authority of Heaven and the sage-kings.

4 I use "epistemic" and "epistemological" here for issues related to the grounds for, assessment of, and agreement regarding judgment and assertion and thus knowledge.

5 See, e.g., 35/1–10. For discussion, see Fraser (2016, pp. 62–69).

6 For a contemporary exploration of how epistemic norms contribute to a properly functioning polity, see the chapter by Fabienne Peter in Part 6 of this volume.

7 On the potential epistemic merits of certain forms of government, see the chapters by Helene Landemore and Robert Talisse in Part 6 of this volume.
8 It may be instructive to compare the Mohist stance with the treatment of reasonable disagreement in contemporary liberal political theory. See the chapters by Richard Rowland, Rob Simpson, and Elizabeth Edenberg in Part 2 of this volume.
9 I thank Eric Schliesser for a thoughtful discussion that influenced this chapter and the editors and an anonymous reader for comments that improved it.

References

Fraser, C., (2002). Mohism. *Stanford Encyclopedia of Philosophy*. <https://plato.stanford.edu/entries/mohism/>

Fraser, C., (2016). *The Philosophy of the Mozi: The First Consequentialists*. New York: Columbia University Press.

Fraser, C., (2020). *The Essential Mozi*. Oxford: Oxford University Press.

Hansen, C., (1992). *A Daoist Theory of Chinese Thought*. New York: Oxford University Press.

Hung, W., (1956). *A Concordance to Mo Tzu*, Harvard-Yenching Institute Sinological Index Series, Supplement no. 21. Cambridge, MA: Harvard University Press.

Lai, K., (2008). *An Introduction to Chinese Philosophy*. Cambridge: Cambridge University Press.

Loy, H., (2007). Mozi (Mo-tzu, c. 400s—300s BCE). *The Internet Encyclopedia of Philosophy*. <https://www.iep.utm.edu/mozi/>

Loy, H., (2008). Justification and debate: thoughts on Moist moral epistemology. *Journal of Chinese Philosophy*. **35**(3), 455–71.

Robins, D., (2012). Mohist care. *Philosophy East & West*. **62**(1), 60–91.

Van Norden, B., (2007). *Virtue Ethics and Consequentialism in Early Chinese Philosophy*. Cambridge: Cambridge University Press.

3

EPISTEMOLOGY AND POLITICS IN ISLAMIC PHILOSOPHY

Anthony Booth

1 Introduction

'Islamic Philosophy', for me, denotes any philosophy that in some way or another engages with the religion of Islam. Islamic Philosophy thus conceived has an old history – beginning at the time of the Prophet Muhammad and continuing on to the present. That's some 1,400 years of thought! Further, relevant to a volume on Political Epistemology, one of the central things about the Prophet Muhammad for Muslims is that he was the antecedent for the role of 'Caliph' – which roughly translates as 'viceregent of God on Earth'. In the concept of a Caliph we see the roles of political and religious leadership inexorably bound. This means that any philosophy which aims to engage with Islam must in some way address a political question.[1] Moreover, the centrality of the role of Prophecy within Islam also raises some essentially epistemological questions: how can we verify genuine Prophecy?[2] What is the difference between the epistemic state of people prior to, and after, receiving the Prophecy (in the Koran, the time preceding the Koranic revelation is referred to as al-*Jāhilīyah* – meaning 'ignorance')? It is therefore not an exaggeration to say that political epistemology is of central importance to all of Islamic Philosophy.

Unfortunately it will be impossible for me to address but a small portion of it. I will focus on two of the most prolific philosophical movements: (i) the school of Falsafa[3] as it was practised in what is sometimes called the 'classical' period of Islamic Philosophy; (ii) the 'Modernist' Movement which arouse in the late nineteenth century and was arguably the progenitor of modern-day 'Political Islam'. I will focus on an epistemological thesis that I believe to be found in both schools of thought: Islamic Moderate Evidentialism (the thesis that while only evidence can give you reason to believe any proposition, some people are exempt from this). I will argue that this (broadly speaking) epistemological thesis leads to a unique political position where the following two things are espoused: A form of Anarcho-Socialism, and a Perfectionist Liberal Account of Political Legitimacy. (Anarcho-Socialism being, roughly, the idea that there should be no state with a monopoly of legitimate violence[4]; a Perfectionist Liberal account of Political Legitimacy is one according to which Liberalism is not justified as a means through which to navigate political disagreement, but rather in its upholding of liberal values[5]).

The central issue of verifying Prophecy is taken up by some of the very first philosophical and theological schools of Islam,[6] who end up endorsing a thesis known as Evidentialism: the thesis that evidence (or 'epistemic reason') solely determines what one ought to believe.[7] I will address Evidentialism within Islam in the next section (2). However, Evidentialism has some serious problems from within an Islamic perspective: most notably the problem of respecting the epistemic uniqueness of Prophecy. I address this problem together with the proposed solution to it as developed by *Falsafa* – Islamic Moderate Evidentialism – in Section 3. In Section 4, I show the political implications of this theory, and how it explains why the Prophet is the ideal political leader. I then move, in Section 5, to discuss the Islamic Modernist Reform movement, and how some of its members married up the thesis of Islamic Moderate Evidentialism with certain Marxist ideas. In Section 6, I discuss how this leads to a Perfectionist Liberal Account of Political Legitimacy, and in Section 7 how it leads to a form of Anarcho-Socialism.

2 Evidentialism and proof of prophecy

Islam is a religion of Prophecy. Its central religious text – the Koran – was revealed to Muhammad via the Angel Gabriel, and is considered to be the unadulterated word of God. The Muslim declaration of faith – the *al-šahāda* – is that 'there is no God but God, and Muhammad is the Messenger of God'. A very natural question that arises from this is: how are we, non-Prophets, to know that Muhammad's message is the genuine word of God? According to the Mutazilite theological tradition what you are required to believe cannot not depend on what tribe you happen to belong to. All people are simply required to believe one thing: the truth. This then gives us an answer as to how to discern the true from the false prophet: verisimilitude. The genuine Prophet's message will accord with the truth, and the false prophet's will not. This, in turn, accords well with the idea that the Prophet's role is a political one, since faith is not then considered a matter for the private sphere, but rather an obligation toward something public: the evidence.

This line of thought is taken up by the inaugurator of the tradition of Philosophy known as *Falsafa* (an Arabized word for the Greek *philosophia*): al-Kindi (c. 801–73). In his work – *On First Philosophy* – he famously writes:

> We ought not be ashamed of appreciating the truth and of acquiring it wherever it comes from, /even if it comes from races distant and nations different from ours. For the seeker of truth nothing takes precedence over the truth, and there is no disparagement of the truth, nor belittling either of him who speaks it or of him who conveys it. (The status of) no one is diminished by the truth; rather does the truth ennoble all. (Al-Kindi *On First Philosophy*, p. 58)[8]

Here, al-Kindi is referencing Greek Philosophy, which had come into the Islamic purview when the Islamic Empire conquered such places as Alexandria. Al-Kindi is here arguing in favour of Muslims studying Greek Philosophy. The argument is premised on epistemic value monism: only the truth is of epistemic value, or is at least of most epistemic value. But more than that, it is premised on the idea that considerations about the truth trump all other considerations when it comes to the question of what we ought to believe ('nothing takes precedence over the truth'). This looks like an endorsement of what is sometimes in contemporary epistemology called 'Evidentialism'[9] – the thesis that there can be no non-epistemic reasons for belief. Put differently, only considerations relevant to whether p is true can settle the normative question of whether you should believe that p.

This view, or something close to it, is sometimes called 'rationalism' in the context of discussing the Mutazilites and al-Kindi.[10] The thought being that for both, Islam was a religion that was to be believed on the ordinances of *reason* and not of faith or blind obedience. I prefer the term 'Evidentialism', however, to set it apart from the issue that was also relevant in this period of Islamic Philosophy as to whether experience was required for knowledge, or if we can know things (or how much we can know) a priori. Evidentialism gives us an answer to the question of how to discern genuine Prophecy. The genuine Prophet, like the genuine expert, speaks the truth, and we can test that against public evidence. This, however, seems to assume then that expertise and Prophecy contain no 'esoteric' knowledge (knowledge that can only be gained by consulting those sources) on pain of reneging on the claim that there is an independent, public test to be had. But of course that raises the question: do we really need Prophecy and experts when we can directly consult the evidence? Evidentialism seems to have a problem, then, with respecting what we can call the epistemic uniqueness of Prophecy – the idea that there are esoteric truths within Prophecy that could not be learned other than by consulting it.

3 Islamic Moderate Evidentialism

By far the most well known of the philosophers of the classical period, following al-Kindi, were al-Farabi (872–950), Ibn Sina (980–1037), and Ibn Rushd (1126–1198). All three of these thinkers endorse versions of a modulated form of Evidentialism, which we can call Islamic Moderate Evidentialism. The celebrated Christian philosopher St. Thomas Aquinas also held a version of Moderate Evidentialism. The way that he moderates Evidentialism is to restrict those propositions to which Evidentialism applies. We can thus formulate a very loosely 'Western' (for ease of exposition) version of Moderate Evidentialism:

Western Moderate Evidentialism: For *all* subjects S and *most* propositions p, only epistemic reasons justify S's belief that p.

Put differently, beliefs in some propositions can be justified by non-epistemic reasons. For example, such propositions, according to Aquinas, as that God is Triune, or propositions about the afterlife – propositions the truth of which (out of principle) can never be settled by the totality of our evidence. To put this back in terms of the issue regarding the epistemic uniqueness of Prophecy: that God is Triune cannot be learned simply by considering the world – we must look to the Christian Bible to learn this.[11] But while this does mean that belief in such matters cannot go *against* our evidence (hence why for Aquinas there can be harmony between 'reason and faith') it cannot be independently verified. So insofar as Prophecy is esoteric, it is impossible for us to discern real Prophecy. The solution to this issue proposed by the Falasifa (al-Farabi, Avicenna, and Averroes) is slightly different from 'Aquinas'. They propose that Evidentialism be moderated not by restricting which propositions it applies to, but by restricting which *subjects* it applies to. We can formulate the position like this:

Islamic Moderate Evidentialism: For *some* subjects S and *all* propositions p, only epistemic reasons justify S's belief that p.

Put differently, only a certain group of people should believe on the basis of truth alone. It is solely appropriate for a cognitive elect, or epistemic elite, to believe just on the basis of epistemic reason. The rest of us are unable to use only reason to come to the beliefs that we need to have, so we can have beliefs that are justified for reasons unrelated to truth. Thus, Prophecy has a unique epistemic purpose: to teach members of the public what they could not have learned had they attempted to use reason alone (perhaps through the use of similes and metaphors which are not strictly true). But at the same time contains nothing that cannot be independently verified.

That rough characterisation of the Falasifa's epistemological position does, of course, raise a number of questions. For instance, if everything that is in Prophecy can be independently verified against our evidence can there really be anything esoteric within Prophecy? If the metaphors contained with it are approximations of *truths* then why cannot there be other approximations or metaphors that will lead people to believe those truths than those contained in Prophecy? If they are the only effective metaphors, then that itself will have to be independently ascertained, so not esoteric after all.

There are nuances in all of the positions of the respective Falasifa that address this. Unfortunately, I will not be able to detail them all here. But I think it is worth saying a bit more about the nuances in al-Farabi's position, since I think they have a very direct relevance for political epistemology (his account of knowledge has a direct bearing on what he thinks should be political leadership). For al-Farabi, the difference between the Prophet's knowledge and our knowledge does not have to do with which propositions we know. Rather, it is the *manner* in which propositions are known that is important. Truth is not the only epistemic value. For al-Farabi, what makes the Prophet epistemically special is that he is able to grasp, or directly intuit, many or all of the *a priori* truths of the world at once, where most of us can at must have an intellectual intuition of such truths one at a time.[12] Try, for example, having the intellectual intuition regarding the law of non-contradiction *together* with the intuition that everything is self-identical! He can do this, explains, al-Farabi due to an enhanced power of the imagination, and because he can then see these truths together, he can see their intimate connection.[13] He thus *understands* the very same truths that can be grasped individually by anyone, but does so much more deeply. It is this wholesale understanding that is esoteric – the individual propositions that are believed by both us and the Prophet can thus be considered verifiable against public evidence without negating the epistemic uniqueness of Prophecy. And, further, it is because the Prophet has these special abilities regarding the understanding that he has a special *rhetorical* ability: he knows how to explain one truth in terms of another. This, in turn, gives him a distinctly political role.

4 The prophet law-maker

Islamic Moderate Evidentialism, then, constitutes what is a unique position in political epistemology. One of the central questions of contemporary political and social epistemology has been about our trust in experts: which ones should be trust? This is a structurally similar question to the one al-Farabi was asking: who among those who call themselves a 'prophet' should we trust? And how do we know the answer to this without putting into question the need for Prophets or experts? In his seminal paper in contemporary political/social epistemology Alvin Goldman calls the issue related to the last question, the 'Expert-Novice problem' (Goldman 2001, p. 96) – how can we, the novices, come to recognise genuine expertise without having to become experts ourselves? According to Goldman, one way in which we might come to recognise an expert is through their rhetorical and dialectical flourish – their testament makes sense to us, they are able to explain the things about which they have expertise. But the obvious objection involves wondering whether one can have knowledge about something and yet be absolutely terrible at explaining it. Or, alternatively, wondering whether someone could be very good at making things seem like they make sense, when in fact they have very little knowledge about the thing they are trying to explain. I'm sure we have all met successful blaggers! There seems to be no principled connection between knowledge that p and the ability to successfully explain p to novices.

Now, because al-Farabi is dealing with Prophecy here, not mere expertise, he has an answer to the correlated question: the Prophet not only has perfect knowledge, but perfect *understanding* – he can see how everything is connected since he sees all the a priori truths *at once*. Indeed, his perfected knowledge (only he can attain the highest level of certainty) is a *function* of his perfected understanding. And this gives him perfect rhetorical and dialectical abilities because he understands, say, how the intricate rules of geometry are related to what you had for breakfast. Thus, if you were ever engaged with a genuine Prophet, it would be impossible for you not to be persuaded by him: in the idealised state of the Prophet, rhetorical and theoretical ability or virtue then fundamentally come together. And the same is true for practical virtue: because the Prophet knows how everything is connected, he knows better than anyone else how to realise the ideal.

As I mentioned, this, for al-Farabi, gives the Prophet a uniquely political role. This is in part developed from Plato's *Republic*. The Falsafa movement was very much concerned with understanding Greek Philosophy, incorporating and seeking to harmonise it with the central tenets of Islam. In the *Republic*, Plato had proposed a tripartite theory of state that mirrored the tripartite division of the human soul. Where the individual human soul comprises an appetitive, a spirited, and a rational element, the city state comprises, correspondingly, workers (appetitive), guardians (spirited), and Philosopher Kings (rational). The individual human soul finds happiness when its various divisions work in harmony, a harmony which can only be guaranteed when the rational element of the soul governs the rest. Likewise then, for Plato, the flourishing city state, or human collective, can only be guaranteed when the theoreticians – the Philosophers – are in charge. But, Plato also tells us in the *Republic* that the harmony can be guaranteed only if the Philosophers invent 'noble lies' – metaphors for people to more easily grasp the truth about why the state is organised as it is, but nonetheless at most only approximate the truth. Al-Farabi's critique of Plato then is to wonder whether those with theoretical knowledge *alone* are the best people to dispatch these noble myths, which surely requires dialectic and rhetoric skill to be done effectively. This is why the Prophet is a better political ruler than those who have mastered Philosophy alone, since the Prophet's perfection is a composite of both practical-rhetorical and theoretical virtue. That is, he is at once both a Philosopher and a Rhetorician – perfectly made for keeping the divisions of the state in harmony. But as others have argued (see Khalidi 2001) the final political question for al-Farabi was about what we should do, given what we have learned about the idealised state, when we find ourselves in less than ideal conditions (i.e. in the aftermath of the death of the Prophet Muhammad). That al-Farabi does not see theoretical knowledge as the governing modality I think has important implications with respect to his overall stance on Political Legitimacy, as we will discuss in Sections 6 and 7.

5 Islamic modernism and neo-Marxism

At the time of the late nineteenth century, the Ottoman Turks still controlled the Islamic Empire. But the Ottoman Empire was thought to have gone into serious decline. The Islamic Modernist Reform movement arose in response to the perceived need to 'modernise' the Islamic world out of this predicament. However, key thinkers of the movement such as Jamal al-Din al-Afghani (1838–1897) and Mohammad Abduh (1849–1905) thought that in order to properly reform, the Islamic world needed to recover its past. It was to modernise by turning back, and recovering the Evidentialist impulses seen in the Mutazilite and Falsafa traditions (for discussion see Kedourie 2014). They felt that the West not only had colonised territorially, but also intellectually. That the ideas of Evidentialism had been taken to the West from Islamic thought, unacknowledged, and they had allowed the West to flourish, embracing Liberalism and Science. Here is Muhammad Abduh, for example:

> The religious leaders of the West successfully aroused their people to make havoc of the eastern world and to seize the sovereignty over those nations on what they believed to be their prescriptive right to tyrannize over masses of men...but...they found freedom in a religion where knowledge, law and art could be possessed with entire certitude. They discovered that liberty of thought and breadth of knowledge were means to faith and not its foes...Then it was that the nations of Europe began to throw off their bondage and reform their condition, re-ordering the affairs of their life in a manner akin to the message of Islam. (Abduh 2006, p. 22)

The Islamic Modernist movement paved the way for what we today call 'Political Islam', and especially the Muslim Brotherhood (founded by Hassan al-Banna in 1928). It very much set up the discourse whereby the Muslim world was to make progress by going backward, reclaiming the 'true' Islam. A very important thinker within the Muslim Brotherhood was Saayid Qutb (1906–1966).[14] His political philosophy and epistemology is really a marriage of the Islamic Moderate Evidentialism of the Falasifa and some Marxist ideas, which are given a Muslim spin.

From Islamic Moderate Evidentialism, Qutb gets the idea that there is an intellectual elite who will need to dispatch 'noble myths' in order to keep the public together. And, from Marx, he gets the idea of ideology, and, especially from Lenin, the idea of a vanguard that needs to lead the masses. Also from Lenin, he gets the idea of a distinction between positive and negative ideology. 'Ideology' in the Marxist tradition denotes something more like 'propaganda' (see Stanley 2015). 'Negative Ideology' is propaganda used by a ruling minority to subjugate the masses, where 'Positive Ideology' is propaganda used by a 'vanguard' who have seen through the negative ideology in order to combat it.

Of course, because ideology is most effective when the fact that it is propaganda is concealed, the masses in the grip of ideology will not know that they are in its grip – 'ideology is self-deception' (Geuss 1984, p. 12). Thus, like with Islamic Moderate Evidentialism, Leninist thought has it that rational arguments will be ineffective in defeating the negative ideology, and hence, we need 'positive ideology' – or, put differently, noble myths. Qutb uses the Koranic term for ignorance – *Jāhilīyah* – to describe what he identifies as the state the majority of Muslims found themselves in: in denial. They think they are living in Muslim countries, but really they are living under puppet regimes designed to promulgate Western Capitalism (worship material things, above the spiritual) and imperial ambition (cultural, economic, territorial). And he thinks that the epistemic elite, i.e. an *ulama*[15] serving the role of the vanguard for Lenin, will see through this state of *Jāhilīyah* combatting it through the use of positive ideology. Thus, we get a bringing together of the Modernist Reform movement, Islamic Moderate Evidentialism, and elements of Marxist thought – and so a revolutionary vision for Islam.

It is not too difficult to see how this revolutionary tenor would appeal to the likes of the more radical Islamists, such as those who formed what came to be known as *Al-Qaeda*: Osama Bin Laden and Ayman al-Zawahiri. They saw this as justification for terrorist acts, especially in the first instance within Muslim countries: putative leaders and the people living under them might claim to be Muslim, but since they are under the spell of *Jāhilīyah* they are not. This makes them apostates in their eyes, and so (according to a precedent in Islamic law) were deserving of the death penalty.[16] Further, it would take much more than rational argument to break them out of *Jāhilīyah* – they needed, instead, to receive a huge shock that would come from terrorist action. Having noted this, I think it is important also to note that while his thought contains revolutionary Marxist elements, it also contains aspects, via Islamic Moderate Evidentialism, that resemble Modern Liberalism. I move to discuss those in the next section.

6 Islamic political legitimacy and perfectionist liberalism

The issue of when a state has political *legitimacy* is currently enjoying a lot of attention within contemporary political philosophy.[17] One popular answer is that a state rules legitimately just in case it rules with the consent of the people it rules over. I think this is broad answer preferred by the so-called 'anti-Perfectionist' Liberals (e.g. Quong 2010). The obvious objection to this involves worrying whether a state is really a legitimate one when the people's consent is unjust. Thus, the broad alternative line – that you find in 'Perfectionist' Liberalism – is to say that what is needed for political legitimacy is not mere consent, but correct *belief*. That is, there are facts of the matter that determine whether a polity acts in line with justice or not. A legitimate state is one that gets us to act in accordance with those facts – or at least more so than had the state not wielded coercive power over us (see Raz 1986). This looks like the Islamic Moderate Evidentialist line on political legitimacy: there are truths about what determines a just polity. A legitimate state is one that governs in such a way to ensure that the various components of the polity are acting as harmoniously as possible. But in order to do this it needs the populace not only to go along with what the government is doing (consent) but to some degree understand why they are doing what they are doing (belief). Thus, not only does the state need to get the people to act in a manner more akin with Justice, it also needs to get them to believe things that are as close to the truth as possible. In other words, it needs to make use of noble lies and positive-sense ideology.

However, for the contemporary Perfectionist Liberal, the independent truths about justice will involve truths about civil liberties: a truly just state, for instance, will be one that guarantees freedom of belief and expression. In the classical view from Islamic Moderate Evidentialism, the truths of justice, as we have presented them here, involve only harmony between different parts of the polity, and seem silent on the issue of civil liberties. Nevertheless, I think that on the Islamic Moderate Evidentialist picture, the fact that the Prophet stands in place for the Philosopher Kings has implications that address the issue of civil liberties. And, certainly for Qutb, an Islamic state is one that is meant to guaranteed liberties like freedom of belief:

> [Islam] strives from the beginning to abolish all those systems and governments which are based on the rule of man over men and the servitude of one human being to another. When Islam releases people from this political pressure and presents to them its spiritual message, appealing to their reason, it gives them complete freedom to accept or not to accept its beliefs…in an Islamic system there is room for all kinds of people to follow their own beliefs, while obeying the laws of the country which are themselves based on the Divine authority. (Qutb 2006, p. 61)

This line of thought is vindicated for Qutb, I think, by the fact that the Koran explicitly tells us that 'There is no compulsion in religion' (Koran 2:256). Thus, Qutb can think that Islam mandates complete freedom of belief despite saying that the laws of any given polity *must* be based on 'the Divine Authority', since a system of laws based on Islam will be one that mandates freedom of belief. It is meant to be a fact, then, that there can be no just society where this human right is not enshrined. As such the view looks very much like a kind of Perfectionist Liberalism. Is this view anti-democratic, however? If the truth is ultimately what generates proper political authority, then what status does popular will and opinion have with respect to the running of a legitimate government? We will address this question in the following section.

7 Graded knowledge and Anarcho-Socialism

A thinker who is often put together with Qutb, as a radical, Islamist political thinker is the Pakistani philosopher Abul A'la Maududi (1903–1979). He addresses, head-on, the issue of how Perfectionism, and especially theological variant of Perfectionism, is compatible with democracy. For example, he says:

> What distinguished Islamic democracy from Western democracy is that while the latter is based on the concept of popular sovereignty the former rests on the principle of popular *Khilafat*. In Western democracy the people are sovereign, in Islam sovereignty is vested in God…[the people] have to follow and obey the laws given by God through his Prophet. (Maududi 1950, p. 16)

What Maududi means by the claim that Western democracy is 'based on the concept of popular sovereignty' is that it is not the truth about justice for Western democracy that grants legitimacy, but the people's will, independent of the truth. This is an idea familiar with anti-perfectionist conceptions of political legitimacy – that because there can be reasonable disagreement regarding the truth about justice (cf. Rawls 1993) only *consensus* can ground legitimate governance, and democracy measures consensus. Conversely, an Islamic Democracy for Maududi is based on the Popular Khilafat – the people are God's deputies to enact His will on Earth. Democracy is an instrument to ensuring that society is a just one, it is not the end in itself by which we measure whether a society is a just one.

But how does the idea of a Popular Khilafat, or a 'Caplihate of Man' (as Andrew March has recently called it) fit together with the political epistemology of Islamic Moderate Evidentialism, according to which the masses and an epistemic elite have divergent statuses? Is not Islamic Moderate Evidentialism really a kind of elitism, rather than a view that mandates democracy? In response, I think we can first wonder whether the impulse to *inform* the public as best one can is not in fact actually a democratic impulse, enabling not just mere consent, but informed consent. Second, we have left it under-specified up to now who the elites are meant to be. While it is tempting to assume that thinkers such as al-Farabi would be naturally inclined to conceive the elite as the *ulama*, I think that would be partially a mistake, at least in the case of al-Farabi. In an essay – *The Conditions of Certainty* – he outlines various grades of knowledge one can have.[18] One can interpret al-Farabi in that essay as saying that only the Prophet's state of knowledge can involve perfect certainty, and, as such, for everyone else, the *ulama* included, there will need to be partially non-epistemic justification for belief. That is, even the beliefs of the most intellectually gifted among us will be in some sense approximations to the truth.

If we put that together with the idea that the Prophet, and not the Philosopher Kings, is the ideal political leader, we get in a position to see the accord with democracy. As Khalidi has persuasively argued (Khalidi 2003) the important political question for al-Farabi concerns how we organize ourselves politically in the absence of a Prophet. Given that the Prophet's perfected state of certainty is an amalgam of both theoretical and practical virtues, and that only the Prophet can achieve this state, neither the philosophers nor the non-philosophers can singularly assume the political role of the Prophet. Thus, in the absence of a Prophet the various parts of the state will need to come together of their own accord in order to be virtuous and sit in harmony. No person, group or institution can engender that harmony for them. This is akin to saying that there really should be no government at all (hence Anarcho-Socialism) – and that is really the force of the 'Popular Khalifat' that Maududi talks about. As Andrew March puts it in his recent, influential book:

> God is the principal agent and actor, and the first response of the people-as-deputy is a passive and receptive one. But the force of God dignifying mankind as His caliph is that He has deputized no one else in between God and man – no kings, no priests, no scholars. (March 2019, p. xviii)

8 Conclusion

I hope I have shown then that the epistemology of the 'Classical' Islamic Philosophers – Islamic Moderate Evidentialism – leads to a unique political position where both Perfectionist Liberal thought and Anarcho-Socialism sit together side by side. I do not know of any contemporary position quite like it, and it deserves the attention of those engaged in political epistemology.[19]

Notes

1 For a good statement of this view see Akhtar (2011).
2 This is made more all the more of a pressing question in (especially Sunni) Islam due to the fact that Muslims are enjoined not just to follow the Prophecy as revealed to Muhammed in the Koran, but to follow the practises and teachings of the Prophet, collected by others in *Hadith* – and it was important when these were being collected that they be authenticated. For an excellent account discussion of this issue see Griffel (2004).
3 *Falsafa* is the generic Arabic word for 'Philosophy', but it also specifically refers to the Classical Islamic Philosophy of the Medieval period. For a remarkable, quick introduction see Adamson (2015).
4 For discussion see Chomsky (2014).
5 See Raz (1986).
6 For good overviews see, among many, Black (2001) and Watt (1987).
7 For the kind of 'Evidentialism' I am here discussing see Shah (2006). In modern Epistemology and Philosophy of Religion, 'Evidentialism' denotes a subtly different view that is meant to distinguish it from so-called 'externalist' accounts of epistemic justification where, very roughly, one does not need to be aware of what one's justifiers are in order to be justified in believing a proposition (see Plantinga 2000). The version of 'evidentialism' I am talking about here is compatible with 'externalist' and 'internalist' accounts of justification.
8 This translation is from Ivry (1974). For an excellent book-length account of al-Kindi's thought, see Adamson (2007).
9 See Booth (2016).
10 See Watt (1987) for example.
11 Of course, we can learn that God is Triune by reading the Christian Bible. In this respect, the Bible on such matters can be thought to be giving us 'evidence'. But how do we know that this bit of the bible is genuine prophecy? We cannot test it against our *public* evidence (so we have to believe it by faith). It is this public notion of evidence that I denoting by the term 'evidence'.
12 See Booth (2016) for a defence of this interpretation.
13 Al-Farabi is also a Neo-Platonist, who sees an affinity between Islam and the Neo-Platonist Emanationist metaphysics, according to which the physical world is an emanation from the One. For an introduction to al-Farabi's thought, see Fakhry (2002). For a good selection of translated texts see Butterworth (2004).

14 See Khatab (2006) for a recent, illuminating study on Qutb.
15 Translates as 'the learned ones', they are, traditionally, the scholars and guardians of knowledge in Islam.
16 For discussion, see Saeed & Saeed (2004).
17 For an excellent introduction see Coicaud (2002).
18 See Black (2006) for a detailed commentary and almost complete translation.
19 With thanks to the two editors of this volume and an anonymous referee for extremely helpful comments on an earlier version of this chapter.

References

Abduh, M. 2006: "Islam, Reason, and Civilisation" in J.J. Donohue & J.H. Esposito (eds) *Islam in Transition: Muslim Perspectives* (New York: Oxford University Press).

Adamson, P. 2007: *Al-Kindī* (Oxford: Oxford University Press).

———. 2015: *Philosophy in the Islamic World: A Very Short Introduction* (Oxford: Oxford University Press).

Akhtar, S. 2011: *Islam as Political Religion: The Future of an Imperial Faith* (New York: Routledge).

Booth, A. 2016: *Islamic Philosophy and the Ethics of Belief* (London: Palgrave Macmillan).

Black, A. 2001: *The History of Islamic Political Thought* (Edinburgh: Edinburgh University Press).

Black, D. 2006: "Knowledge (*'ilm*) and Certitude (*yaqīn*) in al-Fārābī's Epistemology" *Arabic Sciences and Philosophy* **16.1** pp. 11–46.

Butterworth, C. 2004: *Alfarabi: The Political Writings* (translated and annotated by Charles Butterworth) (Ithaca, NY: Cornell University Press).

Chomsky, N. 2014: *On Anarchism* (London: Penguin).

Coicaud, J-M. 2012: *Legitimacy and Politics: A Contribution to the Study of Political Right and Political Responsibility* (Cambridge: Cambridge University Press).

Fakhry, M. 2002: *Al-Fārābī: Founder of Islamic Neoplatonism* (Oxford: One World).

Geuss, R. 1984: *The Idea of a Critical Theory: Habermas and the Frankfurt School* (Cambridge: Cambridge University Press).

Goldman, A. 2001: "Experts: Which Ones Should You Trust?" *Philosophy and Phenomenological Research* **63.1** pp. 85–110.

Griffel, F. 2004: "Al-Ġazālī's Concept of Prophecy: The Introduction of Avicennan Psychology into Aš'arite Theology," *Arabic Sciences and Philosophy* **14** pp. 101–44.

Ivry, A. 1974: *Al-Kindi's Metaphysics* (translation of *On First Philosophy*) (New York: SUNY Press).

Kahlidi, A. M. 2003: "Al-Fārābi on the Democratic City" *British Journal for the History of Philosophy* **11.3** pp. 379–94.

Kedourie, E. 2014: *Afghani and 'Abduh: An Essay on Religious Unbelief and Political Activism in Modern Islam* (London: Routledge).

Khatab, S. 2006: *The Power of Sovereignty: The Political and Ideological Philosophy of Sayyid Qutb* (London: Routledge).

March, A. 2019: *The Caliphate of Man: Popular Sovereignty in Modern Islamic Thought* (Cambridge, MA: Belknap Press, Harvard University Press).

Maududi, A. 1950: in K. Ahmed & K. Murad (eds) *The Islamic Way of Life* (U.K.I.M. Dawah Centre).

Plantinga, A. 2000: *Warranted Christian Belief* (Oxford: Oxford University Press).

Quon g, J. 2010: *Liberalism without Perfection* (Oxford: Oxford University Press).

Qutb, S. 2006: *Milestones* (New Delhi: Islamic Book Service).

Rawls, J. 1993: *Political Liberalism* (New York: Columbia University Press).

Raz, J. 1986: *A Morality of Freedom* (Oxford: Oxford University Press).

Saeed, A. & Saeed, H. 2004: *Freedom of Religion, Apostasy and Islam* (Farnham: Ashgate).

Shah, N. 2006: "A New Argument for Evidentialism" *Philosophical Quarterly* **56** pp. 481–98.

Stanley, J. 2015: *How Propaganda Works* (Princeton, NY: Princeton University Press).

Watt, M. 1987: *Islamic Philosophy and Theology* (Edinburgh: Edinburgh University Press).

4

MILL, LIBERALISM, AND EPISTEMIC DIVERSITY

Paul Kelly

1 Introduction. John Stuart Mill and epistemic liberalism

John Stuart Mill (1806–1873) was the most important British philosopher of the nineteenth century and the most significant theorist of utilitarian liberalism. Today he is mostly read for his short essays *On Liberty* (1859) and *Utilitarianism* (1863) which have become staples of the undergraduate curriculum, but in his lifetime, it was his major works *A System of Logic* (1843), *The Principles of Political Economy* (1848), *Considerations on Representative Government* (1861) and *An Examination of Sir William Hamilton's Philosophy* (1865) on which his significant philosophical reputation rested (Skorupski 1989; Rosen 2013). In these works, he developed a naturalistic philosophy of knowledge and science as well as a naturalistic ethical and political philosophy in which he argued that knowledge was derived from sense experience and inductive generalisation, and value and action was rooted in psychological sensations of pleasure and happiness broadly conceived. In this he followed in the footsteps of the great British empiricists, Locke, Berkeley and Hume and in ethics the naturalism and utilitarianism of David Hume and Jeremy Bentham, his intellectual 'godfather'. Although a great synthesiser and systematiser, seeking wisdom in the ideas of the poet Samuel Taylor Coleridge (1772–1834) and conservative Scottish historian Thomas Carlyle (1795–1881) who were conduits of the German Idealism of Kant, Fichte and Schelling into English thought, as well as French social thinkers such as Saint-Simon (1760–1825) and Comte (1798–1857), Mill remained an original and sophisticated liberal thinker. Whereas David Hume had argued that empiricism collapsed into philosophical scepticism and conservatism in politics, Mill argued that knowledge was possible albeit hard won, and that science progressed towards an expansion of truth and understanding. That scientific and human progress was possible and inevitable led to Mill's liberal and progressive politics, but Mill's liberalism also departed significantly from the natural rights and social-contract tradition that had its roots in John Locke. The progress of knowledge did not converge upon a set of human or natural rights upon which a liberal constitution could be based. Mill's liberalism was derived from the need for epistemic diversity and therefore resulted in a set of institutions that are necessary for maintaining the growth of knowledge. The challenge for political liberals, according to Mill, was not the foundational problem of liberal rights and principles or designing an ideal constitution, but the threat to epistemic diversity as a result of sociological tendencies in modern societies towards social conformity and epistemic homogeneity. Consequently, Mill's political theory proves to be both prescient and increasingly relevant in world that is confronting the populist capture of liberal democratic constitutions.

2 Science, the growth of knowledge and expertise

Mill followed in the empiricist tradition of Locke, Hume and Hartley basing all knowledge on sense perception and the formation of ideas in mental reflection on sensory experiences. Sense perception is the source of impressions from which simple ideas are derived; these ideas are combined in accordance with 'associationist' principles to arrive at more complex ideas which form the basis of reasoning and belief formation. Although Hume had raised significant sceptical arguments against the possibility of certain knowledge being derived from sense experience, empiricism remained the best candidate for the secure basis of knowledge and science according to Mill, especially given his critique of what he described as intuitionism and *a-priorism* which were merely subtle attempts to overcome the difficulty of knowledge acquisition in order to protect the status of revealed religion and traditional morality. Mill was also aware of the problems that a naturalistic epistemology creates in terms of its own philosophical foundations and its application to mathematics and logic. His most sophisticated philosophical treatise *A System of Logic* (1843) seeks to ground the formal canons of logic in inductivism. This attempt to explain logic and mathematics in naturalistic terms fell out of favour during the logical revolution inspired by Russell and Frege in the early twentieth century, but more recently the challenge of logical naturalism has been recovered in the work W.V.O. Quine and Hilary Putnam.

As all knowledge and scientific belief is based ultimately on experience through induction, it is potentially defeasible and therefore authoritative claims to certainty are challengeable. Yet for Mill, this does not mean that scientific progress is not possible, and nor does it mean that we cannot identify false beliefs. All knowledge based on induction is potentially defeasible but equally 'Many of the uniformities existing among phenomena are so constant, and so open to observation, as to force themselves upon involuntary recognition' (Mill 1843: 318). There is a role for expertise and for epistemic authority, but that authority is subject to challenge and revision and it is not a basis for political coercion. Mill was also keen to defend the idea of moral expertise in his account of the distinction between higher and lower pleasures in *Utilitarianism* (1863). Although Mill followed Bentham in explaining value judgements and actions in terms of sensations of pleasure, he rejected Bentham's simple hedonist claim that all pleasure as pleasures are equal differing only in quantity of the sensation. To avoid Carlyle's charge that hedonism is a philosophy only 'fit for swine', Mill argued for qualitative distinctions between pleasures so that some associated with intellectual cultivation were considered higher than those of mere sensual gratification. This raises the question of how such higher values are identified given that moral beliefs and judgements must also be explained by reference to experience. Mill answered this challenge by appealing to moral experts who have experienced both pleasures, or that have an experience that warrants one pleasure to be considered superior or of higher value. This form of moral elitism has been problematic for subsequent utilitarian moralists, but it remained an important part of Mill's experimental ethics and his account of human psychology. The status of moral experts and of epistemic experts within Mill's naturalistic science of man is always defeasible, but as with all knowledge claims it does not follow that defeasibility undermines the claim to epistemic authority. This desire to combine defeasibility with authority was to shape the institutional structure of Mill's epistemic liberalism.

3 Freedom of speech – not expression

The second chapter of *On Liberty*, 'Of the Liberty of Thought and Discussion', is the start of Mill's political defence of epistemic diversity. The main argument of the *On Liberty* is the defence of

> … one very simple principle, as entitled to govern absolutely the dealings of society with the individual in the way of compulsion and control, whether the means used be physical force in the form of legal penalties, or the moral coercion of public opinion. That principle is, that the sole end for which mankind is warranted, individually or collectively, in interfering with the liberty of action of any of their number, is self-protection… …to prevent harm to others. (Mill: 13)

As the essay shows Mill's principle is far from simple, indeed some even question whether there is a single principle given the far more unqualified defence of liberty of thought and discussion than is provided with respect to action by the harm principle (Gray 1984). As Mill's liberty principle is ultimately derived from or shown to be consistent with utilitarianism, as the sole ground of value and obligation, he must show that freedom of speech and discussion is always in the general interest. Whether he succeeds will not be the focus of attention, but given the uncompromising libertarian approach to speech and discussion, this remains an ever-present question. Before outlining his arguments, it is important to emphasise that Mill's concern is speech and discussion as examples of freedom of thought. Thoughts as beliefs have a propositional content and make claims about matters of fact in the world, including claims about what has value and what ought to be done. He does not have a view on non-propositional expression in the way that contemporary discussions of the First Amendment of the US Constitution demand. At the end of the chapter he counsels modesty of expression as it is the belief claim not the mode of that claim which enjoyed the unabridged liberty: this allows Mill to regulate non-propositional speech acts such as shouting fire in a crowded theatre or torts such as slander and libel. What he is primarily concerned with is attempts by the public culture or political institutions to stifle moral and political principles or to censor and deny claims of fact. Censorship, restricting access to ideas and publications, is always wrong and harmful to society for four main reasons.

1   The censored opinion may turn out to be true.
2   Even if an opinion is false it may turn out to contain part of the broader truth or contribute to the discovery of that broader truth.
3   Those opinions which turn out to be the whole truth still need the challenge of other opinions in order to be fully understood and appreciated.
4   The meaning of an opinion loses its contribution to character and conduct unless it is rediscovered in the context of an individual's active reasoning and personal experience.

These four arguments combine the central elements of Mill's account of knowledge and science and his ethical theory and psychology. The acquisition of knowledge and virtue is a constant personal struggle that requires effort and application. The danger to human happiness and culture is when people become lazy, thinking they know the complete truth and there is nothing more to do than protect that truth: for Mill this is illustrated in the relative decline of Catholic southern Europe and the formerly great civilisations of the East in India and China which were being left behind by western intellectual and political progress. Yet what is most striking about these four arguments is not simply an assertion of the importance of diversity of opinions to make the chance of finding the truth more likely, but the lengths Mill goes in defending the rights of error and falsity, precisely the things that traditional western religious cultures deny, claiming 'error has no rights'. The defence of the rights of error is captured in the following famous passage from *On Liberty*:

> ...If all mankind minus one, were of one opinion, and only one person were of the contrary opinion, mankind would be no more justified in silencing that one person, than he, if he had the power, would be in silencing mankind. ...But the peculiar evil of silencing the expression of an opinion is, that it is robbing the human race; posterity as well as the existing generation: those who dissent from the opinion, still more than those who hold it. If the opinion is right, they are deprived of the opportunity of exchanging error for truth: if wrong, they lose, what is almost as great a benefit, the clearer perception and livelier impression of truth, produced by its collision with error. (Mill 2015: 19)

What underpins this defence of error is an ethic of belief which is concerned not only with what beliefs we hold but the way in which we hold them. The danger of mass society is the ease with which (so-called) epistemic elites aspire to do the thinking for us by identifying 'truths' and passing them on by censoring opinions to the contrary. Education has the tendency to indoctrination and even where that education is more likely to track the truth – as the way the world is or as the correct account of morality – unless that is appreciated in the right way its real meaning is lost. One might see Mill's mental crisis as a loss of that appreciation of the truth accompanied by its recovery through the challenge to his naturalistic utilitarianism at the hands of his Coleridgean friends. What Bentham and his father failed to realise in shaping Mill's early education is that ...

> ...He who knows only his own side of the case, knows little of that. His reasons may be good, and no one may have been able to refute them. But if he is equally unable to refute the reasons on the opposite side; if he does not so much as know what they are, he has no ground for preferring either opinion. (Mill 2015: 37)

Whilst the truth may be expressible in a finite number of propositions and we only have true knowledge when our beliefs are true, the quest for knowledge requires the expansion of beliefs and opinions. As we cannot know the truth other than through large scale experience and induction, including not only the observation of events, but experience of the largest numbers of views and claims about matters of fact and value, we need to maintain as large a number of views and opinions as possible. This allows us to refine our beliefs and draw connections that provide a more accurate reflection of the truth but the challenge of sorting through those beliefs and especially constantly countering errors enables us to fully appreciate the truth when we confront it and to be able to understand, explain and defend it to others. Mill provocatively illustrates the way in which elites can stifle truth with the examples of Socrates and Jesus who both were persecuted for insisting on truth that challenged received opinions and traditions in religion and morality. Those who wish to protect moral traditions or religious orthodoxy have precisely the same motivations as those who condemned Socrates and Jesus. Mill was an avowed atheist without religious belief, but even against his most ardent opponents he would insist on maintaining religious beliefs as perhaps partial sources of the truth.

The main outline of the argument is that the broad diversity of opinions is essential for genuine knowledge acquisition and for the psychological benefits of understanding through confronting error, but the most paradoxical part of the argument is the claim that even erroneous beliefs that we know are incorrect – 'that the world is flat' and 'that the universe revolves around the earth' – have a claim to toleration but also, in some respects, protection. The claim is not simply that we should not censor error, but that we should ensure such beliefs persist. These may seem the most problematic cases for a utilitarian libertarianism, after all, do we really lose much if people stop believing in a flat earth? If we consider modern examples of bogus science such as the claims of 'anti-vaxxers' or those who attribute COVID-19 to 5G telecommunications technology, we have examples of beliefs that are positively harmful and must fail in a utilitarian calculus. To understand Mill's defence of these extreme 'rights of error' we need to turn from the epistemic benefits of the diversity of beliefs and focus on his real target which is the politics of elites and their claims to political and epistemic authority.

4 Populism and the threat of democratic conformity

At the beginning of the essay *On Liberty*, Mill described how the political threat in the struggle between liberty and authority has changed from that of government against the people which needed, in a previous age, to be addressed by constitutional protections, to a new threat to liberty from the people themselves in the guise of the 'tyranny of the majority'. Writing after several decades of reform movements and revolution on the European continent, Mill is seen as responding to the threat of mass society unleashed by democratic enfranchisement and the emergence of new industrial society (Skorupski 1989). The working class was engaging in political organisation and revolutionary politics, but the recently enfranchised middle classes were also forming as a people defined by their consumption of new industrial goods and media in the form of newspapers, serialised novels, and pamphlet literature. For Mill, this process of emancipation was double-edged: partly to be welcomed in terms of the extension of literature, culture and well-being but also of concern in the tendency of social classes to be subject to manipulation and direction by self-identifying elites that claim to speak for and give leadership to their real interests. In this, Mill is also reacting against his father's theory of representative government in his 'Essay on Government', where James Mill defended the authority of a representative class as the subject of enfranchisement, who would necessarily act in the interest of the whole of society, but whose emancipation would render unnecessary the extension of the franchise to the majority of men or any women. This class was made up of male property owners of a certain age and economic status who would take the view of the general interest and as either fathers or brothers would also represent all women. When J.S. Mill writes about the 'tyranny of the majority' he does not only mean the levelling of mass opinion, but also mean the elective 'majorities' that emerged in newly democratising constitutions which produced legislative majorities that were anything but the numerical majority of the population or the settled view of the mass of the people. Elective majorities are always institutional constructions that emerge from constitutional rules – think of the 52% vs. 48% split between Leave and Remain in the UK Brexit Referendum. This was based on a 70% turnout of those eligible to vote which is a number larger still. The majority constituted by the rules is not the same as the majority of the eligible voters or of the population at large. Mill was acutely aware of these challenges, but equally of how these temporary legislative majorities could act and speak as if they represented the people in its entirety. The ease with which such 'majorities' could claim their voice for the considered view of the people was precisely the political challenge posed by mass society and democratic emancipation, which as we shall see Mill supported. Such so-called majorities confuse their views and beliefs for those of the people and their 'truth' for the whole of the truth. In this way Mill is concerned with what is now described as the problem of 'populism' or the use of democratic means against democracy.

As we have seen, Mill is not opposed to the existence of expertise and epistemic and moral elites, but he is concerned with the sociological problem of elites that emerge from mass politics who claim to be moral and epistemic elites. In this way his argument echoes themes from Plato's *Republic*, where the argument is that the wisest should rule but the challenge is who identifies the wisest or the philosophers? Mass society either denies the claims of elite experience replacing them with a lowest common denominator view, or more often it allows partial beliefs and party preferences to be claimed as the truth. It is this problem that motivates Mill to defend the widest liberty of opinion even to the most obviously erroneous belief such as a 'flat earth'. The reason for maximal liberty is that conceding a right to censor the most obviously false beliefs and opinions opens the opportunity of political elites to legislate the boundaries of irredeemable error, and whilst there is likely to be some convergence on the most baseless erroneous beliefs it is far from easy to draw a precise boundary around those errors that contribute to the acquisition of the whole truth and whose existence is necessary to support the vital understanding of the actual truth. As there is no transcendental perspective from which to select genuine epistemic and moral expertise modern society will simply produce temporary 'majorities' who mistake their elective status for epistemic authority. Mill had already seen how the elective majorities championed by his father's generation of radicals in the new emancipated Parliaments continued to legislate their own moral prejudices as the truth and permanent wisdom of humanity. Given the importance of knowledge acquisition there is simply no position on a slippery slope of censorship that Mill thought it was safe to occupy, consequently he was happy to give maximal rights to error in the pursuit of truth.

5 Representation and deliberation – the institutions of a liberal democracy

The threat of populism and the importance of epistemic elites or experts come together in Mill's complex institutional political theory in *Considerations on Representative Government* (1861). For those coming to Mill's theory in light of the nineteenth-century development of liberal democracy, this work can seem curious. Whereas Bentham's position on extending the franchise was radical and unequivocal (although not published in his lifetime), Mill's argument seems to obscure the unequivocal defence of the universal franchise, despite his campaign for votes for women, and it reinforces his reputation as a lukewarm defender of democracy. For Mill the question of the franchise had to be seen in light of its benefits and not simply in terms of a rights claim, given his underlying utilitarianism, and considered in this way the benefits of democracy are challengeable. Bentham assumed that government was always a sinister interest that acted against the public interest, and the extension of the franchise and public debate would always be an improvement on elite rule. Mill was sceptical about the ways in which public opinion was malleable and subject to factionalism. For this reason, Mill remained a defender of representative democracy over direct and deliberative democracy associated with Rousseau or Condorcet. Public debate and discussion could be a genuine test of the best policy or legislation but could also reinforce partisanship and prejudice as we saw with his concerns about free speech and publication. If the type of deliberation favoured by Rousseau and Condorcet was to structure politics the characters and beliefs of the deliberators would need to be very different from those found amongst the so-called informed opinion in the real legislatures of European states. The risk was not just that of the untutored masses forming a populist electorate, but rather their supposed more enlightened representatives who sat alongside Mill in the Westminster Parliament. If the task of legislation was to achieve the public good, it was necessary that the conception of the public good was not simply the temporary opinion of a prevailing democratic majority. Mill, like his friend the classicist George Grote (1794–1871), was mindful of the lesson of Thucydides that democracy is essentially self-undermining. The challenge for any representative constitutional government is finding a way of distinguishing the category of expert elites from those that falsely claim expertise.

Democracy seems to suggest that everyone is an expert of the relevant kind, but Mill found that idea highly implausible. But if there are experts then why defer to a majority vote? As we have seen Mill believed in moral as well as epistemic expertise so why bother with a universal franchise? The task of an effective democratic constitution was to be a discovery mechanism for the relevant public experts who were most likely to act and judge in the public interest, and to remove them when they failed to so act. Defending a representative constitution has two important elements. The first concerns the choice of legislators and the executive who will exercise political power, and this is addressed in questions of the franchise, but there is a second question concerning how the legislature works in making policy and passing laws and this is not solved simply by the franchise. Mill's defence of a representative form of government addresses both issues because he saw both posing problems of populism and the tyranny of the majority. With respect to the choice of legislators the challenge is extending the franchise to protect the claims of genuine experts and ensuring that the widest range of opinion is available on legislation and policy making. Mill believed in extending the franchise as widely as possible including the radical for the time idea of enfranchising women, but he did not believe that all votes counted equally. Whereas Bentham, famously according to Mill, argued that 'everyone counts for one and no one for more than one', Mill defended the idea of plural voting based on educational qualifications. The more educated had more votes as an extrapolation of the idea of university votes for graduates of Oxford and Cambridge Universities which continued into the mid-twentieth century. Whilst this is an inegalitarian measure it does allow for those with fewer votes to enhance their standing by acquiring further educational qualifications and in principle everyone might be able to reach the upper threshold of qualification in which case the plural votes cancel themselves out and everyone would count for one as an informed elector. It should be noted that Mill retained the progressive prejudice that the more educated are likely to be the more critical thinkers who converge on a liberal common good. In contrast to this it is also worth remembering that many of Mill's conservative Coleridgean friends were highly educated and not merely prejudiced followers of Church orthodoxy. The central claim is that informed or educated opinion would be more diverse and questioning of tradition and orthodoxy and therefore less subject to the claims of traditional social authorities or sociological or regional factions. For Mill the vote was an exercise of individual informed judgement on the character and performance of representatives who would then be tasked with judging policy proposals and passing laws. As this task is an individual judgement of the character and competence of legislators there was little room for party political platforms which were things Mill disparaged even though he stood as a Liberal candidate for Westminster. Whilst political parties served a role in campaigning and supporting representatives, Mill wished to weaken their claims as authorities and as party platforms. To this end, he was also a supporter of the ideas of Thomas Hare (1806–1891) on proportional representation. Proportional representation had the attraction of broadening the number of views and voices that could be included in the representative and also of expanding the range of parties in the traditional two-party system of the Westminster Parliament. All of the contrary arguments to proportional representation namely its weakening of clear majorities and decisive government were considered precisely its virtues in Mill's view, as the decisive majorities were most often contingent constructions of the electoral system and not genuine majorities at all. Yet Mill's undoubted scepticism of majoritarianism did not entail that there could not be better or worse legislation and policy options. There was policy expertise and evidence for preferring one policy agenda over another. Unlike moral expertise which required experts having experience of higher goods and pleasures, political experts would rely on the evidence of what is now known as the social sciences. Yet this class of experts was not expected to be found amongst the class of elected legislators but rather amongst a professional and highly educated civil service whose task it was to propose legislation and policy for the public good. As the elected legislators where chosen to exercise their judgement on these proposals the executive and civil service functions were distinguished from those of the legislature which was composed of educated and experienced generalists who would pass judgement on the narrowly specialised policy class. This central constitutional structure would, in turn, be supplemented by strong local government which would also exercise most responsibility for social and public policy. It is clear that Mill intended the central government to be focused on a narrow set of great issues which would relate to political economy, trade and national security. It should be remembered that despite his progressive utilitarianism, Mill had a much narrower view of the remit of government and policy than became the norm even amongst liberals in the twentieth century. The challenge for Mill was more from those partial majorities unleashed by electoral reform who would be excessively active in terms of factional interests as opposed to the general interest, than from a reformist liberalism or even the type of socialism that preoccupied many mid-twentieth-century liberals such as Karl Popper (1902–1994) or Friedrich Hayek (1899–1892).

Whilst Mill's commitment to education as a qualification for the vote and his belief in the centrality of experts in the development and implementation of policy suggests that Mill was really an epistocrat (someone who believes that the knowledgeable should rule) he does not use that argument to undermine the claims of democratic majorities as his primary worry is the status of those who claim expertise and who are identified as experts by the population and who try and institutionalise their position. The benefit of democratic institutions is not giving voice to the will of the demos but in limiting the power of temporary majorities and conventional wisdom to close down debates and declare issues settled.

All of this however rests on a faith in the progress of intellect and knowledge through criticism and debate and a belief that this will not distort the growth of public utility and not that opinion will converge on false but widely shared prejudices. Mill's theory ultimately rests on the view that truth has a higher utility than error so that epistemic and moral and political progress converge. The question is how long before that triumph of truth manifests itself?

6 Liberalism, truth and empire – Mill's awkward legacy

Throughout his life Mill managed to combine a role as a senior administrator of the East India Company (which until 1857 ruled Britain's Indian possession and subsequent Empire) with his prodigious intellectual output. But his service of the British East India Company was not only a source of income and insight into the mechanics of government and public administration. His engagement with practical imperialism is also reflected in this ethology and account of the development of cultures and civilisations that raises questions about his commitment to diversity.

Within the British state Mill is committed to the protection of epistemic diversity, error and unpopular views, whereas in the international domain his position is less accommodating or tolerant. He explicitly defends British imperial domination of India on the grounds of India's backwardness and the need for tutelage prior to self-government. This defence of imperialism has been one of the most problematic features of Mill's thought for subsequent liberals, and it involves a departure from the positions of Adam Smith and Bentham who recognised empires as a source of war, domination and a long term threat to freedom even within the imperialist power. Mill's qualified defence of imperial power rests in a view of backward peoples and civilisations whose cultures render them unfit for self-government and suited to the tutelage of more progressive and civilised states such as Victorian Britain. If other civilisations need to be regarded as children in need of tutelage then presumably those civilisations are in moral error of some kind, mere diversity would not merit imperial dominion. Yet, how does he reconcile the rights of error in a domestic context but in an international context allow this to form the basis imperial domination? In the first instance whilst Mill does recognise progress and the growth of knowledge in the domestic realm, he is sceptical of those who want to draw strong political conclusions from that belief by imposing their views of morality or the content of truth through education. His defence of individuality and the right of experiments in living does provide a basis for personal autonomy, and his harm principle also restricts turning erroneous ideas into actions although he does give parents considerable discretion over the content of their education. But if this is to be the basis of his argument for imperialism, he must recognise the claims to hold different cultural beliefs and civilisational standards including the constitution of political power and rule. Mill is not a Lockean or contract theorist who can use arguments about the failure to acknowledge equal rights as a basis for limiting self-rule as he does not use that argument in the domestic realm and as we have seen his epistocratic defence of plural voting is not straight-forwardly egalitarian. In the end the only argument he can provide is that the Indian principalities are so egregiously violent that imperial tutelage will reduce the harm and suffering caused below that of the violence and domination of imperial rule. As we know this is an implausible argument as British imperial domination was not only extraordinarily violent especially during the wars with local powers and imperial rivals in the establishment of the East India Company's dominance, but it was also an economically extractive form of exploitation with little of the civilising and educative mission that Mill's argument rests on. There are no doubt many cultural practices such as *suttee* or the self-immolation of wives on their husband's death which are barbaric, yet these practices though existed alongside many domestic patriarchal conventions that involved violence against women and the denial of their rights and status in British society: conventions that Mill was quick to condemn as a utilitarian feminist under the influence of his wife Harriet. Yet even in these cases the restriction is on the action as the harm is not self-regarding and not upon the holding of the belief. The justification of imperial domination if it can be justified at all is based upon utilitarian calculations about the balance of harm of restricting backward civilisations until they Europeanise. This reinforces a question about the inconsistency of toleration and diversity in Mill's theory. Although he does claim to tolerate and support error as a condition of the growth of knowledge the other parts of his argument for Liberty restrict the consequences of holding erroneous beliefs to, in many cases, the mere expression of them as beliefs divorced from action and practical consequence. In practice his stance is akin to contemporary liberal multiculturalism where diversity is tolerated only if it is consistent with a liberal order and where the consequent expression of unconventional judgement is reduced and practical beliefs that cannot be acted upon are soon abandoned. Preserving such erroneous beliefs becomes akin to preserving the historical and archaeological record where beliefs are available for study but as dead ideas that have passed their usefulness. Whilst scholarship is an important element of the civilising process it is far less clear it has the effect of undermining the tyranny of conventional opinion.

Bibliography

Gordon, J. (1997). 'John Stuart Mill and the Marketplace of Ideas', *Social Theory and Practice*, vol. 23, no. 2, 235–49.

Gray, J. (1984). *Mill On Liberty: A Defence*, (London: Routledge).

———. (1986). *Liberalism*, (Buckingham: Open University Press).

———. (1989). *Liberalisms: Essays in Political Philosophy*, (London: Routledge).

Kelly, P. (2006). 'Liberalism and Epistemic Diversity: Mill's Sceptical Legacy', *Episteme*, vol. 3, no. 3, pp. 248–65.

Mill, J. S. (1843). *Collected Works of John Stuart Mill: A System of Logic*, ed. J. M. Robson, (Toronto: University of Toronto Press), vol. VII–VIII.

———. (2015). On Liberty, in *Utilitarianism and Other Essays*, eds. M. Philp and F. Rosen, (Oxford: Oxford University Press), pp. 5–112.

Rosen, F. (2013). *Mill*, (Oxford: Oxford University Press).

Skorupski, J. (1989). *John Stuart Mill*, (London: Routledge).

5

HANNAH ARENDT AND THE ROLE OF TRUTH IN POLITICS[1]

Yasemin Sari

In response to the publication and publicization of the *Pentagon Papers* in *The New York Times* in 1971, Arendt (1972a: 45) states the following:

> What has often been suggested has now been established: so long as the press is free and not corrupt, it has an enormously important function to fulfill and can rightly be called the fourth branch of government. Whether the First Amendment will suffice to protect this most essential political freedom, *the right to unmanipulated factual information* without which all freedom of opinion becomes a cruel hoax, is another question.

To recall, the *Pentagon Papers* revealed to the American nation that their government was lying to them about the situation after World War II (WWII) leading up to the Vietnam War, and this revelation did imperil the First Amendment for some time when *The New York Times* was banned from publishing.[2]

Arendt's statement addresses two central issues in political theory: (1) the role of the press as a "branch of government," and (2) the question of the relationship between truth and politics, broadly construed. Focusing on the second issue from a politico-philosophical perspective, I will analyze the much-contested role of truth in politics to highlight the importance of a "right to unmanipulated factual information"—a right that, according to Arendt, is crucial for the freedom of opinion.

What does a right to unmanipulated factual information entail? While the OED, in 2016, seized the moment, and deemed "post-truth" the word of that year—looking back at the activists at the Standing Rock, and considering the *Black Lives Matter* protesters—we can see that the political conscience of our times suggests that there is an indispensable role that truth plays in politics. I maintain that such a right to unmanipulated factual information has to be in place—and in practice—for human beings to be able to make sound political judgments about the world.[3] As such, there is a close relationship between truth, politics, and freedom—a relationship that becomes manifest through political action. To make this case, I will reassess Arendt's seemingly contradictory remarks about factual truths in her essay entitled "Truth and Politics" to show how factual truths play a normative role in political action.

Drawing on Arendt's articulation of the world as that which is "in-between" human beings—a space of appearance for plural human existence—that is created in the exchange of opinions and collective action, I demonstrate that factual truths play a key role in politics that brings a new perspective to democratic practice by clarifying the relationship between factual truths and political judgment. By doing so, I aim to elucidate the seemingly rigid distinction Arendt (1968a: 219–20) makes between "truth and knowledge," and "judgment and decision" as stated in her essay entitled "The Crisis in Culture":

> Culture and politics, then, belong together because it is not knowledge or truth which is at stake, but rather judgment and decision, the judicious exchange of opinion about the sphere of public life and the common world, and the decision what manner of action is to be taken in it, as well as to how it is to look henceforth, what kind of things are to appear in it.

For Arendt, politics does not aim at "knowledge and truth" but rather concerns itself with "judgment and decision." There are two reasons for this: First, politics happens in the in-between of human plurality; it happens in the exchange of opinions, and not in being guided by an ideal. As such, there is nothing that is intrinsically political. Second, because of this, politics is related to contingent facts about human affairs, which always have the elements of frailty and unpredictability regarding the achievement of the goals that are set upon political action. This chapter takes up the distinction between rational truths and factual truths, and the question of their validity to demonstrate the role factual truths play in politics.

Rational versus factual truths

Arendt's political thinking is entrenched in interrelated articulations of what she often posits to be clear-cut dichotomies, or distinctions. To begin, I want to take up the seeming contradiction regarding her remarks about factual truths. For this, I would first like to clarify what she understands to be the distinction between a rational truth—a truth based on a so-called determinate concept of what something is (e.g. a square has four equal sides with four right angles, $2 + 2 = 4$), or what it should be—and a factual truth, which can have both a descriptive and a normative content, that is created in political debate and discussion. While the validity of a rational truth is contained in such a truth itself, the validity of a factual truth depends upon articulating the possibility of arriving at the normative content of such truth in the exchange of opinions crucial to judgment in the political realm.

Arendt's most explicit articulation of "factual truth" in relation to politics appears in her essay "Truth and Politics" (Arendt, 1968b). I quote at length:

> Factual truth, is always related to other people: it concerns events and circumstances in which many are involved; it is established by witnesses and depends upon testimony; it exists only to the extent that it is spoken about, even if it occurs in the domain of privacy. *It is political by nature.* Facts and opinions, though they must be kept apart, are not antagonistic to each other; they belong to the same realm. (Arendt, 1968b: 233–34)
>
> The trouble is that factual truth, like all other truth, peremptorily claims to be acknowledged and precludes debate, and debate constitutes the very essence of political life. The modes of thought and communication that deal with truth, if seen from the political perspective, are necessarily domineering; they don't take into account other people's opinions, and taking these into account is the hallmark of all strictly political thinking. (Arendt, 1968b: 236–37)

These statements reveal two distinct characteristics of factual truths: (1) factual truths are political by nature, and (2) they preclude debate, and hence are domineering. Insofar as Arendt understands the essence of politics to be debate, these two characteristics seem to be incompatible with one another. In this section, I want to address this question of their compatibility and offer a reading that renders these two seemingly contradictory statements coherent.

The first of these characteristics suggests that the "status" of factual truths is political, while the second one suggests that their "reception" is antithetical to politics. Taking an epistemic stance regarding the reception of factual truths, that is approaching it as a condition of knowledge can complement the political status of factual truths. This approach allows for an articulation of a more robust account of political action that is not devoid of worldly principles such as equality, public freedom, and justice.[4] My claim is twofold. First, factual truths need to be acknowledged in order to understand a certain situation. That is, these truths cannot be contested. At the same time, factual truths are informative and necessary for opinion-formation.

To be clear, the scope of Arendt's analysis in "Truth and Politics" is specific to what she distinguishes to be rational and factual truths, and the role they can play in politics. For her, rational truths are marked by how they are accessed; whether it be turning of the soul away from appearances to reality in the Platonic sense, or by experimentation and theoretical deduction as in science. While she stresses that the opposite of rational truths in science is "error" or "ignorance," in philosophy, it becomes "illusion and opinion" (Arendt, 1968b: 228). By contrast, the opposite of factual truth is "the deliberate falsehood, or lie" (1968b: 245). A careful analysis of what Arendt's demarcation implies for the formation of political space will be the focus of this chapter.

As Arendt (1968b: 259) does concede explicitly, the political realm is limited, "by those things which men cannot change at will." The stake in the political realm is what gives us, she suggests, our "bearings" in the world, that is, factual truths (1968b: 257). For Arendt, factual truths are necessary in order to provide the concrete conditions of political judgment formation. How do factual truths give us our bearings? This question can be broached by teasing out three alternative ways to understand truth in its relation to (1) knowledge (truth as one of the conditions of knowledge, understood in the traditional sense of "justified true belief," or cognitive content), (2) evidence (which admits of degrees with regard to correspondence), and (3) a claim to (or of) truth (where there is also a claim to authority).[5]

Arendt is not interested in the first two options, for reasons I will briefly explain below. However, in taking up the question of the role of factual truth in relation to political space, she also wants to exclude the third option from becoming relevant to political debate and decision.[6] For a claim to truth that is sufficiently authoritative bears the possibility of destroying the capacity to create a political realm altogether since for Arendt the essence of politics is debate, or simply put, an exchange of opinions.

First, truth understood as a condition of knowledge regards the truth of a statement where a subject can be held to have a justified true belief (hence, knowledge) only so long as there is a state of affair that corresponds to the subject's belief. Such truth, while essential for our basic existence and capacity of action, is not readily relevant for the purposes of understanding political decision in guiding our concerted political action. By contrast, in the context of political discussion, the facts that we are talking about are in need of interpretation. At the same time, this interpretation requires us to have a certain attitude of "disinterestedness" in a world of what Arendt calls "universal interdependence" (Arendt, 1968b: 237). This is to say that knowing a factual truth, insofar as such knowledge can be gathered from one's peers or from the newspaper, only becomes meaningful when it is discussed with others in a manner to understand the world and to form an opinion, that is, by making such an opinion appear in the world.

Next, Arendt brings together the notions of truth and evidence in terms of "factual evidence." And she (1968b: 239) correctly deems that insofar as such evidence is established "through testimony by eyewitnesses—notoriously unreliable—and by records, documents, and monuments, all of which can be suspected as forgeries," it bears within itself the possibility of being denied through "false testimony."[7] To be sure, it is in this sense that neither the internal and external accounts of truth discussed above nor the justificatory articulation of evidence can be readily excluded from an articulation of political discussion, and they are in fact intimately linked to one another. But my interest lies elsewhere.

Central to my aim in this chapter is the third alternative, namely, truth understood in its relation to a claim to (or of) truth. This relationship is more complicated than it at first seems. While Arendt herself does not endorse such a distinction, I argue that a distinction that can be maintained between a claim—that is, the "how"[8] of a claim—and the descriptive and normative content of what is claimed can help us demonstrate the coherence of Arendt's seemingly incompatible statements to which I alluded earlier.

The normativity of factual truths

Factual truths are about what is happening in our "common world" and about the "common world" itself.[9] It is for instance a factual truth that "In August 1914 Germany invaded Belgium" (Arendt, 1968b: 235). Inasmuch as this factual truth describes a historical phenomenon, it keeps open the reasons and the meaning of this invasion for debate that can be tackled by a group of historians who may or may not agree on certain aspects of the invasion, notwithstanding their agreement on the fact of the invasion itself.

By contrast, the statement that "all human beings are equal" is not a factual truth, rather it is a moral ideal to which we aspire and for which we strive. Nonetheless, it is also a statement that appears in our most cherished declarations of human rights and whose truth we do not want to dispute. This brings me to Arendt's critical denial of the factual validity of human rights, not to dismiss them, but to point to the fact that human rights do not entail any enforceable *praxis* on their own—that is, without being taken up and decided to be performed by individuals that make up a community themselves. In this sense, political equality, for instance, is manifested in the actualization of equality of participation.

In her discussion Arendt (1968b: 242) states that "Jefferson declared *certain* 'truths to be self-evident'" to argue further that when he stated that "we *hold* these truths to be self-evident," this claim to truth remains a speech-act that needs to be performed in plurality. This means that the purported self-evidence of his statement "stands in need of agreement and consent" instead of merely being put forth as "the truth" (1968b: 242). There is, then, a performative aspect of articulating certain truths that are purported to be self-evident. The validity of such a claim (to truth), which Arendt (1968b: 243) calls an opinion, "depends upon free agreement and consent; they are arrived at by discursive, representative thinking; and they are communicated by means of persuasion and discussion." In other terms, what Jefferson may have understood as the straightforward utterance of natural law, Arendt contends, can only become what it is when it is understood to rest on a judgment that we can share. It is in this sense that the validity of an opinion depends on a sort of agreement—or judgment. This point is crucial in articulating the normative role that factual truths may play in political debate. Simply put, a mere claim to truth, on its own, does not invite political discussion, due to the complexity of the performative structure of a claim. By contrast, a claim insofar as it is motivated by factual truth can invite further discussion of the decisions to be taken in political debate, and establish a normativity that can be fruitful in guiding action.

Let me give an example of the validity conditions of claims to truth by distinguishing between the performance of "claiming x" and "x (gaining the status of) holding true." For instance, when one asserts that "Life starts at stage X," the statement can be understood at two levels: (1) as a descriptive statement, which, in turn, requires the interpretation of (2) a normative content. The disagreement in this case stems from what one means by the phrase "start of a life" and what normative assumptions these terms carry in relation to one another. The notion of life may imply a plethora of normative valuations: that life must be preserved, or that life is sacred, or that the potential of life requires the articulation of a rights-bearing subject. On the other hand, the start of such life may imply sentience or consciousness following one's presuppositions. Such a claim may preclude the discussion between equal parties, when one imagines pro-life and pro-choice parties involved in a debate as to the right of preserving life in the context of the abortion of a fetus.

While the pro-life party could argue that the life of the zygote should be preserved for the fetus is considered a potential rights-bearing subject; the pro-choice party would contend that life understood as a potential does not have moral force in determining the potential-mother's decision regarding a possible abortion. Since the two parties do not have a "common meaning" of the term "life," their disagreement cannot be resolved for they do not start from similar assumptions. If the statement were instead that "Fetuses feel pain at stage Y," it would have been a "factual truth" rather than a "claim to truth" with a normative ground that can be uncovered in debate. Such a truth then bears the possibility to invite as well as inform a discussion on how this truth can guide our decisions and actions regarding the moral permissibility of abortion. Understood thus, factual truths bring to focus an openness to interpretation and discussion, and they become necessary for opinion-formation.

Central to Arendt's articulation of opinion is a Kantian tenet of thinking, as she makes clear when she states:

> [Kant] believes that the very faculty of thinking depends on its public use; without 'the test of free and open examination,' no thinking and no opinion-formation are possible. Reason is not made to 'isolate itself but to get into community with others'. (Arendt, 1989: 40, 40n92)[10]

In contending thus "no opinion is self-evident" (Arendt, 1968b: 238) opinion-formation is itself a relational act. As Arendt (1963: 268–69) writes:

> Opinions are formed in a process of open discussion and public debate, and where no opportunity for the forming of opinions exist, there may be moods—moods of the masses and moods of individuals, the latter no less fickle and unreliable than the former—but no opinion.

Arendt's point is poignant: a public may have moods, but no opinion. Opinion-formation rests on the conditions of open discussion and public debate which are twofold: (1) that there is a public that has come together to discuss and debate certain issues, and (2) that there are factual truths available to this public, that can render their discussion, and by extension individuals' opinions on the subject matter meaningful and freely formed. Understood thus, the availability of factual truths becomes a necessary condition in a political debate, which involves well-informed parties who practice their freedom of opinion. For Arendt

(1968b: 237), articulated thus, opinion becomes distinct from "interest," understood as a private or collective reality for "the quality of an opinion, as of a judgment, depends upon its impartiality." This articulation of opinion may sound counterintuitive to our modern ears, but Arendt's conviction stems from her re-articulation of the Kantian "enlarged mentality," which she understands as the vehicle of representative thinking to argue that

> [t]he very process of opinion formation is determined by those in whose places somebody thinks and uses his own mind, and the only condition for this exertion of the imagination is disinterestedness, the *liberation* from one's own private interests.[11]

Arendt's contention brings to focus the fact that opinion is not equivalent to one's idiosyncratic conviction about what interests one or one's group. Disinterestedness brings to focus the element of publicness that is required of political judgment. As such, private interests cannot be the proper motivation to enter a public space wherein the free formation of opinion and exchange can happen. Opinion, in this sense, entails a responsibility of thinking, i.e., of thought that which one may reliably defend in contradistinction to something that one may just utter—or believe—without being able to explain one's reasons for believing it. To be sure, one may also be deceived in what they take to be reasons for their opinions, and the possibility of recovering the factual truths that inform opinions is exactly why political discussion matters.

Since opinions are formed in plurality and exchange—which is what create a common world in response to the world itself—interests cannot be what grounds the creation of a common world, or our common responsibility for it. Responsibility here denotes the ability to respond, which can only be preceded by an epistemic stance of combining "factual truths" and understanding so as to be able to judge and initiate action. On my reading, then, opinion-formation not only retains its public status, but also *gains* an essential spatial aspect.

The spatial aspect of political judgment elucidates an element of political discussion in showing that it is not only the possible points of view that count in creating this enlarged mentality; but, rather, the actual discussion and hearing of others' points of view becomes crucial in explaining the import of principled political action that recovers the plurality of human existence.[12] Next, I will explore the question of validity of factual truths, and the role such validity plays in deliberating about our political decisions.

The validity of factual truths

The validity of factual truths is closely linked to the question of the meaningfulness of knowledge of certain factual truths. For Arendt (1994: 310) such meaningfulness is in consonance with understanding: "Understanding is based on knowledge and knowledge cannot proceed without a preliminary, inarticulate understanding." The issue at stake is action. That is, while one can have a basic knowledge of certain facts, these facts on their own do not entail action: the meaning of factual truths relates to what may be relevant to action (either speech or deed or both). In turn, the commitment to respond to the world which takes its bearings from factual truths is what makes room for an understanding that exceeds a preliminary understanding, insofar as it is combined with political judgment that creates meaning in a plurality of others.

Conceding that the role of understanding is to make knowledge meaningful,[13] I argue against Arendt's (1968b: 255) own conviction that the evaluation of factual truths is "one of the various modes of being alone," and that it is a "standpoint outside the political realm" which makes political commitment, in her terms, impossible. The absence of an elucidation of the connection between factual truths, opinion, and action is the reason for Arendt's conviction. If such meaning resides in public debate, then the motivating factor for the public manifestation of a shared meaning corresponds to the relationship between factual truths and participation:

> Facts inform opinions, and opinions, inspired by different interests and passions, can differ widely and still be legitimate as long as they respect factual truth. *Freedom of opinion is a farce unless factual information is guaranteed and the facts themselves are not in dispute. In other words, factual truth informs political thought just as rational truth informs philosophical speculation.* (Arendt, 1968b: 234)

Arendt's claim not only suggests that factual truths are necessary where freedom of opinion is concerned, but also that the legitimacy of opinion is dependent upon an attitude of respect for factual truths. She understands opinion not in terms of validity, as in the case of truths, where, in her terms, the element of coercion corresponds to the validity of any truth claim. "All truths," she (1968b: 235) asserts, "—not only the various kinds of rational truth but also factual truth—are opposed to opinion in their *mode of asserting validity*," for "truth carries within itself an element of coercion."

Arendt elucidates how rational and factual truths are arrived at differently but once established as true, "they are beyond agreement, dispute, opinion, or consent" (Arendt, 1968b: 235). The validity of rational truths is determined by the process by which they are arrived at, which belong to the faculty of cognition aimed at uncovering rational truths. For example, the assertion that "the sum of 2+2 equals 4" can be arrived at by counting, or linear regression, or rational deduction. The process by which this knowledge is established, indeed, has an "element of coercion." For the assertion that "the sum of 2+2 equals 4" is a truth whose validity cannot be contested. One either comes to know the conclusion to be the case, or one simply does not know how to count.

Politically speaking, what is crucial for Arendt is that the validity of rational truths does not require an exchange of opinions. By contrast, the validity of factual truths gains meaning in being discussed. If the essence of political thinking resides in such an exchange, where, in Arendt's terms, "factual truth informs political thought," we must ask where the validity of a factual truth resides. On my view, the most viable candidate here is political judgment, which confers upon this factual truth, meaning. As Arendt (1968a: 217) states, "the capacity to judge is a specifically political ability," as "the ability to see things not only from one's point of view but in the perspective of all those who happen to be present."[14] Judgment, in this sense, is a human capacity that requires the conditions of impartiality and disinterestedness.[15] These conditions underline the normative dimension of political judgment Arendt does not explicitly account for.

Hence, while factuality has a stubborn characteristic of "thereness" (Arendt, 1968b: 253), its validity and meaning comes from how one understands factual truths in relation to others who share one's world. Tracy B. Strong (2013: 360) stresses that "the validity of political judgments depends not so much on the actuality that and of what one knows as on one's capacity to *acknowledge* the opinions of others." Strong rightly wants to emphasize that factual truth by itself is not sufficient to enable one to form a political judgment, but that the capacity to acknowledge (that is, recognize) others' opinions is what enables, so to speak, judgment formation that Arendt deems possible only in a community with others. While I agree with Strong's overall contention, I maintain that this is too quick a leap. The crucial point about the validity of factual truths is that it is not self-evidently coercive. Factual truths demand a response from the individual. It is in this sense that these truths become motivating factors in being willing to partake in the public realm.

A possible objection: the status of the lie

What role does the lie play in politics? While political action as a human performance requires speech in action, which discloses, Arendt suggests, "what [he] [the actor] does, has done, and intends to do" (1958: 179), she states elsewhere that "[he] [the liar] is an actor by nature; he says what is not so because he wants things to be different from what they are—that is, he wants to change the world" (1968b: 246). This attitude is precisely why she contends that to lie is an action and that "our ability to lie—but not necessarily our ability to tell the truth—belong among the few obvious, demonstrable data that confirm human freedom" (Arendt, 1968b: 246). Yet for Arendt, "words can be relied on only if one is sure that their function is to reveal and not to conceal" (Arendt, 1972b: 163).

To recall, the opposite of factual truth is the deliberate falsehood, or the lie. The deliberate falsehood and lie can be seen in cases where political lie/propaganda covers over the emergence of a political space where political debate can happen among equals. I maintain that a lie forecloses the responsible attitude towards our political existence together. Let me explain why. First, the liar is in a quasi-sovereign position to manipulate the truths of the world. This seems like a "response" to the world through and through. The act of lying in this sense still points to the freedom of the human being: the capacity to say/do otherwise, and hence change the world in a certain sense, or present it as it is not. The motive behind lying is to change the world—or an aspect thereof. Isn't this exactly what political action does? Don't political actors aim to change the world when they act? The liar acts in accordance with her self-interest, which is not world-oriented, but rather, if one wills, utility-oriented. Even though the liar's action aims at changing the world, lying cannot be inspired by a "worldly principle," but only by instrumental motives.

Lying cannot create a world of plurality and equality, for it destroys the very foundation on which such a world can rest. This is why the attitude of the liar is irresponsible in a twofold manner: the attitude of liar not only lacks worldly principles, but it also covers over the "factual truths" and incapacitates the individual (or an audience as such) to exercise her freedom of opinion. The lie introduces a rupture in the individual's thinking and opinion-formation[16]; the bridge between factual truth and judgment is thereby corrupted. The act of lying—whether one is the agent of the act itself or the receiving party—does not comply with the element of impartiality, which is necessary to exercise the freedom of opinion. Even though lying manifests the freedom of the individual and hence is called an "action," it cannot be a political action because it lacks worldly principles and cannot admit of a plurality of opinions.

Conclusion

What I have demonstrated thus far is that factual truths cannot be excluded from Arendt's account of political action, and that there is a necessary relationship between factual truths and opinion-formation in political space.

If we are to take seriously a "right to unmanipulated factual information," then the preservation of factual truths themselves is crucial to make possible the basic conditions of freedom of opinion. Having outlined the role that factual truths play in politics, I hope to have arrived at a more robust account of principled political action that established the connection between the knowledge of certain factual truths and the political judgments and decisions of actors in a political space. Based on what gives us our bearings in the world, that is, the validity and meaning of factual truths arrived at by debate and discussion, a responsible decision can capitalize the characteristic of political action as its own end without reducing it to an arbitrary performance without worldly principles.

We are now in a better position to understand what Arendt (1968b: 254) means when she says:

> The political attitude toward facts must, indeed, tread the very narrow path between the danger of taking them as the results of some necessary development which men could not prevent and about which they can therefore do nothing and the danger of denying them, of trying to manipulate them out of the world.

The world, the "space of appearance" as such, is the "in-between" of our existence, which makes community possible in the first place. This "in-between" depends upon our capacity to create meaning through our political judgments rather than to found and be founded by a rational truth. In conclusion, this Arendtian articulation of the relationship between factual truths and political action—where the relationship is manifested through the correspondence of our political judgments—gives us the world as the "place of responsibility."

Notes

1 This chapter is adapted from Yasemin Sari, "Arendt, Truth, and Epistemic Responsibility," *Arendt Studies*, Volume 2, 2018, pp.149–70. https://doi.org/10.5840/arendtstudies20185311. I have updated material for the purposes of publication and modified the argument to exclude the novel claim of the original work, that is, the identification of epistemic responsibility as an action-guiding principle that is implicit in Hannah Arendt's account of political action.
2 The court injunction, to be sure, was overturned by the Supreme Court and the *Times* was able to resume publishing: https://www.nytimes.com/2016/06/30/ insider/1971-supreme-court-allows-publication-of-pentagon-papers.html.
3 Arendt asserts that there is "no right to touch factual matter itself" (Arendt, 1968b: 234), which she leaves undeveloped.
4 For a detailed elaboration on the role of principles in Arendt's account, see (Sari, 2018).
5 This account of truth can admit of both an internal and external account of truth, elucidated in the respective accounts of Plato (1992) and Hobbes (1994), as they are found in the former's *The Republic*, and in the latter's *Leviathan*.
6 This is one reason why an Arendtian decision cannot be read in purely decisionistic terms.
7 In this essay, she alludes to the removal of Trotsky's name from the historical account of the Russian Revolution as an example.
8 By this I mean what philosophers of language underscore as the perlocutionary force of a claim that is the meaning of its performance of as a speech-act.
9 I will limit my discussion here to what may become the topic of public debate—and inspire political action—putting aside the debate about whether these truths may be understood as brute facts or not. Insofar as the concern is politics, the elements of interpretation and debate become crucial.
10 Cf. (Arendt, 1968b: 230).
11 (Arendt, 1968b: 237, my emphasis). The discussion of the element of disinterestedness that accompanies the act of opinion-formation has been one of the central tenets of understanding Arendt's conception of political judgment and has received ample attention by feminist scholars. Cf. (Zerilli, 2005).
12 See also (Benhabib, 1988). For a discussion of "enlarged mentality" see (Arendt, 1989: 42–44).
13 Arendt (1994: 311).
14 For further discussion on judgment, see (Arendt, 1971, 1989). See also (Bernstein, 1989), and (Sari, 2020).

15 The text is revised to retain part of the argument about Arendt's take on "factual truths" and "political judgment" without losing its meaning.
16 I agree with James Phillips' articulation of "opinion as a construct" to be what is at stake for Arendt's defense of opinion against truth (Phillips, 2013: 102).

References

Arendt, H. (1958) *The Human Condition*, Chicago, IL: The Chicago University Press.
———. (1963) *On Revolution*, New York: Penguin Books.
———. (1968a) "The Crisis in Culture: Its Social and Its Political Significance," in *Between Past and Future: Eight Exercises in Political Thought*, New York: Penguin Books, 194–222.
———. (1968b) "Truth and Politics," in *Between Past and Future: Eight Exercises in Political Thought*, New York: Penguin Books, 223–59.
———. (1971) *The Life of the Mind*, San Diego, CA; New York; London: Harcourt Brace & Company.
———. (1972a) "Lying in Politics," in *Crises of the Republic: Lying in Politics; Civil Disobedience; On Violence; Thoughts on Politics and Revolution*, San Diego, CA; New York; London: Harvest Books, 1–47.
———. (1972b) "On Violence," in *Crises of the Republic: Lying in Politics; Civil Disobedience; On Violence; Thoughts on Politics and Revolution*, San Diego, CA; New York; London: Harvest Books, 105–98.
———. (1989) "Lectures on Kant's Political Philosophy," *Lectures on Kant's Political Philosophy*, ed. Ronald Beiner, Chicago, IL: The University of Chicago Press, 7–77.
———. (1994) "Understanding and Politics (The Difficulties of Understanding)," *Essays in Understanding*, ed. Jerome Kohn, New York: Harcourt Brace & Company, 307–27.
Benhabib, S. (1988) "Judgment and the Moral Foundations of Politics in Arendt's Thought," *Political Theory*, Volume 16, No. 1 (February): 29–51.
Bernstein, R. J. (1989) "Judging: The Actor and the Spectator," in *The Realm of Humanitas: Responses to the Writings of Hannah Arendt*, ed. Reuben Garner, New York; Bern; Frankfurt am Main; Paris: Lang, 235–53.
Hobbes, T. (1994) *Leviathan*, ed. Edwin Curley, Indianapolis, IN: Hackett Publishing.
Phillips, J. (2013) "Between the Tyranny of Opinion and the Despotism of Rational Truth: Arendt on Facts and Acting in Concert," *New German Critique*, Volume 40, No. 2 (119): 97–112.
Plato (1992) *The Republic*, trans. G. M. A. Grube, Indianapolis, IN: Hackett Publishing.
Sari, Y. (2018) "Arendt, Truth, and Epistemic Responsibility," *Arendt Studies*, Volume 2: 149–70.
———. (2020) "Towards an Arendtian Conception of Justice," *Research in Phenomenology*, Volume 50, No. 2 (July): 216–39.
Strong, T. B. (2013) *Politics without Vision: Thinking without a Banister in the Twentieth Century*, Chicago, IL: The University of Chicago Press.
Zerilli, L. (2005) *Feminism and the Abyss of Freedom*, Chicago, IL: The University of Chicago Press.

6

POLITICS, TRUTH, POST-TRUTH, AND POSTMODERNISM

Simon Blackburn

1 Epistemology

I believe, and indeed take myself to know, quite a lot of things about political life. I believe that democracy is a better system than tyranny, that freedom under the law and other basic political rights belong equally to everyone, and that they are important and should be defended. I think such things are beyond reasonable doubt, and do not even demand discussion. Fortunately, at least until recently, most of the people with whom I could imagine discussing them thought the same. So they were not themselves matters of political urgency. They were the background against which day-to-day activities of politics took place. For the rest of this essay I shall put them to one side. I shall mean by "politics" only the practical activities of those involved in making and assessing actual projects and decisions, and the thoughts and passions in the foreground of those activities. It should be apparent that what is background at one time may slide into the foreground at another, as presuppositions themselves become contested. But at any moment there will be this difference.

Many people think that there is precious little of either truth or knowledge in practical politics. As I shall explain, in many respects I agree with them, although not because I have much sympathy with the idea of a "post-truth" environment, nor with elements in postmodernism that are supposed to nourish that idea. As I am about to describe, on those matters I am quite conservative. Nevertheless, I do think that truth and knowledge are rare in practical politics. I even find the topic to which this volume is addressed, "political epistemology", quite hard to parse, and I shall start by explaining why.

Epistemology is traditionally the theory of knowledge. It is often said to have started with Plato's account of knowledge as true belief plus logos, this being thought of as some kind of grounding, rationale, or justification. As the second half of the twentieth century showed, it is fiendishly difficult to clarify what this means, and the hangdog failure of those who chose to toil in the salt-mines opened by Edmund Gettier in 1963 suggests that we might do better not to ask what it means. Fortunately, this leaves open a different avenue to understanding the notion. The way was cleared by the long succession of pragmatists, from Hobbes through Berkeley, Hume, to Peirce, Dewey, Ramsey, and Wittgenstein. What these have in common is a direction of approach to philosophical clarity that is not premised on the possibility of straightforward analysis. Instead, it looks at the use of a vocabulary and the concepts it expresses, and asks how that use might have arisen, and what it does for us.

It only became clear how to apply this to the idea of knowledge when Edward Craig wrote his groundbreaking book *Knowledge and the State of Nature* (1990). Craig saw himself as "synthesizing" rather than analysing knowledge: that is, seeing how the notion might have evolved to answer various human needs, and in particular the need to evaluate and grade potential sources of information. We need to do this, first, because as agents in the world we need to select courses of action, and second, because we often have to do so in conditions of uncertainty. This has ever been the human lot, and so we can realistically imagine a genealogy whereby the concept of knowledge grows in this soil. Our ancestors tackled the problem by evaluating our own position and those of would-be informants, since anything that diminishes uncertainty is valuable. This can go on up to the point where we decide our beliefs have become fixed, and when we do this we become able to deem ourselves, or our sources of information, to know something. Knowledge is the limit of an evaluative exercise, but on any particular issue we may fail to reach that limit. With repeated or predictable failures we give up on knowledge, and retreat to opinion, or hunches, or remain in two minds.

As well as concentrating on the rationale for this kind of evaluation, Craig does justice to the various ideas that were excavated in the Gettier literature: causal links, tracking, counterfactuals telling us that had something not been so the information at our disposal would not have been as it is, reliability, and so on—all of them likely symptoms that knowledge is on the way—but he also shows why there is always the threat of cases where such conditions were met, but the purpose of the evaluation is not. It is the same with evaluations in general. A judgement that someone is a good person, for example, is not monotonic, meaning that each additional piece of information will chime in with what has already been established. A new light on someone may throw what hitherto looked likely into complete reverse, and so it is with the features that may be building up the credentials of a person, or a process, as giving us only true informant. Until a final verdict is in, there is always room for the 13th strike of the clock, the one that casts doubt on all the rest.

Deeming that we ourselves, or some informants, know something is the end point, at which we suppose that what was once an open question is now beyond doubt, done and dusted. More inquiry is unnecessary. The answer is fixed. We can, of course, accord an answer this status when in fact it does not deserve it, and conversely we can be too cautious, and refuse to so dignify a source when it is in fact totally reliable, and deserved complete trust. Sound judgement requires both the ability to grade sources of information and a just sense of when to call off inquiry, sometimes because it is predictably futile, but also because it has completed its work.

Armed with this way of positioning our concept of knowledge, what can we say about political epistemology? Politics, as the art of solving real world problems, certainly demands information from many sources, and like any practice we can expect it to go better if these sources are reliable, up to the point we have been describing. But these sources will themselves be diverse and themselves have their own methodologies. A decision, for instance, whether to build a railway line, and then where and when to build it will require input from geography, geology, engineering, economics, population statistics, and more besides, and each of these disciplines has its own epistemological problems, and, one hopes, mature methodologies for solving them. But after these sources have delivered their data and their projections, is there room left for more epistemology—a specifically political one?

I do not think there is. There is room for judgement, certainly. But the question of what to do is not a political one because there is more to know, although there may be, but because there is a decision to make. The best or the right decision is to be found, if possible. But it is often unlikely to be known to be the best. There will be no algorithm for recognizing it, no specifically political mark of truth about it as it rolls into implementation. We might go so far as to say that a question is *only* a political one because it has arisen in a world of trade-offs, opportunity costs, and priorities. And these are not themselves issues where knowledge is likely to be in ready supply. Given the competitive nature of politics, and given the personality traits that take people to the top of the greasy pole, consensus is unlikely. And if consensus is achieved it will often be not because an answer has, as it were, shouted at us, but because of persuasion, preferences in the widest sense, and shared emotions and visions. And all too often shared illusions. Some of these may be the personal property of individual politicians, but others will be share by cliques, and other still may be widely current in the society.

With hindsight it may be possible to know that a decision was disastrous, but it will seldom be possible to know that it was the best that we could have made. The space of possibilities is unlikely to have had definite, and knowable, boundaries. We cannot accurately foresee future events or future needs, and so do well to acknowledge an element of luck, good or bad. And as Plato saw, when luck enters the picture, knowledge departs. In many political contexts it enters very early indeed. A scientist may know that a question is answered, and the answer done and dusted, the last word on the matter. But in human affairs, politics, and history, nobody ever has the last word.

2 Truth or post-truth?

Decisions may legitimately be said to be post-truth, since they are themselves neither true nor false, although sensible, silly, well or ill thought-out, practical or impractical. So when people began to seize on the idea of a "post-truth" environment as new and peculiar to our times, it was quite hard to know what exactly they had in mind. A minimal interpretation was that politicians could no longer be trusted, or could not be trusted as much as they once had been. Perhaps they have become more casual about lying or breaking promises. They can shrug off things that would previously have sunk their careers. We would be talking about a moral change, whereby people become disinclined to hold each other responsible, and reprehensibly so, for things that had previously been taken much more seriously. There may be such a change, just as there has been a notable opposite chance to more severe attitudes in sexual mores. But it is worth remembering that from time immemorial politicians have been charged with infamous trespasses against honesty and truth. Famously, the nineteenth-century politician Joseph Chamberlain said of Prime Minister Benjamin Disraeli what many of us think about Donald Trump that he never told the truth except by accident. Politics, as a domain of hopes, fears, visions, and emotions, is inevitably a cockpit in which truth has to struggle, and not only because of the advantage politicians may hope to gain by deceiving others. As often as not, this only follows on from first deceiving themselves. As Francis Bacon said at the beginning of the seventeenth century "The human understanding is not composed of dry light, but is subject to influence from the will and the emotions, a fact that creates fanciful knowledge; man prefers to believe what he wants to be true" (Jardine and Silverthorne, 2000).

A different aspect of a supposed moral and epistemological decline would be the view that even if politicians, and also news sources, are about as reliable and trustworthy as they have ever been, we the public trust them less. We badly underestimate their integrity. If this is a change, it is easy to sketch how it might have happened. Huge numbers of people get their information or misinformation from the web. And the giants of the web such as Google monetize this by noticing what they like, and directing them to sites that conform to those likes, that they will therefore visit again and again, thereby creating more revenue for Google. This leads to silos or bubbles within which people confine themselves, listening only to voices that confirm their own views of the world. So, to take an example at random, if a mother has heard, from whatever doubtful source, that vaccination is dangerous for her baby, she may seek confirmation from the web and easily find it. Her fear will be echoed and exacerbated, and before long she will be believing that orthodox medical opinion is itself some kind of conspiracy against the people in general, and her baby in particular. She has become untrusting, not because the science is untrustworthy, but because of groundless fears about the safety of vaccines, wickedly exploited.

It has been well said that conspiracy theories flourish so that stupid people can feel smart. A good elementary education in epistemology might do something to protect against them, but it is unfortunately on few school syllabuses. It might start with Hume's great essay on miracles, reminding people to lend very little faith to reports that flatter the passions of the reporter. One might move on to introducing what is in fact the formalization of the structure of Hume's argument, the three components of a Bayesian calculation. This varies directly as the antecedent probability of the story before the evidence came in; the "likelihood", or more accurately the probability of the evidence being as it is if the story is true, and inversely as the probability of the evidence being due to something other than the truth of the story. With conspiracy theories in general the first two are usually very low, and the third, quite high, giving a low probability overall.

Before we lament living in a post-truth world, we might remember that in simple affairs of life we are extremely good at judging what's true, and we would not survive if we could not do so. We have a shrewd sense of how to determine many things about the world around us. We trust our ways of telling if there is butter in the fridge, if it is a sunny day or raining, or if it is safe to cross the road. We have designed, tested, and trusted instruments to help detect whether an electrical circuit is live, whether there is petrol in the car or pressure in the tyres. We make and use good, reliable maps and charts. We also tailor our confidence to the track records of our sources, for as children we learn that not everyone is to be trusted equally about everything. We grow into being good practical epistemologists. Sitting in the study a sceptic may be proud of having seen through and deconstructed truth, objectivity, and reason, but will then turn around and join the rest of the human race in consulting maps and timetables, listening to doctors and finding out whether his brake pads are worn, all of which presuppose both that some descriptions have consequences, and that some sources of information are more trustworthy than others.

We do well enough in routine and proximate matters, but on others we quite quickly go astray. We cannot settle doubts ourselves, and therefore trust authority, sometimes unwisely. Our hopes and fears lead us astray. We are addicted to certainty, and therefore become dogmatic. We hate changing our minds, and therefore dismiss inconvenient facts. Some of us find conspiracy theories irresistible. The will to get things right often has to battle with carelessness, self-deception, vanity, credulity, and the will to power, and it often loses. The philosopher William James was no sceptic about the notion of truth, but he did lament that "Objective evidence and certitude are doubtless very fine ideals to play with, but where on this and dream-visited planet are they found?" (James, 1986, pp. 55–71) – not, at any rate, in the blandishments of advertisers, the assertions of politicians, or the cacophony of social media.

However, these familiar human infirmities give us no cause to doubt the difference between truth and falsity. They just take us into areas in which we are not very good at knowing where truth lies.

I think that more radical scepticism has two main causes. First, people tend not to concentrate on small, worldly, empirical matters but to worry about the so-called big questions:

life, the universe, and everything. And sure enough, if we perplex ourselves about the direction of society, the meaning of liberalism or the rights of the citizen bewilderment is quick to set in.

A, second, deeper cause of worry arises when we pose highly general questions about our categories of thought. How do we know whether our categories faithfully reflect the nature of things? How do we determine when we are describing how things are in reality, and when we are imposing categories of thought on them? Are liberalism and democracy, right and left, race and identity, good categories with which to work? The thought arises that our minds or brains impose interpretations on the world—but how are we to know what distortions they manufacture? How much is discovery, and how much invention?

We seem to have a relentless, but unreliable appetite for finding words, and often enough become entrenched and embattled about their use. In newspapers heated arguments recently broke out about where in Britain the North begins after one academic put Sheffield in the South. Is this merely a matter of definition, or was the academic simply wrong? Here we may suspect that the issue is more verbal than substantive, with people attaching more importance to the labels than they deserve. Similar worries beset almost all the terms we use when we try to describe social and political affairs, complex psychological states, or issues of race and gender. The worry is not new. Indeed, according to Aristotle the problem of finding ways of describing things that truly reflect their real properties so exercised one philosopher, Cratylus, that he was reduced to silence and would only communicate by wagging his finger.

Both problems have an abstract air, and to solve them it is best instead to dig into some detail. My guiding motto here is therefore a saying of the great American philosopher C. S. Peirce, "We must not begin by talking of pure ideas—vagabond thoughts that tramp the public highways without any human habitation—but must begin with men and their conversation". That is, we are not to lose ourselves in abstract thoughts about truth, reason, or objectivity, but have to look at the actual uses of words. We can then find out the practical implications of a description, which means that way it gives rise to systematic inferences and predictions, or whether it just gives rise to verbal disputes and confusions. It may be silly to become exercised whether Sheffield is in the North, but not at all silly to be exercised whether an annoying little lump is a cancer. The second description has definite practical implications that the first lacks. So we do not have to join Cratylus. We can sift out descriptions that have real practical implications from ones that do not.

And then, when an inquiry appears to have settled a question, we deem ourselves to know the answer, and deem the answer to be true. With the notion of truth, we do no more than signal assent to a belief or a claim. So, talking about the truth of an issue is just talking about the issue itself. The importance of this was first noticed by the German logician Gottlob Frege, writing around the beginning of the twentieth century. Frege noticed that if you express a commitment of any kind, you can add "it is true that…" without changing the content of what you have said. I hold that the United States is larger than the United Kingdom. So I equally hold that it is true that the United States is larger than the United Kingdom. If you concur with that judgement, then you can signify agreement by saying "that's true". You could equally have said "right" or you could have just grunted assent. This suggests that saying that a commitment is true is not making a remark *about* it. If it were there would be one question whether the United States is bigger than the United Kingdom, and another different question whether that is true. In fact, there would be an endless list of assertions each saying that the previous one is true, but each introducing a different fact. Since that is flatly unacceptable, it is better to regard the attribution of truth simply as a device for falling in with whatever was claimed. Saying that something is false is simply rejecting it. In this case, so long as we have commitments—which means so long as we have thoughts and beliefs at all—we will have the notions of truth and falsity, in the same way that so long as we have chess at all we will have the notions of a winning position and a good or bad move. This, in turn, means that post-truth life is no more an option than post-winning chess. The notion of truth turns out not to be an optional extra to having beliefs, nor an optional extra to the linguistic performances of communicating those beliefs and concurring with them or rejecting them. It is part and parcel of the very same activities.

A way of putting this that I like is to think of Pontius Pilate, musing "What is truth?" when he was asked to judge Jesus. According to Francis Bacon he was jesting, and would not stay for an answer. I do not know why Bacon thought he was jesting, but Peirce and Frege can help Pilate by counselling that he should not be asking such an abstract question: he should be concentrating on the inquiries he needs to settle. In effect Frege tells us that if Pilate does ask "What is truth?", the right answer is: "you tell me". Not, "you tell me what truth is" but "you tell me what you're trying to judge". If you are trying to judge whether this defendant is guilty of some particular crime, then the truth would just be his being guilty of that particular crime. And it was Pilate's job to find that out. Unfortunately, as far as we are told he did not do that very satisfactorily.

If this leaves the notion of truth in perfectly good standing, what about William James's mistrust of ever-finding objectivity and certainty? Again, if we dig into the detail, there are answers to be found. It is best to think of objectivity not as describing a particular sort of truth, but as characterizing the difference between well-conducted and badly conducted inquiry. There are virtues of good inquiries. They should be sober, open minded, careful and diligent, or to use the familiar phrase, ones that leave no stone unturned. These are the marks of objective inquiry, and an objective truth is simply one that has survived, or would survive, objective inquiry. And after all, there are questions that are answered, and inquiries that are done and dusted. When George Orwell worried that the very idea of objective truth was fading from the world, he would have done better to worry that it was the possibility of objective inquiry that was becoming ever harder, in an age of mass communication, propaganda, and state-sponsored lies.

Of course, as every policeman, or lawyer, or scientist knows, sometimes the best inquiries draw a blank, and we are left in the dark. We may never know who committed the crime, or whether there will one day be a better theory than quantum mechanics. There are also some issues where we have only a poor sense of how inquiries might be mounted. The right methods for settling moral or political uncertainties are as controversial and contested as the issues themselves. When we encounter such issues it is tempting to sit back, shrug our shoulders, and not let them bother us. This was the course of tranquillity, advocated by classical sceptics, and it is in effect the position of modern-day relativists, happy that on such matters each side may have its own truth. But of course such soggy withdrawal leaves the field open for the propagandists, ideologues, dogmatists, and charlatans to run riot. Better is to soldier on, drawing up the costs and benefits, finding what John Stuart Mill called "considerations capable of swaying the intellect". Similarly, the answer to Orwell's worry is not to give up inquiry, but to conduct it with even more care, diligence, and imagination. Even with intractable issues we have to do our best and live in hope.

Where does this leave the concept of truth? If we agree with Frege's deflationism can we any longer say that truth is correspondence with the facts? Yes, we can certainly say it, but it is of little use. We must remember that talk of facts, like talk of knowledge, only comes when inquiry is thought to have been completed. When it is contested whether inquiry has delivered one result or another, or any result at all, wheeling up the notion of a fact adds nothing new. It adds nothing for any of the contestants, except perhaps a rhetorical excuse for thumping the table. It provides no back door from which we can gain an independent view of whatever is left obscure by our best methods of inquiry. This should not be put by saying with Nietzsche that "there are no facts, only interpretations" (Nietzsche, Kaufmann and Hollingdale, 1968). Still less should it be put, as it often is, in the silly assertion that science never discovers facts, only hypotheses. There are facts, and science has discovered many of them. It is a fact that the earth is roughly spherical, that dinosaurs never existed alongside people, and that injecting yourself with disinfectants does not safely confer immunity against the Covid virus. We are perfectly within our rights to conceive of our inquiries as directed towards uncovering facts of the matter, and to say sometimes that they have succeeded. The notion is only of little use in epistemology, because finding what to believe is just the same thing as identifying the facts of the case. Nietzsche was right to think that this requires the interpretation of (what is taken to be) data, but wrong to think that there was an intrinsic opposition between interpretation and fact.[1] There is nothing subjective about interpreting the geological record as showing that the earth is more than 6,000 years old.

3 Postmodernism

Postmodernism named a fairly impenetrable swathe of attitudes and views. Only a few still permeate our culture, and myself I doubt whether the movement brought anything new to political epistemology. For the currents that came together in an apparently nihilistic, ironic attitude that "anything goes" had sources in many older mainstream ideas, especially in epistemology and the philosophy of science.

In 1935 the Polish biologist and historian Ludwik Fleck developed the idea that scientists become locked into a "thought style" (a *Denkstil*) that determined the concepts they would use. A shared *Denkstil* characterized a *Denkkollectiv*, a group, or a sect, locked into the same styles of thought. Fleck's views foreshadowed Thomas Kuhn's (1996) famous idea that normal science proceeds in terms of a shared paradigm, a governing style of thought which, like all governments, will be stable until sufficient pressures generate a revolution, which then, in turn, settles into its own *Denkstil* or paradigm (Fleck, 1979). It was in this vein that postmodernists sometimes wrote as if the sciences dealt with social constructions rather than the real world, or that it invented categories of thought rather than discovering facts about nature.

As well as this less than reverential attitude to science postmodernists were able to feed on other aspects of modern philosophy. After Wilfrid Sellars's attack on the "myth of the given" many epistemologists came to agree that we cannot see knowledge as resting on unassailable foundations in experience and observation (Sellars, 1956). Justification starts only when sense experience is interpreted, even if the interpretation is automatic and instant. Then the flexibility in our powers of observation gives rise to the possibility of error, right at the beginning of our epistemological journeys (apart from forays into pure mathematics and logic, perhaps). A candidate for a basic observation or "given" would be a judgement made in the blink of an eye, without conscious inference or processing, but such immediacy does not by itself ensure that it is true. I might be able to see at a glance that a bird is a chaffinch, but on occasion I might be wrong, and I might even be wrong if I retreat to saying that at any rate it looks like a chaffinch, having forgotten a salient distinguishing feature of these birds. My verdict made in the blink of an eye can be checked, repeated and verified, or discarded or adjusted. It does not stand as an independent rock of truth, immune to relationships of confirmation or disconfirmation.

It is also true that as people gain experience their perceptual capacities change. More things, and different things, can leap to the eye, or the ear or the palate. The experienced tracker can see at a glance that a leopard has passed this way, when the rest of us might be hard put even to notice the dent in the dust. The radiologist sees a tumour where we see only a white and grey pattern. The musician hears that the piece is by Schubert and the tailor can tell by feel that a material is silk or not. Our perceptions select, and they adapt to enable us to be quicker at selecting. But such adaptive mechanisms are far from suggesting an "anything goes" irony about our interpretations of things, for on the contrary they give us an ascending scale of ability, whereby the experts further up the scale are quicker and better at seeing things the rest of us miss.

Even the relativistic or sceptical significance that postmodernists attach to the idea of there being different perspectives on things dissolve here. There are different perspectives, for instance if you look at the Eiffel tower from Montmartre or from the Champ de Mars. But far from conflicting, they work together to give us our sense of the one monument and our different relations to it. The spatio-temporal framework within which the notion of perspective has its place has precisely this objectifying, synthesizing function, uniting what might otherwise have been a bewildering jumble of experiences. If different versions of events and things clash, it is not simply because they represent different perspectives.

A final general point that we can derive from Peirce's counsel to avoid abstractions is that particular worries over meaning only arise within a context in which, at least for the moment, we are not worried. They do not open an avenue to a general scepticism. So suppose we are interpreting a law banning vehicles in the park. We may reasonably be worried whether "vehicle" is supposed to cover lawnmowers or not. But in framing that worry, or any worry like it, we would be relying, for the moment, on our identification of lawnmowers. If that, in turn, raises a problem—are ride-on mowers banned or push mowers as well?—then, in turn, we rely on "ride-on" and "push". We have to stand somewhere. We do not, and could not, raise or solve all possible exegetical problems simultaneously. So there is no context of interpretation in which the insouciant or ironical attitude that anything goes has a proper foothold.

Of course, I see none of this as denial that there are special reasons why epistemology is difficult in connection with politics. To return to my original point, politics is unusual in being an area in which many competing players have an interest in concealing the truth. The government is more or less bound to be addicted to denying that things have gone wrong, while the opposition is equally likely to be addicted to denying that they have gone right. Few of us get behind the scenes to find out which, and those who do, having their own agendas and loyalties, are unlikely to come back speaking with one voice. Sometimes only time will tell, but time only speaks through histories, which themselves are selective, filtered, interpreted, and reinterpreted. A very bare diary or chronicle of events may stand a good chance of being true, but only by steering as clear as possible of whatever it may have been that animated the politics of an era. And as R. G. Collingwood rightly emphasized, such a bare chronicle would scarcely be history at all, for that only starts with sympathetic re-enactment of the thoughts and passions that motivated, or may have motivated, the original actors, who are now known to us only through stories. So it is not unduly sceptical, but more like part of common sense, to take a very cautious view of the epistemological credentials not only of politics in the here and now, but also of annals of political life.

My suspicion is that once postmodernism had enjoyed its day cavorting in the sceptical and ironic playground, it became a more sombre or more adult presence than its reputation suggests. Even the *enfant terrible* Jacques Derrida gave an apparently sincere rebuttal of the idea that his views have nihilistic implications, saying that:

> It must be understood that the value of truth (and all those values associated with it) is never contested or destroyed in my writings, but only reinscribed in more powerful, larger, more stratified contexts. And that within interpretive contexts…that are relatively stable, sometimes apparently almost unshakeable, it should be possible to invoke rules of competence, criteria of discussion and of consensus, good faith, lucidity, rigor, criticism, and pedagogy. (Derrida, 1988, p. 146)

What more should any epistemologist expect?

Note

1 The same mistake can be seen throughout the "slash-and-burn" writings of Richard Rorty.

References

Craig, E. (1990) *Knowledge and the State of Nature*. Oxford: Oxford University Press.

Derrida, J. (1988) *Limited Inc*. Evanston, IL: Northwestern University, p. 146.

Fleck, L. (1979) *Genesis and Development of a Scientific Fact*, Translated by F. Bradley and T. J. Trenn. Chicago, IL and London: The University of Chicago Press.

James, W. (1986) 'The Will to Believe', in McCarthy, G. D. (ed.) *The Ethics of Belief Debate*. Atlanta, GA: Scholars Press, pp. 55–71.

Jardine, L. and Silverthorne, M. (eds.) (2000). *Francis Bacon: The New Organon*. Cambridge, UK: Cambridge University Press.

Kuhn, T. (1996) *The Structure of Scientific Revolutions*, 3rd edn. Chicago, IL: University of Chicago Press.

Nietzsche, F. W., Kaufmann, W., and Hollingdale, R. J. (1968). *The Will to Power*. London: Weidenfeld & Nicolson.

Sellars, W. S. (1956) 'Empiricism and the Philosophy of Mind', in *Minnesota Studies in the Philosophy of Science*, 1. Minneapolis: University of Minnesota Press, pp. 253–329.

7

TYRANNY, TRIBALISM, AND POST-TRUTH POLITICS

Amanda R. Greene

1 Introduction

It has become common to describe our political climate as "post-truth." Post-truth dynamics are evident, according to the Oxford Dictionary, whenever "objective facts are less influential in shaping public opinion than appeals to emotion and personal belief" (Flood 2016). The description is treated as a way of accounting for a social phenomenon by making it more intelligible. Much ink has been spilled about whether the description is true. Here, instead, I offer a diagnosis of why it is compelling to describe our politics in these terms.

In developing my analysis, I will critically examine and build upon the work of Bernard Williams. Although Williams did not use the term "post-truth," his view accounts for its emergence. Williams thinks that allegiance to the idea of truth is more important in politics than having the correct standard of truth. He grants that some truth-telling is needed in order to enable minimal cooperation (Williams 2002: 85), but he thinks that effective methods for truth-seeking "will vary with the kinds of truth in question" (155). So Williams redirects our attention: "The most significant question is not about the truth-status of political or moral outlooks themselves. It is about the importance that those outlooks attach to other kinds of truth, and to truthfulness" (4). Williams thinks that there must be a durable commitment to the idea that truth and truthfulness matter for their own sake. He says, "What is essential for this to be so is that the agent has some materials in terms of which he can understand this value in relation to other values that he holds…," such as friendship and fairness (92). Williams notes that these connections will vary with culture and history, although there are some general patterns (93). In particular, he notes, truthfulness is exhibited through the qualities of sincerity and accuracy.

In what follows I evaluate the implications of this account for a post-truth political climate. Throughout, I rely on a thought experiment in which two different social tribes, the metropolitans and the heartlanders, exhibit sincerity and accuracy in ways that are not recognized by the other side (Section 2). If the two tribes must share one government, I argue, then each tribe comes to think the other is sacrificing truth for the sake of gaining power (Section 3). The lack of a shared political outlook, then, makes it difficult to resist tyranny and the erosion of political order (Section 4). Therefore, I conclude that focusing on post-truth dynamics undermines political legitimacy and that a better way forward is to challenge the strict dichotomy between facts and values (Sections 5 and 6).

2 A tale of two tribes

Here is a story about two kinds of political outlook: metropolitan and heartlander.[1] Heartlanders, on the one hand, are a tribe that values relational integrity. They care that their relationships – with those in their families, neighborhoods, and workplaces – be based on shared values. This outlook leads them to appreciate friendship, family, and loyalty. Heartlanders view social cooperation as association on the basis of shared values, and this model allows them to make sense of authority. Since heartlanders regard social cooperation in light of upholding and enhancing relationships, they understand the virtues of truth – sincerity and accuracy – in terms of maintaining community and loyalty. For heartlanders, all reasoning about what is to be done is personal and connected to values, and they trust and follow leaders that can be seen to deliberate accordingly. They find sincerity in those political leaders who exercise judgment in a way that foregrounds personal values.

Metropolitans, on the other hand, are a tribe that values inward integrity, as it is manifest through individualism and the ideal of self-development. They value their freedom to be a self-authoring person, and they care that their relationships with others be consistent with that freedom. For the metropolitan, social cooperation is about overcoming value differences so that each individual can maintain their integrity. This outlook leads them to appreciate impartiality, diversity, and cosmopolitanism. They resist political coercion that requires individuals to abandon or betray their sincerely held values. They understand the virtues of truth – sincerity and accuracy – in terms of deliberation that avoids or abstracts away from individual values. For metropolitans, reasoning about what is to be done should be impersonal and value-neutral.

When these two tribes form part of the same political community, instances of truthfulness for one group appear to the other group as deliberate neglect and even disavowal of truthfulness.[2] On the one hand, the heartlanders' expectation that the group will coordinate joint action on the basis of shared values leads them to invoke communal identity. In looking for an "us" in contrast to a "them," they often allude to a shared political history that is tied to an ethnicity or religion. They focus on the fidelity and sacrifices of prior generations, in order to fortify the group's sense of itself and inspire further sacrifice. Metropolitans, however, are suspicious of any claims about ethnic or religious identity in political deliberation and justification. In fact, they tend to reject these claims as irrelevant. Metropolitans fear and resent the power that can be unleashed by invoking communal identity, noting how destructive these forces can be. Since metropolitans view these factors as irrelevant and threatening, their invocation by heartlanders seems inaccurate – indeed, recklessly so.

Metropolitans, on the other hand, often invoke cosmopolitan rationales or utilitarian arguments in the quest to respect impartiality. Metropolitans consider natural science and economics to be supremely relevant for answering political questions, concluding that experts in these areas deserve our deference. Treating science and economics as revealing what should be done, politically speaking, ends up depersonalizing these judgments in a way that is alien to the heartlander. Moreover, there are several ways in which this seems insincere. For one thing, metropolitans rarely admit that claims to know scientifically what ought to be done in matters of public policy emerge only from institutions that are populated by metropolitans, such as universities, the civil service, and the financial sector. Furthermore, metropolitans resist the free market some of the time, but seek its expansion at other times, which seems selective and disingenuous. And finally, metropolitans invoke the intrinsic value of diversity to expand bureaucratic oversight, which can appear to be cover for advancing the interests of the professional classes.[3]

The result is that each tribe sees the other side as engaging in practices that are insincere and inaccurate. Consider debates about immigration. Heartlanders are willing to accept outsiders as long as they can affirm and uphold the mores of the community, and so heartlanders seek an admission policy that privileges this criterion. Metropolitans, on the other hand, think that the community ought to admit applicants on the basis of need or merit, making sure to avoid any differential consideration on the basis of religion, culture, or nationality. Thus, each side sees the other as pushing for admission criteria that are inappropriate. The tale of two tribes illustrates how political opinions, viewed as sincere and accurate from within the tribe, can seem politically dangerous to those outside the tribe.

3 Social shaping of beliefs

To better understand this dynamic, Williams explains how truthfulness emerges from shared practices. First, Williams refers us to Diderot's portrait of a man whose declarations are entirely authentic (Diderot 2001). However, the character's declarations are so inconstant that they cannot be taken as expressions of belief by a hearer, since it raises "a question of what kind of thing is in his mind" (Williams 2002: 191). If someone's utterances are noticeably "affected by the weather of the mind," then their statements will be something more like moods than beliefs. In order for us to manage this, Williams argues, we need some assurance of the validity of their utterances over time. Normally, he thinks, we "have [this assurance] in a form that is socially shaped and supported... a practice which socializes people" (192). Engaging with these social practices stabilizes our beliefs, thereby making us steady in the eyes of others.

This stabilizing dynamic, Williams thinks, exhibits two forms of social dependence. One is that sometimes "it can be unclear to us even at the instant what we think we believe," so the mere interaction with another person prompts the crystallization of a belief (Williams 2002: 193). The second is that often we are "speaking in a 'trustful' context in which others rely on us" (193). We may hesitate to commit or present ourselves a certain way, and this awareness of another's reliance on us can affect what we ourselves think. Thus, Williams rejects a simple model on which we each discover what is true and then announce it to others. Instead, "At a more basic level, we are all together in the social activity of mutually stabilizing our declarations and moods and impulses into becoming such things as beliefs and relatively steady attitudes" (193). Williams comes to the striking conclusion that "it is the presence and needs of others that help us to construct even our factual beliefs" (194).

Drawing on Diderot, then, Williams argues that there is necessarily a social dimension in the construction of beliefs (Williams 2002: 200). While the stabilization that social practices provide can have costs, it is nevertheless vital to "human interaction and a manageable life" (200). Thus, Williams concludes, every society needs practices that stabilize the self enough to enable mutual reliance and basic cooperation. These practices, in turn, shape what counts as sincerity and accuracy.[4]

Williams ties the social construction of opinions to the threat of tyranny since the allegiance to truth cannot play its anti-tyranny role, he thinks, if the community is fragmented (more on this below). J.S. Mill comes to the same conclusion while considering a single society with multiple political groupings:

> The influences which form opinions and decide political acts, are different in the different sections... An altogether different set of leaders have the confidence of one part... and of another. The same books, newspapers, pamphlets, speeches, do not reach them.

One section does not know what opinions, or what instigations, are circulating in an-other. The same incidents, the same acts, the same system of government, affect them in different ways; and each fears more injury to itself from the other [groups], than from the common arbiter, the state...the united public opinion, necessary to the working of representative government, cannot exist. (Mill 1977: 187)

Here Mill describes how the same events will be received differently by different groups.[5] The natural result, Mill thinks, is that each group comes to see government power as a weapon to be used against their rivals.

Their mutual antipathies... are generally much stronger than jealousy [dislike] of the government. That any one of them feels aggrieved by the policy of the com-mon ruler, is sufficient to determine another to support that policy. Even if all are aggrieved, none feel that they can rely on the others for fidelity in a joint resistance; the strength of none is sufficient to resist alone, and each may reasonably think that it consults its own advantage most by bidding for the favour of the government against the rest. (187)

Reasoning in this way, Mill concludes that avoiding group fragmentation is necessary in order to maintain healthy representative government. Otherwise, there will not be enough popular resistance to government overreach, including tyranny.

To see why this is the natural result, consider the two tribes again. Suppose the heart-landers value truthfulness because of how it relates to honor. Then they will insist on accuracy and sincerity in politics by punishing leaders whose dishonesty exhibits disregard for honor – for instance, leaders who lie about infidelity. Likewise, suppose that metro-politans value truthfulness because of how it relates to civil liberties. Then they will insist on accuracy and sincerity in politics by punishing leaders whose dishonesty exhibits dis-regard for civil liberties – for instance, leaders who lie about surveillance programs. Both groups are resisting tyranny by upholding standards of truthfulness. But the perceived significance of being untruthful is anchored in their political outlook. If the two tribes share one government, then together they will lack a shared sense of which political ac-tions count as insincere and inaccurate enough to be worth punishing through concerted political action. Unless the government's untruthfulness triggers a reckoning that is polit-ically costly for leaders – as opposed to the untruthfulness being accepted by many as part of the inter-group competition for power – the public's allegiance to truth cannot play its anti-tyranny role.[6]

4 Truthfulness and tribalism

Both Mill and Williams think that truthfulness plays an important role in the avoidance of tyranny. However, they think, truthfulness can play this role only when there is some common ground. Is there any way forward in a case where the two tribes, metropolitans and heartlanders, are under a single government? Perhaps the two tribes could agree on a suitable *method* for seeking the truth. After all, some method must be adopted by the society as a whole in order to deliberate and make decisions. However, each tribe favors a method that reflects their views about the point of cooperation. As we have seen, these views are non-overlapping. Therefore, the two tribes lack a sufficiently common basis from which to derive a single method for seeking truth together.

A second option is to combine multiple methods of truth-seeking. However, combining the methods advocated by each tribe may be worse than using either alone. As Williams observes,

> Multiple methods which are severally effective… cannot necessarily be combined or superimposed, without loss of effectiveness… The joint attempts of A and B to possess, or to express, truth may well mean that both or one has less of it. (Williams 2002: 155)

A third option is to renew trust across tribal lines by taking credible steps to mitigate threats to truthfulness. As Williams observes, two clear threats are wishful thinking and self-deception (156). According to Williams, the boundaries between coming to have a desire and coming to have a belief are blurry. He says,

> Since all practical thinking is full of wishes, in the most general sense of the term in which wishes can occur on the route both to belief and desire, [...an agent] may easily find himself committed to the content in the wrong mode. (197–98)

Thus, Williams argues that all practical deliberation can nudge our beliefs in the direction of our wishes (194). This tendency is likely to be more pronounced for successful leaders.

To address these threats to sound deliberation, leaders might publicly commit themselves to safeguarding against wishful thinking and self-deception. However, I doubt that there is any common ground on what counts as safeguarding. Consider the 2016 Brexit referendum. The metropolitans who opposed Brexit appeared too ready to rely on the opinion of experts when it suited them. Heartlanders suspected that the economic case was not conclusive, and that the metropolitans favored opening the borders regardless.[7] The heartlanders who favored Brexit appeared too ready to rely on the opinion of trusted friends and associates. Metropolitans suspected that interaction with people who were different would expand their circle of concern, and so heartlanders were being insular. Each tribe appeared to outsiders to be engaged in wishful thinking about whether the grounds for their opinions were adequate, thereby deceiving themselves into thinking the correctness of their judgment was obvious.[8] Metropolitans expected heartlanders to safeguard by deferring to experts, while heartlanders thought deferring to experts was a failure of safeguarding. Therefore, one side's safeguarding looks, to the other side, like wishful thinking. As a result, each tribe's subsequent attempts to enact their preferred policy were perceived as a power-grab by the other tribe.

In such circumstances, each side will defend what seems essential by using the means at their disposal. Heartlanders might resort to demographic coercion, utilizing their majority to manipulate the rules of districting and voting. Metropolitans might resort to lawsuits and gatekeeping of elite institutions. These methods of holding onto power are presented as victories for truth, which only enhances mutual suspicion. Moreover, leaders who come to power by exploiting their tribe's suspicions are seen as utterly corrupt by the other tribe. Hence, both sides resonate with a description of this stalemate as a post-truth dystopia.

Now I want to go beyond Williams and suggest that the problem runs deeper. As I understand them, each tribe feels that their values, when presented in the best light, cannot be explicitly rejected by the other side. Who can deny that impartiality matters? Who can deny that community matters? In my opinion, this situation is notably different from other times in history when groups sought to explain to themselves why their political opponents were intransigent. The Protestants thought that the Catholics were blinded by idolatry, and the Marxists thought the bourgeoisie were blinded by ideology. In both cases, their opponents' mode of seeking truth could be seen as mistaken because they had the wrong values. But today, neither tribe can completely reject the values of the other tribe.

On this point, it is useful to consider the analysis of tribalism in terms of universally recognized values proposed by Jonathan Haidt (2012). He claims that partisans draw on six moral taste buds that emerged through evolution. While all of us have all of the taste buds, Haidt argues, some grow to be more sensitive according to group affiliation. Haidt intends to characterize these six moral tastes in such a way that they resonate with everyone – aiming, thereby, to promote mutual understanding.[9] However, Haidt's analysis does not offer a viable way forward. He posits a plurality of moral factors that influence political decisions, where the chief evidence is their explanatory prowess with respect to behavior. However, identifying a set of values that are shared but differentially emphasized can leave us more frustrated: we must share a government with another tribe whose orienting values we oppose but cannot categorically dismiss. Haidt is reluctant to acknowledge that the conflict between values is about more than perceived salience. Thus, I believe there is a limit to an analysis that relies on a plurality of political values.

I have canvassed several possible solutions: finding a common method of truth-seeking, combining multiple methods of truth-seeking, renewing trust through safeguarding, and accepting a plurality of political values. In each case, I argue, there are reasons to be pessimistic. A more promising way forward, I suggest, is to rethink the fact-value distinction.

5 Facts and values

The distinction between facts and values is currently embedded deeply in our culture and media environment (McBrayer 2015). For instance, newspapers strictly separate their reporting from opinion pieces they happen to publish. In response to Donald Trump's election, the *New York Times* doubled-down on its ownership of truth by adopting such slogans as "Truth. It has no alternative." Such a tagline claims neutral status for the value-laden worldview of their writers and readers. As David Bromwich observed soon after, "All the mainstream outlets, with CNN and the *Times* at their head, have now re-emerged as anti-government centres of news, opinion, and news perceptibly mingled with opinion" (Bromwich 2017).

Journalism has been openly political in the past, as it was with the pamphleteers of the French and American revolutions. In Germany a century ago, Max Weber remarks that a person with a calling for politics would do well to start their career as a journalist (Weber 1958). It should not surprise us that public presentation of "facts," by journalists as well as other public figures, is inflected with political views about what matters. While deliberation always involves values, the values are not always suitable for discussion. Consider Socrates's deliberation in the *Crito* on whether to flee his execution. Having affirmed that one should never repay a wrong with a wrong, he says that there can be no common deliberation between people who disagree about this; rather, they despise each other's views.[10] Of course, the verdict on what Socrates should do also turns on whether Socrates would be wronging Athens, a matter that *is* suitable for co-deliberation between those who disagree. The exchange suggests that there are some value clashes too deep for co-deliberation. To see whether this applies to the two tribes, their orienting values must be surfaced and examined through co-deliberation on particular actions, just as Socrates does with Crito.[11]

I suggest that we question the simple dichotomy between facts and values in politics.[12] In order to do this, we may need to entertain new language. In 2016, the phrase "alternative facts" was introduced by Kellyanne Conway, Donald Trump's campaign manager at the time. In a later interview she said the following: "Two plus two is four. Three plus one is four. Partly cloudy, partly sunny. Glass half full, glass half empty. Those are alternative facts" (Nuzzi 2017). If we read Conway charitably, she suggests that different ways of describing the same situation can lead to different postures of deliberation. When we say "glass half full," we mean that we are opting to view the situation from a certain perspective. This perspective frames our deliberation and inclines us towards considering different possibilities and arriving at different conclusions.[13]

Political rhetoric deploys a mixture of facts and values, and it is no surprise that this combination can encode and transmit ideologies. Indeed, this observation often prompts political cynicism (Norris 2012). One might think that giving this ancient problem a novel name such as "post-truth politics" ignores the fact that this dynamic has always been present. For instance, much of the systemic violence against oppressed groups, both tolerated and practiced by the state, has been rationalized on the basis of "alternative facts." Consequently, it is reasonable to think that a lack of concern for truth in politics is nothing new.[14] This is yet another reason to question the sharp dichotomy between facts and values in public deliberation.

6 Truth and political legitimacy

I believe that challenging the fact-value distinction is one way forward for a society consisting of these two tribes. However, taking this route may, in turn, disrupt the political order. To see why, I now return to Williams's claim that allegiance to truth can play an anti-tyranny role. He says, "Political, particularly governmental, truthfulness is valuable against tyranny, but you will get it only as associated with other values and expressed in a set of institutions and practices that as a whole stand against tyranny" (Williams 2002: 208). Williams's understanding of tyranny correlates with his account of political legitimacy. A political system is legitimate, according to Williams, insofar as it makes sense to its subjects as intelligible order – where this order is distinguishable from tyranny (Williams 2005: 10–11).

Whereas I illustrate the threat to political legitimacy with the tale of two tribes, Williams focuses on the "internal economy" of liberalism's political values (Williams 2002: 209). On the one hand, liberalism offers us the "luxury [of discussing] the precise value of truthfulness in politics" (208). On the other hand, as liberals we can question whether free speech promotes the spread of truth, as J.S. Mill argues (Mill 1978; Williams 2002: 212). Williams concludes that "the demand for truthfulness, though it should be an ally of other aspects of liberalism, can nevertheless run into conflict with them" (209).

Despite these tensions, Williams thinks that liberalism's approach to truth is superior overall:

> Liberal societies are more successful in the modern world than others in helping people… to avoid what is universally feared: torture, violence, arbitrary power, and humiliation…The value of the whole enterprise [of liberalism], political truthfulness included, is to be measured against the evils that it resists. (208–9)

In other words, liberal practices and institutions work better than others in checking tyranny, at least in modern conditions. This is an important claim, since Williams calls the anti-tyranny argument "one of the strongest" in favor of truthfulness in politics. The argument is strong, he thinks, because everyone can see and affirm that tyranny is bad.

However, Williams resists the idea that we can get an argument *for* liberalism *in terms of truth*. For one thing, Williams admits that stating an opposition to tyranny – a "truism" – hardly counts as an argument. Williams supplements his theory of political legitimacy with a proviso that allows for the critique of power: provided that the acceptance of political order is not produced by power, then subjects' acceptance can satisfy the basic legitimation demand. The proviso excludes cases in which leaders propagate a legitimation story that would not be believed otherwise. If subjects come to see that the legitimation story is propagated because it is to the advantage of those in power, then their power can no longer be seen as valid (Williams 2002: 227–31). In this way, liberalism forges a robust connection between truthfulness, the debunking of authority claims, and political legitimacy.[15] This connection, according to Williams, shows how truthfulness counteracts tyranny *within* the outlook of liberalism. And this shows, in turn, why liberalism's approach to truth is well-suited for opposing tyranny.[16]

However, a problem remains. This proviso on legitimation is supposed to enable critique of power without presupposing liberalism. But applying the test requires us to make assumptions about what individuals *would* accept if they were suitably reflective about their society. When considering non-liberal societies, we must project onto the individuals some capacity for, and interest in, coming to reject their worldview. Privileging the results of individual reflection over received wisdom, however, is already an implicit rejection of the non-liberal outlook. For this reason, it seems that one must already accept liberal values in order to engage the critical proviso and, by extension, make the anti-tyranny argument count in favor of liberalism. Therefore, it would be circular to claim that the anti-tyranny argument uniquely supports liberalism.[17]

The risk of circularity requires us to be careful in drawing out the implications. When Williams argues that resistance to tyranny is better realized by liberalism's approach to truth, he might appear on the surface to abstract away from the frame of liberalism in order to highlight the value of truth in politics, whether or not it is liberal politics. But this is not what Williams argues. While the avoidance of tyranny is universally appreciated, the role of truthfulness in avoiding tyranny is not similarly universal. Instead, it must be mediated through a particular political outlook; a view of what counts as truthfulness must be shared in order for truth to check tyranny in practice.

Stepping back, it becomes clear that Williams believes that liberalism cannot be defended entirely in terms of the truth of its tenets. In fact, Williams thinks that it would be reasonable to doubt liberalism (Williams 2002: 232). Rather, it can only be appreciated in terms of the evils that it prevents, namely tyranny. For these reasons, truthfulness in politics is a value that is internal to liberalism, not an external, justifying foundation of liberalism. In a sense, therefore, to defend truth against a background of liberalism is to defend liberalism. It is to defend one's political outlook, one's tribe. Perhaps the same holds true for other political outlooks such as socialism or democracy.

And yet, it is no accident that the problem of post-truth politics arose under liberal regimes. Insofar as we are liberals in the sense that Williams has in mind, we will regard the value systems of our political opponents as non-rejectable whenever they are reasonable. In these circumstances, we lack a basis for seeing the other side as a political enemy, even though we feel strongly that their political judgments are wrong and dangerous. So we denounce their indifference to facts, saying that is why they must be opposed. In this way, the denouncing of post-truth politics serves to poison our common discourse.

7 Conclusion

I have argued that describing our political climate as post-truth is both compelling and poisonous. On the one hand, it is compelling because it captures the special diffidence between groups with divergent political outlooks. As we see in the tale of two tribes, heartlanders and metropolitans exhibit the qualities of accuracy and sincerity in ways the other group does not recognize, leading to a loss of confidence that the other side's contributions to public deliberation are made in good faith. The result is that each group interprets the other group's political participation as insincere at best, and at worst domination. I concluded, along with Mill and Williams, that we must have a shared political outlook if truth is to play any role in the resistance of tyranny.

On the other hand, I argued that it is politically poisonous to announce that we live in a post-truth world. Since post-truth politics is a diagnosis that makes sense only within the frame of a shared political outlook, the description expresses and even contributes to an erosion of political legitimacy. I cast doubt on several possible solutions to restoring a common allegiance to truthfulness: agreeing on truth-seeking methods, safeguarding against wishful thinking, and relying on a plurality of non-rejectable political values. I suggested that a more promising way forward was to acknowledge and openly explore the complex relationship between facts and values, rather than impugning each other's commitment to truthfulness. While the strict dichotomy between facts and values seems characteristic of liberalism's appeal, nevertheless it limits us to an appreciation of truthfulness whose anti-tyranny utility presupposes a liberal outlook. In the absence of a widely shared political outlook, I concluded that those of us who care about truth should stop talking about post-truth politics.

Acknowledgments

For helpful discussion, I would like to acknowledge Antón Barba-Kay, Étienne Brown, Alexander Greenberg, Jane Heal, Nikhil Krishnan, Michael Hannon, Jeroen de Ridder, Alex Sarch, Paul Sagar, and Robert M. Simpson.

Notes

1 I do not claim that the tribes exist now or have existed in the past. Rather, they are what Weber called "ideal types" whose artificial simplicity equips us to better understand a complex phenomenon (Weber 1978). Similar ideas have been explored in the United Kingdom by Goodhart (2017) and in the United States by Chua (2018) and Haidt (2012).

2 It is important to distinguish the dynamics I am describing from political relativism. Even if the impasse were to be seen as deep (rationally irreconcilable) disagreement, it is not clear that "there is any plausible path of argument from deep political disagreement to relativism about contested political claims" (Carter 2021: 104).

3 Williams observes that the demand to diversify needs some rationale other than undoing ideological forces:

> One [problem] is that it leaves the critics [of the academic canon, for instance] themselves with no authority, since they need to tell a tale (a lot of detailed tales, in fact) to justify *that* tale: this is the point that, for instance, the denunciation of history needs history. They also need a tale to explain why they are in a position to tell it. Even if they fall back, rather pitifully, on a claim to authority just from minority status, a tale is needed to explain the relevance of that. But if no authority, then only power (Williams 2002: 8).

4 The need for social practices that support sincerity does not mean that *every* communicative act reflects a norm of sincerity, a fallacy he attributes to Habermas (Williams 2002: 225). Individuals as well as institutions face tradeoffs between sincerity and other conditions for deliberative cooperation, such as trust (Greene 2019).

5 Relatedly, Regina Rini argues that higher confidence in the testimony of our fellows can be epistemically reasonable, owing to our greater trust in the judgments of importance made by those who share our values (Rini 2017).

6 It is important that leaders not self-validate that they are honorable or liberty-respecting by rede-fining what these qualities mean. The value system must remain larger than them, so that leaders can be seen as answering to it without dissolving it (Arendt 1961; Thucydides 1989; Weber 1978; Woodruff 2019).
7 I owe this observation to Daniel Y. Elstein.
8 I do not mean to suggest symmetry across the board. As Antón Barba-Kay observes, on any given ques-tion one side can be more susceptible to spates of wishful thinking than the other (Economist 2020).
9 In my opinion, Haidt's authority and sanctity dimensions do not achieve as much resonance as the other four (fairness, harm, loyalty, and liberty). From the inside, one does not value authority so much as the social ordering principles that are upheld by the system of authority. Likewise, it is only from the outside that one appears to be valuing sanctity as such; in many religions, ritual ob-servance arises from love of and devotion to a divine creator. Haidt admits that he relates less well to these dimensions, thereby implying that political values are not easy to integrate for individuals, much less for entire polities.
10 At *Crito* 49c–d, Socrates articulates this precept: "One should never do wrong in return, nor do any man harm, no matter what he may have done to you" (Plato 2005: 44).
11 I take this activity to be compatible with another prescription for overcoming political polariza-tion: participating "in cooperative social engagements that are fundamentally non-political in nature" (Talisse 2019: 131).
12 I owe this suggestion to Antón Barba-Kay.
13 For further discussion of the epistemic significance of Conway's terminology, see (Barba-Kay 2019).
14 Some argue, for instance, that terms like "fake news" and "post-truth" are ideological (Habgood-Coote 2019) and complicit in problematic racial politics (Mejia, Beckermann and Sullivan 2018).
15 Liberalism focuses on the kind of "power over" that is sustained by unwarranted authority claims (Williams 2002: 231–32). As Steven Lukes argues, a definition of power has to make morally sub-stantive assumptions about which effects on others are significant due to the impact on their real interests (Lukes 2005: 30–31).
16 For a fuller discussion of Williams's reliance on the critical proviso in theorizing legitimacy, see (Cozzaglio and Greene 2019).
17 Ben Cross defends Williams's anti-tyranny argument by adding a political analysis that helps citizens decide which deceptive acts to denounce as tyrannical (Cross 2019). While his analysis usefully elaborates the anti-tyranny argument, in my opinion it does not provide an anti-tyranny argument that transcends liberalism.

References

Arendt, H. (1961) *Between Past and Future: Six Exercises in Political Thought*. New York: Viking Press.
Barba-Kay, A. (2019) 'The sound of my own voice', *Eurozine*, 31 January.
Bromwich, D. (2017) 'The age of detesting Trump', *London Review of Books*, 13 July, pp. 9–12.
Carter, J. (2021) 'Politics, deep disagreement, and political relativism'.
Chua, A. (2018) *Political Tribes: Group Instinct and the Fate of Nations*. New York: Penguin.
Cozzaglio, I. and Greene, A. (2019) 'Can power be self-legitimating? Political realism in Hobbes, Weber, and Williams', *European Journal of Philosophy*, 27(4), pp. 1016–36.
Cross, B. (2019) 'Analysing political deception: The virtues of Bernard Williams' anti-tyranny argu-ment', *European Journal of Philosophy*, 27(2), pp. 324–36.
Diderot, D. (2001) *Rameau's Nephew and Other Works*. Indianapolis, IN: Hackett Publishing.
Economist (2020) 'Fake news is fooling more conservatives than liberals. Why?', *The Economist*, 3 June.
Flood, A. (2016) '"Post-truth" named word of the year by Oxford Dictionaries', *The Guardian*, 15 November.
Goodhart, D. (2017) *The Road to Somewhere: The Populist Revolt and the Future of Politics*. London: Hurst & Company.
Greene, A. (2019) 'Is sincerity the first virtue of social institutions? Police, universities, and free speech', *Law and Philosophy*, 38(5), pp. 537–53.
Habgood-Coote, J. (2019) 'Stop talking about fake news!', *Inquiry*, 62(9–10), pp. 1033–65.
Haidt, J. (2012) *The Righteous Mind: Why Good People Are Divided by Politics and Religion*. New York: Random House.

Lukes, S. (2005) *Power: A Radical View*, 2nd ed. Basingstoke: Palgrave Macmillan.

McBrayer, J. (2015) 'Why our children don't think there are moral facts', *New York Times Opinionator*, 2 March.

Mejia, R., Beckermann, K. and Sullivan, C. (2018) 'White lies: A racial history of the (post)truth', *Communication and Critical/Cultural Studies*, 15(2), pp. 109–26.

Mill, J.S. (1977) *The Collected Works of John Stuart Mill*. Edited by John M. Robson. Vol. XIX, Part 2. Toronto: University of Toronto Press.

———. (1978) *On Liberty*. Edited by E. Rapaport. Hackett Publishing.

Norris, A. (2012) "Cynicism, Skepticism, and the Politics of Truth." In *Truth and Democracy*, edited by Jeremy Elkins and Andrew Norris. Philadelphia: University of Pennsylvania Press, pp. 97–113.

Nuzzi, O. (2017) 'Kellyanne Conway is the real first lady of Trump's America', *New York Magazine*, 18 March.

Plato. (2005) *Complete Works*. Edited by J. M. Cooper and D.S. Hutchinson. Indianapolis, IN: Hackett Publishing.

Rini, R. (2017) 'Fake news and partisan epistemology', *Kennedy Institute of Ethics Journal*, 27(2), pp. 43–64.

Talisse, R. (2019) *Overdoing Democracy: Why We Must Put Politics in Its Place*. New York: Oxford University Press.

Thucydides (1989) *The Peloponnesian War*. Edited by D. Grene. Translated by T. Hobbes. Chicago: University of Chicago Press.

Weber, M. (1958) 'Politics as a vocation', in *From Max Weber: Essays in Sociology*. Translated and edited by H. Gerth and C.W. Mills. Oxford: Oxford University Press, pp. 77–128.

———. (1978) *Economy and Society: An Outline of Interpretive Sociology*. Berkeley: University of California Press.

Williams, B. (2002) *Truth & Truthfulness: An Essay in Genealogy*. Princeton, NJ: Princeton University Press.

———. (2005) *In the Beginning Was the Deed: Realism and Moralism in Political Argument*. Edited by G. Hawthorn. Princeton, NJ: Princeton University Press.

Woodruff, P. (2019) *The Garden of Leaders: Revolutionizing Higher Education*. New York: Oxford University Press.

PART 2

Political disagreement and polarization

INTRODUCTION TO PART 2

Disagreement is a permanent and intractable feature of political life. In the United States, nearly half of all Republicans and Democrats say they almost never agree with the other party's positions. Whether the topic is health care, the economy, foreign affairs, education, the environment, privatization, energy, or immigration, it seems nearly impossible for political opponents to agree.

Political disagreement is often a good thing for a healthy democracy. We expect values and preferences to differ in a pluralistic society, and reasonable citizens understand that people of goodwill can disagree about moral and political issues. For this reason, theorizing about liberal democracy has focused largely on disagreements concerning moral and political values, while taking for granted that citizens tend to agree on the facts. However, political disagreements often go beyond political values and even include disputes about matters of fact. Moreover, political debates are increasingly polarized in democratic societies. As a result, political opponents are unable to find agreement and also have highly unfavorable views of each other, regarding one another as immoral, stupid, and lazy. This is a significant problem for democratic politics. Political disagreements are becoming increasingly unreasonable, which makes it difficult to deliberate productively with others and find compromise.

In the first chapter of this section, Shanto Iyengar summarizes a wide range of evidence of increasing levels of polarization, particularly in the United States. Unlike previous research on political polarization, Iyengar's focus is not the ideological extremity of party positions. Instead, he explores a new form of polarization that centers on fear and dislike of one's political opponents. This phenomenon of animosity between the parties is known as *affective polarization*. Iyengar surveys the evidence bearing on the extent of affective polarization, traces its origins to the power of partisanship as a social identity, and explains the factors that have intensified partisan animus. This chapter concludes by reflecting on the implications of heightened partisan animus for the democratic process.

The next chapter, by J. Adam Carter, explores the relationship between political disagreements and political relativism. According to Carter, the question of whether the present trend toward increased political polarization will continue is not just a matter for the social sciences; there are also important philosophical questions to consider. In particular, he considers the idea that both parties to (at least some) political disagreements are right relative to their own perspective. There are two strands of argument for this conclusion: the first involves premises about epistemic circularity; the second diagnoses some political disagreements as 'faultless' on the basis of semantic considerations. This chapter demonstrates how key ideas from epistemology and the philosophy of language (e.g. about deep disagreement, epistemic circularity, semantic relativism) bear on our understanding of political disagreement.

Richard Rowland and Robert Simpson also illustrate how key ideas from epistemology can shed light on foundational issues in political philosophy. In particular, they examine the connection between epistemic permissivism and reasonable pluralism. Intuitively, there is a difference in how we think about pluralism in epistemological vs. political contexts. In politics, it seems perfectly okay to hold one set of political commitments while also thinking it perfectly reasonable for someone in a similar position to have a totally different set of political commitments. Ordinarily, however, it seems problematically arbitrary to hold a particular belief on some issue while also thinking it perfectly reasonable to hold a totally different belief on the same issue given the same evidence. What explains the difference? This chapter considers several explanatory theses that might make sense of this fact.

Elizabeth Edenberg's chapter brings together debates in political philosophy and epistemology over what we should do when we disagree. She argues that we must be cautious about applying one debate to the other because there are significant differences that may threaten this project. For example, there are important differences between civic peers and epistemic peers. Moreover, the scope of the relevant disagreements varies according to whether the methodology chosen falls within ideal theory or non-ideal theory. Further, epistemologists tend to analyze the rationality of individuals' beliefs whereas political philosophers focus on the just governance of a diverse society. Nevertheless, Edenberg claims there are important lessons to learn by considering these debates side by side.

In the next chapter, Daniel Singer and his colleagues use the tools of formal social epistemology to understand how information spreads and how it can influence the beliefs of others. While epistemic network models have been used in philosophy mostly by philosophers of science and social epistemologists, this chapter discusses how epistemic network models can be used to investigate political polarization. It introduces the idea of an epistemic network model and then discusses a series of models for political polarization. The chapter concludes with ideas about how epistemic network models can be used to answer other questions in political epistemology, such as the connection between group beliefs and political legitimacy; how judicial beliefs impact the positions of courts; how social position affects access to knowledge and vice versa; and how epistemic and other injustices are perpetrated and become systematized.

The chapter by Emily McWilliams looks at how political beliefs are formed and maintained in polarized environments. Specifically, she examines how self-serving, directional biases in the ways that people gather and process evidence can make their beliefs resistant to change. By adopting an evidentialist theory of epistemic justification, McWilliams argues that the self-serving biases which influence our beliefs do not actually undermine the justification of these beliefs. This is a counterintuitive result. Thus, McWilliams concludes that evidentialism does not provide us with a complete theory of justification.

In the final chapter of this section, Michael Hannon and Jeroen de Ridder examine the nature, function, and meaning of political beliefs. According to an intuitive and widely accepted view, many citizens have stable and meaningful political beliefs and they choose to support political candidates or parties on the basis of these beliefs. But Hannon and de Ridder call this view into question. They argue that political beliefs differ from ordinary world-modeling beliefs because political beliefs typically do not aim at truth. Moreover, they draw on empirical evidence from political science and psychology to argue that most people lack stable and meaningful political beliefs. Hannon and de Ridder propose that the psychological basis for voting behavior is not an individual's political beliefs but rather group identity, and they briefly reflect on what this means for normative democratic theory.

8

THE POLARIZATION OF AMERICAN POLITICS

Shanto Iyengar

The impeachment trial of U.S. President Donald Trump illustrates vividly the phenomenon of party polarization: intense conflict and ill will across the party divide, and intransigent political preferences that are unresponsive to strong evidence. In this chapter, I will review the political science literature documenting the extent of party polarization and identify possible explanations of the intensified partisan conflict. In closing, I offer some speculative thoughts on how polarization may threaten fundamental democratic norms and institutions.

Defining polarization

Political scientists have typically treated polarization as a matter of ideology, proposing the ideological distance between party platforms as the appropriate yardstick. By this metric, it is clear that elected officials representing the two major American parties have indeed polarized over the past half century (Fleisher and Bond, 2001; Hetherington, 2002; McCarty, Poole and Rosenthal, 2006). However, the jury is still out on whether rank-and-file partisans have followed suit. Some scholars present data showing that most partisans are centrist on the issues despite the movement of their leaders to the ideological extremes (Fiorina, Abrams and Pope, 2008). Others claim that over time party members have gradually emulated the extreme views of party elites (Abramowitz and Saunders, 2008).

Extremity of public opinion on the issues is but one way of defining partisan polarization. An alternative definition, rooted in social psychology, considers mass polarization as the extent to which partisans view each other as a disliked out-group. In the U.S. two-party system, partisanship is about identifying with the "Democrat" group or the "Republican" group (Green, Palmquist and Schickler, 2002; Huddy, Mason and Aaroe, 2015). Once people adopt a partisan identity, they immediately categorize the world into an in-group (their own party) and an out-group (the opposing party) (Iyengar et al., 2018). Psychologists have demonstrated that any in-group versus out-group distinction, even one based on the most trivial of shared characteristics, triggers both positive feelings for the in-group and negative evaluations of the out-group (Billig and Tajfel, 1973). The more salient the group to the sense of personal identity, the stronger these inter-group divisions (Gaertner et al., 1993).

For Americans, partisanship is a particularly salient and powerful identity. It is acquired at a young age and remains stable over the life cycle, notwithstanding significant shifts in personal circumstances (Sears, 1975). Moreover, political campaigns—the formal occasions for expressing citizens' partisan identity—recur frequently, and last for many months. The frequency and duration of campaigns provide individuals multiple opportunities to be reminded of their partisan identity. It is hardly surprising, therefore, that this sense of partisan identity elicits strong feelings of hostility toward political opponents, a phenomenon political scientists refer to as affective polarization.

Affective polarization: the evidence

There is now a burgeoning literature documenting the extent to which partisans treat each other as a disliked out-group. Most of the evidence derives from national surveys, but also includes behavioral indicators of discrimination and measures of implicit or sub-conscious partisan prejudice.

Survey measures of partisan affect

Survey researchers have tracked Americans' feelings toward the parties and their followers since the 1970s. The one indicator with the greatest longevity is the "feeling thermometer" question. Introduced into the American National Election Studies in 1970, the measure has since been widely adopted by other survey organizations (Weisberg and Rusk, 1970). The question asks respondents to rate the two parties or "Democrats" and "Republicans" on a scale ranging from (0) indicating coldness to (100) indicating warmth. Since the measure targets both parties, by dividing the sample into Democrats and Republicans, it is possible to track in-group and out-group affect over the past half century.[1]

As widely reported in scholarly outlets and the popular press, the trends in the feeling thermometer scores reveal substantially increased affective polarization over time. As shown in Figure 8.1, which plots the in-party and out-party thermometer scores in the ANES time series, the gap between the in- and out-party thermometer scores steadily increased from around 23 degrees in 1978 to 41 in 2016 (Iyengar, Sood and Lelkes, 2012). As the figure makes clear, virtually all the increase in affective polarization has occurred because of increased animus toward the opposing party. Warm feelings for one's own party have remained stable across the entire period.

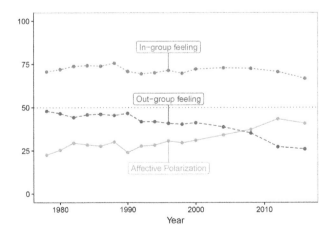

Figure 8.1 ANES party feeling thermometers (1976–2016).

Stronger hostility for the out-party is a recent, but rapidly escalating trend that began at the turn of the century. While the percentage of partisans who rated the out-party between 1 and 49 on the thermometer has increased steadily since the 1980s, the share of partisans expressing intense negativity for the out-party (ratings of 0) remained quite small until 2000. Post-2000, the size of this group has surged dramatically—from 8% in 2000 to 21% in 2016 (Iyengar and Krupenkin, 2018). Thus, the first two decades of the twenty-first century represent an acute era of polarization, in which what was only mild dislike for political opponents now appears to be a deeper form of animus.

A parallel pattern reappears when we track respondents' feelings toward the presidential candidates. Until about 2000, partisans reported only ambivalent feelings toward the opposing party's nominee (average feeling thermometer scores of around 40). However, beginning in 2004, feelings toward the out-party candidate turn colder, with average thermometer scores dropping to around 15 in 2016. As in the case of the party thermometers, partisans' feelings toward their own party nominee are unchanged, the strengthened polarization occurs because of increased hostility toward the opposing party nominee.

The feeling thermometer data show clearly that the party divide elicits affective polarization. It is important, however, to place the findings on partisan affect in some context. How does partisanship compare with other salient cleavages as a source of group polarization? Fortunately, the feeling thermometers have been applied to multiple groups making it possible to compare in-group versus out-group evaluations based on party with evaluations based on race, religion, region, and other relevant groupings. The comparisons reveal that party is easily the most affectively laden group divide in the U.S. Social out-groups including Muslims, Hindus, atheists, Latinos, African Americans, gays, and poor people all elicit much warmer thermometer scores than the out-party (Iyengar, Sood and Lelkes, 2012).

This contrast between the party divide and socio-cultural divides should alert us to a major limitation of self-reported indicators of group affect. Survey responses are highly reactive and susceptible to intentional exaggeration/suppression based on normative pressures. In the case of race, religion, gender, and other social divides, the expression of animus toward out-groups is tempered by strong social norms (Maccoby and Maccoby, 1954). Most individuals are prone to comply with applicable norms when asked sensitive questions. In the case of the party divide, however, there are no corresponding pressures to moderate disapproval of political opponents. If anything, the rhetoric and actions of political leaders convey to their followers that hostility directed at the opposition is not only acceptable, but also appropriate.

Implicit measures

The normative pressures facing survey respondents make it difficult to establish a fair comparison of social with political divides as a basis for out-group animus. Fortunately, psychologists have developed an array of implicit or sub-conscious measures of group prejudice. These implicit measures provide a more valid comparison of the bases for prejudice because they are much harder to manipulate than explicit self-reports and less susceptible to impression management or political correctness (Boysen, Vogel and Madon, 2006).

Iyengar and Westwood (2015) developed a Party Implicit Association Test (Party IAT, based on the brief version of the Race IAT) to document unconscious partisan bias. Their results showed ingrained implicit bias with approximately 70% of Democrats and Republicans showing a bias in favor of their party. Interestingly, implicit bias proved less extensive than explicit bias as measured through survey questions; 91% of Republicans and 75% of Democrats in the same study explicitly evaluated their party more favorably. This is an important reversal from the case of race or religion where social norms restrain the expression of conscious hostility toward out-groups resulting in higher levels of implicit over explicit prejudice.

To place the results from their Party IAT in context, Iyengar and Westwood also administered the Race IAT. Surprisingly, relative to implicit racial bias, implicit partisan bias proved more widespread. The difference in the D-score—the operational indicator of implicit bias across the party divide was 0.50, while the corresponding difference in implicit racial bias across the racial divide was only 0.18. Thus, prejudice toward the out-party exceeded comparable bias directed at the racial out-group by more than 150%!

Indicators of social distance

An even more unobtrusive measure of partisan affect is social distance, the extent to which individuals feel comfortable interacting with out-group members in a variety of different settings. If partisans take their political affiliation seriously, they should be averse to entering into close inter-personal relations with their opponents. The most vivid evidence of increased social distance across the party divide concerns inter-party marriage. In the early 1960s, the percentage of partisans expressing concern over the prospect of their son or daughter marrying someone from the opposition party was in the single digits, but some 45 years later, it had risen to more than 25% (Iyengar, Sood and Lelkes, 2012). Among Republicans, one-half expressed dismay at the prospect of their offspring marrying a Democrat. Today, the party divisions and resulting out-party animus are sufficiently strong to motivate partisans to associate with like-minded others.

More compelling evidence of increased social distance based on party affiliation comes from online dating sites and other available sources of "big data" including national voter files indicating that the party cue does in fact influence the decision to enter into inter-personal relations. In a longitudinal analysis spanning 1965–2015, the authors find that spousal agreement on partisanship moved from 73% to 82%, while disagreement fell from 13% to 6% (Iyengar, Konitzer and Tedin, 2018). Since the 1965 sample of spouses had been married for decades, they had many opportunities to persuade their partner, thus inflating the observed level of agreement. When the researchers limited the focus to younger couples, they found a more impressive shift in spousal agreement; among recently married couples in 1973, spousal agreement registered at 54.3%. For the comparable group of recently married couples in the 2014 national voter file, spousal partisan agreement reached 73.9%. This is an increase of 36% in partisan agreement among couples who have had little opportunity to persuade each other.

Online dating sites are a rich source of data on the politics underlying inter-personal attraction. Huber and Malhotra leverage data from a major dating website where they gained access to both the daters' personal profiles and their messaging behavior (Huber and Malhotra, 2017). They found that partisan agreement increases the likelihood of two people exchanging messages by 10%. To put that difference in perspective, the comparable difference for couples matched on socio-economic status (using education as the indicator) was 11%. Thus, partisanship appears to be just as relevant as social standing in the process of selecting a romantic partner.

The fact that individuals date and marry co-partisans does not necessarily mean that politics was the basis for their choice. Agreement on partisanship may be a byproduct of spousal selection on some other attribute correlated with partisan identity, such as economic status. While some researchers argue that partisan agreement among couples is in fact "induced" or accidental, others provide evidence in favor of an active selection model in which the political affiliation of the prospective partner is the point of attraction. Huber and Malhotra (2017), for instance, show that ideology and partisanship both predict reciprocal online messaging on dating sites even after controlling for alternative bases of spousal attraction. Iyengar et al. (2018) present similar results, showing that spousal agreement in the current era is more attributable to selection based on politics than alternative mechanisms including induced selection, the homogeneity of marriage markets, and agreement due to one spouse gradually persuading the other.

Dating and marriage both entail long-term and more intimate relationships. Does politics also impede the initiation of more casual friendships? Surveys by the Pew Research Center (2017) suggest that it does. About 64% of Democrats and 55% of Republicans say they have "just a few" or "no" close friends who are from the other political party. Thus, partisanship appears to act as a litmus test even at the level of casual social encounters.

Behavioral evidence of partisan bias

Survey measures of partisan affect are subject to several limitations, since people can answer questions in ways that do not reveal their true feelings. In response, scholars have turned to behavioral manifestations of partisan animus in both lab and naturalistic settings. Iyengar and Westwood (2015) have used economic games as a platform for documenting the extent to which partisans are willing to endow or withhold financial rewards from players who either share or do not share their partisan affiliation. In the trust game, the researcher gives Player 1 an initial endowment ($10) and instructs her that she is free to give all, some, or none to Player 2 (said to be a member of a designated group). Player 1 is further informed that any amount she donates to Player 2 will be tripled by the researcher, and that Player 2 is free (although under no obligation to do so) to transfer an amount back to Player 1. The dictator game is an abbreviated version of the trust game in which there is no opportunity for Player 2 to return funds to Player 1 and where the researcher does not add to the funds transferred. Since there is no opportunity for Player 1 to observe the strategy of Player 2, variation in the amount Player 1 allocates to the different categories represented by Player 2 in the dictator game is attributable only to group dislike and prejudice. As Fershtman and Gneezy put it, "any transfer distribution differences in the dictator game must be due to a taste for discrimination" (Fershtman and Gneezy, 2001).

The trust and dictator games provide a consequential test of out-group bias, for they assess the extent to which participants are willing to transfer money they would otherwise receive themselves to co-partisans while simultaneously withholding money from opposing partisans. For both the trust game and the dictator game, partisan bias emerges as the difference between the amount allocated to co-partisans and opposing partisans. The results reported by Iyengar and Westwood show the expected pattern; co-partisans consistently receive a bonus while opposing partisans are subject to a financial penalty (Iyengar and Westwood, 2015). As in the case of implicit bias, the effects of party affiliation on donations exceeded the effects of ethnicity. In fact, the effects of racial similarity proved negligible and not significant—co-ethnics were treated more generously (by eight cents) in the dictator game, but incurred a loss (seven cents) in the trust game. As in the case of the survey data, social norms appear to suppress racial discrimination in the trust and dictator games.

Iyengar and Westwood shed further light on the extent of affective polarization by comparing the effects of partisan and racial cues on non-political judgments (Iyengar and Westwood, 2015). In one study, they asked participants to select one of two candidates for a college scholarship. The candidates (both high school students) had similar academic credentials, but differed in their ethnicity (White or African American) or partisanship (Democrat or Republican). The results indicated little racial bias; Whites, in fact, preferred the African American applicant (55.8%). In contrast, partisan favoritism was widespread; 79.2% of Democrats picked the Democratic applicant, and 80% of Republicans picked the Republican applicant. These results held even when the out-partisan candidate had a significantly higher GPA (4.0 vs. 3.5); in fact, the probability of a partisan selecting the more qualified out-party candidate was never above 30%.

In an important extension to the behavioral literature, researchers have shown that partisanship can distort labor markets. Using an audit design, Gift and Gift (2015) mailed out resumes signaling job applicants' partisan affiliation in a heavily Democratic area and a heavily Republican area. They found that in the Democratic county, Democratic resumes were 2.4% points more likely to receive a callback than Republican resumes; the corresponding partisan preference for Republican resumes in the Republican county was 5.6% points. Whereas Gift and Gift examine employer preferences, McConnell et al. (2018) examine the other side of the labor market and study how partisanship affects employee behavior. The researchers hired workers to complete an online editing task and subtly signaled the partisan identification of the employer. Unlike Gift and Gift, they mainly find evidence of in-group favoritism as opposed to out-group prejudice. The only significant differences occurred between the co-partisan condition and the control group. People exhibited a willingness to accept lower compensation (by 6.5%) from a partisan congruent employer. At the same time, they performed lower-quality work and exhibited less effort. Although the mechanism for this performance deficit is unclear, one possibility is that they perceive the employer to be of higher quality and therefore less likely to make copy-editing mistakes.

In summary, evidence from self-reported feelings toward the parties, sub-conscious partisan prejudice, increased social distance based on political affiliation, and multiple instances of behavioral discrimination against opposing partisans all converge on the finding of intensified party polarization in the U.S. We turn next to consider the factors that may have contributed to this phenomenon.

Possible explanations

The period over which mass polarization has intensified (1980–today) coincides with several major changes in American society and politics, including changes in the media environment, increased social homophily, and partisan sorting or greater differentiation between Democrats and Republicans. In addition to independently inducing hostility toward opponents, each of these factors reinforce the others, further contributing to the rise of affective polarization.

First, in the last 50 years, the percentage of "sorted" partisans, i.e., partisans who identify with the party most closely reflecting their ideology, has steadily increased (Levendusky, 2009). When most Democrats [Republicans] are also liberals [conservatives], they are less likely to encounter conflicting political ideas and identities, and are more likely to see non-identifiers as socially distant (Roccas and Brewer, 2002). Sorting likely leads people to perceive both opposing partisans and co-partisans as more extreme than they really are, with misperceptions being more acute for opposing partisans (Levendusky and Malhotra, 2016).

As partisan and ideological identities have come into alignment, other salient social identities, including race and religion, also converged with partisanship. Democrats are increasingly the party of women, non-whites, professionals, and residents of urban areas, while

Republican voters are disproportionately older white men, evangelical Christians, and residents of rural areas. This decline of crosscutting identities is at the root of affective polarization according to Mason (2018). She has shown that those with consistent partisan and ideological identities became more hostile towards the out-party without necessarily changing their ideological positions, and those that have aligned religious, racial, and partisan identities react more emotionally to information that threatens their partisan identities or issue stances. In essence, sorting has made it much easier for partisans to make generalized inferences about the opposing side, even if those inferences are inaccurate.

A second potential cause of strengthened polarization is social homophily. We have described studies documenting strengthened processes of socialization by which families come to agree on their partisan loyalties. Family agreement creates an inter-personal echo chamber that facilitates polarization. When family members identify with the same party, they also express more extreme positions on the issues and harbor hostile views toward their opponents. In the case of a 2015 national survey of married couples, respondents evaluated the presidential candidates Hillary Clinton and Donald Trump (using the ANES 100 point feeling thermometer). Among spouses who agreed on their party identification, the average difference between the in- and out-party candidate thermometer score was 59 points (70 vs. 11 degrees). Among the few pairs consisting of spouses with divergent loyalties (Democrat-Republican pairings), this margin of difference fell by more than 30 degrees. Partisan agreement within the family strengthens polarization (Iyengar, Konitzer and Tedin, 2018).

Given the importance of family socialization to the development of partisan attitudes, the rate at which any given society undergoes polarization will be conditional on the extent to which partisans grow up in homogeneous environments. Recent simulations by Klofstad, McDermott and Hatemi (2013) suggest that spousal agreement induces ideological polarization within the family fairly rapidly, with most of the increased polarization occurring as early as the fifth generation. We would similarly expect generations to move increasingly apart on their feelings toward the opposing party to the extent family members share these sentiments.

Finally, a third potential contributor to affective polarization is technology. The revolution in information technology has empowered consumers to encounter news on their own terms. The availability of 24-hour cable news channels provided partisans with their first real opportunity to obtain news from like-minded sources (Fox News first for Republicans, and MSNBC later for Democrats). The development of the Internet provided a much wider range of media choices, which greatly facilitated partisans' ability to obtain political information and commentary consistent with their leanings. In a break with the dominant paradigm of non-partisan journalism, a growing number of outlets, motivated in part by the commercial success of the Fox News network, offered reporting in varying guises of partisan commentary. Many of these online partisan outlets depict the opposing party in harsh terms (Berry and Sobieraj, 2014) and focus disproportionately on out-party scandals (real or imagined). The political blogosphere, with hundreds of players providing news and analysis—often vitriolic—developed rapidly as a partisan platform, with very little cross-party exposure (Adamic and Natalie, 2005; Lawrence, Sides and Farrell, 2010). The creation of vast online social networks permitted extensive recirculation of news reports, even to those not particularly motivated to seek out news. Several scholars have thus singled out the technologically enhanced media environment and partisans' ability to encounter "friendly" information providers as an especially influential agent of polarization (Sunstein, 2017).

While there are good reasons to believe that the new media environment has contributed to the growth in partisan animus, by facilitating access to partisan news and commentary, it is possible that enhanced consumer choice also sets in motion processes that weaken polarization. As media platforms have multiplied, consumers gain access not only to more news providers, but also to entertainment providers. The availability of entertainment programming on demand enables some to drop out of the political arena entirely (Prior, 2007). Thus, the net impact of the increased empowerment of consumers is unclear.

In fact, despite the myriad changes in the media environment, the evidence to date demonstrating that news consumption exacerbates polarization is less than unequivocal. While experimental studies of online browsing behavior confirm the tendency of partisans to self-select into distinct audiences (Iyengar and Hahn, 2009; Stroud, 2011) more generalizable real-world studies find few traces of audience segregation. In their pioneering analysis of Americans' web browsing behavior (conducted in 2008), Gentzkow and Shapiro (2011) found that online audiences were only slightly more segregated than audiences for network or cable news. They concluded, "Internet news consumers with homogeneous news diets are rare. These findings may mitigate concerns.... that the Internet will increase ideological polarization and threaten democracy" (p. 1831). However, more recent work—also based on large-scale tracking of online browsing behavior—suggests that the segregation of news audiences is increasing. A 2013 study showed that although most people relied on ideologically diverse online sources such as web aggregators, audience segregation tended to increase among individuals who used search engines to locate news stories and among social media users who encountered links in their news feed (Flaxman, Goel and Rao, 2016). Both these pathways to news exposure feature personalized algorithms, making it more likely that individuals encounter information consistent with their political loyalties. In the case of Facebook, now a major source of news, most individuals find themselves in politically homogeneous networks, increasing the likelihood of exposure to polarizing messages (Bakshy, Messing and Adamic, 2015).

To the extent partisans do gravitate to like-minded news providers, has the diffusion of high-speed Internet facilitated this behavior? Here too, the evidence is mixed. In those parts of the country where broadband is more available, traffic to partisan news sites is greater (Lelkes, Sood and Iyengar, 2017). Moreover, Lelkes, Sood and Iyengar go on to show that broadband diffusion has strengthened partisan affect. Moving from a county with the fewest number of broadband providers to a county with the highest number increased affective polarization by roughly 0.07 (an effect roughly half as large as the effect of partisans' political interest). On the other hand, Boxell, Gentzkow and Shapiro (2017) demonstrate that affective polarization has increased the most among those least likely to use social media and the Internet. Given these inconsistent results, it is too early to conclude that Internet usage (and the availability of a wider array of information) plays a causal role in the growth of affective polarization.

Conclusion

The phenomenon of affective polarization—the tendency of Democrats and Republicans to treat each other as a stigmatized out-group—has far-reaching consequences for the behavior of politicians. For one thing, it creates incentives for politicians to use inflammatory rhetoric and demonize their opponents. The most frequent and enthusiastic chant at Republican rallies in 2016 was "lock her up." Illegal immigrants, in Trump's words, were "rapists and drug dealers." Earlier, during the debate over the passage of the Affordable Care Act, some Republicans likened the mandatory insurance requirement in the law to the forced deportation of Jews by the Nazis. In response, the liberal commentator Keith Olbermann declared that Republicans' opposition to the law was tantamount to racism. Symptomatic of the pressures facing politicians to demonstrate their party colors, a study found that taunting of the opposition party is the most frequent theme in congressional press releases (Grimmer and King, 2011).

At the level of electoral politics, heightened polarization has made it almost impossible for partisans to abandon their party's candidates, no matter their limitations. The release of the Access Hollywood tape—in which Trump made crude references to his willingness and ability to grope women—would surely have ended the candidacy of any presidential candidate in any election cycle from the 1980s or 1990s. Yet the impact on Donald Trump's poll numbers was miniscule. And in Alabama, in the 2017 Senate election, evidence of Republican candidate Roy Moore's inappropriate relations with under-age women hardly caused concern among Republican voters, a mere 7% of whom defected.

Partisans have become so committed to their party that scholars have had to update the standard finding of public opinion research—voter ignorance of current events. Today, partisans are not only uninformed, but also misinformed, and deliberately misinformed (Berinsky, 2017; Flynn, Nyhan and Reifler, 2017). Partisan voters have become reliable team players whose loyalty provides politicians considerable leeway to guide and lead public opinion. As a result, when candidates make claims that are false, there is the very real possibility of voter manipulation. Well before he became a presidential candidate, Donald Trump was the principal sponsor of the conspiracy-oriented "birther" theory concerning former President Barack Obama's place of birth and citizenship. Since taking office, Trump has continued to show little respect for facts and evidence. He claimed that extensive voter fraud was responsible for his loss in the popular vote and that charges of possible collusion between his campaign and the Russian government amount to a "hoax." What's more, he frequently attacks the credibility of the American press by referring to stories critical of his leadership as "fake news." Trump's rhetoric has persuaded Republicans, many of whom believe in Trump's false claims.

All told, intensified affective polarization portends serious repercussions, especially during times of political turmoil. There are multiple parallels between Watergate and the current era, yet polarization has fundamentally altered the political dynamics of scandal. Investigative news reports that brought to light the cover-up in the Nixon White House became widely accepted as credible evidence of official wrongdoing. The media spotlight resulted in a significant erosion of President Nixon's approval among both Democrats and Republicans. In contrast, the multiple investigations swirling around the Trump administration have, to date, done little to undermine his standing among Republicans. Partisans' willingness to ignore information that challenges their sense of political identity is disturbing and undermines the ability of the press to act as the "fourth branch of government." President Trump famously claimed that he could stand in the middle of Fifth Avenue and shoot somebody at no cost to his electoral support. We can only hope that he is mistaken.

Note

1 Following conventional practice, scholars of affective polarization measure party identification using the standard ANES seven-point question ranging from strongly Republican to strongly Democratic. Most scholars classify independent "leaners" as partisans and exclude pure independents from consideration (this group represents less than 15% of the electorate in the 2016 ANES). Democratic and Republican evaluations of their own side constitute the measure of in-group affect while partisans' evaluations of their opponents provide the measure of out-group affect.

References

Abramowitz, A. I. and Saunders, K. L. (2008) 'Is Polarization a Myth?' *Journal of Politics*, 70, pp. 542–55.

Adamic, L. A. and Natalie, G. (2005) 'The Political Blogosphere and the 2004 U.S. Election: Divided They Blog.' Paper presented at the Annual Workshop on the Weblogging Ecosystem, WWW2005, Chiba, Japan, May 10–14.

Bakshy, E., Messing, S. and Adamic, L. A. (2015) 'Exposure to Ideologically Diverse News and Opinion on Facebook.' *Science*, 348, pp. 1130–32.

Berinsky, A. 2017. 'Rumors and Health Care Reform: Experiments in Political Misinformation.' *British Journal of Political Science*, 47, pp. 241–62.

Berry, J. and Sobieraj, S. (2014) *The Outrage Industry: Political Opinion Media and the New Incivility.* Oxford: Oxford University Press.

Billig, M. G. and Tajfel, H. (1973) 'Social Categorization and Similarity in Intergroup Behavior.' *European Journal of Social Psychology*, 3, pp. 27–52.

Boxell, L., Gentzkow, M. and Shapiro, J. M. (2017) 'Greater Internet Use Is Not Associated with Faster Growth in Political Polarization among US Demographic Groups.' *Proceedings of the National Academy of Science*, 114, pp. 10612–17.

Boysen, G. A., Vogel, D. L. and Madon, S. (2006) 'A Public versus Private Administration of the Implicit Association Test.' *European Journal of Social Psychology*, 36, pp. 845–56.

Fershtman, C. and Gneezy, U. (2001) 'Discrimination in a Segmented Society: An Experimental Approach.' *Quarterly Journal of Economics*, 116, pp. 351–77.

Fiorina, M., Abrams, S. and Pope, J. (2008) 'Polarization in the American Public: Misconceptions and Misreadings.' *Journal of Politics*, 70, pp. 556–60.

Flaxman, S., Goel, S. and Rao, J. M. (2016) 'Filter Bubbles, Echo Chambers and Online News Consumption.' *Public Opinion Quarterly*, 80, pp. 298–320.

Fleisher, R. and Bond, J. R. (2001) 'Evidence of Increasing Polarization among Ordinary Citizens,' in Cohen, J. E., Fleisher, R. and Kantor, P. (eds.) *American Political Parties: Decline or Resurgence?* Washington: CQ Press, pp. 55–77.

Flynn, D. J., Nyhan, B. and Reifler, J. 2017. 'The Nature and Origins of Misperceptions: Understanding False and Unsupported Beliefs about Politics.' *Political Psychology*, 38, pp. 127–50.

Gaertner, S., Dovidio, J. F., Anastasio, P. A., Bachman, B. A. and Rust, M. C. (1993) 'The Common Ingroup Identity Model: Recategorization and the Reduction of Intergroup Bias.' *European Review of Social Psychology*, 4, pp. 1–26.

Gentzkow, M. and Shapiro, J. M. (2011) 'Ideological Segregation Online and Offline.' *Quarterly Journal of Economics*, 126, pp. 1799–1839.

Gift, K. and Gift, T. (2015) 'Does Politics Influence Hiring? Evidence from a Randomized Experiment.' *Political Behavior*, 37, pp. 653–75.

Green, D., Palmquist, B. and Schickler, E. (2002) *Partisan Hearts and Minds: Political Parties and the Social Identities of Voters.* New Haven, CT: Yale University Press.

Grimmer, J. and King, G. (2011) 'General Purpose Computer-Assisted Clustering and Conceptualization.' *Proceedings of the National Academy of Science*, 108, pp. 2643–2650.

Hetherington, M. (2002) 'Resurgent Mass Partisanship: The Role of Elite Polarization.' *American Political Science Review*, 95, pp. 619–31.

Huber, G. A. and Malhotra, N. (2017) 'Political Homophily in Social Relationships: Evidence from Online Dating Behavior.' *Journal of Politics*, 79, pp. 269–83.

Huddy, L., Mason, L. and Aaroe, L. (2015) 'Expressive Partisanship: Campaign Involvement, Political Emotion, and Partisan Identity.' *American Political Science Review*, 109, pp. 1–17.

Iyengar, S. and Hahn, K. (2009) 'Red Media, Blue Media: Evidence of Ideological Selectivity in Media Use.' *Journal of Communication*, 59, pp 19–39.

Iyengar, S., Konitzer, T. and Tedin, K. L. (2018) 'The Home as a Political Fortress: Family Agreement in an Era of Polarization.' *Journal of Politics*, 80, pp. 1326–38.

Iyengar, S. and Krupenkin, M. T. (2018) 'The Strengthening of Partisan Affect.' *Political Psychology*, 39, pp. 201–18.

Iyengar, S., Sood, G. and Lelkes, Y. (2012) 'Affect, Not Ideology: A Social Identity Perspective on Polarization.' *Public Opinion Quarterly*, 76(3), pp. 405–31.

Iyengar, S. and Westwood, S. J. (2015) 'Fear and Loathing across Party Lines.' *American Journal of Political Science*, 59, pp. 690–707.

Iyengar, S., Lelkes, Y., Levendusky, M., Malhotra, N. and Westwood S. J. (2019) 'The Origin and Consequences of Affective Polarization in the United States.' *Annual Review of Political Science*, 22, pp. 129–46.

Klofstad, C., McDermott, R. and Hatemi, P. K. (2013) 'The Dating Preference of Liberals and Conservatives.' *Political Behavior*, 35, pp. 519–38.

Lawrence, E. D., Sides, J. and Farrell, H. (2010) 'Self-Segregation or Deliberation? Blog Readership, Participation, and Polarization in American Politics.' *Perspectives on Politics*, 8, pp. 141–58.

Lelkes, Y., Sood, G. and Iyengar, S. (2017) 'The Hostile Audience: The Effect of Access to Broadband Internet on Partisan Affect.' *American Journal of Political Science*, 61, pp. 5–20.

Levendusky, M. S. (2009) *The Partisan Sort: How Liberals Became Democrats and Conservatives Became Republicans*. Chicago, IL: University of Chicago Press.

Levendusky, M. S. and Malhotra, N. (2016) 'Misperceptions of Partisan Polarization in the American Public.' *Public Opinion Quarterly*, 80, pp. 378–91.

Maccoby, E. E. and Maccoby, N. (1954) 'The Interview: A Tool of Social Science,' in Lindzey, G. (ed.) *The Handbook of Social Psychology*. Cambridge: Addison-Wesley, pp. 449–87.

Mason, L. (2018) *Uncivil Agreement: How Politics Became Our Identity*. Chicago, IL: University of Chicago Press.

McCarty, N., Poole, K. and Rosenthal, H. (2006) *Polarized America: The Dance of Ideology and Unequal Riches*. Cambridge: MIT Press.

McConnell, C., Malhotra, N., Margolit, Y. and Levendusky M. (2018) 'The Economic Consequences of Partisanship in a Polarized Era.' *American Journal of Political Science*, 62, pp. 5–18.

Pew Research Center (2017) *The Partisan Divide on Political Values Grows Even Wider*. Technical report Available at: http://pewrsr.ch/2z0qBnt.

Prior, M. (2007) *Post-Broadcast Democracy. How Media Choice Increases Inequality in Political Involvement and Polarizes Elections*. New York: Cambridge University Press.

Roccas, S. and Brewer, M. B. (2002) 'Social Identity Complexity.' *Personality and Social Psychology Review*, 6, pp. 88–106.

Sears, D. O. (1975) 'Political Socialization,' in Greenstein, F. I. and Polsby, N. W. (eds.) *Handbook of Political Science*, Vol. 2. Reading, MA: Addison-Wesley, pp. 93–153.

Stroud, N. J. (2011) *Niche News: The Politics of News Choice*. New York: Oxford University Press.

Sunstein, C.R. (2017) *#Republic: Divided Democracy in the Age of Social Media*. Princeton, NJ: Princeton University Press.

Weisberg, H. F. and Rusk, J. G. (1970) 'Dimensions of Candidate Evaluation.' *American Political Science Review*, 64, pp. 1167–85.

9

POLITICS, DEEP DISAGREEMENT, AND RELATIVISM

J. Adam Carter

1 Introduction

Political disagreements, particularly in Western liberal democracies, are becoming increasingly *polarized*, and they are polarized to an extent that can make political consensus nowadays seem unrealistic, or like a relic of the past.[1]

According to a January 2020 Pew Research study, nine out of ten Americans (91%) hold the view that the disagreements dividing Democrats and Republicans in the United States are either 'strong or very strong', with nearly three quarters of Americans (71%) reporting that they view these disagreements to be 'very strong'. When the same question was posed in the previous presidential election year, 2016, only 56% gave a 'very strong' verdict, which itself was up from 47% in 2012.[2] Meanwhile, in the United Kingdom, 'Brexit identity' (i.e. the mutually exclusive identities of 'Leave' or 'Remain') has become – moreso now than any of the comparatively less well-defined U.K. political party identities – among the most important markers of in-group/out-group self-identification (Hobolt et al. 2018), and this self-identification corresponds with a range of increasingly rigid attitudinal fault lines on issues such as immigration, diversity, globalization, human rights, and trust in experts (Marsh 2020).

These wide divisions are on full display on social media, where political arguments on-line (e.g. on Facebook and Twitter) often have the counterproductive effect of amplifying previously held positions (Carter & Broncano-Berrocal forthcoming; Quattrociocchi et al. 2016; Sunstein 2002). Even more, extreme views are easily exacerbated simply by searching YouTube, whose automated recommender system is programmed to recommend additional content that aligns with a user's previous history (Alfano et al. 2018, forthcoming).

The question of whether the present trend toward increased political polarization in Western democracies will continue to widen is a matter for the social sciences. However, there are important *philosophical* issues in the neighbourhood, especially once we consider what it means for the status of contested political claims if and when political disagreements become *irreconcilable*.

A relativist-friendly template strategy of argument that is familiar from debates about the status of moral, scientific as well as epistemic claims, goes roughly as follows: once disagreements in *any* given area – politics or otherwise – get deep enough, they pass the point at which rational adjudication is possible. This usually occurs when what is contested is not merely some first-order topic or topics in the domain, but also the very *principles* that permit and forbid ways of evaluating those first-order claims (see, e.g., Boghossian 2006a, Ch. 5; Carter 2016, Ch. 4, 2018; Hales 2014; Lynch 2016; Ranalli 2018; Rorty 1979; Siegel 2011). When a disagreement reaches this level, it looks *ex ante* as though all each side can do is appeal to its own principles, including its most fundamental principles, in the service of justifying them.

And it's at this point that the relativist claims a key foothold. As Michael Williams (2007) characterizes the relativist's thread of thinking – once a disagreement moves from the first-order to the second-order:

> the best we can hope for is a justification that is *epistemically circular*, employing our […] framework in support of itself. Since this procedure can be followed by anyone, whatever his […] framework, all such frameworks, provided they are coherent, are equally defensible (or indefensible). (2007, pp. 94–95, *my italics*)[3]

If the above is right, then consider what this all means for your favourite Brexit debate on Facebook. Roughly: you support anti-Brexit policy X. Your interlocutor says 'not-X!'. As the debate progresses, rather than to converge on common ground, you discover that your interlocutor subscribes to different fundamental views about what makes for a reasonable political argument about Brexit, what counts as good evidence for a political position more generally, etc. Of course, you proceed to defend your *own* views about these deeper, 'meta-political' matters, but in the course of doing so, you (obviously) are reasoning in accordance with those *very* kinds of principles now under dispute at the second-order.[4] Enter the relativist:

> Whether you like it or not, you are *both* now on epistemically *equal footing* when it comes to the original Brexit policy X. Both of you can, at most, defend your preferred stance about policy X by appealing to principles that are *circularly* justified – and your circular reasoning lends no better support to your position than theirs does to theirs![5]

In what follows, this chapter will focus in on two distinct philosophical questions that arise out of the above kind of reasoning, and some of the recent debates in the literature surrounding them. These are the *depth question* and the *circularity question*:

- *Depth question*: Are political disagreements really as deep as they seem?
- *Circularity question*: If we can, at best, circularly justify our deeply contested political views, does political relativism follow?

The former question is the focus of Section 2, and the latter of Section 3. The chapter concludes, in Section 4, by showing how political relativism might be motivated in an entirely different way, by appealing to some new insights in the philosophy of language and formal semantics.

2 The depth question

Political disagreements *seem* deep. But might this be illusory?

Here, a comparison with scientific disagreements will be instructive. Consider, for example, the famous seventeenth-century dispute between Galileo and Cardinal Bellarmine about the matter of whether geocentrism (the thesis that the earth is the fixed centre of the universe, around which the sun revolves) is true. Galileo's view was that geocentrism was false, a view he held on the basis of telescopic evidence, and more generally, by appealing to the scientific method. Cardinal Bellarmine maintained that geocentrism was true; however, his appeal was to Scripture. Galileo and Bellarmine accordingly disagreed not only about geocentrism, but also about what kinds of methods constituted good ways of resolving the dispute: science or Scripture?

According to Richard Rorty (1979, pp. 328–29), Galileo and Bellarmine were using entirely different epistemic 'grids'; they were so far apart that rational adjudication was unattainable (as well as pointless to attempt). On a strong way of reading Rorty's assessment of the situation, the 'grid', or framework constituted by Galileo's principles, and that which is constituted by the principles that Bellarmine accepts are *disjoint* – viz., they contain no common principle. Call a disagreement with this feature a 'disjoint deep disagreement'. On a weaker way of unpacking Rorty's assessment, Galileo and Bellarmine's (respective) sets of principles are not disjoint; however, they contain between them no 'Archimedean' principle – viz., that is, no common principle the acceptance of which would be effective in helping them rationally (by both of their lights) break the deadlock (even if there are some common principles).[6] Call a disagreement with this feature a 'non-Archimedean' deep disagreement. All disjoint disagreements are non-Archimedean, but not all non-Archimedean disagreements are disjoint.

It's worth noting at the outset that, at least in the case of this famous scientific dispute – one often used in the service of motivating relativism (by Rorty and others[7]) – a disjoint interpretation of Rorty's assessment is implausible. Consider, for example, a simple logical principle: inferences of the form (X and Y, therefore, X) are justified. This is surely part of Galileo's framework. But, is it really *not* part of Bellarmine's? It most plausibly is, and *mutatis mutandis* for other reasoning principles at a high level of abstraction, viz., the law of the excluded middle, the law of identity, etc.

Rather than to suppose that the depth of Bellarmine and Galileo's dispute is such that they subscribe to disjoint sets of principles when it comes to reasoning about the earth's location, the comparatively more plausible reading is the weaker 'Non-Archimedean' reading on which, in short, it's not that there's no common principle, but there's not a common principle of the 'right kind' (we'll return to this).

But, first, let's return to politics: are some of our most entrenched contemporary political disagreements more plausibly classed as disjoint or non-Archimedean? A moment's reflection suggests at most the latter. Even the most hardline disputes about, e.g., Trump and Brexit take place against at least some shared background about what constitutes rational moves in a political dispute (think again here about the law of the excluded middle and the law of identity). Accordingly, if such disputes are rationally irreconcilable (as opposed to rationally reconcilable), then it is because they are – like the debate between Galileo and Bellarmine – non-Archimedean.

Interestingly, Boghossian (2006) casts doubt on whether even *this* is true in the case of Galileo and Bellarmine. As he puts it:

> For many ordinary propositions, then—propositions about what J. L. Austin called "medium-sized specimens of dry goods"—Bellarmine uses exactly the same epistemic system we use. About the heavens, though, we diverge—we use our eyes, he consults the Bible. Is this really an example of a coherent fundamentally different epistemic system; or is it just an example of someone using the very same epistemic norms we use to

arrive at a surprising theory about the world—namely, that a certain book, admittedly written many years ago by several different hands, is the revealed word of God and so may rationally be taken to be authoritative about the heavens? (2006a, pp. 103–4)

By parity of reasoning, we can imagine an analogous Boghossian-style diagnosis of a Trump/Anti-Trump or a Brexit/Anti-Brexit debate: (i) for many ordinary propositions, the Trump/Brexit supporter uses the *same* epistemic system as we[8] do; (ii) when it comes to the matter of supporting Trump/Brexit, we diverge with them – we consult the Guardian/BBC/CNN, they rely on FoxNews/Breitbart/Quillette, etc.; (iii) (Rhetorical question): "Is this *really* an example of a coherent fundamentally different epistemic system; or is it just an example of someone using the very same epistemic norms we use to arrive at a surprising theory about the world".

If Boghossian is right in his characterization of Galileo versus Bellarmine, then – by parity of reasoning – it becomes much less plausible to suppose that paradigmatic examples of contemporary political disputes are irreconcilable because non-Archimedean. After all, *prima facie*, rational adjudication is possible between interlocutors who share an epistemic system, where an epistemic system is at minimum a set of basic epistemic principles.

But then, if paradigmatic political disputes are *not* irreconcilable either because they are disjoint *or* because they are, more weakly, non-Archimedean, then it becomes increasingly mysterious why we should think that they *really are* rationally irreconcilable at all – and, *a fortiori*, that there is any plausible path of argument from deep political disagreement to relativism about contested political claims.

A potential reply at this juncture might proceed along the following lines: But, we have empirical evidence that such disagreements *are* irreconcilable! Empirical evidence that supports group polarization in the case of political discussions (e.g., Lorentzen 2014; Yardi & Boyd 2010), at the same time, supports the idea that these disagreements tend not toward, but *away from*, consensus.

The counterreply available to this line of thinking, though, is instructive. Evidence that political disagreements have *in fact* not been reconciled is not good evidence that they are irreconcilable. For example, for all we know, individuals who polarize when debating a hot-button political issue *might not have*. That is, it might be a highly contingent fact that such polarization occurs when it does. On one empirical theory that purports to explain political polarization – self-categorization theory (Turner 1982; Wetherell et al. 1986) – the reason that we polarize when we do has do with an underlying need to categorize ourselves in contrast with others. This need for self-categorization, a need that happens to have social benefits, leads us to amplify the kinds of differences that serve the social categorization purpose.

If self-categorization theory were correct, then notice that in a world where such a need was controlled for, we'd have no expectation that a group would polarize as opposed to converge. The matter of what the social-psychological mechanisms are that drive polarization in politics and elsewhere does not presently have consensus among social scientists.[9] This much places an important dialectical burden on one who wants to insist – given what we presently know (and don't know) about these mechanisms – that paradigmatic disagreements are 'deep' in the sense of being rationally irreconcilable. This is the case even if we agree – as we should – that many paradigmatic political disputes are disputes not only about political issues, but about political principles more generally.

3 The circularity question

Let's suppose, from here on out, that the situation is worse than Section 2 suggests. Assume, for the sake of argument, that there are at least *some* irreconcilable political disagreements. What then?

As we saw in Section 1, once an irreconcilability premise is granted, the relativist submits that our attempts to sway our interlocutor will involve appealing to a different system of principles (to wit, *our* system) than the interlocutor with whom we are deeply divided appeals to in an attempt to justify their own. But *this*, the relativist maintains, is best understood as a situation where both parties are on an *equal footing*, epistemically. Sure, we can provide a circular justification for our own epistemic principles. But so can they!

As Howard Sankey (2010, 2011, 2012) captures the relativist's reasoning at this juncture: once the above point about circularity is granted, the relativist thinks the only remaining options are between scepticism and relativism. Scepticism is – as Steven Hales (2014, p. 81) puts it – 'throwing in the towel' and so relativism is really the only remaining choice that can make sense of how any of us can have justified beliefs *at all* in the relevant contested domains.[10]

Two points merit some clarification about the above reasoning. First, note that while irreconcilability is *sufficient* for getting the kind of circularity noted above up and running, it's not *necessary*. Consider, for example, that one might simply – in isolation from the context of an irreconcilable disagreement – aim to justify one's own most fundamental epistemic principles out of intellectual curiosity, or to achieve a kind of grounding for one's knowledge. This was, more or less, what Descartes was up to early in the Second Meditation,[11] when he sought to defend the use of clear and distinct perception as a method for forming beliefs and, in the course of doing so, wound up using that very method he sought to justify.[12]

The second point that deserves some careful thought is actually implicit in the relativist's thinking, rather than explicitly argued for. This concerns the idea that epistemic circularity is always vicious. Or, more accurately, that the kind of circularity that one party to a disagreement faces when justifying her principles by appealing to them is *equally bad*, epistemically, as the other party's (viz., in the case of a deep disagreement).

But there is some precedent for *denying* this implicit premise in epistemology. Here, it will be helpful in particular to consider a line of argument found in Ernest Sosa's (1997) early virtue epistemology.[13]

A question Sosa was grappling with is this: how can we *know* that our faculty of perception is reliable?[14] After all, it looks like we'll inevitably need to rely on perception to establish this. But, if we can't know that perception is reliable on account that we'd have to use it to some extent in coming to a view about its reliability, then aren't we, as perceivers who maintain that perception is reliable, in no better epistemic position (in taking the view we do about the reliability of perception) than would be a crystal ball gazer who comes to the view that crystal ball gazing is reliable *because* the crystal ball says it is?

Sosa encourages us to nip this rhetorical line of thinking in the bud. As he points out, the idea that one would need to use (and in doing so take for granted the reliability of) a given faculty at some point in order to come to have an adequate view of that faculty's epistemic status is implied by the very *possibility* of having 'an adequate theory of our knowledge and its general sources' (2009, p. 201; cf., 1997, p. 422). Put another way, the idea is that no one could provide adequate support of *any* of our sources of knowing, including perception, memory, deduction, abduction, and testimony, without employing those faculties; so the suggestion that we should expect that we ought to be able to is a misguided one.[15]

If Sosa is conceded the above point, then it's false that *all* epistemic circularity of the sort that involves using a way of forming beliefs to come to have a positive view of its epistemic status must be epistemically vicious. However, this still doesn't address the issue of why the kind of circularity one would inevitably rely on in the case of perception, deduction, inference, etc., is on a *better* footing that the kind of circularity that features in the crystal ball gazing case.

At this juncture, the *epistemic externalist* has a special card to play.[16] Suppose, *ex hypothesi*, that to know something, p, what you need is a true belief that p that is appropriately causally related to a reliable belief forming process or disposition; further, suppose that epistemic externalism is true, and thus, that one needn't have any reflective access to facts about the appropriate causal relatedness between one's belief that p and the process that issued it in order for one to know that p when one does.

With this kind of reliabilist externalism in play, Sosa argues, you can straightforwardly, and favourably, distinguish the epistemic status of the reliable perceiver who uses perception to form the belief that perception is reliable from the crystal ball gazer who uses gazing to form the (unreliably produced) belief that crystal ball gazing is reliable. Because perception is *in fact* a reliable belief-forming process, you can come to know, by the lights of the general kind of reliabilist externalism sketched above,[17] *that* perception is reliable through its use. But crystal ball gazing is not, in fact, reliable. And so through its use, you can't. In this respect, the two cases of epistemic circularity are not on an epistemically 'equal footing'.

Bringing things back full circle: we can see that there is at least one straightforward way of resisting the following idea, which looked to be an important one in the relativist's strategy of reasoning from deeply contested disagreements (in politics and elsewhere), through a circularity premise, to relativism; this was, in short, the idea that circular justifications are all epistemically on a par with one another.

Of course, in a heated political debate (e.g. Trump/Brexit), it remains that the matter of which side's circular reasoning – viz., reasoning that will be circular insofar as each side is justifying its ways of forming political beliefs by using those very ways of forming them – is on a better footing than the other *will not be apparent* to both parties to the political dispute. What is the significance, if any, of this fact?

One notable answer to this question is defended by Paul Boghossian (2001). Boghossian, like Sosa, thinks that some of our most basic ways of forming beliefs in any domain of inquiry are such that we *inescapably* will need to appeal to them in the course of any viable attempt to justify them. In Boghossian's case, he gives the example of the basic inference rule *modus ponens*. A thinker who antecedently *doubts* modus ponens will of course object if her interlocutor attempts to reason to the conclusion that modus ponens is true in a way that involves taking one or more reasoning steps in accordance with modus ponens. Does this fact (i.e. one has reasoned at least one step in accordance with modus ponens) bear in any way on the epistemic status of the assessment one makes of modus ponens as an inference rule?

Boghossian thinks the answer is 'no'. If a criterion of epistemic adequacy of a defence of an inference rule is that defence must not beg the question against anyone who happens (even if they have no good reason to) to call the status of that inference rule in to doubt, then we can never satisfactorily justify any epistemic principle. Any actual or possible inference rule could be objected to. Boghossian accordingly reasons that we should reject the idea that a given way of thinking whose defence involves its own application is *thereby* epistemically defective on account of this.[18]

What the discussion in this section suggests, then, is that an argument for relativism about political matters – if it is to appeal to the prevalence of political disagreement – is going to have to do much more than simply to establish that the kind of justification we're in a position to give in defence of our own political principles, in the face of one who challenges them, will be circular.

4 A different kind of political relativism

In this section, the focus will be on a much more recent strategy of argument which takes (a version of) political relativism to gain support from considerations to do with political disagreements. Rather than to appeal to circularity, the strand of argument we consider in this chapter appeals to language, and in particular, to semantics.

Consider the following political disagreement:

> A: *The U.S. President ought to issue an executive order banning fracking – it's bad for the environment, and plus, we have other renewable sources of energy we should focus on developing, including wind and solar.*
> B: *That's not true! The U.S. President ought to encourage fracking, even if it's bad for the environment, because it helps us to not rely so much on foreign energy, which is good economically. Plus, windmills are an eyesore and are overrated.*

It's apparent that A and B are coming from different background perspectives here. (For simplicity, stipulate that A is a Democrat and B is a Republican.) That said, let's zero in on one very specific sentence, which A uttered:

> The U.S. President ought to issue an executive order banning fracking.

It looks like B has just denied the proposition (1) expressed when A used it. So either A or B must be wrong, right? The answer is 'yes' if the extension of the prescriptive[19] 'ought' is – as traditional invariantists maintain – invariant across the contexts in which B is denying what A is asserting. But this is a point that *contextualists* about 'ought' deny. Contextualists about 'ought' maintain that the extension of 'ought' in (1) varies with the context in which (1) *is used*, and thus, that (1) can actually express different propositions (and thus have different truth conditions) in different contexts of use.

For instance, when A uses the sentence (1), the proposition A expresses is something like: *The U.S. President ought$_{Democrat}$ to issue an executive order banning fracking*, where 'ought$_{Democrat}$' means (roughly) 'ought, according to the Democrat worldview that I, the speaker, accept'.[20] But, according to the kind of contextualism we're envisaging here, when B denies that the U.S. President ought to issue an executive order banning fracking, the proposition B denies is actually a different proposition, viz., *The U.S. President ought$_{Republican}$ to issue an executive order banning fracking*, where 'ought$_{Republican}$' means (roughly) 'ought, according to the Republican worldview that I, the speaker, accept'.

It looks as though, if the contextualist offers the right way to think about the meaning of 'ought' in our dispute between A and B, then A and B are not *really* disagreeing in the sense that there is not a single proposition that one is asserting and the other is denying. The idea that contextualists 'lose' disagreement is a long-standing challenge for contextualists about a range of phenomena, and it's beyond what we can do here to evaluate whether and to what extent this turns out to be a genuine problem for the view.[21]

More to the point: is *this* relativism? That is: is embracing the view that what 'ought' means changes across contexts of use – as the contextualist says it does – sufficient for a kind of political relativism, when what the relevant 'ought'-containing sentence is about a political matter?

This is a complex question.[22] There is at least one way of answering it according to which the answer is 'no'. This is the answer given by John MacFarlane (2014), one of the leading contemporary exponents of what is sometimes called a 'relativist semantics' or a 'truth-relativist semantics' for various expressions, including 'ought'.[23] As MacFarlane sees it, a contextualist about 'ought' is not a relativist about 'ought' because the contextualist holds that the propositions expressed by ought-ascribing sentences have the truth values they have *absolutely*. MacFarlane's brand of relativism denies *this*.

In order to appreciate the difference between contextualism about 'ought' and relativism about 'ought', as MacFarlane is framing the issue respect to absolute truth, it's important to distinguish between the *context of use* and the *context of assessment* as follows:

> *Context of use*: a possible situation in which a sentence might be used and where the agent of the context is the user of the sentence.
> *Context of assessment*: a possible situation in which a use of a sentence might be assessed, where the agent of the context is the assessor of the use of a sentence. (2014, p. 60)

Whereas relativizing ought-ascribing sentence truth to merely a context of use is *compatible* with the proposition expressed by the sentence having an absolute truth value, relativizing an ought-ascribing sentence truth to a context of *assessment* is not.[24]

On MacFarlane's view, truth-relativism of the philosophically interesting sort with respect to 'ought' holds that when A utters the sentence "The U.S. President ought to issue an executive order banning fracking", the truth of what A says depends in part on a context of *assessment*, which means that the proposition expressed by that sentence (alternatively: that utterance token) gets a truth value only once the standard of the *assessor* is specified.[25] What this means is that when A says, "The U.S. President ought to issue an executive order banning fracking", this can be *at the same time*, both (i) true relative to a context of assessment in which another Democrat is evaluating A's claim, yet (ii) false relative to a context of assessment in which A's Republican interlocutor, B, is assessing the claim.

Since the very same use of an ought-ascribing sentence (with political content in its scope), such as (1), can be assessed from an *indefinite* number of perspectives, there are only perspective-relative answers to the question whether what A says when A says (1) is true. In this respect, for the MacFarlane-style relativist, A's utterance of (1) does not get its truth value absolutely, but only relatively.

This clearly looks like a form of 'political relativism'. Whether the view is right, however, is something that would depend on whether a relativist semantics for 'ought' does better than the competitors, which include not only traditional invariantism and contextualism, but also interest-relative invariantism, expressivism, and other semantic treatments of 'ought'.[26] And indeed, if it *does*, then this would appear to tell us something interesting about the correctness of our political discourse. Perhaps, among other things, an implication of 'political relativism', derived from semantic motivations, is that there will be a less clear basis for excluding certain political perspectives on the basis of their endorsing false normative claims. However, one may of course embrace a relativist semantics for political 'ought' claims without taking any further (non-semantic) stances about political practice.

It's well beyond our present scope to adjudicate whether a MacFarlane-style semantics for political 'oughts' is viable. For our purposes it's worth – with reference to the above brand of political relativism – drawing attention to two key points. The first has to do with disagreement, and the second has to do with arguments for and against political relativism generally.

First, regarding disagreement. If the relativist about 'ought' is right about the extension of 'ought', and thus, about the truth conditions of ought-attributing sentences, then disagreements of the sort we find between A and B about (1) turn out to be *faultless*.[27] This kind of diagnosis of our example case is interestingly distinct from the diagnosis of the traditional invariantist as well as the contextualist offers. The traditional invariantist's assessment of the disagreement between A and B about (1) is that the disagreement is genuine in the sense that A's use of (1) expresses a proposition that A affirms and B denies; second, the traditional invariantist is committed to the view that at least one party to the dispute has made a mistake; they can't both be right. The contextualist generates the opposite result: whereas, if contextualism is true, there is no mistake being made by either side, there is also no genuine agreement, given that the proposition A affirms is different from the proposition B denies.

The relativist's assessment combines – in a way that MacFarlane thinks is optimal[28] – the 'disagreement' aspect of the invariantist's diagnosis with the 'no-mistakes' aspect of the contextualist's diagnosis. Because the truth conditions of the proposition A express when using (1) is assessment-sensitive, it is true when assessed by A, false when assessed by B. Both are right, and yet, they *do* disagree – albeit, about a proposition with assessment-sensitive truth conditions. An appreciation of this 'combinatory result' (viz., disagreement + no-mistakes) gives us a perspective from which to see how a MacFarlane-style relativist semantics about 'ought', one widely applicable to normative political disagreements, has ramifications for the very *status* of those disagreements.

Regarding the second point concerning political relativism generally. It's important to notice that the kinds of philosophical motivations that underpin the circularity-based argument from political disagreements to political relativism (Sections 2 and 3) are *entirely distinct* from the kinds of philosophical motivations – mostly linguistic – driving the species of political relativism discussed in this section, one that involves a truth-relativist semantics for 'oughts' whose scope include political claims. What this means is that arguments *against* one of these species of political relativism do not, at the same time, count as arguments against the other. The matter of which form of political relativism is more viable remains contested and is a question for ongoing research across several subdisciplines of philosophy, including epistemology, ethics, political philosophy, and the philosophy of language.[29]

Notes

1 For discussion of eras of greater political consensus in previous decades of Western politics, with a focal point being the U.S. Congress, see for example Adler & Wilkerson (2013) and Maass (1983). See, however, Campbell (2018) for a defence of the view that U.S. polarization in politics goes back at least to the 1960s civil rights movement.
2 See Schaeffer (2020).
3 See also Green (this volume) for a discussion of epistemic circularity in justifying norms of truthfulness in politics.
4 This might involve explicitly stating these principles and reasoning from them in order to justify them – what is called *premise circularity* (Psillos 1999). Or, more subtly, it might involve reasoning in accordance with contested rules or norms without explicitly endorsing them, viz., *rule circularity*. For a helpful discussion of rule circularity in reasoning, see Boghossian (2001).
5 It is worth noting that a potential explanation for some of these epistemic commitments is a difference in fundamental non-epistemic commitments. Even more, on some views, apparent deep epistemic disagreements are better understood as disagreements in fundamental moral values. For the present purposes and space, I will be focusing on cases where the epistemic divergence is assumed to be genuine. Thanks to Michael Hannon for discussion on this point.
6 For a discussion of Archimedean principles in the context of deep disagreements, see Carter (2016, Ch. 4, 2018). Cf., Baghramian & Carter (2015).
7 For alternative arguments for relativism that use the Galileo/Bellarmine dispute as a reference point, see Kusch (2019) and MacFarlane (2008).
8 For neatness with the analogy with Boghossian's diagnosis of Bellarmine versus Galileo, I'm using 'we' inclusively to refer to those who adopt an anti-Trump/anti-Brexit stance. But nothing hangs on this. If the reader is a either a Trump or a Brexit supporter, simply swap out the 'anti'-qualifiers.

9 For an alternative empirical explanation of polarization in group deliberative settings, framed in terms of an abundance of persuasive arguments, see Burnstein & Vinokur (1977). For critical reviews of this literature, see Isenberg (1986) and Carter & Broncano-Berrocal (forthcoming, Ch. 1).
10 For criticisms of this line of argument, see Carter (2016, Ch. 3) and Seidel (2013).
11 Descartes (1641/1975, p. 24).
12 As Sosa (1997) discusses in some detail, the kind of epistemic circularity Descartes engages in in the third paragraph of the Second Meditation is distinct from the wider form of circularity often described as the 'Cartesian Circle', which involves an appeal to God as a guarantor. Sosa accordingly refers to this circle in the Second Meditation as a 'smaller circle' (1997, p. 415).
13 Note that a slightly amended and expanded presentation of the arguments from this paper appears as a chapter, with the same title, in Sosa's later (2009) book on reflective knowledge and circularity, the second of the two books on virtue epistemology that arose from his 2005 John Locke Lectures 'A Virtue Epistemology'.
14 For an extended discussion of this question, from the perspective of virtue epistemology, see Sosa (2009).
15 For a detailed assessment of Sosa's reasoning here, and how it is in tension in important ways with the thinking of Barry Stroud (1989, 2004) on these issues, see Carter (2020).
16 Epistemic externalism, minimally, involves the denial of *epistemic internalism*, the view that what makes a belief epistemically justified is something a justified believer has reflective access to (or supervenes on the subject's internal mental states). For general discussions of epistemic externalism in epistemology, see, e.g., Alston (1986); BonJour (2002); BonJour & Sosa (2003); Carter et al. (2014); Goldberg (2007); Pappas (2005).
17 Sosa opts for a *virtue reliabilist* externalism (e.g. Sosa 1991, 2007), however, the argument considered here does not turn on this fact and is available to a process reliabilist externalist (e.g. Goldman 1999) more generally.
18 Of course, Boghossian's point also applies, mutatis mutandis, to those who would attempt to reason from rule circularity to scepticism rather than relativism. For discussion, see Carter (2016, Ch. 5).
19 Prescriptive 'oughts' of the kind that are principally of interest in moral and political philosophy (and the sort that will be the focus here) differ importantly from *predictive* 'oughts' – viz., the bank ought to be open by now. For discussion, see Von Wright (1986).
20 Note that this is just a toy version of contextualism about 'ought'. Different contextualists can fill in the relevant parameter that is fixed by the context of use in different ways. For example, rather than to use individual worldviews, one could use local cultures. Such a position would be a form of cultural contextualism.
21 See DeRose (2009) for some general strategies to responding to this objection from the perspective of contextualism. See also McKenna (2015).
22 For discussion, see Carter (2016, Ch. 7). Cf., Boghossian (2006b) and Harman (1975).
23 This kind of position, alternatively, is referred to as 'New Relativism' (Baghramian & Carter 2015, Sec. 5) and sometimes as 'New Age Relativism' (Wright 2007). For an overview of this view across a range of areas of discourse, see Baghramian & Carter (2015, Sec. 5) and Baghramian & Coliva (2019).
24 For a related discussion about the distinction between contextualism and relativism, see Carter (2017, pp. 294–95).
25 What I am describing here is the basic template structure of MacFarlane's proposal, on which 'ought'-ascriptions are modelled as assessment-sensitive as opposed to merely use-sensitive. There are also some further substantive elements of MacFarlane's view (including to do with how the view is meant to reconcile subjective and objective uses of 'ought') which I'm not discussing here, as these points are independent of the key structural feature of his proposal which distinguishes it as a relativist (as opposed to, e.g., a contextualist) proposal.
26 For a discussion of various competitors to relativism in semantics, see Baghramian & Carter (2015, Sec. 5).
27 For discussion, see Kölbel (2004), MacFarlane (2007), and Baghramian & Carter (2015, Sec. 5).
28 On MacFarlane's view, this combination best accords with our patterns of 'ought' attributions than the combinations implied by invariantism and contextualism.
29 This paper was written as part of the Leverhulme-funded 'A Virtue Epistemology of Trust' (#RPG-2019-302) project, which is hosted by the University of Glasgow's COGITO Epistemology Research Centre, and I'm grateful to the Leverhulme Trust for supporting this research. Thanks also to Michael Hannon and Jeroen de Ridder for helpful feedback.

References

Adler, E. S., & Wilkerson, J. D. (2013). *Congress and the Politics of Problem Solving*. Cambridge: Cambridge University Press.

Alfano, M., Carter, J. A., & Cheong, M. (2018). 'Technological Seduction and Self-Radicalization'. *Journal of the American Philosophical Association* 4(3): 298–322.

Alfano, M., Fard, A. E., Carter, J. A., Clutton, P., & Klein, C. (forthcoming). 'Technologically Scaffolded Atypical Cognition: The Case of YouTube's Recommender System'. *Synthese*. https://doi.org/10.1007/s11229-020-02724-x

Alston, W. P. (1986). 'Internalism and Externalism in Epistemology'. *Philosophical Topics* 14(1): 179–221.

Baghramian, M., & Carter, J. A. (2015). 'Relativism'. In E. N. Zalta (Ed.), *Stanford Encyclopaedia of Philosophy* (Fall 2015, pp. 1–46). http://plato.stanford.edu/entries/relativism/.

Baghramian, M., & Coliva, A. (2019). *Relativism*. London: Routledge.

Boghossian, P. (2001). 'How Are Objective Epistemic Reasons Possible?'. *Philosophical Studies* 106(1): 1–40.

Boghossian, P. (2006a). *Fear of Knowledge: Against Relativism and Constructivism*. Oxford: Oxford University Press.

Boghossian, P. (2006b). 'What is Relativism?'. In P. Greenough, & M. P. Lynch (Eds.), *Truth and Realism* (pp. 13–37). New York: Oxford University Press.

BonJour, L. (2002). 'Internalism and Externalism'. In Paul K. Moser (Ed.), *The Oxford Handbook of Epistemology* (pp. 234–64). New York: Oxford University Press.

BonJour, L., & Sosa, E. (2003). *Epistemic Justification: Internalism vs. Externalism, Foundations vs. Virtues*. London: Wiley-Blackwell.

Burnstein, E., & Vinokur, A. (1977). 'Persuasive Argumentation and Social Comparison as Determinants of Attitude Polarization'. *Journal of Experimental Social Psychology* 13(4): 315–32.

Campbell, J. E. (2018). *Polarized: Making Sense of a Divided America*. Princeton, NJ: Princeton University Press.

Carter, J. A. (2016). *Metaepistemology and Relativism*. Basingstoke: Palgrave Macmillan.

Carter, J. A. (2017). 'Epistemological Implications of Relativism'. In J. J. Ichikawa (Ed.), *The Routledge Handbook of Epistemic Contextualism* (292–301). London: Routledge.

Carter, J. A. (2018). 'Archimedean Metanorms'. *Topoi*: 1–11. https://doi.org/10.1007/s11245-018-9586-9.

Carter, J. A. (2020). 'Virtue Perspectivism, Externalism, and Epistemic Circularity'. In M. Massimi (Ed.), *Knowledge from a Human Point of View* (pp. 123–40). Dordrecht: Springer.

Carter, J. A., & Broncano-Berrocal, F. (forthcoming). *The Philosophy of Group Polarization*. London: Routledge.

Carter, J. A., Kallestrup, J., Palermos, S. O., & Pritchard, D. (2014). 'Varieties of Externalism'. *Philosophical Issues* 24(1): 63–109.

DeRose, K. (2009). *The Case for Contextualism: Knowledge, Skepticism, and Context, Vol. 1: Knowledge, Skepticism, and Context*. Oxford: Oxford University Press.

Descartes, R. (1975). In J. Cottingham, R. Stoothoff, & D. Murdoch (Eds.), *The Philosophical Writings of Descartes*, 2 vols. Cambridge: Cambridge University Press.

Goldberg, S. C. (2007). *Internalism and Externalism in Semantics and Epistemology*. Oxford: Oxford University Press on Demand.

Goldman, A. (1999). *Knowledge in a Social World*. Oxford: Oxford University Press.

Hales, S. D. (2014). 'Motivations for Relativism as a Solution to Disagreements'. *Philosophy* 89(1): 63–82.

Harman, G. (1975). 'Moral Relativism Defended'. *Philosophical Review* 84(1): 3–22.

Hobolt, S. B., Leeper, T., & Tilley, J. (2018). *Divided by the Vote: Affective Polarization in the Wake of Brexit*. Boston, MA: American Political Science Association.

Isenberg, D. J. (1986). 'Group Polarization: A Critical Review and Meta-analysis'. *Journal of Personality and Social Psychology* 50(6): 1141.

Kölbel, M. (2004). 'Faultless Disagreement'. *Proceedings of the Aristotelian Society* 104(1): 53–73.

Kusch, M. (2019). 'II—Relativist Stances, Virtues And Vices'. *Aristotelian Society Supplementary Volume* 93(1): 271–91.

Lorentzen, D. G. (2014). 'Polarisation in Political Twitter Conversations'. *Aslib Journal of Information Management* 66(3): 329–41.

Lynch, M. P. (2016). 'After the Spade Turns: Disagreement, First Principles and Epistemic Contractarianism'. *International Journal for the Study of Skepticism* 6(2–3): 248–59. https://doi.org/10.1163/22105700-00603010.

Maass, A. (1983). *Congress and the Common Good*. New York City: Harpercollins.

MacFarlane, J. (2007). 'Relativism and Disagreement'. *Philosophical Studies* 132(1): 17–31.

MacFarlane, J. (2008). 'Boghossian, Bellarmine, and Bayes'. *Philosophical Studies* 141(3): 391–98.

MacFarlane, J. (2014). *Assessment Sensitivity: Relative Truth and Its Applications*. Oxford: Oxford University Press.

Marsh, D. (2020). 'Populism and Brexit'. In Crewe I., & Sanders D. (Eds.), *Authoritarian Populism and Liberal Democracy* (pp. 73–86). Cham: Palgrave Macmillan. https://doi.org/10.1007/978-3-030-17997-7_5.

McKenna, R. (2015). 'Epistemic Contextualism Defended'. *Synthese* 192(2): 363–83.

Pappas, G. (2005). 'Internalist vs. Externalist Conceptions of Epistemic Justification'. In E. N. Zalta (Ed.), *Stanford Encyclopedia of Philosophy*. https://plato.stanford.edu/archives/fall2017/entries/justep-intext/.

Psillos, S. (1999). *Scientific Realism: How Science Tracks Truth*. London: Routledge.

Quattrociocchi, W., Scala, A., & Sunstein, C. R. (2016). 'Echo Chambers on Facebook'. Available at SSRN 2795110.

Ranalli, C. (2018). 'What is Deep Disagreement?'. *Topoi*: 1–16. https://doi.org/10.1007/s11245-018-9600-2.

Rorty, R. (1979). *Philosophy and the Mirror of Nature*. Princeton, NJ: Princeton University Press.

Sankey, H. (2010). 'Witchcraft, Relativism and the Problem of the Criterion'. *Erkenntnis* 72(1): 1–16.

Sankey, H. (2011). 'Epistemic Relativism and the Problem of the Criterion'. *Studies in History and Philosophy of Science Part A* 42(4): 562–70.

Sankey, H. (2012). 'Scepticism, Relativism and the Argument from the Criterion'. *Studies in History and Philosophy of Science Part A* 43(1): 182–90.

Schaeffer, K. (2020). 'Far More Americans See 'Very Strong' Partisan Conflicts Now than in the Last Two Presidential Election Years'. Pew Research Centre, 4 March, 2020. https://www.pewresearch.org/fact-tank/2020/.

Seidel, M. (2013). 'Why the Epistemic Relativist Cannot Use the Sceptic's Strategy: A Comment on Sankey'. *Studies in History and Philosophy of Science Part A* 44(1): 134–39.

Siegel, H. (2011). 'Epistemological Relativism: Arguments Pro and Con'. In S. D. Hales (Ed.), *A Companion to Relativism* (pp. 199–218). London: Wiley Online Library.

Sosa, E. (1991). *Knowledge in Perspective: Selected Essays in Epistemology*. Cambridge, UK: Cambridge University Press.

Sosa, E. (1997). 'Reflective Knowledge in the Best Circles'. *The Journal of Philosophy* 94(8): 410–30.

Sosa, E. (2007). *A Virtue Epistemology: Apt Belief and Reflective Knowledge, Volume 1*. Oxford: Oxford University Press.

Sosa, E. (2009). *Reflective Knowledge: Apt Belief and Reflective Knowledge, Volume 2*. Oxford: Oxford University Press.

Stroud, B. (1989). 'Understanding Human Knowledge in General'. In M. Clay, & K. Lehrer (Eds.), *Knowledge and Skepticism* (pp. 31–50). Boulder, CO: Westview Press.

Stroud, B. (2004). 'Perceptual Knowledge and Epistemological Satisfaction'. In J. Greco (Ed.), *Ernest Sosa and His Critics* (pp. 165–73). Malden, MA: Blackwell.

Sunstein, C. R. (2002). 'The Law of Group Polarization'. *Journal of Political Philosophy* 10(2): 175–95.

Turner, J. C. (1982). 'Towards a Cognitive Redefinition of the Social Group'. In H. Tajfel (Ed.), *Social Identity and Intergroup Relations* (pp. 15–40). Cambridge, UK: Cambridge University Press.

Wetherell, M., Turner, J. C., & Hogg, M. A. (1986). 'A Referent Informational Influence Explanation of Group Polarization'. University of St Andrews and Macquarie University, Unpublished Paper.

Williams, M. (2007). 'Why (Wittgensteinian) Contextualism Is Not Relativism'. *Episteme* 4(1): 93–114.

Von Wright, G. H. (1986). 'Is and Ought'. In M. C. Doeser, & J. N. Kraay (Eds.), *Facts and Values* (pp. 31–48). Martinus Nijhoff Philosophy Library, Vol. 19. Dordrecht: Springer. https://doi.org/10.1007/978-94-009-4454-1_3.

Wright, C. (2007). 'New Age Relativism and Epistemic Possibility: The Question of Evidence'. *Philosophical Issues* 17(1): 262–83.

Yardi, S., & Boyd, D. (2010). 'Dynamic Debates: An Analysis of Group Polarization Over Time on Twitter'. *Bulletin of Science, Technology & Society* 30(5): 316–27.

10

EPISTEMIC PERMISSIVISM AND REASONABLE PLURALISM

Richard Rowland and Robert Mark Simpson

1 Pluralism and arbitrariness

For a wide variety of questions we think every reasonable person should agree. The earth is not flat. Killing for fun is wrong. Pigs don't fly. But for many other things – perennial ethical debates, questions about aesthetic value, or questions about what it's reasonable to believe on (at least some) philosophical, religious, and scientific questions – we think informed people can rationally disagree. We will call this ethos, as loosely characterised, *pluralism.*[1]

Permissivism is a position in epistemology that seems to express a pluralistic ethos. It says there is sometimes more than one rational doxastic attitude that one may hold on some proposition, P, given a particular body of evidence, E.[2] In political theory we find another expression of a pluralistic ethos in the position Rawls and his followers call *Reasonable Pluralism*. Reasonable Pluralism says that given the exercise of human reason under conditions of political freedom, people won't all converge upon a single world-view or life plan. They will, rather, adopt a diverse plurality of worldviews and related commitments.[3]

In this chapter we aim to make sense of some differences in how pluralism works in these two domains, the epistemic and political. In order to describe these differences, we need to distinguish two ways of expressing a pluralistic ethos in one's attitudes. One can either be *abstemiously* pluralistic or *indulgently* pluralistic. An abstemious pluralist thinks informed people can rationally adopt different stances on various questions, but he refrains from taking a stance on any such questions, and only takes stances where he thinks there is just one rationally acceptable attitude. An indulgent pluralist also thinks people can rationally adopt different stances on various questions, but she *does* take a stance on some of these contested questions. She thinks people can rationally disagree about God's existence, but she is a firm atheist. She thinks people can rationally disagree about the credibility of evolutionary psychology, but she sees it as hogwash. She thinks people can rationally disagree on whether reparations are owed to descendants of enslaved and colonised peoples, but she is in favour.

Indulgent pluralism in an epistemic context encounters a serious challenge, one that abstemious pluralism in an epistemic context seemingly doesn't. Suppose we have two incompatible propositions, p_1 and p_2. The worry is that there seems to be something rationally dubious about simultaneously thinking:

1   On the available information, it's reasonable to believe either p_1 or p_2, and
2   For my part, I believe that p_1.

Suppose you think there are apprehensible factors that speak in favour of believing p_1 instead of p_2. In that case it is difficult to make sense of (1), because by your own lights accepting p_2 would mean failing to take account of apprehensible factors that impugn this option, and that seems irrational. Conversely, suppose you think there aren't any apprehensible factors that favour believing p_1 instead of p_2. In that case it seems like any reason you might have for (2), i.e. believing p_1 instead of p_2, must be an arbitrary pseudo-reason, like you simply 'taking a shine' to p_1, and it seems irrational to believe on such bases.[4] Several authors have discussed whether this arbitrariness worry ultimately makes Permissivism untenable.[5] Permissivism sounds appealing in the abstract. But if you are a Permissivist on any question where you have your own views – if you're at all indulgent, rather than abstemious, in your Permissivism – then this dilemma instantly arises. Any reason for favouring your own view over others that you see as rationally permissible either undermines your meta-view about the rational permissibility of rival views, or else seems irrationally arbitrary.[6]

Intuitively, though, arbitrariness-based objections don't create the same worry for (indulgent) Reasonable Pluralism as for (indulgent) Permissivism. Upon honest reflection, most people recognise that they have arrived at their worldview – and the practical life projects they are undertaking, in light of their worldview – via accidents of circumstance, and hence that these commitments are arbitrary in an important sense. And while it can create a feeling of unease to acknowledge this arbitrariness, it generally doesn't seem to undermine people's sense of being committed to their projects. Unlike with beliefs, it can seem not only reasonable but indeed virtuous to be indulgently pluralistic in your worldview-based projects. Forswearing any projects or political commitments that are 'tainted' by arbitrariness seems somehow hyper-rationalistic, to the point of error. It's a little bit like adopting an explicitly utilitarian mindset while trying to make friends, or choosing a football team to support based on its forecasted win ratio next season, rather than accidents of geography. Much like your friendships or sporting allegiances, your worldview-based projects seem like commitments that you can be virtuous in holding fast to, irrespective of the contingency in how you acquired them.

But does this double standard withstand scrutiny? Maybe we *should* see the influence of arbitrary factors in our worldview-based projects as a source of concern, much the same as we think of arbitrary factors in our beliefs. Here we examine three ways that one might seek to defend the discrepancy in how we think about arbitrary commitments across the two domains. Arbitrariness might be relatively unobjectionable in our worldview-based projects, because:

1   Practical rationality is *desire-dependent*, in a way that epistemic rationality isn't,
2   We have reasons to be *resolute* in our practical commitments, but no analogous reasons to be resolute in our doxastic commitments, or
3   Compromise in the face of epistemic disagreement generally *mitigates controversy*, whereas compromise in the face of practical disagreement doesn't.

We discuss these proposals in §2, §3, and §4, respectively.

2 Desire-dependence

Many authors argue that what it is practically rational for you to do depends on your desires. Bernard Williams (1981), for instance, defends *reasons internalism*: some fact is a reason for you to φ only if you could come to φ by deliberating from your current motivations. A number of authors have held that our reasons for action are ultimately explained by our desires, or the desires of somewhat idealised versions of ourselves.[7] If one of these views is right, then we can be indulgent practical pluralists. For we can hold that it is rational for us to φ because φ-ing promotes our desires but that it is not rational for another to φ because φ-ing does not promote their desires. It seems that we can explain the rationality of indulgent practical pluralism in this way even if we do not think that all our reasons are dependent on our desires: so long as we hold that sometimes one person has a reason to do one thing, which another does not have, we can hold that sometimes it is rational for us to do one thing while it is reasonable that others do another. And the actions that it is rational for us to perform do seem to vary with our desires in this way. Suppose that dancing will promote your desires but not your friend's because you want to dance and they don't. Intuitively, you have a good reason to go to a dance party, which they do not have. The desire-dependence of practical reasons and rationality straightforwardly explains this.[8]

But epistemic rationality and reasons are not desire-dependent in the same way, so we might think. Whether or not it's rational for you to believe p is primarily a matter of whether or not your evidence supports p, and your desires don't have a bearing on what your evidence supports. If some piece of evidence is a reason to believe p, then, so we ordinarily think, that evidence tells in favour of you believing p regardless of whether believing that p promotes one of your desires. We might think that even if A and B's desires are completely different, if their evidence is the same, their epistemic reasons and what it is rational for them to believe are the same.[9]

Some hold that epistemic reasons and rationality are entirely explained by our desires. But the most plausible versions of this view can still preserve an asymmetry between the desire-dependence of practical rationality and the desire-dependence of epistemic rationality. We might think that (a) everyone has the goal of believing the truth and avoiding error, because to be engaged in the activity of forming beliefs is just to have a goal along these lines, or that (b) whatever we desire, forming beliefs in line with our evidence promotes our desires better than not forming beliefs in line with our evidence, because having correct beliefs helps us get other things that we want.[10] If either (a) or (b) holds, then – holding our evidence and background-beliefs fixed – epistemic reasons and rationality will not differ from person to person. But practical reasons and rationality depend on our particular contingent desires (e.g. a desire to dance) and what would promote these particular contingent desires. In this case, indulgent epistemic pluralism would not be epistemically rational because holding our evidence fixed what's rational for one of us to believe is what it is rational for another to believe, but the actions that it is rational for us to perform can vary from person to person based on our different particular desires: indulgent practical pluralism can be rational.[11]

This difference in the desire-dependence of practical and epistemic rationality may explain why indulgent practical pluralism is rational in some cases. But some of those who hold that indulgent practical pluralism is rational (such as at least some Rawlsians) hold that it is rational in cases in which the practical rationality of our actions does not seem to depend on our desires. What we have most moral reason to do does not seem to depend on our particular desires. For instance, regardless of our (particular) desires, we have most moral reason to save a drowning child when we could easily do so. But practical indulgent pluralists think that there are many cases in which we can rationally hold fast to and pursue our moral views while insisting that other incompatible moral views are reasonable. For instance, according to some, it is rational to stand by and act in line with one's moral commitment that euthanasia is permissible while acknowledging that it is reasonable for others to hold that it is wrong and act accordingly.[12] But the rationality of our moral commitments must be independent of our particular desires. So, the explanation of why such cases of practical indulgent pluralism are rational cannot be that the rationality of such practical commitments depends on our desires.

One option here would be to give up the view that moral reasons do not depend on our particular desires. Such a view may provide a good explanation of the contrast between indulgent practical pluralism and indulgent epistemic pluralism. However, we will set this aside as holding that moral reasons depend on our contingent desires is a controversial – and for many people, extremely counterintuitive – view. Another option would be to hold that although indulgent practical pluralism is sometimes rational, it is not in moral cases like the one discussed above. But in the rest of this chapter we will investigate whether we can explain how a more capacious practical indulgent pluralism is rational even though indulgent epistemic pluralism is not.

3 Resoluteness vs. readiness to revise

In general, you have a good reason to revise your beliefs upon receipt of evidence that tells against them. We speak of epistemic or doxastic *commitments*, but that term is slightly misleading, because in forming some token belief you aren't binding yourself to a mental state. You are forming a working, but ever-ready-to-be-revised, picture of how things stand in the world. Rationality requires you to adjust this when you gain information that indicates an inaccuracy in it. And as a Permissivist you don't want to deny any of this. You may think there is more than one rational doxastic attitude to take towards P given E, but you should still be (or had better be) working to get your picture right, vis-à-vis P, and so you will still want to make your belief on P dynamically responsive to evidence.[13]

Practical commitments – including the projects people take on, in light of their worldviews – are different to this, in that they really are *commitments*. They are a matter of resolution in ways that beliefs are not, or at any rate shouldn't be. To live as a devout Catholic, or an environmental campaigner, or a socialist reformer, isn't just to assent to some theses, or adopt a representation of how things stand, metaphysically and morally. It is to adopt a suite of projects that reach across an extended duration, and which displace rival projects.[14] With worldview-based projects you resolve to follow a certain way of life, not just by having a specific to-do list in the present, but by trying to guide yourself along a long-range trajectory, and live a life with a particular shape and pattern. Revision is not forbidden, but you shouldn't change course every time you come across a *pro tanto* good reason to prefer another course. After all, if you undertake a continually revised succession of projects, you're thereby abandoning the effective pursuit of any long-range projects.

This suggests another explanation of why we needn't see arbitrariness in people's political projects as a worry, the same as arbitrariness in beliefs. In order to have any long-range practical commitments at all you have to throw your lot in, in some sense, with one project or another among the range of projects that you see as rationally eligible for you at the point where you are deciding. If you think you could live your best life by pursuing either project

A or B, and you can't pursue both, then you had better find a way to choose one over the other. And if you can't see any deep-seated reason to favour A over B or *vice versa*, then it seems inevitable that arbitrary factors – e.g. accidents of location, time, or acquaintance – will have an influence in this. By contrast, in forming and revising your beliefs there is no need for anything like this sort of arbitrary leap of faith: one where non-rational inputs into the choice itself lead to commitments which you then have a reason (a defeasible one, but a reason all the same) to see through.

Ru Ye (2020) offers an intriguing challenge to this position. She thinks practical and epistemic rationalities are basically the same with respect to the involvement of arbitrary factors in determining where we end up. The main worry with positing this equivalence, for Ye, is that allowing your beliefs to arbitrarily shift direction, sans evidence, seems to place you at risk of carrying out disadvantageous or pointless acts, given how your beliefs guide your actions over time.[15] But Ye thinks this problem can be dealt with. She argues that it can be rational for you to choose to undergo something like a *transformative experience*, in L. A. Paul's (2014) sense. Specifically, you can undergo a *doxastically* transformative experience, in whose wake you expect that you will come to believe things that you now think false, or *vice versa* – similar to the results of undergoing a Kuhnian paradigm shift.[16]

How does this suggestion undermine the asymmetry we're positing? The life projects you embark upon are unavoidably subject to arbitrary influences, and so the presence of arbitrary influences doesn't seem to impugn the rationality of your projects. You embark upon some projects, and then you have a (defeasible) reason to see them through, although you may be moved to undergo a transformative experience that orients you towards a whole different set of projects. Ye is claiming that things are similar with your beliefs. Our claim is that practical commitments involve leaps of faith, followed by resolute adherence, whereas beliefs involve continual revision, as the believer dynamically updates her doxastic representation of the world in response to incoming evidence. Ye is saying that beliefs are more like practical commitments than we are suggesting, vis-à-vis the involvement of rationally arbitrary jumping-off points.

The main worry with Ye's proposal is that the motivation for undergoing a doxastically transformative experience is hard to understand. Unless it's the evidence that's compelling you, why should you be open to ricocheting around through a variety of mutually incompatible sets of beliefs? If you think rival sets of beliefs have as much to rationally recommend them as your current set, then you have ways of doxastically capturing your ambivalence about this. And if you don't think other sets of beliefs are as good as your current set, then undergoing experiences that shift your views, sans evidence, seems perverse. The difference with practical commitments is that it is much more difficult to hedge your bets across different options. We don't have effective ways of capturing our ambivalence about different projects we might choose to undertake. Being resolute about the projects we do undertake is a natural response to the fact that we have to choose in the face of ambivalence, in order to have any long-range projects at all.

In sum, then, there are good reasons to be resolute in your practical, worldview-based commitments, despite the (often inescapable) influence of arbitrary factors in determining which worldview-based commitments you adopt in the first place. There don't seem to be analogous reasons to be similarly resolute in your beliefs. If your beliefs are dynamically responsive to the evidence, then over time arbitrary initial influences in your belief system can and should be 'washed out' of significance, as with a rational Bayesian agent who has eccentric priors, but who has conditionalised on many pieces of evidence.

4 Compromise and mitigating controversy

According to a popular type of conciliatory view about the epistemology of disagreement, when we find ourselves with a belief that we believe others can reasonably disagree with, rationality requires that we suspend belief or significantly lower our confidence in our beliefs, that we do not court controversy but rather retreat to more neutral ground.[17] Often when we are confronted with disagreement about how to act we cannot shift to a less controversial practical stance, or pursue a less controversial course of action. For example, suppose you're a member of parliament voting on a bill to raise inheritance tax. You are in favour of the hike, but others disagree with you, and you regard their dissenting views as reasonable. Suppose that it's a free vote, and you don't know if the bill will pass without your vote, because parliament is roughly split. In this case there is no practical option available to you that's less controversial than voting in line with your own view. Voting against the tax is equally controversial, and abstaining will be practically equivalent to voting against it. So, perhaps the contrast between indulgent practical pluralism and indulgent epistemic pluralism is that when there is reasonable disagreement rationality requires that we retreat to less controversial ground. But although this is possible with beliefs – we can suspend or lower our credences – it is often impossible with our actions.

Practical choices do sometimes allow a compromise option, unlike the above case. But even where there is a compromise option, pursuing it might not be less controversial than sticking with a non-compromise position. Suppose in a legislative debate the left-leaning politicians are pushing to relax immigration controls, while those on the right, backed by a majority of their constituents, are pushing to tighten controls. A compromise policy is tabled which tightens restrictions a little, but less than the right-leaning cohort was pushing for. Both the left *and* the right might end up just as unhappy with the compromise as they were with their opponents' initial proposal. The left may believe that the compromise still infringes the rights of would-be immigrants and damages industries reliant on migrant labour. The right may believe that the policy fails to do justice to their constituents' preference for stricter controls. If the compromise policy is enacted, everyone will oppose it, whereas at least with one of the initial rival policy positions, a large cohort of people would have been satisfied. The compromise option is, in one important respect, more controversial than either non-compromise option.[18]

Not all cases of practical disagreement have this feature. But many do. Adopting a compromise policy around restrictions on abortion won't be acceptable to either pro-lifers *or* pro-choicers. Adopting a compromise policy on animal rights won't satisfy either vegan activists *or* eager carnivores. Or consider ethically significant lifestyle choices. Suppose you're trying to decide whether to follow your family's devout religious lifestyle or be a thrill-seeking hedonist. Or suppose you're wrestling with being a well-paid professional and settling down in the suburbs, or being a bohemian artist with nothing tying you down. Middle-ground options may be worse than either extreme, by your own lights. You can try to leave all your options open, but this means postponing the pursuit of any long range projects, and that is a lifestyle choice in its own right – one that seems excessively reticent, to the point of being inferior to the options which you thereby refrain from pursuing.

Examples like these indicate another significant difference between Permissivism and Reasonable Pluralism. In practical contexts being an abstemious pluralist sometimes isn't an option, or else it is an option but pursuing it does nothing to mitigate controversy between parties who hold rival views. But in epistemic contexts hedging options are always available. If you cannot tell which of two inconsistent propositions, p_1 or p_2, is more likely true, you have ways to represent this ambivalence in your doxastic attitudes. You can withhold belief, or divide your credences between p_1 and p_2. And using one of these hedging options – e.g. saying "it's reasonable to believe either p_1 or p_2, and I'm withholding judgement on it" – generally *is* an effective way to mitigate controversy. Suppose you believe there will be a second Covid-19 outbreak, but you hear some thoughtful people making a persuasive case to the contrary. You might continue to lean towards your initial stance, while also thinking it entirely possible that you assessed the evidence incorrectly. (After all, those who disagree with you seem credible, and you already thought it could be reasonable, given the evidence, to believe that there wouldn't be a second outbreak.) Here it seems rationally permissible to withhold belief on the question of whether there will be a second outbreak, and adopting this view seems to lessen the controversy between you and others.

We think this provides another good explanation of why one needn't find arbitrariness in practical commitments as concerning as arbitrariness in beliefs. In cases where you recognise a range of rational doxastic attitudes that you might take on a proposition, given certain evidence, without any decisive consideration favouring one above the others, you have the option of suspending belief or distributing your credences, and this will lead you to have a doxastic attitude that's no less rationally acceptable by your own lights, and (typically) more acceptable to others.[19] Being conciliatory mitigates controversy, whereas arbitrarily sticking to your guns perpetuates it, and when you think that there are a range of reasonable alternative positions, rationality requires not courting controversy by picking one rather than the other.

By contrast, in cases where you see a range of incompatible, practically rational courses of action, without any good reason recommending one above the others, arbitrarily pursuing one of them will often be better, since compromise options may be less agreeable than any individual course of action. In a practical context, arbitrarily preferring one course of action seems acceptable, because being conciliatory leads towards compromise options that no-one likes, thus *increasing* – or at least not mitigating – controversy. Although rationality requires that we do not court controversy, in the practical case compromising courts controversy more than sticking to one's guns; the same is not true of epistemic commitment.

Against this sort of thinking, Daniel Weinstock (2013: 545–46) argues that compromises like in the immigration policy example actually do mitigate controversy. An example will help illustrate. Suppose Libertarian Liz regards any taxation beyond what's strictly needed for a minimal state as unacceptable, while Socialist Sophie thinks we should tax 100% of income over £30k, the national average. Liz and Sophie have strong views, but suppose they aren't arrogant, and they regard each other's views as reasonable. Suppose they're trying to agree upon an income tax policy. A centrist compromise policy taxing 50% of income over £30k seems to assign some weight to the two conflicting ideals, liberty and equality, which underpin Liz and Sophie's rival views. If Sophie accepts that Liz's view is reasonable, then presumably she must think there is something to be said for an ideal of liberty that recommends massive tax cuts. And if Liz sees Sophie's view as reasonable, then it seems like she must think there is something to be said for an ideal of equality that recommends tax hikes. While neither Liz nor Sophie would individually support the centrist compromise policy, both can recognise this policy as one that assigns some weight to both ideals, whereas either of their individually preferred policies accord total priority to one ideal or the other. The compromise policy may therefore be less controversial, in a certain sense, insofar as it is more ecumenical with respect to the ideals to which it assigns some weight. Hence, if you take the epistemic credentials of those with whom you disagree seriously, this can lead you to regard a practical compromise as less controversial, even if it is an option that neither you nor your opponent would individually favour.[20]

Weinstock, however, does not think that we can always practically compromise in this way. Furthermore, we might think that although there is a way in which the centrist compromise tax policy is less controversial in the sense that it takes into account both the ideal that Liz prioritises and the ideal that Sophie prioritises, it is no less controversial in an important sense. When we suspend belief about whether p in light of disagreement in belief about whether p, we no longer take a stance on the issue. If Liz or Sophie accepts the centrist policy, they do not refrain from taking a stance; they merely take a different stance. So, even if Weinstock is right that there is a sense in which compromise policies mitigate controversy, this fact does not challenge the explanation of the difference between indulgent epistemic pluralism and indulgent practical pluralism that we have been providing. There is still an important sense in which we cannot mitigate practical controversy in the way that we can mitigate epistemic controversy.

Ultimately these issues are all about how ready we should be to agree to disagree on controversial matters. We should be pluralistic about people's political commitments, and this doesn't mean we have to let go of our own substantive political commitments. This can generate a sense of arbitrariness, granted, but this is the lesser of two evils, since the alternatives are either to give up most of one's practical commitments, or (worse) to give up on political pluralism. On the other hand, we shouldn't be too eager to agree to disagree on purely epistemic matters. Beliefs needn't be resolute, and adopting ambivalent or hedged doxastic attitudes around controversial claims is often a way to mitigate epistemic controversy. The upshot of our discussion is that we shouldn't let our worries about the arbitrariness of being an epistemic indulgent pluralist infect our thinking about indulgent pluralism in people's political commitments.[21] There are differences between the epistemic and practical domains, which justify us in being more tolerant of arbitrariness in the latter case.[22]

Notes

1 One can have a pluralistic ethos without being a relativist. To think people can rationally disagree about e.g. ethical questions isn't necessarily to think ethical questions don't have objectively true answers. You may believe that there's a lot of uncertainty about what the answers are, such that people can rationally arrive at different conclusions.

2 For recent defences of Permissivism see Schoenfield (2019) and Jackson (2020). Many accounts of Permissivism distinguish interpersonal and intrapersonal versions of the view. The former says that there is sometimes more than one doxastic attitude that two agents can hold on proposition P given evidence E; the latter says there is sometimes more than one doxastic attitude that the same agent can hold on P given E.

3 This characterisation of Reasonable Pluralism is paraphrased from Rawls (1993: xvi). In this context being reasonable means, roughly, seeking to abide by fair terms of social cooperation. A reasonable worldview isn't just one that's supported by reasons, then, it's a worldview that evinces a commitment to cooperating with others in the face of ongoing disagreement. There is a significant connection for Rawls, though, between reasonableness and the potential for rational disagreement. Roughly, reasonable people think political decisions shouldn't be based on judgements about which rational, informed people disagree (ibid: 60, 138).

4 This is how the arbitrariness objection to Permissivism is presented in Simpson (2017), building on White's (2005) account. There are some problems that must be addressed by abstemious and indulgent Permissivists alike. For example (see Schultheis 2018), if you believe there's a range of permissible credences you might have in P, then you could hold a credence on the range's edge. But that credence will be rationally dominated by other credences nearer the middle of the range, because (a) you don't know the permissible range's exact boundaries, and (b) a credence nearer the edge seems at greater risk of falling outside the range. Therefore, one might argue, *pace* Permissivism, we aren't rationally permitted to hold any credence in a range of credences for a given proposition and body of evidence.

5 Further to the above, see also Schoenfield (2014), and Stapleford (2019).
6 What we're calling *abstemious* Permissivism is similar to what Sharadin (2017: 65) calls *lower-case* permissivism. Smith (2020) argues that Permissivists rationally ought to be abstemious, in something like our sense.
7 For discussion see Finlay and Schroeder (2017).
8 See Schroeder (2007).
9 See e.g. Shah (2006: 481) and Rowland (2012: 4–5).
10 See e.g. Schroeder (2007: ch. 6) and Cowie (2014).
11 Thanks to Joshua DiPaulo for pressing us on this.
12 See, for instance, Quong (2010: ch. 7).
13 Some of the debate around Permissivism focuses on these sorts of issues, about the connection between (a) being rational and (b) having true beliefs or accurate credences. Because Permissivists think we can see other beliefs as less eligible than our own, and yet still rational, they're at risk of severing the conceptual link between rationality and truth/accuracy. Greco and Hedden (2016) and Horowitz (2019) focus on the rationality-truth connection in criticising Permissivism. Schoenfield (2019) focuses on the rationality-accuracy connection in defending Permissivism.
14 When Rawls and his supporters identify the *burdens of judgement*, i.e. the factors which explain why reasonable people diverge in their practical, worldview-based commitments, they advert to some factors that pertain to rational belief-formation (e.g. the fact that empirical data are conflicting, or that our concepts are vague and subject to various interpretations), but also several factors that primarily relate to people's goals or ideals (e.g. the fact that values can be shaped by different experiences). Our point isn't to deny that worldviews involve doxastic commitments. Our point is that worldviews involve practical commitments beyond these doxastic commitments, and that different people's goals or ideals will reflect their varying experiences, allegiances, desires, etc.
15 For example, if at time t_0 you believe route A is a better way to your destination than route B, and if you know you won't get any new, relevant evidence between t_0 and t_1, then you should intend to keep believing that A is best at t_1. Flip-flopping that isn't prompted by evidence is instrumentally irrational. But if you know that at t_0 you *arbitrarily* chose to regard A as better than B – if either was rationally permissible, so you just decided randomly – it seems like you aren't rationally bound to keep believing that A is best at t_1. Rationality doesn't require this, because you arbitrarily decided in the first place, which by your own lights should be seen as irrelevant (Ye 2020: 21).
16 Thanks to Josh DiPaolo for this suggestion.
17 For an introduction see Christensen (2009).
18 See May (2005: 339). And even if we modify the example so that some people favour the compromise policy, the compromise policy may still be the most controversial option available, if many on the right and left oppose it as strongly as they oppose their opponents' policy.
19 One might doubt whether suspending belief in response to reasonable disagreement about p is really a less controversial response than believing either p or not-p. We can imagine a debate where two sides disagree about what the evidence supports, but both are adamant that it supports a belief one way or the other, and that suspension of belief is irrational. In such a case suspending belief will be more controversial than believing p or not-p, similar to adopting a compromise policy in the immigration case.
20 See Kappel (2018: 88–89), and for discussion, Rowland (2020, ch. 8). The kind of public reason liberalism espoused by Rawls and others aims at controversy-mitigation in something like the sense that Weinstock describes. But critics of public reason liberalism may of course argue that this kind of controversy-mitigation isn't as effective as it seems, since, as per our analysis in the previous paragraph, it can easily result in compromise policies that everyone regards as second-best, at best.
21 However, certain kinds of indulgent practical pluralism, such as certain forms of public reason liberalism, may have epistemic commitments and commitments regarding epistemic pluralism, see van Wietmarschen (2018).
22 Thanks for Josh DiPaolo, Elizabeth Edenberg, and two anonymous referees, for feedback on an earlier draft of this chapter.

References

Cowie, Christopher (2014), "In Defence of Instrumentalism about Epistemic Normativity", *Synthese* 191: 4003–17.

Christensen, David (2009), "Disagreement as Evidence: The Epistemology of Controversy", *Philosophy Compass* 4 (5): 756–67.

Finlay, Stephen and Mark Schroeder (2017), "Reasons for Action: Internal vs. External", in Edward N. Zalta (Ed.), *The Stanford Encyclopedia of Philosophy* (Fall 2017 Edition). https://plato.stanford.edu/archives/fall2017/entries/reasons-internal-external/.

Greco, Daniel and Brian Hedden (2016), "Uniqueness and Metaepistemology", *The Journal of Philosophy* 113 (8): 365–95.

Horowitz, Sophie (2019), "The Truth Problem for Permissivism", *The Journal of Philosophy* 116 (5): 237–62.

Jackson, Elizabeth (2020), "A Defense of Intrapersonal Belief Permissivism", forthcoming in *Episteme*.

Kappel, Klemens (2018), "How Moral Disagreement May Ground Principled Moral Compromise", *Politics, Philosophy & Economics* 17 (1): 75–96.

May, Simon Cabulea (2005), "Principled Compromise and the Abortion Controversy", *Philosophy & Public Affairs* 33 (4): 317–48.

Paul, L. A. (2014), *Transformative Experience* (Oxford: Oxford University Press).

Quong, Jonathan (2010), *Liberalism without Perfection* (Oxford: Oxford University Press).

Rawls, John (1993), *Political Liberalism* (New York: Columbia University Press).

Rowland, Richard (2012), "Moral Error Theory and the Argument from Epistemic Reasons", *Journal of Ethics and Social Philosophy* 7 (1): 1–24.

——— (2020), *Moral Disagreement* (Abingdon: Routledge).

Schoenfield, Miriam (2014), "Permission to Believe: Why Permissivism Is True and What It Tells Us about Irrelevant Influences on Belief", *Noûs* 48 (2): 193–218.

——— (2019), "Permissivism and the Value of Rationality: A Challenge to the Uniqueness Thesis", *Philosophy and Phenomenological Research* 99 (2): 286–97.

Schultheis, Ginger (2018), "Living on the Edge: Against Epistemic Permissivism", *Mind* 127 (507): 863–79.

Schroeder, Mark (2007), *Slaves of the Passions* (Oxford: Oxford University Press).

Shah, Nishi (2006), "A New Argument for Evidentialism", *Philosophical Quarterly* 56 (225): 481–98.

Sharadin, Nathaniel (2017), "A Partial Defence of Permissivism", *Ratio* 30 (1): 57–71.

Simpson, Robert Mark (2017), "Permissivism and the Arbitrariness Objection", *Episteme* 14 (4): 519–38.

Smith, Julia Jael (2020), "Unacknowledged Permissivism", *Pacific Philosophical Quarterly* 101 (1): 158–83.

Stapleford, Scott (2019), "Intraspecies Impermissivism", *Episteme* 16 (3): 340–56.

Weinstock, Daniel (2013), "On the Possibility of Principled Moral Compromise", *Critical Review of International Social and Political Philosophy* 16 (4): 537–56.

White, Roger (2005), "Epistemic Permissiveness", *Philosophical Perspectives* 19: 445–59.

Williams, Bernard (1981), "Internal and External Reasons", in *Moral Luck: Philosophical Papers 1973–1980* (Cambridge: Cambridge University Press): 101–13.

van Wietmarschen, Han (2018), 'Reasonable Citizens and Epistemic Peers: A Skeptical Problem for Political Liberalism', *Journal of Political Philosophy* 26 (4): 486–507.

Ye, Ru (2020), "The Arbitrariness Objection against Permissivism", forthcoming in *Episteme*.

11

POLITICAL DISAGREEMENT

Epistemic or civic peers?

Elizabeth Edenberg

Introduction

Disagreement is a persistent problem in our shared political lives. Many political disagreements strike at the heart of our most cherished values and impact the shape of our society. Political epistemology brings epistemology and political philosophy together to shed light on such issues as the deep disagreements that characterize contemporary political discourse.

Political philosophers focus on intractable disagreements about our deeper worldviews, religious beliefs, morality, and the good life. Much of this literature grows out of Rawls's *Political Liberalism*, which seeks to find fair terms of cooperation in the face of deep and persistent reasonable disagreement about the good.[1] Rawls explains that the wide diversity of views in society is a predictable and welcome outcome of institutions that protect citizens' freedom. He asks, "how is it possible for there to exist over time a just and stable society of free and equal citizens, who remain profoundly divided by reasonable religious, philosophical, and moral doctrines?" (Rawls 2005, 4). Rawls's question has been at the center of a wide set of debates about moral and political disagreement. Furthermore, contemporary investigations of the epistemology of democracy, many of which focus on disagreement, grow out of Rawlsian influences (e.g., Cohen 1986, Bohman and Rehg 1997, Gutmann and Thompson 1998).

More recently, social epistemologists have begun to ask questions about the epistemic significance of disagreement (e.g., Feldman and Warfield 2010, Christensen and Lackey 2013). Debates center on questions about responsible epistemic agency when encountering an epistemic peer who disagrees and whether a given body of evidence justifies one or more rational epistemic states.[2]

This chapter brings together debates in political philosophy and epistemology over what we should do when we disagree. While it might be tempting to think we can readily apply one debate to the other, significant differences between the two threaten this project. After outlining different factors that might cause disagreement among citizens, I will examine how peerhood is specified in each literature and which idealizations are relevant when defining who qualifies as a peer. Next, I show how the two literatures focus on different units of analysis that diverge according to the philosophical purpose behind their respective investigations of disagreement. Epistemologists analyze the rationality of individuals' belief states, whereas political philosophers focus on the just governance of a diverse society. Despite these many differences, political epistemologists can learn valuable lessons by considering these debates side by side in order to provide insights that address a host of different challenges posed by political disagreement. The core lesson to draw from the disanalogies outlined in this chapter is that to make progress, careful attention should be paid to specifying the goal of any particular project within political epistemology.

What causes disagreement?

When considering why people disagree about politics, a variety of factors may explain this disagreement. According to Rawls, disagreement is inevitable among well-motivated citizens who respect one another as free and equal, and who seek terms of cooperation that protect basic democratic rights and are fair to all.[3] Rawls refers to the many "sources of disagreement" between reasonable individuals as the burdens of judgment (Rawls 2005, 55). The burdens of judgment explain how well motivated individuals who are reasoning responsibly could nevertheless come to incompatible (but equally reasonable) positions (Rawls 2005, 54–58).[4] While the burdens of judgment is a convenient way to reference the many influences on people's political views, one need not be a Rawlsian to recognize similarly complex influences on individuals that explain why disagreement arises between morally upright and responsible citizens (e.g., Mason 1993, Gutmann and Thompson 1996).

For those who seek to analyze political disagreement typical in ordinary societies, the causes of disagreement expand greatly (Gutmann and Thompson 1996, 18–26). In addition to morally upright and rational individuals disagreeing while doing their best to reason responsibly, society is filled with a more complex range of incompatible values. Many actual citizens do not embrace the liberal values that underlie Rawls's ideal conception of reasonable citizens. Not everyone views politics as a means for seeking just and fair terms of cooperation; instead, some people aim to ensure their own moral views become the law of the land. Some also view politics as tool for gaining power and influence in society. In addition, citizens' knowledge about politically relevant issues varies significantly.

Herein, I will consider four salient reasons why two people may find themselves disagreeing about politics.

1   *Evidence.* Sometimes disagreement arises because the parties to the disagreement draw on different *sources* of evidence for their beliefs. For example, if there are conflicting reports about a particular event in different newspapers, and we form our beliefs on the basis of our trusted news source—unaware that it is contested—we might hold different views about the event in question. Our disagreement, however, can be traced to the different sources of evidence that ground our beliefs. Revealing these sources could illuminate why we disagree; however, resolving the disagreement may require further questions to establish which (if either) source is accurate.

2   *Interpretation.* Disagreement may also arise because we *interpret* shared evidence differently. When faced with new information, people naturally try to assimilate it into their worldviews. Preexisting commitments and past life experiences can significantly impact how any particular proposition is interpreted by an individual. Furthermore, a host of well-documented cognitive biases can impact belief formation, from confirmation bias to the availability heuristic to framing effects—i.e. the ways and order in which information is presented can have an outsized impact on how the same piece of evidence is interpreted (see Kahneman 2011).

3   *Values.* People frequently disagree about which values are relevant to particular cases that arise in political life. But even if they agree about the relevant values, they often disagree about how to properly weigh and prioritize relevant values. Many moral and political concepts are also open to a range of reasonable interpretations.[5] In politics, we are frequently faced with genuinely difficult cases that require individuals to exercise judgment. And for these variety of factors, our judgment about what is best may vary greatly.

4   *Experiences and Circumstances.* Our moral, religious, and political stances are often influenced by our life circumstances, including our upbringing, education, family, community, work, and geographic location, among many other factors. Our experiences and circumstances also impact what we know, what new experiences and information we encounter, and how we assess new information in light of all of this.

In short, "citizens' total experiences are disparate enough for their judgments to diverge, at least to some degree, on many if not most cases of significant complexity" (Rawls 2005, 57). Given the various reasons why disagreement might arise between people, the way in which we specify the types of disagreements that are of philosophical interest is important. Are we analyzing any form of political disagreement that can arise between citizens, or only disagreement among some subset of citizens who qualify as peers? If so, how should we specify this basic qualification?

What makes two people "peers"?

When investigating the epistemological significance of disagreement, epistemologists often focus on the degree of belief revision, if any, required to maintain the rationality of belief in the face of disagreement. Of course, not just any disagreement is epistemically significant. When there is a clear asymmetry of information, expertise, and/or capacities, disagreement need not threaten the epistemic bona fides of the well-justified believer. To know whether to revise beliefs when faced with disagreement, we should consider the capacities, source of information, and expertise of the person with whom we disagree. Do they have roughly equal intellectual capacities to our own? Are they victim to any distorting epistemic factors, e.g. fatigue or inebriation that could temporarily impair their cognitive function? Are they misinformed or did they overlook a significant piece of evidence? Do they have the same level of expertise in the disputed area?

If both parties to the disagreement share the same evidence on the disputed proposition, have roughly equal intellectual capacities for assessing this evidence, and there are no other distorting factors, they are *epistemic peers.*[6] Epistemic peers are symmetrically situated with regard to the disputed proposition. So defined, it should be clear that disagreement between epistemic peers cannot be sorted out by identifying a mistake in reasoning or a piece of evidence that was overlooked.

By contrast to epistemologists, political philosophers tackle a different type of question about disagreement. Their concern is not what is rational to believe when encountering peer disagreement. Rather, they seek principles of justice that can govern a political community characterized by deep disagreements between members. For this project, the question of epistemic parity between parties is not a primary concern. Instead, *civic* peers are members of the same political community.[7] Civic peers are members of a shared political community, and have certain rights and duties accordingly. Civic peers are governed by the same laws, part of a shared distributive scheme, and often share political power.

What role do idealizing assumptions play in discussions of disagreement?

As we've seen, the debates about disagreement in epistemology are framed differently from those in political philosophy. At first glance, it might be tempting to see the differences as differences between an *idealized* conception of disagreement between epistemic peers and the more practically grounded disagreement that characterizes politics. But that would be too quick. The divide is not simply between ideal theory and nonideal theory; rather, the difference lies in *what* is idealized. There are different idealizations at play in both literatures and more clarity around which ideals are used for which purposes will help us avoid pitfalls that can arise by simply bringing the two debates together.

In epistemology, idealizations help focus the inquiry on the rational response to the purest case of disagreement between peers. The central idealizations stipulate symmetry between the parties. That is, epistemologists stipulate that (1) both parties are intellectual peers—they have similar (or, more idealized, the same) capacities for assessing the evidence and arguments relevant to the question at hand, (2) both parties have access to the same evidence bearing on the proposition about which there is disagreement, and (3) neither party has any antecedent reason to assume that they rather than their peer are more likely to be right or wrong in this domain. They have a similar track record such that they regard each other as epistemic peers for the case at hand.[8] While responses to peer disagreement differ in the literature, most sides to the debate share a similarly idealized conception of what qualifies two individuals as epistemic peers.

By contrast, the question of which idealizations are helpful to stipulate when tackling disagreement between civic peers is subject to extensive debate in political philosophy (see, e.g., Mills 2005, Simmons 2010, Anderson 2010, Estlund 2020). This question is frequently methodological. Should we first clarify an ideal of justice to offer a *telos* that can guide our work to improve existing unjust social arrangements? Or should we turn first to the unjust and messy world to diagnose existing injustices and seek to rectify them as we progress? Ideal theorists argue that insofar as any effort to identify injustice implicitly relies on some as of yet unrealized ideal of justice, it will be practically best to make that ideal explicit from the get-go. Nonideal theorists critique ideal theorists for failing to address injustices in society or, worse, structuring their theory in a way that it is unable to recognize clear injustices. They argue that many injustices are well established and easily identifiable, so a project that seeks justice should start with the messy world and find ways of improving it.

How do ideal and nonideal theorists each think about civic peers? Nonideal theorists are more likely to look at people as they are, with complex motivations, implicit and explicit biases, and various degrees of willingness to comply with just social orders. By contrast, ideal theorists often build in idealizing assumptions about citizens and society, which vary according to the aims of their political project. For example, to establish the possibility of a just social order that remains stable despite deep and persistent disagreement between citizens (Rawls 2005), it is helpful to stipulate that all parties to the disagreement are committed to cooperating on fair terms. The challenge is then focused on how to specify principles of justice and legitimacy when people disagree. The idealizations relevant to this project have little to do with epistemic symmetry between parties. Instead, the central idealizations stipulate a shared commitment to the aim of the project, seeking a just social order that respects individuals.

Determining which (if any) idealizations are used to specify the qualification of civic peerhood makes a significant difference to the ultimate theory. An idealized conception of disagreement between civic peers who are motivated to cooperate on just and fair terms is a very different problem, and may require a different response than disagreements between civic peers who are not so well motivated. Should the qualification for civic peers be defined in terms of a basic moral threshold or are epistemic qualifications also important? Should the moral threshold be set low to rule out only psychopaths and tyrants? How should common forms of injustice and discrimination fit into idealizing assumptions about disagreement? Theorists vary widely on all of these questions. Nevertheless, the debate about how to co-operate on fair terms with those who disagree is unified in treating the question as a moral problem to be adjudicated between members of a political community.

The different idealizations used to specify peerhood in the epistemology and political philosophy of disagreement are ultimately tied to core differences concerning the philosophical purpose of investigating disagreement. Should we assume peers are epistemic equals (in terms of capacities, access to the evidence, justification, etc.) in order to clarify what a rational individual should believe? Or should we assume peers are moral equals (showing equal moral respect for one another and agreeing to cooperating on fair terms that secure individuals' basic rights) to clarify how to structure a just society? Or, should we reject ideal theory and tackle questions of disagreement between any members of a shared political community? Political epistemologists who seek to bridge the epistemology and political philosophy of disagreement should keep track of the different idealizing assumptions in each literature and should carefully specify how they define peerhood for specific projects within political epistemology.

What is the basic unit of analysis?

So far, we have looked at different factors that may cause two people to disagree and the specific requirements and idealizations used to establish whether that disagreement is between peers. This might suggest that the core differences are in how peer disagreement is specified. But there are deeper differences in the basic unit of analysis for each theory: epistemologists focus on individuals' belief states, whereas political philosophers focus on the just governance of society.

While the epistemology of disagreement is a thriving area of social epistemology, the focus remains squarely on the appropriate epistemic stance individuals should take toward their own beliefs when faced with peer disagreement. The social elements come in because the individual is considering the epistemic impact of their peer's contrary belief. Yet it matters little *who* the peer is, provided symmetry between the parties has been established. In fact, the interpersonal element can drop away altogether; the same intuitions apply to differences between just one individual's views over time.[9] The conclusions drawn about the epistemic impact of peer disagreement, thus fit within a much larger literature about responsible belief, epistemic agency, and the acquisition of knowledge and understanding. In all of these cases, the core unit of analysis is the individual and her epistemic states, and the conclusions drawn primarily concern responsible individual epistemic agency.

By contrast, when political philosophers consider disagreement between citizens, the focus is not on what each person believes. Rather, it is on how to structure legitimate governance of a diverse society. The primary unit of analysis is the terms of justice, structure of legitimate government, and/or specific political policies and laws. They ask: which principles of justice can govern a society in which moral, religious, philosophical, and political views are deeply contested? How can we ensure coercive power is legitimate when citizens hold a wide variety of opposing beliefs? What can be justified to a diverse political community, evaluating policies against a wide variety of viewpoints?

This does not imply that individuals' viewpoints are irrelevant. To figure out what might be acceptable to a community, we must figure out what is acceptable to the individual members of the community. But the core focus is not individuals' justified epistemic states. Rather, the focus is on which proposals survive contestation from the many members of a political community and how political processes (e.g., deliberation, debate, voting) are structured to allow disagreeing parties to debate, vote, and find fair terms of cooperation in spite of persistent disagreement between citizens. Some epistemic democrats add that certain deliberative or aggregative procedures have epistemic value either for individuals (who learn from deliberation with others) or for society (improving the epistemic quality of democratic decisions). Nevertheless, the problem of disagreement is generally framed as a collective problem for social governance.

Should disagreements be resolved or managed?

The last major difference between epistemology and political philosophy that I will survey in this chapter lies in how each theory approaches solutions to the problem posed by disagreement. Should disagreements be resolved or managed?

Epistemologists seek to determine how a responsible epistemic agent should respond to the prima facie challenge peer disagreement poses to the rationality of her beliefs. They seek a rational resolution to disagreement to ensure that individuals maintain justified epistemic states. Should an individual revise her confidence in her belief, suspend judgment on the issue at stake, or is it rationally permissible to set aside the significance of the disagreement and stick to her guns? No matter which response is deemed appropriate, the assumption in the literature is that there is a rational resolution to the challenge of peer disagreement. The response hinges on whether and to what degree peer disagreement is epistemically significant for an individual.

By contrast, political philosophers do not seek rational resolution to the disagreement. Instead, they view disagreement as a persistent problem in political life and thus seek fair terms according to which we can manage our disagreements. Unlike the cases discussed in the epistemology of disagreement, political disagreement is not a problem that can be overcome. While some disagreements may be resolved over time and many political debates are aimed at trying to convince others of one's view, disagreement is a permanent feature of democratic politics. In any society that protects basic democratic rights to freedom of conscience and expression, a diversity of incompatible but nevertheless reasonable views will remain (Rawls 2005, 37). Given the "intractable sources of disagreement," theorists should not only offer ways of adjudicating political disagreements, their theory should also enable citizens to learn to live with persistent disagreements (Gutmann and Thompson 1996, 360). Thus, the project is not about resolution but management. We must enable citizens to live with disagreements that persist, and do so in a way that still fosters just social institutions and fair modes of government. For many political philosophers, this means finding ways to structure productive political discussions in spite of disagreement and find procedures that can secure legitimate rule for a diverse society in which citizens continue to disagree with one another. Furthermore, on most democratic or political liberal theories, it is permissible for individuals to object to the outcome of any political decision and believe that it is incorrect, irresponsible, immoral, or unjust. Agreement on specific policies is unlikely and not expected for a proposal to be legitimate. The core question is what makes proposals legitimate despite individuals' objections.

Lessons for political epistemologists

As we've seen, many of the differences between epistemic and political approaches to disagreement grow out of the differences between each inquiry's aim: whether the goal is evaluating individuals' epistemic states or finding just political principles to govern society. The different aims explain many subsidiary differences concerning: the specification of peerhood, which factors contribute to peer disagreement, the idealizations used in theorizing, whether the analysis focuses on individuals or society, and whether disagreement should be seen as a problem to resolve or manage. These differences may pose some difficulties for political epistemologists who seek to bring together these two literatures in order to evaluate political disagreement.[10] Nevertheless, there are lessons to be drawn from considering these differences in order to carve out fruitful paths forward for political epistemology.

Lessons drawn from the peer disagreement literature may not directly apply to political disagreements between citizens who may or may not be epistemic peers. The variety of factors that contribute to political disagreements extend beyond the more narrow conception of epistemic peers. Epistemic parity between citizens is often difficult to determine, even more so with the splintering of information spheres and the hyper-personalization of digital access to politically relevant information. In cases of uncertainty about the epistemic status of our interlocutor, it is still important to consider how to resolve disagreement in an epistemically responsible manner.

In addition, people's political beliefs are often adopted in a cluster of positions, such that co-partisans have many beliefs in common, whereas members of different political parties may have very few overlapping commitments. This leads many people to have greater default trust in people who share their political views.[11] To establish two parties' status as epistemic peers, epistemologists look for a similar track record of performance in the domain in question. While we can establish an agreed upon track record of success in one's past performance in many fields, this is far easier when faced with issues where there is more settled consensus on shared standards for assessment. This is less available in political disagreements. The standards for assessing one's track record about political disputes are often just as controversial as a disagreement about any particular issue. It may be difficult for citizens from different political parties to see one another as epistemic peers in the relevant domain because our disagreements about political issues come in clusters such that we may not find a core area of agreement by which to judge each other epistemic peers.[12]

In this fractured context, trying to approach political debate as if we're talking about epistemic peers will be no less divisive than politics as usual. We may be apt to downgrade the epistemic standing of individuals who do not share our commitments, judging them to be insufficiently responsive to the evidence we take to justify our own beliefs. Once the parties to the disagreement have exchanged reasons, they might conclude—on the basis of the continued disagreement in light of this exchange—that they were not talking to their epistemic peer. If I explain reasons I think decisively support my position and you hear those reasons, yet draw a different conclusion or fail to see the weight of the evidence, it seems I have new evidence you are not my epistemic peer after all. So much the better for my view.

The challenges that arise when attempting to resolve political disagreements are not incidental. Political disagreements often hinge on deeper disagreements about moral or religious values, the order of priority assigned to shared values, and disagreements about the proper role of government in promoting valuable aims. In addition, many people's views about politics relate to diverse aspects of their identity, social location, and experience. In these cases, it is difficult to clearly establish all of the information and evidence that bear on the belief in question, and thus, assessing parity of evidence and information bearing on the views will be difficult to parse. Resolution to the disagreement is often unlikely, even if both parties share their own reasoning behind their political views and approach the conversation with intellectual humility, seeking to learn from one another. Instead, we should figure our productive ways to live with the disagreements that are a persistent feature of politics.

Yet even if we approach political debate as a problem to be managed over time, analyzing the epistemic positions embedded in political theories is important for making progress. Uncovering the epistemological and metaphysical assumptions that undergird different political theories and defending these commitments is fruitful ground for philosophical inquiry. For example, what forms of political justification are epistemically as well as morally robust? How should an epistemically responsible agent reconcile the persistence of political disagreement with their own desire to hold well-justified beliefs about these contested questions?

The core lesson to draw from the disanalogies outlined in this chapter is that to make progress, careful attention should be paid to specifying the goal of any particular project within political epistemology. Before beginning a project that simply meshes together the two literatures, political epistemologists should first establish what insights they hope to attain in a particular project. The aim of the inquiry shapes many features of the precedent literature in the epistemology and political philosophy of disagreement. So too, the aim of specific projects within political epistemology should inform the choices about who qualifies as a peer, which disagreements are relevant, which (if any) idealizations are useful, and what level of analysis is appropriate to that aim.

Overall, future directions may turn on how idealized the political epistemology of disagreement ought to be. Moving forward, political epistemologists may divide themselves into ideal and nonideal theory camps. Yet no matter where one falls on the question of idealization, clarity about the aim of the inquiry is important for framing the core concept of peerhood at stake.

For those who seek to tackle disagreements between citizens as we find them, it might be time to take a nonideal turn within the epistemology of disagreement. All of the diverse causes of disagreement between citizens would need to be taken into account if we aim to determine the epistemically appropriate response to political disagreement. Citizens whose views all have legitimate political standing in the debate may vary widely in terms of their epistemic credentials, evidence they draw on, and the grounding beliefs that undergird their political positions. Political epistemologists who seek insights that will help us navigate the types of disagreements that people face in contemporary society will need to clarify how peerhood should be defined for this project.

For those who seek to use idealizations to clarify the philosophical stakes of disagreement, careful attention should be paid to which questions about disagreement the theory aims to solve. Different idealizations may be relevant to understanding what citizens ought to believe and which theories of justice could govern a society characterized by deep disagreements. Likewise, when analyzing the epistemic underpinnings of political theories or political implications of epistemic theories, clarity about which idealizations are relevant to the joint project may shed light on how existing models might need to change to accommodate insights from political epistemology. Idealizations are likely to remain helpful for clarifying the issues at stake, but only if these are clearly articulated and defended in relation to the ultimate goal of the project.

More broadly, expert disagreement and more general disagreement among citizens may require different approaches no matter which methodological approach one chooses. Expert disagreement mirrors the peer disagreement debate in epistemology, but there may be new lessons to draw from shifting the debate from what experts should believe to the impact of expert disagreement on public policy. Likewise there are questions about disagreement between citizens that impact what each person is justified in believing as well as questions about how to structure the social order to find ways to cooperate in spite of persistent disagreements. Both sets of questions are relevant for political epistemology.

Ultimately, I do not seek to come down on either the side of ideal theory or nonideal theory in political epistemology. Rather, I hope to encourage open debate about the role of ideal theory in political epistemology. No matter which method is chosen, it is essential to carefully consider the aims, purpose, and limits of specific projects within political epistemology, and the precedent literature in both the epistemology and political philosophy of disagreement.[13]

Notes

1 Rawls's turn toward political liberalism began in his 1980 Dewey lectures at Columbia University, culminating in the publication of *Political Liberalism* in 1993. He continued to revise and expand political liberalism in response to critiques of the work. I have included the citation to the expanded edition (2005).
2 The latter issue concerns the "uniqueness thesis" and is the subject to of a separate chapter in this handbook. As such, I largely set it aside herein.
3 Rawls refers to such disagreements as 'reasonable' disagreements, using 'reasonable' as a technical term, with specific qualifications, to specify the range of disagreements he considers in *Political Liberalism*. Rawls contrasts reasonable pluralism with simple pluralism, which may also include unreasonable, irrational, "and even mad" comprehensive doctrines (Rawls 2005, xvi). In this paper, I bracket discussions of how we should understand Rawlsian reasonableness to keep the focus on more general lessons for the disagreement literature in political epistemology.
4 Rawlsians will recognize many of the factors I survey in this section as examples of the types of disagreements that Rawls includes in the burdens of judgment.
5 For example, what kind of equality are we trying to establish and why? How should freedom be interpreted: is this negative freedom, positive freedom, freedom from domination?
6 This specification of who qualifies as an epistemic peer is widely shared by epistemologists on different sides of the debate about the rational response to peer disagreement. See, e.g., Kelly (2005), Christensen (2007), Elga (2007), Lackey (2010), and Goldman (2010).
7 Many political philosophers use the term 'citizens' to describe this relationship. Citizen refers to people in their capacities as political agents in a particular community and, when used in political philosophy, is not intended to track immigration status. Since immigrants are often times important civic peers and members of the political community, I opt for this more inclusive term.
8 I've stated this somewhat loosely as it might make a difference whether we are stipulating that two people are in fact epistemic peers, or whether each is believed to be a peer, or whether each party is justified in believing that they are peers (see Enoch 2010, 970–74).
9 Thomas Kelly, for example, asks us to consider parallels between an individual's own justified belief at different points in time and the classic cases of peer disagreement (Kelly 2013, 32–33).
10 I do not mean to overstate the challenges in bringing these two literatures together. Some political philosophers have drawn on the epistemology of disagreement in order to defend their political theories (see, e.g., Peter 2013), while others have used the epistemology of disagreement to critique public reason theorists (see, e.g., Enoch 2017 and van Wietmarschen 2018).
11 If Regina Rini is right greater trust in co-partisans may even be rational (Rini 2017).
12 For example, Adam Elga offers a helpful case of two friends who disagree about abortion and a related cluster of positions. They are unlikely to judge the other party to be their epistemic peer on any of the related cases because of the full cluster of moral and political options (Elga 2007). This problem may also extend to our ability to see one another as moral peers. For a great illustration of how clusters of values can impact how citizens view one another, see Amanda Greene's chapter in this volume.
13 Thanks to Michael Hannon, Jeroen de Ridder, and Rebecca Tuvel for their helpful comments, which improved this chapter significantly.

Works cited

Anderson, Elizabeth. 2010. *The Imperative of Integration*. Princeton, NJ: Princeton University Press.

Bohman, James and William Rehg (eds.). 1997. *Deliberative Democracy: Essays one Reason and Politics*. Cambridge: MIT Press.

Christensen, David. 2007. "The Epistemology of Disagreement: The Good News." *Philosophical Review* 116(2): 187–217.

Christensen, David and Jennifer Lackey (eds.). 2013. *The Epistemology of Disagreement: New Essays*. Oxford: Oxford University Press.

Cohen, Joshua. 1986. "An Epistemic Conception of Democracy." *Ethics* 97(1): 26–38.

Elga, Adam. 2007. "Reflection and Disagreement." *Nous* 41(3): 478–502.

Enoch, David. 2010. "Not Just a Truthometer: Taking Oneself Seriously." *Mind* 119(476): 953–97.

———. 2017. "Political Philosophy and Epistemology: A Case of Public Reason." In *Oxford Studies in Political Philosophy*, vol. 3, David Sobel, Peter Valentine, and Steven Wall (eds.), 132–65. Oxford: Oxford University Press.

Estlund, David. 2020. *Utopophobia: On the Limits (If Any) of Political Philosophy*. Princeton, NJ: Princeton University Press.

Feldman, Richard and Ted Warfield. 2010. *Disagreement*. Oxford: Oxford University Press.

Goldman, Alvin. 2010. "Epistemic Relativism and Reasonable Disagreement." In *Disagreement*, Richard Feldman and Ted A. Warfield (eds.), 187–215. Oxford: Oxford University Press.

Gutmann, Amy and Dennis Thompson. 1996. *Democracy and Disagreement*. Cambridge, MA: Harvard University Press.

Kahneman, Daniel. 2011. *Thinking Fast and Slow*. New York: Farrar, Straus and Giroux.

Kelly, Thomas. 2005. "The Epistemic Significance of Disagreement." In *Oxford Studies in Epistemology*, vol. 1, John Hawthorne and Tamar Szabó Gendler (eds.), 167–96. Oxford: Oxford University Press.

———. 2013. "Disagreement and the Burdens of Judgment." In *The Epistemology of Disagreement: New Essays*, David Christensen and Jennifer Lackey (eds.), 31–53. Oxford: Oxford University Press.

Lackey, Jennifer. 2010. "A Justificationist View of Disagreement's Epistemic Significance." In *Social Epistemology*, Alan Haddock, Adrian Miller, and Duncan Pritchard (eds.), 298–325. Oxford: Oxford University Press.

Mason, Andrew. 1993. *Explaining Political Disagreement*. Cambridge: Cambridge University Press.

Mills, Charles. 2005. "'Ideal Theory' as Ideology." *Hypatia* 20(3): 165–84.

Peter, Fabienne. 2013. "Epistemic Foundations of Political Liberalism." *Journal of Moral Philosophy* 10(5): 598–620.

Rawls, John. 2005. *Political Liberalism: Expanded Edition*. New York: Columbia University Press.

Rini, Regina. 2017. "Fake News and Partisan Epistemology." *Kennedy Institute of Ethics Journal* 27(2): 43–64.

Simmons, A. John. 2010. "Ideal and Nonideal Theory." *Philosophy & Public Affairs* 38(1): 5–36.

Van Wietmarschen, Han. 2018. "Reasonable Citizens and Epistemic Peers: A Skeptical Problem for Political Liberalism." *The Journal of Political Philosophy* 26: 486–507.

12

EPISTEMIC NETWORKS AND POLARIZATION

Daniel J. Singer, Patrick Grim, Aaron Bramson, Bennett Holman,
Jiin Jung, and William J. Berger

Introduction

Much of applied epistemology asks questions about how information moves in groups of individuals and institutions and how that dynamic influences individuals' and institutions' beliefs and actions. *Political* epistemology focuses on that dynamic with the aim of advancing our understanding of questions in political philosophy, but similar and related questions have been addressed by social epistemologists, philosophers of science, complex systems theorists, sociologists, political scientists, social psychologists, and marketing and management researchers. Among social epistemologists and philosophers of science, thinking in terms of epistemic network models has been fruitful for understanding the ways in which individuals' beliefs can influence the beliefs of others and groups. This chapter will introduce the notion of an epistemic network model and discuss some of the ways that epistemic network models and implementations of them in computer simulations have contributed to our understanding of political polarization. In doing so, this chapter will serve as a non-comprehensive introduction to these topics that aims to inspire future work in political epistemology.

In Section I, we'll introduce epistemic network modeling and contrast epistemic network approaches to thinking about political epistemology with more general aggregative approaches. Section II will introduce a result from Zollman (2007) about how the structure of epistemic networks influences how quickly and how accurately members of groups can come to have true beliefs. Section III begins to investigate polarization in epistemic networks by first looking at models of divided networks from Grim and Singer et al. (2015). Those models do not produce polarization despite seeming like they should. We'll then turn to a model from Hegselmann and Krause (2002) that does produce polarization in similar networks. Section IV looks at two recent applications of the epistemic network approach to thinking about polarization in non-divided networks, those from Singer et al. (2019a) and Weatherall and O'Connor (forthcoming). The chapter concludes by briefly discussing some ways this framework can contribute to future work in political epistemology.

I What is an epistemic network?

To a first approximation, the guiding ideas of the epistemic network approach to questions in social epistemology are that

1 Beliefs, information, evidence, and other epistemic elements are held by *agents*, where "agents" is broadly understood to include individuals, but also families, small groups (like a Parent–Teacher Association), scientific lab groups, companies, journals, and other institutions;
2 The agents are connected to other agents in a (not necessarily fixed) network structure; and
3 The beliefs, information, evidence, and other epistemic elements are shared via network connections with other agents.

Let's consider two simple examples.

Example 12.1: A racially divided city

Suppose there is a city that is so deeply racially divided between White and Black people that there is literally no communication between the two races. The epistemic network of this city will contain two disconnected parts. Perhaps it looks something like Figure 12.1.

Here the individual agents (represented by dots) are connected to other agents (with the connections represented by lines). In this setup, beliefs, information, and evidence can move within the two racial groups, but because there are no links between the racial groups, no beliefs, information, or evidence is shared between them. Of course, the idea that two

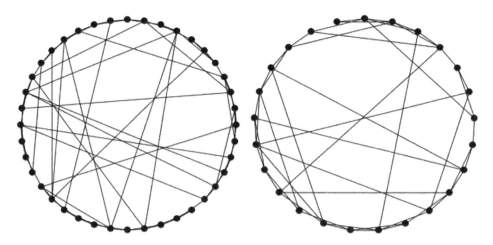

Figure 12.1 Two disconnected epistemic networks.

subgroups of a population would be this disconnected is unrealistic, but here we're simplifying. For a more realistic epistemic network model of a racially divided city, see Grim et al. (2012).[1]

Example 12.2: High school gossip

Charlie starts a rumor that Alex likes Sandy. Charlie tells one friend. That one friend tells the most popular person in the school, who proceeds to tell everyone else. In this situation, there's an epistemic network on which the (misleading) information about Alex and Sandy travels. Figure 12.2 represents the network through time.

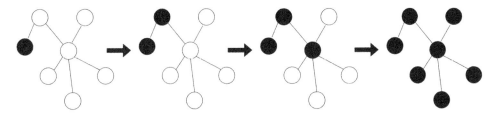

Figure 12.2   Illustration of a high school gossip epistemic network through time.

On the left, we see Charlie, who uses a piece of (mis)information to start the rumor. In the next step, that information has spread to Charlie's friend. In the time step after that, the misinformation is spread to the popular student, who shares it with the rest of the group. Here the color of the agent represents whether the rumor has spread to that agent.

Both of these examples illustrate epistemic networks in which there are (1) nodes (agents) who have or do not have some information, belief, or evidence, and (2) links between agents that represent the connections between them. The second example also involves changes in the epistemic states of the group through time, which is another common element of epistemic network models. That particular example also uses a diffusion or infection dynamic, where information travels in the network by "infecting" neighboring nodes. Although that dynamic is commonly used in epistemic networks, it is not the only possibility, as we'll discuss below.

Epistemic network models are a subspecies of the broader class of *agent-based models*. Agent-based modeling is an approach to modeling complex high-level phenomena in terms of simple interactions of the small parts of systems that give rise to the phenomena. We can contrast agent-based models with more traditional kinds of models that we call "aggregative models." In aggregative models, the relevant features of the smaller parts of the phenomena are typically summed up and represented as a single unit. For example, simple macroeconomic models of the sales price of goods might represent the price as a function of the aggregated supply and aggregated demand for the good. Facts about how much individual agents will pay for the good or how much individual suppliers will supply are aggregated into supply and demand curves that represent the collection of buyers and the collection of sellers. An agent-based model of the same phenomenon would disaggregate the individual buyers and sellers and treat each as an independent actor that can contribute to changes in the good's price.

Agent-based models (and epistemic network models, in particular) have made important contributions to our understanding of questions in political epistemology.[2] To introduce the reader to some of these contributions and hopefully inspire future ones, we'll use the next section to review an important general result about how the structure of epistemic networks can influence how quickly and how accurately members of groups of truth-seeking agents come to have true beliefs. After that, we'll look at more recent work using epistemic network models to try to understand polarization.

II The impacts of epistemic network structure

It's common in philosophical reasoning (and in scientific reasoning) to employ idealized abstract models of complex phenomena. Lottery and urn cases are used as paradigmatic idealized models of uncertainty in epistemology, for example, and Rawls uses a highly idealized model of group decision-making in his veil of ignorance argument. Similarly, one might think that political epistemologists can avoid the complexities of epistemic networks by idealizing them to completely connected networks. Work by Kevin Zollman (2007) shows this would be a mistake.

Zollman gives a model in which agents are trying to figure out which of two slot machines has a higher payoff. They do this by playing the two machines, collecting the outputs, and sharing their results with their neighbors in an epistemic network. Zollman uses this as a model of scientific inquiry, but it can easily be seen as a model of information sharing about the effectiveness of government policies, the justness of police action, and many other kinds of information. In Zollman's model, agents start out with random credences (degrees of belief) about which of the two slot machines is better. They then play the slot machines in ways that balance maximizing their expected payoff (by playing the machine they think is best) and exploring the other machine (to get more information in case they are wrong). The agents share their information with their neighbors and update their credences based on their experience and the experience of those with whom they are connected. Zollman compares how different communities of researchers perform on different types of epistemic networks, including ring networks (where agents are connected in a circle), wheel networks (where agents are connected in a circle but also to a central hub), and complete networks (where all agents are connected).

Using computer simulations of this model, Zollman shows that the more connected a network is, the *worse* the agents can be expected to perform in the long run. In the complete network, even though the agents tend to converge on an answer quickly, they tend to converge more commonly on the wrong answer, since the group tends to react too quickly to misleading information. In less connected networks, when part of the group is misled, the more distant parts of the group still have a chance to turn the misled part around. This general point was explored in more detail and with a different model by Grim and Singer et al. (2013). What these arguments show is that the structure of epistemic networks might have an important effect on outcomes of interest to political epistemology. For example, if epistemic democrats are right that democracies are stronger partly as a function of how epistemically good they are (e.g. Landemore 2013), these epistemic network models point toward thinking that less connected democracies might be better. Care must be taken in working from highly theoretical and idealized models like Zollman's to real-world implications, and unfortunately, exploring that further is beyond the scope of this chapter.

Epistemic network models are often too complex to explore from the (computer-free) armchair. So analyses of epistemic network models are typically done with computer simulations. The way this works is that the model is implemented in a simple program-ming language like Python (a general-purpose high-level programing language) or NetLogo (a program designed specifically for agent-based model simulation). A "run" of the model starts with some initial conditions. In Zollman's model, these would include the network of agents, facts about the payoffs of the slot machines, and an initial distribution of beliefs about the payoffs among the agents. The simulation then proceeds in "time steps," in which the model's primary dynamic is repeated. In Zollman's model, in each time step, the agents play the slot machines to collect new data, share that data with their network neighbors, and update their beliefs about which machine is best. Many runs are performed, and data from those runs is statistically analyzed. Typically thousands to millions of different runs are per-formed (depending on the complexity of the model and available computational resources) so contingent initial conditions and stochastic elements of the model don't affect the analysis.

It's common to discuss epistemic network models as though they just are computational simulations, but we think it's important to at least conceptually distinguish the models from their computational instantiations. Flaws or peculiarities in implementations of models need not be flaws or peculiarities in the models themselves, and often our understanding of the phenomena of interest (such as the spread of some idea or political polarization) comes from understanding the models and arguments about the models, not the details of their com-putational instantiations. So the simulations should be seen as a tool that helps us explore these models, not as the models themselves. We'll turn now to discussing epistemic network models of polarized groups, but we encourage the reader to see Zollman (forthcoming) for a much deeper introduction to epistemic network research.

III Polarization in divided ("homophilous") networks

The reader of this volume is probably aware of the polarization that characterizes contempo-rary political climates in most democratic countries. This polarization consists in persistent (and sometimes even violent) disagreement between groups, often two, and typically across an array of different issues regarding both factual and policy matters. For one recent collec-tion of case studies, see Carothers and O'Donohue (2019). It's a complex technical question how to define and measure polarization (see Bramson et al. 2016), but those technicalities won't affect the discussion here. We'll focus on models that purport to model very clear-cut cases of group polarization.[3]

In modeling polarization, it's natural to think we should start with a divided epistemic network, perhaps representing connections inside and between different social groups. In "Germs, Genes, and Memes," Grim and Singer et al. (2015) explore how information travels on divided networks of this sort. Grim and Singer et al. use five different types of sub-networks connected by varying numbers of bridging links. Figure 12.3 shows examples of these networks.

Their paper wasn't about polarization. It was about the dynamics of different types of information transfer, including infection dynamics (like in the gossip example above), split-the-difference belief averaging, and the sexual reproduction dynamics of genes. They started the models with different information on each side of the network and explored how that information moved.

Although they weren't focused on polarization, there's a lesson for polarization in their work: every kind of information dynamic led to convergence across every network type. That is, given enough time, all of the forms of information dynamics destroyed any polar-ization that was originally there. What this means is that if we want to get a model that helps

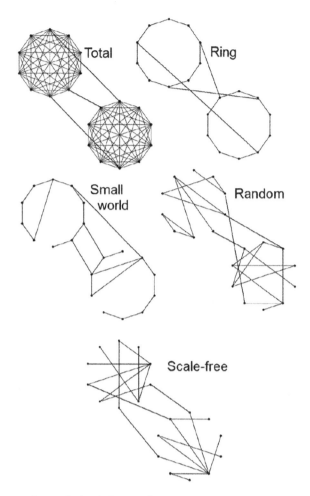

Figure 12.3   Pictures of example divided networks.

us understand how groups can become and stay polarized, starting with a divided network and a simple dynamic isn't going to get us as far as we might have thought.

Another approach comes from Hegselmann and Krause's (2002) Bounded Confidence model (and related relative agreement models, e.g. Deffuant et al. 2002). Hegselmann and Krause generate polarization with agents who update on others' opinions only when those opinions are already close enough to their own. Opinions in the model are mapped onto the [0, 1] interval, with initial opinions spread uniformly at random. Belief updating is done by taking a weighted average of the opinions that are close enough to the agent's own. What counts as "close enough" is determined by a variable threshold in the model. As agents' beliefs change, so do the other agents that count as close enough. In practice, what this means is that the Hegselmann–Krause model has a *dynamic epistemic network*, since who listens to whom changes as the model runs. Unlike the static network models of Grim and Singer et al., Hegselmann and Krause's model does generate polarization for some thresholds.

When the threshold is too small (like 0.01), agents only talk to others who have beliefs very close to their own. In this case, the group doesn't become polarized so much as divided into lots of tiny groups. On the other hand, if the threshold is too big (like 0.25),

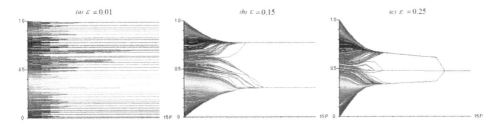

Figure 12.4   Example beliefs through time with threshold values (ε) of (a) 0.01, (b) 0.15, and (c) 0.25 in the Hegselmann and Krause (2002) model.

everyone's beliefs end up influencing everyone else's, so the group converges onto a single average belief. In the middle though, there are some thresholds that give rise to polarized groups. When the threshold is 0.15, for example, the agents tend to divide into two groups both of which consolidate within themselves but to not eventually converge. Figure 12.4 illustrates this.

Hegselmann and Krause's models (and relative agreement models generally) use the simple belief updating mechanism of averaging with one's interlocutors. One might worry that averaging of beliefs is neither realistic nor obviously rational, but averaging does capture the reinforcement learning effects and dissonance weakening effects that are characteristic of many forms of belief updating. To see that, imagine that you and your friends are discussing the weather last month. If you start out thinking it was unusually hot and your friends disagree, that will likely undermine your confidence in your own belief, making you less sure. This is dissonance weakening. On the other hand, if your friends agree with you, that agreement is likely to reinforce your original attitude. This is reinforcement learning. In models that use a belief averaging mechanism, the more an agent's beliefs are like those of their interlocutors on the network, the less pressure there will be to change those beliefs, and the flip holds as well. So even though belief averaging is too simplistic to accurately represent belief change, it is convenient and methodologically advantageous because it captures key dynamics of belief change in a manageable way. For these reasons, it is probably the most common mechanism used in epistemic network models, and it's definitely one of the earliest, dating back to some of the first epistemic network models from French (1956) and DeGroot (1974). Belief averaging is also one of the dynamics explored in the Grim and Singer et al.'s study discussed above. That mechanism fails to produce polarization in Grim and Singer et al.'s models, although it does produce it in the Hegselmann–Krause model. The difference is the flexible and changing network in Hegselmann–Krause as opposed to the static networks in Grim and Singer et al.'s work. The dynamic network of the Hegselmann–Krause model essentially disconnects each of the polarized subgroups from the other. While averaging continues to occur in the model, agents in each of the subgroups no longer have any averaging-connection to the agents in the other subgroup.

Bramson et al. (2017) critique the Hegselmann–Krause model and similar relative agreement models as being too unrealistic to be useful in understanding real polarization. This is because these models use a "peeling-back-from-the-edges" mechanism. Polarization occurs in these models (when it does) because agents at the extremes of the belief spectrum (very close to 0 or 1) don't have neighbors who are more extreme than them. So those agents get "pulled" toward a more moderate position when they update with their more moderate neighbors. This results in there being two clusters of agents on either side of the mean belief, which form the basis of the polarized groups. So when polarization is produced in this model, it's because of the artificial edges of the belief spectrum in the model. This dynamic can be seen in Figure 12.4b. Bramson et al. argue that this mechanism doesn't correspond to real-world mechanisms of polarization (2017:148). Despite this, the model might be able to help us understand polarization in other ways, as we'll discuss more below.

We started this section thinking that we should use divided networks in models of polarization, and we saw that while Grim and Singer et al.'s divided models didn't produce polarization, Hegselmann and Krause's models did. There's a methodological worry for any divided-network model of polarization though: If the goal is to understand polarization, models that start with a divided network will have a harder time producing any explanatory insight. That's because the dividedness of polarization that we seek to explain is baked into the model from the beginning. Since the goal is to explain a kind of dividedness, the explanation will produce more insight if it doesn't treat division as one of the explanans. In the next section, we'll look at two epistemic network models of polarization where polarization is produced by how agents respond to each other, rather than division in the epistemic network.

IV Recent epistemic network approaches to polarization

Singer et al.'s (2019a) epistemic network model aims to be a general model of group deliberation. They use that model to show that for agents with limited memories, a deliberating group can become polarized simply by agents rationally managing their limited memory. They argue that because the polarization arises from what is epistemically rational for agents in light of their cognitive limitations, the polarization produced is, in that sense, epistemically rational. In their model, the epistemic network is a static and complete network (where everyone is connected to everyone else). So, the epistemic network being divided isn't what explains the polarization. Instead, the agents polarize because of how they respond to each other.

Singer et al.'s model of group deliberation takes inspiration from Rawls's conception of group discussion as "a way of combining information and enlarging the range of arguments" (1999:315). In Singer et al.'s model, agents have reasons for their beliefs, and they share those reasons with other agents. Reasons are modeled in terms of a content that is supported by that reason (e.g. that the defendant is guilty or that a particular tax policy will lead to less unemployment) and a (positive real-valued) strength of that reason. In the main kind of model run that Singer et al. consider, they assume that there are only two opposing contents in play in the discussion (e.g. the guilt or innocence of some defendant). They also assume that what reasons support and how strongly they support those contents doesn't vary over time or between agents. They treat the agent's over-all belief as the weighted sum of their reasons – i.e. agents believe the content that's on balance supported by the reasons they have, which is required if the agents are to be epistemically rational. In the model, each agent starts with a random assortment of reasons. Agents are then chosen in a random order to share one of their reasons with the rest of the group. In their original model (2019a), agents choose reasons at random, but in the later version of the model (Singer et al. 2019b), the model is expanded to include different strategies agents might use to share reasons. When an agent hears a new reason, they add it to their stock of reasons and update their belief accordingly. If the agents' memories and cognitive processing abilities are unlimited, as they are in the simplest versions of the model, then the agents eventually converge to the belief that's supported by the total collection of held reasons.

When agents' memories are limited, agents need a strategy to manage their memory. The authors consider several strategies. One strategy, which they call "coherence-minded," has agents retain reasons with a slight preference for reasons that cohere with their collection of reasons as a whole. Although this model of memory isn't intended to be descriptively accurate, it's worth noting the similarity in mechanisms between coherence-minded agents and those posited by Lord et al. (1979) and discussed in the "myside bias" literature.

What Singer et al. show is that in many circumstances, groups of coherence-minded agents will polarize into subgroups and those subgroups will get tighter within themselves over time. Unlike in Hegselmann and Krause's model, this happens in Singer et al.'s model even though every agent continues to be connected to (and listen to) every other agent. So, in this model, the polarization arises from how the individual agents react to new reasons, not a division in the network. Coherence-minded agents listen to any reason presented, one at a time, decide what's most plausible on the basis of the reasons they already have and the newly presented ones, and then discard the weakest reason for the apparently misleading view. When agents manage their memory like this, they'll disproportionately (but definitely not always) stick with the view they had before receiving new reasons.

Singer et al. argue that for epistemically limited agents, the coherence-minded memory management strategy is epistemically rational. If they're right, then their model gives us a mechanism for understanding how groups of epistemically rational agents can get together, share their arguments for their views, but then end up more polarized than they were when they started. What the model brings out is a connection between individually rational management of one's epistemic limitations and the distribution of beliefs in a group, and in doing so, it undermines a natural line of thought that polarization will be reduced by everyone calmly and collectively sharing their views.

This model, and the rest of the models discussed here, can be used in different ways to understand polarization. Singer et al. use the model for *normative* theorizing, since it's supposed to tell us something about groups of *rational* agents. Singer et al. don't argue that their model is empirically descriptively correct, but were it sufficiently similar to real groups, the model could also be used to try to understand some real cases of polarization. That is, the model could be used in *descriptive* research, similar to models in physics and biology, which help us understand and describe real systems. Finally, these models can serve a *theoretical* role. Rather than offering a way to understand particular real systems, the models can be used to help us understand what *could* happen by bringing out a mechanism for how polarization might arise. That is, they can offer what is sometimes called "how possibly" explanations.

Let's consider another model of polarization that can also be used in each of these three ways. In real political polarization, individuals within polarized groups often agree with others in their group on a range of topics including apparently unrelated topics. In U.S. politics, for example, conservatives tend to share views on the permissibility of abortion as well as proper tax policy. The models discussed so far can't account for cross-topic grouping, but that is the focus of Weatherall and O'Connor's model of what they call "epistemic factionalization."

To understand the model of epistemic factionalization from Weatherall and O'Connor (forthcoming), let's start with the simpler model from O'Connor and Weatherall (2018). In the simpler model, agents gather and share evidence about the world. How much weight individual agents put on evidence shared with them is a function of how much they trust the sharer, and the amount of trust agents have in others varies over time. The model starts with a collection of agents in a complete network who are all trying to determine which of two slot machines has a higher payoff (following Zollman 2007). Agents start with a random credence between 0 and 1 about whether the second machine is better than the first. On each round of the model, each agent plays the machine they think is best and updates their belief about which machine is best. When they update their beliefs, however, they don't only use the evidence they collected. They also use evidence from their network neighbors (everyone, in this case, since it's a complete network). If it's a model run where everyone fully trusts everyone else, the group quickly converges onto a stable consensus (and so is not polarized). In runs where agents don't fully trust their neighbors, agents treat the shared evidence as uncertain and the uncertainty increases the more the sharer's belief differs from their own.[4] So when an agent with a belief very different from their own offers them information, these agents don't give it as much weight in their updating.

In the first paper, O'Connor and Weatherall show that using this kind of updating on a single issue can lead to agents polarizing when there is enough mistrust between agents. In their later paper, Weatherall and O'Connor show how polarization can arise across multiple topics when hearers adjust their trust of sharers as a function of how much the sharer agrees with the hearer's antecedent views on various topics.

In the model from the second paper, agents have beliefs about more than one set of slot machines. Which slot machine is best in one pair has no connection to which is best in another pair, so the second model can be thought of as a model of agents having beliefs about independent topics. Again here, agents play the slot machines they think are best and share their results with the group, and they again discount the input of those who disagree with them. This time though, disagreement is measured as disagreement across all of the beliefs, not just a single belief.

Interestingly, Weatherall and O'Connor show that with enough mistrust between agents, coordinated polarization can arise in this model – that is, the model can give rise to groups of agents who are polarized into subgroups that internally agree about unrelated issues. Why does the coordinated polarization arise? The correlation happens because once there is polarization about one set of slot machines, the disagreement between those polarized groups affects how the agents think of input about the other slot machines, representing other questions. In other words, since there is agreement about the first set of slot machines in one subgroup, members of that subgroup take insiders' opinions about other questions more seriously than the opinions of outsiders. That results in correlation on the issues about which agents are polarized, even when the issues don't bear any theoretical connection to each other. The upshot, the authors tell us, is that mistrust can lead to what they call "epistemic factionalization" even when there is no common cause for that factionalization such as a shared group ideology or desire to maintain group boundaries.

Like Singer et al.'s model, this model explains how polarization (and epistemic factionalization) can happen in virtue of how agents respond to each other's input, rather than in terms of a communicatively divided network.[5] Both of these epistemic network models can provide ways of understanding how political polarization might arise in highly connected societies.

V The prospects for epistemic network approaches for political epistemology

As the above examples make clear, epistemic network approaches are well-poised to help answer important questions about political epistemology. Here we've focused on group polarization in particular, but epistemic network models have already been used in many other areas of political epistemology, including (but certainly not limited to) understanding the epistemic aspects of democracy (Landemore 2013), the epistemic aspects of representative democracies (Grim et al. 2018a), the role of diversity and expertise in group deliberation (Grim et al. 2019; Hong and Page 2004; Singer 2019), the influence of minorities in groups (Jung et al. 2018), the stability of political institutions (Grim et al. 2018b), and the impact of fraudulent actors and misinformation on groups (Holman and Bruner 2015; Weatherall et al. forthcoming). This methodology could easily contribute further to our understanding of other topics in political epistemology as well, such as the connection between group beliefs and political legitimacy, how judicial beliefs impact the positions of courts, how representative and constituent beliefs influence each other and policy, how social position affects access to knowledge and vice versa, and how epistemic and other injustices are perpetrated and become systematized.

The examples we discussed here were of relatively simple models with relatively high-level normative and theoretical implications. The question of how to apply the lessons from the models to real-world policy is complex, and in many ways, it's analogous to the question of how to apply lessons from other parts of highly idealized and theoretical political philosophy to real-world policy. In both cases, doing so is hard, and it must be done only with a careful eye toward empirical results and the potential impacts of missteps. The goal of this chapter was to introduce epistemic network models and discuss some of the ways they have contributed to our understanding of political polarization. We hope this discussion has also inspired some readers to use these tools for further research in political epistemology.

Notes

1 We don't use this model for this here, but this model also shows how polarization can be produced from opposing information from religious, friend, and government sources.
2 For general history and defense of agent-based modeling, see Railsback and Grimm (2019).
3 We'll discuss models of group polarization, the formation of groups of like-minded individuals. This is different from belief polarization, the phenomenon discussed by social psychologists involving two individuals' opinions diverging after sharing evidence.
4 Weatherall and O'Connor actually consider two kinds mistrust, but we're simplifying the model here.
5 One might worry that the O'Connor and Weatherall model implicitly uses a divided network like the Hegselmann and Krause model. That may be right, but it's at least a degreed version of division.

Bibliography

Bramson, A., Grim, P., Singer, D. J., Berger, W. J., Sack, G., Fisher, S., Flocken, C., & Holman, B. (2017) "Understanding polarization: Meanings, measures, and model evaluation," *Philosophy of Science, 84*(1):115–59.

Bramson, A., Grim, P., Singer, D. J., Fisher, S., Berger, W., Sack, G., & Flocken, C. (2016) "Disambiguation of social polarization concepts and measures," *The Journal of Mathematical Sociology, 40*(2):80–111.

Carothers, T. & O'Donohue, A. (2019) *Democracies Divided*, Washington, DC: Brookings Institution Press.

Deffuant, G., Amblard, F., Weisbuch, G., & Faure, T. (2002) "How can extremism prevail? A study based on the relative agreement interaction model," *Journal of Artificial Societies and Social Simulation, 5*(4).

DeGroot, M. H. (1974) "Reaching a consensus," *Journal of the American Statistical Association, 69*:118–21.

French Jr, J. (1956) "A formal theory of social power," *Psychological Review, 63*(3):181–194.

Grim, P., Bramson, A., Singer, D. J., Berger, W. J., Jung, J., & Page, S. E. (2018a) "Representation in models of epistemic democracy," *Episteme*, 1–21.

Grim, P., Liu, M., Bathina, K. C., Liu, N., & Gordonf, J. W. (2018b) "How stable is democracy? Suggestions from artificial social networks," *Journal on Policy and Complex Systems, 4*(1):87–108.

Grim, P., Singer, D. J., Bramson, A., Holman, B., McGeehan, S., & Berger, W. J. (2019) "Diversity, ability, and expertise in epistemic communities," *Philosophy of Science, 86*(1):98–123.

Grim, P., Singer, D. J., Fisher, S., Bramson, A., Berger, W. J., Reade, C., & Sales, A. (2013) "Scientific networks on data landscapes," *Episteme, 10*(4):441–64.

Grim, P., Singer, D. J., Reade, C., & Fisher, S. (2015) "Germs, genes, and memes: Function and fitness dynamics on information networks," *Philosophy of Science, 82*(2):219–43.

Grim, P., Thomas, S. B., Fisher, S., Reade, C., Singer, D. J., Garza, M. A., & Chatman, J. (2012) "Polarization and belief dynamics in the Black and White communities," *Artificial Life Conference Proceedings, 12*:186–93.

Hegselmann, R. & Krause, U. (2002) "Opinion dynamics and bounded confidence models, analysis, and simulation," *Journal of Artificial Societies and Social Simulation, 5*(3):1–33.

Holman, B. & Bruner, J. (2015) "The problem of intransigently biased agents," *Philosophy of Science, 82*(5):956–68.

Hong, L. & Page, S. (2004) "Groups of diverse problem solvers can outperform groups of high-ability problem solvers," *Proceedings of the National Academy of Sciences, 101*(46):16385–89.

Jung, J., Bramson, A., & Crano, W. D. (2018) "An agent-based model of indirect minority influence on social change and diversity," *Social Influence, 13*(1):18–38.

Landemore, H. (2013) *Democratic Reason*, Princeton, NJ: Princeton University Press.

Lord, C. G., Ross, L., & Lepper, M. R. (1979) "Biased assimilation and attitude polarization," *Journal of personality and social psychology, 37*(11):2098.

O'Connor, C. & Weatherall, J. O. (2018) "Scientific polarization," *European Journal for Philosophy of Science, 8*(3):855–75.

Railsback, S. F. & Grimm, V. (2019) *Agent-Based and Individual-Based Modeling: A Practical Introduction,* Princeton, NJ: Princeton University Press.

Rawls, J. (1999) *A Theory of Justice*, Cambridge, MA: Harvard University Press.

Singer, D. J. (2019) "Diversity, not randomness, trumps ability," *Philosophy of Science, 86*(1):178–91.

Singer, D. J., Bramson, A., Grim, P., Holman, B., Jung, J., Kovaka, K., Ranginani, A., & Berger, W. (2019a) "Rational social and political polarization," *Philosophical Studies, 176*(9):2243–67.

Singer, D. J., Bramson, A., Grim, P., Holman, B., Kovaka, K., Jung, J., & Berger, W. (2019b) "Don't forget forgetting: the social epistemic importance of how we forget," *Synthese*.

Weatherall, J. & O'Connor, C. (forthcoming). "Endogenous epistemic factionalization," *Synthese*.

Weatherall, J., O'Connor, C., & Bruner, J. (2020). "How to beat science and influence people: Policymakers and propaganda in epistemic networks," *The British Journal for the Philosophy of Science, 71*(4): 1157–1186.

Zollman, K. (2007) "The communication structure of epistemic communities," *Philosophy of Science, 74*(5):574–87.

Zollman, K. (forthcoming) *Network Epistemology*. Manuscript.

13

AFFECTIVE POLARIZATION, EVIDENCE, AND EVIDENTIALISM

Emily C. McWilliams

1 Introduction

This chapter concerns some ways that political beliefs are formed and maintained in polarized political environments. Specifically, it examines how self-serving, directional biases in the ways that agents gather and process evidence can make their beliefs resistant to change. It argues that although our intuitive judgment is that these mechanisms undermine the justification of resulting beliefs, this is not so according to an *evidentialist* theory of epistemic justification, which says the epistemic justification of a subject's doxastic attitude toward a proposition at a time strongly supervenes on the evidence that the person has at the time. It then argues that this gives us some reason to doubt that evidentialism gives us a complete theory of epistemic justification.

Affective polarization occurs when partisan groups experience strong and persistent negative affect or sentiment towards opposing groups, while having positive sentiment towards their own group. In political landscapes structured by affective polarization, distance between groups can move beyond issue-based differences to a *social identity*. I will focus on how such polarization impacts the ways that individuals form and maintain political beliefs. I argue that affective polarization can impact individuals' motivation to maintain their political beliefs, and motivation mediates information processing in a way that shields those beliefs from contrary evidence.

How might affective polarization impact motivation? The heuristic-systematic model (HSM) of information processing is widely recognized in psychology as a model of how people process information relevant to their beliefs, depending on their motivation (Chaiken et al. 1996).[1] It distinguishes states in which the subject's primary motivation is to form an accurate and unbiased understanding of some matter (*accuracy-motivation*) from states of *goal-oriented, directional* information processing, such as *defense-motivation*, in which the subject's primary motivation is to defend her pre-existing beliefs. These motivations can affect encoding, organization, and use of new information that bears on a subject's inquiry.[2] HSM also distinguishes two different modes of information processing: *systematic processing*, in which subjects thoroughly scrutinize the quality of relevant information and arguments, and *heuristic processing*, in which they rely on cognitive shortcuts.[3] When a subject is defense-motivated, they process information in the way that best meets their defensive needs.

These processing strategies are not consciously chosen; rather, the process is mediated by the affective dimension of information processing. Defense-motivation is particularly likely to arise with respect to self-definitional attitudes and beliefs (Chen & Chaiken 1999). So, it is likely to arise with respect to our political beliefs in an environment structured by affective polarization, where such beliefs function as part of one's social identity.

I will argue that defense-motivation mediates information processing in a way that can shield our beliefs from contrary evidence, regardless of whether contrary information is available in the subject's informational environment. In *§2*, I argue that since evidentialist-justification supervenes on a subject's evidence, these beliefs count as justified on common understandings of evidentialism. In *§3*, I argue that this gives us some reason to doubt that evidentialism gives us a complete theory of epistemic justification.

2 An evidentialist analysis of (certain) polarized beliefs

This section argues that, *contra* intuitive judgments, certain polarized beliefs come out evidentialist-justified. This leaves us with the question of whether our judgment, or the analysis, is correct. *§3* argues in favor of the intuitive judgment – not because such judgments are infallible, but because, I argue, evidentialist-justification fails to capture some of the things we should want it to.

I will use a specific example of a belief whose content is prototypical of the far-right oeuvre in the contemporary United States.[4] My argument focuses on the cognitive and perceptual mechanisms by which it is produced and maintained. I take these mechanisms to be common to defense-motivated subjects, but since there is not space to detail all of the relevant psychological literature, I make no specific claims about exactly how common they are. However, I intend this example to be realistic, rather than merely possible:

Climate hoax

Suppose that Fred believes that 'climate change is a hoax' (hereafter, 'CCH'). This belief is part of his sociocultural identity, and he is defense-motivated with respect to it. Like most people, Fred is not aware of the research on defense motivation. From his perspective, he simply feels confident that CCH is true. Fred has substantial evidence in support of this belief. Almost everyone in his social circles seems to believe it, and their views have been robust across time. They also believe that their views are widely held, and only a small minority of liberal elites disagree. Fred's contacts often share articles supporting CCH on social media, which he skims when time permits. He has also heard arguments for CCH on a popular radio station in his town. Fred has found these written and verbal arguments convincing – they seemed internally consistent, and he could not think of contravening evidence (*i.e.,* defeaters).

Suppose, moreover, that the articles Fred has skimmed and the verbal arguments he has heard contain flaws that, if he noticed them, would defeat at least some of the support these arguments lend to CCH from Fred's perspective. Fred is intelligent enough to appreciate these flaws, but doing so would require careful focus, not just skimming. And Fred is not motivated to engage in careful scrutiny of arguments for CCH – in fact, he is motivated *not* to.[5] Since Fred isn't aware of his defense motivation, from his perspective the arguments simply seem convincing, so do not call for further scrutiny.

Fred does not often encounter arguments against CCH. On the few occasions where he has seen liberal relatives share articles that seem to support ~CCH, or overheard snippets of such conversations, he experiences negative affect – he feels annoyed. He scrolls past them, or directs his attention elsewhere. He is not making an intentional decision to do this, but if someone were to point it out, he would say that it is not worth engaging with such arguments – there must be something wrong with them, since he's confident their conclusion is false.

The remainder of *§2* argues that Fred's belief is evidentialist-justified.[6] According to Conee and Feldman, the bedrock evidentialist view about justification is:

> ES   The epistemic justification of anyone's doxastic attitude toward any proposition at any time strongly supervenes on the evidence that person has at that time. (2004, p. 101)

There are a few important things to note about this. First, it is a theory of *propositional justification*, which is the sort of justification that a proposition p enjoys for an agent, even if the agent does not actually believe p. *Doxastic justification* – a property of the subject's belief – is more complex. Evidentialists agree that a necessary condition on doxastic justification is that the subject must believe p on the basis of the evidence that ES describes, but it is difficult to work out necessary and sufficient conditions.[7] I will focus on Fred's propositional justification in *§2*, and return to the question of doxastic justification in *§3*.

Second, evidentialist-justification turns on the evidence that the subject has *at that time*. It is a *synchronic*, or *time-slice* notion of justification.[8] In addition to Conee and Feldman's formulation, McCain (another prominent evidentialist) agrees that "propositional justification strongly supervenes on the non-factive mental states that one has at a particular time (2004, p. 119)." The debate between time-slice and historical theories of justification is long standing.[9] Some philosophers go further, extending time-slice theories beyond justification. Moss (2015) defends *time-slice epistemology*, which says that what is rationally permissible or obligatory for you at some time is entirely determined by what mental states you are in at that time, and that the fundamental facts about rationality are exhausted by these temporally local facts. Hedden (2015) defends *time-slice rationality*, which says that all requirements of rationality are synchronic. These broader theses are not my focus, but if my argument is correct, it cuts against them.[10]

Since justification turns entirely on the subject's evidence, evidentialism must say more about what that evidence consists in. Otherwise, ES is not a fleshed-out theory of justification, but a schema. I will argue that regardless of how evidentialism answers this question, Fred's belief comes out evidentialist-justified.

A significant part of what seems intuitively wrong with Fred's belief is that it results from bad evidence-gathering on his part. But since evidentialist-justification is synchronic, this does not undermine his justification, so long as the evidence thus gathered supports his belief.

A number of philosophers have challenged this by offering cases in which a subject's evidence supports some proposition p, but *only because* they have been negligent in their evidence-gathering. Evidentialists respond by insisting that, *contra* our intuitive judgments, this does not undermine the justification of resulting beliefs.

Kornblith (1983) describes a case of what he calls 'epistemically culpable ignorance,' in which a headstrong young physicist is unable to tolerate criticism. After presenting a paper, this physicist pays no attention to the devastating objection of a senior colleague, which therefore fails to impact his belief in his theory because he has not even heard it. While

Kornblith argues that the physicist's continued belief is unjustified, Conee and Feldman (2004, p. 90) contend that if the physicist remains ignorant of the fact that his senior colleague is offering an objection, then his evidence remains just as it was, and his belief remains justified. While this may show that the physicist lacks intellectual integrity, this is an evaluation of his character, which does not bear his belief's epistemic status.

More recently, Baehr (2011) offers a number of cases in which subjects gather evidence in ways that are characterized by intellectual vices like laziness, apathy, and obliviousness. They end up in situations where their evidence supports their belief. Had their evidence-gathering not been characterized by intellectual vice, it would not. Baehr argues that their evidence is not what it should be, and is therefore *defective* or *contaminated*. He thus finds it implausible that these subjects do well from an epistemic standpoint to believe on the basis of the evidence that results from their cognitive failings.

McCain (2016) responds to Baehr (2011) in much the same way that Conee and Feldman (2004) respond to Kornblith (1983). He accommodates Baehr's intuitive judgment by offering that there *is* something amiss with the subjects Baehr describes, *qua* epistemic agents. But he says this does not affect their beliefs' justification, which depends on the evidence they *have*, not on the evidence they *might* have had.

Like Fred, Kornblith and Baehr's subjects exhibit a pattern prototypical of defense-motivation: a self-serving, directional bias in how they gather evidence that bears on their beliefs. Fred's present evidence supports CCH because he has unknowingly avoided evidence that contravenes it. The evidentialist responses to Kornblith and Baehr's cases illustrate that since evidentialist-justification is synchronic, diachronic assessments of subjects' inquiries do not undermine the justification of resulting beliefs. For the same reason, evidence that a subject could gather in the future – even the immediate future – is not relevant. So it does not matter for a belief's justification whether contravening evidence is readily available in a subject's informational environment. Insofar as Fred's case is typical of how our cognitive and perceptual mechanisms, dispositions and biases interact with ideology in a polarized political environment, many politically polarized beliefs come out evidentialist-justified despite irresponsible evidence-gathering practices.

Although Fred successfully avoided evidence that was uncongenial to his belief, this is not always possible. When we do encounter uncongenial evidence, must we reduce our credence in order for our beliefs to remain evidentialist-justified? To answer this, consider the following modification of Fred's case:

★Climate hoax

The origin and maintenance of ★Fred's belief in CCH has been exactly the same as Fred's. The difference between them is that ★Fred has a liberal nephew he is fond of. Though they generally have an unspoken agreement not to talk politics, the nephew makes a special request to show ★Fred a video he produced as a final project for his environmental studies course. Out of fondness for his nephew, ★Fred agrees. Suppose that the video presents an excellent argument for ~CCH, pitched at a level that ★Fred is capable of understanding.

In watching the video, has ★Fred acquired defeaters of at least some of his previous evidence in favor of CCH, such that he must lower his credence to remain evidentialist-unjustified? Not necessarily. It depends on how we fill in the case, and on what it means for a subject to possess evidence.

I will argue that because evidentialist-justification is synchronic, it must understand evidence possession such that on plausible ways of filling in the case, ★Fred does not acquire defeaters of his evidence for CCH. Evidentialism is an internalist theory of justification. The two main types of internalism are *accessibilism* and *mentalism*. I will discuss how accessibilist and mentalist evidentialists understand evidence possession, and then consider how those understandings interact with plausible ways of filling in ★Fred's case.

Accessibilism says that something counts as part of a subject's evidence only if it is actually or potentially accessible to introspection or reflection. What counts as *potentially accessible* can be understood more or less restrictively with respect to how much is required of a subject S in order to count as having proportioned her beliefs to the accessible evidence. For instance: Is S's accessible evidence at time t comprised simply of how things evidentially *seem* to her when she turns inward at t? Does it include things that are stored in memory, but that might take a moments' effort to recall? Does it include evidential support relations she would be able to appreciate upon a few moments' reflection?[11]

The synchronic requirement forces the accessibilist evidentialist's hand towards a restrictive answer: S's evidence is limited to what is immediately before her mind at the moment of belief. Any information that S can only access via a temporally extended cognitive process is not *now* within her purview. So, things like currently unrecalled memories and unappreciated evidential support relations are not part of S's synchronic evidence. On this restrictive account of evidence possession, evidentialist-justification is easy to come by. There is little room for the possibility of unappreciated evidence, since if evidence was immediately before S's mind, she would almost certainly have appreciated it. So accessi*ble* evidence becomes nearly synonymous with access*ed* evidence.

Many prominent defenders of evidentialism – including Conee and Feldman (2004), and McCain (2016) – are mentalists. Mentalism says that a subject's total *possible* evidence includes all and only the information that the subject has 'stored in her mind' at the time – including everything that she actively believes, and everything stored in her memory. Feldman points out that given the synchronic requirement, this excludes things that S no longer has stored in her mind, as well as information that she has not taken in, or deduced, even if such information is readily available in her informational environment. Her total evidence is some subset of that. Feldman's view about what that subset includes is more restrictive than McCain's.

McCain calls Feldman's view of the subset of S's total possible evidence that counts as her total evidence the *restrictive view of evidence possession (RVP)*. RVP says that S has p available as evidence at t iff S is currently thinking of p. Feldman defends RVP from an objection similar to Baehr's. It points out that intuitively, S's belief is unjustified when there is convincing counter-evidence that she could have thought of, but failed to because of inattentiveness, poor concentration, or other epistemic failings. In response, Feldman distinguishes what he calls *current-state epistemic rationality* from *methodological epistemic rationality*. Given the synchronic requirement, evidentialism is only concerned with the former. Feldman says

> There are many ways in which one might behave over the long term that will help one gain knowledge of important facts…Evidentialism is silent about such practices. It focuses on the epistemic value to be obtained immediately from the adoption of an attitude toward a proposition. (Feldman 2000, p. 686)[12]

McCain (2016) argues that RVP is too restrictive. One issue he raises is that intuitively, there are cases where S has a defeater that she is not currently thinking of. For instance, suppose S was just told something that she takes to be a straightforward defeater of her belief that p.

Moments later, S is thinking about what she will have for lunch, and not about the defeater. According to RVP, this means the defeater is not part of her evidence. McCain opts instead for a *moderate view of evidence possession* (*MVP*). *MVP construes evidence possession as a three-place relation between S, her evidence p, and a proposition q. It says that "S has *p* available as evidence relevant to *q* at *t* iff at *t* S is currently aware of *p* or S is disposed to bring *p* to mind when reflecting on the question of *q*'s truth (p. 51)." This solves the problem of currently unaccessed defeaters. But the synchronic requirement on evidentialist-justification limits *MVP. First, it cannot include thoughts that S is disposed to have for the first time when reflecting on the question of q's truth, such as thoughts about how different parts of her evidence bear on one another, since those are not even included in one's total possible evidence. Second, it can only include evidence that S is disposed to bring *immediately* to mind when reflecting on q's truth. Otherwise, it is not clear how it could be relevant, on a notion of justification that is meant to capture the epistemic value to be obtained immediately from adopting an attitude towards q.

How do RVP and *MVP answer the question of what evidence *Fred has for CCH, on plausible ways of filling in the case? There are many ways of filling it in at various levels of detail. But given *Fred's defense motivation, the most plausible general description is one consistent with HSM's *least effort principle*, which says that generally, people will spend only as much cognitive effort as is required to satisfy their goal (in *Fred's case, of defending his pre-existing belief). My description of the case stipulated that the video is pitched at a level that *Fred is capable of understanding. But suppose that, as with most complex empirical arguments, understanding the video's argument, and thinking through how it bears on his antecedent evidence would require deliberate attention and cognitive effort. In the language of HSM, it would require *systematic* rather than *heuristic* processing. Although *Fred is perfectly capable of this, HSM explains that he is not motivated to put in this effort – in fact, he is positively motivated *not* to. The general empirical point is that by using processing styles that fit their defensive goals, defense-motivated subjects can avoid *taking in* uncongenial evidence, even when they cannot avoid *encountering* it.[13]

Had *Fred been accuracy motivated when he watched the video, he would have paid careful attention to its arguments, thought through how they bear on his antecedent evidence for CCH, and gained defeaters of some of that evidence. But his defense-motivated avoidance of systematic processing prevented this. I will argue that this means he has not gained any defeaters, according to evidentialism.

Consider the moment just after *Fred has watched the video. His memory is fresh enough that with effort, he would be able to recall some details of the video's arguments that he did not originally attend to. Even so, RVP would not count these as part of his evidence, since he is not *currently* thinking of them. This echoes McCain's worry about currently unaccessed defeaters. But *MVP does not include them either, since it includes only what *Fred is *disposed* to bring to mind when reflecting on the question of CCH's truth. And dispositions vary with motivation. Given *Fred's defense motivation, HSM explains that he will not be disposed to exert cognitive effort to bring these arguments to mind. Even if we changed *MVP to focus on what S is *able* (rather than *disposed*) to bring to mind, or we incentivized *Fred to induce accuracy-motivation, the arguments would not be *immediately* available. Calling them up from memory and thinking through how they bear on his antecedent evidence would be an effortful, diachronic cognitive *process*. So, insofar as defense-motivation prevents *Fred from *taking in* evidence that he cannot avoid *encountering*, the synchronic requirement on evidentialist-justification has it that he thus avoids acquiring defeaters of his antecedent evidence for CCH.

One might object that I am making things too easy. Surely, it is not *always* the case that subjects who encounter uncongenial evidence can avoid taking it in. Sometimes, evidence 'smacks one in the face,' as it were. For instance, suppose that ★Fred's nephew's video presents a compelling illustration of statistical evidence that it is extremely likely that human influence is the dominant cause of recent warming of earth's atmosphere and oceans. The illustration is compelling enough, and ★Fred understands statistics well enough that he cannot help but take it in. Would he thus acquire a defeater of some of his antecedent evidence for CCH? Again, not necessarily. We can see this by introducing Tom Kelly's (2008) distinction between *narrow* and *broad* evidence. Narrow evidence consists of relevant information about the world – things that it would be natural to call *data*. *Broad* evidence includes narrow evidence, plus anything else one is aware of that makes a difference to what she is justified in believing. Subjects might have the same narrow evidence, but differ in what they are evidentialist-justified in believing, because they have different broad evidence. Broad evidence includes the space of alternative hypotheses of which one is aware. Kelly argues that "the mere articulation of a plausible alternative hypothesis can dramatically reduce how likely the original hypothesis is on one's present evidence (p. 620)." This matters because defense-motivated ★Fred will be particularly motivated to find alternative explanations of the statistical evidence that seems to tell against CCH. For instance, he might question the source of the statistical data, and come up with various specific ways that they might result from politically motivated professional misconduct. Depending on his antecedent evidence for CCH, he might already have these to hand. So when he finishes watching the video, ★Fred may not have any undefeated new defeaters of his antecedent evidence for CCH.[14]

Another objection offers that surely ★Fred has evidence *of* evidence against CCH, since even if he paid no attention to the video's arguments, he knows they exist. One reason to think he has nonetheless not gained a defeater is that he already knew there were people arguing against CCH, so this is not new information. The objector might nonetheless think it matters that it is now salient, and part of his synchronic evidence. Even so, since Fred's evidence for CCH is substantial, he can reasonably conclude that there must be *something* wrong with these arguments, since their conclusion is false.

Plainly, my Fred and ★Fred examples do not cover all trajectories by which political beliefs are formed and maintained. Nonetheless, the empirical literature on HSM supports the idea that they are realistic – even typical – examples of how our cognitive and perceptual mechanisms, dispositions, and biases interact with ideology in a polarized political environment. So it is striking that their beliefs come out evidentialist-justified, despite the large extent to which self-serving, directional biases shape the mechanisms by which they are formed and maintained.

3 What does synchronic evidentialist account of justification leave out?

This section argues that the evidentialist account does not capture everything we should want from a complete account of epistemic justification. In one sense, this is obvious: since evidentialism is, in the first instance, a theory of propositional (rather than doxastic) justification, it is incomplete on its own. But evidentialists think we can generate a theory of doxastic justification by adding a requirement that S's belief is properly based on her evidence.[15] I argue that the resulting theory does not give us everything we should want from a theory of justification, either.

First, note that the evidentialist concept of justification is not our ordinary concept. We saw that defense-motivated subjects are motivated to shape their broad evidence to support antecedent beliefs, while accuracy-motivated subjects are motivated to discover the truth, and they seek evidence accordingly. The analysis of §2 put us in a position to see that our intuitive judgments about justification respond to these differences. But because these differences show up diachronically, evidentialist-justification cannot capture them.

Perhaps *justification* as a theoretical concept need not capture our ordinary notion exactly. Still, one reason to think something important is lost is that the evidentialist notion gives up on one of the main social and cognitive functions of our ordinary concept. Namely, we use the ordinary concept to offer criticism, hold one another accountable for aspects of the belief-forming process in which our doxastic agency is involved, and push one another to do better. By labeling someone's belief *unjustified*, I communicate that the way the belief was formed or revised is unacceptable on epistemic grounds. Where we have control over the relevant control, such disapproval encourages us to do better.

Even if we forego the idea that our theoretical notion of *justification* should preserve the ordinary concept's main functions, I argue that the evidentialist concept falls short. At bottom, epistemologists should want a theoretical notion of justification that is capable of evaluating the beliefs of human doxastic agents, as such. We have seen that evidentialist-justification is not concerned with agents' diachronic doxastic conduct or epistemic responsibility. It aims instead to give a theory of the epistemic goodness or fittingness of a state of affairs in which an agent with certain broad evidence has a particular belief. But one important lesson from §2 was that human doxastic agents are creatures whose doxastic agency can be actively involved in shaping and constituting the broad evidence on which these evaluations turn.[16] It is therefore deeply mysterious that a concept of justification designed to assess the beliefs of such creatures – especially one that turns on an assessment of their evidence – should not take account of the role(s) of their agency in producing it.

What more might we want from a complete theory of epistemic justification? Space considerations preclude giving adequate argument for the two claims, but I submit that given the ways we shape our evidence diachronically, we should want a complete account to be able to (1) *evaluate* ways that we as subjects have been involved in shaping our evidence through inquiry, and (2) *provide guidance* on how we can become better inquirers (since ultimately, our political goal is not simply to depolarize, but to depolarize as a result of *doing better epistemically*).[17]

The evidentialist concept of justification can neither evaluate nor provide guidance about (A) the perceptual and cognitive processes that determine what information we take in from the world, or (B) the ways in which we interpret and shape the information that we have taken in.[18] The analysis of §2 illustrated specific examples of (A) and (B) in Fred's case. I will close by offering more general examples of the *kinds* of things that fall under (A) and (B). This will help systematize things that came up in §2, and serve as a preliminary list of diachronic processes that may be relevant to a complete theory of justification.

First, here are examples of the kinds of perceptual and cognitive processes that determine what information we take in from the world:

Salience structures: Jessie Munton defines a salience structure as a subject's dispositions to find certain stimuli salient. Such dispositions are driven both by bottom-up elements like stimulus contrast, and top-down elements like conceptual associations. While not directly manipulable at will, they may be manipulable via top-down elements. We might think them epistemically evaluable since they impact epistemic outcomes by determining what information we take in.

Patterns of attention: Agents can shape what information we take in by choosing to pay deliberate attention to certain informational features of the world. For instance, an accuracy-motivated version of *Fred might will himself to pay attention to the video in the same way that students will themselves pay attention to information that will be on an exam.

Active search for information: Agents can shape the ways that they actively seek out information during inquiry. Baehr (2011) frames this as an exercise of intellectual virtues during inquiry.

Here are two examples of the ways our agency is involved in constituting the broad evidence to which evidentialism says our beliefs should be proportioned:

Determining how to weigh various pieces of one's complex evidence: This process can involve choices, for instance, about how thoroughly to scrutinize arguments that seem to tell for and against one's belief. As Kelly (2008) says, it can also involve generating and considering alternative possible explanations of the information one has taken in.

Judgments about whether and how various pieces of one's evidence bear on one another: Sometimes it is not obvious how different pieces of evidence bear on one another. If one has some evidence that seems to support p, and some that seems to support ~p, then inquiry into whether p may involve thinking through whether and how they bear a defeat relationship to one another. It might involve complex judgments about whether arguments rely on similar information or rhetorical strategies, whether that bears on judgments about their relative strength, etc.

These processes are the very sorts of things that are impacted by motivation during inquiry. I submit that a complete theory of the epistemic evaluation of our beliefs should have the resources to take account of this.

Notes

1 HSM is one example of a *dual process* model in psychology. While dual process theory provides a general account of how thought can arise as a result of two different processes, HSM is a specific theory of how different kinds of thinking lead to attitude change.
2 For a review, see Srull and Wyer (1986).
3 See McWilliams (2019) for a more detailed description.
4 According to Uscinski and Olivella (2017), about 40% of Americans reject the scientific consensus that climate change is real and manmade.
    Choosing this example does not imply that there are no examples of prototypical far-left beliefs that have the same key features. These cognitive and social epistemic mechanisms are involved in forming and maintaining beliefs on both political poles.
5 This is based on Lord et al. (1979), a well-known empirical study in which subjects avoid scrutinizing information that appears to support their antecedent views. More generally, Gawronski and Bodenhausen explain that if a subject's automatic affective response to new information aligns with their preferred attitude, then the search for additional relevant information may be truncated, and evaluative judgments based largely on affirmation of the automatic effect (Baumeister & Newman, 1994; Ditto & Lopez, 1992).
6 Kelly (2008) makes a similar argument that the beliefs that subjects have at the end of a specific study on attitude polarization by Lord et al. (1979) are evidentialist-justified. My argument is broader, and focused on the details of what evidentialism must mean by 'possessing evidence.'
7 See Conee and Feldman (2004, p. 93).
8 It is possible to remove the synchronic requirement on justification-conferring evidence without abandoning evidentialism's core idea that justification turns on evidence. But the originators and main defenders of evidentialist accounts of justification understand it as a time-slice theory.

9 Goldman (1979) argues that time-slice theories of justification cannot do justice to the epistemic role of preservative memory. In addition to Goldman's process reliabilism, standard Bayesians also treat conditionalization as a diachronic norm of belief revision.

10 Fantl (2020) argues that evidentialism should not be understood as an instance of time-slice epistemology. Since there is no space here to respond to his argument, I simply note that I am understanding evidentialist-justification the way that its main proponents do.

11 In McWilliams (2019), I refer to this as *the hard question* about accessibilism, and argue that answers at both extreme ends of the spectrum are implausible.

12 Kelly (2003) goes further, framing the distinction as being not between two different kinds of epistemic rationality, but between *epistemic* and *instrumental* rationality. On this way of thinking, to understand things that we do diachronically as evaluable by standards of epistemic rationality would be a category mistake. Such things bear only on one's instrumental rationality (insofar as one has a goal of believing the truth about p).

13 For further explanation of how defense- and accuracy-motivation interact with heuristic versus systematic processing, see McWilliams (2019).

14 In terms of Lackey's (2006) distinction between *psychological* and *normative* defeaters, I am talking about psychological defeat. But importantly, part of my criticism is that given the synchronic requirement, evidentialism does not have room for a robust concept of normative defeaters, since to say there are defeaters a subject ought to have had is to criticize her diachronic process of gathering and processing evidence.

15 See Conee and Feldman (2004, p. 93), and McCain (2016, Ch. 5).

16 See McWilliams (2019) for more on how our agency is actively involved in constituting our broad evidence.

17 One might question whether we have specific reason to call a theory that includes the desiderata I articulate in this section *justification*. I think the argument of the previous paragraphs makes a *prima facie case* that we do, but we should also remain open to suggestions for satisfying these desiderata elsewhere in our repertoire of normative epistemic concepts.

18 In practice, there may not be a strict division between (A) and (B).

References

Baehr, J. (2011). *The Inquiring Mind: On Intellectual Virtues and Virtue Epistemology*. Oxford: Oxford University Press.

Baumeister, R.F., & Newman, L.S. (1994). Self-regulation of cognitive inference and decision processes. *Personality and Social Psychology Bulletin, 20*, 3–19.

Chaiken, S., Giner-Sorolla, R., & Chen, S. (1996). Beyond accuracy: Defense and impression motives in heuristic and systematic information processing. In P. Gollwitzer & J. Bargh (Eds.), *The Psychology of Action: Linking Cognition and Motivation to Behavior* (pp. 553–78). New York: Guilford.

Chen, S., & Chaiken, S. (1999). The heuristic-systematic model in its broader content. In S. Chaiken & Y. Trope (Eds.), *Dual Process Theories in Social Psychology* (pp. 73–98). New York: Guilford.

Conee, E., & Feldman, R. (2004). *Evidentialism*. New York: Oxford University Press.

Ditto, P.H., & Lopez, D.F. (1992). Motivated skepticism: Use of differential criteria for preferred and nonpreferred conclusions. *Journal of Personality and Social Psychology, 63*, 568–84.

Fantl, J. (2020). Evidentialism as an historical theory. *Australasian Journal of Philosophy*. https://doi.org/10.1080/00048402.2019.1699127.

Feldman, R. (2000). The ethics of belief. *Philosophy and Phenomenological Research, 60*, 667–95.

Goldman, A. (1979). What is justified belief? In G. Pappas (Ed.), *Justification and Knowledge* (pp. 1–24). Dordrecht: Riedel Publishing Company.

Hedden, B. (2015). *Reasons without Persons: Rationality, Identity, and Time*. Oxford: Oxford University Press.

Kelly, T. (2003). Epistemic Rationality as Instrumental Rationality: A Critique. *Philosophy and Phenomenological Research, 66*(3), 612–40.

Kelly, T. (2008). Disagreement, dogmatism, and belief polarization. *The Journal of Philosophy, 105*, 611–33.

Kornblith, H. (1983). Justified belief and epistemically responsible action. *The Philosophical Review, 92*(1), 33–48.

Lackey, J. (2006). Introduction. In Lackey, J. & Sosa, E. (Eds.) *The Epistemology of Testimony*. Oxford: Oxford University Press.

Lord, C., Ross, L., & Lepper, M. (1979). Biased assimilation and attitude polarization: The effects of prior theories on subsequently considered evidence. *Journal of Personality and Social Psychology, 37*, 2098–109.

McCain, K. (2016). *Evidentialism and Epistemic Justification*. New York: Routledge.

McWilliams, E.C. (2019). Evidentialism and belief polarization. *Synthese*. https://doi.org/10.1007/s11229-019-02515-z.

Moss, S. (2015). Time-slice epistemology and action under indeterminacy. In T. Gendler & J. Hawthorne (Eds.), *Oxford Studies in Epistemology* 5 (pp. 172–94). Oxford: Oxford University Press.

Munton, J. Unpublished MS. Prejudice as the Misattribution of Salience.

Srull, T.K., & Wyer, R.S. (1986). The role of chronic and temporary goals in social information processing. In R.M. Sorrentino & E.T. Higgins (Eds.), *Handbook of Motivation and Cognition* (pp. 503–49). New York: Guilford Press.

Uscinski, J., & Olivella, S. (2017). The conditional effect of conspiracy thinking on attitudes toward climate change. *Research & Politics, 4*(4), 1–9.

14

THE POINT OF POLITICAL BELIEF

Michael Hannon and Jeroen de Ridder

1 Introduction

On the face of it, lots of people hold political beliefs. Some people even hold lots of them, often with seemingly great confidence. Let's understand political beliefs quite broadly as beliefs that concern, on the one hand, descriptive facts about the workings and development of political systems at various levels (from international to local) and, on the other, normative beliefs about the right course for politics, ranging from very general beliefs about what a just society would look like, to more specific beliefs about what policy proposals would be good to implement, what laws would need to be passed, how best to realize one's political vision, and what candidates to vote for.[1] Also included are beliefs that are, or have become, politically charged, i.e. seen as relevant to one's political choices and action, even if they are not political *per se*; for instance, the belief that Barack Obama was not born in the United States.

Here is an intuitive and commonsensical picture of the point of political beliefs, loosely based on what Christopher Achen and Larry Bartels (2016) call the 'folk theory of democracy'. Imagine a citizenry of individuals who enjoy spending some portion of their leisure time reading newspapers, magazines, and books; consuming news on TV and the internet; debating political issues in various public and private forums; weighing the arguments and evidence for particular policies, laws, and other political options; and then forming and updating their political beliefs in light of the evidence. This uplifting picture of democracy has its roots in the Enlightenment tradition of rational choice. Voters seek reliable information, formulate their political views on the basis of that information, assess where candidates stand on the issues, and then choose to support the candidate or political party that best embodies their own preferences and values.

This folk theory of democracy is a *belief-first* model of political behavior.[2] It assumes a model of voter political psychology that is cognitive, doxastic, and epistemically rational. On this theory, then, the point of political beliefs is to form an accurate picture of (a) political reality, (b) one's personal political values and preferences, and (c) the courses of action that are most likely to realize (b) given (a). Political beliefs subsequently form the basis of political actions like voting, activism, or other political engagement. This account of political belief fits with the broader commonsense view that beliefs and desires together cause and explain behavior.

Drawing on various strands of literature from cognitive and social psychology, as well as political science, this chapter asks whether this portrayal of political belief is accurate. Spoiler alert: for many people, it is not. At best, it is accurate for a select few highly informed and reflective political buffs. For many others, political beliefs fulfill different roles and it is even doubtful whether we should call the mental states playing these roles 'belief' in the first place.

2 Political beliefs as socially adaptive beliefs

All humans need true beliefs to survive and flourish. We must truly believe that our bodies need water in order to stay alive; we must figure out which foods are poisonous in order to avoid death; and if we falsely believe that we are performing well at our job, we are likely to get fired. If our minds were filled with false beliefs, human life would be frustrating, unpleasant, and short. Indeed, it would probably have ended long ago. As Quine once said, "Creatures inveterately wrong in their inductions have a pathetic but praiseworthy tendency to die before reproducing their kind" (1969: 126).

In the philosophical literature, it is commonly held that beliefs 'aim at truth' (Williams 1973; Velleman 2000; Shah 2003). Precisely how to interpret this claim is a matter of controversy. Our framework will be a *teleological* conception of belief according to which the functional goal of cognitive systems is the formation and maintenance of true beliefs. Thus, an attitude counts as a belief if it is formed and regulated by cognitive processes that are truth-conducive (Fassio 2015: §2a). There are many reasons to think that beliefs are deeply connected to truth. It is a truism to say that to believe something is to believe that it is true. And as soon as we regard something as false, we stop believing it. Furthermore, we have no direct choice in the matter. It is not up to us to decide whether to retain the belief or not. We cannot believe directly at will, no matter how convenient that might be (Williams 1973). Finally, there are normative constraints on belief that imply the goal of truth. For example, it seems *irrational* to hold beliefs without evidence, and evidence is needed because it increases the probability of truth. False beliefs seem defective.

Yet many beliefs do *not* seem to aim at truth. Our focus is on political beliefs, but similar points could be made about moral, religious, and other beliefs. In all these cases, humans tend to evaluate evidence and form beliefs in non-truth-conducive ways. For example, we tend to seek out, uncritically accept, and better remember evidence that is favorable to our view, whereas we tend to avoid, forget, and be more critical of counterevidence (Lord et al. 1979). This general human tendency is known as *motivated reasoning*. (For more details, see the chapters by Keith Stanovich and Robin McKenna in this handbook.) We also tend to discuss our political beliefs primarily with people who agree with us, and those who care most about politics often choose to receive political information through like-minded media (Mutz 2006). In political contexts, people also misinterpret simple data that they easily interpret correctly in other contexts (Kahan et al. 2017).

All this fits poorly with the idea that truth is the aim of belief. We humans regularly engage in motivated reasoning, identity-protective cognition, confabulation, and we succumb to a variety of positive illusions that make us feel better about our own lives—all at the expense of truth. This is not to deny that beliefs formed through biased and unreliable processes may still *seem* true to us from the inside, but from an external perspective it is hard to maintain that such beliefs aim at truth in any meaningful sense.

A plausible hypothesis is that *false beliefs are often adaptive* (see Stich 1990; Kahan et al. 2017). They can provide us with psychological comfort, foster group loyalty and belonging, and serve a variety of other ends unrelated to truth. A primary function of political beliefs, we submit, is *social bonding.*[3] A lot of evidence shows that people tend to conform their beliefs and attitudes to those around them, particularly when they view others as similar to themselves (Cialdini 1993). In politics, for example, people often prefer to hold the same beliefs as those they want to associate with (Huemer 2016).[4] It is a way to satisfy their emotionally charged group loyalties. Somin makes a similar observation:

> Both sports fans and political fans tend to be dogmatic and closed-minded in large part because seeking truth is not the main reason why they choose to pursue these activities in the first place. Instead, they have motives such as entertainment, confirming their pre-existing views, enjoying the camaraderie of fellow fans, and so on. (Somin 2013b)

When information threatens our sense of self or our social identity, our "psychological immune system" is programmed to adjust our beliefs to ward off such threats (Mandelbaum 2019). This often requires avoiding harsh truths and believing pleasant falsehoods.

We can incorporate these observations by bifurcating the concept of belief. Borrowing from Williams (2020), we can distinguish between *ordinary world-modeling beliefs* and *socially adaptive beliefs.* The functional properties of these two types of beliefs are sufficiently different to warrant status as different kinds of cognitive attitude.[5] Whereas ordinary world-modeling beliefs are geared towards truth, socially adaptive beliefs aim at social-psychological goods. For both types of belief, mechanisms for belief production can be said to function *properly* (that is, doing what ancestral tokens of that type were selected for doing). Imagine someone who falsely believes *that Hillary Clinton gave classified information to Russia in exchange for donations.* This may not be an error in their belief-system's processing. Rather, it may stem from the system functioning as it should. This is because the *point* of such beliefs is not to be true, but to be socially adaptive.

This distinction may help illuminate the sort of mental states that political beliefs often are. In general, deeply held political beliefs seem unresponsive to evidence, driven by affect, and formed on largely non-evidential grounds (Achen and Bartels 2016). For these reasons, political beliefs (and other identity-constitutive beliefs) seem to be a different cognitive attitude than many ordinary world-modeling beliefs. In politics, we often care more about belonging and team loyalty than truth because, for many, politics *is not really about truth.* This is likely because it is often far more important for our ordinary world-modeling beliefs to be true than it is for our political beliefs.[6]

That last point might sound counterintuitive. Political beliefs are often assumed to be very important, while many ordinary beliefs are mundane. But Paul Bloom nicely illustrates the importance of having accurate ordinary beliefs over political beliefs:

> If I have the wrong theory of how to make scrambled eggs, they will come out too dry; if I have the wrong everyday morality, I will hurt those I love. But suppose I think that the leader of the opposing party has sex with pigs, or has thoroughly botched the arms deal with Iran. Unless I'm a member of a tiny powerful community, my beliefs have no effect on the world. This is certainly true as well for my views about the flat tax, global warming, and evolution. They don't have to be grounded in truth, because the truth value doesn't have any effect on my life. (...) To complain that someone's views on global warming aren't grounded in the fact, then, is to miss the point. (Bloom 2016: 236–37)

When a false belief provides us with *social benefits* and comes with *almost zero practical costs*, our cognitive processing seems geared toward promoting and sustaining such beliefs. This also explains why it is often so difficult to correct false beliefs. If a belief is (strongly) socially adaptive, then providing people with correct information may do little to change their minds.[7]

None of this should deter us from accepting the plausible claim that it is *usually* valuable to avoid falsity (Street 2009: 235; Cowie 2014: 4007). It would clearly not be adaptive to believe that we are immortal, or infallible, or capable of flying, even though acknowledging these limitations may cause us negative affect. However, the simple view that construes beliefs as oriented toward truth alone ignores the many forms of cognitive processing that serve functions other than truth.

3 Political 'beliefs' as expressive behavior

A different and arguably more radical response to the evidence that many political beliefs are produced and sustained in biased ways and often unresponsive to evidence is to reject that they are beliefs in the first place. What look like assertions of political belief are really expressions of different underlying attitudes.

According to new research on political attitudes, people often deliberately misreport their beliefs as a way to *express their attitudes*. This is called "expressive responding" or simply "cheerleading" (Bullock et al. 2015). Consider what Trump supporters said when asked to compare a photo of his 2017 inauguration crowd with a photo of Obama's inauguration crowd in 2009. In a survey of almost 700 American adults, participants were shown both photos and asked a very simple question: "Which photo has more people?" Although only one answer is clearly correct, almost 15% of Trump supporters (n = 218) said that the half-empty photo of Trump's inauguration had more people, compared to only 2% of Clinton voters (n = 275) (Schaffner and Luks 2018).

Did these Trump supporters really *believe* there are more people in an obviously half-empty photo? It would be mistaken to interpret their responses in this way. Instead, some Trump supporters clearly decided to *express their support* for Trump rather than to answer the question factually. These expressions still reliably correspond to an underlying trait or fact about the sender (e.g. a pro-Trump attitude). In this sense, deliberately misreporting one's belief is not necessarily a deceptive act. But expressive proclamations are *misleading* when they are interpreted as genuine belief reports. Here's another example: expressive responding may explain why approximately one in seven Americans says that Obama is "the antichrist" (Harris 2013). Do they really believe this? More likely, such reports reflect partisan cheerleading rather than genuine belief.

How often do people misreport their beliefs? Recent research in political behavior suggests that what seems like factual disagreement is often just partisan cheerleading. For example, John Bullock and colleagues (2015) find that partisans tend to give more accurate (and less partisan) responses to politically charged questions when offered monetary incentives to answer correctly. As a result, the gap between Democrats and Republicans in response to factual questions sharply decreases. Small payments for correct answers reduced partisan divergence by at least 60%. They reduce by 80%–100% when participants are paid both for correct responses and a smaller amount for admitting they do not know the correct response. Multiple independent studies report similar findings (Prior et al. 2015; Huber and Yair 2018; Khanna and Sood 2018).[8]

If these survey responses reflected actual beliefs, then paying partisans to answer correctly should not affect their responses. Yet it does. The observed gaps between Democrats and Republicans are substantially reduced with relatively small payments. This suggests that partisans "do not hold starkly different beliefs about many important facts" (Bullock et al. 2015: 522). Further, it indicates that partisans have the capacity to acknowledge inconvenient truths and are willing to report them when motivated to do so. Without adequate incentives, however, the motivation to give an answer that supports one's political party may outweigh the motivation to give an accurate response. As Gary Langer (2010), former chief pollster for ABC News, remarks: "Some people who strongly oppose a person or proposition will take virtually any opportunity to express that antipathy... not to express their 'belief', in its conventional meaning, but rather to throw verbal stones".

Public opinion polls are consistently showing that partisans are unable to agree on the facts (Bartels 2002; Sinnott-Armstrong 2018). These patterns are ordinarily taken as evidence that partisanship affects factual *beliefs* about politics. But, given the above findings, we should be wary of taking answers to factual questions with partisan implications at face value, since they are often contaminated by the motivation to root for one's team. An alternative explanation is that such patterns merely reflect a desire to praise one's own party or condemn another. People believe one answer, but express a different answer to support their party. This is potentially good news. Expressive responses tend to mask shared, bipartisan beliefs about factual matters. Thus, people are not seeing "separate realities" (Kull et al. 2004). Rather, these political disagreements reflect partisan bad-mouthing and the joy of cheerleading.

4 Political beliefs as 'in-between' beliefs or acceptances

Let's recap. In Section 2, we distinguished socially adaptive beliefs from ordinary factual beliefs, and we claimed that socially adaptive beliefs do not aim at truth, but at securing social benefits. In Section 3, we explored the idea that political 'beliefs' may not really be beliefs at all, but rather expressions of partisan allegiance. In the current section, we introduce yet another way of thinking about political 'beliefs', which steers a middle course between the options from Sections 2 and 3. In the case of some political attitudes, it neither seems accurate to describe a person as *believing* nor to describe them as *not believing*. Schwitzgebel (2001) calls these cases of "in between" believing.

According to Achen and Bartels,

> voters choose political parties, first and foremost, in order to align themselves with the appropriate coalition of social groups. Most citizens support a party not because they have carefully calculated that its policy positions are closest to their own, but rather because 'their kind' of person belongs to that party. (2016: 307)

The true psychological basis for voting behavior, they claim, is not formed by an individual's political beliefs but rather by group identity. As a result, many partisans are not deeply committed to their proclaimed ideologies.

To illustrate, consider how many Republicans switched their views on numerous economic issues when Trump was elected. For example, they went from pro-free trade to protectionist very quickly during the 2016 campaign.[9] This suggests that even apparently key issues like free trade are, at bottom, proclamations intended to demonstrate group membership. Similarly, when Democrats say "I'm pro-regulation", it is unclear whether they are expressing a firmly held belief about appropriate responses to market failure; instead, they may just be expressing a commitment to seeing the Democrats win (see Brennan 2021).

Indeed, people will support whatever policy or platform they think is backed by their party. Geoffrey Cohen's (2003) work provides a striking example of this. He ran a study in which participants were told about two welfare programs: a harsh (extremely stingy) welfare program and a lavish (extremely generous) one. When Democrats were told that their in-group party supported the harsh policy, they approved of it. When Democrats were told that their party supported the lavish policy, they approved of that instead. The same thing happened with Republican participants. All that mattered was which party was said to support the program; it made little difference what the actual content of the policy was. Moreover, the participants were unaware of their bias. Indeed, they denied having it when asked.

This doesn't detract from the fact that people might experience these 'beliefs'—if that's what we want to call them—as genuine, report that they truly believe them when asked, and even stand by them when incentivized to give answers that accurately reflect their internal convictions, in contrast with the merely expressive model from the previous section. Instead of deciding whether or not these are cases of full belief, perhaps we can regard them as "in-between beliefs" (Schwitzgebel 2001). When it seems neither accurate to describe a person as believing p nor correct to describe them as not believing p, we can say it is a case of "in between" believing. Such cases do not force a yes-or-no intuition about whether the agent possesses a (full) belief. Schwitzgebel offers the following examples: a person who asserts that white people are not superior to black people, and yet displays behavior indicative of racist bias (Schwitzgebel 2010: 532); a person who receives an email that a bridge will be out, and yet takes the route to that bridge and only recalls the email upon approaching the bridge (ibid.: 533).

Similarly, when Republicans switched their 'views' when Trump was elected, it neither seems clear that they now *believe* that protectionism is better for the economy, nor does it seem clear that they don't. On the one hand, it does not seem to be a full-fledged belief because it is not associated with the dispositions constitutive of full belief. This belief does not guide behavior in the robust way that full beliefs do. On the other hand, it also doesn't seem to be a merely expressive attitude. Indeed, these beliefs are sincerely professed by the agent: they are *taken to be beliefs*.[10]

Alternatively, one might follow Jonathan Cohen's (1992) distinction and argue that many political opinions are 'accepted' rather than believed. To accept that p is to have or adopt a policy of positing or postulating that p. In contrast to belief, acceptance is under direct voluntary control. Moreover, the reasons for acceptance are often practical rather than evidential. This seems more in keeping with the sort of political beliefs mentioned in this section, where voters adopt whatever opinions are endorsed by their party and then go on to proclaim these 'beliefs' (e.g. "I'm pro-regulation").[11] Thus, it may be that the positive attitude that voters have toward *many* central doctrines of their political party is best understood as accepting such views rather than believing them.

5 Evidence for political beliefs?

We have presented three models for thinking about political 'beliefs', all of them suggesting that many people's political beliefs are not quite—or not at all—like ordinary beliefs. In this section, we will consider two ways of resisting this suggestion and show that both fail.

Isn't there substantive empirical evidence from survey research that the electorate is increasingly polarized along ideological lines? (We focus on the U.S. political context, but claims about increasing polarization have been made about the U.K. and various European countries too.) Republicans are allegedly becoming more conservative and Democrats are reportedly more liberal. Political opinions have shifted towards the more extreme ends of the political spectrum, leaving the middle ground mostly vacated. Surely, this suggests that people have stable, but increasingly extreme political beliefs?

This assumes that surveys reliably get at people's stable political beliefs. There is reason to doubt this. John Zaller's (1992) seminal book, *The Nature and Origins of Mass Opinion*, argues that a substantial portion of respondents to political surveys tend to construct their responses on the spot (see also Zaller and Feldman 1992). For example, the person who reports believing *that Hillary Clinton gave classified information to Russia in exchange for donations* may not really believe (or have ever thought about) any such thing prior to being asked. When citizens are at a loss as to what their view is on a political issue, they often form improvised 'beliefs' that are based on whatever considerations become salient to them in the moment.[12]

Consider another example: a taxpayer might initially oppose increased school funding because high property taxes come to mind (Kuklinski 2001: 243). However, they may later support increased school funding because another consideration, such as low teachers' salaries, gains their attention. According to Kuklinski, "the taxpayer is ambivalent, and thus her expressed attitude at any point in time depends on whether she is cued to think principally about the pro or con considerations" (ibid.). In short, she is simply making up her mind as she goes.

The precise extent to which this occurs is debated. According to Zaller, "most people, on most issues, do not 'really think' any particular thing" (1994: 194); and "most people really aren't sure what their opinions are on most political matters" (Zaller 1992: 76). Sniderman et al. (2001) offer a more moderate interpretation. We do not aim to settle this issue here. Whether the situation is *extremely* bad or just *pretty* bad, it is widely agreed that individuals lack stable beliefs on many political issues.

One might think, however, that this doesn't quite settle things yet. Maybe many people lack stable political beliefs *on specific, particular issues*, but nonetheless possess a stable set of core political convictions, a *political ideology*, which they unfortunately have a hard time applying consistently to specific political issues. An ideology is, roughly, a configuration of beliefs that express what people take to be right and proper. Following Kinder and Kalmoe (2017: 12–3), we can say that ideologies have the following characteristics: their subject is society, economics, and politics; they are comprised of ideas that form an organized structure (i.e. the ideas are arranged in ordinarily, predictable patterns); these ideological structures are shared (i.e. an ideology organizes politics for many, not just one); rival ideologies compete over plans for public policy (i.e. they provide the justificatory basis for particular social and political arrangements and process of a political community); and the beliefs that constitute an ideology are held sincerely and steadfastly (i.e. they are resistant to change). The reason people make up survey answers is that they don't always see immediately what their ideology means for a novel political question.

However, Converse (1964) famously argued that few people are ideological; most citizens simply lack any recognizable ideology. Building on Converse's work, Kinder and Kalmoe (2017) argue that the American electorate is very far from polarized in ideological terms.[13] While political *elites* are strongly ideologically divided, ordinary voters are not. Most people are indifferent to—or confused about—liberalism and conservatism as political ideas. Indeed, according to Converse (1964), five in six Americans lacked understanding of what it even means to be a liberal or a conservative. Thus, the typical citizen's opinions on government policy display little evidence of coherent organization (or polarization) along ideological lines.[14]

But the narrative about polarization is not entirely false. The American electorate is increasingly divided along *partisan* lines. In particular, citizens are polarized in the sense that Republicans and Democrats feel more anger, fear, and loathing toward each other than in previous decades (Iyengar et al. 2012). In other words, the electorate is *affectively* polarized, but not *ideologically* polarized (Mason 2018).

The existence of affective polarization without ideological polarization indicates how unimportant ideology is to partisanship. For the most part, voters do not base their political identities on systems of stable core ideological beliefs. When deciding whom to elect or which policy to support, ideology is not the organizing principle. Rather, as we saw above, political preferences arise from group attachments, which are affective rather than cognitive in nature. As Kinder and Kalmoe put it, public opinion mostly reflects the "attachments and antipathies of group life" (2017: 136), not our ideological convictions about politics, society, or economics. Thus, the American public is increasingly partisan, but for identity-based reasons rather than ideologically-based ones.

Ideological innocence has profound implications for the nature and significance of political beliefs. An ideology provides an intellectual framework, a system of belief that "supplies citizens with a stable foundation for understanding and action" (Kinder and Kalmoe 2017: 12–3). When one lacks an ideology, one tends to express policy preferences that change randomly over time and reflect almost no liberal-conservative coherence across issue domains.[15] As a result, the majority of people lack stable, consistent, meaningful beliefs about political issues.

6 Conclusion

When thinking about the point of beliefs, we tend to think their function is to represent the world. Beliefs aim at truth. This line of thought, however, is a poor fit with many people's political 'beliefs'. These often appear to serve different functions: bolster group loyalty, protect identities, or receive psychological gratification. We have discussed three different models to make sense of this: political beliefs as socially adaptive beliefs, as expressions of non-cognitive attitudes, and as in-between beliefs.

We have not tried to decide which of these three models is the most plausible or promising. As we see it, they may co-exist peacefully: perhaps some political beliefs are best understood as socially adaptive, whereas others are better seen as expressive attitudes, and yet others as in-between beliefs. We are also not that interested in taking a stand on whether the attitudes described by these models deserve the label 'belief'. Some may prefer to call them political 'opinions' or 'attitudes'. As long as it is clear that there is a rich variety of mental attitudes relevant to understanding political behavior, it is largely immaterial which of those get to be called 'belief'.

All of this raises important and fundamental questions for normative democratic theory. If many people's political beliefs aren't stable, consistent, and indicative of underlying ideology, this throws into doubt the folk theory of democracy with which we started this chapter. Political disagreement shouldn't obviously be thought of as cognitive and evidence-based, but rather as affective and identity-based. The function and normative assessments of various forms of political engagement, such as voting and deliberation, need to be revisited, as they are premised on a belief-first model of politics. Answering these questions is far beyond the scope of this chapter, but clearly there is plenty of work left to do at the intersection of political philosophy, epistemology, political science, and political psychology.[16]

Notes

1 By including normative beliefs, our characterization is broader than what political scientists measure when they investigate citizens' political knowledge (Zaller 1992; Delli Carpini and Keeter 1996; Somin 2013a). This is typically limited to factual issues about the political system.
2 Simler and Hanson (2017: 264) describe a 'belief-first' model of *religious* behavior, according to which one's religious beliefs explain their religious behavior.
3 According to Graham and Haidt (2010), this is the function of religious belief and practice.
4 As Huemer (2016) points out, this likely explains why political beliefs cluster together around logically unrelated topics.
5 Funkhouser (2017) makes a similar distinction. He says that beliefs serve a *navigational* function (which requires truth) and a *social signaling* function (which may conflict with truth). We will return to the social signaling function shortly.
6 As Papineau (2013) argues, we ought to form true beliefs when something important hinges on "getting it right", but we can relax the standard if nothing important hinges on the matter.
7 A model for thinking about beliefs that is highly congenial to the line of thought presented here is to conceive of beliefs as *social signals* (Funkhouser 2017). Social signals enable people to fit in, stand out, or advertise their loyalty to communities. Their point is not to model the world accurately, it is to get you invited to barbecues, dinner parties, camping trips, and so on. (For similar thoughts about beliefs as social tools, see Simler and Hanson 2017.)
8 For a dissenting voice, see Berinsky (2018).
9 According to Pew (2017), Republican support for free trade dropped from 56% in 2015 to 36% in 2017.
10 As Rose et al. (2014) show, frequent assertion is the single most powerful cue for belief attribution by ordinary people, even when these assertions are inconsistent with the agent's behavior.
11 We do not claim that political beliefs will meet all the conditions for 'acceptance'. For example, Cohen says that accepting p is being disposed to employ p in one's deliberations and to act upon it to guide one's behavior by relying on it in theoretical and practical reasoning. However, many political opinions do not even meet this dispositional requirement. Our main claim is that political opinions often meet conditions for attitudes that are distinct from beliefs.
12 Zaller claims that people tend to have many relevant considerations in their mind for any given policy domain, so an individual's preference will depend on which of these considerations prevail at any given time. Precisely which considerations prevail will depend on innumerable factors, such as what they saw on the news recently, the wording of the question, the question order, race of the interviewer, social cues they happen to receive, and numerous other internal and external considerations. This differs from Converse's explanation of political attitudes, as we'll describe below.
13 There is some evidence that the electorate is 'inching' toward ideological division, but this is happening very gradually and most people still occupy ideological middle ground (Kinder and Kalmoe 2017: 80–1).
14 According to Lenz (2012), then many voters will easily change even their views about even core commitments to their political party. For example, in 1971, Republican President Richard Nixon imposed a 90-day freeze on wages and prices to halt inflation. This decision ran strongly against conservative economic policy. Nevertheless, a Columbia survey found an increase from 32% to 82% "virtually overnight" among Republican activists—precisely the people who should have resisted the policy shift on ideological grounds (see Resnick 2018).
15 According to Kinder and Kalmoe (2017), about one in six voters (17%) think in ideological terms. Moreover, this number has not changed in 50 years. These voters tend to pay close attention to politics and have consistent opinions from year to year.
16 Thanks to Elias Antilla, Valentin Arts, Roland den Boef, Catarina Dutilh Novaes, Rik Peels, and René van Woudenberg for comments on an earlier version of this chapter. Jeroen de Ridder's work on this chapter was made possible by a Vidi grant from the Dutch Research Council (NWO, project 276-20-024).

Works cited

Achen, C. and L. Bartels (2016) *Democracy for Realists*. Princeton, NJ: Princeton University Press.
Bartels, L.M. (2002) "Beyond the Running Tally: Partisan Bias in Political Perceptions." *Political Behavior* 24(2): 117–50.

Berinsky, A. J. (2018) "Telling the Truth about Believing the Lies? Evidence for the Limited Prevalence of Expressive Survey Responding." *The Journal of Politics* 80: 211–24.

Bloom, P. (2016) *Against Empathy: The Case for Rational Compassion.* New York: Ecco.

Brennan, J. (2021) "Does Public Reason Liberalism Rest on a Mistake? Democracy's Doxastic and Epistemic Problems." In E. Edenberg and M. Hannon (eds.), *Politics and Truth: New Perspectives in Political Epistemology.* Oxford: Oxford University Press.

Bullock, J., A. Gerber, S. Hill and G. Huber (2015) "Partisan Bias in Factual Beliefs about Politics." *Quarterly Journal of Political Science* 10(4): 519–78.

Cialdini, R. B. (1993) *Influence: The Psychology of Persuasion.* New York: Morrow.

Cohen, G. (2003) "Party over Policy: The Dominating Impact of Group Influence on Political Beliefs." *Journal of Personality and Social Psychology* 85: 808–22.

Cohen, L. J. (1992) *An Essay on Belief and Acceptance.* New York: Clarendon Press.

Converse, P. E. (1964) "The Nature of Belief Systems in Mass Publics." In D. E. Apter (ed.), *Ideology and Discontent.* New York: The Free Press, 206–61.

Cowie, C. (2014) "In Defence of Instrumentalism about Epistemic Normativity." *Synthese* 191(16): 4003–17.

Delli Carpini, X. M. and S. Keeter (1996) *What Americans Know about Politics and Why It Matters.* New Haven, CT: Yale University Press.

Fassio, D. (2015) "The Aim of Belief." *Internet Encyclopedia of Philosophy.* Accessed at: https://iep.utm.edu/beli-aim/.

Funkhouser, E. (2017) "Beliefs as Signals: A New Function for Belief." *Philosophical Psychology* 30(6): 809–31.

Graham, J. and J. Haidt (2010) "Beyond Beliefs: Religions Bind Individuals into Moral Communities." *Personality and Social Psychology Review* 14(1): 140–50.

Harris, P. (2013) "One in Four Americans Think Obama May Be the Antichrist, Survey Says." *The Guardian.* Accessed at: https://www.theguardian.com/world/2013/apr/02/americans-obama-antichrist-conspiracy-theories.

Huber, G. A. and O. Yair (2018) "How Robust Is Evidence of Perceptual Partisan Bias in Survey Responses? A New Approach for Studying Expressive Responding." Presented at the Midwest Political Science Association Annual Meeting, April 5–8, Chicago, IL.

Huemer, M. (2016) "Why People Are Irrational about Politics." In J. Anomaly, G. Brennan, M. C. Munger and G. Sayre-McCord. (eds.), *Philosophy, Politics, and Economics: An Anthology.* New York: Oxford University Press.

Iyengar, S., G. Sood and Y. Lelkes (2012) "Affect, Not Ideology: A Social Identity Perspective on Polarization." *Public Opinion Quarterly* 76: 405–31.

Kahan, D. M., A. Landrum, K. Carpenter, L. Helft and K. Hall Jamieson (2017) "Science Curiosity and Political Information Processing." *Political Psychology* 38: 179–99.

Khanna, K. and G. Sood (2018) "Motivated Responding in Studies of Factual Learning." *Political Behavior* 40(1): 79–101.

Kinder, D. and N. Kalmoe (2017) *Neither Liberal Nor Conservative: Ideological Innocence in the American Public.* Chicago, IL: University of Chicago Press.

Kuklinski, J. (2001) *Citizens and Politics: Perspectives from Political Psychology.* Cambridge: Cambridge University Press.

Kull, S., C. Ramsay, S. Subias and E. Lewis (2004) "The Separate Realities of Bush and Kerry Supporters." *Program on International Policy Attitudes.* Accessed at: http://hdl.handle.net/1903/10533.

Langer, G. (2010) "This I Believe." *ABC News*, August 30 (blog post). Accessed at: http://blogs.abcnews.com/thenumbers/2010/08/this-i-believe.html.

Lenz, G. (2012) *Follow the Leader?* Chicago, IL: University of Chicago Press.

Lord, C. G., L. Ross and M. R. Lepper (1979) "Biased Assimilation and Attitude Polarization: The Effects of Prior Theories on Subsequently Considered Evidence." *Journal of Personality and Social Psychology* 37(11), 2098–109.

Mandelbaum, E. (2019) "Troubles with Bayesianism: An Introduction to the Psychological Immune System." *Mind & Language* 34(2): 141–57.

Mason, L. (2018) *Uncivil Agreement: How Politics Became Our Identity.* Chicago, IL: University of Chicago Press.

Mutz, D. (2006) *Hearing the Other Side.* Cambridge: Cambridge University Press.

Papineau, D. (2013) "There Are No Norms of Belief." In T. Chan (ed.), *The Aim of Belief.* New York: Oxford University Press, 64–79.

Pew (2017) "Continued Partisan Divides in Views of the Impact of Free Trade Agreements". Accessed at: https://www.pewresearch.org/fact-tank/2017/04/25/support-for-free-trade-agreements-rebounds-modestly-but-wide-partisan-differences-remain/.

Prior, M., G. Sood and K. Khanna (2015) "You Cannot Be Serious: The Impact of Accuracy Incentives on Partisan Bias in Reports of Economic Perceptions." *Quarterly Journal of Political Science* 10(4): 489–518.

Quine, W. V. (1969) "Natural Kinds." In *Ontological Relativity and Other Essays*. New York: Columbia University Press, 114–38.

Resnick, B. (2018) "Trump Is a Real-World Political Science Experiment." *Vox*. Accessed at: https://www.vox.com/science-and-health/2017/10/11/16288690/trump-political-science-psychology-follow-the-leader.

Rose, D., W. Buckwalter and J. Turri (2014) "When Words Speak Louder than Actions: Delusion, Belief, and the Power of Assertion." *Australasian Journal of Philosophy* 92(4): 683–700.

Schaffner, B. F. and S. Luks (2018) "Misinformation or Expressive Responding? What an Inauguration Crowd Can Tell Us about the Source of Political Misinformation in Surveys." *Public Opinion Quarterly* 82(1): 135–47.

Schwitzgebel, E. (2001) "In-between Believing." *The Philosophical Quarterly* 51(202): 76–82.

Schwitzgebel, E. (2010) "Acting Contrary to Our Professed Beliefs or the Gulf between Occurrent Judgment and Dispositional Belief." *Pacific Philosophical Quarterly* 91(4): 531–53.

Shah, N. (2003) "How Truth Governs Belief." *The Philosophical Review* 112(4): 447–82.

Simler, K. and R. Hanson (2017). *The Elephant in the Brain: Hidden Motives in Everyday Life*. New York: Oxford University Press.

Sinnott-Armstrong, W. (2018) *Think Again*. London: Penguin.

Sniderman, P. M., P. E. Tetlock and L. Elms (2001) "Public Opinion and Democratic Politics: The Problem of Non-attitudes and the Social Construction of Political Judgment." In J. Kuklinski (ed.), *Citizens and Politics: Perspectives from Political Psychology*. Cambridge: Cambridge University Press, 254–88.

Somin, I. (2013a) *Democracy and Political Ignorance*. Stanford, CA: Stanford Law Books.

Somin, I. (2013b) "Why (Most) Political Ignorance Is Rational and Why It Matters: Reply to Jeffrey Friedman." *Cato Unbound*. Accessed at: https://www.cato-unbound.org/2013/10/22/ilya-somin/why-most-political-ignorance-rational-why-it-matters-reply-jeffrey-friedman.

Stich, S. P. (1990) *The Fragmentation of Reason: Preface to a Pragmatic Theory of Cognitive Evaluation*. Cambridge, MA: MIT Press.

Street, S. (2009) "Evolution and the Normativity of Epistemic Reasons." *Canadian Journal of Philosophy* 39: 213–48.

Velleman, J. D. (2000) *The Possibility of Practical Reason*. New York: Oxford University Press.

Williams, B. (1973) "Deciding to Believe." In *Problems of the Self*. Cambridge: Cambridge University Press, 136–51.

Williams, D. (2020) "Socially Adaptive Belief." *Mind & Language*. Online First: https://doi-org.ez-proxy.nottingham.ac.uk/10.1111/mila.12294.

Zaller, J. (1994) "Elite Leadership of Mass Opinion." In W. L. Bennett and D. L. Paletz (eds.), *Taken by Storm: The Media, Public Opinion, and US Foreign Policy in the Gulf War*. Chicago, IL: University of Chicago Press.

Zaller, J. R. (1992) *The Nature and Origins of Mass Opinion*. Cambridge: Cambridge University Press.

Zaller, J. and S. Feldman (1992) "A Simple Theory of the Survey Response: Answering Questions versus Revealing Preferences." *American Journal of Political Science* 36(3): 579–616.

PART 3

Fake news, propaganda, and misinformation

INTRODUCTION TO PART 3

Fake news and misinformation have attracted a great deal of attention in recent years. One might even worry that we are getting to a point where there is more talk of misinformation than actual misinformation. Regardless, there is plenty of reason to worry about the quality of our information environment. Figuring out where to find reliable information, whom to trust, and how to verify one's sources is no easy job when there is a world of misinformation at your fingertips. Social media platforms have made it easy for tech-savvy actors to boost sensationalistic and inflammatory content and ideologically driven political actors make extensive use of the possibilities to influence the public opinion offered by the internet. On the international geopolitical stage, covert information warfare is rumored to be intensifying, even though this is inherently hard to verify.

We shouldn't naïvely assume that fake news appeared out of the blue before the 2016 American elections or the Brexit vote. Misinformation has deep roots. Even Plato's criticisms of democracy hinged on the fact that people are susceptible to being deceived by misleading information. Arguably our individual psychologies, as well as the ways in which we interact and exchange information, are generally conducive to acquiring true beliefs, but under certain circumstances they also make us vulnerable to biased thinking, lies, and deception. When we consider contemporary misinformation, we should therefore also think about how it relates to more familiar and older concepts such as lies, bullshit, propaganda, and systematically manufactured doubts about science induced by Big Tobacco, Big Pharma, and the fossil fuel industry.

Axel Gelfert tackles the question of what fake news is head on. His chapter reviews extant definitions of the term 'fake news', identifies four dimensions that dominate attempts to define what fake news is, and argues that the term is best understood as an exploratory concept which can be clarified only by engaging with the empirical phenomena and dynamics that motivated its introduction in the first place. These, he argues, are first and foremost systemic aspects of converging social, political, and technological developments, which render existing processes of creating, disseminating, and consuming news reports vulnerable to exploitation by 'bad actors', who intend to pass off their own fabrications as trustworthy news.

Neil Levy and Robert Ross investigate the consumption side of misinformation by providing a survey of recent work in the cognitive sciences on the psychology of fake news in the political domain. The focus is on whether and why people believe fake news. They argue that the proportion of people who believe fake news might be significantly smaller than is usually thought (and smaller than suggested by surveys). This is because people are prone to assert belief insincerely, merely to express support for their political party or simply for fun. Moreover, respondents tend to report believing things about which they had no opinion prior to being probed. Levy and Ross also consider rival accounts that aim to explain why people believe in fake news when they do. Partisan explanations that turn on motivated reasoning are probably best known, but Levy and Ross argue that they face serious challenges from accounts that explain belief by reference to analytic thinking.

In addition to the production and consumption of misinformation, there are questions about its distribution and spread. The next two chapters address those. A common concern about online misinformation is that it bounces around and is reinforced in filter bubbles and echo chambers. Hanna Gunn's chapter investigates these phenomena more closely. It is widely assumed both that filter bubbles and echo chambers are necessary consequences of online platforms, and that they are the product of our online actions causing us to be isolated in cyber-enclaves of like-minded individuals. Gunn looks at the epistemic and political risks of this, focusing her discussion around four themes: selective exposure, homophily, polarization, and responsibility.

Given that misinformation is undesirable, what can and should we do about it? This is the question Étienne Brown takes up in his chapter. He considers four reasons to worry about misinformation, having to do with its likely impact on people's political opinions, emotions, physical safety, and personal autonomy. Next, he assesses three strategies for regulating misinformation: individual self-regulation, platform-based innovations, and governmental action. Brown suggests that the most effective strategies are those that spare human agents from having to successively review individual pieces of content.

Megan Hyska's chapter turns to propaganda and proposes a novel group-based account of it. It is traditionally claimed that propaganda undermines individuals' rationality, but Hyska argues against this. Instead, she outlines an alternative account of propaganda inspired by Hannah Arendt, on which propaganda characteristically creates or destroys group agency. Propagandists should have an interest in both creating and suppressing group agency, she argues, both because groups have capacities that individuals do not, and because participation in group action can have a transformative effect on individuals. Her account also has significant implications for thinking about how to resist propaganda.

15

WHAT IS FAKE NEWS?

Axel Gelfert

1 Fake news as an exploratory concept

Worries about the reliability of the news and reports we receive from others have been with us for as long as reporting itself. Modern journalism is only the latest institution that has been found to be vulnerable in this way. Historians are well aware of the vicissitudes of how information travels, and how it can be shaped – through omission as well as elaboration, deliberately as well as tacitly – to fit virtually any narrative. When Athens, during the Peloponnesian War, was hit by the plague, the Athenians quickly blamed the Spartans for poisoning the wells at Piraeus, or so Thucydides tells us; most likely, they were simply the victims of a haemorrhagic fever that had spread from its port of arrival. More than 2,000 years later, as the world is struggling to contain the Covid-19 pandemic in early 2020, fake news about the alleged military origins of the SARS-CoV 2 virus is being re-tweeted by political leaders aiming to shore up domestic support. In between, disinformation campaigns have been regularly deployed by adversaries in times of war and struggle, and political actors have often taken liberties with the truth when it suited their goals. Such goals were not always selfish: When Greenpeace, in 1995, misstated the facts about the oil platform *Brent Spar* – which was to be sunk in a controlled way in the deep waters of the North Atlantic (not the North Sea, as Greenpeace reported), along with a moderate amount of oil (far short of the 5,500t – a third of the total weight of the structure! – that Greenpeace claimed was remaining in the storage tanks), they presumably did so in the hopes of protecting the environment. Were these, and similar, cases of false or untruthful reports instances of 'fake news', and what distinguishes fake news from other forms of deception, such as outright lying? The question 'What is Fake News?', in recent years, has received considerable philosophical attention, and the present chapter aims to take stock.

The very question, however, may raise eyebrows: Is there even a unified category of problematic claims, or news content, that is picked out by the term 'fake news', and are we warranted in speaking of 'the rise of fake news'? As with any philosophical question, there is bound to be disagreement, and some of this will be taken up in a later section. Given that more and more countries have begun to enact 'anti-fake news legislation', sometimes deploying their own proprietary definitions, simply agreeing to disagree about definitional issues no longer seems a viable option; hence, even as one laments (over-)use of the term, one must confront the very real need for careful analysis. As a starting point, it is worth reviewing the recent history of the term. The first systematic use of 'fake news' dates to the early 2000s, in connection with fake *news shows* such as the Colbert Report (2004–2015), which satirized the biases and dysfunctions of an increasingly 'fact-free' political discourse in the United States, especially under George W. Bush's presidency. The implicit goal was to call out biased reporting and sensitize viewers to the biases, mistakes, and deficiencies of traditional network and cable TV news. This concern for media literacy, which informed much of satirical 'fake news', quickly evaporated, however, and from around 2014 onward, the term slowly came to be applied to false or misleading statements, published mostly (though not exclusively) on websites specifically set up for this purpose, which often had an established ring to them ('National Report', 'Denver Guardian'). During the 2016 U.S. presidential election campaign, such websites rose to prominence and were accused of peddling false claims about political actors (notably, about Democratic candidate Hillary Clinton), either as clickbait (i.e. attention-grabbing online content that drove internet traffic, thereby generating online ad revenue) or for political purposes. Some of the website operators were found to have links with foreign lobby groups (e.g. the Internet Research Agency, which is thought to be run by Russian oligarchs with support of the Kremlin), though the exact extent of electoral meddling and the role it may have played in the election of Donald Trump as U.S. president remains disputed.

Since late 2016, there has been much public and academic debate about the nature and character of 'fake news', not least due to the rapid co-opting of the term as a partisan label for any form of inconvenient reporting (as in Trump's use of the phrase 'the *fake news* media' as an umbrella term for established news sources such as the *New York Times* and *CNN*). Perhaps unsurprisingly, given the novel role of social networks such as Facebook and Twitter, more analytical approaches to the term have sometimes taken the medium of dissemination to be constitutive, as in the proposed definition of fake news as "the online publication of intentionally or knowingly false statements of fact" (Klein & Wueller 2017). Others have equated fake news simply with 'false news' or characterized it as "invented entirely from thin air", "completely fabricated", with "no factual basis".[1] While most definitions agree that producers of fake news must possess some kind of intention to deceive, the precise character and extent of such deceptive intentions is hotly contested, ranging from intentions to deceive about the content of the claims in question (Rini 2017) to the intention to "manipulate an audience's well-formed expectations about the baseline processes of news aggregation and presentation in systematic and misleading ways" (Gelfert 2021). Some critics have denied the need for introducing the novel term 'fake news', on the basis that it has at best "a use as a catch-all for bad information" and at worst is radically polysemic, with each usage having "a radically different extension" (Habgood-Coote 2019: 1047). While it is certainly true that any survey of the actual usage of the term 'fake news' turns up a range of different meanings, this does not, however, entail that the term is redundant or cannot be clarified in productive ways. Instead, one response to such worries has been the suggestion that 'fake news' may be best understood as an *exploratory concept* (Gelfert 2021), the precise meaning and extension of which is to be determined by paying close attention to the phenomena that first motivated the introduction of the associated term. Especially in the social sciences, it is not at all uncommon that novel concepts are introduced, even as researchers are still in the process of figuring out whether a stable, genuinely new phenomenon has been identified. In such a situation, concepts may be "imported from every-day language, which typically inform the ways in which scientists think about the concept's referent", with inquiry being understood as a process by which "these everyday intuitions are put on a more rigorous and explicit footing" (Feest 2012: 172). This sentiment is echoed by Pepp, Michaelson and Sterken (2019), who note that "extensional and intensional uncertainties" are to be expected whenever we deal with complex social phenomena, and that it may overall be beneficial "to live with such uncertainties" (Pepp, Michaelson & Sterken 2019: 4), as long as one aims for making linguistic and conceptual progress over time. It is in this spirit that the discussion in this chapter proceeds.

2 Four dimensions of fake news

News reports, in their written or spoken form (e.g. as reports published on a website or in a newspaper, or as announced in a radio or TV broadcast), are assertions about recent events; as such, they are directed at an audience, which, at least implicitly, is invited to trust the source for the veracity of the reports in question. On a widely held view, assertion is governed by the knowledge norm, according to which we must assert only what we know. While, in the context of news reporting, it may be too much to demand that the speaker be able to *guarantee* the truth of her claims – perhaps especially so in the case of 'developing stories' and 'breaking news' – at the very least such reporting should be constrained by the reporter's vouching for her *belief* that her claims are veridical. Regarding the content of news reports, recency of the events in question is usually considered essential to the nature of 'news' (even if this may sometimes consist in new evidence overturning previous findings, e.g. in criminal cases), as is relevance to the target audience's range of interests. At a societal level, the modern concept of 'the news' was tied up with the historical emergence of a 'public sphere', such that certain social and political events and developments are typically deemed newsworthy without much further argument.

This sketch of what characterizes the concept of 'the news' already suggests various ways in which reporting can fail – unintentionally, or by deliberate manipulation – and thus points to several potential dimensions of the concept of 'fake news'. Broadly speaking, four such dimensions may be distinguished, which, to varying degrees, are reflected in extant definitions of 'fake news' (to be discussed in the next section). These concern the *epistemic* standing of the claims in question (in particular, whether they are false or misleading), the *intentional* dimension (whether the speaker intends to deceive or manipulate the audience), the *functional* role of fake news (e.g. the extent to which it aims at being circulated and succeeds at being taken up and believed), and its *medium* (where this is to be understood broadly, not just as relating to the platform via which information is received – e.g. online or in printed form – but also to the way in which a report is presented *as* news, e.g. by mimicking contextual markers of prima facie trustworthiness).

Regarding the first of these four dimensions, the conception of the 'epistemic' intended here is a fairly broad one, so a report can be epistemically defective in several ways: e.g. by being false, unreliable, contravening the best available evidence, giving a false impression, or in other ways that lead away from the truth of the matter. Simply settling for the issue of truth vs. falsity – which would amount to equating 'fake news' with 'false news' (which, interestingly, social media giant Facebook has opted for) – will not do, as it ignores the possibility of certain types of selective presentation and bias resulting in fake news. The second dimension, concerning the extent to which fake news is intended to pass off epistemically defective claims as news, not only relates to the issue of insincerity on the part of the producers of fake news, but also to their more distal goals – e.g. their intention to instil particular beliefs in others or to bring about certain desired outcomes. The absence of any intention to deceive or manipulate might then explain why honest journalistic mistakes – which, after all, give rise to epistemically defective reports – do not count as cases of 'fake news'.

The third dimension to be distinguished concerns the *functional* role of fake news, as aiming at wide dissemination within its intended target audience. Which degree of circulation (if any) must, in fact, be achieved, and whether an 'innocent' falsehood may turn into a piece of 'fake news' once it is taken up by the media, is a matter of contention; if actual dissemination must be achieved, this would place fake news into roughly the same category as rumour (which, arguably, cannot be dissociated from its circulation). In order to ensure widespread circulation, fake news often is first published in (online and/or offline) venues that mimick familiar 'markers' of trusted mainstream news sources. This is especially easy to achieve online, where it only takes a few mouseclicks to register a domain name (e.g. "buffalochronicle.com"), set up a blog and replicate, say, the *New York Times* layout. The final (fourth) dimension – the manner and *medium* of presentation – is intended to reflect this. A verbal or written statement need not explicitly include a reference to its (purported) status as news, in order for it to be presented as such. Typically, reports are presented *as news* in virtue of the context, in which they appear; this requires (usually tacit) cultural background knowledge on the part of their audience.

Linking all four dimensions together are *systemic* considerations relating to the specific convergence of ongoing social, political, and technological developments, which render existing processes of creating, disseminating, and consuming news reports vulnerable to their exploitation by 'bad actors', who intend to pass off their own fabrications as believable and trustworthy news reports. The systemic nature of such developments is what, arguably, has led to the popularization of the (problematic) phrase 'post-truth', which reflects the recognition that "[w]e now find ourselves in an informational environment where technology enables psychometric targeting, information floods, and filter bubbles; a political environment typified by escalating polarization, extremism, and distrust"; and a media environment "marked by economic pressure" (Levi 2018: 236). Fake news is often taken to be a manifestation of these dynamics. Arguably, then, whether a term such as 'fake news' is fruitful – whether it meets a genuine conceptual need – is partly determined by whether the overall changes in how news reports are generated, and how we consume information that represents itself as news, are sufficiently uniform and genuine enough to warrant a new label.

3 Defining 'fake news': a brief survey

Since 2016, when the term 'fake news' began to receive widespread usage by journalists, media scholars, political pundits, and cultural critics, a plethora of definitions have been proposed. While some of these, including those mentioned in the first section, have been somewhat casual and were sometimes intended as easy-to-grasp tools for educating the public about the need to 'check their sources', philosophers – and especially social epistemologists – soon entered the fray. This section discusses a subset of philosophical definitions that have been proposed. Since, for lack of space, completeness is not a realistic goal, the selection is based partly on priority, partly on the need for a certain degree of coverage of the available conceptual possibilities. Rather than explore every definition in detail – some borderline cases and counterexamples are discussed in the next section – the emphasis is on elucidating how each definition relates to the dimensions of 'fake news' discussed in the previous section.

Many of the definitions that have been proposed combine broad (defeasible) characterizations with one or two necessary conditions that are thought to form the core of the concept of 'fake news'. Thus, Regina Rini defines fake news as any 'news story' that

> purports to describe events in the real world, typically by mimicking the conventions of traditional media reportage, yet is known by its creators to be significantly false, and is transmitted with the two goals of being widely re-transmitted and of deceiving at least some of the audience. (2017: E45)

Rini explicitly speaks of 'news stories', which may or may not turn out to be instances of fake news, suggesting that often – though not always – this presentation of a claim *as news* is achieved by mimicking the trappings of legitimate news. Others have taken a stronger position on this: For example, Neil Levy describes fake news as "the presentation of false claims that purport to be about the world in a format and with a content that resembles the format and content of legitimate media organisations" (2017: 20). By contrast, Rini explicitly allows for fake news to be spread also through "email chains, posters on streetlamps, etc." (2017: E45), so the *medium* dimension is less central than the *functional* aspect of fake news aiming at wide re-transmission. The latter appears to derive largely from the intentions of the fake news creators, who *knowingly* put "significantly false" stories into circulation. Clearly, then, the *epistemic* and *intentional* dimensions are at the core of Rini's definition: Fake news consists of false stories that are circulated as news with the intention to deceive (some of) the audience.

In an earlier paper (Gelfert 2018), I defined fake news as "the deliberate presentation of (typically) false or misleading claims *as news*, where the claims are misleading by design" (108). This definition, too, places the *epistemic* defectiveness at the heart of the concept, though it allows for the possibility of fake news being not literally false, but misleading – e.g. through the omission of relevant facts or contextual information. This is more than a matter of mere rhetoric and framing, since, for a report to be misleading, it must be "likely to create false beliefs" (105) about the matter in question. Whether or not a fake news report ends up 'going viral', it must have at least some "measure of success in *realizing* the goal of widespread circulation and uptake" (102). This is less a matter of the intentions of the producers and conveyors of fake news, but instead is a *functional* point that ties in with the observation that systemic features of the processes of news aggregation and dissemination are what gives fake news its conceptual novelty. A number of criticisms have been levelled against this definition: that it overstates the degree to which fake news reports must be *intentionally* false or misleading; that the phrase 'by design' remains vague; and that the restriction to verbal claims leaves out other forms of news content. This is partly due to the ambiguity of the phrase 'by design', which can be taken to refer to systemic features as well as intentions ('he has designs on…'). Importantly, however, the proposed definition restricts the role of intention to the presentational aspect, whereas the epistemic defectiveness may arise solely due to the utilization of problematically designed news processes. An updated version of the definition, broadened to include non-verbal news content (e.g. news footage) and also acknowledging the effects fake news is intended to have on its audience (e.g. revise a belief, click a link, cast a vote), would thus run as follows: "Fake news is the deliberate presentation of manipulative and misleading content as news, where the content is manipulative and misleading by design" (Gelfert 2021).

A different approach to the project of defining 'fake news' is adopted by Nikil Mukerji (2018), who defines fake news as "bullshit asserted in the form of a news publication". On the face of it, this definition is appealing in virtue of its simplicity, in that it contains three conditions, which are taken to be necessary and jointly sufficient: the bullshit condition (B), the assertion condition (A), and the publication condition (P). For (B), a broadly Frankfurtian conception of 'bullshit' is adopted, according to which the publisher of fake news has to (B1) be indifferent to the truth of the claim and (B2) cover up this fact. (A) excludes claims that are merely inferred by conversational implicature, whereas (P) excludes statements uttered in private. Yet, upon closer inspection, the definition is anything but simple. Take (P), for example: Mukerji writes that "for a story to qualify as fake news, it has to be made available publicly, for example, in paper form, on the radio, on the internet etc." (2018: 930), yet unless more is said about what counts as a "news publication" in these various media, the definition would overgenerate cases of fake news, counting harmless online banter as publicly asserted bullshit and, therefore, fake news. It also undercounts instances of fake news, e.g. when misleading falsehoods are asserted as fake news, not because the publisher is indifferent to the truth value of the claim – as would be required of Frankfurtian 'bullshit' – but because he is putting out a deliberately false claim in order to mislead or divert attention. Published bullshit may be an important subclass of fake news, but it is not constitutive of it.

The latter point is reflected in Romy Jaster and David Lanius's definition of fake news as "news that does mischief with the truth in that it exhibits both (a) a lack of truth and (b) a lack of truthfulness" (Jaster & Lanius 2018: 213). Lack of truth (a) is construed here as a claim's being objectively false or misleading, while (b) lack of truthfulness covers not only an informant's intention to deceive, but also bullshitting (in the sense discussed earlier) and cases such as that of the Macedonian teenagers who, during the 2016 U.S. presidential elections, ran websites spreading false claims about Hillary Clinton – not because they wanted to actively mislead their audience, but simply because they found Trump supporters to be more susceptible to such clickbait, thereby driving internet traffic and generating ad revenue for the website operators. The conjunction of conditions (a) *and* (b) elegantly avoids counting honest journalistic mistakes (which lack truth but not truthfulness) as fake news, though it does so at the cost of having to distinguish between actual fake news and *merely attempted* fake news (where the latter, presumably, would obtain if an untruthful source fabricated a claim which, by happenstance, turned out to be true).

Don Fallis and Kay Mathiesen have called this distinction into question, arguing that attempts at fake news that happen to result in truths are just as detrimental as 'typical' cases, in that they undermine the institution of the news media, thereby "harm[ing] everyone who consumes the news" (2019: 13). Just as the circulation of counterfeit money can undermine trust in the monetary system, so the existence of fake news undermines legitimate trust in the aggregation and dissemination of news reports. Fake news, on this account, is "counterfeit news"; that is, a story is fake news "if and only if it is not genuine news, but is presented as genuine news, with the intention and propensity to deceive" (2019: 8). By emphasizing how fake news 'piggy-backs' on established institutions and processes of news aggregation and dissemination, Fallis and Mathiesen's definition is more aligned with those accounts that emphasize the *systemic* nature of 'fake news' than with those that take individual intentions of the producers and/or the specific content of individual reports to be constitutive of fake news.

Thomas Grundmann (2020) has argued against the general preference for 'hybrid' views that combine essentially subjective aspects pertaining to the source of fake news (e.g. the intention to deceive) with additional objective aspects of the effects of its consumption (e.g. giving rise to false beliefs). In his "purely consumer-oriented explication" of the term, 'fake news' is defined entirely in terms of its robust disposition to bring about, under normal conditions, a significant number of false beliefs in a significant share of the audience that is being addressed. Whether this is done with the intention to deceive a specific target audience or happens merely as the unintended by-product of an algorithm gone haywire is of secondary importance. By bracketing any questions concerning the motivations and intentions of purveyors of fake news, Grundmann's definition aims to focus on the purely epistemic shortcomings of fake news. While this approach is compatible with acknowledging the systemic nature of fake news production and consumption (cf. Grundmann 2020: fn. 14), it remains silent, by choice, on the issue of whether fake news is always, or typically, associated with some sort of dereliction of epistemic duty.

4 Borderline cases and other worries

Any term that purports to describe a new (or newly relevant) phenomenon will inevitably face challenges from borderline cases, and paying close attention to such cases will be important for properly delineating the extension of the term. While this is not the place to thoroughly test each of the definitions surveyed in the previous section, the borderline cases and related conceptual worries raised in this section should help convey a sense of further challenges and complexities that await any definitional project.

First, it is worth re-iterating that honest journalistic error alone never counts as fake news. More than mere falsity is required for a report to be considered fake news; in turn, for a report to constitute legitimate news it is not a necessary condition that it consists only of true statements. A false report that originated from normally reliable processes of news aggregation, was (at the time of publication) based on sufficient objective evidence, and was generated with the aim of getting to the truth of the matter, would count as genuine news, in spite of its failings – even if it went viral and had similar effects as corresponding fake news. The journalistic practice of publishing corrections and noting discrepancies between the current and previous versions of an article attests to the overall truth-orientation of genuine news. Yet, evidently, journalistic practices vary considerably, and not all processes of news aggregation and dissemination are equally reliable. An interesting question is whether, with increasing unreliability, legitimate news may degenerate into fake news. What if, for example, journalists use methods they could easily recognize to be unreliable (and, therefore, likely to lead to false or misleading reports), yet – perhaps due to economic pressure or time constraints – they continue to deploy them unquestioningly? It may well be argued that, if a process of news production "is so flawed (and is recognized as flawed by those who would be in a position to make adequate improvements, but fail to do so) that it can legitimately be regarded as being misleading *by design*" (Gelfert 2018: 110), it should be considered a source of fake news.

A similar point applies to aspects of the presentation of (otherwise legitimate) news reports, such as selective *overreporting* of certain states of affairs (at the expense of other facts that, if reported appropriately, would give a more balanced view of reality) and more generally biased reporting. Scott Aikin and Robert Talisse discuss the example of a news source that reports – accurately – a violent crime committed by a minority group, say immigrants, in the vicinity of its target audience, but gives it excessive air time "throughout a news cycle, underreports cases of similar crimes committed by people who are not immigrants, and reports the incident in a manner that could give a casual member of the audience" the impression that several distinct crimes of this sort took place (Aikin & Talisse 2020: 71). Though nothing about the report, considered in isolation, is false or misleading, they consider this "clearly an instance of fake news" (ibid.). By adding an institutional dimension to Fallis and Mathiesen's (2019) criterion of fake news posing as genuine news, adopting Gelfert's (2018) systemic notion of fake news being misleading "by design", and limiting the intentional dimension to the political realm, Aikin and Talisse arrive at what they call an *institutional view*, according to which "'fake news' characterizes the activities of institutions that pose as journalistic, which by design feed and codify the antecedent biases of a preselected audience [...] with a view to facilitating some decidedly political objective" (Aikin & Talisse 2020: 73).

The various political uses to which the term 'fake news' has been put have also been the source of philosophical controversy. While much of the discussion so far has focused on developing a definition of 'fake news' – assuming, at least implicitly, that the term offers some potential analytical or explanatory benefit – a small, but vocal, number of critics have argued that "the problem is not fake news, it is the term 'fake news'" (Coady 2019: 40). 'Fake news', so the argument goes, has no determinate meaning, and is increasingly being hijacked as a political slur to discredit unfriendly reporting. This development is associated with a distinct shift in usage, since it no longer singles out problematic claims for criticism, but instead casts doubt on the legitimacy of whole *news organizations* – as when, notoriously, former U.S. president Donald Trump made it a habit to refer to established domestic news outlets, such as the *New York Times*, the *Washington Post*, and *CNN*, as "the fake news media". This move, it has been argued, serves "as a power-shifting governance mechanism to delegitimize the institutional press as a whole" (Levi 2018: 234), thereby rendering the label 'fake news' a "rhetorical device used by the powerful to crush dissent" (Dentith 2017: 65). At the same time, it is not at all obvious that the mere risk of such a 'hostile takeover' of a term necessarily invalidates its potential usefulness as an analytical tool. Neither does the fact that there already exist neighbouring, and partly overlapping, concepts – such as 'bullshit' or 'propaganda' – conclusively show that the novel term 'fake news' is redundant (rather than a successful step towards an even more fine-grained taxonomy of social-epistemic dysfunctions). Consider the example of 'propaganda', which has itself been defined in various ways, but which at its root involves communications designed to manipulate a target audience with the goal of bringing about alignment with a certain set of political or ideological commitments. Such commitments may be embodied in centralized power structures (e.g. the Communist state) or political movements (e.g. fascism), but always go beyond individual views or preferences; by contrast, fake news may well be created and disseminated by individuals – with or without a coherent political or ideological agenda – not least due to the new technological possibilities of online social media. (On this point, see also Dutilh Novaes & de Ridder 2021.)

In short, what gets called 'fake news' varies considerably with ideology and worldview, but as long as there are good reasons for thinking that the term 'fake news' meets a valid conceptual need, social epistemologists would be well-advised to push back against attempted takeovers – rather than surrendering – and develop analytically intuitive and explanatorily fruitful definitions and characterizations of their own.

5 Reacting to fake news

Fake news, this much seems clear, has become an important tool for influencing public debate – not necessarily by convincing the audience of the truth of any particular claim, but by stoking resentment, putting up smokescreens, and generating uncertainty. Estimates of the reach of individual fake news stories are notoriously difficult; according to an early investigation, the five leading fake news stories on Facebook during the three months preceding the 2016 U.S. presidential election (including a story by the bogus *Denver Guardian*, titled "FBI Agent Suspected in Hillary Email Leaks Found Dead in Apparent Murder-Suicide") were shared or liked by about three million users (Berghel 2017). Some fake news stories may achieve even wider circulation (especially if one's definition includes fabricated official stories, such as the purported intelligence findings alleging the deployment of weapons of mass destruction by Saddam Hussein in the run-up to the Iraq War in 2003), whereas others may fail to catch on.

By now, a sizeable, though by no means fully consistent, body of empirical findings regarding the spread and the efficacy of fake news exists. Some of the more robust results include the finding that false news stories – partly as the result of their content being perceived as, on average, more novel – spread "significantly farther, faster, deeper, and more broadly than the truth in all categories of information" (Vosoughi, Roy & Aral 2018: 1146), especially so for political news (as compared with news about natural disasters, urban legends, or financial information). Regarding online social media as an important medium for the dissemination of fake news, it has been found that the sharing of articles from fake news websites is not evenly distributed across the population, but instead is modulated by age effects and political affiliation. No doubt reflecting highly contingent aspects of the U.S. political situation, studies have found that the most politically conservative users were also the most active when it came to sharing fake news stories; at the same time, "older Americans were more likely to share articles from fake news domains" – a finding that was robust even with respect to educational attainment, party affiliation, ideological outlook, and degree of online activity (Guess, Nagler & Tucker 2019: 2).

Arguably, this wide circulation and differential susceptibility to fake news raises important questions about how best to react, both individually – when confronted with a claim that, for all we know, may or may not constitute fake news – and collectively, in order to minimize the circulation of fake news. Two standard types of proposals are (1) to focus on the individual responsibilities of consumers (thereby neglecting the systemic aspects of informational environments) and (2) to urge technological tweaks, especially in the way online information is presented, in an attempt to reduce the cognitive burden on the individual. The former is often associated with calls for better media literacy and with complaints about the decline of critical thinking in civic education, which has allegedly left young people "not only less informed than we might have expected", but also "less interested in applying what little they might have learned to their responsibilities of citizens" (Nichols 2017: 138). Such a view, however, is in tension with the finding that often it is older, not younger, consumers who uncritically share fake news; it also neglects the fact that better reasoning skills may be used in self-serving ways, and it underestimates, at the collective level, the role of so-called 'backfire effects', which occur when individuals, upon being criticized, cling to their beliefs more strongly. Regarding technological tweaks, such as automated fact-checking or labelling of dubious claims (e.g. on Twitter), while such measures may have some effect, there remains a risk of an 'arms race' between producers of fake news and the operators of the relevant platforms, given that any plausible algorithm for spotting fake news lends itself to being gamed and outsmarted.

Given that there seems to be no easy solution, perhaps we need to acknowledge that fake news has become part of our epistemic predicament in the highly complex sociotechnical environments we live in, and that we need to cultivate truth-conducive "epistemic routines" (Gelfert 2021) that help us navigate our informational environment, while at the same time pushing for responsible systems and reliable processes of news aggregation and dissemination.

Note

1 All quotes from actual sources, cited after (Gelfert 2018: 96).

References

Aikin, S. F., and Talisse, R. B. (2020) *Political Argument in a Polarized Age: Reason and Democratic Life*, Cambridge: Polity Press.

Berghel, H. (2017) "Lies, Damn Lies, and Fake News", *Computer*, 50 (2), 80–85.

Coady, D. (2019) "The Trouble with 'Fake News'", *Social Epistemology Review and Reply Collective*, 8 (10), 40–52.

Dentith, M. R. X. (2017) "The Problem of Fake News", *Public Reason*, 8 (1–2), 65–79.

Dutilh Novaes, C., and de Ridder, J. (2021) "Is Fake News Old News?", in S. Bernecker, A. K. Flowerree, and T. Grundmann (eds.) *The Epistemology of Fake News*, Oxford: Oxford University Press.

Fallis, D., and Mathiesen, K. (2019) "Fake News is Counterfeit News", *Inquiry*, online first at https://doi.org/10.1080/0020174X.2019.1688179, accessed 24 June 2020.

Feest, U. (2012) "Exploratory Experiments, Concept Formation, and Theory Construction in Psychology", in U. Feest, and F. Steinle (eds.) *Scientific Concepts and Investigative Practice*, Berlin: de Gruyter, 167–89.

Gelfert, A. (2018) "Fake News: A Definition", *Informal Logic*, 38 (2), 84–117.

Gelfert, A. (2021) "Fake News, False Beliefs, and the Fallible Art of Knowledge Maintenance", in S. Bernecker, A. K. Flowerree, and T. Grundmann (eds.) *The Epistemology of Fake News*, Oxford: Oxford University Press.

Grundmann, T. (2020) "Fake News: The Case for a Purely Consumer-Oriented Explication", *Inquiry*, online first, https://doi.org/10.1080/0020174X.2020.1813195.

Guess, A., Nagler, J., and Tucker, J. (2019) "Less Than You Think: Prevalence and Predictors of Fake News Dissemination on Facebook", *Science Advances*, 5 (1), 1–8.

Habgood-Coote, J. (2019) "Stop Talking about Fake News!", *Inquiry*, 62 (9–10), 1033–65.

Jaster, R., and Lanius, D. (2018) "What Is Fake News?", *Versus*, 127 (2), 207–24.

Klein, D. O., and Wueller, J. R. (2017) "Fake News: A Legal Perspective", *Journal of Internet Law*, 20 (10), 5–13.

Levi, L. (2018) "Real 'Fake News' and Fake 'Fake News'", *First Amendment Law Review*, 16 (Symposium issue), 232–327.

Levy, N. (2017) "The Bad News about Fake News", *Social Epistemology Review and Reply Collective*, 6 (8), 20–36.

Mukerji, N. (2018) "What Is Fake News?", *Ergo: An Open Access Journal of Philosophy*, 5, 923–46.

Nichols, T. (2017) *The Death of Expertise: The Campaign against Established Knowledge and Why It Matters*, New York: Oxford University Press.

Pepp, J., Michaelson, E., and Sterken, R. (2019) "Why We Should Keep Talking about Fake News", *Inquiry*, online first, https://doi.org/10.1080/0020174X.2019.1685231.

Rini, R. (2017) "Fake News and Partisan Epistemology", *Kennedy Institute of Ethics Journal*, 27, E43–E64.

Vosoughi, S., Roy, D., and Aral, S. (2018) "The Spread of True and False News Online", *Science*, 359 (6380), 1146–51.

16

THE COGNITIVE SCIENCE OF FAKE NEWS

Neil Levy and Robert M. Ross

Introduction

Fake news is, roughly, the set of reports of events of public interest ("news") that purport to be or which mimic reliable news sources but which intend to deceive or are indifferent to truth.[1] Fake news is very widely disseminated: for example, during the 2016 US presidential election, the most popular fake stories were shared more widely than the most popular genuine new stories (Vosoughi et al., 2018). While the extent of its consumption and its influence over behaviour is often exaggerated (Allen et al., 2020; Guess et al., 2020b, 2020c; Mercier, 2020), it is plausible that it is big enough to be decisive when matters are finely balanced (in close elections, for instance). Some people credit, or blame, fake news with swinging the Brexit referendum (Grice, 2017) and the 2016 election of Donald Trump (Gunther et al., 2018).

While there are a range of purely conceptual questions raised by fake news, fully understanding and addressing its rise, reach and influence requires grappling with a range of empirical findings. The cognitive science of fake news specifically is in its infancy, but there is a rich literature on related topics – on misinformation and its effects, conspiratorial ideation, and so on – on which to draw. The questions asked by cognitive scientists are often continuous with those raised by philosophers, and also provoke further philosophical reflection. In this chapter, we will survey and critically assess some of this rich literature. We note at the outset that our discussion is heavily skewed to the US context, because most of the available research concerns the United States. That is an important limitation of this discussion, since the United States may have features that entail that fake news has different effects in that context than elsewhere.

There are at least five questions concerning the spread and influence of fake news that might be addressed by, or with the help of, cognitive science: (1) why do people share fake news? (2) to what extent do they believe it? (3) on the assumption they do believe it, what explains their belief? (4) what influence does it have over their behaviour? (5) to the extent to which its influence is negative, either epistemically or behaviourally, how can we reduce these impacts? In the interest of space, we will concentrate on (2), (3) and (5); even so restricted, our discussion will necessarily be highly selective.

Do people believe fake news?

A surprisingly high number of people express agreement with some of the more widely disseminated fake news items. For instance, one survey found that approximately a third of Americans reported believing the "Birther" theory that Barack Obama was not born in the United States (Uscinski and Parent, 2014). However, while assertion is usually a very reliable guide to belief (and may be the most powerful cue to belief attribution; Rose et al., 2014), it is not infallible. There is evidence of a belief/behaviour mismatch on politically charged topics, which calls into question the sincerity of people's belief reports. McGrath (2017) found little evidence that political partisans changed their economic behaviour in line with their assertions about the effects of preferred and non-preferred candidates on the economy. However, other studies have found evidence that people do tend to behave in ways that conform to their professed beliefs. For instance, Lerman et al. (2017) found that Republicans do not merely say that "Obamacare" is undesirable; they also enrol in it at lower rates than those who express more favourable attitudes. Because these data are difficult to interpret and remain sparse, we will not say more about them here. Note, though, that our discussion of survey responses has direct relevance to claims about how we ought to interpret behavioural evidence. That is as it should be: assertion is, after all, behaviour.

Political attitudes and beliefs, including beliefs in misinformation, have primarily been probed through survey instruments. Surveys have long documented large partisan gaps in beliefs, with each side perceiving the world in a way that seems to conform to their normative views (Jerit and Barabas, 2012; note, however, that Roush and Sood, 2020, have recently provided evidence that partisan knowledge gaps might be much smaller than previously thought). Thus, Republicans and Democrats report diverging beliefs about factual claims (e.g. the unemployment rate). However, there is an alternative explanation of these reports: perhaps they are not sincere reports of beliefs at all, but more akin to partisan cheerleading (Bullock and Lenz, 2019). That is, rather than report their sincere beliefs, people may seek to *express* their allegiance to a party, a policy or a person. Someone might assert "Obama is a secret Muslim" not because they believe he is a Muslim, but rather to express their dislike of him. Since these responses have an expressive function, we will adopt the terminology used by other researchers (Berinsky, 2018; Bullock et al., 2015) and call this kind of behaviour *expressive responding.*

There is persuasive evidence that people engage in expressive responding (Hannon, 2021). The Trump administration notoriously claimed that the crowd at the incoming president's inauguration was the largest ever, claims that flew in the face of the photographic evidence that clearly showed that Obama's inauguration in 2009 was much larger. On the days immediately following the controversy, Schaffner and Luks (2018) presented participants with photos of the two events and asked which depicted a larger crowd, knowing that many participants would recognize them as photos of the Trump and Obama inaugurations. A very small proportion of non-voters and Clinton voters identified the photo of the Trump inauguration as depicting a larger crowd (3% and 2%, respectively). This contrasts with the response of Trump voters: 15% of them identified the photo of his inauguration as depicting a larger crowd. This strongly suggests that some individuals are willing to report a belief they do not hold in order to express support for their preferred party or candidate. Schaffner and Luks suggest that this figure may represent a lower bound for expressive responding: some Trump supporters were probably unaware of the controversy, and therefore did not see the task as presenting them with an opportunity for an expressive response.

Evidence from other studies, using different methodologies to attempt to estimate the prevalence of expressive responding, seems to indicate this study is an outlier in terms of the magnitude of the effect (perhaps because conditions are rarely so ideal for expressive responding). Prior et al. (2015) found that the possibility of small monetary rewards for correct responses halved partisan bias (from 12% to 6%). Bullock et al. (2015) report similar results and an apparent dose dependence of reduction: the larger the incentive, the bigger the reduction in bias; and a combination of treatments eliminated partisan differences altogether. In contrast, Berinsky (2018) found little or no evidence of expressive responding, despite offering an incentive (albeit one of a different type: a reduction in time spent on the survey), and Peterson and Iyengar (2020) found that a partisan gap about two thirds of the unincentivized gap persisted with financial incentives. Taken together, and despite some failures to narrow the partisan gap via the provision of incentives, the evidence strongly suggests that a substantial number of respondents express attitudes, rather than report beliefs, in surveys (see Bullock and Lenz, 2019 for a comprehensive review). It is important to note, however, that only Berinsky probed beliefs of the kind that tend to feature in fake news (e.g. 9/11 "truther" claims) so we should be wary of generalizing from evidence of expressive responding in other contexts to the contexts of fake news more specifically.

However, there are reasons to suspect that studies that utilize incentives to measure the prevalence of expressive responding underestimate their extent. Most obviously, people may misrepresent their true beliefs if they know they are controversial, in order to secure the monetary reward. In addition, incentives for accuracy might have perverse effects: someone who wants to express strong support for a politician or a party may do so by spurning the opportunity to receive monetary compensation for reporting their true belief. We might therefore worry that many partisan participants might be difficult to shift by modest monetary reward. Moreover, if participants count support for a person, policy or stance as a sacred value, they may reject the opportunity for financial reward for accuracy: sacred values are usually held to be incommensurable with and tainted by financial reward (Tetlock, 2003). Berinsky's study might fail to demonstrate expressive responding for one or both these reasons.

In addition, incentivization (and polling more generally) may have the effect of *producing* the very beliefs that are reported. As well as expressive responding, participants may use partisan heuristics (rules of thumb sensitive to cues of party affiliation or of identities and activities valued by or associated with their side of politics), biased sampling methods (e.g. searching memory – or the internet – for evidence that bears on a question, but in a way that is more sensitive to supporting than disconfirming evidence) or other motivated ways of drawing inferences to generate a response, in the absence of a prior belief and without being confident in the truth of the proposition they assert. While this isn't expressive responding – participants do not report a belief they do not hold, in order to express an attitude – nor is it the veridical report of a *pre-existing* belief (of course, tricky issues to do with dispositional beliefs arise at this point, but we think it is reasonable to restrict the latter to beliefs that are entailed by agents' representations, and thus to exclude beliefs like this, generated by inference from prompts).

Political scientists have long recognized that a substantial proportion of respondents to surveys on political issues construct their responses on the spot (Zaller and Feldman, 1992). Thus, surveys of public opinion play a role in producing the responses they aim to probe. The person who reports believing *that Obama is a secret Muslim* or *that Hilary Clinton gave uranium to Russia in exchange for donations* may not have believed these things prior to being asked. Rather, they may have engaged in biased memory search or biased inference procedures, or applied heuristics, to construct the belief on the spot (while this route to response is less likely to be employed when a claim is widely circulated – agents can be expected to have attitudes on many familiar fake news stories – their current attitude might reflect an earlier reliance on such routes to response). Some support for this view is provided by Bullock et al. (2015) who found that when a "don't know" response was incentivized (at a lower level than for correct responses), use of this option increased dramatically. Similarly, Clifford et al. (2020) found that offering participants realistic alternative options decreased endorsement of conspiratorial explanations markedly. While beliefs constructed for the purposes of response may sometimes persist, surveys that fail to discourage the construction of such beliefs over-report their prevalence in the population.[2]

Between expressive responding and overreporting as a consequence of belief construction, the extent to which people believe fake news is probably exaggerated by surveys. Nevertheless, there can be little doubt that substantial numbers of people do come to give sufficient credence to fake news for it to affect their behaviour. For instance, in 2017 a false story that the founder of Ethereum had died in a car accident caused the market value of the company to drop by $4 billion (Dunning, 2019). More disturbingly, a number of Sandy Hook "truthers" – conspiracy theorists who allege that the mass shooting was a false flag operation – have escalated their harassment of parents who lost children at the elementary school beyond online trolling to confronting and threatening them in person (Robles, 2016), and the survivors and relatives of survivors of other mass shootings have also been victims of this kind of activity (Raphelson, 2018). This pattern of behaviour strongly suggests some people come to be convinced of the veracity of some fake news.[3] Given that some people come to believe fake news, often in the face of apparent implausibility, and some of them go on to act on these beliefs in ways that are significant and sometimes even harmful to themselves or to loved ones, it is important to understand the mechanisms that explain their acceptance. We turn to this issue next.

Why do people believe fake news?

A natural hypothesis for why people believe fake news, especially when it is prima facie implausible, cites cognitive limitations or ignorance (or, of course, both). However, this deficit model for belief in the implausible or the irrational has come under challenge from a number of researchers, most influentially Dan Kahan. Kahan focuses specifically not on fake news, but on questions like climate change and evolution. These are topics on which there is a large partisan divide, but one side is at odds with the scientific consensus. They therefore provide an opportunity for probing the processes whereby people come to reject a view that is strongly supported by evidence. On these topics, Kahan (2015) find evidence that a deficit model apparently struggles to explain: while liberals who score higher on the Ordinary Science Intelligence scale (which measures both basic science literacy and thinking dispositions) are more likely to accept the science of climate change and the truth of evolution, conservatives who score higher are *less* likely to accept both than conservatives who score less well. Kahan argues that the Ordinary Science Intelligence scale reliably measures cognitive capacity: what matters is not just what capacities agents have, but also how they are deployed. He argues that our values – specifically, our sense of belonging to a particular culture – biases our cognition, such that we reject information sources when they conflict with the beliefs central to that identity (Kahan, 2016). Individuals with greater cognitive capacities also have a greater capacity to explain away inconvenient data. It is easy to see how the deployment of what Kahan terms *identity protective cognition* (Kahan, 2017) might explain acceptance of fake news (or rejection of genuine news).

Kahan's hypothesis appears to be supported by evidence from elsewhere in cognitive science. For instance, there's evidence that better education interacts with political orientation, such that (for example) it predicts higher levels of belief that Barack Obama is a secret Muslim among better educated Republicans (Lewandowsky et al., 2012) and that motivated cognition may enable those with greater capacity or knowledge more effectively to dismiss evidence they find uncongenial (Taber and Lodge, 2006; see Rust and Schwitzgebel, 2009; Schwitzgebel, 2009, for a similar hypothesis in the context of explaining the behaviour of professional philosophers). Recently, however, Kahan's hypothesis has faced a challenge from theorists who have offered a new version of something like a deficit hypothesis.

Pennycook and Rand (2019a) argue that if susceptibility to fake news were explained by motivated cognition, we ought to see a positive association between belief in politically congenial fake news headlines and cognitive capacities (measured using the Cognitive Reflection Test, CRT). But they found that higher CRT scores correlate with correctly rating fake news as less accurate and genuine news stories as more accurate, regardless of its fit with political leanings. In further work, the same group of researchers provide evidence that higher CRT scores are associated with updating of beliefs about factual political statements closer to Bayesian norms (Tappin et al., 2020a). The focus on belief *updating* is an important innovation because a shortcoming of other study designs is that they do not disentangle political identities from pre-treatment information exposure and issue-specific prior beliefs (Tappin et al., 2020b).

A potential worry for this rival to Kahan's view can be motivated by other work by the very same group of researchers. Their data on voters in the 2016 US presidential election shows an association not only between lower CRT scores and higher support for Trump, but also that lower CRT scores are correlated with lower levels of engagement with politics (Pennycook and Rand, 2019b). Given this association between lower levels of engagement and lower CRT scores, one possible explanation for a decreased capacity to identify fake news (assuming, that is, that those with lower CRT scores genuinely lack such a capacity) is that this subgroup lacked the background knowledge required for assessing the plausibility of the headlines presented (few were so obviously fake that those without the requisite background could easily dismiss them).

The relative influence of motivated reasoning versus bad reasoning and ignorance on susceptibility to fake news therefore remains an open question for the moment. While there is much more to be said regarding the mechanisms whereby people come to accept fake news, we suggest that the relevant perspectives might best be covered by considering them under the third heading we will discuss next.

How might belief in (and spread of) fake news be prevented or reduced?

As well as looking to cognitive science for explanation of the mechanisms that underlie acceptance of fake news, we might hope to mine cognitive science for strategies to inoculate media consumers against misinformation, or to correct beliefs (or perhaps to reduce reliance on its claims in decision-making).

Obvious candidate interventions for combating fake news are explicit corrections of information reported in fake news and warning labels attached to fake news indicating that the information is not true. There is a large literature examining corrections of misinformation. Meta-analyses of this literature show that corrections do have an effect, but beliefs often continue to be influenced by the misinformation (Chan et al., 2017; Walter et al., 2019; Walter and Tukachinsky, 2020). Given the frequency of belief perseverance, an important focus of research is the properties of corrections that are most effective. Some research suggests that more effective corrections do not simply inform the consumer that some information is incorrect, but also provide new information that plays the same role as the old (Levy, 2017). For example, one study found that people continue to rely on rebutted information when they have no alternative explanation of an event, but reliance is greatly reduced (though not eliminated) if an explanation is provided (Lewandowsky et al., 2012).

Recent studies have found that a corrective article (Porter et al., 2018) and a warning label (Pennycook et al., 2020a) can reduce belief in fake news. Nonetheless, concerns have been raised about the possibility that corrections and warnings might have negative consequences. At least three classes of negative outcomes have been discussed. First, corrections might elicit a "backfire effect", with people becoming more committed to a claim following presentation of strong evidence against it. For example, an influential study found that a correction of George W. Bush's false statement about there being weapons of mass destruction in Iraq before the American invasion increased belief in the false claim among American conservatives (Nyhan and Reifler, 2010). However, follow-up research failed to replicate the backfire effect (Clayton et al., 2019; Porter and Wood, 2019; Wood and Porter, 2019), and a broader reading of the literature suggests that if this phenomenon is real, it is not as common as was initially feared (Swire-Thompson et al., 2020). It should be noted, however, that Merkley (2020) has recently provided evidence of a backfire effect among those high in anti-intellectualism. A second concern about corrective messages is that they might create an "implied truth effect" where fake news headlines that fail to get tagged as inaccurate are considered validated and more accurate (Pennycook et al., 2020a). This could create significant challenges for fact checking because it isn't practical for professional fact checkers to check all fake news that is produced. Happily, this research also provides evidence for a solution. The authors also find that attaching verifications to a subset of true headlines eliminates, and might even reverse, the implied truth effect for untagged headlines. Third, invalid corrections might create a "tainted truth effect" whereby informative news that is wrongly labelled as inaccurate can result in a reduction in the credibility of informative news (Freeze et al., 2020). This could be exploited by bad actors by intentionally creating invalid corrections.

As discussed earlier, individuals high in analytic cognitive ability appear to be better at identifying fake news (Pennycook & Rand, 2019b). A hypothesis that follows naturally from this is that encouraging people to deliberate could reduce belief in fake news. A recent study provides evidence for this (Bago et al., 2020). Participants were presented with a series of partisan news headlines and were asked to make intuitive judgements about the accuracy of the headlines under time pressure and while completing a task designed to tax working memory. They were then given an opportunity to rethink their responses with no constraints, thereby permitting more deliberation and correction of intuitive mistakes. Participants believed fewer false headlines (but not true headlines) when making their final responses. Moreover, other studies from this research group provide evidence that bringing an accuracy motive to the front of people's minds (by asking them to rate the accuracy of a non-political headline) reduces intention to share fake news on social media (Pennycook et al., In press, 2020b) and actual sharing of misinformation on Twitter (Pennycook et al., In press). Together, these studies suggest that interventions that facilitate deliberation on social media platforms, such as bringing an accuracy motive to mind by periodically asking users if a randomly selected headline is accurate, could reduce the spread of fake news.

Another potential intervention for reducing belief in fake news is to equip people with skills to identify it. Lutzke et al. (2019) provide experimental evidence that asking oneself four questions can significantly reduce trusting, liking and intending to share of fake news: (1) *Do I recognize the news organization that posted the story?*; (2) *Does the information in the post seem believable?*; (3) *Is the post written in a style that I expect from a professional news organization?*; and (4) *Is the post politically motivated?* Another study found that digital media literacy intervention increased discernment between mainstream and fake news in both the United States and India (Guess et al., 2020a). However, other research failed to find that making publisher information visible had any influence on the perception of accuracy of unreliable sources or in reducing intention to share fake news (Dias et al., 2020).

Another approach uses "inoculation", on the hypothesis that psychological resistance against deceitful persuasion attempts can be conferred by exposing people to a weakened version of the misinformation. Inoculation theory has been extensively studied in the context of building resistance to misinformation in particular domains, such as climate science (Banas and Rains, 2010; Compton, 2013) and vaccines (Jolley and Douglas, 2017), but only recently has research begun to examine the effectiveness of "broad base" misinformation inoculation. A series of studies investigated this in the context of a recently developed fake news game (Basol et al., 2020; Roozenbeek and Linden, 2019). In this game, players take the role of a news editor whose goal is to build a media empire using fake news articles. In playing this game, participants are exposed to "weakened doses" of misinformation techniques with the aim that this will improve their ability to spot misinformation techniques and, thus, they will become "inoculated" against misinformation. These studies found a significant reduction in the perceived accuracy of fake news presented in the form of Twitter "tweets" irrespective of education, age, political ideology and cognitive style.

A further avenue worth exploration is utilization of the wisdom of crowds. A recent study found that crowdsourced judgements of news source quality by laypeople correlated strongly with the judgements of professional fact checkers (Pennycook and Rand, 2019c). If this result is reliable, the wisdom of crowds might be harnessed by algorithms on social media to identify reliable news and make it much more visible than less reliable news.

Summary

In the interests of space, the survey of work on the cognitive science of fake news has been brief and partial. It leaves us with many open questions. To that extent, however, it is an accurate reflection of the state of our knowledge here: many central questions remain for future research. To mention just two: (1) to what extent does analytic thinking (which appears to predict the capacity to distinguish fake news from real) reduce the propensity to *share* fake news? Intuitively, reduced acceptance would predict a reduced likelihood of sharing, but this remains controversial, with Pennycook and colleagues finding the expected relation (e.g. Pennycook et al., 2020b) but others failing to find an association (e.g. Osmundsen et al., 2020). (2) To what extent do these lab-based experiments capture real-world behaviour? There is much greater need for researchers in different disciplines and subdisciplines to take account of one another's work: too few take into account the prevalence of expressive responding and trolling, for example. We often decry the extent to which people are siloed into filter bubbles on the internet, but researchers may need to burst bubbles of their own.[4]

Notes

1 Note that cognitive scientists tend to define fake news more narrowly (the single most cited paper on the topic (Lazer et al., 2018) defines it as "fabricated information that mimics news media content in form but not in organizational process or intent" (1094). We follow philosophers like Mukerji (2018) in encompassing 'bullshit' information – produced by those indifferent to truth – as well as information produced with the intention to deceive.

2 In addition to the use of motivated inference and expressing responding, survey respondents may simply fail to respond sincerely for fun or to troll researchers (Lopez and Hillygus, 2018). Our own unpublished research indicates that this kind of response is surprisingly common.

3 We acknowledge that there are alternative explanations available. Public affirmations of belief, especially with high costs attached, provide an opportunity for an especially powerful expression of one's attitudes, along similar lines to the ways in which costs can enhance the strength of signals (Sosis, 2003) or increase credibility (Henrich, 2009). Arguably, the states that underlie such a signal could count as beliefs (Funkhouser, 2017), but this remains an open question. Since the states play many of the same functional roles as beliefs – in particular, generating behaviour of much the same kind as the belief would – we take them to raise many of the same questions and therefore suggest that we need not wait until their doxastic status has been settled to take them as an important target.

4 We are grateful to the editors of this volume and a reviewer for helpful comments. We acknowledge the generous support of the Australian Research Council (DP180102384).

References

Allen, J., Howland, B., Mobius, M., Rothschild, D., Watts, D.J., 2020. Evaluating the Fake News Problem at the Scale of the Information Ecosystem. *Science Advances* 6, eaay3539. https://doi.org/10.1126/sciadv.aay3539.

Bago, B., Rand, D.G., Pennycook, G., 2020. Fake News, Fast and Slow: Deliberation Reduces Belief in False (But Not True) News Headlines. *Journal of Experimental Psychology: General.* https://doi.org/10.1037/xge0000729.

Banas, J., Rains, S. 2010. A Meta-Analysis of Research on Inoculation Theory. *Communication Monographs* 77, 281–311.

Basol, M., Roozenbeek, J., van der Linden, S., 2020. Good News about Bad News: Gamified Inoculation Boosts Confidence and Cognitive Immunity against Fake News. *Journal of Cognition* 3, 2. https://doi.org/10.5334/joc.91.

Berinsky, A.J., 2018. Telling the Truth about Believing the Lies? Evidence for the Limited Prevalence of Expressive Survey Responding. *The Journal of Politics* 80, 211–24. https://doi.org/10.1086/694258.

Bullock, J.G., Gerber, A.S., Hill, S.J., Huber, G.A., 2015. Partisan Bias in Factual Beliefs about Politics. *Quarterly Journal of Political Science* 10, 519–78. https://doi.org/10.1561/100.00014074.

Bullock, J.G., Lenz, G., 2019. Partisan Bias in Surveys. *Annual Review of Political Science* 22, 325–42. https://doi.org/10.1146/annurev-polisci-051117-050904.

Chan, M.-P.S., Jones, C.R., Hall Jamieson, K., Albarracín, D., 2017. Debunking: A Meta-Analysis of the Psychological Efficacy of Messages Countering Misinformation. *Psychological Science* 28, 1531–46. https://doi.org/10.1177/0956797617714579.

Clayton, K., Blair, S., Busam, J.A., Forstner, S., Glance, J., Green, G., Kawata, A., Kovvuri, A., Martin, J., Morgan, E., Sandhu, M., Sang, R., Scholz-Bright, R., Welch, A.T., Wolff, A.G., Zhou, A., Nyhan, B., 2019. Real Solutions for Fake News? Measuring the Effectiveness of General Warnings and Fact-Check Tags in Reducing Belief in False Stories on Social Media. *Political Behavior.* https://doi.org/10.1007/s11109-019-09533-0.

Clifford, S., Kim, Y., Sullivan, B.W., 2020. An Improved Question Format for Measuring Conspiracy Beliefs. *Public Opinion Quarterly.* https://doi.org/10.1093/poq/nfz049.

Compton, J. 2013. Inoculation theory, In J.P. Dillard & L. Shen (eds). *The SAGE Handbook of Persuasion: Developments in Theory and Practice.* SAGE Publications, Los Angeles, pp. 220–236.

Dias, N., Pennycook, G., Rand, D.G., 2020. Emphasizing Publishers Does Not Effectively Reduce Susceptibility to Misinformation on Social Media. *Harvard Kennedy School Misinformation Review* 1. https://doi.org/10.37016/mr-2020-001.

Dunning, D., 2019. Gullible to Ourselves, in: Alcoff, L. & Potter, E. (eds.), *The Social Psychology of Gullibility: Conspiracy Theories, Fake News and Irrational Beliefs.* Routledge, Abingdon, pp. 217–33.

Freeze, M., Baumgartner, M., Bruno, P., Gunderson, J.R., Olin, J., Ross, M.Q., Szafran, J., 2020. Fake Claims of Fake News: Political Misinformation, Warnings, and the Tainted Truth Effect. *Political Behavior.* https://doi.org/10.1007/s11109-020-09597-3.

Funkhouser, E., 2017. Beliefs as Signals: A New Function for Belief. *Philosophical Psychology* 30, 809–31. https://doi.org/10.1080/09515089.2017.1291929.

Grice, 2017. Fake News Handed Brexiteers the Referendum – And Now They Have No Idea What They're Doing. *The Independent.*, January 18, 2017.

Guess, A.M., Lerner, M., Lyons, B., Montgomery, J.M., Nyhan, B., Reifler, J., Sircar, N., 2020a. A Digital Media Literacy Intervention Increases Discernment between Mainstream and False News in the United States and India. *Proceedings of the National Academy of Sciences of the United States of America* 117, 15536–45. https://doi.org/10.1073/pnas.1920498117.

Guess, A.M., Lockett, D., Lyons, B., Montgomery, J.M., Nyhan, B., Reifler, J., 2020b. "Fake News" May Have Limited Effects Beyond Increasing Beliefs in False Claims. *Harvard Kennedy School Misinformation Review* 1. https://doi.org/10.37016/mr-2020-004.

Guess, A.M., Nyhan, B., Reifler, J., 2020c. Exposure to Untrustworthy Websites in the 2016 US Election. *Nature Human Behaviour* 4, 472–80. https://doi.org/10.1038/s41562-020-0833-x.

Gunther, R., Nisbet, E.C., Beck, P.A. 2018. Trump may owe his 2016 victory to 'fake news,' new study suggests. The Conversation February 15. https://theconversation.com/trump-may-owe-his-2016-victory-to-fake-news-new-study-suggests-91538.

Hannon, M., 2019. Political Disagreement or Partisan Cheerleading? The Role of Expressive Discourse in Politics.

Henrich, J., 2009. The Evolution of Costly Displays, Cooperation and Religion: Credibility Enhancing Displays and Their Implications for Cultural Evolution. *Evolution and Human Behavior* 30, 244–60. https://doi.org/10.1016/j.evolhumbehav.2009.03.005.

Jerit, J., Barabas, J., 2012. Partisan Perceptual Bias and the Information Environment. *The Journal of Politics* 74, 672–84. https://doi.org/10.1017/S0022381612000187.

Jolley, D., Douglas, K.M., 2017. Prevention Is Better than Cure: Addressing Anti-Vaccine Conspiracy Theories. *Journal of Applied Social Psychology* 47, 459–69.

Kahan, D.M., 2015. Climate-Science Communication and the Measurement Problem. *Political Psychology* 36, 1–43.

Kahan, D.M., 2016. The Politically Motivated Reasoning Paradigm, Part 1: What Politically Motivated Reasoning Is and How to Measure It – Kahan – Major Reference Works – Wiley Online Library, in: RA Scott, SM Kosslyn, (eds.), https://doi.org/10.1002/9781118900772.etrds0417 *Emerging Trends in Social and Behavioral Sciences*, New York: Wiley, pp. 1–16. https://doi.org/10.1002/9781118900772.etrds0417.

Kahan, D.M., 2017. Misconceptions, Misinformation, and the Logic of Identity-Protective Cognition (SSRN Scholarly Paper No. ID 2973067). Social Science Research Network, Rochester, NY.

Lazer, D.M.J., Baum, M.A., Benkler, Y., Berinsky, A.J., Greenhill, K.M., Menczer, F., Metzger, M.J., Nyhan, B., Pennycook, G., Rothschild, D., Schudson, M., Sloman, S.A., Sunstein, C.R., Thorson, E.A., Watts, D.J., Zittrain, J.L., 2018. The Science of Fake News. *Science* 359, 1094–96. https://doi.org/10.1126/science.aao2998.

Lerman, A.E., Sadin, M.L., Trachtman, S., 2017. Policy Uptake as Political Behavior: Evidence from the Affordable Care Act. *American Political Science Review* 111, 755–70. https://doi.org/10.1017/S0003055417000272.

Levy, N., 2017. The Bad News about Fake News. *Social Epistemology Review and Reply Collective* 6, 20–36.

Lewandowsky, S., Ecker, U.K.H., Seifer, C.M., Schwarz, N., Cook, J., 2012. Misinformation and Its Correction: Continued Influence and Successful Debiasing. *Psychological Science in the Public Interest* 13, 106–31.

Lopez, J., Hillygus, D.S., 2018. Why So Serious?: Survey Trolls and Misinformation (SSRN Scholarly Paper No. ID 3131087). Social Science Research Network, Rochester, NY. https://doi.org/10.2139/ssrn.3131087.

Lutzke, L., Drummond, C., Slovic, P., Árvai, J., 2019. Priming Critical Thinking: Simple Interventions Limit the Influence of Fake News about Climate Change on Facebook. *Global Environmental Change* 58, 101964. https://doi.org/10.1016/j.gloenvcha.2019.101964.

McGrath, M.C., 2017. Economic Behavior and the Partisan Perceptual Screen. *Quarterly Journal of Political Science* 11, 363–83. https://doi.org/10.1561/100.00015100.

Mercier, H., 2020. *Not Born Yesterday: The Science of Who We Trust and What We Believe.* Princeton University Press, Princeton, NJ.

Merkley, E., 2020. Anti-Intellectualism, Populism, and Motivated Resistance to Expert Consensus. *Public Opinion Quarterly.* https://doi.org/10.1093/poq/nfz053.

Mukerji, N., 2018. What Is Fake News? *Ergo: An Open Access Journal of Philosophy* 5, 923–46. https://doi.org/10.3998/ergo.12405314.0005.035.

Nyhan, B., Reifler, J., 2010. When Corrections Fail: The Persistence of Political Misperceptions. *Political Behavior* 32, 303–30. https://doi.org/10.1007/s11109-010-9112-2.

Osmundsen, M., Bor, A., Vahlstrup, P.B., Bechmann, A., Petersen, M.B., 2020. Partisan Polarization Is the Primary Psychological Motivation Behind "Fake News" Sharing on Twitter (Preprint). PsyArXiv. https://doi.org/10.31234/osf.io/v45bk.

Pennycook, G., Bear, A., Collins, E., 2020a. The Implied Truth Effect: Attaching Warnings to a Subset of Fake News Headlines Increases Perceived Accuracy of Headlines without Warnings. *Management Science*. https://doi.org/10.1287/mnsc.2019.3478.

Pennycook, G., Epstein, Z., Mosleh, M., Arechar, A. A., Eckles, D., & Rand, D. G. In press. Shifting attention to accuracy can reduce misinformation online. *Nature*. https://doi.org/10.31234/osf.io/3n9u8/.

Pennycook, G., McPhetres, J., Zhang, Y., Rand, D., 2020b. Fighting COVID-19 Misinformation on Social Media: Experimental Evidence for a Scalable Accuracy Nudge Intervention. *Psychological Science* 31, 770–80. https://doi.org/10.31234/osf.io/uhbk9.

Pennycook, G., Rand, D.G., 2019a. Lazy, Not Biased: Susceptibility to Partisan Fake News Is Better Explained by Lack of Reasoning than by Motivated Reasoning. *Cognition, The Cognitive Science of Political Thought* 188, 39–50. https://doi.org/10.1016/j.cognition.2018.06.011.

Pennycook, G., Rand, D.G., 2019b. Cognitive Reflection and the 2016 U.S. Presidential Election. *Personality and Social Psychology Bulletin* 45, 224–39. https://doi.org/10.1177/0146167218783192.

Pennycook, G., Rand, D.G., 2019c. Fighting Misinformation on Social Media Using Crowdsourced Judgments of News Source Quality. *Proceedings of the National Academy of Sciences of the United States of America* 116, 2521–26. https://doi.org/10.1073/pnas.1806781116.

Peterson, E., Iyengar, S., 2020. Partisan Gaps in Political Information and Information-Seeking Behavior: Motivated Reasoning or Cheerleading? *American Journal of Political Science* n/a. https://doi.org/10.1111/ajps.12535.

Porter, E., Wood, T.J., 2019. *False Alarm: The Truth about Political Mistruths in the Trump Era*. Cambridge: Cambridge University Press, S.l.

Porter, E., Wood, T., Kirby, D., 2018. Sex Trafficking, Russian Infiltration, Birth Certificates, and Pedophilia: A Survey Experiment Correcting Fake News. *Journal of Experimental Political Science* 5, 1–6. https://doi.org/10.1017/XPS.2017.32.

Prior, M., Sood, G., Khanna, K., 2015. You Cannot Be Serious: The Impact of Accuracy Incentives on Partisan Bias in Reports of Economic Perceptions. *Quarterly Journal of Political Science* 10, 489–518. https://doi.org/10.1561/100.00014127.

Raphelson, S., 2018. Survivors of Mass Shootings Face Renewed Trauma from Conspiracy Theorists [WWW Document]. NPR.org. https://www.npr.org/2018/03/20/595213740/survivors-of-mass-shootings-face-renewed-trauma-from-conspiracy-theorists (accessed 7.3.19).

Robles, F., 2016. Florida Woman Is Charged with Threatening Sandy Hook Parent. *The New York Times*, December 7.

Roozenbeek, J., Linden, S. van der, 2019. Fake News Game Confers Psychological Resistance against Online Misinformation. Palgrave Communications 5, 1–10. https://doi.org/10.1057/s41599-019-0279-9.

Rose, D., Buckwalter, W., Turri, J., 2014. When Words Speak Louder than Actions: Delusion, Belief, and the Power of Assertion. *Australasian Journal of Philosophy* 1–18. https://doi.org/10.1080/00048402.2014.909859.

Roush, C.E., Sood, G., 2020. A Gap in Our Understanding? Reconsidering the Evidence for Partisan Knowledge Gaps. Presented at the Annual Meeting of the Southern Political Science Association, p. 73.

Rust, J., Schwitzgebel, E., 2009. Ethicists' and Nonethicists' Responsiveness to Student E-mails: Relationships among Expressed Normative Attitude, Self-Described Behavior, and Empirically Observed Behavior. *Philosophical Psychology* 22, 711–25.

Schaffner, B.F., Luks, S., 2018. Misinformation or Expressive Responding? What an Inauguration Crowd Can Tell Us about the Source of Political Misinformation in Surveys. *Political Opinion Quarterly* 82, 135–47.

Schwitzgebel, E., 2009. Do Ethicists Steal More Books? *Philosophical Psychology* 22, 711–25. https://doi.org/10.1080/09515080903409952.

Sosis, R., 2003. Why Aren't We All Hutterites? *Human Nature* 14, 91–127. https://doi.org/10.1007/s12110-003-1000-6.

Swire-Thompson, B., DeGutis, J., Lazer, D., 2020. Searching for the Backfire Effect: Measurement and Design Considerations (Preprint). PsyArXiv. https://doi.org/10.31234/osf.io/ba2kc.

Taber, C.S., Lodge, M., 2006. Motivated Skepticism in the Evaluation of Political Beliefs. *American Journal of Political Science* 50, 755–69. https://doi.org/10.1111/j.1540-5907.2006.00214.x.

Tappin, B.M., Pennycook, G., Rand, D.G., 2020a. Bayesian or Biased? Analytic Thinking and Political Belief Updating. *Cognition* 204, 104375. https://doi.org/10.1016/j.cognition.2020.104375.

Tappin, B.M., Pennycook, G., Rand, D.G., 2020b. Thinking Clearly about Causal Inferences of Politically Motivated Reasoning: Why Paradigmatic Study Designs Often Undermine Causal Inference. *Current Opinion in Behavioral Sciences* 34, 81–87. https://doi.org/10.1016/j.cobeha.2020.01.003.

Tetlock, P.E., 2003. Thinking the Unthinkable: Sacred Values and Taboo Cognitions. *Trends in Cognitive Sciences* 7, 320–24. https://doi.org/10.1016/S1364-6613(03)00135-9.

Uscinski, J.E., Parent, J.M., 2014. *American Conspiracy Theories.* New York: Oxford University Press.

Vosoughi, S., Roy, D., Aral, S., 2018. The Spread of True and False News Online. *Science* 359, 1146–51. https://doi.org/10.1126/science.aap9559.

Walter, N., Cohen, J., Holbert, R.L., Morag, Y., 2019. Fact-Checking: A Meta-Analysis of What Works and for Whom. *Political Communication.* https://doi.org/10.1080/10584609.2019.1668894.

Walter, N., Tukachinsky, R., 2020. A Meta-Analytic Examination of the Continued Influence of Misinformation in the Face of Correction: How Powerful Is It, Why Does It Happen, and How to Stop It? https://doi.org/10.1177/0093650219854600.

Wood, T., Porter, E., 2019. The Elusive Backfire Effect: Mass Attitudes' Steadfast Factual Adherence. *Political Behavior* 41, 135–63. https://doi.org/10.1007/s11109-018-9443-y.

Zaller, J., Feldman, S., 1992. A Simple Theory of the Survey Response: Answering Questions versus Revealing Preferences. *American Journal of Political Science* 36, 579. https://doi.org/10.2307/2111583.

17

FILTER BUBBLES, ECHO CHAMBERS, ONLINE COMMUNITIES

Hanna Kiri Gunn

1 Introduction

In Neal Stephenson's fictional novel, *Diamond Age* (1995), the protagonist Nell acquires a prototype of what we might today recognise as a highly sophisticated e-reader with a voice-assistant. This e-reader, the "Young Lady's Illustrated Primer", uses artificial intelligence to serve as Nell's personal teacher.

What is key to the Primer is how it is designed to respond *to Nell*. The Primer has a theory of Nell – her needs, her real-world situation, her abilities – and it tailors its lessons for her. The Primer is a *highly personalised* artificially intelligent device. For many readers – myself included – the Primer was a utopian vision of the bespoke digital tutors of the future. The appearance of new media and technologies in the early 2000s all pointed to the near-term reality of devices like Primers.

The real-life experience of personalised digital media, though, is so far from Stephenson's vision that it is hard to imagine we will ever get there. Nell's time with the Primer develops her intellectually, emotionally, and physically. Our "bespoke" media experience, by contrast, is more likely to turn us in on ourselves rather than guide us to live well in our societies. Personalised media is making us more like Narcissus: our consumption is driven by personal choices and automated algorithms that reflect what we already want to hear, see, and consume, and we are captivated.

Central to our understanding of the problems with the personalisation of digital media are filter bubbles and echo chambers. These phenomena are used interchangeably by some, but in distinct ways by others. I take the position that filter bubbles and echo chambers are distinct phenomena, but ones that raise similar epistemic worries.

I begin with a general discussion of filter bubbles and echo chambers, and I introduce the concept of "selective exposure" as central to both phenomena. There is minimal uniformity across uses of the terms "filter bubble" and "echo chamber". Consequently, I divide the later discussion into two more precise topics: homophily and polarisation. I conclude with some future-looking comments about responsibility and the epistemic risks posed by digital personalisation.

1.1 What are filter bubbles and echo chambers?

We now know with great certainty what writers of all stripes have long bemoaned: left unchecked, we gravitate towards information that reinforces what we already believe and what we want to hear. Terry Pratchett explains this disposition in his novel, *The Truth*, in the words of Lord Vetinari:

> Be careful. People like to be told what they already know … They like to know that, say, a dog will bite a man. That is what dogs do. They don't want to know that man bites a dog, because the world is not supposed to happen like that. In short, what people think they want is news, but what they really crave is olds…Not news but olds, telling people that what they think they already know is true. (Pratchett, 2000)

In principle, there's nothing wrong with wanting to have one's beliefs reaffirmed. What is problematic, though, is when we're excluding new information because it justifiably challenges the beliefs we already have. The phrases "filter bubbles" and "echo chambers" are both metaphors designed to express ways that we surround ourselves with – or find ourselves surrounded with – "olds" and not "news". The olds that we're after might be particular beliefs, or a more general ideological picture or world view.

1.2 Filter bubbles

Our collective awareness of the risks of filter bubbles increased with the publication of Eli Pariser's (2011) book, *The Filter Bubble*. According to Pariser, "filter bubble" describes digital media curation gone wrong because algorithms that are designed to present us with content we are likely to be interested in are causing us to be enclosed in "a unique universe of information for each of us". The concern is that as we are increasingly informationally isolated, either at the level of groups or individuals, we lose important common ground that is essential for a well-functioning society.

The filter bubble idea is related to several other slightly older terms used to describe ways that our online experience is increasingly personalised, including both "cyberbalkanization" and "splinternet" (Bozdag and van den Hoven, 2015). Preferred metaphors aside, these terms all express a collection of epistemic, social, moral, and political concerns about what might happen if digital personalisation causes us to be isolated from those with whom we don't share much common ground.

Prior to Pariser's book on filter bubbles, Cass Sunstein had published *Republic.com* in 2001, followed by *Republic.com 2.0* (2009) and *#Republic* (2017). In each of these three publications, Sunstein explores how the Internet is making it easier to close ourselves off from one another, and to informationally isolate ourselves into a "Daily Me" newsfeed of content that reflects our own values, beliefs, and desires. This alienates us from those other members of our political community who do not share our worldview.

While both Pariser and Sunstein agree on a range of the political and epistemic risks from filter bubbles (and echo chambers), they differ in their identification of the cause. For Pariser, the issue is how the *algorithms* behind social media platforms and search engines filter our online experience. For Sunstein, the concern is how these same platforms better enable *us* to choose what content we want to see. A full picture of the epistemic risks posed by new media will surely have to appeal to both our personal choices and automated personalisation algorithms.

Crucial to both Pariser and Sunstein's different diagnoses about our apparently fracturing public sphere is a concept in social science known as "selective exposure". Selective exposure describes our preference for "olds", or, put more precisely, the fact that "given the chance, individuals will choose to consume media that reinforces their previous beliefs" (Cardenal et al., 2019a). Selective exposure is arguably made worse by new technologies including personalised search engines and social media. This claim, however, is ambiguous about exactly how new technologies and selective exposure interact.

First, it might be that, given a widespread and natural tendency to consume content we want to see, new media makes it far easier to engage in more radical forms of selective exposure. Cardenal et al. (2019a) refer to this as "voluntary exposure" to reflect that it is ultimately our personal choices that are the cause of filter bubbles (466). Second, it might be that the new technologies that utilise personalisation algorithms are exacerbating the voluntary exposure that we are otherwise engaging in – what Cardenal et al. call "involuntary exposure" by algorithmic filtering.

As Cardenal et al. (2019a) note, it is common to find the filter bubble hypothesis in the literature framed in terms of this second claim that involuntary exposure amounts to being in a filter bubble (see, e.g., Dubois and Blank, 2018). Exactly how much of our new media experience is the product (or cause) of selective exposure of either kind is a contested issue.[1]

C. Thi Nguyen has a slightly modified account of filter bubbles that is widely gaining traction in philosophy. For Nguyen, a filter bubble is a special case of an epistemic bubble. An epistemic bubble is "a social epistemic structure which has inadequate coverage through a process of exclusion by omission" (Nguyen, 2018, 3). To some degree, epistemic bubbles are just our epistemic reality – we simply can't attend to all of the relevant information out there.

The unintentional nature of omission is important, as Nguyen points out, because the lack of exposure to other relevant information can easily be corrected by simply "popping" one's epistemic bubble.

This ameliorative action, though, can only be taken by those who know that they are in an epistemic bubble. Boaz Miller and Isaac Record (2013) have more fully developed the epistemic problems that lie in "secret Internet technologies" like those described by Pariser. Miller and Record argue that a lack of awareness or understanding of digital personalisation undermines our ability to get fully justified beliefs online. Miller and Record's piece is a useful starting place for reconsidering our epistemic theories of concepts like justification and knowledge in the context of new media.

1.3 Echo chambers

Echo chambers are plausibly similar to filter bubbles in both their causes and their epistemic consequences. However, the strength of these similarities, unsurprisingly, depends on one's chosen characterisation of both types of structures. It is not uncommon – particularly in popular media – to find the two terms used interchangeably for the same underlying phenomenon. In many cases, this is the siloeing of ourselves into epistemic bubbles by voluntary exposure.

What makes echo chambers distinct, according to Nguyen (2018), is that membership in an echo chamber undermines one's epistemic trust in either some or all non-group testifiers. Echo chambers are "a social epistemic structure in which other relevant voices have been actively discredited".[2] One, therefore, can't simply "pop" an echo chamber by diversifying one's sources. Nguyen's fairly specific definition of echo chambers is not widely shared, particularly not in the social science research that models social information networks. I will use "exclusionary-type echo chamber" to refer to the specific definition provided by Nguyen and just "echo chamber" elsewhere with appropriate caveats.

Echo chambers are commonly identified as groups of homophilous ("like-minded" or "similar") individuals, where members have mostly interactions with other members, and make choices about what information to attend to that amounts to varieties of voluntary exposure. It is also common for "echo chamber" to refer specifically to politically homophilous groups, for example "Democrats", "Liberals", or "Conservatives".

Another commonality across uses of the echo chamber metaphor in discussions of digital personalisation is the *amplifying* nature of what is said inside the echo chamber. Choi et al. (2020), for example, examined how "rumour echo chambers" (defined by the properties of voluntary exposure and political homophily) amplify rumours by causing them to propagate more widely than rumours spread by non-members. Another relevant idea and metaphor in the neighbourhood is that of "information cascades", Sunstein's (2017) discussion of cyber-cascades is a useful introduction to this phenomenon.

1.4 Pre-existing concerns about epistemic segregation and identity

It is worth priming ourselves with some general comments about why echo chambers and filter bubbles are problematic. One epistemic response is simply that we are not infallible, and neither are the like-minded individuals that we will be inclined to surround ourselves with. So, selective exposure makes it likely that we may miss out on knowledge.

A fuller response isn't easily separated from both social epistemic concerns and political epistemic concerns. Nor are the epistemic risks easily separated from identity facts about Internet users – something that Anglo-analytic epistemology has tended to shy away from. Relevant identity facts may include, e.g., race or ethnicity, gender identity, or political affiliation. At the dystopian end of the spectrum of the consequences of filter bubbles and echo chambers is the worry that we will end up "living in different political universes—something like science fiction's parallel worlds" (Sunstein, 2017, Chapter 1). A possibility on the table, then, is that we risk taking a path that leads us to a society divided by political communities of "alternative facts".[3]

The idea that our identities are structurally significant for our epistemic lives has been a core theme in epistemologies of ignorance and feminist epistemology. As we've just seen, our identities – our values, beliefs, desires – determine the trajectory of selective exposure.

Charles Mills paper, "White Ignorance" (2007), might not strike one as relevant for understanding filter bubbles and echo chambers. However, the project is one of understanding how group identity, in this case racial groups, leads to patterns of false belief and a lack of true belief within particular groups, i.e., the white American community. Mills' characterisation of the social-structure of white ignorance is similar to characterisations of media echo chambers. For epistemologists, Mills' critiques of theorising about ideal cognition are especially relevant for future normative work on digital personalisation.

Lorraine Code (1993) similarly criticises mainstream analytic epistemology for erasing epistemically significant properties from knowers, i.e., their gender. Both Mills and Code argue that we must understand that our everyday epistemic actions are differently enabled and constrained by our (perceived) identities. Recent work by Kristie Dotson (2011) and Jose Medina (2012) develops the importance of identity for shaping our testimonial communities, including normative arguments about the failures to live up to our duties to one another as knowers. These works lay important foundations for theorising about what we ought to be aiming for in reforming online communities to avoid the more dystopian possibilities that could result from filter bubbles and echo chambers.

Concerns about the segregation of epistemic life on the basis of group identity have long been with us. Moreover, philosophers working on epistemic ignorance and related subjects recognise and highlight the interaction between epistemic and political agency. There is certainly room for exploring how these literatures overlap with major themes in research on filter bubbles and echo chambers with respect to topics like polarisation, homophily, and trust networks.

Recall that it's not necessarily bad that we engage in selective exposure, and the sheer volume of content online means that we are going to have to be selective in some way about what we look at. Aiming for truth is one goal we can optimise for, but the social-historical context that creates the groups that we are likely to align with are not created by such a goal. It is likely that the ignorance that prevails in some communities will not be overcome by actions as simple as popping filter bubbles, so understanding ignorance in context is crucial.

2 Bespoke or biased?

The idea of personalised media has widespread appeal. The epistemic (and moral and political) concerns arise when the resulting diet of information has some other problematic property. Exacerbating or causing cognitive biases is one such problematic property. A second is the tailoring of the very communities that we have online conversations with – not many of us are designing our social media friends bubbles with lofty aims of truth and wisdom in mind.

Confirmation bias is one of the most studied clusters of cognitive biases and generally describes the "seeking or interpreting of evidence in ways that are partial to existing beliefs, expectations, or a hypothesis in hand" (Nickerson, 1998). If the experience of being in filter bubbles or echo chambers leads to higher levels of confirmation bias, then that would be epistemically problematic because it undermines the goal of rational cognitive action.

Similarly, if confirmation bias is playing a role in causing filter bubbles or echo chambers, e.g., by voluntary exposure, then we have a situation where people are choosing to attend to and exclude information for irrational reasons. One study supporting this concern is Geschke et al. (2018), who found via agent-based modelling that confirmation bias analogues in their models were sufficient for generating echo chambers.

Homophily is a widespread theme in research and discussions of filter bubbles and echo chambers, and describes the tendency of individuals to form groups with like-minded others. The causal arrows between homophily and digital personalisation run in both directions in discussions of these phenomena: a filter bubble is caused by homophily, or homophily is a cause of filter bubbles.

Cyberbalkanization refers to a concern that, in some loose similarity with the real-world division of the Balkan Peninsula (and other regions), the Internet will in practice be divided into a number of small and politically (or ideologically) aligned groups. Bozdag and van den Hoven (2015) provide a detailed discussion of how cyberbalkanization and filter bubbles threaten different democratic models.

The filter bubble and echo chamber hypotheses are often presented as claims about the basic nature of the online epistemic ecosystem. While it seems right to be concerned about the consequences of homophilous groups online, it is a jump to assume that all online discourse takes place in siloes. Furthermore, we don't have good reasons yet to believe that cyberbalkanization is a necessary end point for online communities. We do have some good reasons, though, for being worried that particular features of our online experience interact with our tendency to form like-minded groups in epistemically problematic ways.

Yosh Halberstam and Brian Knight (2016) investigated both the effect of homophily and group size on the spread of political information on Twitter. They note that "the degree of homophily in the political network is similar to that documented in other social networks" (74). This is important context given the frequently made observation that filter bubbles and echo chambers are not wholly "new". Halberstam and Knight's results suggest that homophily in social networks does cause restricted access to political information.

Barberá et al. (2015) found that conversations about national events that are not political issues were better characterised as "national conversations" – conversations between people of a diverse range of political and ideological leanings. They found that political topics of conversation typically took place within echo chambers, which they define as being characterised by "selective exposure, ideological segregation, and political polarization" (2015, 1532).

Results from both Barberá et al. (2015) and Williams et al. (2015) suggest that the politicisation of an issue changes the social epistemic structure of the online community. Barberá et al. (2015) observed shifts from national conversations to echo chambers. Williams et al. (2015) found that Twitter conversations about climate change were likely to occur in both echo chambers (like-minded groups with similarly positive or negative attitudes), and "open forums" (mixed user groups with mixed attitudes, similar to national conversations).[4]

Flaxman et al. (2016) looked at ideological segregation in US online news consumption. They found the people who consume the most news consume a broad range of mostly reliable sources. Thus, new media are in some ways increasing the diversity of news consumption. However, they also found that reading news through primarily social networks and search engines is associated with an increase in ideological segregation not reflected in consumption via online news outlets.

Cardenal et al. (2019b) found no evidence of online partisan media echo chambers with their analysis of the Spanish media system, but they found that voluntary exposure increases with individual interest in news consumption. So, we may need to look more closely at what kinds of online platforms lead to undesirable social epistemic structures, and that negatively affect belief-formation.

While the subject is still contested, there is a growing body of research into whether filter bubbles and echo chambers are more concentrated among certain political groups. The majority of the present research into partisan differences focuses on the United States and their associated two-party partisan system, so cross-cultural analysis will be an interesting development for this work in the future. One such study has already been mentioned in the work of Jamieson and Capella (2008) who argue that the US conservative media establishment is an exclusionary-type echo chamber.

Andrei Boutyline and Robb Willer (2017) examines homophily in online networks. They found that among Twitter users, individuals with extreme political beliefs across political affiliations, but also conservative individuals in particular, were more homophilous than other groups. Interestingly, Barberá et al. (2015) found that liberal Twitter users were more likely to engage in cross-ideological re-tweeting than their conservative counterparts.

Benkler et al. (2018) look directly at partisan differences in news consumption. If "the Internet" is the problem, and not anything peculiar to particular online communities, then we should expect to see "a symmetric pattern of segmentation, assuming that users on the left and the right operate under similar social psychological dynamics and algorithms decisions" (2018, 291). In other words, if "the internet" is constituted by filter bubbles and echo chambers, then we should see the same patterns across the partisan spectrum.

From their analysis of readership trends, around 70% of the US population "exists in a mixed-media ecosystem that is not fragmented and is more or less normally distributed in its attention around a core of traditional professional media outlets" (ibid.). The remaining 30%, however, is primarily consuming right-wing media that exhibits problematic filter bubble and exclusionary-type echo chamber dynamics. Importantly, these asymmetric tendencies on the left and right pre-date the Internet (2018, 341–51).

3 Polarisation of beliefs, politics, or communities?

Polarisation is another key phenomenon in this area of research and is often used as a measurable proxy for filter bubbles and echo chambers. It is also another concept that deserves precisification, as there are a range of distinct polarisation processes under study, and many are plausibly relevant for understanding filter bubbles and echo chambers – which might be either the cause or the consequence of polarisation. We should note, too, that across disciplines there are varied uses of "polarisation". To a greater degree than usual, then, it is important to closely evaluate the detailed description of the process under discussion or analysis than just the label. I begin with some remarks on the epistemic concerns underlying polarisation, then discuss some examples of polarisation research.

The primary epistemic concern about polarisation concerns its underlying cause. In almost all cases this is that what is driving the poles apart is not truth, rational argument, or evidence, but some irrational or non-rational processes. Note that we do not yet know what these poles are and so we also do not know what the distance between them signifies. These poles could be the beliefs of a particular individual, the beliefs of some sports team, the population of an entire country in 2020, or even the same population measured 50 years apart. It is still a fair enough description, though, to say that the core epistemic concerns behind polarisation and filter bubbles and echo chambers is a concern about rationality.

A useful guide for disambiguation of "polarisation" (and the associated formal measures) can be found in Bramson et al. (2016) who distinguish nine kinds. Bramson et al. take the position that "polarisation" is a conceptual cluster denoting a broad range of properties and processes. As a property, polarisation research might look at the distribution of some belief across a population. As a process, polarisation might refer to the change of an individual's or community's beliefs over time given some event.

Two forms of polarisation include "spread" and "dispersion". Spread provides a fairly simplistic model of the difference in attitudes within a population. If we take their sample question, "What percentage of the federal budget should be spent on education?", the spread of our sample of results will be the distance between our two most extreme answers (2016, 83).

As a measure of polarisation, spread will illuminate discussions of filter bubbles and echo chambers for some fairly simple measures of understanding, e.g., changes in one population over time. If we ran a study surveying people's opinions on the education budget twice, we might see that the most extreme attitudes have grown much further apart.

What it won't tell us is how *many* people endorse the extreme positions at the "poles". Dispersion would be a more informative measure of polarisation in that case (Bramson et al., 2016, 84). Where spread is concerned only with tracking the distance between the most extreme attitudes in our sample, dispersion is a measure which accounts for the distribution of attitudes of the whole population.

It is not uncommon to hear that filter bubbles or echo chambers are making us "more polarised" about politics, as is shown by polling data. This quick survey gives us good grounds to wonder what that means! We might also be interested, for example, in the number of different attitudes that are present in our society, i.e., "coverage" (ibid., 84); or even the overlap (or lack thereof) between the attitudes of particular groups in our society about some important topic like climate change, i.e., "distinctness" (ibid., 89).

A philosophical carving of the polarisation terrain is provided in *Overdoing Democracy* by Robert B. Talisse (2019). Echo chambers and filter bubbles factor into Talisse's discussion as enablers of polarisation. This is in line with other research investigating how the diversity of opinions available in a group is correlated with the degree of polarisation in that group over time (see, e.g., Flache and Macy, 2011; Turner and Smaldino, 2018).

Talisse presents three kinds of "political polarization" and distinguishes these from "belief polarisation". "Belief polarisation" here refers to processes that shift one's existing beliefs to more extreme versions of them as a consequence of interacting with primarily like-minded individuals (2019, 97). This is commonly referred to as "group polarisation". This is a central subject in discussions of filter bubbles, where the concern is that filter bubbles are causing our beliefs to become more extreme.

There is important ambiguity in the idea of "extreme" belief as mentioned earlier, and Talisse discusses this in some detail (2019, 106). A belief may be extreme because of its contents, because of how it was formed, because of its evidentiary basis, because of its relationship to the mainstream beliefs of some relevant group, or a range of other factors. Talisse has us consider if extremeness refers to the commitment one has to one's existing beliefs, a change in belief from a previous belief to a more extreme version of that belief, or whether it refers to the degree of confidence in a newly adopted belief.

Alfano et al. (2020) tested the widely held belief that online recommender systems that prompt users to watch or read further content can cause radicalisation. Radicalisation describes a process of belief polarisation for an individual, namely, one whose beliefs become more extreme in content as a consequence of watching the recommended videos. Alfano et al. found that the recommender system promotes increasingly extreme content, supporting the idea that it scaffolds belief polarisation.[5]

Political polarisation can be subdivided into at least three measurable kinds: platform polarisation, partisan polarisation, and affective polarisation (Talisse, 2019, 99). Platform polarisation describes the ideological distance between political parties. Partisan polarisation describes the ideological "purity" within a group, where we can understand this as the degree of homophily between members. For example, the current Democratic Party in the United States exhibits high levels of partisan polarisation with the split between moderate or centrist democratic members and progressive members.

Finally, affective polarisation describes the (typically, negative) emotional attitudes of one partisan group towards other groups, e.g., levels of antipathy and animosity. A recent Pew poll, for example, finds that US partisan attitudes towards the opposing party are more negative than they have been in a quarter of a century (Pew Research Center, 2016).

Thus, when we come across claims that filter bubbles or echo chambers are "polarising" us we should ask for further clarification. The metaphor at work in polarisation provides the image of two poles being drawn further and further apart. The first part of understanding a polarisation claim, then, is to understand what the poles are and what the nature of the distance between them is a measurement of.

4 Future directions: epistemic responsibility

Insofar as it is a personal choice to use any particular online platform or technology, we might think that it is up to each individual to decide to expose themselves to the risks that it brings. However, this overlooks the opaqueness of many of these technologies and removes all accountability from companies or developers. Part of the complication is that there is a mixture of personal choices (e.g., voluntary exposure) alongside that choices of developers who create personalised digital media (e.g., involuntary exposure). The ethical exploration of such issues will be helped with the existing work in computer ethics, information ethics, and more generally bioethics.

A second sense of "epistemic responsibility" that's also important in this discussion has to do with broader questions about what we owe to one another as members of epistemic communities. If membership in an epistemic community generates responsibilities to other members, then we may think there is action to be taken to reduce epistemic risks even though the causal claims about accountability and responsibility are not clear cut. A full list of the epistemic risks we face from filter bubbles or echo chambers might be very long, I wager that it will at least include being caused to have false beliefs, hermeneutical lacunae and failures to acquire true beliefs as a consequence of things like homophily, an undermining of one's reasonable trust in the testimony of others, and the development vices like close-mindedness and arrogance.

Lorraine Code's (1987) *Epistemic Responsibility* is one of the few book length treatments of these issues. Code's vision of an epistemically responsible community builds up a theory of intellectual virtue, and connects this with the ethics of belief. There is certainly a public sentiment that we are responsible for forming our beliefs in epistemically rational ways, and that new media is challenging our ability to meet this demand. Whether a philosophical analysis of the situation will affirm this sentiment remains to be seen, though we have precedence for it in the literature on the ethics of belief.

Discussions of filter bubbles and echo chambers are complex, and much nuance can be found in exploring these phenomena in detail. Our present understanding of how new media and technological personalisation affects epistemic and political life is still incomplete. While we continue to develop our descriptive understanding, philosophers can make significant parallel progress on the normative dimensions of these phenomena. In particular, I have suggested that we attend to how existing work on identity and ignorance may help us understand and respond to epistemic segregation online. Further, I have proposed that understanding the many faces of responsibility in this area is critical for shaping online epistemic communities in line with our social epistemic goals and values.

Notes

1 Cardenal et al. (2019a) have a fairly thorough discussion about research on the prevalence of selective exposure. They find that personalised search engines, i.e., Google, can reduce selective exposure, and that some social media websites, i.e., Facebook, have no direct effect on selective exposure. Gentzkow and Shapiro (2011) report that online news consumption is both more segregated than offline news consumption and less segregated than our face-to-face interactions on a daily basis.

2 This particular proposal for defining echo chambers by Nguyen is a development of work by Kathleen Hall Jamieson and Frank Capella about American right-wing media in their *Echo Chamber: Rush Limbaugh and the Conservative Media Establishment (2008)*. Jamieson and Capella's thesis is that certain aspects of the conservative media establishment are in essence echo chambers that intentionally discredit other media sources.

3 In 2017, former Counsellor to the President Kellyanne Conway claimed that former White House Press Secretary, Sean Spicer, was appealing to "alternative facts" in an attempt to justify Spicer's false claims about the crowd size at the presidential inauguration. Conway's comments were widely criticised with explicit connections being drawn to George Orwell's concept of "doublethink" in his book, *1984.*

4 See also Jasny et al. (2015) for a detailed exploration of echo chambers in the climate change debate in the United States.
5 In previous work, Alfano et al. (2018) coined the term "technological seduction" to describe how algorithms can lead people to consume content they otherwise would not have consumed.

Bibliography

Alfano, M.; Carter, J. A. & Cheong, M. (2018). 'Technological Seduction and Self-Radicalization', *Journal of the American Philosophical Association*, 3, pp. 298–322.
Alfano, M.; Fard, A. E.; Carter, J. A.; Clutton, P. & Klein, C. (2020). 'Technologically Scaffolded Atypical Cognition: The Case of YouTube's Recommender System', *Synthese*, pp. 1–24. https://doi.org/10.1007/s11229-020-02724-x.
Barberá, P.; Jost, J. T.; Nagler, J.; Tucker, J. A. & Bonneau, R. (2015). 'Tweeting from Left to Right', *Psychological Science*, 26, pp. 1531–42.
Benkler, Y.; Faris, R. & Roberts, H. (2018). *Network Propaganda: Manipulation, Disinformation, and Radicalization in American Politics*. Oxford: Oxford University Press.
Boutyline, A. & Willer, R. (2016). 'The Social Structure of Political Echo Chambers: Variation in Ideological Homophily in Online Networks', *Political Psychology*, 38, pp. 551–69.
Bozdag, E. & van den Hoven, J. (2015). 'Breaking the Filter Bubble: Democracy and Design', *Ethics and Information Technology*, 17, pp. 249–65.
Bramson, A.; Grim, P.; Singer, D. J.; Fisher, S.; Berger, W.; Sack, G. & Flocken, C. (2016). 'Disambiguation of Social Polarization Concepts and Measures', *The Journal of Mathematical Sociology*, 40, pp. 80–111.
Cardenal, A. S.; Aguilar-Paredes, C.; Galais, C. & Pérez-Montoro, M. (2019a). 'Digital Technologies and Selective Exposure: How Choice and Filter Bubbles Shape News Media Exposure', *The International Journal of Press/Politics*, 24, pp. 465–86.
Cardenal, A. S.; Aguilar-Paredes, C.; Cristancho, C. & Majó-Vázquez, S. (2019b). 'Echo-Chambers in Online News Consumption: Evidence from Survey and Navigation Data in Spain', *European Journal of Communication*, 34, pp. 360–76.
Choi, D.; Chun, S.; Oh, H.; Han, J. & Kwon, T. (2020). 'Rumor Propagation is Amplified by Echo Chambers in Social Media', *Scientific Reports*, 10, p. 310. https://doi.org/10.1038/s41598-019-57272-3
Code, L. (1987). *Epistemic Responsibility*. Hanover, NH: University Press of New England.
Code, L. (1993). 'Taking Subjectivity into Account', in Alcoff, L. & Potter, E. (eds.), *Feminist Epistemologies*. New York: Routledge, pp. 15–48.
Dotson, K. (2011). 'Tracking Epistemic Violence, Tracking Practices of Silencing', *Hypatia*, 26(2), pp. 236–57.
Dubois, E. & Blank, G. (2018). 'The Echo Chamber Is Overstated: The Moderating Effect of Political Interest and Diverse Media', *Information, Communication & Society*, 21, pp. 729–45.
Flache, A. & Macy, M. W. (2011). 'Small Worlds and Cultural Polarization', *The Journal of Mathematical Sociology*, 35(1–3), pp. 146–76.
Flaxman, S.; Goel, S. & Rao, J. M. (2016). 'Filter Bubbles, Echo Chambers, and Online News Consumption', *Public Opinion Quarterly*, 80, pp. 298–320.
Gentzkow, M. & Shapiro, J. M. (2011). 'Ideological Segregation Online and Offline', *The Quarterly Journal of Economics*, 126, pp. 1799–839.
Geschke, D.; Lorenz, J. & Holtz, P. (2018). 'The Triple-Filter Bubble: Using Agent-Based Modelling to Test a Meta-theoretical Framework for the Emergence of Filter Bubbles and Echo Chambers', *British Journal of Social Psychology*, 58, pp. 129–49.
Halberstam, Y. & Knight, B. (2016). 'Homophily, Group Size, and the Diffusion of Political Information in Social Networks: Evidence from Twitter', *Journal of Public Economics*, 143, pp. 73–88.
Jamieson, K. H. & Capella, J. N. (2008). *Echo Chamber: Rush Limbaugh and the Conservative Media Establishment*. New York: Oxford University Press.
Jasny, L.; Waggle, J. & Fisher, D. R. (2015). 'An Empirical Examination of Echo Chambers in US Climate Policy Networks', *Nature Climate Change*, 5, pp. 782–86.
Kidd, I. J. (2019). 'Epistemic Corruption and Education', *Episteme*, 16(2), pp. 220–35.
Medina, J. (2012). *The Epistemology of Resistance*. New York: Oxford University Press.
Miller, B. & Record, I. (2013). 'Justified Belief in a Digital Age: On the Epistemic Implications of Secret Internet Technologies', *Episteme*, 10, pp. 117–34.

Mills, C. (2007). 'White Ignorance', in Sullivan, S. & Tuana, N. (eds.), *Race and Epistemologies of Ignorance*. Albany, NY: SUNY, pp. 13–38.

Nickerson, R. S. (1998). 'Confirmation Bias: A Ubiquitous Phenomenon in Many Guises'. *Review of General Psychology*, 2(2), pp. 175–220.

Nguyen, C. T. (2018). 'Echo Chambers and Epistemic Bubbles', *Episteme*, 7, pp. 141–61.

Pariser, E. (2011). *The Filter Bubble: How the New Personalized Web Is Changing What We Read and How We Think*. New York: Penguin Press.

Pew Research Center (2016). 'Partisanship and Political Animosity in 2016'. Accessed 23/12/2020: https://www.pewresearch.org/politics/2016/06/22/partisanship-and-political-animosity-in-2016/.

Pratchett, T. (2000). *The Truth*. New York: Doubleday.

Stephenson, N. (1995). *The Diamond Age, Or, Young Lady's Illustrated Primer*. New York: Bantam Books.

Sunstein, C. (2001). *Republic.com*. Princeton, NJ: Princeton University Press.

Sunstein, C. (2007). *Republic.com 2.0*. Princeton, NJ: Princeton University Press.

Sunstein, C. R. (2017). *#Republic: Divided Democracy in the Age of Social Media*. Princeton, NJ: Princeton University Press.

Talisse, R. B. (2019). *Overdoing Democracy: Why We Must Put Politics in Its Place*. New York: Oxford University Press.

Turner, M. A. & Smaldino, P. E. (2018). 'Paths to Polarization: How Extreme Views, Miscommunication, and Random Chance Drive Opinion Dynamics', *Complexity*, pp. 1–17. https://doi.org/10.1155/2018/2740959.

Vallor, S. (2016). *Technology and the Virtues: A Philosophical Guide to a Future Worth Wanting*. New York: Oxford University Press.

Williams, H. T.; McMurray, J. R.; Kurz, T. & Lambert, F. H. (2015). 'Network Analysis Reveals Open Forums and Echo Chambers in Social Media Discussions of Climate Change', *Global Environmental Change*, 32, pp. 126–38.

18

MODELING HOW FALSE BELIEFS SPREAD

Cailin O'Connor and James Owen Weatherall

Introduction

Effective political decision-making, like other decision-making, requires decision-makers to have accurate beliefs about the domain in which they are acting. In democratic societies, this often means that accurate beliefs must be held by a community, or at least a significant portion of a community, of voters. Voters are tasked with scrutinizing candidates and possible policy proposals and, considering their own experiences, interests, goals, knowledge, and values, with deciding which of various ballot measures is most likely to bring about their desired outcomes.

For this process to make sense, voters need to have access to reliable information about what the current state of affairs is like – for instance, what problems need to be solved – and what the likely outcomes of policies will be. And yet, observation of contemporary political environments reveals widespread disagreement and polarization, not only about political values, but also about matters of fact, on topics ranging from the status of anthropogenic climate change, to the relative sizes of the crowds at Trump and Obama's inaugurations, to whether unemployment and the U.S. national debt increased or decreased under various U.S. presidential administrations. Irrespective of one's own beliefs or political affiliations, these disagreements reveal that false beliefs about matters of fact must be rampant, since after all, both sides cannot be correct on these matters.

Widespread false belief is often explained by appeal to individual epistemic factors, such as personal cognitive and epistemic biases, ignorance, and media illiteracy. But these individual factors can be at most only part of the story. The information needed to form good beliefs is difficult to come by, and generally requires a broad range of experiences and domain-specific knowledge that no individual can hope to achieve alone. In virtually all cases, individuals cannot gather and evaluate all, or even most, of the evidence and information that they need to make the sorts of decisions that democracy implicitly demands. Instead, they rely on others. Most of what we know, or believe, we have learned from other people.

Over the past four decades, observations of this sort, i.e. most of our beliefs come from other people, have motivated the development of the field of social epistemology (see Goldman and O'Connor, 2019, for more details). Social epistemology seeks to understand how social factors do and should influence belief. Insights gleaned in this field are of special importance for political epistemology, both because political decision-making is often distributed across many members of a community and because, in democratic societies, voters must make decisions about matters on which they have no personal experience, which may then affect others' lives more significantly than their own.

More recently, philosophers have begun to use formal methods, including mathematical models and computer simulations based in game theory, decision theory, and network science, to explore various aspects of social epistemology. A topic of particular focus has been the (formal) social epistemology of *false belief* (O'Connor and Weatherall, 2019): that is, how do social factors contribute to the persistence and spread of false beliefs within a community, even in cases where evidence of their falsehood is available? Formal models are a particularly useful way of exploring this question because they allow one to step away from disputed and politically fraught questions concerning actual matters of fact, and ask how even ideal agents, in a context where there is no ambiguity regarding what the truth is, may nonetheless come to believe falsehoods.

This chapter will review the recent literature in formal social epistemology related to false belief. We will begin by introducing some further background on social epistemology. We will then introduce some basic ideas from the formal modeling literature, explaining how researchers use models to address the questions at hand and discussing various results. We then move on to what these models tell us about how politically or economically motivated actors shape public belief by exploiting social factors.

Social epistemology

Traditional philosophical approaches to epistemology were largely individualistic in focus. But in the late 1980s, the field of social epistemology emerged, with a core mission to investigate social aspects of knowledge. A central tenet of this field is that belief and knowledge are deeply shaped by our social contexts and connections, and that to understand doxastic states in humans we need to attend to these social considerations (Goldman and O'Connor, 2019).

The key debates in social epistemology have been largely normative, in that they consider how beliefs or knowledge should be adopted in social contexts. For instance, the "problem of testimony" concerns what beliefs an agent should form in light of testimony from others, and whether these beliefs are justified. (See, for instance, Coady, 1992; Fricker, 1994.) The peer disagreement literature considers how individuals should change beliefs in light of disagreement (Christensen, 2007), and the judgment aggregation literature concerns how a group of agents should combine judgments (List and Petit, 2011). The "two experts, one novice" problem asks what an uninformed individual should do in the face of expert disagreement (Goldman, 2001). Other debates, such as that over collective agents, are less normative, but ask questions such as: what is it for a *group* to hold a belief, as opposed to an individual (Gilbert, 1989)?

Relatively less explored in this area are more empirically focused questions about how, in fact, beliefs spread between individuals. Why, for instance, do individuals actually make the judgment to trust some testimony, but not others? How do they decide what to believe when experts disagree? How do groups, in fact, aggregate their judgments when making decisions? These sorts of questions have been widely addressed in the social sciences, and especially in psychology and behavioral economics. It will be beyond the purview of this chapter to survey this literature, though it has been deeply influential in shaping the work we will discuss in the rest of the chapter.

As noted, one off-shoot from social epistemology is the subfield sometimes called formal social epistemology. This subfield uses modeling methods and formal paradigms to address social aspects related to knowledge and belief. Much of this work addresses more descriptive/ empirical questions such as: how does information flow in social networks? And, how do aspects of social learning influence this spread? In addition, it often seeks to make normative recommendations about the organization of epistemic communities by appeal to our empirical understanding of these communities, such as: how can we organize groups so as to best preserve accurate belief, given what we know about human social learning?

Much of the work in this subfield has been done by philosophers of science, who start with questions related to the spread of knowledge and theories in science. Given the interdisciplinary nature of the field, it is unsurprising that there is a great deal of overlap with work in the social sciences on belief and sociality. For the purposes of this chapter, we will curtail our focus to one corner of this literature. In particular, we will look at some of the work using networks to consider the spread of true and false beliefs.[1]

Modeling the spread of false beliefs

One key insight into human knowledge is that most people derive most of their beliefs from others in their community. We all learn some things on our own – for instance that one's child reacts badly to grapefruit, or that the local squirrel likes to steal birdseed. But we learn a tremendous amount via social channels. There are different ways this happens. First, we learn from the testimony of others. I might tell you that a particular caterpillar is poisonous and if you trust my testimony you will adopt (and maybe pass on) this belief. Second, we share evidence with others. For instance, I might pass on a graph of a model charting the spread of a virus under different interventions. Given this socially spread evidence, your beliefs may change.

There are several approaches to modeling belief transmission. In some models, one has a collection of "agents" – mathematical representations of idealized inquirers – all of whom may interact with others to exchange information (e.g. Hegselman and Krause, 2002). In other cases, the agents are arranged in a network, so that each agent can share information only with certain others, representing social connections. A *network* in this context consists in a collection of *nodes*, associated with the models' agents. These nodes are connected by *edges* which represent social ties across which information might pass. (Singer et al., 2020 in this volume give a more in-depth introduction to epistemic networks.)

Two dominant network approaches to epistemology approximately track the two sorts of scenarios described in the first paragraph of this section. On one of these approaches, network models treat beliefs/ideas as virus-like. They pass from person to person directly, as an infection might. This best corresponds to a scenario where a belief spreads via testimony. The relevant modeling paradigm is sometimes referred to as the *diffusion* or *contagion approach*. (There are a number of variations and subtleties here, which we largely ignore.) The second approach models agents who both gather and share evidence with those in their social networks. This is sometimes called the *network epistemology approach* and corresponds to a scenario where beliefs spread socially, but the spread depends on the transmission of evidence rather than just testimony.[2]

The contagion/diffusion approach has proved a useful paradigm for modeling many aspects of belief spread (Rogers, 2010). It is particularly well-tuned for things like rumors (or "memes"): units of belief that are accepted and shared relatively non-reflexively, rather than subject to reasoning. We will not spend much time on this literature here, but will mention some findings to give the reader a sense of what it can do. A number of authors, such as Jackson and Rogers (2007), look at how network structure influences the diffusion of ideas.

Golub and Jackson (2012), for example, consider how homophily – disproportionate connectivity with in-group members – could slow information spread. (They use a variation on the diffusion idea, where agents adopt beliefs that average those of their neighbors.) Some use this paradigm to consider the formation of epistemic networks. Barrett et al. (2019), for instance, consider what happens when epistemically focused agents choose to listen to good inquirers in a diffusion-type network. Still others consider variants on learning rules. Granovetter (1978), for instance, presents an influential diffusion model where individuals only pick up new beliefs when a threshold percentage of neighbors hold them.

In this chapter we focus more on the second type of model, where agents share evidence. This is particularly germane in thinking about the spread of scientific beliefs, which are often supported by data. An influential version of this sort of model was introduced by economists Bala and Goyal (1998). Kevin Zollman (2007, 2010) imported it to philosophy of science to study theory change in scientific communities.

How do these models work? They involve two elements: a network and a decision problem, called a *multi-armed bandit problem*. This sort of problem is analogous to choosing between slot machine (or "bandit") arms that pay off at different rates. It is assumed that the agents involved are unsure about which choice (or "arm") is the best one. They make this decision by actually testing their choices and seeing what happens. Over time their theories about the success of the arms change as they gather evidence.

The social epistemology aspect of this model involves the sharing of this data through the network. Over subsequent rounds, agents gather data and share it with their neighbors, always updating their beliefs about the arms in light of their own results and the results shared with them by their neighbors. Many versions of the model involve what we might call "myopic Bayesians". The agents are myopic because they tend to choose whichever arm they think best. They are Bayesians because they have credences about the arms, and use Bayes' rule to update these credences in light of evidence. In other words, they display a sort of bounded rationality.

In these models, the social sharing of evidence means that individuals tend to converge with respect to belief. If I favor a poorer action, I do not personally gather data about better ones. But I may receive this data from my neighbors, and it will eventually be enough to guide me towards better actions. Then the evidence generated by my behavior may, in turn, convince my (other) neighbors to try a better action.

This sort of process means that in baseline versions of this model, communities always end up sharing beliefs. Consider the simple case where agents choose between two actions, A and B. These might represent doctors administering two different treatments for a given ailment. The doctors' choices are guided by credences about which treatment succeeds more often. Suppose B has a higher probability of success than A.[3] A typical model will start with agents who have random credences about whether B is better than A. In successive rounds, they try their preferred action, record the frequency with which that action succeeds (where those successes occur with some fixed probability, unknown to the agents), and share those results, always updating beliefs in light of that evidence and the evidence shared with them by their neighbors. Sometimes the community will end up with all agents having high credence that B is, in fact, better. In other cases (though less often) the community ends up preferring A.

Why might they settle on the worse action – in this case the treatment that works less often? This can result from strings of misleading data. Real evidence is often probabilistic, just like the evidence in the model. A medication that is generally successful may not work for everyone, whereas one that is less successful may still work sometimes. Likewise, action B may pay off less frequently than action A in a particular set of trials. This might cause all the agents in the community to turn to action A. If this happens, because all agents stop performing action B, they fail to learn more about it and remain in a suboptimal belief state.

What does this model tell us about social epistemology? First, it makes clear how evidence sharing can get a community on the same page, and how it can be beneficial. Without social influence, all individuals develop beliefs separately. Those who start with poor beliefs are never even exposed to evidence that might change them. This means that the actors in the network model tend to do better together than they do alone. But the model also illuminates why failures can happen. Group influence can lead an entire community to pre-emptively settle on a poor theory (even though individually some of them might have gotten things right).

In the rest of this section, we will describe some results derived from these models in the discipline of formal social epistemology. These results look at various features of the model, and at how those features influence, on average, the success of communities. They sometimes provide guidance into how real communities can fail (or succeed) in spreading belief.

Zollman (2007, 2010) considers the effect of connectivity on community success. In particular, he runs simulations of the models just described and compares those where actors are linked to relatively many vs. relatively few neighbors. In general, for such models, one might suppose that the more connections the better. Each neighbor shares only real data which, in general, tends to push one towards true beliefs. Paradoxically, Zollman finds that, in fact, less connected networks do better. This *Zollman effect* happens because tightly connected networks share data widely, meaning that a string of misleading evidence can convince everyone of the wrong belief. Less connected groups tend to preserve pockets of accurate belief, which can then lead the rest of the community to a better theory. Rosenstock et al. (2017) show that this effect only occurs for certain parameter values of the model, corresponding to cases where inquiry is difficult. In other words, when a community actually struggles to find truth, too much communication can be harmful.

Mayo-Wilson et al. (2011) use this model to defend a thesis central to the discipline of social epistemology, which is that the rationality of individuals and the rationality of communities can come apart. This *Independence Thesis* holds that sometimes irrational individuals can constitute effective communities of learners, while rational individuals fail to form a successful group. For example, if theory A is the most promising in a community, it may make sense for every individual to test it. But the community will do better if labor is divided and individuals test many diverse possibilities and then share their knowledge. (See also Kitcher, 1990.) Alternatively, irrationally stubborn actors can make a group more successful, by focusing on many different plausible theories and sharing knowledge about them.

O'Connor and Weatherall (2018) add to the base model a tendency of human learners that has been widely documented by psychologists. They suppose that the individuals place greater trust in data shared by those with similar beliefs. As noted, the base model always tends to consensus. But once this aspect of social trust is introduced, polarization or the emergence of stable, opposing beliefs becomes common. In particular, feedback loops emerge where individuals with different beliefs do not fully trust each other's evidence, and form increasingly distant beliefs until they no longer influence one other. Previous models have found similar feedback loops can lead to polarization (e.g. Hegselmann and Krause, 2002; Olsson, 2013), but, perhaps surprisingly, O'Connor and Weatherall show how this can happen even in the face of evidence gathering and otherwise rational belief updating. (For more on polarization models, including relevant variants, see Singer et al., 2020, from this volume.)

In a follow-up paper, Weatherall and O'Connor (2020b) study how the same trust dynamics work when they are applied over multiple domains of belief. In this variation on the model, agents who agree on one topic place more trust in one another's evidence concerning other topics, even if there is no intrinsic relationship between the topics. They find that agents can form "epistemic factions", which are subcommunities with highly correlated beliefs, where those beliefs are polarized over the community as a whole. Remarkably, this occurs endogenously in the model, with no coordination. It suggests that some cases of correlated political polarization over multiple matters of fact, a phenomenon often attributed to shared values or ideology among members of the factions (e.g. by Lakoff, 2010), can arise without any such common cause. This can perhaps explain how, for instance, during the COVID-19 pandemic, beliefs about whether the antiviral hydroxychloroquine was an effective treatment for COVID-19 – a matter with high stakes for the belief-holders and with no clear ideological basis – became polarized in the United States along existing political lines.

Weatherall and O'Connor (2020a) look at another typical social behavior – conformity bias – and see how it influences these models. Agents who conform are more likely to engage in the behavior favored by their neighbors, even if it is not the one they would usually prefer. As Weatherall and O'Connor show, this addition to the model significantly hurts the knowledge-producing capacity of the community. Conforming individuals with accurate beliefs fail to spread useful data to their peers. And due to conformity, social networks with cliques can end up with polarization as well. Likewise Mohseni and Williams (2019) find that conformity bias in a network of Bayesian updaters hurts their ability to settle on accurate beliefs. In particular, they find that highly connected individuals who constitute hubs in the network cause problems because many others try to conform with them, while they are strongly influenced by their connections.

As we have seen, these models have been used to inform a number of questions: What is the optimal communication structure? Do rational individuals necessarily make rational communities? How do social biases impede the spread of good beliefs in an epistemic network? These investigations, as noted, have a descriptive character. They seek to illuminate the workings of real communities (or at least to direct research towards plausible effects in real communities). Like more traditional work in social epistemology, though, they also answer normative questions, but at the community level. How do we design better epistemic communities?

Propaganda in epistemic communities

Many widespread false beliefs appear to emerge and spread endogenously – that is, without any kind of intervention by actors who wish to influence public belief. For instance, during the late nineteenth century, there was a widespread belief in the northeastern United States that the so-called "tomato worm" was highly venomous, and that it could kill someone merely by "spitting" its venom onto their skin. Stories about the dangers of the worm, which was actually the (harmless) larva of the hawkmoth, spread in newspapers, and some deaths were attributed to it. This belief apparently originated in error, but then propagated independently for years afterward (Smith, 2001).

Such beliefs are often, though not always, harmless. (As an example of a harmful one, during the COVID-19 epidemic in Iran, viral rumors spread that drinking pure alcohol could cure COVID, leading to hundreds of deaths.) But many of the most politically salient examples of widely held false beliefs appear to have a different character. In these cases, there are often powerful politically and economically motivated actors who have a vested interest in the public holding certain beliefs (or failing to come to hold certain beliefs).

For instance, although today there is broad scientific consensus, generally shared by the public, that tobacco products cause cancer, this has not always been the case. In fact, as historians of science Naomi Oreskes and Eric Conway (2010) describe, when evidence began to come to the public's attention in the early 1950s that tobacco use may have severe adverse health effects, the tobacco industry responded with a number of interventions designed to combat public uptake of this evidence. (See also Brandt, 2007, and Michaels, 2008, for further material on this case and several others.)

There is considerable reason to think that these efforts succeeded. For instance, cigarette sales briefly dipped (for the first time in decades) following the publication of a widely read *Reader's Digest* article, "Cancer by the Carton", in 1952. They rebounded, however, following a massive public relations push by industry-supported groups and continued to grow for decades, even as the tobacco firms themselves established (internally) that the hypothesized link between tobacco and cancer was real. Moreover, efforts to regulate tobacco sales, including advertising and sales to minors, stalled for decades.

In this case, industry agents succeeded in propagating the false belief that cigarette smoke is not harmful, and, equally importantly, that the scientific record on the harms of tobacco was not conclusive. Their attempts directly impeded democratic functioning inasmuch as political bodies failed to appropriately protect public health from the dangers of tobacco as a result. Oreskes and Conway (2010) argue that these same methods were used to promote falsehood and manufacture uncertainty regarding a large number of politically salient issues, often with significant public health impacts, including the causes and harms of acid rain; the effects of chlorofluorocarbons on ozone; and the status of anthropogenic climate change.

Several philosophers have used the formal methods discussed in the previous section to better understand the various strategies employed by the tobacco industry and other such groups to manipulate public belief and influence political outcomes.[4] In the first work along these lines, Holman and Bruner (2015) consider a modification of the basic model described above in which one agent – whom they call an "intransigently biased agent", but whom we will call a "propagandist", for consistency in what follows – shares evidence drawn from a sample biased towards action A, i.e. the worse of the two actions. The idea here is that the propagandist wishes to convince other agents in the network that A is, in fact, better; to do so, they share spurious evidence that supports their preferred hypothesis, but which does not reflect the true success frequencies of the two arms. This agent is epistemically "impure" in the sense that they perform their preferred action, and report biased results, irrespective of what other evidence they have seen.

Holman and Bruner show that with this simple modification, the model will no longer converge to a true consensus in general, because the biased evidence generated by the propagandist will prevent the rest of the community from reaching consensus on whether the better arm is in fact better. They also consider agents in the network who attempt to identify propagandists by comparing the distributions of results shared by other agents with their own beliefs. They find that this strategy for rooting out propagandists can succeed, though it will be more effective in some cases than others – for instance, when the number of "draws" per round of the model is low (corresponding roughly to a situation in which members of a scientific community tend to perform experiments with low statistical power).

Weatherall et al. (2018) consider a different modification to the basic model described above. Whereas in the Holman-Bruner model, the propagandist seeks to influence their "epistemic peers", i.e. other agents who are gathering and sharing evidence, Weatherall et al. consider what happens when a propagandist seeks to influence outside observers who form beliefs on the basis of evidence shared by others, but do not collect evidence themselves; such agents might represent the public or policy makers who learn from scientists, but are not engaged in research. In this model, the observers receive evidence both from agents who are performing experiments ("scientists") and sharing (all) of their data as usual in model, and from an additional agent – the propagandist – who shares evidence in a manner intended to convince the observers that the incorrect action is, in fact, better.

Weatherall et al. consider two different strategies that the propagandist might adopt. The first strategy is what they call "biased production". This strategy, which is similar in spirit to the one considered by Holman and Bruner, consists in performing a number of trials of the worse arm, and then reporting only those results that happen to (spuriously) suggest it is better.

On the second strategy, which they call "selective sharing", the propagandist does not perform any experiments at all. Instead, the propagandist merely searches the results generated each round by the network of scientists and shares results produced "organically", that is, by the scientists themselves, that happen to support action A. This strategy works because given the probabilistic nature of evidence in these models, in any given round a certain number of results apparently supporting the worse action may be generated by the scientists themselves – with more such results appearing in large networks of scientists, especially when the number of trials (again, a proxy for the "power" of studies) is small.

In both cases, the effect of the propagandist's strategy is that the observers see more data supporting action A than they would if the propagandist were not operative. The result is that under a wide range of parameters the observers come to hold the false belief, even as the scientists converge to the true belief. In this sense, both strategies can succeed. That said, Weatherall et al. also argue that, perhaps contrary to intuition, selective sharing is often more effective and less costly than biased production. This is because this strategy does not require the propagandist to perform their own experiments at all, saving costs and effort, and obscuring their influence on public understanding.

A key insight from all of these models is this. Real scientific evidence can be noisy, with results sometimes pulling in different directions. Agents come to form the correct belief only by considering a representative sample, which will typically include both some results supporting the worse action and (generally more, stronger) results supporting the better one. By sharing a disproportionately large sample of results supporting action A, propagandists can shift this balance.

A second, perhaps even more important insight is that a propagandist can influence public belief without manipulating individual results or violating the standard "norms" of science. Under the selective sharing strategy, the propagandist shares only "legitimate" science, in the sense of science produced by unbiased, truth-seeking agents without outside influence. The strategy works by "curating" that evidence. Of course, the propagandist is effectively cherry-picking in the model, but they are not sharing fraudulent evidence.

This theme, that propagandists can influence scientific communities and public belief without committing "fraud" or other norm-violations, is further emphasized by another model studied by Holman and Bruner (2017). The set-up of this model is somewhat more complicated, but the basic idea is that within a research community, there may be a diversity of methods, operationalizations, working hypotheses, etc. It is assumed that scientists adopt these methods for their own reasons, free of outside influence. And yet, a propagandist may have reason to believe that some of these methods – for instance, emphasis on particular forms of evidence or specific research questions – may be more likely to favor the propagandist's preferred outcome than others.

In this model, the propagandist adopts the following strategy, which Holman and Bruner dub "industrial selection": they identify agents who have independently adopted research methods they consider favorable, and they "promote" those agents, essentially by increasing the amount of evidence they can share. For present purposes, one may think of this as lav-ishing those researchers with funding, enabling them to publish more papers or share their results more widely at conferences or in the press. The net result is, once again, that the propagandist increases the number of industry-favorable results that are shared within the network – now without producing any experiments of their own, or even sharing any results themselves. Instead, they do so by shifting the balance of how much research of different kinds can be produced.

Industrial selection is especially pernicious, because the scientists who are "selected" can honestly claim that they have continued to do precisely the research they would have done anyway, even without industry funding. The propagandist does not ask them to change their methods or bias their results. They are, in a certain sense, "independent". And yet by dis-proportionately amplifying some methods over others, the propagandist achieves their aim, again, by biasing the total body of evidence seen by other agents in the network.

Once again, we have seen these models used to investigate a number of questions related to false belief. How do propagandists use social factors to manipulate public belief? What strategies are most effective, and why? It is clear that these questions are of direct interest to political epistemology in that, as noted, the aims of these propagandists are often politi-cal ones. In misleading the public, and policy makers, on matters of science, propagandists achieve desired legislative and regulatory outcomes, such as lax tobacco regulation and a lack of action to prevent climate change. In addition, it should be noted that the influence strate-gies outlined in these models may be at play in more directly political cases. For instance, in lavishing funding on only some political think tanks, so that their work is more widely in-fluential, political actors can engage in a direct analog of industrial selection. In emphasizing only selective cases related to legislative outcomes, political actors do something very akin to selective sharing. One promising avenue for further work is to further elucidate the connec-tions between strategies for influencing scientific beliefs and for influencing political ones.

Conclusion

Formal social epistemology provides a rich toolbox for studying the mechanisms by which false beliefs persist and spread within a community. It can also help identify the conditions under which falsehoods spread most readily – and, perhaps, those conditions under which the truth is more likely to prevail. In this chapter we have reviewed a recent body of work that uses methods from network theory and decision theory to tackle these questions. We have highlighted what we take to be the key insights of these models. This literature has clear implications for those interested in political epistemology, and especially in the success-ful functioning of democracy.

There are many promising avenues for future work employing this methodology. For instance, future models might explore in more detail how various social psychological rea-soning biases – confirmation, recency, etc. – impede or influence the social spread of belief. As noted, the work surveyed in this chapter mostly focuses on agents who display at least a bounded level of rationality, but in thinking about real false beliefs it is very important to recognize the important role of such reasoning biases. Another possible avenue might look at special sorts of community structures that influence the social spread of belief, such as the effect of scientific advisory boards to political actors, and the impacts of expert testimony in legal and political settings. In sum, the type of model presented here provides a flexible framework for asking and answering many diverse questions related to social and political epistemology.[4]

Notes

1 There is a related literature in formal epistemology that mostly uses proof-based methods to consider normatively ideal learning in social conditions. While we will not discuss this literature, interested readers can find an overview in Goldman and O'Connor (2019).

2 Some models include aspects of both elements. Golub and Jackson (2010), for instance, consider agents who gather evidence, but who develop beliefs by averaging those of their neighbors rather than by sharing evidence directly.

3 See O'Connor and Weatherall (2019, Chapter 3) for a more detailed overview of this work.

4 This material is based upon work supported by the National Science Foundation under Grant No. 1922424.

Bibliography

Bala, V., and Goyal, S. (1998). 'Learning from neighbours'. *The Review of Economic Studies*, 65(3), 595–621.

Barrett, J. A., Skyrms, B., and Mohseni, A. (2019). 'Self-assembling networks'. *The British Journal for the Philosophy of Science*, 70(1), 301–25.

Brandt, A. (2007). *The Cigarette Century: The Rise, Fall, and Deadly Persistence of the Product that Defined America*. New York: Basic Books.

Christensen, D. (2007). 'Epistemology of disagreement: The good news'. *Philosophical Review*, 116(2), 187–217.

Coady, C. A. J. (1992). *Testimony: A Philosophical Study*. Oxford: Clarendon Press.

Fricker, E. (1994). 'Against gullibility' in Matilal, B. K. and Chakrabarti, A. (eds.) *Knowing from Words*. Dordrecht: Springer Netherlands, 125–61.

Gilbert, M. (1989). *On Social Facts*. New York: Routledge.

Golub, B., and Jackson, M. O. (2010). 'Naive learning in social networks and the wisdom of crowds'. *American Economic Journal: Microeconomics*, 2(1), 112–49.

Golub, B., and Jackson, M. O. (2012). 'How homophily affects the speed of learning and best-response dynamics'. *The Quarterly Journal of Economics*, 127(3), 1287–338.

Goldman, A. (2001). 'Experts: Which ones should you trust?', *Philosophy and Phenomenological Research*, 63(1), 85–110.

Goldman, A., and O'Connor, C. (2019). 'Social epistemology' in Zalta, E. N. (ed.) *The Stanford Encyclopedia of Philosophy* (Fall 2019 Edition). https://plato.stanford.edu/archives/fall2019/entries/epistemology-social/.

Granovetter, M. (1978). 'Threshold models of collective behavior'. *American Journal of Sociology*, 83(6), 1420–43.

Hegselmann, R., and Krause, U. (2002). 'Opinion dynamics and bounded confidence models, analysis, and simulation'. *Journal of Artificial Societies and Social Simulation*, 5(3), 2.

Holman, B., and Bruner, J. P. (2015). 'The problem of intransigently biased agents'. *Philosophy of Science*, 82(5), 956–68. doi:10.1086/683344.

Holman, B., and Bruner, J. (2017). 'Experimentation by industrial selection'. *Philosophy of Science*, 84(5), 1008–19.

Jackson, M. O., and Rogers, B. W. (2007). 'Relating network structure to diffusion properties through stochastic dominance'. *The BE Journal of Theoretical Economics*, 7(1), 1–16.

Kitcher, P. (1990). 'The division of cognitive labor'. *Journal of Philosophy*, 87(1), 5.

Lakoff, G. (2010). *Moral Politics: How Liberals and Conservatives Think*. Chicago, IL: University of Chicago Press.

List, C., and Petit, P. (2011). *Group Agency: The Possibility, Design, and Status of Corporate Agents*. Oxford: Oxford University Press.

Mayo-Wilson, C., Zollman, K. J. S., and Danks, D. (2011). 'The independence thesis: When individual and social epistemology diverge'. *Philosophy of Science*, 78(4), 653–77.

Michaels, D. (2008). *Doubt Is their Product: How Industry's Assault on Science Threatens Your Health*, 1 ed. Oxford and New York: Oxford University Press.

Mohseni, A., and Williams, C. R. (2019). 'Truth and conformity on networks'. *Erkenntnis*, 1–22.

O'Connor, C., and Weatherall, J. O. (2019). *The Misinformation Age: How False Beliefs Spread*. New Haven: Yale University Press.

O'Connor, C., and Weatherall, J. O. (2018). 'Scientific polarization'. *European Journal for Philosophy of Science*, 8(3), 855–75.

Olsson, E. J. (2013). 'A Bayesian simulation model of group deliberation and polarization' in Zenker, F. (ed.) *Bayesian Argumentation*. Dordrecht: Springer, pp. 113–33.

Oreskes, N., and Conway, E. M. (2010). *Merchants of Doubt: How a Handful of Scientists Obscured the Truth on Issues from Tobacco Smoke to Global Warming*. New York: Bloomsbury Press.

Rogers, E. M. (2010). *Diffusion of Innovations*. New York: Simon and Schuster.

Rosenstock, S., Bruner, J., and O'Connor, C. (2017). 'In epistemic networks, is less really more?'. *Philosophy of Science*, 84(2), 234–52.

Singer, D., Grim, P., Bramson, A., Holman, B., Jung, J., and Berger, W. (2020). 'Epistemic network and polarization' in de Ridder, J. and Hannon, M. (eds.) *Routledge Handbook of Political Epistemology*. Abingdon: Routledge.

Smith, A. F. (2001). *The Tomato in America: Early History, Culture, and Cookery*. Urbana and Chicago: University of Illinois Press.

Weatherall, J. O., and O'Connor, C. (2020a). 'Conformity in scientific networks'. *Synthese*. doi:10.1007/s11229-019-02520-2.

Weatherall, J. O., and O'Connor, C. (2020b). 'Endogenous epistemic factionalization'. *Synthese*. doi:10.1007/s11229-020-02675-3.

Weatherall, J. O., O'Connor, C., and Bruner, J. (2018). 'How to beat science and influence people: Policymakers and propaganda in epistemic networks'. *British Journal for Philosophy of Science*. doi:10.1093/bjps/axy062.

Zollman, K. J. (2007). 'The communication structure of epistemic communities'. *Philosophy of Science*, 74(5), 574–87.

Zollman, K. J. (2010). 'The epistemic benefit of transient diversity'. *Erkenntnis*, 72(1), 17–35.

19

REGULATING THE SPREAD OF ONLINE MISINFORMATION

Étienne Brown

1 Introduction

Since the Russian attempt to influence the outcome of the 2016 U.S. Election, there is a growing fear that the circulation of made-up news and misleading information on social media disrupts the democratic process by inciting citizens to make political judgments based on false beliefs. According to a 2019 survey by the Pew Research Center (Mitchell et al., 2019), 50% of U.S. adults believe that misinformation is a critical problem that needs to be fixed, and 79% of them consider that steps should be taken to restrict it. In Western Europe, countries such as Germany and France have enacted legal measures which authorize public officials to order the removal of pieces of misinformation from social media. While a growing number of legal measures against misinformation are currently being implemented, some researchers remain unconvinced that misinformation fundamentally threatens democracy. In their recent study of exposure to untrustworthy websites in the 2016 Election, Andrew Guess, Brendan Nyhan and Jason Reifler (2020) suggest that "the widespread speculation about the prevalence of exposure to untrustworthy websites has been overstated."

These two perspectives on misinformation—the alarmist and the deflationary—raises philosophical questions that are worth considering. Deflationary perspectives invite us to consider whether liberal democracies truly have reasons to worry about misinformation and, if they do, what these reasons are. By way of contrast, concerned citizens and public officials who conceive of misinformation as a problem that ought to be fixed invite us to reflect upon the regulatory options that are available to us. This chapter takes up these two tasks. First, I define key terms such as misinformation, disinformation and fake news, and offer a brief explanation of how misinformation circulates in online contexts. I then assess the reasons we have to limit its spread. Lastly, I consider three possible ways to combat misinformation in liberal democracies—individual self-regulation, platform-based innovations and governmental action—and suggest that the most effective ones are those that spare human agents from having to successively review individual pieces of content.

2 What is misinformation and how does it spread?

Let us begin by broadly defining misinformation as the communication of false or misleading information. How does it compare to related terms such as disinformation and fake news? The simplest way to contrast *mis*information with *dis*information is to use the former as a broad category under which we can subsume the latter.[1] In this light, disinformation amounts to *intentional* misinformation, i.e. the communication of false or misleading claims by actors who believe that such claims are false or misleading. As for fake news, I suggest that a news story qualifies as fake when (i) it contains false or misleading claims, (ii) it imitates the format of traditional news media (Brown, 2019a) and (iii) its originators do not intend to communicate true claims.[2] As false information can have a negative impact on the belief and behaviour of individuals whether or not it counts as *disinformation* or *fake news*, this chapter focuses on misinformation *per se* as opposed to its subsets.

Different actors are involved in the spread of misinformation. To see this, consider how misinformation spreads online in a chronological manner. First, individuals or automated accounts (i.e. "bots") create the content and originally publish it on social media. In general, the motive behind intentional misinformation is either political or financial. Foreign actors sometimes attempt to influence rival countries' politics by diffusing false information which supports a particular cause or creates antagonism between citizens. In 2016, for instance, Russia's Internet Research Agency created thousands of "sock puppet" social media accounts (that is, accounts based on false identities) which posed as radical American political groups and published fabricated articles in an attempt to destabilize the country. In other cases, originators of misinformation create and diffuse it to make financial gains. Indeed, misinformation often functions as clickbait, that is, content which is designed to trigger internet users' interest and make them click on a thumbnail link. This generates traffic to the linked website, which itself translates into profit through advertising revenue.

Once misinformation has been created, posted and diffused, it is often relayed by inadvertent users who do not perceive it as misleading or, alternatively, know that it is misleading but nonetheless have reasons to share it. For instance, social media users might write posts about false rumours they have encountered online or simply "reshare" misleading posts and fake news articles. As Starbird (2019) underlines, misinformation campaigns often include "a majority of 'unwitting agents' who are unaware of their role" in amplifying content. That said, the role of bots in the spread of online misinformation should not go unnoticed. According to a recent study published in *Nature* (Shao et al., 2019), bots play a "disproportionate role in spreading articles from low-credibility sources," especially in the early spreading moments before an article goes viral. One strategy bots are programmed to use amounts to targeting "users with many followers through replies and mentions" in order to maximize exposure. In a nutshell, the spread of misinformation on social media is usually a joint endeavour between humans who desire to misinform others, careless social media users and automated accounts.

3 Why worry about misinformation?

Although there is evidence that falsehood diffuses "significantly farther, faster, deeper, and more broadly than the truth" on social media (Vosoughi et al., 2017), it may still be the case that misinformation has little influence on the beliefs and reasoning process of its consumers.[3]

Yet, if this influence turns out to be substantial, there are several reasons that count in favour of limiting its spread. This section briefly considers four of them.

3.1 Misinformation prevents democratic citizens to make good political judgements

Scholars interested in freedom of expression often argue that the free flow of quality information is essential to democratic self-government as citizens need to form true beliefs in order to make good political judgements (Barendt, 2007, pp. 18–21). This is the rationale behind Alexander Meiklejohn's (1961, p. 255) famous quote according to which the First Amendment protects "the freedom of those activities of thought and communication by which we govern." From this perspective, it is quite easy to see why we might want to regulate misinformation. Here, the worry is that forming false beliefs can impair people's capacity to make good political decisions. The assumption which undergirds such reasoning is that political judgements which exclusively rely on true beliefs are more likely to produce good normative outcomes than those that rely on false beliefs. A straightforward example of this is defamatory misinformation that besmirches electoral candidates. For instance, one frequently cited fake news stories—commonly know is "Pizzagate"—connected Hilary Clinton and other well-known members of the Democratic Party to a fictitious child sex ring hidden in the basement of a Pizza restaurant in Washington, D.C. If one believes that a presidential candidate is a sex trafficker, one is significantly less likely to vote for her (and this independently of the quality of her policy proposals).

As some political theorists have suggested that (at least part of) the legitimacy of democracy derives from its ability to promote good normative outcomes (Estlund, 2007; Landemore, 2013), the worry that misinformation will prevent citizens from making good political judgements can also foster uncertainty about the value of democratic self-government (Brown, 2018). In twentieth-century political epistemology, the thought that misinformation undercuts the people's ability to govern itself has been influential. The scholar who best expressed this worry remains Walter Lippman (1922, p. 249), who wrote that "under the impact of propaganda [...] it is no longer possible, for example, to believe in the original dogma of democracy."[4]

3.2 Misinformation makes politics more antagonistic

Misinformation also risks eroding civic friendship. To see this, consider echo chambers, that is, online spaces in which an inside group denies the status of potential truth tellers to outsiders through epistemic discrediting.[5] Simply put, epistemic discrediting amounts to assigning "some epistemic demerit, such as unreliability, epistemic maliciousness, or dishonesty" to others (Nguyen, 2018, p. 6), and misinformation often plays a central role in it. If one's goal is to convince an audience to reject all claims made by outsiders, an available strategy is to denigrate the latter by falsely claiming that they have malicious intentions or committed evil deeds. This represents a second manner in which misinformation can hurt democracy: even if it does not directly lead citizens to make bad political judgements, it can strengthen epistemic structures which themselves fosters distrust between political, religious and racial groups.[6]

Interestingly, the spread of misinformation online might also be a *consequence* of political antagonism. In a study of partisan polarization on Twitter, Osmundsen et al. (2020) found that people who report hating their political opponents are the most likely to share fake news.[7] Their interpretation of this finding is that "when strong partisans decide what to share on social media, they place less value on the veracity of information as long as it satisfies their partisan motivations: derogating the out-party." In other words, the spread of online misinformation might be partisan business as usual, a fact which itself suggests that polarization, echo chambers and the spread of low-quality information should be studied jointly.[8]

3.3 Misinformation leads to physical harm

A third reason to fight online misinformation is that people can get hurt as a result of its spread. Consider, for instance, false rumours that circulate on private encrypted messenger services. On July 1, 2018, five men belonging to a nomadic group in India were beaten to death by a mob in Rainpada, India, after having handed a biscuit to a young girl (McLaughlin, 2018). Before the killings, rumours warning of kidnappers and organ-harvesters roving in the area had circulated on WhatsApp. As Mark Zuckerberg—the CEO of Facebook—himself recognized, fake news stories diffused by state-sponsored sock-puppet accounts have also played an important role in the genocidal killings and displacement of the Rohingya people in Myanmar (Mozur, 2018). In such cases, photographs taken out of context are often mixed with hate speech that targets minority groups. For instance, the Rainpada rumours included photos of lifeless children laid out in rows who were not the victims of a "murderous kidnapping ring" but rather of a "chemical attack on the town of Ghouta, Syria, five years earlier and thousands of miles away." This demonstrates that misinformation sometimes works through what I propose to call *pictorial implicature*, that is, the act of showing a photograph that is a representation of something other than what is implied by the showing.[9]

Misinformation can also lead to harm when it fools people into taking decisions that compromises their health or that of others. Misleading information that fosters vaccine hesitancy by suggesting that vaccines cause autism is a clear example of this. Lastly, misinformation about climate change may turn out to be a deadly killer if we take the lives of future generations into accounts, for it risks slowing down attempts at mitigation and adaptation that could protect densely populated areas from catastrophic effects.

3.4 Misinformation hinders personal autonomy

Lastly, misinformation sometimes hinders our capacity to pursue the goals we freely set for ourselves by impairing our capacity to appreciate reasons. Consider once again the case of parents who have been misinformed about vaccines. Presumably, such parents have a desire to protect their children's health and, because of this, have a reason to have their children vaccinated (assuming that the vaccine went through normal phases of testing). Yet, misinformation may prevent them from appreciating this reason by suggesting that vaccines do not protect their children's health, but in fact endanger it. This particular example illustrates two general points about practical rationality and testimony. First, we need to appreciate reasons to effectively pursue our goals. Second, we continuously rely on information provided to us by others in order to appreciate reasons. When our informational landscape is polluted by claims that are false or misleading, however, our capacity to appreciate reasons is impaired and our desires are more likely to be frustrated as result.

A different way of making this claim is to point out that misinformation undermines personal autonomy. On a reasons-responsive account of autonomy, the level of personal autonomy a person enjoys depends on her capacity to appreciate reasons. As Buss and Westlund (2018) underline:

> If doing *Y* is constitutive of doing *Z*, then if I authorize myself to be moved by the desire to do *Y* because I mistakenly believe that doing *Y* is a way of *not* doing *Z*, then there is an obvious sense in which I have not authorized myself to do what I am now doing when I am moved by the desire to do *Y*.

The vaccine sceptic example—in which a person considers that having their children vaccinated is a way of *not* protecting their children's health—is a simple illustration of this idea. Arguments in favour of regulating misinformation that focus on autonomy will be especially appealing to Kantian deontologists. In Kant's (2012) view, lying is morally wrong precisely because it robs others of their freedom to choose rationally. It is also quite easy to see how intentionally deceiving others often amounts to treating them as means rather than as ends. If I trick you into doing something that furthers my interest through deliberate misinformation, then I use you as a tool that can help me better fulfil my desires while disregarding your need to rely on quality information in order to satisfy your own.[10]

4 How should misinformation be regulated?

Assuming that we have reasons to limit the spread of online misinformation, what regulatory options are available to us? In the remainder of this chapter, I assess three ways of doing so. A first option amounts to allowing or helping internet users modify their online habits to minimize the chance that they will form false beliefs on the basis of misleading claims. A second option is to let social media companies modify their platform so that fewer people are exposed to it. A third option is to demand that governments enact laws that punish individuals who wittingly engage in misinformation or disincentivize them from doing so.

4.1 Individual self-regulation

Do internet users have a duty to inoculate themselves against online misinformation? Given that misinformation and epistemic discrediting often go together, should they not exclude all individuals who defame others from their epistemic network? Moreover, do they have the epistemic responsibility to ensure that information to which they are exposed is reported by multiple sources before allowing it to influence their beliefs? Individual self-regulation is an appealing option to philosophers who consider that individuals are primarily responsible for their poor epistemic habits, and that it is unfair to impose the costs of misinformation on others. In *Know-it-all Society* (2019, p. 4), for instance, Michael Lynch criticizes our tendency to "dismiss evidence for victory and truth for power" in online contexts. In his view, our arrogance and carelessness with regard to truth is not a technical problem, but a human one: "if we want to solve it […] we have to change our attitudes" (2019, p. 5).

Self-regulation is arguably the less costly option in terms of both financial resources and liberties compared with platform-based innovations (which entail financial costs for technology companies) and government regulation (which carries the risk of censorship). Yet, some deep-seated psychological tendencies appear to stand in the way of cognitive self-improvement in the fight against misinformation.[11] For instance, fake news is often published on relatively unknown websites and psychological studies suggest that "when people know little about a source, they treat information from that source as credible" (Rapp, 2016). A second relevant psychological tendency that can limit our attempt to immunize ourselves against misinformation is misattribution. Put simply, people sometimes initially categorize some claims as false because they encountered them in (what they know to be) a fake news article, but eventually misattribute this claim to a reliable source and re-categorize such claims as true (Marsh, Cantor and Brashier, 2016).

The very architecture of social media platforms also presents some obstacles for users who desire to improve their epistemic habits. Indeed, even internet users who make the conscious choice to become intellectually virtuous and reduce their consumption of misinformation might struggle to do so as a result of algorithmic filtering. If such users have a history of consuming conspiracy theories stemming from sources of dubious quality, for instance, such content will continue to appear in their feed for the near future. Even if they stop engaging with such theories or report them as misinformation, they may still be exposed to misleading stories if their epistemic network is mainly composed of users who like sharing them.

Of course, exposure is not all there is to the story. When individuals have formed false beliefs as a result being exposed to misinformation, can they not correct them at a later point in time? Empirical evidence about corrections is mixed. While meta-analyses of fact-checks suggest that they improve the accuracy of belief (Chan et al., 2017), a central worry is that internet users will not be exposed to them. Consider first what psychologists have dubbed the confirmation (or myside) bias. People have a tendency to seek "evidence in ways that are partial to existing beliefs," and they are therefore not likely to attempt to disconfirm their false beliefs by seeking corrections (Nickerson, 1998). This hypothesis is supported by the finding that corrections almost never reach their targeted audience. For instance, Guess, Nyhan and Reifler (2020, p. 476) found that less than "half of the 44.3% of Americans who visited an untrustworthy website" during the length of their recent research "also saw any fact check from one of the dedicated fact-checking websites."

Moreover, people are generally overconfident and have a "bias blind spot," that is, tend to rate themselves as less susceptible to cognitive biases compared to the average individual and their peers (Pronin, Lin and Ross, 2002). The worry here is that this will prevent them from seeking new information that corroborates or contradicts their beliefs. Nathan Ballantyne has also argued that we often engage in *debunking reasoning*. When others present us with evidence that contradicts our opinions, we tend to attribute biases to them "in order to prevent their dissent from lowering our confidence in our view" (2015, p. 142). This has led some epistemologists to argue that the prospects for epistemic self-improvement are dire (Ahlstrom-Vij, 2013).

If self-motivated cognitive improvement is trickier than it appears at first sight, can we not foster such self-improvement through external constraints such as media literacy education programs? Some philosophers have recently suggested that we teach intellectual virtues such as scepticism and intellectual humility to middle school and high school students to decrease the likelihood that misinformation will affect their beliefs (Brown, 2019b). For instance, they could be tasked with identifying instances of reliable journalism and misinformation as well as situations in which epistemic discrediting impairs the rational evaluation of claims and arguments. Admittedly, the empirical evidence which supports the claims that critical thinking or intellectual virtue education is an effective solution to misinformation is not robust. One encouraging finding comes from Rozenbeek and van der Linden (2019), who designed a fake news game that "confers psychological resistance against misinformation." In the game, players take on the role of a fake news producer who employs different strategies to deceive its audience: "polarisation, invoking emotions, spreading conspiracy theories, trolling people online, deflecting blame, and impersonating fake accounts."[12] According to the researchers, playing the game "significantly reduced the perceived reliability of tweets that embedded several common online misinformation strategies." In general, it would be relatively simple for instructors to integrate modules on misinformation developed by cognitive psychologists to their teaching (provided that they have access to the right technology). Even if such modules do not fulfil their promises in the end, the costs of *attempting* to inoculate students against misinformation remain low.

4.2 Platform-based innovations

A second regulatory option is to let social media companies modify their platform so that fewer people are exposed to misinformation or, at least, exposed to it without knowing that they are. Such an option will be appealing to those who consider that technology companies are partly responsible for the spread of online misinformation and should take on the burden of eliminating it. Consider two different ways to conceive of social media platforms. According to the first conception, such platforms are akin to public squares. If someone spreads false information while standing on a public square, it would be strange to hold urban planners who designed the square responsible for this person's behaviour. After all, the very function of public squares is to allow people to publicly express their views, and we normally judge that people are responsible for what they say. Yet social media platforms do not truly function like public squares. One important difference is that unlike neutral spaces in which people can express their views, they promote and demote content through algorithmic filtering. This gives us reason to consider that social media companies are more akin to publishers. According to this second conception, social media companies design algorithms which determine what content individual users encounter just as an editor decides what content will be published on the front page of a newspaper. If a fake news story finds itself at the top of millions of users' feed, it therefore seems reasonable to claim that social media companies share at least part of the responsibility for this.

What can technology companies concretely do to limit the spread of online misinformation? We can situate the options available to them on a paternalism continuum. At the least paternalistic end of the continuum are transparency requirements. Indeed, platforms can provide users with information about the content to which they are exposed. When users encounter a news story on Facebook, for instance, they have the opportunity to click on a context button and learn more about the source which published the article. The social media giant has also announced that it will start labelling content "that has been rated false or partly false by a third-party fact-checker" (Rosen et al., 2019). For its part, Twitter has introduced labels to help users identify misleading information and disputed claims.[13] A more radical proposal comes from philosopher Regina Rini (2017), who suggests that social media platforms give reputation scores to their users. Such scores "could be displayed in a subtle way, perhaps with a colored icon beside user photos." Users could then choose to have content posted from users with low reputations scores downranked or filtered out, but they would not be obligated to do so. This innovative proposal is worth considering, but it could be exploited by sophisticated deceivers. For instance, an organization could gradually build an excellent reputation score and then use it as leverage to launch a misinformation campaign that may become even more effective than if epistemic trustworthiness scores had not been made available in the first place.

Moving up the paternalism spectrum, social media companies could remove or demote content reported as misinformation by their community of users or by third-party fact-checkers. For instance, Facebook both employs fact-checkers and allows its users to report news stories they encounter as "false news." While removing and demoting misleading content is more paternalistic than simply increasing transparency, it is arguably not more paternalistic than how social media platforms function generally given that *all* content to which social media users are exposed is ranked by algorithms. There is, however, an important risk tied to this measure. When users expect that false information will be flagged, false information that *fails* to be flagged can be seen as more accurate than it would otherwise have been. This is what Pennycook et al. (2020) call the "implied truth effect." Another moderately paternalistic measure amounts to redirecting users to quality information when they are about to engage with news stories. During the coronavirus outbreak, for instance, Twitter has combated rumours that oregano oil proves effective against coronavirus by steering U.S. users searching for coronavirus-related hashtags to the website of Center for Disease Control and Prevention.

As for pragmatic challenges that social media companies face in their attempts to fight misinformation, one worry is that the amount of third-party fact-checkers they currently employ pales in comparison of the vast amount of content that needs to be evaluated. In January 2020, Rodrigo (2020) estimated that Facebook's six fact-checking partners "have 26 full-time staff and fact-checked roughly 200 pieces of content per month," an amount which many experts find insufficient. To solve this problem, social media giants can rely on user reports, but these risk not being accurate. For instance, nothing prevents a user to report a perfectly accurate news story which contradicts its ideological beliefs as "false news." What is more, letting social media companies self-regulate is unlikely to lead them to enact measures that would significantly hurt their business model, which consists of promoting content in exchange for advertising revenues. In 2020, Facebook has faced severe criticisms for refusing to remove political advertisements that have been found to contain false claims by its third-party fact-checking partners.[14] This explains why some governments have recently decided to step in the fight against misinformation.

4.3 Governmental action

By far, the most controversial way to regulate the spread of online misinformation is through law and policy, for speech restrictions always come with the reasonable worry that public officials will abuse them or that they will amount to undue censorship. Nevertheless, some Western European countries have chosen this route. In Germany, the Network Enforcement Act allows the government to impose fines of up to 50 million euros on social media companies if they fail to remove illegal content including fake news. In late 2018, the Macron government in France also passed the "law against the manipulation of information," which authorizes judges to order the removal of pieces of misleading content from social media platforms in a period of three months leading up to a national election. Such a law was heavily criticized by the French Senate on the grounds that it amounts to a violation of citizens' right to freedom of expression.

Let us consider this objection in more detail. To refute it, one might point out that influential theories of freedom of expression rest on the idea that (at least part of) the value of speech derives from its ability to promote truth. As misinformation and fake news are unlikely to do so, this provides us with reason to believe that they do not amount to the kind of speech that we ought to protect in liberal democracies. Yet these arguments are unlikely to convince Millians who consider that truth is more likely to emerge when we refrain from regulating speech and let it collide with error. This is an empirical claim that remains difficult to assess, but disagreement over it may yield radically different views about the limits of freedom of expression. Proponents of the so-called autonomy defence of free speech are also likely to argue against the French law.[15] Even if the legal prohibition of misinformation proved effective at hindering the formation of false beliefs, they would condemn it on the grounds that governmental attempts to preselect the evidence on which citizens base their judgements are unduly paternalistic and incompatible with our right to autonomy (Scanlon, 1972).

Beyond free speech worries, it is worth asking whether the French law is likely to prove effective at reducing the amount of misinformation which circulates on social media. Let us imagine a situation in which judges mostly defer to judgements made by third-party fact-checkers when deciding which pieces of content should be removed. As we have seen, fact-checkers may not be available in sufficient numbers to review the vast amount of content that might amount to misinformation. Of course, the situation would only worsen if judges themselves took up the task of evaluating content. What is more, even if fact-checkers and judges identified most misleading content, there is no guarantee that they would be able to do so *before* pieces of misinformation have spread and influenced users' beliefs.

Laws against misinformation have also been proposed in the American context. For instance, Senator Mark Warner (2018) has proposed to pass laws that require social media companies to "clearly and conspicuously identify and label bots" as well as accounts based on false identities. An alternative proposal is to make social media platforms liable for state-law torts (defamation, false light, public disclosure of private facts, etc.).[16] Such a law would provide technology companies with a strong incentive to remove deep fakes (the content of which is generally defamatory), but once again presupposes that such companies have the resources to review an enormous amount of content.

Before concluding, let us therefore consider a proposal that avoids this pitfall. Unfortunately, social media provide organizations that wilfully engage in misinformation with highly effective tools. Perhaps the most effective is targeted advertising, which allows organizations to ensure that their posts will be seen by individuals who share specific characteristics with each other (age, gender, geographical location, political orientation, etc.). Here, the underlying assumption is that specific instances of misinformation will be of interest to a particular demographic. Indeed, it seems reasonable to suppose that a fake news story which defames high-ranking Democrats is more likely to be believed by Republicans who have shown interest for conspiracy theories than by Democrats who have not. For this reason, one way to decrease the efficacy of misinformation without having to review specific instances of it would be to prohibit targeted advertising altogether, that is, to make it impossible for originators of misinformation to direct it at the individuals they think are the most likely to believe it (or be interested by it). While a prohibition against targeted advertising might be a step in the right direction, it would not be a panacea, for there are myriad other means by which misinformation can spread and influence people's beliefs. Perhaps the most daunting way in which it does is by permeating closed and encrypted communicative spaces such as WhatsApp groups, which remain extremely difficult to monitor and, as we have seen, can spread rumours which lead to physical harm. Such a prohibition would also significantly hurt the business model of social media platforms.

Is misinformation a serious enough public issue for the government to interfere with the freedom of private businesses to organize and operate for profit in a competitive market? My final suggestion is that we will not be able to answer such a question before answering some of those considered in this chapter. First, how likely is it that misinformation will influence our beliefs? Second, assuming that it does, to what extent do false beliefs threaten our capacity to be safe, to pursue our personal goals and to fulfil our democratic duties? Third, what other regulatory options are available to us? Regarding the latter, it remains possible that rapid advances in machine learning will make regulations against misinformation superfluous. If we develop artificial agents that are capable of swiftly and accurately identify pieces of misinformation, it will become possible for technology companies to use them and better review the vast amount of information (and misinformation) which currently circulates on their platform.[17] Until they do, however, it is likely that worries about misinformation will incite political epistemologists to doubt the people's capacity to self-govern. As we have seen, rapid advancements in communications technology usually give rise to Lippmannian misgivings about democracy. This is why philosophical reflection upon misinformation ultimately matters. In the end, assessing the political dangers posed by false beliefs can lead us to regain confidence in the rule of the many or—if we fail to do so—to seek viable alternatives to it.

Notes

1 This broad definition of misinformation entails that honest mistakes, factual errors in reporting and even some instances of political satire count as instances of it. I do not see this as a problem if we use narrower concepts (disinformation, fake news, etc.) to refer to different kinds of misinformation. If we define misinformation broadly, not all forms of misinformation will be legitimate targets of regulation. For instance, some might consider that it would be a mistake to attempt to regulate satirical news website like *The Onion* on the grounds that contributors to the website have no wrongful intention. That said, communication scholars have recently argued that we should at least label satirical misinformation as such on the grounds that "too many people think satirical news is real." See Garrett, Bond and Poulsen (2019).

2 Some philosophers have offered definitions of fake news which focus on the reliability of the production process instead of on the intention of publishers. See, for instance, Michaelson, Pepp and Sterken (2019). For an extensive discussion of the definition of fake news, see Axel Gelfert's chapter in this handbook.

3 For an extensive discussion of psychological studies which suggest that misinformation can be effective, see Levy (2017) as well as Levy and Ross's chapter in this handbook ("The cognitive science of fake news").

4 On the relationship between propaganda and misinformation, see Megan Hyska's chapter in this handbook.

5 On epistemic bubbles and echo chambers, see Hana Kiri Gunn's chapter in this handbook.

6 Highly selective one-sided information that does not contain false claims can also make politics more antagonistic, and my claim here is not that we should worry about misinformation *more than we do* about other types of political communication that risk pitting citizens against each other like spin, dog-whistles or straightforward insults ("crooked Hilary," etc.).

7 I thank Michael Hannon and Jeroen de Ridder for drawing my attention to this study and, more generally, for their insightful remarks on this chapter.

8 It is worth noting that "making politics more antagonistic" is a contingent feature of misinformation, not a necessary one. In fact, misinformation could even be used to *lessen* partisan antipathy. For instance, political actors who seek to create alliances between groups that have traditionally shown hostility toward each other could falsely portray the members of one group as having committed heroical deeds that benefit the other group.

9 This "something else" can be a real event that happened in a different context (as in the Rainpada case) or a fictional event.

10 See *On a supposed right to lie from philanthropy* in the Cambridge edition of Kant's *Practical Philosophy* for his influential discussion of lying.

11 Levy and Ross's contribution to this handbook offers a more detailed discussion of this point.

12 Some limitations of this study should be pointed out. First, it has not been replicated. Second, it is hard to tell how long the "inoculation effect" will last. Third, the sample of experimental subjects was self-selected.

13 According to Twitter's policy, misleading information (but not disputed claims) can be removed from the platform if its propensity for harm is considered severe rather than moderate. In May 2020, Twitter applied this "propensity for harm" criterion to a tweet by Donald Trump (in which he remarked that "when the looting starts, the shooting starts") by labelling it as "glorifying violence."

14 This policy stands in stark contrast with Twitter's 2019 to ban all political advertisements from its platform. That said, both Facebook and Twitter have banned content featuring politicians making false claims about COVID-19 that were deemed harmful. In August 2020, for instance, Facebook removed a video interview with Donald Trump in which he claimed that children are "almost immune" to the virus.
15 See (Brison, 1998) for a discussion of the autonomy defence of free speech.
16 Section 230 of the Communications Decency Act currently immunizes social media platforms from state tort and criminal liability in the United States.
17 Andersen and Søe (2019) have argued that we should refrain from using automated fact-checking on the grounds that it would be difficult (if not impossible) for artificial agents to understand the intentions behind posts, and the precise meaning of such posts.

References

Ahlstrom-Vij, K. (2013) 'Why We Cannot Rely on Ourselves for Epistemic Improvement', *Philosophical Issues*, 23(1), pp. 276–96.
Andersen, J. and Søe, S. O. (2019) 'Communicative Actions We Live by: The Problem with Fact-Checking, Tagging or Flagging Fake News – The Case of Facebook', *European Journal of Communication*, 35(2), pp. 126–39.
Ballantyne, N. (2015) 'Debunking Biased Thinkers (Including Ourselves)', *Journal of the American Philosophical Association*, 1(1), pp. 141–62.
Barendt, E. (2007) *Freedom of Speech*. 2nd Edition. New York: Oxford University Press.
Brison, S. J. (1998) 'The Autonomy Defense of Free Speech', *Ethics*, 108(2), pp. 312–39.
Brown, É. (2018) 'Propaganda, Misinformation, and the Epistemic Value of Democracy', *Critical Review*, 30(3–4), pp. 194–218.
Brown, É. (2019a) '"Fake News" and Conceptual Ethics', *Journal of Ethics and Social Philosophy*, 16(2), pp. 144–54.
Brown, É. (2019b) 'Civic Education in the Post-Truth Era: Intellectual Virtues and the Epistemic Threats of Social Media', in Macloed, C. and Tappolet, C. (eds) *Philosophical Perspectives on Education: Shaping Citizens*. New York: Routledge, pp. 45–67.
Buss, S. and Westlund, A. (2018) 'Personal Autonomy', in Zalta, E. N. (ed) *Stanford Encyclopedia of Philosophy*. https://plato.stanford.edu/entries/personal-autononmy.
Chan, M. P. S., Jones, C. R., Jamieson, K. H. and Albarracín, D. (2017) 'Debunking: A Meta-Analysis of the Psychological Efficacy of Messages Countering Misinformation', *Psychological Science*, 28(11), pp. 1531–46.
Estlund, D. M. (2008) *Democratic Authority: A Philosophical Framework*. Princeton, NJ: Princeton University Press.
Garrett, R. K., Bond, R. and Poulsen, S. (2019) 'Too Many People Think Satirical News Is Real', *The Conversation*. Available at: https://theconversation.com/too-many-people-think-satirical-news-is-real-121666.
Guess, A. M., Nyhan, B. and Reifler, J. (2020) 'Exposure to Untrustworthy Websites in the 2016 Election,' *Nature Human Behaviour*, 4(5), pp. 472–80.
Kant, I. (2012) 'Groundwork of the Metaphysics of Morals', in Gregor, M. J. (ed) *Practical Philosophy*. Cambridge: Cambridge University Press, pp. 37–108.
Landemore, H. (2013) *Democratic Reason: Politics, Collective Intelligence, and the Rule of the Many*. Princeton, NJ: Princeton University Press.
Levy, N. (2017) 'The Bad News about Fake News', *Social Epistemology Review & Reply Collective*, 6(8), pp. 20–36.
Lippman, W. (1922) *Public Opinion*. New York: Harcourt, Brace and Company.
Lynch, M. P. (2019) *Know-It-All Society: Truth and Arrogance in Political Culture*. New York: Liveright Publishing Corporation.
Marsh, E. J., Cantor, A. D. and Brashier, N. M. (2016) 'Believing that Humans Swallow Spiders in Their Sleep: False Beliefs as Side-Effects of the Processes that Support Accurate Knowledge', *Psychology of Learning and Motivation*, 64, pp. 93–132.
Meiklejohn, A. (1961) 'The First Amendment Is an Absolute', *The Supreme Court Review*, 1961, pp. 245–66.

Mclaughlin, T. (2018) 'How WhatsApp Fuels Fake News and Violence in India', *Wired*. Available at: www.wired.com/story/how-whatsapp-fuels-fake-news-and-violence-in-india.

Michaelson, E., Pepp, J. and Sterken, R. K. (2019) 'What Is New about Fake News?', *Journal of Ethics and Social Philosophy*, 16(2), pp. 67–94.

Mitchell, A., Gottfried, J., Stocking, G., Walker, M. and Fedeli, S. (2019) 'Many Americans Say Made-Up News Is a Critical Problem That Needs to Be Fixed', *Pew Research Center*. Available at: www.journalism.org/2019/06/05/many-americans-say-made-up-news-is-a-critical-problem-that-needs-to-be-fixed.

Mozur, P. (2018) 'A Genocide Incited on Facebook with Posts from Myanmar's Military', *The New York Times*. Available at: www.nytimes.com/2018/10/15/technology/myanmar-facebook-genocide.html.

Nguyen, C. T. (2018) 'Echo Chambers and Epistemic Bubbles', *Episteme*, 17(2), pp. 1–21.

Nickerson, R. S. (1998) 'Confirmation Bias: A Ubiquitous Phenomenon in Many Guises', *Review of General Psychology*, 2(2), pp. 175–220.

Osmundsen, M., Bor, A., Vahlstrup, P. B., Bechmann, A. and Petersen, M. B. (2020) 'Partisan Polarization Is the Primary Psychological Motivation Behind "Fake News" Sharing on Twitter', *PsyArXiv*. Available at: https://psyarxiv.com/v45bk/.

Pennycook, G., Bear, A., Collins, E. T. and Rand, D. G. (2020) 'The Implied Truth Effect: Attaching Warnings to a Subset of Fake News Headlines Increases Perceived Accuracy of Headlines without Warnings', *Management Science*. Available at: https://pubsonline.informs.org/doi/pdf/10.1287/mnsc.2019.3478.

Pronin, E., Lin, D. Y. and Ross, L. (2002) 'The Bias Blind Spot: Perceptions of Bias in Self Versus Others', *Personality and Social Psychology Bulletin*, 28(3), pp. 369–81.

Rapp, D. N. (2016) 'The Consequences of Reading Inaccurate Information', *Current Directions in Psychological Science*, 25(4), pp. 281–85.

Rini, R. (2017) 'Fake News and Partisan Epistemology', *Kennedy Institute of Ethics Journal*, 27(2), pp. 43–64.

Rodrigo, C. M. (2020) 'Critics Fear Facebook Fact-Checkers Losing Misinformation Fight', *The Hill*. Available at: https://thehill.com/policy/technology/478896-critics-fear-facebook-fact-checkers-losing-misinformation-fight.

Rosen, G., Harbath, K., Gleicher, N. and Leathern, R. (2019) 'Helping to Protect the 2020 US Election', *Facebook*. Available at: https://about.fb.com/news/2019/10/update-on-election-integrity-efforts.

Rozenbeek, J. and van der Linden, S. (2019) 'Fake News Game Confers Psychological Resistance against Online Misinformation', *Palgrave Communications*, 5(65). Available at: www.nature.com/articles/s41599-019-0279-9.

Scanlon, T. (1972) 'A Theory of Freedom of Expression', *Philosophy & Public Affairs*, 1(2), pp. 204–26.

Shao, C., Giovanni, L. C., Varol, P., Yang, K-C., Flammini, A. and Menczer, F. (2018) 'The Spread of Low-Credibility Content by Social Bots', *Nature Communications*, 9(4787). Available at: https://www.nature.com/articles/s41467-018-06930-7.pdf.

Starbird, K. (2019) 'Disinformation's Spread: Bots, Trolls and All of Us', *Nature*, 571(7766), p. 449. Available at: https://media.nature.com/original/magazine-assets/d41586-019-02235-x/d41586-019-02235-x.pdf.

Vosoughi, S., Roy, D. and Aral, S. (2018) 'The Spread of True and Fake News Online', *Science*, 359(6380), pp. 1146–51.

Warner, M. R. (2018) 'Potential Policy Proposals for Regulation of Social Media and Technology Firms'. Available at: www.warner.senate.gov/public/_cache/files/d/3/d32c2f17-cc76-4e11-8aa9-897eb3c-90d16/65A7C5D983F899DAAE5AA21F57BAD944.social-media-regulation-proposals.pdf.

20

PROPAGANDA, IRRATIONALITY, AND GROUP AGENCY

Megan Hyska

1 Introduction

Propaganda is an attempt to change the world. But to say this much is evidently not to have given a full theory—it remains to say what aspect of the world propaganda aims to change. The position I stake out in this chapter is that, contrary to a widespread view, propaganda does not characteristically target the individual's beliefs or rationality. Propaganda's characteristic effect is not at the level of the individual at all, but at the level of the *group-agency landscape*.

2 Against the belief account

A natural first thought is this: the parts of the world that propaganda targets are agents, with all their associated faculties. But many thinkers have been keen to pinpoint some specific facet of the agent as propaganda's characteristic target. One tradition says (or can be reconstructed as saying) that it is the agent's needs and desires that propaganda targets, either by changing the desires the agents in fact has (Wimberly 2017, 2020), or else by alienating the agent from their true ones (Marcuse 1964; Marx and Engels 1972; Horkheimer and Adorno 2002). Others identify propaganda as aiming to change the individual's ideology—but ideology has been specified variously as consisting of beliefs (Shelby 2016), material institutions (Althusser 1971), and practices (Haslanger 2017), among other things which may or may not collapse the propaganda as targeting-ideology view down to the targeting-desire or targeting-belief views. In any case, the position that will interest us is that propaganda aims at individuals' *beliefs*.

That beliefs and desires should be proposed as targets for propaganda is natural, given that these are often taken as the antecedents of action. Indeed, we will regard the idea that propaganda's function is to influence action as a core insight into its nature. This by itself might suggest a decentering of beliefs in the account. As Ellul notes,

> Very frequently propaganda is described as a manipulation for the purpose of changing ideas or opinions, of making individuals 'believe' some idea or fact... This is a completely wrong line of thinking...The aim of modern propaganda is no longer to modify ideas, but to provoke action. (1973: 25)

And as Wimberly judiciously adds, "Propagandists are not epistemologists and are not fo-cused on a battle to prove things true or false; they are governors seeking to alter the conduct of the public" (2017: 115).

However, the need to center action in our account is not by itself a knock-down objection against belief accounts. While the production of (in-)action may be the end goal of the pro-pagandist, this doesn't rule out that some kind of belief change is the distinctive mechanism by which propaganda influences action.

My objection to the belief account is instead that it has no plausible precisification. A view on which every attempt to alter someone's beliefs counted as propagandistic would be both counterintuitive and theoretically useless, and so the question becomes which attempts at belief change a plausible version of the belief account should count as propagandistic. We will review two possible answers to this question: that propaganda creates false beliefs, and that it creates irrational beliefs. Neither of these accounts will be satisfying.

The first proposal is that propaganda seeks to create false beliefs. In rejecting this view, theorists often cite cases like "there are muslims among us," uttered by an Islamophobic poli-tician (Stanley 2015: 42) or "93 percent of blacks [in America] are killed by other blacks," ut-tered by one seeking to deflect inquiry into police violence against black Americans (Táíwò 2017: 1); such statements are strictly true, while also plausibly instances of propaganda.

Notable about these cases is that, while not themselves false, their propagandistic effect seems dependent in some way on the audience's acceptance of further falsehoods, which they somehow bring along to supplement themselves: that there are Muslims among us manages to stoke fear only supposing that Muslims' being unusually prone to violence is already accepted. And the "black-on-black" crime deflection characteristically relies for the per-ception of its relevance upon the falsehood that intracommunal violence is unique to black Americans, whereas in fact the vast majority of all crime is intracommunal.

I offer a further counterexample to the false belief account, which is different from the above in that it doesn't seem to rely for its effect on some proximate proposition that *is* false. Consider a workplace in which employees are attempting to unionize. Deeply opposed to this, management circulates pamphlets highlighting cases where attempts at unionization prompted similar workplaces to outsource, and the would-be unionizers lost their jobs.

I take this sort of messaging to be, intuitively, a case of propaganda. A few observations about it: we may stipulate that management's anecdotes about unsuccessful unionization attempts past are all true. We may even suppose that the inference they encourage employees to make on the basis of these anecdotes—that any unionization effort will be both diffi-cult and high-stakes—is true. One might press that management isn't just saying that the unionization effort will *likely* fail but that it *will* fail—and it's not so clear that this is true. A response may seem to turn on the alethic status we take statements about the future to have. On the one hand, if we take it that there is some fact of the matter about the truth of such statements, we may stipulate that, in our case, management's statement is true, and it so happens that unionization efforts really will fail—but this does not, to my mind, change whether it counts as propaganda. On the other hand, if we take it that there is no fact of the matter about the truth value of statements about the future, then management's statements still aren't false, and so still amount to a counterexample.

The direction that most belief theorists actually head in is saying that propaganda en-courages beliefs that are irrational, whether or not they're false. On such accounts, pro-paganda has been described as the "manipulation of the *rational will* to close off debate"; as "speech that *irrationally closes off* certain options that should be considered" (Stanley 2015: 48, 49 on the 'classical' sense of propaganda, italics mine); as "the organized attempt through communication to affect belief or action or inculcate attitudes in a large audience in ways that *circumvent or suppress an individual's adequately formed, rational, reflective judgment*" (Marlin 2002: 22, italics mine); and as "an *epistemically defective message* used with the intention to persuade a socially significant group of people" where epistemically defective persuasion stretches to cover falsehoods, instances of misleading and the use of "spurious" means, like emotional arousal, to persuade (Ross 2002: 24 *et passim*, italics mine).

The discussion in Stanley (2015) I take to be in the spirit of the irrationality account, if not strictly an endorsement of it, as Stanley does not claim to offer a fully general analysis of what propaganda is. But he regards it as possible that his conception of propaganda is a version of the 'classical' view articulated above (2015: 48) and, accordingly, inclines toward the view that "propaganda runs counter to rational principles," focusing on a variety of propaganda ("undermining demagoguery") which conspires to use liberal democratic ideals against themselves, with the contradiction here unnoticed by the audience (an obvious irrationality) because of their pre-existing flawed ideology (2015: 57–58 *et passim*).

I object to the class of belief-irrationality accounts of propaganda very generally, rather than to any one theorist's particular version. So I aim to formulate the irrationality condition quite loosely. Where x is a putative case of propaganda:

> **Irrationality Condition (IC)**: x incites the individual to form beliefs in an irrational manner.

I take it as obvious that IC could not be a sufficient condition on x's being a case of propaganda; it is a familiar observation that a huge range of conditions that seem to trigger cognitive biases, and where such biases are instances of genuine irrationality (*pace* e.g. Dorst 2020) then we see that this account would massively overgenerate.

What is left open to the irrationality theorist is to posit IC as necessary. But I don't think this version of the view fares any better, because I think there are instances of propaganda that don't clearly function by inducing irrationality. In fact, I think the anti-union pamphlets discussed above are such a case. We recall that what the pamphlets do is provide evidence in favor of a particular assessment of the likely outcome of labor organizing. And evidence that my intended plan is high risk with a low probability of success is clearly relevant to deliberations about whether to adopt that plan[1]—there is nothing irrational about being influenced by these considerations.

A remaining option to the irrationality theorist is to just deny that the anti-union pamphlet is an instance of propaganda. My response will involve marshaling a few further cases, any one of which individually, if regarded as propaganda, is a counterexample to the necessity of IC, and the collective exclusion of which from the category of propaganda dooms the concept to something near political irrelevance.

One class of propaganda that I want to draw attention to is brought out in Lisa Wedeen's ethnography of late twentieth-century Syrian political life:

> In official Syrian political discourse, President Hafiz al-Asad is regularly depicted as omnipresent and omniscient…[But] no one in modern Syria, neither those who orchestrate official praise nor those who are forced to consume it, believes that Asad is the country's "premier pharmacist," that he "knows all things about all issues," or that he actually garners 99.2 percent of the vote in elections. (Wedeen 1999: 1)

Haifeng Huang, whose own work primarily concerns contemporary China, dubs the sort of propaganda that Wedeen draws our attention to "hard propaganda" (Huang 2015, 2018). Hard propaganda involves messages that are "crude, heavy-handed, or preposterous," which can be "seen through by citizens" and which therefore "do not induce persuasion" (2018: 1034). The puzzle that Huang raises is what could be gained through propaganda that persuades no one—must we just understand such cases as miscalculations, symptomatic of autocratic hubris? Huang says not. Instead, he argues that we must nuance our understanding of what such propaganda could be trying to persuade its audience *of*. While it might abjectly fail to persuade anyone of that which it strictly speaking *says*, that may be beside the point—it may function to *offer evidence* of the state's power, and with significant persuasive strength. Huang, for instance, argues that "Chinese citizens frequently dislike and ridicule the state's flagship TV news program *Xinwen Lianbo*, [but] the fact that the regime easily bombards the nation with the program daily at 7:00 p.m. manifests its power" (Huang 2018: 1034–35). In other words, hard propaganda is a *flex*.

If Huang and Wedeen are right, the content of the belief that an instance of hard propaganda aims to create is not the same as the content of the propagandistic speech act itself, even given an expansive notion of speech act contents that includes implicata, not-at-issue content and other such phenomena. That the Chinese state has a strength and appetite for control such that one should think twice before publicly dissenting with its policies, for instance, needn't be among the propositions speaker-meant by the anchors on *Xinwen Lianbo* on a given evening[2]—but the broadcast may nonetheless *show this to be so*, and showing this may be part of its purpose.

It will pay later dividends to ask in passing what the hard propagandist gains via their demonstration of power. Not necessarily approval or admiration; Huang notes that

> Chinese college students who are more familiar with the government's propaganda messages…are not more satisfied with the government, but they are more likely to believe that it has a strong capacity in maintaining political order and are, hence, less willing to express dissent. (2015: 421, italics mine)

And importantly, dissent should not be understood sheerly as a matter of individual expressions of disagreement, but of *joining with others in acts of protest*; hard propaganda targets the capacity for this collective action. As a result of state hard propaganda:

> [individuals] may also be reminded that other citizens know the state is powerful too, given the prevalence of such propaganda and the lack of overt opposition in their daily lives. Since failed protest in an authoritarian setting would incur punishment by the regime, participation in such actions depends on not just individuals' opinions of the government but also their assessment of the state's power and the likely outcome of protest. Therefore…it will also decrease their willingness to protest. (Huang 2018: 1035)

While Huang is concerned with authoritarian contexts, I leave it to the reader to decide whether propaganda purporting to demonstrate the futility and risk of, say, radical left social movements might not also be a salient presence in the legal and political lives of liberal democratic polities too. In any case, since many such polities fail to extend democratization to work places, either fully or at all, hard propagandistic intimidation certainly remains a presence in the economic lives of many outside of authoritarian states.

In discerning that an instance of propaganda may *constitute* evidence of a fact, we can see that hard propaganda has a certain amount in common with a second class of propaganda relevant to our argument against the necessity of IC: so-called "propaganda of the deed." Propaganda of the deed is a notion which originated in nineteenth-century anarchist thought, tracing its name to an 1877 article by Paul Brousse and Peter Kropotkin (Fleming 1980: 4). It involves acts of insurrection against the state, including assassinations and bombings, where the accomplishment of such acts is comprehended not just as doing immediate damage to the state, but as an article of evidence concerning both the ruling class's fallibility and the power of the working class. Like hard propaganda, propaganda of the deed is a *demonstration* of power, not just an assertion of it.

Let's finally make clear why hard propaganda and propaganda of the deed are troublesome for accounts upholding the necessity of IC: the evidence such propaganda offers in favor of the propagandist's strength really does seem like evidence. That is, the Chinese state's ability to restrict dinner-hour television to a single jingoistic, self-consciously censored news program is a demonstration of power, and there is nothing irrational about inclining toward the belief that the Chinese state is powerful on its basis. Likewise, there is nothing irrational about allowing a suitably elaborated-upon instance of spontaneous industrial sabotage to incline one toward the belief that working people would hold the power to threaten currently powerful institutions, should they choose to do so. It seems therefore that both hard propaganda and propaganda of the deed are excluded from the category of propaganda altogether if one maintains IC as a necessary condition.

To come full circle, let's consider what hard propaganda and propaganda of the deed have in common with the union-busting tactics cited as a counterexample to the necessity of IC above: all three cases concern the viability of a possible future political formation. Anti-labor management and an authoritarian state seek to demonstrate that political formations opposing them are futile and risky while the insurrectionary anarchist seeks to demonstrate that organizing against the state can be fruitful; these cases share an orientation toward the future and toward group-formation. One determined to hold onto the necessity of IC is forced to deny that the above cases are propaganda, and in doing so to shrink the ambit of their theoretical project. Here we may recall the insight of Wimberly and Ellul: that the essential task of propaganda is to prime individuals for (in-)action, not just for belief. A theory of propaganda that systematically excludes the cases where this priming for (in-)action is most explicit parts ways with this insight. And this exclusion will indeed be somewhat systematic; one of the reasons that the above cases fall short of clear incitement to irrationality is that, when it comes to forming beliefs about what the future may bring, a huge range of facts about the past will be count as among the set of salient considerations, and so a huge range of messages, serving a huge range of political goals, will be compatible with rational reflection. But it would be an error to overlook all of these messages as possible instances of propaganda.

In what follows I present a characterization of propaganda that makes room for a wide variety of cases, including those explicitly oriented toward future group-formation possibilities. On my view, propaganda may frequently incite people to irrationality and bias; it may also frequently act upon their desires. But none of these individual-agent-level effects are what is characteristic of propaganda. The effect which is characteristic of propaganda exists only at the level of the group, and more specifically what I will call the group-agency landscape.

3 An Arendtian positive account

In fleshing out a positive account of propaganda's characteristic, group-level effects, I'll be taking at least initial inspiration from Hannah Arendt's characterization of propaganda in *The Origins of Totalitarianism* (1994). While Arendt is concerned primarily with the totalitarian propaganda of Nazi Germany and a Stalinist USSR, I think that a view based on her observations applies to liberal democracies as well.

Arendt discerns a role for propaganda among other tools of political control, like physical coercion, the terror imposed by threat of this, and indoctrination, which she sees as distinct from propaganda.[3] And she doesn't think that what is distinctive of propaganda is the power to incite beliefs of any kind; the "true goal of totalitarian propaganda is not persuasion," she asserts, "but organization of the polity" (1994: 361).

Whereas indoctrination consists of the dissemination of "ideological doctrine for the initiated in the movement," propaganda is what organizes the "outside world" into a movement in the first place (1994: 343). Propaganda precedes indoctrination and is what makes it possible. And in the extreme case where a totalitarian movement takes total control of a polity "it replaces propaganda with indoctrination" (1994: 341). We may then think of propaganda, on the Arendtian account, as *group-forming speech*, whereas indoctrination is *group-addressing speech*.

What I take from Arendt is the idea that the characteristic effect of propaganda has to do with the formation of groups. In this respect I also draw from Wimberly's argument (2020: 31–50 *et passim*) that, since the profession's inception in the Progressive Era, the mission of public relations (i.e. professionalized propaganda production) has been to *produce the publics* needed to sustain corporate power. In addition to organizing people into groups, I emphasize that propaganda may also disorganize people, by destroying groups or pre-empting their formation.

So far I have said that propaganda creates or destroys groups. However, this isn't quite my fully refined view, since, if *any* collection of people counts as a group, then the mildest utterance might seem to have created a group—say, of people who were in hearing range of the utterance! Here I will be sidestepping some tricky questions around the metaphysics of groups,[4] because my concern is in fact not with groups simpliciter but with group *agency*. My account of propaganda can be understood as positing a message's creation or destruction of group agency, rather than of groups simpliciter, as a condition on that message counting as propaganda.

Now, accounts of group agency place differing requirements on which intentional states need be present at the level of the individual in order for an event involving many individuals to count as a group action. For instance, some theorists posit agents who each intend to make certain contribution to the joint action, and commonly know one another to have these intentions concerning their respective conducts (e.g. Tuomela and Miller 1988; Bratman 1993), whereas others insist that individuals' intentions to act as part of a collective are irreducible to any suite of beliefs and standard intentions (e.g. Searle 1990). Note, however, that a fully fleshed-out account of what it is to modify group-agential capacities—per our account, the hallmark of propaganda—may be somewhat ecumenical concerning these debates, as our question is not what individual intentional states and actions taken together constitute group action, but rather what it looks like to cultivate, or extinguish, the *antecedents* to these states, as propaganda does. Some of these antecedents will be quite banal; one step toward being able to work together, for instance, is simply finding one another—no wonder, then, that propaganda frequently works just to make like-minded individuals identifiable by one another. By way of noting how the group-agency account brings discussion of propaganda into contact with other literatures, we can observe that other plausible candidates for these antecedents will include many robustly theorized epistemic and affective relations—relations, perhaps, like love, different varieties of trust, and solidarity, among others.

The group action account of propaganda deals well with those cases that troubled the irrational belief account. Union-busting pamphlets and Chinese state television attempt to disrupt the formation of groups capable of action (a union, capable of withholding labor and collective bargaining; a pro-democracy movement capable of making authoritarian rule untenable); classical instances of propaganda of the deed aim to demonstrate the capacity of working people to disrupt the operations of capital, and to inspire the formation of groups that can accomplish this.

With the basics of my view now on the table, we should ask why would-be wielders of political power would sometimes reach into their toolbox and pull out propaganda, if propaganda is really as I characterize it. We start by once more recalling Wimberly and Ellul's idea that propaganda fundamentally aims to alter actions. That insight by itself leaves open the possibility that propaganda could be meant to cultivate the capacity for individual rather than group action, even if individual action at a mass scale. What's required is the additional insight that groups can do things that an individual can't—I alone can't instigate or prevent a political revolution, or make or break a corporation's third quarter earnings. And while non-group collections of individuals can also do things individuals can't (e.g. I can't make 500 phone calls in an hour, but for any given hour we could no doubt find 100 people whose collective number of phone calls adds up to 500), only group or joint action allows for coordination and control over what gets done—whether this control is exerted in a top-down manner, or determined and enforced by distributed processes of deliberation and accountability.

In addition to the insight that shaping group action is the only practical route to the large-scale effects they desire, the would-be propagandist functions also within the reality that people are often transformed by participation in group action. This contention has both negative and positive manifestations. It is an old idea (Marx and Engels 1972) that engaging in collective struggle allows for the achievement of insight into one's society, into oneself, and into one's relationships with others. And so propaganda, in its most salutary forms, may even be what makes certain epistemic achievements possible. We are also well-acquainted with the profoundly negative alterations in individual conduct that group-participation can sometimes induce; Arendt, considering the transformative effects of totalitarian movements, noted that "without the force of the movement, its members cease at once to believe in the dogma for which yesterday they were willing to sacrifice their lives" (Arendt 1994: 363).

Techniques of political influence and control, like propaganda, are adapted to function in a world characterized by the realities of human sociality. A depiction of the propagandistic calculation is then as follows: If I aim to steer the public's actions, I must contend with the possibility that the individuals I want to reach will be deeply influenced, not only by me, and not only by their own material conditions, but also by the epistemic and emotional entanglements they have in virtue of their membership in their families, schools, workplaces, neighborhood associations, political parties, churches, sports teams, frequented subreddits, and so on. If I want to alter the conduct of large groups of people, I must decide how to make an ally out of the joint-action-enabling structures that already have a hold on them, or I must figure out a way to sever their ties to these competing relationships. If I opt for the latter, I must bear in mind that a totally atomized individual is highly volatile, and if my attention slips for a moment I may find that they have thrown themselves into the group least suited to my purposes. And so I may ultimately decide that it is better to invite my targets into a group whose influences upon the individual, and collective action as a group, will be acceptable for my purposes, than to try to sustain their isolation.

Propaganda is one of the tools that attempts to address this essential predicament of the would-be-molder of mass action, and its group-destroying and group-creating declensions simply reflect different tactical choices at different moments.

I have posited it as a necessary condition on a case's being one of propaganda that it creates or destroys group agency. At this point a misunderstanding might result in the following question: mustn't any attempt to shape group action proceed by influencing the beliefs of the individuals *in* the group? How then could propaganda be said not to aim at individual beliefs, even if the end goal is to affect group action? The short response is: of course, propaganda alters the group by altering the intentional states of the individuals in the group—a rejection of the belief account of propaganda, as above, does not require denying this. Rather, the upshot of the previous section is that there is nothing *distinctive* about the intentional states that propaganda creates in order to influence group action; some of the individual beliefs that propaganda creates will be false and some won't; some will rest on a flawed ideology and some won't; some will be the consequence of brute unreasoned inculcation, and some will be the result of considering evidence. So propaganda has individual belief formation as one of its effects, but this is hardly distinctive of propaganda. Its characteristic effect is only discernible at the level of group action.

Strictly speaking then, I am open to the idea that a very generic belief condition is a necessary condition on a case's being one of propaganda—i.e. all instances of propaganda must target individuals' beliefs somehow. But where two theories each offer only a necessary condition, and each seems true as far as it goes, we can arbitrate between them by asking which has theoretical utility—a theory which posits only the necessity of the generic belief condition does not illuminate the nature of propaganda. The group-agency account does.

One might attempt to construct a more precise, and therefore more theoretically useful belief account by saying that what is characteristic of propaganda is the creation of those individual beliefs which, when acted upon by the individual at the same time that certain other individuals engage in certain other actions, constitute the execution or absence of group action. I suppose I am fine with this formulation, but that's because it reflects the fact that propaganda's characteristic effect on individual beliefs can be articulated only with prior reference to group action; group action is what is theoretically fundamental.

4 Conclusion

One consequence of regarding propaganda as operating fundamentally on the level of groups, rather than individuals, is that it suggests a new set of social operations as propaganda's next of kin: organization, mobilization, and polarization, rather than lying and manipulating.[5]

A further consequence of shifting from a view of propaganda within the irrational-belief class to one based on modification of group agency is a different picture of what it is to resist propaganda—and while, on my account, propaganda is not something that need always be resisted, it surely remains so sometimes. The vision of resistance that flows from at least some recent irrational-belief accounts centers the individual's attempts to purify their own reasoning by purging the flawed ideology that undergirds it as best they can. Coupling this with an understanding that ideologies are of, and propagated by, the ruling class, some critics have discerned in Stanley (2015) a tendency to focus on the capacity of educated elites to analytically dissect the flawed ideologies that function as apologetics for their unearned privileges, rather than on non-elites' achievement of insight into the systems that oppress them via lived experience and liberatory action (Srinivasan 2016; McKinnon 2018).

Certainly, the irrational-belief theorist's view of resistance does not require engagement with one's possible participation in social and political collectives. Their vision may require one to have certain humane beliefs about others, or to engage in reflection that triangulates with others' hypothetical reasoning.[6] But it is compatible with the agent's never seriously deliberating about actually participating in joint action. Indeed, to the extent that there is a lingering inclination to regard the highly reflective isolated individual as a model of rationality, and the epistemic and affective entanglements of group memberships only as threats to proper reasoning, some forms of this view of what it is to resist propaganda may be actively hostile to wholehearted participation in a group.

An alternative vision of resistance, and the one that I endorse, involves an individual meeting instances of group-agency-forming propaganda with an eye to whether the group they are being invited into has a structural insensitivity, or even hostility, to their questions, priorities, and opinions, or else whether it draws them into a collective deliberative process. Resistance of group-agency-destroying propaganda may look somewhat different: particularly in those cases where the audience's membership in a group is pre-empted, and where the negative propaganda in question seems to provide evidence of the danger or futility of joining, I don't think that the task of resistance can be an individual matter at all. I think it requires an infusion of optimism that can only come from evidence that the group in questions can successfully organize after all—which is to say, it requires group-agency-forming propaganda. The most effective type of such propaganda will be evidence that the group already has successfully organized, even if for a transient moment. And naturally, this successful instance of organizing requires many agents beyond the one whose resistance to negative propaganda was in question, to execute it. We see then that propaganda often cannot be resisted alone.

Notes

1 Discussion of the rationality of plan adoption suggests that the notion of rationality relevant here is practical rationality. I am, however, trying to be ecumenical about the sort of irrationality which might be invoked by the IC, and I take it that the same point can be put in terms of theoretical rationality.
2 This observation relies on some familiar discussion in the philosophy of language about where or whether to draw the line between actions that speaker-meant that p, and actions that show that p. Classically, see Grice (1957); but for dissenting views see e.g. Schiffer (1972); Récanati (1986); Neale (1992); Sperber and Wilson (1986, 2015). Insofar as the propagandistic effect will not, on my account, be traceable to some expressed content, I am on the same page as Táíwò (2017) who discerns a class of "trojan horse" propaganda. However, unlike Táíwò, nor do I think that such cases' status as propaganda is based in their undermining a standard of reasonableness.
3 For more discussion on the relation between these tools, see e.g. Hyska (2018).
4 See e.g. Ritchie (2013, 2015) for a discussion of the groups-as-realized-social-structures account, designed to rein in this overgeneration.
5 That propaganda needn't involve manipulation will follow most clearly from my arguments against the necessity of IC in combination views on which manipulation itself requires some incitement to irrationality (see e.g. Baron 2003; Greenspan 2003; Cave 2007), though not everyone holds this view (see e.g. Gorin 2014).
6 See Stanley's discussion (2015: Chapter 3) on how propaganda undermines public reason.

References

Althusser, L. (1971), "Ideology and ideological state apparatuses (Notes towards an investigation)", trans. Ben Brewster, *Lenin and Philosophy and Other Essays.* New York and London: Monthly Review Press, 127–188.
Arendt, H. (1994), *The Origins of Totalitarianism*, New York: Harcourt.

Baron, M. (2003), "Manipulativeness", *Proceedings and Addresses of the American Philosophical Association* 77(2), 37–54.

Bratman, M. (1993), "Shared intention", *Ethics* 104, 97–113.

Cave, E. (2007), "What's wrong with motive manipulation", *Ethical Theory and Moral Practice* 10(2), 129–44.

Dorst, K. (2020), "The rational question", *The Oxonian Review*, viewed May 2020. http://www.oxonianreview.org/wp/the-rational-question/.

Ellul, J. (1973), *Propaganda: The Formation of Men's Attitudes*, Vintage Books. Online.

Fleming, M. (1980), "Propaganda by the deed: Terrorism and anarchist theory in late nineteenth-century Europe", *Studies in Conflict and Terrorism* 4(1–4), 1–23.

Gorin, M. (2014), "Do manipulators always threaten rationality?", *American Philosophical Quarterly* 51(1), 51–61.

Greenspan, P. (2003), "The problem with manipulation", *American Philosophical Quarterly* 40(2), 155–64.

Grice, H. P. (1957), "Meaning", *Philosophical Review* 66(3), 377–88.

Haslanger, S. (2017), "Racism, ideology, and social movements", *Res Philosophica* 94(1), 1–22.

Horkheimer, M. and Adorno, T. W. (2002), "The culture industry: Enlightenment as mass deception", trans. Edmund Jephcott, in Gunzelin Schmid Noerr (ed.), *Dialectics of Enlightenment*, Stanford: Stanford University Press, pp. 94–136.

Huang, H. (2015), "Propaganda as signaling", *Comparative Politics* 47(4), 419–37.

Huang, H. (2018), "The pathology of hard propaganda", *The Journal of Politics* 80(3), 1034–38.

Hyska, M. (2018), "Of martyrs and robots: Propaganda and group identity", *The Yale Review* 106(4), 1–11.

Marcuse, H. (1964), *One-Dimensional Man: Studies in the Ideology of Advanced Industrial Society*, Boston, MA: Beacon Press.

Marlin, R. (2002), *Propaganda and the Ethics of Persuasion*, Peterborough: Broadview Press.

Marx, K. and Engels, F. (1972), *The German Ideology*, International Publishers, New York.

McKinnon, R. (2018), "The epistemology of propaganda", *Philosophy and Phenomenological Research* 96(2), 483–89.

Neale, S. (1992), "Paul Grice and the philosophy of language", *Linguistics and Philosophy* 15, 509–559.

Récanati, F. (1986), 'On defining communicative intentions', *Mind & Language* 1, 213–42.

Ritchie, K. (2013), "What are groups?", *Philosophical Studies* 166(2), 257–72.

Ritchie, K. (2015), "The metaphysics of social groups", *Philosophy Compass* 10(5), 310–21.

Ross, S. T. (2002), "Understanding propaganda: The epistemic merit model and its application to art", *Journal of Aesthetic Education* 36(1), 16–30.

Schiffer, S. (1972), *Meaning*, Oxford: Clarendon Press.

Searle, J. (1990), "Collective intentions and actions", in *Intentions in Communication*, eds. P. Cohen, J. Morgan, and M. Pollack. Cambridge: MIT Press, 401–15.

Shelby, T. (2016), *Dark Ghettos: Injustice, Dissent, and Reform*, Cambridge, MA: Harvard University Press.

Sperber, D. and Wilson, D. (1986), *Relevance: Communication and Cognition*, Oxford: Blackwell.

Sperber, D. and Wilson, D. (2015), "Beyond speaker's meaning", *Croatian Journal of Philosophy* 15(44), 117–49.

Srinivasan, A. (2016), "Philosophy and ideology", *Theoria: An International Journal for Theory, History and Foundations of Science* 31(3), 371–80.

Stanley, J. (2015), *How Propaganda Works*, Princeton, NJ: Princeton University Press.

Táíwò, O. (2017), "Beware of schools bearing gifts: Miseducation and trojan horse propaganda", *Public Affairs Quarterly* 31(1), 1–18.

Tuomela, R. and Miller, K. (1988), "We-Intentions", *Philosophical Studies* 53, 367–89.

Wedeen, L. (1999), *Ambiguities of Domination: Politics, Rhetoric, and Symbols in Contemporary Syria*, Chicago, IL: University of Chicago Press.

Wimberly, C. (2017), "The job of creating desire: Propaganda as an apparatus of government and subjectification", *Journal of Speculative Philosophy* 31(1), 101–18.

Wimberly, C. (2020), *How Propaganda Became Public Relations*, New York: Routledge.

PART 4

Ignorance and irrationality in politics

INTRODUCTION TO PART 4

A critical component of democratic citizenship is knowledge about politics. As James Madison once said, a popular government without an informed public "is but a prologue to a farce or a tragedy, or perhaps both." But are citizens knowledgeable enough to vote responsibly? Will they competently exercise their political power over others?

One of the most consistent findings in political science over the past 60 years is the staggering degree to which citizens are ignorant about politics. The average voter is ignorant of even the most basic political information, such as who their elected officials are, what their opponents believe, and which important laws or policies were passed in the past two years. This level of ignorance poses a significant challenge for democracy. When voters make poor decisions out of ignorance, they harm the common good. For example, the false belief that climate change is not the result of human activity has blocked policies that would reduce global emissions, and mistaken convictions about the health risks of vaccines can endanger public health. This illustrates that citizens often lack the knowledge necessary to make informed political decisions. It is for this reason that Plato said democracy is defective. In the *Gorgias*, he criticized democracies for adopting policies based on the views of the ignorant common citizens and neglecting the better informed counsel of experts.

But political ignorance may actually be rational. After all, the vast size and complexity of modern government make it almost impossible for ordinary citizens to be adequately informed on most issues. Moreover, an individual voter has virtually no chance of influencing electoral outcomes. In the 2008 US presidential election, for example, the chance of an individual vote having a decisive impact was approximately 1 in 60 million. As a result, the incentive to become a smarter voter is vanishingly small. What does this mean for democracy?

In the first chapter of this section, Ilya Somin explains why most political ignorance is rational. The theory of rational ignorance says that citizens know (at least implicitly) that the costs of acquiring political knowledge outweigh the benefits of possessing it. He argues that this hypothesis is more compelling than two alternative hypotheses: inadvertent ignorance and irrational ignorance. Inadvertent ignorance occurs when an individual simply has no idea that a particular body of information exists (or that it might be useful for their purposes); irrational ignorance occurs when an individual avoids learning information that would be useful because of cognitive biases that lead them to take actions running counter to their own goals. After finding these two alternative hypotheses unsatisfactory, Somin summarizes some of the implications of widespread rational ignorance for democratic theory.

Ken Boyd's chapter looks specifically at the relationship between political ignorance and pragmatic encroachment. Pragmatic encroachment is the view that whether one knows something is partly determined by practical factors, such as the costs of being wrong. Boyd considers some consequences of this thesis for political knowledge and political ignorance. For example, he argues there will be cases in which it is not practically rational to acquire political knowledge because the stakes surrounding one's political actions are high. Moreover, it seems that political knowledge can be more easily acquired when one values the welfare of others less. Finally, pragmatic encroachment may fail to account for a form of epistemic injustice when it comes to evaluating the political knowledge of members of marginalized groups. These consequences are undesirable, according to Boyd, but the extent to which the pragmatic encroacher is committed to them will depend both on the details of the theory and the extent to which one considers political knowledge to be important.

The chapters by Jeffrey Friedman, Keith Stanovich, and Robin McKenna shift the focus from political ignorance to political irrationality. According to Friedman, we are too quick to describe our opponents' political beliefs as irrational. This form of explanation is implausible, says Friedman, because it fails to acknowledge the possibility that others have rational, yet quite possibly mistaken, grounds for their beliefs. When we impute irrationality to others, we are mistakenly treating our own knowledge as though it were self-evident. But intellectual charity demands that we reject this naïve assumption. Instead, we should think that human knowledge is mediated by fallible processes of information gathering, interpretation, and communication, which may produce mistaken (yet rational) beliefs.

Along similar lines, Stanovich claims that attempts to impute irrationality to one's political opponents may reflect a cognitive bias. His chapter provides an extensive review of evidence suggesting there are no partisan differences in rational thinking. This goes against a prominent line of argument in social science, where several researchers have claimed to find cognitive differences between American conservatives and liberals. Against this idea, Stanovich claims that such researchers themselves likely suffer from a "bias blind spot," which is a meta-bias which makes people think that psychological biases are more prevalent in others than in themselves. As a result of this, liberal social scientists mistakenly feel that their political opponents display irrationality and other epistemically problematic psychological traits, when Stanovich says that no such difference in rational thinking has been proven.

McKenna continues this theme by investigating two questions: first, why are we so polarized about certain issues, and, second, does this mean that our views about these issues are all equally ir/rational? Drawing on the literature on ideologically motivated reasoning, McKenna argues that we exhibit "directional biases" in our information processing: we try to assimilate new information into our existing webs of beliefs. Moreover, he claims that we *all* exhibit such biases in our thinking, so in this sense we are all equally rational (or irrational).

21

IS POLITICAL IGNORANCE RATIONAL?[1]

Ilya Somin

Introduction

Surveys from countries around the world indicate that political ignorance is widespread, and that voters often do not know even very basic information about government and public policy.[2] To take just one striking example, a recent study found that only 26% of Americans can even name the three branches of the federal government: legislative, executive, and judicial (Annenberg Public Policy Center 2017).[3]

It may seem strange to claim that such ignorance is rational. But most of it is. Because of the extremely low odds of any one vote having an impact on the outcomes of elections, it is in fact rational for most voters to devote little or no time and energy to learning about political issues – at least if their goal in seeking out political information is to cast better-informed votes. Those that do acquire more than modest amounts of political information usually do so for other reasons, often ones that are in tension with seeking out truth.

Section I of this chapter outlines the logic of rational ignorance and how it applies to political information. In Section II, I outline evidence indicating that rational ignorance is indeed the best explanation for most, even if not all, of the widespread political ignorance we see in modern society. This part also explains why rational ignorance is a more defensible explanation for this phenomenon than inadvertent or irrational ignorance. Finally, Section III describes some potential implications of widespread rational ignorance for democratic theory.

I The logic of rational ignorance

For social scientists, the idea of rational ignorance has a specific meaning that is distinct from the way the term "rational" is generally used in ordinary language. A person is rationally ignorant whenever he or she has decided not to learn some body of knowledge because the costs of doing so exceed the benefits, based on the decision-maker's own objectives.

Finding, studying, and assimilating information is a costly activity. The time we spend studying philosophy or seeking out information about the best possible deal on a new car could instead be used on other activities. Going through information that one does not find interesting can also be boring, tedious, and otherwise distasteful, which imposes an additional cost. The rational decision-maker therefore will try to expend resources on searching for it only up to the point where expected returns no longer exceed expected costs (Stigler 1961). "Costs" are broadly defined to include time, effort, and psychological discomfort, as well as pecuniary expenditures. While the idea of rational ignorance was not formalized by scholars until the twentieth century,[4] it is based on a simple intuition that many people implicitly acted on long before: because information-seeking is costly, it often makes good sense to forego additional learning in order to concentrate on other, more useful activities.

Rational behavior in this sense need not be precisely calculated behavior. Often, it would actually be *irrational* to precisely calculate the potential costs and benefits of learning a particular piece of information, because calculation itself requires more time and effort than it is worth. A person who knows she has little interest in the doings of celebrities, can rationally decide not to give careful consideration to the question of whether she should try to read every new article in a tabloid publication. She can simply make what Herbert Simon (1959) called a "satisficing" decision to avoid tabloids altogether, without scrutinizing each new issue in detail.

Rational behavior decision-making is also distinct from morally praiseworthy behavior. For present purposes, rationality is defined in terms of maximizing the decision-maker's own objectives (Becker 1976), regardless of whether those objectives are morally good, bad, or indifferent. A crime boss focused on increasing his wealth and power acts rationally when he devotes time and effort to learning information that enables him to operate a more successful protection racket, rather than that which might make him a better person.

Rational ignorance may be usefully distinguished from two other types of ignorance: *inadvertent* ignorance and *irrational* ignorance. Inadvertent ignorance occurs when an individual simply has no idea that a particular body of information exists, or that it might be useful for her purposes (Friedman 2005).[5]

Rational ignorance is also distinct from irrational ignorance. The latter occurs in situations where an individual avoids learning information that would be useful to him because of cognitive biases that lead him to take actions that run counter to his own goals. For example, "motivated skepticism" might lead an individual to avoid information that cuts against his preexisting beliefs (Taber and Lodge 2006), even though the new information might be very useful in achieving his goals. Motivated skepticism is a subset of the broader problem of "motivated ignorance," where people choose to avoid certain information not because it is too costly to acquire, but because there are psychic costs associated with knowing it (Williams 2020).

Rejecting or undervaluing information that runs counter to one's preexisting views is not always irrational. If the information was sought out for purposes other than learning the truth, then evaluating it in a biased way is not irrational, in the sense that it runs counter to the decision-maker's objectives.[6] But such behavior does become irrational in cases where ascertaining truth is a key objective of the person evaluating the information. A variety of other psychological biases might similarly lead people to avoid or deny the validity of new information.[7]

A voter whose only purpose in acquiring political knowledge is to be a better voter has little reason to devote more than minimal time and effort to the task. The likelihood that his vote will make a difference to the outcome of an election is infinitesimally small – about 1 in 60 million in an American presidential election, for example Gelman et al. (2012).[8] While few voters know these exact odds, it is likely that most have at least an intuitive sense that there is little point to spending substantial amounts of time following politics in order to be a better voter (Somin 2016, ch. 3).

It is more rational to devote one's time to acquiring information that is relevant to decisions that are actually likely to make a difference. As former British Prime Minister Tony Blair puts it,

> most people, most of the time, don't give politics a first thought all day long. Or if they do, it is with a sigh…., before going back to worrying about the kids, the parents, the mortgage, the boss, their friends, their weight, their health, sex and rock 'n' roll….. (Blair 2010, 70–71).

Decades of survey data bear out Blair's conjecture that most voters prioritize other activities over learning about politics. Since the beginning of modern survey research in the 1930s, voter knowledge levels in the United States have been fairly stable, and consistently low (e.g. Delli Carpini and Keeter 1996; Althaus 2003; Somin 2016, ch. 1). Political knowledge levels have stagnated despite major increases in educational attainment and increased availability of information thanks to modern technology, such as the internet and cable television news. Majorities are often ignorant of such basic facts as the distribution of spending in the government budget, the nature of opposing liberal and conservative ideologies, which party controls the two houses of the US Congress, and which government officials are responsible for which issues (Somin 2016, ch. 1).

It is important to recognize that political ignorance is rational even for highly altruistic voters whose main purpose in life is to help others. For such altruists, it is more rational to spend time and effort on activities that are actually likely to effectively help others than to devote the time to studying political information in order to be a better voter – an activity which only has a tiny chance of effectively advancing altruistic purposes (ibid., 78). The large potential "payoff" that the altruist will get in the vanishingly rare scenario where her vote does turn out to be decisive justifies a modestly greater expenditure on getting the vote "right" than would otherwise be rational; but still only a small one, given the much greater likely efficacy of devoting time and effort to other ways of helping people.[9]

Political scientist Jeffrey Friedman claims the theory of rational ignorance requires voters to be "effectively omniscient" (Friedman 2019, 279–80). Otherwise, he contends, they could not know valuable the information they forego might be, or how likely it is that their vote could change the outcome of an election. At the very least, Friedman claims they would need to make complicated calculations about the likelihood of their vote having an impact (ibid., 278–79). He points out that social scientists did not develop the theory of rational ignorance until the 1950s, so it is unlikely that ordinary voters could have realized that ignorance is rational without familiarity with the relevant scholarship (ibid., 277–79).

But no such omniscience, complex calculation, or knowledge of social science is needed for people to rationally decide to devote only minimal time and effort to learning about political issues. As already noted, people can and do intuitively – and rationally – weigh the costs and benefits of acquiring more information about a given subject, every day. Similarly, precise calculations are not needed to understand that there is little chance one vote will make a difference in an election with many thousands or millions of voters.

People who know little or no social science routinely decide not to take costly actions that are unlikely to make a decisive difference to an outcome, because the latter depends on the actions of large numbers of people. This, for example, is why unpopular oppressive authoritarian regimes persist despite the fact that they would collapse if a majority of the population refused to obey (Kuran 1995).

To claim that voters need to understand the formal theory of rational ignorance in order to act in accordance with its tenets is much like claiming that consumers and businesses need to understand the formal economic theory of comparative advantage in order to understand that it makes sense to buy goods and services from the lowest cost producers. Obviously, international trade developed in accordance with comparative advantage long before economists developed the formal theory of the phenomenon in the nineteenth century. The same goes for rational ignorance, which also existed long before scholars developed a formal analysis of the phenomenon. Widespread political ignorance was a serious problem long before the twentieth century, which is an indication that citizens in those eras were already making marginal decisions about how much time to spend acquiring political knowledge and often choosing to make only minimal efforts to do so – including with respect to very basic knowledge.[10]

The value of formal social science analysis of rational ignorance is not to guide the decisions of individual voters, but to help us understand the systemic implications of such individual decisions. Similar, market actors do not need the theory of comparative advantage to help decide which products to buy, but that theory can help analysts understand patterns of trade and economic development.

Finally, some critics of the rational choice explanation for public ignorance contend that it may be rational for voters to acquire substantial political information after all. For example, even voters who know they are unlikely to cast a decisive ballot may want to acquire political knowledge in order to increase or decrease the size of the winner's "mandate" (Mackie 2012). The problem with this theory is that the odds of one vote influencing perceptions of a "mandate" are likely even lower than the odds of one vote determining an electoral outcome (Somin 2016, 86–87).

Political theorist Richard Tuck argues that conventional rational choice theory underestimates the likelihood that one vote will make a difference, because it can do so as long as it is part of a "causally efficacious set" (Tuck 2008, ch. 2).[11] Such a set is the number of votes necessary to ensure victory in an election. For example, if Candidate A defeats Candidate B by 10,000 votes to 9,000, then 9,001 votes were needed to form the "causally efficacious set" needed for A to prevail. Tuck contends that there is a substantial likelihood that any given vote will be part of the relevant set. In this case, for example, just over 90% of the voters supporting A were part of the set.

The problem with Tuck's argument is that, in all but vanishingly rare cases, a single voter's decision has only an infinitesimal chance of determining whether a given candidate gets enough votes to form a set large enough to ensure victory. For the potential voter interested in assuring victory for the "right" candidate, the important question is not the likelihood that she will be part of a causally efficacious set, but the likelihood that her efforts will make a decisive difference in ensuring that the causally efficacious set will come into existence at all. If her preferred candidate will get enough votes to win without her, or will lose even with her support, her vote does not make any difference to the outcome, regardless of whether it is part of a causally efficacious set or not.

Some voters, of course, acquire political information for reasons other than improving their ballot box decisions. Just as sports fans enjoy learning about their favorite teams and cheering them on against the opposition irrespective of whether they can influence the outcome of games, so "political fans" enjoy learning about their preferred ideologies, candidates, and parties regardless of whether they can influence electoral results (ibid., 93–96). Unfortunately, people who acquire political information for the purpose of enhancing their fan experience often process new data in a highly biased away, overvaluing any evidence that supports their preexisting views and undervaluing or ignoring anything that cuts the other way (ibid., 95–96). Those most interested in politics also have a strong tendency to discuss political issues only with those who hold similar views, and follow political news only in like-minded media (Mutz 2006, 29–41).

Such behavior is irrational if the goal is to find the truth. As John Stuart Mill famously pointed out, a rational truth-seeker should make a special effort to consult information sources with viewpoints different from his or her own (Mill 1975 [1859], 36). But it makes perfect sense if the goal is not truth-seeking, but entertainment, validation of one's preexisting views, or a sense of camaraderie with fellow political fans. Economist Bryan Caplan calls this phenomenon "rational irrationality" (Caplan 2001, 2007). When the goal of acquiring information is something other than truth-seeking, it may be rational to be biased in the selection of information sources, and in the evaluation of new information that is learned.

Thus, rational ignorance creates a two-level problem for democracy. Most voters pay little attention to politics and government policy, and therefore know very little about it. A minority – the "political fans" – are much more engaged. But their motivations are often at odds with truth-seeking and therefore result in highly biased evaluation of the information they learn.

II Inadvertent ignorance and irrational ignorance

Rational behavior is far from the only possible explanation for widespread political ignorance. Two of the most prominent competing explanations are what I refer to as "inadvertent ignorance" and "irrational ignorance." Each of them probably accounts for at least some of the ignorance we observe, though probably not as much as rational ignorance does.

Inadvertent ignorance

The most obvious alternative to the rational ignorance explanation for widespread political ignorance is the idea that widespread political ignorance is just an honest mistake. Given the complexity of the political world, it is possible that voters are "inadvertently" ignorant. They could be simply unaware that there is a body of information out there that might improve the quality of their political decisions if they learned it (Friedman 2005; Friedman 2019, 277–82).[12] Either they don't know that the relevant information exists, or they do not realize it might be useful to understanding political issues. Instead of rational ignorance, low levels of political knowledge could be the result of just plain simple ignorance.

The biggest difficulty with the inadvertent ignorance theory is that it fails to explain why so many people are ignorant even of very basic facts about politics. Simple intuition suggests that, to be an adequately informed voter, it might help to know the names of the opposing candidates, the major policies adopted by the government in recent years, and which officials are responsible for which issues. If one is planning to cast a vote based on the state of the economy, it should not be hard to figure out that it might help to check the data on whether the economy has grown or shrunk recently. Such basic information is readily available in the media and, now, on the internet. Today's denser media environment and the ready availability of an enormous range of information on the internet make it harder than ever to remain completely unaware that there are whole bodies of knowledge that are relevant to political decisions. Yet a large percentage of the public, often a majority, fail to learn it. If you are planning to purchase a TV, it's not difficult to figure out that you will make a better decision if you acquire some basic information about the price, reliability, and picture quality of competing brands. Even a person with little knowledge of the TV market can readily grasp that much. The TV consumer who fails to get that basic information is unlikely to do so simply through mere "inadvertence." If she remains ignorant on such points, it is likely because she doesn't care very much about the choice of a TV and prefers to devote the time and effort needed to acquire that information to other pursuits that she considers more important. The same point applies to voters' failure to acquire basic political information.

Moreover, if political ignorance is inadvertent, one would expect knowledge levels to increase substantially over time as education levels have risen and political information becomes more widely available at lower cost, thanks to modern technology. The more education one has and the more political information is readily available, the higher the likelihood that individuals will be exposed to the idea that there are bodies of knowledge available that could help them inform their voting decisions. Yet political knowledge levels have risen little if at all over the last several decades, despite major increases in education and the availability of information (Somin 2016, ch. 1).

Another telling point of evidence against the inadvertent ignorance theory is the very different behavior of jurors relative to voters, even though both groups are drawn from the same population, with jurors usually being selected from voter rolls. When citizens decide a case as jurors, they typically make far greater effort to acquire relevant information and evaluate it in an unbiased way than ballot box voters do at election time.[13] The key difference between the two situations is that jurors have a far greater chance of making a difference to the outcome than ballot box voters do. In most trials, there are only somewhere between 6 and 12 jurors, thereby magnifying the importance of each vote (Somin 2014, 1175). In many cases, every single juror, in effect, casts a decisive vote, because the law requires a unanimous verdict. As a result, they take their responsibilities far more seriously than most ballot box voters do (ibid., 1174–89).

If political ignorance were largely inadvertent, we would expect jurors to behave similarly, despite the great difference in incentives. They too might ignore or forget relevant information – including that presented to them by lawyers or the judge – just as voters routinely ignore or quickly forget information available from candidates in the media. But the very different behavior of jurors relative to voters strongly suggests that many voters would make greater efforts to inform themselves if their votes had a comparably high probability of influencing outcomes.

Indeed, this is exactly what happened in a rare instance where a failed attempt at gerrymandering ensured that college student Jen Henderson would be the sole eligible voter in a referendum on whether to raise a local sales tax. Upon learning she would be the only voter, Henderson studied the issue far more carefully than she had previously, and concluded that the sales tax increase was not a good idea (Somin 2016, 79). In this rare case, a voter was put in a position similar to that of jurors, and she acted accordingly.

Jeffrey Friedman argues that the inadvertent ignorance theory is backed by survey data indicating that majorities of voters believe that voting "really matters" and that influencing the outcome of an election is an important reason to choose to vote (Friedman 2019, 278–79).

But one can believe that an activity "matters" and that a very low probability of achieving a goal is enough reason to do it, while still recognizing that the odds of the latter are low, and therefore don't justify devoting more than minimal effort to acquiring information about.

The key point here is the fact that casting a vote is – for most people – a very low-cost activity, while acquiring more than minimal information about the issues takes far more time and effort. If an activity is very low-cost, even a small chance of making a difference is enough incentive to rationally do it, and you might even consider it "important" to do it, because of its role in the political process. It "really matters" enough to devote the small amount of effort needed to cast a ballot. But things change when we consider the much higher-cost activity of devoting significant time and effort to learning about political issues.[14]

The fact that voters are often unaware of even very basic political information and that this ignorance has persisted in the face of rising education levels and the information technology revolution is hard to reconcile with the idea that political ignorance is merely inadvertent. The same is true of the divergence in behavior between voters and jurors. On the other hand, it is clearly consistent with rational ignorance. Demand for information, not supply, is the main constraint on political learning in a world where most people are rationally ignorant about politics.

Friedman also argues that a rationally ignorant voter would have no basis for voting nonrandomly, since she would know she doesn't have adequate epistemic basis for choosing one party or candidate over another (Friedman 2019, 281–82). But his analysis overlooks the difference between a decision that has a low likelihood of decisiveness and one that has much higher odds of impacting outcomes. It is entirely rational to reach conclusions on the basis of very limited information, when the costs of error are low. We do so all the time, in fact. For example, many people have opinions on who is the best basketball or soccer player of all time, even though they have not carefully studied all the relevant contenders for that title, or analyzed their statistics. It is perfectly rational to hold opinions on such a subject, based on very limited information, because the costs of error are low. At the same time, however, you do have some knowledge (even if very little) and that creates a basis for holding an opinion on the subject, even if you know that learning more might change your mind.[15]

It is undeniable that at least some political ignorance is likely to be inadvertent, particularly ignorance about many small details of policy that most nonexperts are unlikely to even think to consider. But widespread ignorance about basics is unlikely to be the result of mere inadvertence.

Irrational ignorance

Some political ignorance is neither rational *nor* inadvertent. It could actually be irrational, in the sense described in Section I. In some cases, people choose to remain ignorant of information that they know might be helpful to making a decision, even though the costs of learning are smaller than the potential benefits. For example, "motivated reasoning" leads many to avoid or reject information that can cause psychological discomfort because it goes against preexisting views (Taber and Lodge 2006). More generally, it is common for voters to make serious cognitive errors in assessing political information, and such errors are, on average, more severe than similar mistakes in assessing other data.[16]

Much of this is readily explicable within the framework of rational political ignorance. As noted in Section I, there is little incentive to seek out and objectively evaluate political information when the costs of error are very low; as a result, "rational irrationality" (Caplan 2007) is ubiquitous: people seek out and evaluate political information for reasons other than establishing the truth, such as reinforcing their preexisting views.

In additional, like inadvertent ignorance theory, irrational ignorance cannot easily explain widespread ignorance of very basic information. It should not require much in the way of rigorous thought to realize that such basics are useful to evaluating candidates and parties. Thus, if people still choose not to acquire such information, it is unlikely to be because they irrationally underestimate its usefulness, and more likely that they avoid it because the costs of acquisition outweigh the benefits of improving the quality of a voting decision that has so little chance of making a difference.

But it is likely that some bias in seeking out and evaluating political information goes beyond rational ignorance and "rational irrationality." Given the number and extent of cognitive biases (e.g. Ariely 2008; Kahneman 2011),[17] it would be surprising if they did not result in any irrationality in the use and acquisition of political information. The extent to which that is true is an important subject for future research.

III Implications for democratic theory

The extent to which political ignorance is a serious problem for democracy is much-debated among social scientists and political theorists. Some scholars argue that rational political ignorance can be overcome by "information shortcuts," small bits of information that can be used as stand-ins for larger bodies of knowledge that voters are not familiar with.

For example, "retrospective voting" might enable voters to make good choices at the ballot box without knowing much about the details of policy (Fiorina 1981). The retrospective voter can simply look to see whether things have gotten better or worse under incumbent political leaders, and then reward or punish them at the polls accordingly. Knowing that they will be held accountable for results, in turn, gives elected officials strong incentives to choose good policies.

Other possible information shortcuts include relying on cues from trusted opinion leaders (Lupia 1994; Lupia and McCubbins 1998; Lupia 2015) such as pundits and interest group leaders, and utilizing politically relevant knowledge acquired from everyday life (Popkin 1991). Each of these shortcuts can potentially enable rationally ignorant voters to vote as if they were much more knowledgeable than they actually are.

Critics of the shortcut literature argue that effective use of shortcuts often requires preexisting knowledge that the majority of voters do not possess. For example, retrospective voters may not be able to use this shortcut effectively if they do not know which policy outcomes incumbents can actually affect (Somin 2016, 117–22). They also contend that shortcuts fail to effectively overcome rational irrationality (ibid., ch. 4; Caplan 2007; Brennan 2016). Shortcuts may also be less effective if government policy addresses a large number of complex issues that are difficult to boil down to a few simple cues, and perhaps impossible for rationally ignorant voters to monitor effectively (cf. Somin 2016, 160–63).

A different case for optimism about political ignorance is advanced by advocates of the "miracle of aggregation," which holds that the electorate collectively makes better decisions than individual voters can (e.g. Converse 1990; Wittman 1995; Surowiecki 2004; Landemore 2012). Even if most individual voters know very little and are prone to error, this need not lead to poor collective decision-making if ignorance-induced errors in one direction are offset by errors that cut the other way. For example, if 40% of the electorate votes for the Democrats out of ignorance, and another 40% has ignorant reasons for voting for the Republicans, these errors will offset each other, and the outcome will actually be determined by the knowledgeable minority. Another version of aggregation theory contends that cognitive diversity within the electorate may increase its collective knowledge above that possessed by a smaller, more expert group (e.g. Landemore 2012).

Miracle-of-aggregation theories have been criticized as overoptimistic on several grounds,[18] most notably because they depend on the assumption that ignorance-induced errors are relatively uncorrelated, and will tend to cancel each other out. Critics claim that nonrandom, intercorrelated errors are extremely common (e.g. Althaus 2003; Caplan 2007; Caplan et al. 2013).

Finally, some critics of rational ignorance theory contend that it may be rational for voters to acquire substantial political information after all. For example, even voters who know they are unlikely to cast a decisive ballot may want to acquire political knowledge in order to increase or decrease the size of the winner's "mandate" (Mackie 2012).[19]

The extent to which rational ignorance undermines democracy depends in part on one's normative theory of democratic participation. Some standards for evaluating the democratic process demand greater knowledge and sophistication on the part of voters than others.[20] "Pure proceduralist" theories of democracy could potentially dispense with the need for knowledge altogether, in so far as they justify democracy purely based on fair procedures rather than the production of good policy outcomes (Kelly 2012, 47–48). On the other hand, John Stuart Mill (1958 [1861]), and some modern political theorists (e.g. Brennan 2011) argue that voters have a moral duty to be well-informed, because electoral decisions influence the rights and interests of all of society, not just those who vote for the winning candidate. Mill argued that voting is the exercise of "power over others" and is therefore not a "right" but a "trust" that must be exercised responsibly (1958, 155).

Occasionally, rational political ignorance might actually lead to beneficial political outcomes rather than harmful ones. For example, an electorate with "bad" values might cause less harm if it is also factually ignorant about the effects of different government policies and thereby less able to incentivize elected officials to implement its preferences effectively (Somin 2016, 65–68). In some situations, ignorance on some issues can offset the negative effects of ignorance on others (ibid., 68–70). But such cases are unlikely to be typical.

If rational ignorance does turn out to be a serious problem for democracy, there are many possible potential solutions, including using public education or the media to increase political knowledge, transferring greater political power to knowledgeable experts or to a knowledgeable subset of the general population (e.g. Breyer 1993; Sunstein 2002; Brennan 2016), and limiting and decentralizing government (Caplan 2007; Somin 2016). Assessment of these ideas is beyond the scope of the present chapter.[21]

Some of these approaches can potentially work regardless of whether political ignorance is primarily rational or not. But others are less likely to succeed if voters are, for the most part, rationally ignorant rather than inadvertently so. For example, approaches that rely on increasing the availability of good political information – such as through media reform – are unlikely to succeed if most voters will rationally choose to ignore high-quality political information and instead focus their attention elsewhere. Rational ignorance might even be an obstacle to its own alleviation, if it prevents the electorate from effectively monitoring government policies intended to increase voter knowledge, and thus reduces the likelihood that such policies will be effective and will avoid "capture" by interest groups (Somin 2016, ch. 7).

Conclusion

Not all political ignorance is rational. But a great deal likely is. How much of a problem that is for democracy depends on a number of factors, including the amount of knowledge needed for informed voting, the effectiveness of various information "shortcuts," and the scope and complexity of government policy. But, at the very least, the rational nature of most political ignorance is a notable finding that makes it harder to increase knowledge by some of the conventional methods often advocated for that purpose.

Notes

1 Some of the material in this chapter is adapted, with permission, from Somin (2016, ch. 3); and Somin (2015).
2 For recent overviews of the relevant evidence, see, e.g., Achen and Bartels (2016); Somin (2016, ch. 1); Ipsos-Mori (2014); and Duffy (2018).
3 Other studies find modestly higher estimates for this figure, ranging up to 39%, which is still very low in absolute terms. See Somin (2016, 20); Annenberg Public Policy Center (2019).
4 For an important early statement, see Downs (1957, ch. 13).
5 Friedman has since switched to calling this kind of ignorance "radical ignorance." See Friedman (2019). I find "inadvertent" a more intuitive term than "radical" in this context, so will continue to use the former.
6 See discussion of "rational irrationality" later in this chapter.
7 For discussion of various cognitive biases, see, e.g., Ariely (2008) and Sunstein and Thaler (2008).
8 The theory of rational ignorance was first formally applied to voting decisions by Anthony Downs (1957, ch. 13).
9 For a more detailed discussion, see Somin (2016, 77–78).
10 For an overview of the evidence on political ignorance in the nineteenth-century United States, see Altshuler and Blumin (2000).
11 For a more detailed critique of Tuck's argument, see Brennan (2011, 28–34).
12 See also Friedman and Bennett (2008) and Friedman (2007, 11–13).
13 For an overview of the evidence on this point, see Somin (2014).
14 This distinction and its relevance to rational political ignorance are analyzed in much greater detail in Somin (2016, 79–84).
15 For a more detailed discussion of this point and its relevance to voting, see Somin (2016, 84–86).
16 For a discussion of relevant studies and evidence, see Somin (2016, 143–44, 154–56).
17 For an extensive recent argument that cognitive biases are not as common or as severe as is often claimed, see Rizzo and Whitman (2020).
18 For a review of several potential weaknesses, see Somin (2016, 127–34).
19 For an argument that the probability of decisively influencing the size of a "mandate" is even lower than that of casting a decisive vote, see ibid., 86–87.
20 For reviews of the different theories and their knowledge prerequisites, see Kelly (2012, ch. 4), and Somin (2016, ch. 2).
21 I have, however, outlined reasons for skepticism about the likely effectiveness of education and some other solutions in Somin (2016, ch. 7).

Bibliography

Achen, Christopher, and Larry Bartels. 2016. *Democracy for Realists*. Princeton, NJ: Princeton University Press.
Althaus, Scott. 2003. *Collective Preferences in Democratic Politics*. Cambridge: Cambridge University Press.
Altshuler, Glenn C., and Stuart C. Blumin. 2000. *Rude Republic: Americans and Their Politics in the Nineteenth Century*. Princeton, NJ: Princeton University Press.
Annenberg Public Policy Center. 2017. "Americans are Poorly Informed about Basic Constitutional Provisions." Available at https://www.annenbergpublicpolicycenter.org/americans-are-poorly-informed-about-basic-constitutional-provisions/.
Annenberg Public Policy Center. 2019. "Americans' Civic Knowledge Increases." Available at https://www.annenbergpublicpolicycenter.org/americans-civics-knowledge-increases-2019-survey/.
Ariely, Dan. 2008. *Predictably Irrational: The Hidden Forces that Shape Our Decisions*. New York: Harper Collins.
Becker, Gary S. 1976. *The Economic Approach to Human Behavior*. Chicago, IL: University of Chicago Press.
Blair, Tony. 2010. *A Journey: My Political Life*. New York: Alfred A. Knopf.
Brennan, Jason. 2011. *The Ethics of Voting*. Princeton, NJ: Princeton University Press.
Brennan, Jason. 2016. *Against Democracy*. Princeton, NJ: Princeton University Press.

Breyer, Stephen. 1993. *Breaking the Vicious Circle: Toward Effective Risk Regulation*. Cambridge: Harvard University Press.

Caplan, Bryan. 2001. "Rational Ignorance vs. Rational Irrationality." *Kyklos* 53: 3–21.

Caplan, Bryan. 2007. *The Myth of the Rational Voter: Why Democracies Choose Bad Policies*. Princeton, NJ: Princeton University Press.

Caplan, Bryan, Eric Crampton, Wayne Grove, and Ilya Somin. 2013. "Systematically Biased Beliefs about Political Influence: Evidence from the Perceptions of Political Influence on Policy Outcomes Survey." *PS* 46: 760–67.

Converse, Philip. 1990. "Popular Representation and the Distribution of Information." in *Information and Democratic Processes*, eds. John Ferejohn and James Kuklinski. Urbana: University of Illinois Press. 369–88.

Delli Carpini, Michael X., and Scott Keeter. 1996. *What Americans Know about Politics and Why It Matters*. New Haven, CT: Yale University Press.

Duffy, Bobby. 2018. *The Perils of Perception: Why We're Wrong about Nearly Everything*. London: Atlantic Books.

Downs, Anthony. 1957. *An Economic Theory of Democracy*. New York: Harper & Row.

Fiorina, Morris. 1981. *Retrospective Voting in American National Elections*. New Haven, CT: Yale University Press.

Friedman, Jeffrey. 2005. "Popper, Weber, and Hayek: The Epistemology and Politics of Ignorance." *Critical Review* 17(1–2): 1–58.

Friedman, Jeffrey. 2007. "Ignorance as a Starting Point: From Modest Epistemology to Realistic Political Theory." *Critical Review* 19: 1–22.

Friedman, Jeffrey. 2019. *Power without Knowledge: A Critique of Technocracy*. New York: Oxford University Press.

Friedman, Jeffrey, and Stephen E. Bennett. 2008. "The Irrelevance of Economic Theory to Understanding Economic Ignorance," *Critical Review* 20: 195–258.

Gelman, Andrew, Nate Silver, and Aaron Edlin. 2012. "What Is the Probability that Your Vote Will Make a Difference?" *Economic Inquiry* 50: 321–26.

Hayek, F.A. 1945. "The Use of Knowledge in Society." *American Economic Review* 4: 519–30.

Ipsos-MORI. 2014. *Perils of Perception: A Fourteen-Country Study*. London: Ipsos-MORI.

Kahneman, Daniel. 2011. *Thinking Fast and Slow*. New York: Farrar, Straus & Giroux.

Kelly, Jamie Terence. 2012. *Framing Democracy: A Behavioral Approach to Democratic Theory*. Princeton, NJ: Princeton University Press.

Kuran, Timur. 1995. *Private Truths, Public Lies: The Social Consequences of Preference Falsification*. Cambridge, MA: Harvard University Press.

Landemore, Hélène. 2012. *Democratic Reason: Politics, Collective Intelligence, and the Rule of the Many*. Princeton, NJ: Princeton University Press.

Lupia, Arthur. 1994. "Shortcuts vs. Encyclopedias: Information and Voting Behavior in California's Insurance Reform Elections." *American Political Science Review* 88: 63–76.

Lupia, Arthur. 2015. *Uninformed: Why People Seem to Know So Little about Politics and What We Can Do about It*. New York: Oxford University Press.

Lupia, Arthur, and Matthew McCubbins. 1998. *The Democratic Dilemma: Can Citizens Learn What They Need to Know?* New York: Cambridge University Press.

Mackie, Gerry. 2012. "Rational Ignorance and Beyond." in *Collective Wisdom: Principles and Mechanisms*, eds. Jon Elster and Helene Landemore. Cambridge: Cambridge University Press. 290–318.

Mill, John Stuart. 1958 [1861]. *Considerations on Representative Government*. Indianapolis, IN: Bobbs-Merrill.

Mill, John Stuart. 1975 [1859]. *On Liberty*, ed. David Spitz. New York: Norton.

Mutz, Diana. 2006. *Hearing the Other Side: Deliberative versus Participatory Democracy*. New York: Cambridge University Press.

Popkin, Samuel. 1991. *The Reasoning Voter*. Chicago, IL: University of Chicago Press.

Rizzo, Mario, and Glen Whitman. 2020. *Escaping Paternalism: Rationality, Behavioral Economics, and Public Policy*. Cambridge: Cambridge University Press.

Somin, Ilya. 2014. "Jury Ignorance and Political Ignorance," *William and Mary Law Review* 55: 1167–93.

Somin, Ilya. 2015. "Rational Ignorance." in *Routledge International Handbook of Ignorance Studies*, eds. Matthias Gross and Linsey McGoey. London: Routledge. 274–81.

Somin, Ilya. 2016. *Democracy and Political Ignorance: Why Smaller Government Is Smarter*, 2nd ed. Stanford, CA: Stanford University Press.

Simon, Herbert A. 1959. "Theories of Decision-Making in Economics and Behavioral Science." *American Economic Review* 49: 253–83.

Stigler, George J. 1961. "The Economics of Information." *Journal of Political Economy* 69: 213–25.

Sunstein, Cass R. 2002. *Risk and Reason: Safety, Law and the Environment.* New York: Oxford University Press.

Sunstein, Cass R., and Richard H. Thaler. 2008. *Nudge.* Princeton, NJ: Princeton University Press.

Surowiecki, James. 2004. *The Wisdom of Crowds: Why the Many Are Smarter than the Few.* New York: Doubleday.

Taber, Charles S., and Milton R. Lodge. 2006. "Motivated Skepticism in the Evaluation of Political Beliefs." *American Journal of Political Science* 50: 755–69.

Tuck, Richard. 2008. *Free Riding.* Cambridge: Harvard University Press.

Wittman, Donald. 1995. *The Myth of Democratic Failure.* Chicago, IL: University of Chicago Press.

Williams, Daniel. 2020. "Motivated Ignorance, Rationality, and Democratic Politics." *Synthese.* Available at https://link.springer.com/content/pdf/10.1007%2Fs11229-020-02549-8.pdf.

22

PRAGMATIC ENCROACHMENT AND POLITICAL IGNORANCE

Kenneth Boyd

1 Pragmatic encroachment

Pragmatic encroachment is the view that whether one knows a proposition is, at least in part, a function of the practical factors that surround the truth or falsity of that proposition.[1] The kinds of practical factors that are discussed most often are the *stakes* in being right or wrong such that, paradigmatically, the higher the stakes surrounding the truth of p, the more difficult it is to know that p.[2] Three main types of support have been put forth for the view: appeals to intuitive cases, empirical studies, and an argument that relies on a principled connection between knowledge and action.

The first kind of support involves appealing to cases in which it seems that one's willingness to ascribe knowledge varies with the relevant stakes. For example, say that you want to get to Spadina Avenue in order to check out a new ramen restaurant. While you have been to Spadina Avenue several times before, you are not an infallible city navigator; regardless, with very little at stake we may be happy to say that you know where Spadina Avenue is on the basis of your experience and memory. Consider now instead that getting to Spadina Avenue is a matter of life or death: the only pharmacy that carries your life-saving medicine is on that street, and it is closing soon. We then might have the following intuition: while your memory and experience are good enough to allow you to know where Spadina Avenue is when you are looking for a restaurant, it is not good enough when you are trying to get to the pharmacy. Given that you have the same memories and experiences in both cases, the argument goes, what stands in the way of your knowing are the high stakes. This is not to say that you could not come to know where the pharmacy is; indeed, you could come to know this after asking your friend who has been there many times for directions, or by using an app on your phone to plan a route, etc. The point is not that high stakes make knowledge impossible, but rather that when the stakes are high, the standards for acquiring knowledge can become more demanding.

While cases like these are ubiquitous in the pragmatic encroachment literature, they will do little to convince those who do not share the relevant intuitions. Some have thus appealed to empirical studies that investigate whether non-philosophers evaluate cases like the above in the same way as the pragmatic encroacher, or whether pragmatic encroachment can best explain certain patterns of knowledge ascriptions. Thus far, however, the results are inconclusive. While some studies have reported that the intuitions elicited by pragmatic encroachers are shared by non-philosophers (Sripada and Stanley 2012), others have failed to corroborate these results (Feltz and Zarpentine 2010; May et al. 2010; Schaffer and Knobe 2012; Buckwalter and Schaffer 2015; Rose et al. 2019). Other types of experiments are perhaps more promising. For instance, Pinillos (2012) conducted "evidence-seeking experiments" in which subjects were asked how much evidence one thought someone would need in order to count as knowing when the stakes varied (see also Francis et al. 2019), and Dinges and Zakkou's (2020) study looked at patterns of retractions of knowledge attributions, providing results that support the view that such patterns shift when certain practical factors shift. While these new approaches provide support for pragmatic encroachment, it is still up for debate how best to interpret the various kinds of empirical results (see for discussion Buckwalter and Schaffer 2015; Boyd 2016; Weatherson 2017).

The third and perhaps strongest form of support for pragmatic encroachment is a conceptual argument that relies on a principled relationship between knowledge and action. Say that knowledge is the norm of practical reason, such that if one knows that p then it is rational to act as if p. It then follows that since practical factors determine whether it is rational to act, so too can they determine whether one knows. Again, consider the case of needing to get to Spadina Avenue when the stakes are high: since in this case it is not rational to act solely on the basis of what one remembers, then given the relationship between knowledge and action, neither will it be the case that one knows on that basis.[3]

Pragmatic encroachment is thus appealing in that it can explain a range of intuitive cases, and is closely tied to what many see as a plausible relationship between knowledge and action. What has yet to be explored, however, are the consequences of applying the view to issues of political knowledge and ignorance. Before doing this, however, we need to get a sense of what some of these issues are.

2 Political knowledge and political ignorance

What constitutes political knowledge? Boudreau and Lupia (2011) argue that,

> A common analytic definition of political knowledge is that it is a measure of a citizen's ability to provide correct answers to a specific set of fact-based questions. Typical political knowledge questions include "What is the political office held by [name of current vice president, British prime minister, or chief justice of the United States]" and "Which party has the most seats in the U.S. House of Representatives?". (p. 171)

This definition is that which is often employed in empirical studies of the level of political ignorance of a populace (Barabas et al. 2014; Bischof and Senninger 2018). More broadly, though, we can define political knowledge not in terms of any specific content, but instead in terms of the role that knowledge plays in political actions. For instance, Cameron Boult (Forthcoming) characterizes political knowledge as involving "any belief that is of direct relevance to decision making on political issues" including issues like "whether to increase the national deficit, foreign aid, or to have public health care" (p. 5). On this broader definition, while any proposition may be the object of political knowledge, whether it constitutes such knowledge will depend on the relevant context in which that knowledge is employed. While more can be said to make this notion more precise, I will here accept this broader conception.

Many have argued that political knowledge is important for a well-functioning democracy. For instance, De Vreese and Boomgaarden (2006) argue that,

> Public knowledge of and participation in politics are at the core of democratic processes. The quality of citizenship and the health of the collective are preconditioned by political knowledge and there is a positive relationship between knowledge and the act of voting. (p. 317)

At the same time, it has been widely recognized that people are, by and large, politically ignorant (see Brennan 2016 and Somin 2016 for summaries of recent data). Given that an individual is likely to be politically ignorant, a question then becomes under what conditions it is practically rational[4] for them to make the effort to acquire the political knowledge they lack, given that doing so comes at a practical cost. One argument for *rational political ignorance* concludes that it will often not, in fact, be worth it. Consider the case of voting in a large democracy: given that an individual vote is very unlikely to make a difference to the outcome, then even if it is the case that political knowledge allows one to make better voting decisions, it may not be worthwhile for one to acquire it for the purposes of voting, as the costs outweigh the expected benefits.

There are, however, reasons to be worried about rationalizing political ignorance. As Ilya Somin (2006) argues,

> The theory of rational ignorance implies not only that voters will acquire little or no political knowledge, but also that they will make little effort to use the knowledge they do have in a consistent and effective manner. It is not just that they might be apathetic; far worse, they sometimes use their knowledge in a way that increases the danger of making serious errors. (p. 256)

Somin argues that one problem surrounding political ignorance is that there will be a gap between the practical rationality of voting and that of reducing one's political ignorance. To show this, Somin first appeals to Derek Parfit's (1984) argument that it can be rational for one to vote in a large democratic system "so long as the voter perceives a significant difference between candidates and cares even slightly about the welfare of fellow citizens, as well as [their] own" (Somin 2010, p. 205). Somin defends this view via an expected utility calculation:

$$D \star \left(300 \text{ million}/1{,}000\right)/(100 \text{ million}) - C_v = U_v$$

where U_v is the expected utility of voting, C_v the practical cost of voting, and D the expected difference in welfare per person if the voter's preferred candidate defeats their opponent, along with the assumption that one is participating in a system with 300 million voters, that one's ballot has a 1/100 million chance of being decisive, and that the voter values the welfare of their fellow citizens 1,000 times less than their own. Somin argues that on plausible values of these variables (i.e. given that one does, in fact, value the welfare of one's fellow citizens at least a bit, that the difference in welfare that would result from electing different candidates is non-trivial, and that the practical cost of voting is not too high) it will, in fact, turn out to be rational for one to vote (i.e. it will be the case that $U_v > 0$).

Somin's concern, however, is that it is much *less* likely to be practically rational to acquire political knowledge. To see why, he presents a similar calculation:

$$D \star \left(300\,\text{million}/1000\right)/\left(100\,\text{million}\right)\text{-}C_{pi} = U_{pi}$$

where U_{pi} is the expected utility of acquiring enough information to make the "right" decision when voting, and C_{pi} is the practical cost of reducing one's political ignorance. The problem, Somin argues, is that the practical costs of acquiring political knowledge can be higher than the costs of voting.[5] As such, on plausible values of the relevant variables, it will often turn out that it is not practically rational to reduce one's political ignorance (i.e. it is likely that $U_{pi} < 0$). Somin ultimately argues that given that widespread political ignorance is a problem, we then need to better incentivize individuals to take measures to reduce said ignorance. How we might do this is a matter of ongoing debate.[6]

We now have a general overview of pragmatic encroachment, as well as some problems surrounding political knowledge and ignorance. Next, I consider some consequences of accepting pragmatic encroachment when thinking about these problems.

3 Three consequences of pragmatic encroachment

In this section I consider three consequences of pragmatic encroachment when it comes to issues of political knowledge and ignorance. These consequences center on a general consequence of pragmatic encroachment, namely that just as the standards for knowledge become more demanding, so too do the practical costs of acquiring it. Thus, given that the paradigmatic case of pragmatic encroachment is one in which high stakes increases the demands on knowledge, so too will they increase the cost of acquiring political knowledge.[7]

Consider an example. Say that I am trying to decide what to order at a restaurant, and that I have a terrible peanut allergy.[8] Despite the menu stating that a dish does not contain peanuts, if we accept pragmatic encroachment then I may not know that the dish does not contain peanuts on the basis of the available evidence, given that the stakes are high. In order to acquire this knowledge, then, I need to do some extra work, perhaps by acquiring additional evidence: I could, e.g. ask a waiter to verify, or check with the chef, or run a detailed chemical analysis of the dish, etc. While acquiring this additional evidence may then put me in a position to know, it also comes at a practical cost. A consequence of accepting pragmatic encroachment, then, is that an increase in stakes leads not only to increased epistemic demands on acquiring knowledge, but also to increased practical costs in acquiring that knowledge.

Of course, how significant these costs are will vary depending on how much work one needs to do in order to meet the standards required for good decision-making (e.g. checking with the chef is a small cost, running a scientific analysis looking for peanut traces is a large one). Regardless, given that increased standards for knowledge bring along increased costs in acquiring it, pragmatic encroachment has three consequences for thinking about political knowledge and ignorance: first, that political ignorance can become more practically rational as the stakes surrounding one's political actions go up; second, that one can acquire political knowledge by valuing the welfare of others less; and third, that pragmatic encroachment may warrant the epistemically unjust treatment of members of marginalized groups. I address these consequences in turn.

3.1 *Rationalizing (even more) political ignorance*

The first consequence of accepting pragmatic encroachment is that doing so can widen the gap between the practical rationality of political action and that of acquiring political knowledge. To see why, we need to get a sense of which factors determine the stakes when it comes to political actions. Consider again the above calculation of the expected utility of voting: here we see that the greater the expected difference in welfare and the higher the chances of one's vote being impactful, the more rational it will be to vote, given that the cost of voting remains constant (e.g. it will take just as long to wait in line and cast a vote regardless of any other factors). However, these factors also determine, at least in part, the stakes involved in voting. For example, an election will be higher stakes if candidates have radically different policies with very different expected outcomes in terms of welfare for oneself and those one cares about, and lower stakes if the candidates have very similar policies, or have policies that have little impact on oneself and those one cares about. Thus, as the values of expected difference in welfare, concern for the welfare of others, and chance of one's actions making a significant impact go up, so too (*ceteris paribus*) do the stakes.[9]

The result is that accepting pragmatic encroachment also means accepting that there can be a larger gap between the practical utility of participating in a political process and that of acquiring political knowledge. For instance, say that you are going to vote in an election, the results of which will have significant practical importance to you. As the cost of voting is the same regardless of the stakes, it will become more rational to vote the more significant the practical consequences of that vote. However, on a pragmatic encroachment view, more significant political actions can present more significant obstacles to acquiring political knowledge: as it will be more difficult to know when the stakes are higher, one will be required to acquire more evidence in order to possess that knowledge, which brings along a higher practical cost. The consequence is that it may be more practically rational for one to refrain from acquiring political knowledge when it comes to voting in high-stakes elections.[10]

To illustrate this consequence a different way, consider an extension of the above restaurant case. Say that one has a peanut allergy, but is also extremely hungry; furthermore, given the high stakes, one is not in a position to know that one's dish does not contain peanuts solely on the basis of the menu description. If the demands for knowledge are high enough, it can be practically rational for one to order the dish – given that one needs to satiate one's hunger – despite it not being practically rational for one to do the work to acquire the relevant knowledge. The same, I argue, can be the case when it comes to voting in high-stakes elections: if the demands for knowledge are too high, it can remain practically rational for one to vote, despite it not being practically rational for one to acquire the relevant political knowledge.

Of course, this will not always be the case: if the expected difference in welfare is very high, then the increased expected benefits of acquiring political knowledge may swamp the associated costs. Nevertheless, there will still be cases in which the stakes surrounding one's political actions will be high, but in which it would be less practically rational to acquire political knowledge than if the stakes were lower. This consequence is undesirable insofar as it seems that possessing political knowledge is most important in high-stakes voting situations (although I consider a response to this in Section 4). For example, while it may not be terribly important for one to possess political knowledge when it comes to an election in which there is only a marginal difference between the candidates, when these differences are significant it seems that it is much more important that voters possess political knowledge in order to make the best decisions. We thus get the conclusion that a pragmatic encroachment view of political knowledge may rationalize political ignorance when it comes to decisions regarding participation in important political processes.

3.2 Selfishness as a means to acquiring political knowledge

A consequence of pragmatic encroachment generally is that when practical factors stand in the way of knowing, one can acquire knowledge if those factors become less significant. For example, if the stakes surrounding the presence of peanuts in my dish prevent me from knowing whether there are peanuts in my dish, then one way I could acquire this knowledge would be if the stakes were lowered, e.g. if someone gave me an epi-pen. Critics of pragmatic encroachment have argued that the view thus warrants odd ways of acquiring knowledge, as well as a concept of knowledge that is unstable, given that practical factors can change in unexpected ways (see Russell and Doris 2008; Kim 2017).

Similar worries arise when considering political knowledge. For example, say that there are large potential differences in welfare for me given the results of an upcoming election, as one of the key issues pertains to increasing minimum wage, and I have very little money. Say also that I have collected some evidence with regard to the policies of the respective candidates, but, given that the stakes are high, I do not qualify as knowing which candidate is the right choice. One way that I could acquire political knowledge, then, would be if the stakes were to become lower as a result of my financial situation improving, e.g. if I get a new, well-paying job. It is prima facie odd, however, that my employment status can have a direct impact on how much political knowledge I possess.

There are additional ways that one can lower the stakes when it comes to one's political knowledge; specifically, by valuing the welfare of others less. For instance, Edlin et al. (2007) argue that voting is likely not practically rational for someone who has purely selfish motives, given that a reduction in the concern for the welfare of others will result in a reduction in the overall expected utility. In general, then, the more one values the welfare of others, the more rational it will be to vote; at the same time, an increased concern for others will also raise the stakes surrounding one's actions, thus making it more difficult and practically costly to acquire relevant political knowledge. Accepting pragmatic encroachment thus has the additional consequence that there is a seemingly implausible relationship between one's concern for the welfare of others and the rationality of acquiring political knowledge, such that if one values the welfare of others *too* much then it may no longer be practically rational for one to acquire that knowledge.

3.3 Political ignorance and epistemic injustice

A final consequence of pragmatic encroachment is that it may warrant the epistemically unjust treatment of members of marginalized groups when it comes to ascriptions of political knowledge. For example, consider a member of a minority group who has to choose between two white men in an election: both have histories of policy decisions that tend not to be favorable toward minorities, although one may end up making slightly more favorable policy decisions than the other. In this case the stakes for the minority voter may be much higher than a white male voter. As we have seen, a consequence of pragmatic encroachment is that as a result of these higher stakes, the standards for knowing, and hence the practical costs of acquiring knowledge, will be higher for the minority voter.

While the pragmatic encroacher will not take issue with any of this, a concern with this consequence is that it may run afoul of what seem to be instances of epistemic injustice. For instance, Mikkel Gerken (2019) argues that a consequence of pragmatic encroachment in general is that it can warrant a form of *discriminatory epistemic injustice*, i.e. discrimination against others as knowers in virtue of paradigmatically unjust features.[11] Gerken provides an example in which one's financially dire circumstances can make the practical consequences surrounding the truth of some proposition more significant, which, according to the pragmatic encroacher, can prevent one from knowing it: pragmatic encroachment would thus warrant treating individuals in such circumstances as knowing less, given that they in fact *do* know less according to the theory. The worry, however, is that such treatment is not, in fact, warranted: if it is an *injustice* to treat such individuals as knowing less, then this is because they do, in fact, possess knowledge, but are being treated as if they do not.

When applied to the domain of political knowledge, then, pragmatic encroachment has the consequence not only of potentially failing to account for the epistemically unjust treatment of marginalized groups, but also of deeming it less practically rational for members of marginalized groups to acquire said knowledge, given that doing so will be costlier. Again, consider the above case where a member of a minority group needs to decide between which of two white male candidates she will vote for. Given that the stakes are higher for her than for someone who will not be affected nearly as much by the outcome, the demands of knowing which candidate is the better choice will be much higher, and hence it will also be much more practically costly for her to acquire that knowledge. Given the increased practical costs, however, it may be less practically rational for her to acquire that political knowledge. Pragmatic encroachment may then warrant an additional kind of injustice, one that deems it practically irrational for a member of a minority to acquire political knowledge.

In this section I have traced three consequences of applying pragmatic encroachment to problems of political knowledge and ignorance, all of which appear to run afoul of commitments one might have with regard to the value of political knowledge, appropriate means of acquiring political knowledge, and epistemic injustice. In the next and final section, I will consider a possible response on behalf of the pragmatic encroacher.

4 Pragmatic encroachment and the value of political knowledge

Does the pragmatic encroacher have any recourse for dealing with these worries? Possibly. Consider first that in discussing political knowledge and ignorance, I have assumed that there is an important connection between them, such that in reducing political ignorance one aims to acquire political knowledge. However, one might deny this, and thereby call into question whether there is any particular value in possessing political *knowledge* when it comes to making good political decisions. For instance, some have argued that individuals can make good political decisions solely on the basis of heuristics (such as party affiliation) and other kinds of information cues (i.e. "bits of information that enable people to make judgments and decisions about an attitude object without in-depth knowledge" (Bowler and Nicholson 2018, p. 382)), while others have argued that individual-level ignorance is not necessarily a barrier to good decision-making at the group level. For instance, Hélène Landemore (2013) argues for what she calls the "strong epistemic argument for democracy": despite there being widespread political ignorance at the level of individual members of a democratic society, decisions made in a democracy will typically be better than those made in other political systems, given the epistemic benefits of cognitive diversity (i.e. that in the right circumstances, due to differences in the ways that individuals interpret the world, mistakes in reasoning will systematically cancel each other out, resulting in overall better decision-making in the aggregate (p. 160)). If the aim of reducing political ignorance is to attempt to make good political decisions, either at the individual or societal level, then it may be the case that political knowledge is, strictly speaking, not very important in achieving this goal.

What the pragmatic encroacher might argue, then, is that even if political knowledge becomes more difficult to acquire as the stakes go up, the costs of reducing political ignorance may not, given that one does not need to meet the standards of political knowledge for one to contribute to a good decision-making at the societal level. This response may be available especially for a view of pragmatic encroachment in which it is only the standards for knowledge, but not one's epistemic position otherwise, that is affected by political considerations (see Fantl and McGrath 2009). Whether this response is enough to immunize the pragmatic encroacher against the three consequences I have presented here will depend both on how one interprets the details of pragmatic encroachment, as well as what one takes the relationship between political ignorance and knowledge to be.

Notes

1 Here I will focus on the metaphysical thesis (i.e. one that pertains to the nature of knowledge), and will not have anything to say about a strictly semantic version of the view (i.e. one that pertains solely to the truth value of knowledge ascriptions).

2 Other factors, such as time constraints with regard to forming a belief or acting, have also been proposed as a potentially relevant practical consideration (see Shin 2014). It is also up for debate as to whether practical factors affect knowledge *directly*, or only *indirectly* in virtue of affecting belief. For example, one might argue that one is simply less likely to believe that p when the stakes surrounding p are high, and thus may fail to know only in virtue of failing to believe (see Ganson 2008; Nagel 2010; Gerken 2017). Here I will take pragmatic encroachment to be the view that practical factors are relevant to knowledge regardless of their effects on belief.

3 Versions of this argument can be found in Hawthorne (2004), Stanley (2005), Fantl and McGrath (2009), and elsewhere. They have, as one might suspect, also received their share of objections (see, e.g. Williamson 2005; Brown 2008; Gerken 2017).

4 There are, of course, other kinds of value that one might consider when determining whether one should acquire political knowledge, especially epistemic or moral value. Here, however, I will only be concerned with practical value associated with decision-making. However, depending on what one takes the relationship between stakes and standards for epistemic rationality to be, discussions of others kinds of value may be relevant, as well.

5 How costly it is to acquire political knowledge will of course not be uniform for everyone. Indeed, there will be cases in which acquiring such knowledge will be easy and low cost, e.g. cases in which one can acquire some relevant political knowledge just by Googling. That being said, what is important for Somin's view is that there can be some political matters that require more effect to be known, say by requiring in-depth research, consulting experts, etc.

6 Somin's own solutions focus on measures meant to provide individuals with more effective ways of participating in a political system, and by significantly reducing the size of government (see Somin 2010; see Page 2015 for criticism).

7 I say this is the *paradigmatic* case as I leave it open that it is not *necessarily* the case that for every proposition and every practical consequence, high stakes increase the demands on knowledge (for instance, Anderson and Hawthorne (2019) argue that there can be cases in which higher stakes result in the standards for knowledge being *less* demanding). However, it is also the case that the pragmatic encroacher ought not to be satisfied with a *bare* existential claim (i.e. merely that there is some proposition, in some possible circumstance, in which practical factors affect the demands of knowing it) lest they pull all the teeth from the theory.

8 Cases like this are common throughout the literature; for an empirical study of similar cases, see Sripada and Stanley (2012).

9 One might wonder whether in such a situation the stakes surrounding one's vote should be considered "high", given that one still has only a very small chance of making a difference in the outcome of the election. There are a few potential responses to this worry. First, given that the chance of making a difference is only one variable among many that determine what is at stake for someone, merely having a low chance of making a difference does not preclude a situation from being high stakes. Second, I am here making a comparative claim, i.e. that more significant differences in candidates make stakes *higher*, even though they may not be overall very high. Finally, there are additional consequences beyond the outcome of an election that can be taken into account when determining the stakes surrounding one's voting, for instance, those pertaining to one's political interests.

10 Again, consider the above equation for the utility of reducing political ignorance, i.e. $U_{pi} = D \star (300$ million/1,000)/(100 million) $- C_{pi}$. There can then be cases in which U_{pi} is positive, given that $D\star(300$ million/1,000)/(100 million) $> C_{pi}$. A consequence of pragmatic encroachment is that just as the left side increases, so too does the right side. However, there is no reason to think that the increases will be uniform. For instance, it can be the case that the costs of meeting the standards for knowledge according to pragmatic encroachment will swamp the expected difference in expected welfare, depending on how difficult it is to meet the increased epistemic standard.

11 These and related notions of epistemic injustice originate in Fricker (2007).

Works cited

Anderson, C & Hawthorne, J 2019, 'Knowledge, practical adequacy, and stakes', in Gendler, TS & Hawthorne, J (eds.), *Oxford Studies in Epistemology* (Vol. 6), Oxford University Press, Oxford, pp. 234–57.

Barabas, J, Jerit, J, Pollock, W & Rainey, C 2014, 'The question (s) of political knowledge', *American Political Science Review*, vol. 108, no. 4, pp. 840–55.

Bischof, D & Senninger, R 2018, 'Simple politics for the people? Complexity in campaign messages and political knowledge', *European Journal of Political Research*, vol. 57, no. 2, pp. 473–95.

Boudreau, C & Lupia, A 2011, 'Political knowledge', in Druckman, JN, Green, DP, Kuklinski, JH & Lupia, A (eds.), *Cambridge Handbook of Experimental Political Science*, Cambridge University Press, Cambridge, pp. 171–83.

Boult, C Forthcoming, 'The (virtue) epistemology of political ignorance', *American Philosophical Quarterly*.

Bowler, S & Nicholson, SP 2018, 'Information cues and rational ignorance', in Congleton, R, Grofman, B & Voigt, S (eds.), *The Oxford Handbook of Public Choice*, Oxford University Press, Oxford, pp. 381–94.

Boyd, K 2016, 'Pragmatic encroachment and epistemically responsible action', *Synthese*, vol. 193, no. 9, pp. 2721–45.

Brennan, J 2016, *Against Democracy*, Princeton University Press, Princeton, NJ.

Brown, J. 2008, 'Subject-sensitive invariantism and the knowledge norm of practical reasoning', *Nous*, vol. 2, no. 42, pp. 167–89.

Buckwalter, W & Schaffer, J 2015, 'Knowledge, stakes, and mistakes', *Noûs*, vol. 49, no. 2, pp. 201–34.

De Vreese, CH & Boomgaarden, H 2006, 'News, political knowledge and participation: The differential effects of news media exposure on political knowledge and participation', *Acta Politica*, vol. 41, no. 4, pp. 317–41.

Dinges, A & Zakkou, J 2020, 'Much at stake in knowledge', *Mind & Language*, pp. 1–21.

Edlin, A, Gelman, A & Kaplan, N 2007, 'Voting as a rational choice: Why and how people vote to improve the well-being of others', *Rationality and Society*, vol. 19, no. 3, pp. 293–314.

Fantl, J & McGrath, M 2009, *Knowledge in an Uncertain World*, Oxford University Press, Oxford.

Feltz, A & Zarpentine, C 2010, 'Do you know more when it matters less?', *Philosophical Psychology*, vol. 23, no. 5, pp. 683–706.

Francis, K, Beaman, P & Hansen, N 2019, 'Stakes, scales, and skepticism', *Ergo*, vol. 6, no. 16, pp. 427–87.

Fricker, M 2007, *Epistemic Injustice: Power and the Ethics of Knowing*, Oxford University Press, Oxford.

Ganson, D 2008, 'Evidentialism and pragmatic constraints on outright belief', *Philosophical Studies*, vol. 139, no. 3, pp. 441–58.

Gerken, M 2017, *On Folk Epistemology: How We Think and Talk about Knowledge*. Oxford University Press, Oxford.

Gerken, M 2019, 'Pragmatic encroachment and the challenge from epistemic injustice', *Philosophers' Imprint*, vol. 15, pp. 1–19.

Hawthorne, J 2004, *Knowledge and Lotteries*, Oxford University Press, Oxford.

Kim, B 2017, 'Pragmatic encroachment in epistemology', *Philosophy Compass*, vol. 12, no. 5, pp. 1–14.

Landemore, H 2013, *Democratic Reason: Politics, Collective Intelligence, and the Rule of the Many*, Princeton University Press, Princeton.

May, J, Sinnott-Armstrong, W, Hull, J & Zimmerman, A 2010, 'Practical interests, relevant alternatives, and knowledge attributions: An empirical study', *Review of Philosophy and Psychology*, vol. 1, no. 2, pp. 265–73.

Nagel, J 2010, 'Knowledge ascriptions and the psychological consequences of thinking about error', *The Philosophical Quarterly*, vol. 60, no. 239, pp. 286–306.

Page, B 2015, 'That same old song: Somin on political ignorance', *Critical Review*, vol. 27, no. 3–4, pp. 375–79.

Parfit, D 1984, *Reasons and Persons*, Clarendon Press, Oxford.

Pinillos, NA 2012, 'Knowledge, experiments and practical interests', in Brown, J & Gerken, M (eds.), *Knowledge Ascriptions*, Oxford University Press, Oxford, pp. 192–219.

Rose, D, Machery, E, Stich, S, Alai, M, Angelucci, A, Berniūnas, R, Buchtel, EE, Chatterjee, A, Cheon, H, Cho, IR & Cohnitz, D 2019. 'Nothing at stake in knowledge', *Noûs*, vol. 53, no. 1, pp. 224–47.

Russell, GK & Doris, JM 2008, 'Knowledge by indifference', *Australasian Journal of Philosophy*, vol. 86, pp. 429–37.

Schaffer, J & Knobe, J 2012, 'Contrastive knowledge surveyed", *Noûs*, vol. 46, no. 4, pp. 675–708.

Shin, J 2014, 'Time constraints and pragmatic encroachment on knowledge", *Episteme*, vol. 11, no. 2, pp. 157–80.

Somin, I 2006, 'Knowledge about ignorance: New directions in the study of political information', *Critical Review*, vol. 18, nos. 1–3, pp. 255–278.

Somin, I 2010, 'Foot voting, political ignorance, and constitutional design', *Social Philosophy and Policy*, vol. 28, no. 1, pp. 202–27.

Somin, I 2016, *Democracy and Political Ignorance: Why Smaller Government is Smarter*. Stanford University Press, Stanford.

Somin, I 2003, 'Political ignorance and the countermajoritarian difficulty: A new perspective on the central obsession of constitutional theory', *Iowa Law Review*, vol. 89, pp. 1287–372.

Sripada, CS & Stanley, J 2012, 'Empirical tests of interest-relative invariantism', *Episteme*, vol. 9, no. 1, pp. 3–26.

Stanley, J 2005, *Knowledge and Practical Interests*, Oxford University Press, Oxford.

Weatherson, B 2017, 'Interest-relative invariantism', in Jonathan Ichikawa (ed.), *The Routledge Handbook of Epistemic Contextualism*, Routledge, New York, pp. 240–253.

Williamson, T 2005, 'Contextualism, subject-sensitive invariantism and knowledge of knowledge', *The Philosophical Quarterly*, vol. 55, no. 219, pp. 213–35.

23

IS POLITICAL IRRATIONALITY A MYTH?

Jeffrey Friedman

I am writing this chapter in the midst of a pandemic that led to many examples of the propensity I wish to address. This is the propensity to ascribe beliefs we do not understand—or with which we simply disagree—to the irrationality of those who hold them. However, nothing particularly suits a pandemic to the expression of this propensity, which is of very long standing. The brief list of pandemic-related examples provided in Section I, then, is intended only to suggest that the propensity itself is pandemic. Section II provides a critical analysis of the examples, producing some basic principles of political epistemology. Section III applies these principles to three influential areas of research: the "heuristics and biases" research program, the motivated-reasoning paradigm, and the theory that voting in a large electorate is irrational. Finally, Section IV sketches three stances one might take toward the critique of irrationalism, or "political psychologism," presented in Sections II and III.

I Four pandemic examples

1   A global health reporter, addressing the failure of "some of the most seasoned infectious diseases experts to recognize the full threat of what was bearing down on the world" in January and February 2020, concludes that the experts were victims of "magical thinking" (Branswell 2020).

2   A conservative pundit argues that the pandemic is not as severe as generally thought, and that the liberal media are victims of "hysteria" in failing to recognize this. In response, a liberal pundit lobs back the charge of irrationality, citing a psychologist claiming that "in a crisis event, one thing people do is engage in sense-making—seeking out facts and coming up with explanations," as "a way of psychologically coping with the uncertainty and anxiety of the event, and of having agency in the response." By blaming the media, the conservative pundit was responding, in effect, to *his own* hysteria (Warzel 2020).

3   The "Interpreter" columnist of the *New York Times* finds it puzzling that in the initial weeks of the pandemic, political leaders around the world became more popular—regardless of how well their governments were responding to the crisis. The solution to the puzzle, he suggests, is that "rallying around the flag" makes us feel "sane and stable during terrifying times" (Fischer 2020).

4   A political scientist tells a writer for *Politico* that conspiracy theories about whether the Chinese government or some other nefarious agent caused the crisis were popular because in a pandemic, "a lot of the psychological elements that give rise to conspiracy theories are heightened: powerlessness and anxiety and uncertainty" (Stanton 2020).

I hope readers will register how commonplace this type of political psychologizing is. To anyone who follows the news, I suspect, none of the examples will come across as the least bit unusual. That, I will maintain, is a problem.

II Principles of (rationalist) political epistemology

One objection to political psychologism is that it has the effect of infantilizing those whose beliefs and behavior are being explained. Political psychologism, one might say, fails to accord those being psychologized the respect that political theorists tend to think should be accorded to our fellow citizens. However, one might reply that however much we should, normatively, treat our fellow citizens with the respect due to rational adults, in particular cases they may not "deserve" this respect, empirically: their beliefs or behavior may just be too infantile, or otherwise irrational, to warrant respect. So I will bracket the ethical objection and, taking the perspective of empirical political epistemology, suggest that at the very least, political psychologism poses serious risks of inaccuracy; and that, more radically, it may *always* be inaccurate, as it is untrue to the phenomenology of human belief—which is ineluctably rationalistic.

Thus, I will seek to establish that the examples presented above bespeak a particular type of error—a neglect of the ideational causes of beliefs and actions—and that this error is peculiarly anti-epistemological, as it is predicated on the tacit assumption that the truth, in a given case, is self-evident, such that only an irrational psychological mechanism can explain why someone might not acknowledge it. In short, political psychologism tends to ignore the very possibility of mistaken, false, or illusory knowledge—the starting point of epistemologists from Plato to Hobbes, Descartes, and Hume; and of philosophers of science from Popper to Kuhn, Quine, and Feyerabend. To sloganize my message: psychology is not epistemology. And the two may inherently be at odds.

Consider the examples in turn.

Example 1. The epidemiologists accused of engaging in magical thinking, it turns out— according to the article that makes this accusation—had good reason to doubt the likelihood of a pandemic. Initially, according to the article, the disease did not "appear to be behaving as explosively outside of China as it had inside it." Moreover, "the world had experience controlling coronavirus outbreaks" such as SARS and MERS (Branswell 2020). Thus, there is nothing irrational, on its face, about the fact that the scientists erred in this case, so long as we recognize that scientists, being human, are not omniscient. The epistemologist does not deem people irrational merely by virtue of their being ignorant or mistaken. Instead she deems them human, i.e., fallible and, ab initio, ignorant.

Example 2. Contrary to the quoted psychologist, people "seek facts and come up with explanations" all the time, not just in crisis situations. The psychologist, and the liberal pundit quoting her, overlook the *epistemic* reason to seek facts and come up with explanations: not to achieve emotional security, but to transcend one's initial position of ignorance so as to learn the truth. This epistemic reason is the engine of science, and would be irrational only if the truth were self-evident: that is, only if we were *not* initially ignorant of the truth, and thus had no need to discover it by seeking facts and coming up with explanations.

The conservative pundit, too, ignores the epistemic dimension by suggesting that journalists were "hysterical" merely because they thought they had discovered an alarming truth (i.e., that the contagion was of nearly unprecedented severity). The pundit's psychologizing of the journalists explains nothing about their behavior that cannot more readily be explained by their search for truth. I say "*more* readily" because once we take account of the epistemic motive, there remains no puzzle to be resolved; while if we insist on an irrational motive, we need evidence that this motive, not the epistemic one, is in play. As with Example 1, then, I am suggesting, at the very least, that our default explanation for human beliefs should be epistemological, and thus rational.

In support of this suggestion, consider that we are not really capable of explaining any specific belief *of our own* as due to our need for psychological comfort, our hysteria, etc. To form and maintain a belief requires what appear to us—perhaps mistakenly, of course—to be sound reasons. If one actually thought that a certain belief of one's own were due to a psychological factor, rather than due to one's recognition of a good reason for the belief, one would not accept the belief. If one does accept it, it must be for some reason that, if sound, would warrant the belief.

We impose a double standard, then, when we psychologize others' beliefs: we never psychologize our own. Arguably, then, our default approach to understanding others' beliefs should be to assume that they, like us, have rational (yet possibly mistaken) reasons for their beliefs. This would not preclude the possibility that in a given case the double standard is warranted, but it would caution us to do what is too rarely done: try to *understand* beliefs with which we disagree before we explain them away as irrational.

Our pandemic propensity to instead use the irrationalist default setting may be due to our uncritical consumption of badly interpreted psychological findings (Section 3) and to an underemphasis on human *fallibility*, by which I mean both people's frequently flawed logical abilities and people's simple, innocent ignorance. Those who underestimate fallibility may fail to recognize that rational truth-seeking is an imperfect process that can produce, in the minds of other rational truth seekers, conclusions with which we do not agree—because either they or we are ignorant of evidence of which the other party is aware; or because either they or we are evaluating the same evidence differently, or even illogically. The irrationalist view—ironically, since it is an attempt at hardheaded realism—treats everyone as not only a truth seeker but a truth attainer: that is, as effectively omniscient. Once the truth is treated, in effect, as self-evident to one and all, what would, for an epistemologist, count as a failure of some (or all) of the parties to a disagreement to know the truth *must* count as some parties' perverse rejection of the *known* truth—which can only be deemed irrational.

Cognitive psychologists (as opposed to social and political psychologists) have a useful term for the view that one's own opinions are self-evidently true, i.e., that they are unmediated by fallible human processes of data gathering, interpretation, and communication: *naïve realism* (Ross and Ward 1996). Naïve realists treat their own beliefs as if they were self-evidently true emanations of reality itself, such that anyone who disagrees with their beliefs must, ipso facto, be irrational. I am suggesting that irrationalist explanations of others' beliefs may manifest naïve realism, such that the naïve realist attributes irrationality to the Other by neglecting the possibility that the Other—or the naïve realist herself—is simply mistaken.

Example 3. The methodological consequence of naïve realism is a failure of *intellectual charity.* By that I mean a failure to put oneself into the shoes of those whose belief one is tempted to diagnose as irrational so as to see why, from the Other's perspective, the belief might actually be rational (even if we continue to see it as mistaken).

Intellectual charity is not the same thing as *interpretive* charity (e.g. Davidson 1973–1974). Interpretive charity has come to mean, among analytic philosophers, the attribution to the Other of the *best* arguments that one can think of for the conclusions advocated by the Other. This procedure is merited if one is interested in arguing against the strongest possible opponent. However, if one is interested not in arguing, but in understanding—that is, understanding real people, not imaginary interlocutors—interpretive charity goes too far. Unlike interpretively charitable interpretations, intellectually charitable interpretations do not credit the Other with the best arguments for her conclusions, but with arguments, other ideas, and (putative) knowledge that may *actually* be present in the Other's web of belief, and that, if present, would make the Other's conclusions rational—even if they are mistaken. Intellectual charity, then, allows for the possibility that the Other might be making bad arguments that seem plausible to her, whether because she is unwittingly making logical errors, is ignorant of something that the observer thinks relevant, or is interpreting some (putative) fact differently than the observer interprets it.

Consider "rallying around the flag." If we try to put ourselves in the shoes of the survey respondents in various countries who believed that their leaders' performance warranted the respondents' approval, it is fairly easy to come up with epistemological, non-psychological, non-irrationalist explanations for this belief—even if we think the belief mistaken. Perhaps they saw the pandemic as a difficult situation to deal with, such that they set a low bar for adequate performance and focused only on whether their leaders cleared it, regardless of by how much. And perhaps even respondents who were inclined to compare leaders' performance across countries did not know about the statistics that, in the *Times* Interpreter's mind, clearly identified some leaders, such as Boris Johnson, as relative failures in comparison to others, such as Angela Merkel. A third possibility is that even respondents who were aware of these statistics, and who found them relevant to judging their own leaders' performance, disagreed with the Interpreter's assessment of which leaders were performing better. They might have thought, for example, that German culture was more conducive to an effective response to the pandemic than British culture because German culture fosters obedience to authority; this stereotype might have been seen as excusing Johnson's poor performance vis-à-vis Merkel's. The stereotype may be mistaken, as may the judgment to which it leads, but we have no reason to assume that these mistakes are irrational—rather than stemming from different beliefs than our own.

Thus, intellectual charity corrects the default inclination to psychologize the survey results. They present no puzzle so great that we must resort to irrationalist explanations if we do not treat *our own* assessment of the leaders' relative performance as self-evidently warranted, and if we therefore do not project this assessment into the heads of survey respondents (on the tacit grounds that if it is self-evident to us, it must be self-evident to them). This is not to say, of course, that any one of the intellectually charitable explanations that we might come up with in a given case is accurate; that is an empirical question that would require investigation by empirical political epistemologists. It is to say, however, that the naïve realist may produce an inaccurate explanation of the behavior in question if, blinded by naïve realism, she does not even attempt to be intellectually charitable.

The *New York Times* Interpreter, for example, in imputing to the survey respondents his own knowledge about different leaders' relative statistical performance, credits even people who do not carefully read, say, the *New York Times*, or who do not read it at all, with knowing in detail what is reported there. Such *imputations of knowledge* are characteristic of naïvely realistic approaches to understanding human beliefs and actions. An intellectually charitable analyst would pause, before imputing knowledge (or putative knowledge) to the Other, to ask where the Other might have gotten this knowledge (or putative knowledge), given that the truth is *not* self-evident—i.e., given that the human starting point is ignorance, not knowledge. An empirical political epistemologist might then investigate the Other's sources of knowledge, or rather belief (e.g., her media diet). In most cases, this simple step will go a long way toward explaining any seemingly irrational political belief.

It may seem paradoxical that intellectual "charity" encourages a recognition of others' *mistakenness*. But the intellectually charitable view that British survey respondents might have seen German culture as cultivating obedience to authority does not entail *agreement* with this belief; it is thus consistent with a recognition that the respondents are rational even if mistaken. Accordingly, an important principle of political epistemology is the injunction to operate only at the second order, bracketing one's own agreement or disagreement with the first-order beliefs one is investigating.[1] Intellectual charity, then, is not a prescription for relativism. It is simply a recognition of the fact that human fallibility may afflict either oneself or the Other one is trying to understand, and that one should not treat one's own beliefs as truths so self-evident that one is licensed to impute one's own knowledge and logic, or putative knowledge and logic, to the Other. If we fail to follow this injunction, we become unable to understand the Other on her own terms, i.e., as a rational being, and this will leave us little recourse but to seek irrationalist explanations of our disagreements with the Other. We cannot put ourselves in the Other's shoes if all we can imagine standing there is somebody with our own (self-evidently true) beliefs, such that her failure to act as if she shares those beliefs indicates her irrationality—rather than indicating our failure to grasp that she simply has different beliefs than we do, beliefs we consider mistaken. Our naïve realism may thus feed into our *psychologizing of disagreement* with the Other and, thus, our inability to understand accurately those with whom we disagree. We can avoid this trap only if we bracket our first-order beliefs, and thus our potential disagreements with the Other—which are, after all, utterly irrelevant, causally, to the Other's beliefs (at least when the Other is unaware of us and our beliefs).

First-order belief bracketing probably entails the abandonment of not just naïvely realistic psychologizing but also of the philosophical attempt to *moralize* disagreement by treating beliefs with which a given philosopher disagrees as violations of epistemic "norms," and thus as exemplifying epistemic "vices." In treating the Other as violating *our* (beliefs about) epistemic norms in a culpable (vicious) manner, we are failing to recognize that the Other might rationally (if, perhaps, mistakenly) disagree with us about the normativity of those norms or about whether, in the case at hand, she has violated them. We are then treating *our* norms and *our* understanding of the reasons for the Other's beliefs as if they are so self-evidently true that they *must be* agreed upon by the Other (at the first order)—who then contradicts herself, viciously acting as if she does *not* agree with them. We do better to recognize that the contradiction between the "knowledge" we impute to the Other and the behavior in which she engages may indicate not the viciousness of her habits but the inaccuracy of our imputation.

That, in turn, suggests that the epistemological perspective is *ideationally deterministic*. It recognizes that mistake is involuntary—one never deliberately errs—and thus cannot be explained as a culpable choice, any more than it can be explained as psychologically determined. Rather, if the Other is mistaken, the cause is whatever items in her web of belief combine to form the judgment with which we disagree; or an error in the logic by which these items have been combined. The middle ground between perfect knowledge and irrationality is thus the ground of beliefs that are determined not by choice, nor by psychological forces, but by fallible processes of rational belief formation.

Example 4. Even philosophers pursuing the "epistemic norms" project have failed to come up with a persuasive reason to think that conspiracy theorists, as such, are epistemically vicious, let alone irrational. For (on the whole) they have recognized that in principle, any given conspiracy theory, or perhaps even all of them, might be true; and that conspiracy theorists tend to be such assiduous and rigorous investigators of the empirical evidence *that they consider plausible* that they may "amass sufficient evidence to *rationally* believe certain conspiracy theories" (Harris 2009, 240). When there is a problem with a *particular* conspiracy theory (from the perspective of any given observer), it usually comes down to the observer's first-order disagreement with the plausibility of, the importance of, or the interpretation of the evidence adduced by the conspiracy theorist. Such disagreement can be assumed to indicate a psychological problem (for the conspiracy theorist) only if the observer treats her own first-order position as so self-evidently true that the conspiracy theorist *must* be irrational to disagree with it.

Thus, what the *Politico* writer treats as incorrect or preposterous conspiracy theories—e.g. "that the coronavirus was spread deliberately; that the pandemic is over-exaggerated in an attempt to hurt President Trump's reelection; [or] that this whole thing was some sort of bioweapon created in a Chinese lab" (Stanton 2020)—are *plainly* incorrect, or *inherently* preposterous, only from a naïvely realistic standpoint, from which one treats the conspiracy theorists as knowing, in some sense, that what they believe is incorrect or preposterous. But if one is to put oneself into the Other's shoes, one must not efface the empirical otherness of the Other, i.e., the differences between her web of belief and our own—erasing her in the process. (This is the problem with interpretive charity, as opposed to intellectual charity.) This erasure begins when we impute (what we consider to be) our knowledge to her. Having made such an imputation, we cannot possibly understand why she behaves as if a conspiracy we "know" to be preposterous is credible. Similarly, our judgment that certain sources of information are *inherently* suspect and thus should not be trusted by the conspiracy theorist comes down to a disagreement with the Other about whether these sources really are inherently suspect: she plainly thinks that they aren't.

The attribution of irrationality is, in the end, a refusal to countenance the possibility that one's own beliefs, about trustworthiness or anything else, are not self-evidently true, such that other rational beings may disagree with them.

III Naïve realism in the academy

The problem of naïve realism, leading to intellectually uncharitable attributions of knowledge to others, and to unjustified attributions of irrationality to them when they disagree with us, is ubiquitous not just in political culture but academic psychology and other disciplines. For reasons of space, I confine myself to three examples before reflecting on their implications.

Consider first the "motivated-reasoning" framework for understanding dogmatism. In political psychology, the most widely cited application of this framework has been Charles Taber and Milton Lodge's (2006) paper, "Motivated Skepticism in the Evaluation of Political Beliefs" (cited 2,823 times by mid-2020). The authors gave subjects the opportunity to read arguments that were congruent or incongruent with the subjects' initial beliefs about affirmative action and gun control. Most subjects then became more persuaded of the veracity of their prior beliefs than they had been before the experiment—even if they read incongruent arguments, which, the authors assume, should have weakened their priors rather than strengthening them. This effect was predominantly found among subjects who were likely to be relatively well-informed about affirmative action and gun control and among those who had stronger initial beliefs about these issues. The authors conclude that "rather than moderating or simply maintaining their original attitudes, citizens—especially those who feel strongly about the issue and are the most sophisticated—strengthen their attitudes *in ways not warranted by the evidence*" (Taber and Lodge 2006, 756, my emphasis).

Only if the emphasized words were true would the subjects' dogmatic behavior warrant the inference that they were in the grip of a non-epistemic motive, such as ego defense, that steered them away from the clear—self-evident—implication of incongruent evidence for their priors, namely that this evidence should reduce their confidence, not increase it. Yet their gains in confidence may have stemmed from the subjects' disagreement with the authors' assumptions about the appropriate procedure for rationally updating their beliefs. In the authors' view, apparently, the rational procedure is not to judge the incongruent evidence in light of previously assimilated evidence. That is, incongruent evidence is not to be screened for its plausibility. It is far from obvious that this is the most rational way to proceed, let alone that it is self-evidently the best way. Surely there can be legitimate differences of opinion as to whether any evidence thrown one's way in a laboratory experiment should be treated as a good reason to doubt one's priors. It may, in fact, be rational for incongruent evidence to strengthen one's priors once the evidence is placed into the wider context of one's extant web of belief. Thus, Lee Ross (2012, 236), a coauthor of the classic article on naïve realism, suggests that Taber and Lodge's subjects may have said to themselves, in effect: "'If that's the best [the other side] can do to support their argument, I'm even more certain [than before] that they are wrong.'" This interpretation is all the more compelling since the most dogmatic subjects were those with the strongest and (evidentially) best-supported priors. The evidence and logic for their priors may, from their perspective, have rationally justified a rejection of the arguments presented in the lab as implausible. If this response to the arguments is a mistake, it surely is not such an obvious mistake that the subjects must somehow have realized (unconsciously) that they were violating authoritative epistemic norms, which only an extra-epistemic motive could explain.[2]

My next example is drawn from behavioral economics—the branch of psychology that surely provides the most popular irrationalist framework in the academy today. The list of "heuristics and biases" that behavioral economists have come up with is, of course, quite long and it keeps growing. All I can do is select an example of the genre that lends itself to abbreviated exposition and epistemological critique. In Section 4, I will address the fact that we are not in a position to know if such examples are representative of the quality of research in the field as a whole.

My example is a landmark experiment that gets its own chapter in Daniel Kahneman's popularization of behavioral economics, *Thinking: Fast and Slow* (2011). Kahneman and Amos Tversky (1973, 238–39) presented subjects with a character sketch of "Tom W." that portrays him as an intelligent, socially awkward science fiction reader. The subjects were then asked to rank various fields of graduate specialization "in order of the likelihood that Tom is now a graduate student in each of these fields." Ninety-five percent of the subjects believed that Tom was likelier to be studying computer science than "the humanities or education." This belief is irrational, according to the authors, because the subjects "*were surely aware* that there are many more graduate students in the latter field" (my emphasis), such that the odds are greater that Tom is in the latter field.

Thus, the authors attribute to the subjects accurate knowledge of a topic to which most of them had probably never given a moment's thought before the experiment began: the statistical distribution of graduate students across academic disciplines in the United States circa 1973. Surely such statistics are not self-evident. Yet if the subjects were simply ignorant of them, there is no reason to assume that they irrationally preferred to use the stereotype of a computer geek *rather than* using the statistics. According to the authors, "base-rate neglect" is one of the most important human biases, but without their naïvely realistic attribution of base-rate knowledge to the subjects, base-rate neglect would have to be seen as ignorance of obscure statistics, which is in no sense irrational—except from the perspective of an omniscient being.

Third and finally, consider a theory that commands widespread assent among political scientists: the theory that citizens who vote in an election with a large electorate, and who intend thereby to help achieve an outcome—such as the adoption of the policies favored by their candidate or party (as opposed to citizens who vote from a sense of duty)—are irrational, because the odds against any one vote being decisive are so high that it is extremely improbable that the outcome will be affected by one's vote (Downs 1957). The theory naïvely attributes knowledge of those odds to the voters—with no evidence to justify the attribution. Indeed, survey research suggests that people tend to think that their votes *are* likely to make a difference, such that they could not possibly know the odds against this (Friedman 2019, 277–78). This stands to reason, as the depressing mathematics of voting are rarely discussed in popular culture (where it is repeatedly maintained, in fact, that "every vote counts"). Moreover, the theory is falsified every time people do vote in large electorates, which happens without fail when mass elections are held: people vote, by the millions, despite the odds.

The naïve attribution to voters of knowledge of these odds is foundational to arguments for both the *rationality* of voters' ignorance of political affairs and public policy (e.g. Somin 2013; Brennan 2016) and the rationality of holding *plainly irrational* beliefs about these matters (e.g. Caplan 2007).[3] Here the theorist attributes voters' failure to acquire knowledge that *the theorist* considers important, and voters' consequent endorsement of policies that *the theorist* considers irrational, to voters' (assumed, not demonstrated) knowledge of the odds against their votes mattering. *If* voters knew these odds, they would rationally decide not to spend resources on informing their (inefficacious) votes. And in the void created by their rationally chosen ignorance, they might feel licensed to indulge in irrational "emotion and ideology," as they recognize that their underinformed, emotional, ideological votes are unlikely to make any difference (Caplan 2007, 2). All of this, however, is predicated on the assumption that voters know that their votes are highly unlikely to matter—an assumption that is never defended, and is inconsistent with both the survey evidence and the fact that voters vote. Once again, naïve realism leads to an unwarranted ascription of irrationality that prevents the theorist from exploring reasons for the Others' behavior that do not rest on the congruence between their knowledge and that of the theorist.[4]

IV How mythical is political irrationality?

One cannot possibly establish the prevalence of false attributions of irrationality with a few examples. How, then, should we treat the examples I have adduced?

One possibility would be to treat them *positivistically:* that is, as suggesting that social scientists should test rationalist, interpretively charitable hypotheses against the irrationalist interpretations that are hegemonic in the psychology literature. For example, they could try to replicate the "Tom W." experiment but tell the subjects what the base rates are. Supposing that they were to embark upon this endeavor, however, political epistemologists would need to know, in the meantime, how to treat the vast ocean of findings that have not yet been re-tested, which is pretty much coextensive with the truly gigantic literature of social and political psychology. Should we, as consumers of this literature, treat it as innocent until proven guilty, or vice versa?

The most conservative positivist tack would be to treat the examples of badly interpreted psychological findings as anomalous, such that all the other irrationalist findings continue to guide our thinking until social scientists get around to re-testing them. More radically, we could treat all of those findings with suspicion, pending re-testing, on the following grounds: our introspective experience of our own rationality counts as empirical evidence against the irrationalist double standard common to all such findings (although not indefeasible evidence). Thus, if we ask ourselves if we *ever* "ignore" base rates that we know about and understand the relevance of; if we ourselves ever trust media sources that we find inherently untrustworthy, or—one might add (to begin a very long list of other irrationalist findings)—whether we ourselves ever believe something because we *want to* "identify" with a social group by accepting its beliefs as true (e.g. Achen and Bartels 2016; Kahan 2016), rather than simply agreeing with its beliefs because they rationally seem to us to be true, the answer appears to be that we don't. For scientific reasons, then, we should treat others as rational until we have evidence to the contrary, where "evidence" refers to positivist findings from research in which rationalist and irrationalist explanations for particular behavior are tested against each other. For we have introspective empirical evidence in favor of the rationalist conclusion, and science should never ignore empirical evidence.

However, there are several reasons to think that the more radical positivist approach, which would merely deprive irrationalist findings of the benefit of the doubt prior to re-testing them, is not radical enough.

First, it may not be fruitful to re-test, because what is often at issue is not the behavior revealed in the laboratory but its interpretation. In the case of motivated reasoning, for example, Ross simply offered an alternative interpretation of Taber and Lodge's findings. It may be impossible to test the two interpretations against each other, because Ross is saying that people who behave *precisely as Taber and Lodge's dogmatic subjects behave* may do so not from a non-epistemic "motive" but an epistemic motive pursued in a manner that Taber and Lodge find "obviously" irrational. In his interpretation of the subjects' behavior, Ross appeals to our introspectively derived knowledge of what would "make sense" of the behavior for putatively rational beings such as ourselves. Taber and Lodge prefer, in effect, to assign control over our behavior to a homunculus secreted in our unconscious, which manipulates our behavior to defend our egos by protecting our beliefs from falsification (Friedman 2019, 243–47). Conflicting independent variables are being invoked to explain the same dependent variable, but the independent variables are metaphysical, not empirically observable.

(It is worth repeating that one would only resort to the metaphysical homunculus because one assumes that there can be no rational explanation for the behavior.)

At the very least, then, it would seem to follow that political theorists and philosophers should end the practice of taking empirical researchers' interpretations of their findings at face value. Empirical researchers are not selected and trained for introspective sensitivity (or metaphysical insight) but, rather, for statistical rigor and inventiveness in operationalizing hypotheses. This would explain why, as connoisseurs of their efforts will recognize, their findings are dazzling but their interpretations of the findings often fly in the face of introspection (ibid., 210–28). Therefore, we should never cite the interpretations as if they *were* findings, we should never fail to report the experimental procedures whose results are being interpreted, and we should never fail to look for intellectually charitable alternative interpretations.

Further grounds for caution about any positivistic approach, no matter how radically it questions empirical findings, are suggested by the *reason* that empirical researchers are not selected or trained for interpretive acuity. Those who select and train them are looking for scholars who will carry on the work of unearthing or refining laws or regularities of human behavior (ibid., chapter 4). That entails treating one's research subjects (people) as predictable and largely homogeneous, which almost necessarily militates against a consideration of causal factors, such as beliefs, that may vary unpredictably, but not randomly, from person to person (ibid., chapter 3). This may explain the emphasis in the social sciences on people's *motives*, such as self-interest, ego defense, or group identification: the number of motives that would apply across large populations is minuscule compared to the number of beliefs the members of those populations might have about which actions to take in pursuit of a given motive. The homogenizing, ahistorical, universalist ambitions of social scientists would also explain their emphasis on biases that are supposed to hold across all populations, regardless of the particular beliefs the individual members of a population might have. The very purpose of psychology, as a field of academic study, is to predict common and lasting phenomena, not those that are unpredictable or historically specific, as beliefs are. It is much easier to predict commonality by focusing on people's (putative) motives or biases, in short, than by allowing that their behavior is the result of heterogeneous and fallible yet rational beliefs.

This last point, I think, tells in favor of a third, anti-positivist stance toward irrationalist social science: that we should neither treat it as innocent until proven guilty, nor as guilty until proven innocent, but as fundamentally incorrect. This is because unpredictable belief heterogeneity may occur not only among the populations in which social scientists are positing behavioral regularities, but between the observer and the observed. This is what may have happened in all the cases cited in both Sections I and III: in each case, the observers *could not imagine* beliefs that might rationally have prompted behavior that they therefore treated as irrational. By putting my imagination (and Lee Ross's) to work, I hope to have shown that the observers may have overlooked rational beliefs that would have explained the behavior. But what happens if no observer happens to imagine what is going on in the minds of those whose behavior is being observed?

It is only to be expected that fallible, ideationally heterogeneous creatures will sometimes be unable to think of accurate explanations for the behavior of other such creatures. However homogeneous we are in our emotional and cognitive architecture, the beliefs populating that architecture are likely to vary, to some extent, from person to person. Because these beliefs, as mental phenomena, are inaccessible to observers, I may be unable to put myself into your shoes in a particular case. That, however, does not justify assuming that you have no reasons for your beliefs, rather than allowing that I am simply ignorant of what they are.

If this line of thought is correct, we should treat irrationalist explanations as illegitimate in principle. Even if the behavior they attempt to explain *cannot* be explained rationally—by us—this may mean nothing more than that we cannot read other people's minds. Our own failures of mind reading, however, do not justify the attribution of irrationality to those whose minds we cannot read.

Notes

1 See Friedman (2019, 61–75).
2 For a fuller critique of the motivated-reasoning literature, see ibid., 232–47.
3 For critiques, see ibid., 277–83 on Somin; Gunn (2019) on Brennan; Bennett and Friedman (2008) on Caplan.
4 I attempt such an exploration of "ignorant voters" in Friedman (2019, 264–301).

References

Achen, C. H., and L. M. Bartels (2016) *Democracy for Realists*, Princeton, NJ: Princeton University Press.
Bennett, S. E., and J. Friedman (2008) "The Irrelevance of Economic Theory to Understanding Economic Ignorance," *Critical Review* 20: 195–258.
Branswell, H. 2020. "The Months of Magical Thinking: As the Coronavirus Swept over China, Some Experts Were in Denial," *Stat*, 20 April.
Brennan, J. (2016) *Against Democracy*, Princeton, NJ: Princeton University Press.
Caplan, B. (2007) *The Myth of the Rational Voter*, Princeton, NJ: Princeton University Press.
Davidson, D. (1973–1974) "On the Very Idea of a Conceptual Scheme," *Proceedings and Addresses of the American Philosophical Association* 47: 5–20.
Downs, A. 1957. *An Economic Theory of Democracy.* New York: Harper & Row.
Fischer, M. (2020) "How Fear and Psychology Explain Rising Support for Leaders," *New York Times*, May 25.
Friedman, J. (2019) *Power Without Knowledge*, New York: Oxford University Press.
Gunn, P. (2019) "Against Epistocracy," *Critical Review* 31(1): 26–82.
Harris, K. (2009) "What's Epistemically Wrong with Conspiracy Theorizing?" in S. Barker, C. Crerar, and T. S. Goetze (eds.), *Harms and Wrongs in Epistemic Practice*, Cambridge: Cambridge University Press.
Kahan, D. M. (2016) "The Expressive Rationality of Inaccurate Perceptions," *Behavioral & Brain Sciences* 40: 26–28.
Kahneman, D. (2011) *Thinking: Fast and Slow*, New York: Farrar, Straus, and Giroux.
Kahneman, D., and A. Tversky (1973) "On the Psychology of Prediction," *Psychological Review* 80(4): 237–51.
Ross, L. (2012) "Reflections on Biased Assimilation and Belief Polarization," *Critical Review* 24(2): 233–46.
Ross, L., and A. Ward. (1996) "Naïve Realism in Everyday Life," in E. S. Reed, E. Turiel, and T. Brown (eds.), *Values and Social Knowledge*, Mahwah, NJ: Lawrence Erlbaum.
Somin, I. (2013) *Democracy and Political Ignorance*, Stanford, CA: Stanford University Press.
Stanton, Z. (2020) "You're Living in the Golden Age of Conspiracy Theories," *Politico*, June 17.
Taber, C. S., and M. R. Lodge (2006) "Motivated Skepticism in the Evaluation of Political Beliefs," *American Journal of Political Science* 50: 755–69.
Warzel, C. (2020) "What We Pretend to Know about the Coronavirus Could Kill Us," *New York Times*, April 3.

24

THE IRRATIONAL ATTEMPT TO IMPUTE IRRATIONALITY TO ONE'S POLITICAL OPPONENTS

Keith E. Stanovich

In the wake of the surprising 2016 election results—Brexit in the United Kingdom and the presidential election in the United States—the prevailing opinion among political elites in both Europe and America was that the winning electorates in both of these cases were characterized by psychological defects. They were thought to be uninformed and/or xenophobic. They were said to be unintelligent. Subsequent to the 2016 election in the United States, high-caliber publications, from *The Atlantic* (Serwer, 2017) to *The New Republic* (Heer, 2016) to *The Wall Street Journal* (Stephens, 2016), were nearly uniform in their relentless portrayal of the Trump voter as racist, sexist, and xenophobic. In *Foreign Policy* magazine, we were told that "Trump owes his victory to the uniformed" and that his victory was due to "the dance of the dunces" (Brennan, 2016). In the United Kingdom, the portrayal of the Brexit voter in the elite media was largely similar (see Fuller, 2019). The agenda here was sometimes baldly displayed, as in Traub's (2016) essay titled "It's Time for the Elites to Rise Up Against the Ignorant Masses."

The list of psychological defects ascribed to these voters extended to my own specialty area—individual differences in rational judgment and decision-making. In September of 2016, I published, in collaboration with my colleagues Richard West and Maggie Toplak, a book titled *The Rationality Quotient*. As the author of a rationality test, I began to receive many communications that assumed I was the perfect person to prove what my interlocutors thought was beyond doubt: that both the Brexit voters and the Trump voters were irrational. I was in a good position to engage with these queries at the time because I had already moved on from the 2016 book and was working on a book on mysided reasoning (Stanovich, 2021). Many of the main convictions that fuel mysided thinking derive from partisanship and ideology. However, my examination of this literature did not provide comfort for my correspondents. In this chapter, I will outline my two discomforting conclusions. The first is that I find no strong converging evidence that the partisan *opponents* of the largely left-wing social science researchers who study voter psychology (Duarte et al., 2015) are any less rational than are their partisan supporters (not only the Trump voters, but other ideological opponents as well). This null finding regarding partisan differences in rationality suggests a second, somewhat ironic, conclusion: that the social scientists who study partisan differences are subject to a particularly virulent version of the so-called bias blind spot (Pronin, 2007).

1 Instrumental and epistemic critiques of the Trump voters

Partisan overlap in voting patterns at the presidential level is quite high from election to election in the United States. Thus, when we talk about the Trump voters, the first thing to understand is that the vast majority of them were Romney voters in the previous election and McCain voters in the election before that. Statistically, most Trump voters were standard-issue Republicans. Some analyses, such as that of Ganzach et al. (2019) attempt to analyze whether there were characteristics on the margin (that is, over and above party affiliation) that were different among the Trump voters, but it is important to realize that analyses such as these are isolating a tiny sliver of voters on the margins (al-Gharbi, 2018). The small sliver who may have tipped the election toward Trump in the Electoral College are not the same as the much, much larger entity "Trump voters." Ganzach et al. (2019) analyzed affective warmth ratings of Trump (and other presidential candidates) in a regression equation using a number of predictor variables. They found that the dominant beta weight (a statistic indicating the strength of a variable independent of others with which it is correlated) when predicting ratings of Trump was for party affiliation (0.610). That predictor was orders of magnitude stronger than other significant predictors such as sex (-0.091) and verbal ability (-0.061).

It follows, then, that when the claim is that the Trump voters were irrational, statistically, it entails that the Romney voters and the McCain voters were irrational too. Thus, when I analyze the evidence on rationality in this chapter, I will use research which looks at partisan affiliation and ideology as well, because it has a 90% overlap with comparisons based strictly on the Trump vs. Clinton voters in 2016.

Another caveat is that my focus is on the comparison between voters of different types (Clinton voters vs. Trump voters)—not the more global question of the absolute level of rationality among voters, which is a much larger and more difficult issue. The absolute level question is, in fact, much more conceptually complex (see Caplan, 2007; Fuller, 2019; Lomasky, 2008).

A common complaint about less-affluent Republican voters (and by implication, Trump voters) among Democratic critics is that they were irrational because they were voting against their own interests. Over a decade ago, this was the theme of Thomas Frank's (2004) popular book *What's the Matter with Kansas?* and it has recurred frequently since. The idea is that lower income people who vote Republican are voting against their interests because they would receive more government benefits if they voted Democratic. Many of these critiques contain the presumptions that, to be instrumentally rational, preferences must be self-interested and that people's primary desires are monetary. But theories of utility maximization contain no such presumptions. Utility refers to the good that accrues when people achieve their goals—and a person's goal is not always to maximize pleasure. More important for discussions of voter rationality, however, is that utility does not just mean monetary value. For instance, people gain utility from holding and expressing specific beliefs and values (more on this below). Utility theory also does not dictate that every goal has to reflect strict self-interest in a narrow sense. We can have as our goal that other people achieve their goals.

These *What's the Matter with Kansas?* critiques of working-class Republican voters are thus misplaced. They gratuitously insult their targets by assuming that these voters *should* care only about their material interests. For example, liberals who work for nonprofit organizations are often choosing their values over monetary reward. And likewise, conservatives joining the military are often also choosing their values over monetary reward. The *What's the Matter with Kansas?* argument seems to ignore or deny this symmetry. Even if part of the *Kansas* critique is correct (Republicans are voting against their purely economic interests), these voters are not necessarily irrational because they may be sacrificing monetary gain in order to express their values or worldview.

If you are particularly ill-disposed toward Trump voters, at this point you may still be feeling that, deep down, there is something else wrong with them that was not covered in my discussion of instrumental rationality. You might feel that something in the domain of knowledge is wrong with the Trump voters: they don't know enough, or they seem to be misinformed, or they don't seem to listen to evidence. You would be right that there is another aspect of rationality that we must assess: epistemic rationality.

Concern with Trump voters in the epistemic domain is, however, not unique because this is a charge (the charge of epistemic irrationality) that Democrats have made about Republicans for some time now. We have become accustomed to critiques of conservative Republicans who do not accept the conclusions of climate science, or of evolutionary biology. These critiques are correct, of course. The role of human activity in climate change is established science, and evolution is a biological fact. Thus, it would be very tempting to say: well, the Democrats get climate science right, and Republicans get it wrong; the Democrats get evolution right, and conservative Republicans get it wrong; so therefore we liberal Democrats are getting everything factually right about all of the other charged topics that figure in political disputes—crime, immigration, poverty, parenting, sexuality, etc. Such an argument is essentially the claim that Democrats are epistemically more rational than Republicans—that they acquire knowledge in better ways.

Some years ago, this type of thinking prompted the Democratic Party to declare itself the "party of science" and to label the Republican Party as the science deniers. That stance spawned a series of books with titles like Mooney's *The Republican War on Science* (2005). As a political strategy, this "party of science" labeling might be effective, but epistemic superiority cannot simply be declared on the basis of a few examples. In fact, any trained social scientist would be quick to point out the obvious selection effects that are operating. The issues in question (climate science and creationism/evolution) are cherry-picked for reasons of politics and media interest. In order to correctly call one party the party of science and the other the party of science deniers, one would of course have to have a representative sampling of scientific issues to see whether members of one party are more likely to accept scientific consensus (Lupia, 2016).

In fact, it is not difficult at all to find scientific issues on which it is liberal Democrats who fail to accept the scientific consensus. Ironically, there are enough examples to produce a book parallel to the Mooney volume cited above titled *Science Left Behind: Feel-Good Fallacies and the Rise of the Anti-Scientific Left* (Berezow & Campbell, 2012). To mention an example from my own field, psychology: liberals tend to deny the overwhelming consensus in psychological science that intelligence is moderately heritable and that the tests are not biased against minority groups (Deary, 2013; Haier, 2016; Plomin et al., 2016; Rindermann et al., 2020). They become the "science deniers" in this case.

Intelligence is not the only area of liberal science denial, though. In the area of economics, liberals are very reluctant to accept the consensus view that when proper controls for occupational choice and work history are made, women do not make 20% less than men for doing the same work (Bertrand et al., 2010; Black et al., 2008; CONSAD, 2009; Kolesnikova & Liu, 2011; O'Neill & O'Neill, 2012; Solberg & Laughlin, 1995). Liberals tend to deny or obfuscate the data indicating that single-parent households lead to more behavioral problems among children (Chetty et al., 2014; McLanahan et al., 2013; Murray, 2012). Overwhelmingly liberal university schools of education deny the strong scientific consensus that phonics-based reading instruction facilitates most readers, especially those struggling the most (Seidenberg, 2017). Many liberals find it hard to believe that there is no bias at all in the hiring, promotion, and evaluation of women in STEM disciplines and other departments in universities (Jussim, 2017; Madison & Fahlman, 2020; Williams & Ceci, 2015). Gender feminists routinely deny biological facts about sex differences (Baron-Cohen, 2003; Buss & Schmitt 2011; Pinker, 2002, 2008). I will stop here because the point is made.[1] Each side of the ideological divide finds it hard to accept scientific evidence that undermines its own ideological beliefs and policies.

However, beyond scientific knowledge, possessing information relevant to social and political issues is also part of epistemic rationality. Perhaps the Trump/Republican voters have a deficit here, compared to the Clinton/Democratic voters. Most studies have indicated, however, that there are few differences in factual knowledge between Republicans and Democrats (Pew Research Center, 2013, 2015).

Similar findings are obtained in specific areas of knowledge related to voting, such as economics. Klein and Buturovic (2011) gave a 17-item questionnaire on knowledge of economics to over 2,000 online respondents. They found that individuals labeling themselves libertarian or very conservative scored higher than individuals labeling themselves as liberal or progressive. Importantly, their major conclusion was not that conservatives were more economically knowledgeable than liberals. Instead, they stressed how such surveys can be tilted by the selection of questions (see Lupia, 2016, for an extensive discussion). For example, the item "rent-control laws lead to housing shortages" (correct answer: true) is more difficult for liberals because it challenges their ideology; whereas the item "a dollar means more to a poor person than it does to a rich person" (correct answer: true) is more difficult for conservatives because it challenges their ideology. Measures of so-called "knowledge" in such a domain are easily skewed in a partisan manner by selection effects. This is a version of the "party of science" problem discussed previously. Whether the Democrats or the Republicans are the "party of science" depends entirely on how the issue in question is selected.

Similar sampling problems plague studies of conspiracy beliefs. These are important to study because perhaps the problem with the Trump voters is not that they have acquired too little knowledge but that they have acquired too much *misinformation*. The early research literature on the relation between ideology and conspiracy belief seemed to suggest that conspiratorial thinking was, in fact, more strongly associated with the political right. However, more recent research has suggested that this finding was simply a function of the distribution of specific conspiracy beliefs that were studied. Research using more balanced items has suggested that conspiracy beliefs are equally prevalent on the political right and left (Enders, 2019; Oliver & Wood, 2014; Stanovich et al., 2016).

Although there is no strong evidence that there are differences in the knowledge that liberal and conservative voters have accumulated, it might be that the problem with conservatives (and Trump voters) is in the *process* of knowledge accumulation (in belief *forming* mechanisms). There are right and wrong ways to acquire knowledge. A person can acquire a true fact in the wrong manner. If a person acquired a true political fact by a process of searching exclusively for things that support their political position, they may well be acquiring knowledge in the technical sense, but the knowledge base will be skewed and selective. The degree of myside bias is a direct measure of this general tendency. Myside bias occurs when people evaluate evidence, generate evidence, and test hypotheses in a manner biased toward their own prior beliefs, opinions, and attitudes.

In a recent paper, Ditto et al. (2019) meta-analyzed 41 experimental studies of partisan differences in myside bias that involved over 12,000 subjects. After amalgamating all of these studies and comparing an overall metric of myside bias, Ditto and colleagues concluded that the degree of partisan bias in these studies was quite similar for liberals and conservatives.[2] Thus, the lack of partisan differences found in actual acquired knowledge discussed previously is mirrored by a lack of partisan differences in the biasing process of myside thinking.

In summary, both in terms of the knowledge acquisition process and in terms of knowledge content, there is no strong evidence that the Republicans who were the bulk of those who voted for Trump were less epistemically rational than the Democrats who were the bulk of the Clinton voters. In terms of both components of rationality—instrumental and epistemic—there is no support in the empirical literature for attributing a unique problem of rationality to Trump voters. However, there remain broader types of rationality to consider.

2 Myside bias in critiques of the expressive rationality

Many human communications are not aimed at conveying information about what is true (Tetlock, 2002). They are, instead, signals to others and sometimes signals to ourselves. Such communications are *functional* signals because, when sent to others they bind us to a group that we value (Haidt, 2012; Kahan, 2013; Kahan et al., 2017), and when sent to ourselves they serve motivational functions. These signals are sometimes termed exemplars of expressive rationality (or symbolic utility, see Nozick, 1993) to reflect the fact that they are not aimed at maximizing first-order desires or immediate consumption utility (see Abelson, 1996; Akerlof & Kranton, 2010; Anderson, 1993; Stanovich, 2004, 2013).

We are quite prone to view acts of expressive rationality as irrational (at least in our political opponents) in cases where the lack of a causal link between the action and the actual outcome has become manifestly obvious yet the symbolic action continues to be performed. Some anti-drug measures possibly fall in this category. In some cases, evidence has accumulated to indicate that an anti-drug program does not have the causal effect of reducing actual drug use (or the effect is minimal, or it is not cost-effective), but the program is continued because it has become the symbol of our concern for stopping drug use. In the present day, many actions signaling a concern for global warming are expressive (their immediate efficaciousness is less important than the meaning of the signal being sent by the signaler). Likewise, analyses of voting as an expressive act de-emphasize the instrumental utility of the voting and emphasize the signaling and psychological benefits (Brennan & Lomasky, 1993; Johnston et al., 2017; Lomasky, 2008). The buying of books that we know we will never read is perhaps another example. Expressive rationality encompasses Kahan's (2013, 2015) and Kahan et al.'s (2017) concept of identity protective cognition.

Evaluations of the expressive rationality of our partisan opponents are invariably saturated with myside bias (Stanovich, 2021). Why your own side would choose to signal a value at a utility cost seems perfectly obvious—yet when your political opponents do it, it seems utterly irrational. Republicans can clearly see the irrationality of Democratic city councils divesting themselves of investments in corporations disliked by the left (often at a cost in real return on city-invested dollars). Democrats likewise denigrate the enthusiasm of Republicans for "just say no" campaigns surrounding drugs and sex and point out the irrationality of the Republicans not caring if the programs work or not. Such judgments are overwhelmingly determined by myside bias. The other side is judged deeply irrational when they abandon cost-benefit analysis to signal a value choice, but when my own side sacrifices utility, money, or outcome goals in order to signal a value, that is OK because our values are the right ones (seems to be the reasoning!).

In short, each side accuses the other of epistemic irrationality when the opposing side switches from purely epistemic modes to expressive modes. Even if we were to stipulate that expressive modes are less rational, there is no extant evidence that they are more prevalent among Trump voters than they are among Clinton voters.

3 Blindness to bias in the study of political psychology

The overwhelmingly left/liberal professoriate has been on a quest to find psychological defects in their political opponents for quite some time, but the intensity of these efforts has increased markedly in the last two decades. The intensity of the quest has led Shermer (2011) to quip that

> much as medical scientists study cancer in order to cure the disease, liberal political scientists study political attitudes and voting behavior in order to cure people of the cancer of conservatism. This liberal bias in academia is so deeply entrenched that it becomes the political water through which the liberal fish swim—they don't even notice it. (p. 233)

The classic psychological work linking authoritarian thinking to conservatism (Adorno et al., 1950; Altemeyer, 1981) was given new impetus by the much-cited Jost et al. (2003) literature review reviving the "rigidity of the right" theme in modern social and political psychology. In the years subsequent to the Jost et al. (2003) review, it has not been hard to find in the literature many correlations linking conservatism with intolerance, prejudice, low intelligence, close-minded thinking styles, and just about any cognitive and personality characteristic that is undesirable.

The problem is that most of these relationships have not held up when subjected to critiques that used frameworks different from the ideological assumptions that fueled much of the earlier research (Brandt & Crawford, 2019; Chambers et al., 2013; Crawford & Jussim, 2018; Reyna, 2018; Stanovich, 2021). Despite the low yield of the psychological research attempting to link conservatism with negative psychological traits, the impetus to find such relationships became magnified by the surprising US presidential election results of 2016. Trump's victory made political and cognitive elites even more sure that their political opponents were cognitively defective. However, the search for the deficient cognitive characteristics of the Trump voters has backfired. You can say whatever you want about the irrationality of Trump *himself*, but cognitive science does not support the claim that his *voters* were irrational—or, more precisely, that they were any less rational than the Clinton voters. The judgment that these voters were irrational was, ironically, driven by convictions of just the type that cause intense myside bias (Stanovich, 2021). Politics is a bad place to look for the validation of our beliefs. Our judgments in this domain are uniquely susceptible to myside bias.

In a recent book (Stanovich, 2021), I reviewed evidence indicating that myside bias was not attenuated by cognitive sophistication indicated in a variety of ways: by high cognitive ability; by education; or by well-developed rational thinking dispositions. In this concluding section, I will describe how these facts about myside bias interact to create a particularly virulent form of metacognitive failure among cognitive elites in the political domain.

The bias blind spot is an important meta-bias demonstrated in a paper by Pronin et al. (2002). They found that people thought that various motivational biases were much more prevalent in others than in themselves, a much-replicated finding (Pronin, 2007; Scopelliti et al., 2015). Bias turns out to be relatively easy to recognize in the thinking of others, but often difficult to detect in our own judgments.

In two studies, my research group (see West et al., 2012) demonstrated that there is a bias blind spot regarding most of the classic cognitive biases in the literature (anchoring bias, outcome bias, base rate-neglect, etc.)—people think that most of these biases are more characteristic of others than of themselves. We found *positive* correlations between the blind spots and cognitive sophistication—more cognitively skilled people were more prone to the bias blind spot. This makes some sense, however, because most cognitive biases in the heuristics and biases literature *are* negatively correlated with cognitive ability—more intelligent people are less biased (Stanovich, 1999, 2011; Stanovich & West, 1998, 2000; Stanovich et al., 2016). Thus, it would make sense for intelligent people to say that they are less biased than others—because they are!

However, one particular bias—myside bias—sets a trap for the cognitively sophisticated. Regarding most biases, they are used to thinking—rightly—that they are less biased. However, myside thinking about your political beliefs represents an outlier bias where this is not true (Drummond & Fischhoff, 2019; Kahan & Corbin, 2016; Kahan et al., 2012; Kahan et al., 2017; Stanovich, 2021; Stanovich & West, 2008; Van Boven et al., 2019). This may lead to a particularly intense bias blind spot among cognitive elites. Specifically, they may be prone to think that traits such as intelligence (which they have) and experiences such as education (which they will also have in abundance) provide them with very generalizable inoculations against biased political thinking. In many areas of thinking this is true, but not in the domain of myside bias about politics.

If you are a person of high intelligence, if you have lots of education, and if you are strongly committed to an ideological viewpoint, you will be especially prone to think that you thought your way to your viewpoint. You will be even less likely than the average person to be aware that you derived your beliefs from the social groups around you and because they comported with your temperament and innate psychological propensities (see Haidt, 2012; Stanovich, 2021). There is in fact a group of people who tick all of these boxes: people who are highly intelligent, highly educated, and are strongly committed to an ideological viewpoint. That group happens to be the group of social scientists who have been looking for psychological deficiencies in their political opponents!

The university professoriate is overwhelmingly left/liberal. This demographic fact has been demonstrated in numerous studies (Abrams, 2016; Lukianoff & Haidt, 2018; Peters et al., 2020; Turner, 2019). The trend is particularly strong in the social sciences (sociology, political science, etc.), and it is especially strong in psychology, the source of many of the studies looking for cognitive differences among voters (Buss & von Hippel, 2018; Ceci & Williams, 2018; Clark & Winegard, 2020; Duarte et al., 2015).

I am not suggesting here that all areas of research in psychology have this problem, or even a majority of them. However, we know that ideological beliefs lead to the unwarranted projection of prior attitudes on the evidence concerning a variety of issues, for example, topics such as: sexuality, morality, the psychological effects of poverty, family structures, crime, child care, productivity, marriage, incentives, discipline techniques, educational practices, and many more such topics where distal political attitudes are intertwined with people's beliefs on specific issues. Of course, the place where we would most expect ideology to skew experimental findings is in the study of ideology itself!

A combustible brew of facts accounts for the existence of a massive myside bias blind spot among university faculty studying the psychological characteristics of voters. The first consists of the studies showing that academics are largely of one ideological persuasion (e.g. Clark & Winegard, 2020; Duarte et al., 2015). The second is the Ditto et al. (2019) meta-analysis demonstrating that the particular ideological position they hold is equally susceptible to myside bias (see also, Guay & Johnston, 2021). The social sciences in academia are full of people who believe that they have *thought* their way to their positions, whereas their ideological opponents have not—*and* this group of social scientists are not characterized by the kind of ideological variability that would help them to ferret out myside bias in conclusions. This myside bias blind spot in the academy is a recipe for disaster when it comes to studying the psychology of political opponents.

The highly educated professoriate seems to have a hard time accepting the fact that voting is largely a matter of value conflicts and not differential rationality, intelligence,[3] or knowledge. The thinking seemed to have been that "well, as an academic, I am a specialist in rationality and knowledge, and therefore that expertise confers on me special wisdom in the domain of politics." Lupia (2016, p. 116) terms this stance the error of transforming value differences into ignorance—that is, mistaking a dispute about legitimate differences in the weighting of the values relevant to an issue for one in which your opponent "just doesn't know the facts." Cognitive elites think that if a dispute can be resolved by reasoning about facts, then they will always win because they are the experts on facts and reasoning. This leads them to overestimate the extent to which political disputes are about differential possession of factual knowledge and underestimate how much they are actually based on a clash of honestly held values.

Industrialized nations have ameliorated an enormous number of societal problems that have solely empirically based solutions (Pinker, 2011, 2018). All of the non-zero-sum problems where we can easily find a Pareto improvement (where some people can gain from a policy without anyone else in society losing) likely tend to be problems that have already been ameliorated. The contentious issues that we are left with are those that are particularly refractory to solution via the use of knowledge that we already have. If an issue is squarely and contentiously in the domain of politics, it is probably *not* "just a matter of facts." Thinking that your political opponents have knowledge deficits across the incredibly wide range of (often uncorrelated, see Joshi, 2020) issues that define modern ideological stances is itself a form of irrationality.

Notes

1 The point here being only the weak conclusion that a claim for a partisan difference in science denial would have to be based on a study with representative sampling of the domains of policy-related science. Such a study has not been conducted.

2 Baron and Jost (2019) have criticized the conclusions of Ditto et al. (2019). However, Guay and Johnston (2021) have recently conducted a more refined meta-analysis focused on the Baron and Jost criticisms and have come to the same conclusion as Ditto et al. (2019).

3 Partisan differences and voter differences in intelligence are either nonexistent or miniscule (Ganzach, 2016; Ganzach et al., 2019; Stanovich, 2021).

References

Abelson, R. P. (1996). The secret existence of expressive behavior. In J. Friedman (Ed.), *The Rational Choice Controversy* (pp. 25–36). New Haven, CT: Yale University Press.

Abrams, S. (2016, January 9). Professors moved left since 1990s, rest of country did not. *Heterodox Academy.* https://heterodoxacademy.org/professors-moved-left-but-country-did-not/.

Adorno, T. W., Frenkel-Brunswik, E., Levinson, D. J., & Sanford, R. N. (1950). *The Authoritarian Personality.* New York: Harper.

Akerlof, G., & Kranton, R. (2010). *Identity Economics*. Princeton, NJ: Princeton University Press.

al-Gharbi, M. (2018). Race and the race for the White House: On social research in the age of Trump. *The American Sociologist, 49*, 496–519.

Altemeyer, B. (1981). *Right-Wing Authoritarianism*. Winnipeg: University of Manitoba Press.

Anderson, E. (1993). *Value in Ethics and Economics*. Cambridge, MA: Harvard University Press.

Baron, J., & Jost, J. T. (2019). False equivalence: Are liberals and conservatives in the United States equally biased? *Perspectives on Psychological Science, 14*, 292–303.

Baron-Cohen, S. (2003). *The Essential Difference: The Truth about the Male and Female Brain*. New York: Basic Books.

Berezow, A., & Campbell, H. (2012). *Science Left Behind: Feel-Good Fallacies and the Rise of the Anti-scientific Left*. New York: Public Access.

Bertrand, M., Goldin, C., & Katz, L. (2010). Dynamics of the gender gap for young professionals in the financial and corporate sectors. *American Economic Journal: Applied Economics, 2*, 228–55.

Black, D., Haviland, A., Sanders, S., & Taylor, L. (2008). Gender wage disparities among the highly educated. *Journal of Human Resources, 43*, 630–59.

Brandt, M. J., & Crawford, J. T. (2019). Studying a heterogeneous array of target groups can help us understand prejudice. *Current Directions in Psychological Science, 28*, 292–98.

Brennan, J. (2016, November 10). Trump won because voters are ignorant, literally. *Foreign Policy*. https://foreignpolicy.com/2016/11/10/the-dance-of-the-dunces-trump-clinton-election-republican-democrat/.

Brennan, G., & Lomasky, L. (1993). *Democracy and Decision: The Pure Theory of Electoral Preference*. Cambridge: Cambridge University Press.

Buss, D. M., & Schmitt, D. P. (2011). Evolutionary psychology and feminism. *Sex Roles, 64*, 768–87.

Buss, D. M., & von Hippel, W. (2018). Psychological barriers to evolutionary psychology: Ideological bias and coalitional adaptations. *Archives of Scientific Psychology, 6*, 148–58.

Caplan, B. (2007). *The Myth of the Rational Voter: Why Democracies Choose Bad Policies*. Princeton, NJ: Princeton University Press.

Ceci, S. J., & Williams, W. M. (2018). Who decides what is acceptable speech on campus? Why restricting free speech is not the answer. *Perspectives on Psychological Science, 13*, 299–323.

Chambers, J. R., Schlenker, B. R., & Collisson, B. (2013). Ideology and prejudice: The role of value conflicts. *Psychological Science, 24*, 140–49.

Chetty, R., Hendren, N., Kline, P., Saez, E., & Turner, N. (2014). Is the United States still a land of opportunity? Recent trends in intergenerational mobility. *American Economic Review, 104*, 141–47.

Clark, C. J., & Winegard, B. M. (2020). Tribalism in war and peace: The nature and evolution of ideological epistemology and its significance for modern social science. *Psychological Inquiry, 31*, 1–22.

CONSAD Research Corporation. (2009, January 12). An analysis of the reasons for the disparity in wages between men and women. *U.S. Department of Labor*, Contract Number GS-23F-02598.

Crawford, J. T., & Jussim, L. (Eds.). (2018). *The Politics of Social Psychology*. New York: Routledge.

Deary, I. J. (2013). Intelligence. *Current Biology, 23*, R673–76.

Ditto, P., Liu, B., Clark, C., Wojcik, S., Chen, E., Grady, R., Celniker, J., & Zinger, J. (2019). At least bias is bipartisan: A meta-analytic comparison of partisan bias in liberals and conservatives. *Perspectives on Psychological Science, 14*, 273–91.

Drummond, C., & Fischhoff, B. (2019). Does "putting on your thinking cap" reduce myside bias in evaluation of scientific evidence? *Thinking & Reasoning, 25*, 477–505.

Duarte, J. L., Crawford, J. T., Stern, C., Haidt, J., Jussim, L., & Tetlock, P. E. (2015). Political diversity will improve social psychological science. *Behavioral and Brain Sciences, 38*, e130. doi:10.1017/S0140525X14000430.

Enders, A. M. (2019). Conspiratorial thinking and political constraint. *Public Opinion Quarterly, 83*, 510–33.

Frank, T. (2004). *What's the Matter with Kansas?* New York: Metropolitan Books.

Fuller, R. (2019). *In Defence of Democracy*. Cambridge: Polity.

Ganzach, Y. (2016). Cognitive ability and party identity: No important differences between Democrats and Republicans. *Intelligence, 58*, 18–21.

Ganzach, Y., Hanoch, Y., & Choma, B. L. (2019). Attitudes toward presidential candidates in the 2012 and 2016 American elections: Cognitive ability and support for Trump. *Social Psychological and Personality Science, 10*, 924–34.

Guay, B., & Johnston, C. (2021). Ideological asymmetries and the determinants of politically motivated reasoning. *American Journal of Political Science, 65*, 1–21.

Haidt, J. (2012). *The Righteous Mind*. New York: Pantheon Books.

Haier, R. J. (2016). *The Neuroscience of Intelligence*. Cambridge: Cambridge University Press.

Heer, J. (2016). Are Donald Trump's supporters idiots? *New Republic*. https://newrepublic.com/minutes/133447/donald-trumps-supporters-idiots.

Johnston, C. D., Lavine, H. G., & Federico, C. M. (2017). *Open versus Closed: Personality, Identity, and the Politics of Redistribution*. Cambridge: Cambridge University Press.

Joshi, H. (2020). What are the chances you're right about everything? An epistemic challenge for modern partisanship. *Politics, Philosophy & Economics, 19*, 36–61.

Jost, J. T., Glaser, J., Kruglanski, A. W., & Sulloway, F. J. (2003). Political conservatism as motivated social cognition. *Psychological Bulletin, 129*, 339–75.

Jussim, L. (2017, July 14). Gender bias in science? Double standards and cherry-picking in claims about gender bias. *Psychology Today*. https://www.psychologytoday.com/us/blog/rabble-rouser/201707/gender-bias-in-science.

Kahan, D. M. (2013). Ideology, motivated reasoning, and cognitive reflection. *Judgment and Decision Making, 8*, 407–24.

Kahan, D. M. (2015). Climate-science communication and the measurement problem. *Political Psychology, 36*, 1–43.

Kahan, D. M., & Corbin, J. C. (2016). A note on the perverse effects of actively open-minded thinking on climate-change polarization. *Research & Politics, 3*(4), 1–5. doi:10.1177/2053168016676705.

Kahan, D. M., Peters, E., Dawson, E., & Slovic, P. (2017). Motivated numeracy and enlightened self-government. *Behavioural Public Policy, 1*, 54–86.

Kahan, D. M., Peters, E., Wittlin, M., Slovic, P., Ouellette, L., Braman, D., & Mandel, G. (2012). The polarizing impact of science literacy and numeracy on perceived climate change risks. *Nature Climate Change, 2*, 732–35.

Klein, D. B., & Buturovic, Z. (2011). Economic enlightenment revisited: New results again find little relationship between education and economic enlightenment but vitiate prior evidence of the left being worse. *Econ Journal Watch, 8*(2), 157–73.

Kolesnikova, N., & Liu, Y. (2011, October). Gender wage gap may be much smaller than most think. *The Regional Economist*. Federal Reserve Bank of St. Louis. https://www.stlouisfed.org/Publications/Regional-Economist/October-2011/Gender-Wage-Gap-May-Be-Much-Smaller-Than-Most-Think?hc_location=ufi#endnotes.

Lomasky, L. (2008). Swing and a myth: A review of Caplan's "The Myth of the Rational Voter". *Public Choice, 135*(3/4), 469–84.

Lukianoff, G., & Haidt, J. (2018). *The Coddling of the American Mind*. New York: Penguin.

Lupia, A. (2016). *Uninformed: Why People Know So Little about Politics and What We Can Do about It*. New York: Oxford University Press.

Madison, G., & Fahlman, P. (2020). Sex differences in the number of scientific publications and citations when attaining the rank of professor in Sweden. *Studies in Higher Education*, 1–22. doi:10.1080/03075079.2020.1723533.

McLanahan, S., Tach, L., & Schneider, D. (2013). The causal effects of father absence. *Annual Review of Sociology, 39*, 399–427.

Mooney, C. (2005). *The Republican War on Science*. New York: Basic Books.

Murray, C. (2012). *Coming Apart*. New York: Crown Forum.

Nozick, R. (1993). *The Nature of Rationality*. Princeton, NJ: Princeton University Press.

Oliver, J. E., & Wood, T. (2014). Conspiracy theories and the paranoid style(s) of mass opinion. *American Journal of Political Science, 58*, 952–66.

O'Neill, J., & O'Neill, D. (2012). *The Declining Importance of Race and Gender in the Labor Market*. Washington, DC: AEIPress.

Peters, U., Honeycutt, N., De Block, A., & Jussim, L. (2020). Ideological diversity, hostility, and discrimination in philosophy. *Philosophical Psychology, 33*(4), 511–48.

Pew Research Center. (2013, September 10). What the public knows – In words, pictures, maps and graphs. https://www.people-press.org/2013/09/05/what-the-public-knows-in-words-pictures-maps-and-graphs/.

Pew Research Center. (2015, April 28). What the public knows – In words, pictures, maps and graphs. https://www.people-press.org/2015/04/28/what-the-public-knows-in-pictures-words-maps-and-graphs/.

Pinker, S. (2002). *The Blank Slate: The Modern Denial of Human Nature*. New York: Viking.

Pinker, S. (2008). *The Sexual Paradox: Men, Women, and the Real Gender Gap*. New York: Scribner.

Pinker, S. (2011). *The Better Angels of Our Nature.* New York: Viking.

Pinker, S. (2018). *Enlightenment Now: The Case for Reason, Science, Humanism and Progress.* New York: Viking.

Plomin, R., DeFries, J. C., Knopik, V. S., & Neiderhiser, J. M. (2016). Top 10 replicated findings from behavioral genetics. *Perspectives on Psychological Science, 11,* 3–23.

Pronin, E. (2007). Perception and misperception of bias in human judgment. *Trends in Cognitive Sciences, 11,* 37–43.

Pronin, E., Lin, D. Y., & Ross, L. (2002). The bias blind spot: Perceptions of bias in self versus others. *Journal of Personality and Social Psychology Bulletin, 28,* 369–81.

Reyna, C. (2018). Scale creation, use, and misuse: How politics undermines measurement. In J. T. Crawford & L. Jussim (Eds.), *The Politics of Social Psychology* (pp. 81–98). New York: Routledge.

Rindermann, H., Becker, D., & Coyle, T. R. (2020). Survey of expert opinion on intelligence: Intelligence research, experts' background, controversial issues, and the media. *Intelligence, 78,* 101406. doi:10.1016/j.intell.2019.101406.

Scopelliti, I., Morewedge, C. K., McCormick, E., Min, H. L., Lebrecht, S., & Kassam, K. S. (2015). Bias blind spot: Structure, measurement, and consequences. *Management Science, 61,* 2468–86.

Seidenberg, M. (2017). *Language at the Speed of Sight.* New York: Basic Books.

Serwer, A. (2017, November 20). The nationalist's delusion. *The Atlantic.* https://www.theatlantic.com/politics/archive/2017/11/the-nationalists-delusion/546356/.

Shermer, M. (2011). *The Believing Brain.* New York: Times Books.

Solberg, E. & Laughlin, T. (1995). The gender pay gap, fringe benefits, and occupational crowding. *ILR Review* 48(4): 692–708.

Stanovich, K. E. (1999). *Who is Rational? Studies of Individual Differences in Reasoning.* Mahwah, NJ: Erlbaum.

Stanovich, K. E. (2004). *The Robot's Rebellion: Finding Meaning in the Age of Darwin.* Chicago, IL: University of Chicago Press.

Stanovich, K. E. (2011). *Rationality and the Reflective Mind.* New York: Oxford University Press.

Stanovich, K. E. (2013). Why humans are (sometimes) less rational than other animals: Cognitive complexity and the axioms of rational choice. *Thinking & Reasoning, 19,* 1–26.

Stanovich, K. E. (2021). *The Bias that Divides Us: The Science and Politics of Myside Thinking.* Cambridge: MIT Press.

Stanovich, K. E., & West, R. F. (1998). Individual differences in rational thought. *Journal of Experimental Psychology: General, 127,* 161–88.

Stanovich, K. E., & West, R. F. (2000). Individual differences in reasoning: Implications for the rationality debate? *Behavioral and Brain Sciences, 23,* 645–726.

Stanovich, K. E., & West, R. F. (2008). On the relative independence of thinking biases and cognitive ability. *Journal of Personality and Social Psychology, 94,* 672–95.

Stanovich, K. E., West, R. F., & Toplak, M. E. (2016). *The Rationality Quotient: Toward a Test of Rational Thinking.* Cambridge: MIT Press.

Stephens, B. (2016, February 29). Staring at the conservative gutter. *The Wall Street Journal.* https://www.wsj.com/articles/staring-at-the-conservative-gutter-1456791777.

Tetlock, P. E. (2002). Social functionalist frameworks for judgment and choice: Intuitive politicians, theologians, and prosecutors. *Psychological Review, 109,* 451–71.

Traub, J. (2016, June 28). It's time for the elites to rise up against the ignorant masses. *Foreign Policy.* https://foreignpolicy.com/2016/06/28/its-time-for-the-elites-to-rise-up-against-ignorant-masses-trump-2016-brexit/.

Turner, J. H. (2019). The more American sociology seeks to become a politically-relevant discipline, the more irrelevant it becomes to solving societal problems. *The American Sociologist, 50,* 456–87.

Van Boven, L., Ramos, J., Montal-Rosenberg, R., Kogut, T., Sherman, D. K., & Slovic, P. (2019). It depends: Partisan evaluation of conditional probability importance. *Cognition, 188,* 51–63.

West, R. F., Meserve, R. J., & Stanovich, K. E. (2012). Cognitive sophistication does not attenuate the bias blind spot. *Journal of Personality and Social Psychology, 103,* 506–19.

Williams, W. M., & Ceci, S. J. (2015). National hiring experiments reveal 2:1 faculty preference for women on STEM tenure track. *Proceedings of the National Academy of Sciences, 112,* 5360–65.

25

ASYMMETRICAL IRRATIONALITY

Are only other people stupid?

Robin McKenna

1 Introductory remarks

My topic is public irrationality about political issues and certain scientific issues that have become politically contentious, like climate change (I call these "hot" scientific issues). More specifically, my question is: are there partisan asymmetries in the rationality (or lack thereof) of views about these sorts of issues? In the literature on this question it is common to frame things in terms of the "political divide" between liberals and conservatives. So the question becomes: are conservatives *more* irrational than liberals, or vice versa?[1] If there are such asymmetries, then the *epistemic asymmetry thesis* is true:

> The epistemic asymmetry thesis: One side of the "political divide" generally has rational views about political and "hot" scientific issues, whereas the other side generally has irrational views about such issues.

In the empirical literature some claim that the epistemic asymmetry thesis—or something like it—is true (Baron and Jost, 2019; Hodson and Busseri, 2012; Iyengar et al., 2008; Jost et al., 2003; Kanazawa, 2010; Nisbet et al., 2013). But others reject it (Ditto et al., 2019; Kahan et al., 2011a; Lewandowsky and Oberauer, 2016; Stanovich, this volume). In this chapter I give an overview of the empirical and philosophical literature pertaining to the epistemic asymmetry thesis. I focus on arguments *against* the epistemic asymmetry thesis because my impression is that the "standard" view in the empirical literature is that the epistemic asymmetry thesis is false (see Ditto et al., 2019). It therefore makes sense to consider whether the case against it stands up. I don't take a stance on whether the epistemic asymmetry thesis is true but I point to some places where philosophy—and in particular epistemology—can offer resources for defending the epistemic asymmetry thesis. Thus, this chapter should have something to offer both to those who reject the epistemic asymmetry thesis and to those who accept it.

Here is the plan. First, I clarify the epistemic asymmetry thesis (Section 2). Second, I run through two arguments against it and identify lacunae in both arguments (Sections 3 and 4). I finish by considering some recent work by Dan Kahan which suggests that, while there may not be partisan asymmetries in rationality, there are some interesting asymmetries in rationality between those who possess and those who lack certain character traits (Section 5).

2 Epistemic and cognitive asymmetries

You might think the epistemic asymmetry thesis is clearly true because conservatives are more "anti-science" than liberals. Just consider climate change denial, which is largely the preserve of conservatives (Hardisty et al., 2010; Kahan et al., 2011a; Tranter and Booth, 2015). Now, one way of responding to this would be by simply denying that conservatives are more anti-science than liberals (this is the route taken by Keith Stanovich in his chapter in this handbook). While this possibility cannot be dismissed, I want to set it to one side. This is because some critics of the epistemic asymmetry thesis think the thesis is false even if conservatives are more anti-science than liberals. As two critics put it:

> [T]he rejection of specific scientific evidence across a range of issues, as well as general-ized distrust in science, appears to be concentrated primarily among the political right. It does not follow, however, that there are any fundamental differences in the cognition between people of differing political attitudes and values. Quite to the contrary, the cognitive shortcuts that drive the rejection of scientific evidence appear to be politically symmetrical. (Lewandowsky and Oberauer, 2016, p. 218)

While "science denialism" may be more prevalent among conservatives than liberals, this is not due to "fundamental differences in cognition". Both conservatives and liberals utilise the same heuristics in their thinking and are subject to the same sorts of biases. But these heuris-tics and biases lead them in different directions. It leads conservatives to (often) reject science, whereas it leads liberals to (generally) accept science. As Lewandowsky and Oberauer put it:

> [T]he basic cognitive processes implicated in the rejection of science—namely, cog-nitive shortcuts, differential risk perception, and conspiracist cognition—appear to be universal and engaged on both sides of the political aisle. (2016, p. 220)

Thus, while there may be a kind of epistemic asymmetry between liberals and conservatives when it comes to their views about issues like climate change—one side has largely true beliefs, whereas the other has largely false beliefs—this is not an asymmetry in rationality. So the epistemic asymmetry thesis is false. Further, it is false because there is a sort of *cognitive symmetry* between liberals and conservatives. Members of both groups form their views about these issues in the same sorts of ways.

What do I mean when I say there is a cognitive symmetry? Here are two—simplistic but suggestive—ways of understanding it. First, as inquirers, we need to make decisions about how to gather the information and evidence we need to make judgements and form beliefs. This includes decisions about who to ask for information, and who to trust. These are de-cisions about how to structure our inquiries. We can say that there is a cognitive symmetry between two inquirers (or groups of inquirers) with respect to some issue when their inqui-ries into that issue are structured in the same sort of way.

Second, we are all biased in various ways, if not to the same extent (e.g. some of us are more likely to "pause" and engage in reflective System 2 reasoning than others). We can say that there is a cognitive symmetry between two inquiries with respect to some issue when they exhibit the same sort of biases in their thinking about that issue.

Putting this together, one reason why the epistemic asymmetry thesis might not be true, even though one side of the partisan divide seems to have more false beliefs about sci-ence than the other, is that there are underlying cognitive symmetries between liberals and conservatives. While one side happens to get things right more often than the other, both sides form beliefs about these issues in the same sort of way. In the next two sections I will look at attempts to cash this line of thought out.

3 Kahan on ideologically motivated reasoning

Empirical work on motivated reasoning suggests our judgements are influenced by our wants, desires and preferences (Kahan, 2016; Lord et al., 1979; Molden and Higgins, 2012; Taber and Lodge, 2006). I am interested in the impact of our political ideologies on our assessment of arguments pertaining to political and "hot" scientific issues. Call this *ideologically* motivated reasoning (IMR for short). In particular, I focus on Dan Kahan's work on IMR, because he is a vocal critic of the epistemic asymmetry thesis (Kahan, 2014, 2016; Kahan et al., 2011a, 2011b).[2]

Here is Kahan explaining the basic idea:

> Even among modestly partisan individuals, shared ideological or cultural commitments are likely to be intertwined with membership in communities of one sort or another that furnish those individuals with important forms of support … If a proposition about some policy-relevant fact comes to be commonly associated with membership in such a group, the prospect that one might form a contrary position can threaten one's standing within it. Thus, as a form of "identity self-defense," individuals are unconsciously motivated to resist empirical assertions … if those assertions run contrary to the dominant belief within their groups. (Kahan, 2013, p. 408)

Kahan has found that ideologies influence our information-processing when it comes to several political and scientific issues, including climate change, nuclear power, concealed carry laws, nanotechnology and perceptions of protestors (Kahan et al., 2009, 2011a, 2012). When it comes to these sorts of issues, we all tend to make judgements and form beliefs that cohere with our ideologies. The way in which we process information pertaining to political and "hot" scientific issues exhibits a "directional bias": we happily take on board information that coheres with our existing beliefs and values, but look for ways to reject information that conflicts with them.

There are two crucial points to note about Kahan's work on IMR. The first is that he thinks *both* liberals and conservatives engage in it. So, for instance, conservatives tend to under-estimate the risks posed by global warming, whereas liberals tend to over-estimate the risks posed by nuclear power (Kahan et al., 2011a). Thus, both liberals and conservatives exhibit directional biases in their information-processing.

Second, one might expect the influence of IMR to decrease as scientific comprehension, scientific literacy and numeracy increase. Kahan finds that, in fact, it is more like the reverse: the influence of IMR increases as scientific comprehension, scientific literacy and numeracy increase. Importantly, this goes for both liberals and conservatives (Kahan, 2013; Kahan et al., 2011a, 2017b).[3] Thus, conservatives who score highly on scientific comprehension, scientific literacy and numeracy are *more* sceptical about global warming than conservatives who score lower on these things.

Putting this together, Kahan doesn't deny there are important differences between liberal and conservative attitudes towards science. He may even agree that conservatives generally have more false beliefs about "hot" scientific issues than liberals and so there is a kind of partisan epistemic asymmetry. But the crucial point is that this is not an asymmetry in rationality because it is not due to cognitive asymmetries between liberals and conservatives. Rather, there is an underlying symmetry between the ways in which liberals and conservatives make judgements and form beliefs about "hot" scientific issues: both engage extensively in IMR. So the epistemic asymmetry thesis is false.

I want to finish this section by highlighting a lacuna in Kahan's argument against the epistemic asymmetry thesis. One might argue that, while both liberals and conservatives engage in IMR, conservatives engage in it *more* than liberals, or that it has more of an impact on the thinking of conservatives than of liberals. This may be borne out in the fact that Kahan's studies generally find that conservative scepticism about issues like climate change is more pronounced than liberal scepticism about issues like the safety of nuclear power (Kahan et al., 2011a). So while there may be no *cognitive asymmetry in kind* between liberals and conservatives, there is an *asymmetry in degree*.

Crucially, this cognitive asymmetry in degree may support a range of epistemic asymmetries between the attitudes of liberals and conservatives about "hot" scientific issues. For instance, it may be that liberal acceptance of the scientific consensus on climate change is *more* rational than conservative rejection of it, because liberal acceptance is less influenced by IMR than conservative rejection. Now, to say that some belief A is more rational than some belief B is not to say that A is rational, whereas B is irrational. Rationality comes in degrees, and A can be more rational than B while still being irrational. But one could supplement what I have said here with an argument that the influence of IMR on liberal political cognition does not impugn the rationality of beliefs liberals form about issues like climate change, whereas conservative political cognition is influenced by IMR to such a degree that conservative views about issues like climate change are irrational.[4]

4 Levy and Rini on partisan epistemology

In this section I look at two recent papers in political epistemology, Neil Levy's "Due Deference to Denialism" (Levy, 2019) and Regina Rini's "Fake News and Partisan Epistemology" (Rini, 2017). I focus on these papers because they are prime examples of empirically informed political epistemology and because I think they usefully complement each other. We can start with Levy, who tells us:

> While we are apt to accept testimony—to defer to others—we reject testimony from sources that signal unreliability by evincing cues of incompetence or lack of benevolence. When science becomes politicized, expression of the scientific consensus may itself come to serve as a signal of lack of benevolence to those on one side of the issue, leading to rejection of the testimony. On all sides, filtering mechanisms may be working as designed, but for reasons beyond the purview of the individuals involved, warrant may accrue to one side alone. (2019, p. 314)

We use two criteria to assess the reliability of testimony: the competence of the testifier, and the extent to which they are benevolent towards us. Levy thinks we often use political affiliation as a proxy for benevolence. If someone agrees with us on fundamental political issues, we will (all else being equal) regard them as benevolent; if they disagree with us on these issues, we (all else being equal) won't. Applying these criteria leads individuals with divergent political positions to form divergent views on "hot" scientific issues. Given the divergent attitudes of liberals and conservatives towards scientific expertise, we find that:

Liberals are epistemically luckier: they are disposed to defer to the most competent individuals and institutions, because these individuals and institutions pass tests for benevolence as well as for competence. Liberals defer to sufficiently large groups of sufficiently expert deliberators to ensure that their beliefs have a high degree of warrant; conservatives defer to a much smaller group of genuine experts and their chains of deference trace back as much or more to non-experts. These facts (which are outside the purview of the individuals at the end of each chain) entail that one set of beliefs is very much better warranted than the other. Biased assimilation may thus be individually rational, whether it leads toward better or worse warranted beliefs. (pp. 322–23)

Levy says that both liberals and conservatives are "individually rational". But his argument is based on the descriptive claim that we *have* a general tendency to trust people we share a political outlook with (cf. Marks et al., 2019). The fact that we have a tendency does not show that it is *rational*. So why think that the tendency Levy highlights is rational?

This is where Rini comes in. In her paper she defends this claim:

It is sometimes reasonable to assign more credibility to testifier A than testifier B just because you agree with A (but do not agree with B) on a range of central political issues. (Rini, 2017, p. 50)

If this claim is true, then the partisan patterns of deference highlighted by Levy are rational. Of course, it is clearly not reasonable for a liberal to listen to a liberal journalist and ignore a conservative physicist when it comes to testimony about physics. Rini's view is rather that it is reasonable when the testimony either concerns a straightforwardly normative issue (such as the morality of abortion), or an issue with a normative dimension. It is plausible that many "hot" scientific issues have a normative dimension, though what that dimension is will depend on the issue at hand. Rini's example is crime rates. Is crime rising or falling? To answer this question, we need to first define "crime", and then figure out how to measure how much of it there is. It is hard to see how this could be done without taking any stance on some normative issues. Rini's thought is that it may be reasonable for me to regard A's testimony about crime rates as more credible than B's testimony because I agree with A on these normative issues.

Rini doesn't discuss issues like climate change. But one can argue that, while the question whether human activity is causing the Earth's climate to change is a scientific question, the more general issue has a clear normative dimension. We need to decide *inter alia* the extent to which we are *morally* responsible for protecting the Earth's climate, whether the evidence we have is sufficient to warrant action (and, if it is, which courses of action are appropriate), on whom the greatest burdens should be placed (all countries? all developed countries?), and whether the potential benefits outweigh the risks of economic catastrophe. However clear you may think the answers are to these questions, they are clearly normative, not purely scientific.[5]

If we combine Rini's claim with Levy's, we get this argument:

1   We—both liberals and conservatives—tend to defer to our fellow partisans about political and "hot" scientific issues [from Levy].
2   It is (often) rational to defer to fellow partisans about such issues [from Rini].
3   Therefore, while we generally end up with divergent views about such issues, these divergent views are (often) rational.

Take Catriona, who thinks crime rates are rising, and Laurie, who thinks they are falling. They have formed these beliefs because they have listened to what like-minded partisans say about the issue. But Catriona leans conservative, whereas Laurie leans liberal. Catriona agrees with the conservative narrative on law and order; Laurie agrees with the liberal narrative. If the above argument is correct, it may well be that they are both reasonable in doing so. Now, it must be the case that one of them is wrong: crime can't be both rising and falling. But it is less clear there is any asymmetry in rationality here. Both Laurie and Catriona have formed their beliefs in much the same way (by listening to like-minded partisans). This point will generalise beyond Catriona and Laurie. Many disagreements about political issues, or scientific issues with a political resonance, will have the form of Catriona and Laurie's.

How does this fare as an argument against the epistemic asymmetry thesis? Even if we grant that there is a sense of "rational" in which liberals and conservatives are equally rational (for critical discussion, see Worsnip, 2018), there is a potential lacuna here, which Levy notes. He allows that there may be a sort of epistemic asymmetry between liberals and conservatives—an asymmetry in what he calls "warrant". We can explore this point further by considering the literature on epistemic rationality. I am going to suggest that whether the argument goes through might depend on what we mean by "rational".

It is standard to distinguish between *internalist* and *externalist* approaches to epistemic rationality (Pappas, 2017). Put roughly, on an internalist approach, whether one's beliefs are rational depends only on facts that are cognitively accessible to one whereas, on an externalist approach, whether they are rational depends on a combination of cognitively accessible and cognitively inaccessible facts. Put crudely, for the internalist, it matters whether you are in a position to recognise when you have got it wrong, whereas, for the externalist, what matters is whether you generally get things right or wrong.

My suggestion is that the tendencies adverted to by Rini and Levy are rational in the internalist sense of epistemic rationality. As Levy puts it, facts "outwith the purview of the individual" mean that, while liberal views about "hot" scientific issues are (largely) correct, conservative views about such issues are often incorrect. Both liberals and conservatives look for indications of competence and benevolence, and judge of these things as best they can. But one side often gets it wrong, whereas the other often gets it right. Thus, while both liberals and conservatives defer to individuals they take to exhibit signs of competence and benevolence, liberals tend to form correct beliefs about "hot" scientific issues, whereas conservatives tend to form incorrect views about such issues.

You might ask: why care if liberal and conservative views about political and "hot" scientific issues are rational by the lights of internalist conceptions of rationality? The short answer is: because such conceptions capture the idea that rationality is connected with the notion of *blame* (Steup, 1999). On an internalist conception of rationality, you must, at least in principle, be able to recognise what it is about the way in which you formed the belief that makes it irrational. This seems to permit blaming you when you form irrational beliefs. After all, you were in a position to recognise that your beliefs are irrational. If it turns out that many climate sceptics—and sceptics about science in general—are rational in the internalist sense, then it makes no sense to blame them for having these attitudes.

You might also ask: what about the externalist sense of rationality? Can we argue that there are important partisan asymmetries in this sense? I lack the space to fully answer this question here, but I want to make a few preliminary points.

First, on an externalist conception of rationality, anyone who generally forms false beliefs in some domain is not going to have rational beliefs about that domain. This is because, for the externalist, what matters is whether one (generally) gets things right. So, in virtue of the fact (which we are assuming) that many conservatives have a lot of false beliefs about "hot" scientific issues, those beliefs are going to be irrational. The crucial question is whether liberals (who we are assuming generally have true beliefs) satisfy externalist conditions on rationality.

Second, "externalism" isn't a single view, but a family of views. Whether liberals (generally) have rational beliefs is going to depend on the specific conditions we put on rationality. It is important to note that, for the externalist, it isn't enough that one generally form true beliefs about some domain. After all, one can form true beliefs through pure luck. Different externalists try to capture this point in different ways. Here are two ways:

1   S's true belief B is rational just in case, were it false, S wouldn't have B.[6]
2   S's true belief B is rational just in case, if things had been (a bit, but not too) different, S would still have had B.[7]

The idea behind the first proposal is that, if you would have had the belief if it were false, then your belief isn't sufficiently sensitive to what is actually the case. As for the second proposal, there are many other ways the world could be that are consistent with your belief being true. The idea behind this proposal is that, if you wouldn't have had the belief if things had been one of these ways, then it is a happy accident that you nonetheless managed to form a true belief about the world. Of course, the crucial question is: how different? In the present case, it might look like things would have to be very different for liberals to have different beliefs about, say, climate change. The point of the empirical work discussed above that it is in an important sense *no accident* that liberals accept the science on climate change: it fits with their political predispositions.

Can we argue that there are partisan asymmetries in rationality using either of these externalist accounts? On the one hand, I doubt we have any empirical evidence that could directly decide the issue. On the other, we can perhaps extrapolate from the existing work and argue that it is (at best) unclear whether liberal beliefs about science satisfy the first externalist condition. If you take someone with liberal political dispositions and ask what they would believe if climate change were in fact a myth, then it is plausible to say that they would still believe as they do.

When it comes to the second externalist condition, things are less clear. We can also extrapolate from the existing work and argue that, if you took someone with liberal dispositions and somehow managed to fundamentally shift their dispositions, then their beliefs about climate change would shift accordingly. But does this mean they fail to satisfy the second condition, given that we are now imagining that the individual in question is very different to how they in fact are?[8]

5 Asymmetries in intellectual virtue?

I finish by looking at some recent empirical work by Dan Kahan which suggests that there is an intellectual virtue that minimises the impact of IMR. Thus, individuals who exhibit this virtue may be at an epistemic advantage when it comes to political and "hot" scientific issues. But, as we will also see, it is not clear that this virtue has a partisan dimension. If this is right, then there is an important class of epistemic asymmetries that do not neatly line up with a partisan political divide.

In a recent paper Kahan and collaborators present evidence that individuals who score highly in *science curiosity* are less prone to IMR. They define science curiosity as "a general disposition, variable in intensity across persons, that reflects the motivation to seek out and consume scientific information for personal pleasure" (Kahan et al., 2017a, p. 180). They found that subjects who scored highly on science curiosity had more accurate risk perceptions (e.g. about global warming), regardless of their political ideology. They also found evidence that this is because subjects who scored highly on science curiosity were more willing to expose themselves to information running contrary to their political views and values. Thus, science curiosity appears to be a trait that de-activates one of the central biases that drives IMR: a preference for attitude-congruent over attitude-incongruent information (Taber and Lodge, 2006). They therefore hypothesise that the scientifically curious: "have a reason to engage information for truth seeking that those who are low in science curiosity don't have: to experience the pleasure of contemplating surprising insights into how the world works" (2017a, p. 195).

While this is just one study, it is worth reflecting on its ramifications. First, it suggests there may be asymmetries in tendencies to rely on IMR between groups that can't be characterised in simple political terms. There may be an important class of epistemic asymmetries that don't have a clear political dimension. While this isn't the epistemic asymmetry thesis, it is clearly in the same ballpark.

The second reason is that it allows us to draw some connections between the empirical literature on political cognition and the burgeoning field of *virtue epistemology*.[9] This field can be split into two camps. The first camp focuses on what are called "faculty virtues", such as perception, intuition and memory (Sosa, 2007). The second camp focuses on character traits such as open-mindedness and curiosity (Baehr, 2011; Zagzebski, 1996). The connection that will concern me here is between the literature on political cognition and the second camp, which is called "responsibilist virtue epistemology" (RVE).

What connections can we draw between Kahan's work on science curiosity and RVE? First, in the RVE literature curiosity is construed as a character trait that involves a disposition to seek out new and worthwhile information (Watson, 2019). We can view science curiosity as a species of curiosity so understood. The scientifically curious person is characteristically motivated to acquire new and worthwhile scientific information.

Second, within RVE there is a debate about whether the intellectual virtues need to be *truth-conducive*: if you are intellectually virtuous, must you thereby be more likely to get things right (Carter and Gordon, 2014; Kwong, 2017)? This issue is surely amenable to empirical investigation: is the intellectually virtuous individual more likely to get things right? We can see Kahan et al.'s study as a small part of that investigation: they present evidence that (scientifically) curious, open-minded individuals are more likely to form accurate views about issues like climate change.

Third, a central question in the RVE literature is why be intellectually virtuous. One striking feature of this literature is that it focuses on the benefits that might accrue to the virtuous individual (Baehr, 2011). Kahan et al.'s work might be used as a corrective to this individualistic focus. One might think that virtues which mitigate against a tendency to engage in IMR and other forms of bias are particularly important for the well-being of society at large, given that they lead to a reduction in polarisation about political "hot" scientific issues, thereby increasing the potential of reaching consensus on public policy decisions. We can thus view science curiosity (and perhaps curiosity in general) as a *civic-intellectual virtue*: it has a civic aspect insofar as its cultivation is important for the well-being of society at large. Thus, there is an answer to the question of why be intellectually virtuous at the societal level.

6 Conclusion

In this chapter I have looked at some arguments against the thesis that there are asymmetries in rationality between liberals and conservatives. I have also looked at some recent work by Dan Kahan and collaborators, which suggests there may be some asymmetries in rationality that lack a clear political dimension. My aim has been to show that philosophical reflection can reveal potential lacunae in arguments against the epistemic asymmetry thesis. First, while it may be the case that we all engage in IMR, this is consistent with there being asymmetries in the extent to which we rely on IMR. This may have implications for the rationality of our beliefs. Second, while there may be a sense of "rational" in which liberal and conservative attitudes are equally rational, there are other senses of "rational" on which the status of the epistemic asymmetry thesis is a little less clear.[10]

Notes

1 Because most of the literature has a US-focus, I use these labels in their US senses, and assume a US-centric framing of political debate.
2 Classic papers on motivated reasoning include (Kunda, 1990) and (Lord et al., 1979). For overviews see Jost et al. (2013) and Molden and Higgins (2012).
3 This result fits with the general result that more knowledgeable individuals are more rather than less prone to engage in motivated reasoning (Taber and Lodge, 2006).
4 For an attempt to resist this move, see McKenna (2019).
5 For an accessible discussion of different varieties of climate scepticism see Walker and Leviston (2019). For a more academic discussion, see Hobson and Niemeyer (2013).
6 This is modelled on "sensitivity" accounts of knowledge (Nozick, 1981).
7 This is modelled on "safety" accounts of knowledge (Sosa, 2007), though I've expressed the basic idea in a rather crude way for the sake of simplicity.
8 Making progress on this question will require looking into the details of how "safety" conditions should be formulated. For relevant literature, see Hirvelä (2019), Pritchard (2012), and Williamson (2009).
9 For an overview of this field, see Turri et al. (2018).
10 Thanks to Cameron Boult, Jeroen de Ridder, Mikkel Gerken, Michael Hannon, and to audiences in Liverpool, London and Nottingham for comments on earlier versions of this paper.

Bibliography

Baehr, J., 2011. *The Inquiring Mind: On Intellectual Virtues and Virtue Epistemology.* Oxford: Oxford University Press.
Baron, J., Jost, J.T., 2019. False Equivalence: Are Liberals and Conservatives in the United States Equally Biased? *Perspectives on Psychological Science* 14, 292–303.
Carter, J.A., Gordon, E.C., 2014. Openmindedness and Truth. *Canadian Journal of Philosophy* 44, 207–24.
Ditto, P.H., Liu, B.S., Clark, C.J., Wojcik, S.P., Chen, E.E., Grady, R.H., Celniker, J.B., Zinger, J.F., 2019. At Least Bias Is Bipartisan: A Meta-analytic Comparison of Partisan Bias in Liberals and Conservatives. *Perspectives on Psychological Science* 14, 273–91.
Hardisty, D.J., Johnson, E.J., Weber, E.U., 2010. A Dirty Word or a Dirty World? Attribute Framing, Political Affiliation, and Query Theory. *Psychological Science* 21, 86–92.
Hirvelä, J., 2019. Global Safety: How to Deal with Necessary Truths. *Synthese* 196, 1167–86.
Hobson, K., Niemeyer, S., 2013. "What Sceptics Believe": The Effects of Information and Deliberation on Climate Change Scepticism. *Public Understanding of Science* 22, 396–412.
Hodson, G., Busseri, M., 2012. Bright Minds and Dark Attitudes: Lower Cognitive Ability Predicts Greater Prejudice through Right-Wing Ideology and Low Intergroup Contact. *Psychological Science* 23, 187–95.

Iyengar, S., Hahn, K.S., Krosnick, J.A., Walker, J., 2008. Selective Exposure to Campaign Communication: The Role of Anticipated Agreement and Issue Public Membershio. *Journal of Politics* 70, 186–200.

Jost, J.T., Glaser, J., Kruglanski, A.W., Sulloway, F.J., 2003. Political Conservatism as Motivated Social Cognition. *Psychological Bulletin* 129, 339–75.

Jost, J.T., Hennes, E.P., Lavine, H., 2013. "Hot" Political Cognition: Its Self-, Group-, and System-Serving Purposes, in: Carlston, D., *The Oxford Handbook of Social Cognition*. Oxford University Press, New York, pp. 851–75.

Kahan, D., 2013. Ideology, Motivated Reasoning, and Cognitive Reflection. *Judgment and Decision Making* 8, 407–24.

Kahan, D., 2014. Making Climate-Science Communication Evidence-Based--All the Way Down, in: Boykoff, M., Crow, D. (Eds.), *Culture, Politics and Climate Change*. Routledge, New York, pp. 203–20.

Kahan, D., 2016. The Politically Motivated Reasoning Paradigm, Part 1: What Politically Motivated Reasoning Is and How to Measure It, in: Scott, R. A., Kosslyn, S. M., Buchmann, M. C. (Eds.), *Emerging Trends in the Social and Behavioral Sciences*: : An Interdisciplinary, Searchable, and Linkable Resource. doi:10.1002/9781118900772.etrds0417

Kahan, D., Braman, D., Slovic, P., Gastil, J., Cohen, G.L., 2009. Cultural Cognition of the Risks and Benefits of Nanotechnology. *Nature Nanotechnology* 4, 87–91.

Kahan, D., Hoffman, D., Braman, D., Evans, D., Rachlinski, J., 2012. "They Saw a Protest": Cognitive Illiberalism and the Speech-Conduct Distinction. Cornell Law Faculty Publications Paper 400, 851–905.

Kahan, D., Jenkins-Smith, H., Braman, D., 2011a. Cultural Cognition of Scientific Consensus. *Journal of Risk Research* 14, 147–74.

Kahan, D., Landrum, A., Carpenter, K., Helft, L., Jamieson, K.H., 2017a. Science Curiosity and Political Information Processing. *Political Psychology* 38, 179–99.

Kahan, D., Peters, E., Dawson, E.C., Slovic, P., 2017b. Motivated Numeracy and Enlightened Self-Government. *Behavioural Public Policy* 1, 54–86.

Kahan, D., Wittlin, M., Peters, E., Slovic, P., Ouellete, L.L., Braman, D., Mandel, G.N., 2011b. The Tragedy of the Risk-Perception Commons: Culture Conflict, Rationality Conflict, and Climate Change. Temple University Legal Studies Research Paper No. 2011–26; Cultural Cognition Project Working Paper No. 89; Yale Law & Economics Research Paper No. 435; Yale Law School, Public Law Working Paper No. 230.

Kanazawa, S., 2010. Why Liberals and Atheists Are More Intelligent. *Social Psychology Quarterly* 73, 33–57.

Kunda, Z., 1990. The Case for Motivated Reasoning. *Psychological Bulletin* 108, 480.

Kwong, J., 2017. Is Open-Mindedness Conducive to Truth? *Synthese* 194, 1613–26.

Levy, N., 2019. Due Deference to Denialism: Explaining Ordinary People's Rejection of Established Scientific Findings. *Synthese* 196, 313–27.

Lewandowsky, S., Oberauer, K., 2016. Motivated Rejection of Science. *Current Directions in Psychological Science* 25, 217–22.

Lord, C.G., Ross, L., Lepper, M.R., 1979. Biased Assimilation and Attitude Polarization: The Effects of Prior Theories on Subsequently Considered Evidence. *Journal of Personality and Social Psychology* 37, 2098–109.

Marks, J., Copland, E., Loh, E., Sunstein, C.R., Sharot, T., 2019. Epistemic Spillovers: Learning Others' Political Views Reduces the Ability to Assess and Use Their Expertise in Nonpolitical Domains. *Cognition* 188, 74–84.

McKenna, R., 2019. Irrelevant Cultural Influences on Belief. *Journal of Applied Philosophy* 36, 755–68.

Molden, D.C., Higgins, E.T., 2012. Motivated Thinking, in: Holyoak, K. J., Morrison, R. G. (Eds.), *The Oxford Handbook of Thinking and Reasoning*, pp. 390–409. Oxford: Oxford University Press.

Nisbet, E.C., Hart, P.S., Myers, T., Ellithorpe, M., 2013. Attitude Change in Competitive Framing Environments? Open-/Closed-Mindedness, Framing Effects, and Climate Change. *Journal of Communication* 63, 766–85.

Nozick, R., 1981. *Philosophical Explanations*. Cambridge, MA: Harvard University Press.

Pappas, G., 2017. Internalist vs. Externalist Conceptions of Epistemic Justification, in: Zalta, E. N. (Ed.), *The Stanford Encyclopedia of Philosophy* (Fall 2017 Edition). https://plato.stanford.edu/archives/fall2017/entries/justep-intext/

Pritchard, D., 2012. Anti-Luck Virtue Epistemology. *Journal of Philosophy* 109, 247–79.

Rini, R., 2017. Fake News and Partisan Epistemology. *Kennedy Institute of Ethics Journal* 27, 43–64.

Sosa, E., 2007. *A Virtue Epistemology: Apt Belief and Reflective Knowledge*, Volume I. Oxford: Oxford University Press.

Stanovich, K., 2021. The Irrational Attempt to Impute Irrationality to One's Political Opponents, in: deRidder, J., Hannon, M. (Eds.), *Routledge Handbook of Political Epistemology*. Abingdon: Routledge.

Steup, M., 1999. A Defense of Internalism, in: Pojman, L. (Ed.), *The Theory of Knowledge: Classical and Contemporary Readings*. Wadsworth, Belmont, CA, pp. 310–21.

Taber, C.S., Lodge, M., 2006. Motivated Skepticism in the Evaluation of Political Beliefs. *American Journal of Political Science* 50, 755–69.

Tranter, B., Booth, K., 2015. Scepticism in a Changing Climate: A Cross-National Study. *Global Environmental Change* 33, 154–64.

Turri, J., Alfano, M., Greco, J., 2018. Virtue Epistemology, in Zalta, E. N. (Ed.), *The Stanford Encyclopedia of Philosophy* (Summer 2018 Edition). https://plato.stanford.edu/archives/fall2019/entries/epistemology-virtue/

Walker, I., Leviston, Z., 2019. There are Three Types of Climate Change Denier, and Most of Us Are at Least One. The Conversation. https://theconversation.com/there-are-three-types-of-climate-change-denier-and-most-of-us-are-at-least-one-124574

Watson, L., 2019. Curiosity and Inquisitiveness, in: Battaly, H. (Ed.), *Routledge Handbook of Virtue Epistemology*. Routledge, Abingdon, pp. 155–66.

Williamson, T., 2009. Reply to John Hawthorne and Maria Lasonen-Aarnio, in: Greenough, P., Pritchard, D. (Eds.), *Williamson on Knowledge*. Oxford University Press, Oxford, pp. 313–29.

Worsnip, A., 2018. The Obligation to Diversify One's Sources: Against Epistemic Partisanship in the Consumption of News Media, in: Fox, C., Saunders, J. (Eds.), *Media Ethics: Free Speech and the Requirements of Democracy*. Routledge, Abingdon, pp. 240–264.

Zagzebski, L., 1996. *Virtues of the Mind: An Inquiry into the Nature of Virtue and the Ethical Foundations of Knowledge*. Cambridge: Cambridge University Press.

PART 5

Epistemic virtues and vices in politics

INTRODUCTION TO PART 5

Successful government of any kind requires knowledge. Reflection on democratic government in particular has tended to emphasize the need for both evidence-based political decisions and a well-informed citizenry. Citizens need to know facts about the natural world and society, they need to have knowledge of how government works, knowledge about laws, policy plans, the performance of politicians and other elected officials, and so on. Achieving this is far from easy and there are reasons for doubting that citizens generally do a good job, as the previous section has documented.

Even so, the democratic ideal of a well-informed citizenry is one worth striving for. This is where intellectual virtues enter the picture: being well-informed requires thinking well, and thinking well is thinking virtuously. Virtue epistemology has become widely popular and influential in epistemology in recent decades. A lot of effort has gone into analyzing the concept of virtue, addressing traditional problems in epistemology with the help of virtue theory, as well as analyzing more specific virtues such as intellectual humility, open-mindedness, epistemic justice, and many more. Virtue epistemological theorizing has also recently turned its gaze to the dark side by exploring intellectual vices, or qualities that make one a poor or bad cognizer, such as prejudice, arrogance, and closed-mindedness.

The chapters in this section focus on intellectual virtues and vices in politics and government. On the one hand, they use examples from those realms to elucidate the nature of virtues and vices, and, on the other, they chart the analytical and explanatory potential of virtue and vice theory for understanding the world of politics.

In a noticeable departure from his own earlier work on vice epistemology, Quassim Cassam's chapter presents a critical take on vice explanations that are used to explain political behavior of individuals. According to him, such explanations tend to underestimate the significance of other factors, and are at odds with the principle that a democratic culture is one in which citizens assume that their fellow citizens have good reasons, or at any rate reasons, for acting as they do. Even worse, vice explanations can themselves be epistemically vicious to the extent that they make it harder to understand people whose lives, values, and political preferences are very different from our own. Vice explanations imply that the epistemically vicious suffer from a form of false consciousness.

Heather Battaly's chapter has an ameliorative outlook and considers whether closed-mindedness, typically considered an intellectual vice, can actually be permissible, or even salutary under certain circumstances. In particular, she argues that closed-minded engagement with one's social media feeds is epistemically good when these feeds are ridden with misinformation and fake news. In situations like these, Battaly argues, we should dismiss and report false posts, advocate for structural reform of content algorithms, and flood the epistemic environment with truths and critical thinking. We should also be alive to opportunities where closed-minded engagement with people who believe the posts can produce good epistemic effects overall.

The next chapter, by Alessandra Tanesini, revisits oft-repeated pessimistic claims about people's inability to change their minds in response to counter-evidence and arguments from the opposite side. Against this, she argues that motivation makes a significant difference to individuals' ability to rationally evaluate information. Empirical work on group deliberation shows that the motivation to learn from others, as opposed to a desire to win arguments, promotes good quality group deliberation. This then leads to an overview of some epistemic virtues and vices crucial to the politico-epistemic activities of arguing, debating, and listening to a contrary point of view.

The final two chapters in the section explore the potential of virtue and vice theory at the level of collectives. José Medina analyzes the epistemic behavior of groups by contrasting the epistemic vices found in privileged groups with epistemic virtues found in the collective thinking of oppressed or mixed groups. The chapter discusses psychological, epistemic, and discursive models of epistemic bubbles and echo chambers, focusing on the epistemic vice of critical insensitivity as it appears in the group dynamics of homogeneous, racially privileged groups that become echo chambers. Medina's analysis highlights the specifically collective form that the vice of critical insensitivity with respect to racial bias takes. The chapter also points the way to improvement by discussing how critical insensitivity can be resisted through the epistemic empowerment of oppressed groups and epistemic activism.

Institutions take center stage in Ian James Kidd's contribution. His chapter explores the claim that political institutions can be bearers of epistemic vices. His inroad is a characterization of epistemic corruption and the various processes that can corrupt the epistemic ethoi of political institutions. The discussion then focuses on recent work by Miranda Fricker and select examples from recent British political experience. The chapter ends with suggestions for further work on the corruption and repair of the epistemic ethoi of political institutions.

26

EPISTEMIC VICES, IDEOLOGIES, AND FALSE CONSCIOUSNESS

Quassim Cassam

1 Introduction

Virtues are praiseworthy personal qualities that are beneficial to us and to our fellow human beings. Vices are blameworthy personal qualities that are harmful to us and to our fellow human beings. Among our virtues and vices are *intellectual* or *epistemic* virtues and vices. Their main impact is on our intellectual or epistemic flourishing. Open-mindedness, intellectual humility and sensitivity to evidence are epistemic virtues. Some corresponding epistemic vices are closed-mindedness, intellectual arrogance and imperviousness to evidence. Epistemic vices are character traits, attitudes or ways of thinking that systematically obstruct the gaining, keeping or sharing of knowledge.[1] As long as we have the requisite degree of control over these qualities we can be blamed or criticised for them. *Vice epistemology* is the branch of philosophy that studies the nature, identity and significance of epistemic vices.[2]

A *vice attribution* is the judgement that another person has a specific epistemic vice.[3] The judgement that another person is closed-minded or dogmatic or has some other epistemic vice can serve a number of different purposes. It can be explanatory, evaluative or cautionary.[4] We suppose that a person's epistemic conduct can sometimes be explained by their epistemic vices. In attributing an epistemic vice to someone we are also implicitly evaluating them, and the implicit evaluation is negative. Finally, the judgement that someone is epistemically vicious can serve as a warning to others.

The focus here will be on the explanatory role of vice attributions. The point at which such attributions are made is the point at which an individual's epistemic conduct is taken to be defective in some way, and the vice attributor seeks to explain the attributee's supposedly defective conduct by reference to an underlying epistemic vice. This makes vice attributions potentially problematic in any of the following ways:

1   Their assumption that the attributee's conduct is epistemically defective is open to question, especially in cases where this assumption is grounded in partisan political differences between the attributer and attributee.
2   Even if the attributee's conduct is epistemically defective, there may be better ways of explaining its defectiveness than by pinning it on an underlying epistemic vice.

3   Vice attributions potentially underestimate the extent to which epistemically vicious thinking can nevertheless be rational. Even in epistemically vicious thinking there must be some semblance of cogency.

In this context, epistemic conduct includes judging or belief-formation, as well as reasoning or inferring.

The first two of these difficulties are illustrated by much commentary on the Brexit vote in the United Kingdom and the election of President Trump in the United States. The judgements that Brexit was best for Britain and that Donald Trump was a better candidate for President than Hillary Clinton were seen by many liberal commentators as deeply flawed.[5] As a result, they took it for granted that the thinking or reasoning that led voters to these judgements must also have been defective. This defectiveness was explained in terms of a range of epistemic vices, including gullibility, imperviousness to evidence, wishful thinking and stupidity. On a different reading, however, the judgements in favour of Brexit and Trump were grounded in the values, life experiences and genuine preferences of the relevant groups of voters. The fact that another person's political preferences are diametrically opposed to one's own does not justify the assumption that the person in question must be epistemically vicious.[6] However, the temptation to take political or ideological disagreements as a sign that one's political opponents must be epistemically vicious is hard to resist.

Even in cases of conduct that *is* epistemically defective vice attributions can lead to a neglect of other potentially more relevant factors. For example, hardened conspiracy theorists who circulate anti-Semitic conspiracy theories are both ethically and epistemically defective but it is questionable whether conspiracy thinking is best explained by the epistemic vices of the thinker. What leads a person to subscribe to a particular conspiracy theory is usually their broader ideological commitments.[7] This does not mean, of course, that epistemic vices do not also play a role. This raises a deeper question about the relationship between *vice explanations* – explanations of a person's epistemic conduct by reference to their supposed epistemic vices – and explanations of their conduct by reference to their ideologies or values.

The issue of rationality is brought into focus by a remark of Jason Stanley's. According to Stanley, 'a democratic culture is one in which citizens assume that their fellow citizens have good reasons for acting as they do' (2015: 104). When one citizen assumes that others could only have acted as they did as a result of their stupidity or some other epistemic vice, they are precisely *not* abiding by what might be called Stanley's Principle of Charity.[8] Is this principle sound? The assumption that other people generally have *good* reasons for acting as they do is over-optimistic. This does not mean that other people are *irrational* since, as Alan Millar notes, 'rationality is compatible with a lot of bad thinking' (2004: 7). However, even in such cases, 'cogency, or at least some semblance of cogency, must be discernible' (2004: 11). To the extent that vice explanations make it harder to detect a semblance of cogency in their thinking, they make other people harder to understand. Hannon argues that in order to understand others, 'we need to empathize with their thinking' (2019: 8). Dismissing another person's thinking as defective or explaining it by reference to their supposed epistemic vices hardly counts as empathising with their thinking. The question this raises is whether, in some circumstances, vice explanations might *themselves* be epistemically vicious, by obstructing our knowledge or understanding of other perspectives.

Vice explanations of a person's epistemic conduct might seem to imply that the person in question suffers from a type of false consciousness.[9] A form of false consciousness is when a person is mistaken about the basis of his own beliefs and choices. Vice explanations might be thought to imply that people are mistaken in this way when their political beliefs and choices have more to do with their epistemic vices than with the good reasons that they take themselves to have. In such cases, their 'real reasons' are different from the ones they take themselves to have. Yet this description of their predicament is open to challenge. It might even be argued that in many cases vice explanations of a person's epistemic conduct can *themselves* be regarded as embodying a form of false consciousness.

The following discussion is divided into three sections. The next section will focus on when it is, and when it is not, advisable to give vice explanations of other people's epistemic conduct. Section 3 will have more to say about the Principle of Charity and the importance, even from a vice perspective, of seeing other people as having good reasons, or at least reasons, for their actions. Section 4 will return to the issue of false consciousness. Two key questions here are: do vice explanations imply that people are systematically deluded about their reasons, and are vice epistemologists themselves deluded in many cases about *their* own reasons and motives?

2 The limits of vice explanations

For an example in which a vice explanation seems appropriate, consider the following: on 6 October 1973, Egyptian and Syrian forces launched a surprise attack on Israel. Israel's military was taken by surprise despite the availability of intelligence indicating an impending attack. A study by Uri Bar-Joseph and Arie Kruglanski blamed the intelligence failure on the closed-mindedness of Israel's Director of Military Intelligence and his senior Egyptian Affairs specialist.[10] The study concluded that these individuals had ignored evidence of an impending attack because they had a particularly high need for cognitive closure and had already made up their minds that Egypt and Syria would not attack. The 'because' in this formulation is causal and explanatory. Bar-Joseph and Kruglanski's hypothesis is that attributing the epistemic vice of closed-mindedness to two senior intelligence officers explains their lapses.

It is useful to keep this case in mind when considering the circumstances in which vice explanations are appropriate. A vice explanation is appropriate in this case because it is hard to deny that the conduct of the two intelligence officers was epistemically defective and prevented them from knowing what they could and should have known – that Israel was going to be attacked. Furthermore, quite apart from the arguments presented by Bar-Joseph and Kruglanski, there is a strong intuitive case for conceptualising the explanatory epistemic vice in this case as the vice of closed-mindedness. This is not to deny the relevance of other factors. Closed-mindedness only led the two officials to ignore evidence of an attack because they had a prior commitment to a doctrine about the how Israel's neighbours would proceed. In addition, the fact that the failings of the two officials had such a major influence on Israel's planning and decision-making is indicative of institutional as well as personal failings. These institutional failings can be described as *institutional vices*, a remedy for which is the introduction of the appropriate institutional safeguards.[11] Still, epistemic vices are clearly a significant part of the explanatory story.

When it comes to vice analyses of more recent and still controversial political events, matters are much more complicated. On the issue of whether the thinking or reasoning that led voters to back Trump in the United States and Brexit in the United Kingdom was defective, much will depend on the perceived merits and demerits of these political choices. For commentators who view Brexit as 'utterly, utterly stupid' (Wren-Lewis 2019), it will be hard not to regard the thinking that led people to vote for it as flawed in ways that call for a vice explanation. Yet, unlike the judgement that the decision-making in Israeli intelligence prior to the Yom Kippur surprise was flawed, the judgement that a vote for Brexit or Trump was a vote for something utterly stupid is plainly political. By the same token, it is a partly *political* judgement to opt for a vice explanation of these political choices. This is problematic on the assumption that the primary concern of vice epistemology should be to provide a philosophical analysis of a person's epistemological failings. It should not be, or give the impression of being, a way to attack one's political opponents.[12]

Even politically motivated judgements can still be correct. Regardless of whether the judgement that certain voters were gullible or insensitive to evidence is politically motivated, it could still be true. However, this cannot be decided without testing vice explanations against other possible explanations. A number of the most compelling alternatives are a good deal more charitable than vice explanations. Two key notions in non-vice explanations of recent trends in the United States and Europe are those of *class* and *ideology*. Both play a key role in contrarian analyses by Thomas Frank, David Goodhart and Michael Lind.[13] These analyses are contrary to the received wisdom and challenge the assumption that voters are 'gullible dimwits who are easily manipulated by foreign propaganda or domestic demagogues' (Lind 2020: 91). Gullibility and susceptibility to manipulation are epistemic vices but contrarians regard attempts to explain voter behaviour by reference to such vices as patronising and misguided.

For Lind, the Cold War has been followed by a transatlantic class war in many Western countries. This is a war between 'elites based in the corporate, financial, government, media, and education sectors and disproportionately native working-class populists' (2020: 1). The ideology of the 'overclass' of college-educated managers and professionals is *technocratic liberalism*. Its main tenets are a commitment to free market economics, cultural liberalism and labour arbitrage.[14] It sees economic inequality as an inevitable consequence of differences in educational attainment. According to Lind, what we have been witnessing in recent years is a 'populist counterrevolution from below' against 'minoritarian rule by enlightened technocrats' who see themselves as 'insulated from mass prejudice and ignorance' (2020: 84).

Frank's analysis focuses on what he sees as the 'inherently undemocratic' ideology of 'professionalism' (2016: 24).[15] A basic tenet of this ideology is that 'the successful deserve their rewards, that the people on top are there because they are the best' (2016: 31). The dominance of this ideology has resulted in large-scale economic and social inequalities that have, in turn, opened the door to populist demagogues. *Technocracy* refers to the reign of professionalism in which important decisions are made in distant offices by unaccountable experts. Frank quotes J. K. Galbraith's description of economists as having been 'on the wrong side of every important policy issue, and not just recently but for decades', and argues that those who succeed in a professional discipline are simply 'those who best absorb and apply its master narrative' (2016: 39).[16]

In Goodhart's analysis, the two upsets of 2016 – Brexit and Trump – were a reflection of what he calls 'the new value divisions in developed democracies' (2017: vii). Specifically:

> A large minority group of the highly educated and mobile – the Anywheres – who tend to value autonomy and openness and comfortably surf social change have recently come to dominate our society and politics. There is also a larger but less influential group – the Somewheres – who are more rooted and less well educated, who value security and familiarity and are more connected to group identities than Anywheres. Somewheres feel that their socially conservative intuitions have been excluded from the public space in recent years, which has destabilised our politics and led to the Brexit and Trump backlashes. (2017: vii)

Anywheres see themselves as the voice of reason and look down on Somewheres, who they regard as irrational and xenophobic. Anywheres are more socially tolerant than Somewheres but less politically tolerant. When Somewheres complain about the impact of globalisation and free trade on their jobs and communities, Anywheres respond, as Tony Blair did in 2005, that debating the merits of globalisation is like debating whether autumn should follow summer.[17] Against this background, it isn't hard to understand why Somewheres took the opportunities of the 2016 Brexit vote and US Presidential Election to send a message to Anywhere elites. Voting for Trump or Brexit was an exercise of political agency by people who 'feel buffeted by external events with little political agency, social confidence or control over their destinies' (2017: 7–8).

The point of these analyses is not to defend Trump or Brexit but to make their victories intelligible. Crucially, these analyses make Somewhere voting patterns intelligible without any suggestion that those who voted for Trump or Brexit were gullible or irrational. The question whether these analyses are *correct* cannot be settled here. What is clear is that the explanatory work in these analyses is done by class and ideology. The counterrevolution from below has its own ideology and the name of that ideology is populism, the 'ideology of popular resentment against elites' (Rovira Kaltwasser et al. 2017: 6). Vice and ideological explanations are not incompatible, but one should not assume that people must be irrational or otherwise epistemically vicious if their conduct can be explained without this assumption.

Those who give vice explanations of recent trends might object that the discussion so far misses their point. The focus has been on whether it is appropriate to accuse *voters* of being epistemically vicious but the targets of many vice analyses are leaders rather than the led.[18] In the last few years there has been a torrent of columns and articles on the epistemic vices of populist politicians in the United Kingdom and America. These politicians have been described as arrogant, stupid, lacking any concern for truth and insensitive to evidence. Yet they have been successful in electoral terms. This might show that epistemic vice is no barrier to political success, but there is another possibility: focusing on the epistemic vices of demagogues leaves one with no explanation of their political effectiveness. Effective political leaders cannot afford to be insensitive to evidence in their political calculations or to lack a concern for truth when it comes to polling and other evidence of the most effective lines to take with voters.

The lesson is that if we are serious about wanting to understand the strategies and tactics of populist leaders it is unwise to assume that they are intellectually incompetent or irrational, though Trump might be special case. Their manifest ability to take on board polling information and adjust their methods in the light of such information does not support this assumption. For all the populist rhetoric about the supposed incompetence of experts, they themselves rely on experts, including experts at developing winning political strategies. They may talk about 'alternative facts' but the facts that count for them are hard facts: facts about what works for the people they represent and about what resonates with voters. Analysts who focus on their real or imagined epistemic vices risk underestimating them. The real story is about a group of populist demagogues who have won and, in some cases, held on to power. If we look to vice epistemology in its current evolving forms to explain their political successes, we are likely to be disappointed. Vice epistemology is feel-good political epistemology for liberals but a more hard-headed analysis is called for.

3 Acting for a reason

A person is instrumentally rational insofar as 'she adopts suitable means to her ends' (Kolody and Brunero 2020). In this context, 'suitable' means are efficacious, that is, means that deliver desired end. If the end is to convince people to vote for Brexit, then describing it as a way for the United Kingdom to 'take back control' proved highly efficacious. In the same way, the promise that Trump would 'drain the swamp', that is, root out corruption in Washington, was highly efficacious in attracting voters to his cause. The issue is not whether Brexit would actually enable Britain to take back control or whether Trump had the intention or the capacity to drain the swamp but whether these promises would resonate with voters. It was anticipated by the relevant strategists that they would and they were right about this.

Why did these promises resonate with many voters? Did those making these promises have any serious intention of carrying them out, and did the voters to whom the promises were made believe them? If there is an explanatory role for vice attributions in connection with the twin political upsets of 2016 then one might hope to detect it in relation to one or more of these questions. In reality, the scope for vice explanations in relation to any of these questions is limited. The attractions of 'take back control' and 'drain the swamp' can be easily explained by reference to the contrarian analyses described above. It is easy to understand why those with little political agency should be attracted by the idea of taking control. In the same way, 'drain the swamp' exploited the ideology of popular resentment against elites. To the extent that this ideology was itself a response to inequality and the marginalisation, it was not irrational for politically and economically marginalised voters to favour candidates who at least 'talked the talk' about draining the swamp. If actually draining the swamp would mean the expulsion from Washington of highly paid political consultants and corrupt lobbyists then what's not to like?

These are all ways of making the obvious point that those who voted for populist causes in 2016 had their reasons for doing so. It is less obvious that, in line with Stanley's principle, they had *good* reasons for acting as they did, and this might conceivably create an opening for vice explanations. If economic inequality and a perceived lack of political agency were the considerations which led voters to act as they did, then it is relevant whether they had good reason to expect Brexit and a Trump presidency to tackle these problems. On the face of it, they did not. There was really never any prospect of political demagogues doing anything to address inequality and marginalisation, and one would have to be naïve or gullible or both to suppose otherwise. If the promises made by populist leaders were patently insincere then a failure to spot their insincerity can perhaps be explained in vice terms. Gullibility and naivety are, after all, epistemic vices. Wishful thinking is another epistemic vice that might have played a role in inducing the economically marginalised and powerless to vote for populist demagogues.

Even so, it is important to proceed with caution in proposing such an analysis. A point to bear in mind is that many votes are protest votes. The desire to express one's unhappiness with the status quo is not just a reason but arguably a good reason to vote for anti-establishment candidates even if one has little faith that they have one's best interests at heart. The function of such a vote is *expressive*, and expressive voting has its own rationale. There would be better grounds for attributing epistemic vices to voters who genuinely believed, in the face of all the evidence, that populist demagogues would make a positive difference to their lives. However, it is one thing to describe or evaluate such voters as epistemically vicious and another to explain their conduct by reference to such vices. Vice attributions are not necessarily vice explanations. It might be the case that voters must have been gullible or naïve to believe the promises made by a populist demagogue but it is a further question whether they voted for the demagogue *because* they were gullible or naïve. On an alternative interpretation, they voted as they did because the demagogue spoke to their concerns. This was their reason for voting the way their voted, the consideration upon which they acted.[19]

This is not a vice *explanation* even if it does not preclude a vice *attribution*; it does not preclude evaluating such voters as naïve or gullible. Despite such an evaluation, it is still possible to detect at least a semblance of cogency in their thinking.

What is the vice epistemological significance of the insincerity of populist leaders? For example, suppose that there was never any intention on Trump's part to drain the swamp. This would make the promise to do so morally suspect but not *epistemically* vicious. Suppose that many pro-Brexit politicians were aware that Brexit would reduce rather than increase the UK's economic and political autonomy. In that case, Brexit was sold on a false prospectus, and those doing the selling can be criticised for moral misconduct, but not necessarily for epistemic misconduct. A vice attribution is more plausible in the case of populist politicians who believed what they were saying. There is certainly no lack of evidence that things would not turn out as they promised. If they still believed their own words, were they not guilty of wishful thinking? Or of being too lazy to brief themselves properly, or too dogmatic to be swayed by evidence?

Wishful thinking, intellectual laziness, dogmatism and imperviousness to evidence are certainly epistemic vices. Bearing in mind the distinction between a vice attribution and a vice explanation, the real issue is not whether demagogues who believed their own predictions and propaganda can properly be *described* as epistemically vicious but whether they believed these things *because* they were epistemically vicious. A way to assess this is to ask: if they had not been epistemically vicious would they still have believed their own predictions? It is hard to be sure that the answer to this question is negative. Belief in the benefits of Brexit can also be explained by a person's anti-EU ideology, in which EU bureaucrats are identified as the bad guys. Such an ideology might be misguided but it is a further question whether acceptance of a misguided ideology is a sure sign of epistemic vice.

Aside from any philosophical doubts about vice explanations of recent events there are also sound practical reasons for not insisting that large numbers of voters are, if not downright irrational, then at least epistemically vicious to some degree. The point has been well made by Michael Ignatieff in a review of a book by Nick Clegg, the pro-EU former leader of the Liberal Democrat party in the United Kingdom. Clegg's description of Brexit as one of the greatest acts of national self-immolation in modern times leads Ignatieff to reflect on the tendency of liberals to regard themselves as 'apostles of sweet reason, the clear quiet voice in a bar room of brawlers'. Yet Brexiters 'had their reasons', and 'presenting yourself as the voice of reason isn't smart politics. It's elitist condescension' (2016: 3–4). The parallel worry is that sitting in judgement on the supposed epistemic vices of Brexiters and Trump voters can just as easily come across as elitist condescension. This is not only inadvisable on political grounds but also brings into focus the possibility that vice epistemological political analyses are themselves epistemically vicious. It is to this possibility that I now turn.

4 False consciousness

A form of false consciousness is when a person is mistaken about the basis of his own beliefs and choices. Vice explanations might be thought to imply that people are mistaken in this way when their political beliefs and choices have more to do with their epistemic vices than with the good reasons that they take themselves they have. Consider the following case: Sally voted for Trump because, according to her, he cares about people like her. Let us suppose, also, that in fact he doesn't care about people like her and that his policies favour people like him rather than people like her. By voting for Trump Sally is voting against her own economic interests. Marxists would regard Sally as suffering from false consciousness.

The Marxist view, as described by Denise Meyerson, is that both rulers and the ruled in cap-italist societies suffer from this condition. Rulers misinterpret their own motives and provide rationalisations of their actions that misrepresent their motives to themselves and the people they rule. The ruled vote for people who do not have their best interests at heart because they have 'a poor perception of their interests' (1991: 7).

What, if anything, does vice epistemology have to add to this analysis? Sally's poor per-ception of her own interests and failure to grasp that Trump doesn't care about people like her are both cognitive failings. The more obvious it is that Trump really doesn't care about people like her, the greater the cognitive failing. From a vice epistemological perspective, these failings call for an explanation, and the proposed explanation is in terms of Sally's epis-temic vices. For example, it might be suggested that she fails to see facts about Trump that are staring her in the face because of some combination of wishful thinking, gullibility, and intellectual naivety. If she were epistemically virtuous, she would be less likely to be conned by people like Donald Trump and would have a better grasp of her own interests. On this account, her false consciousness is explained, at least in part, by her epistemic vices, and the antidote is the cultivation of epistemic virtues that would enable her to arrive at a better understanding of her choices and interests.

This explanation of Sally's false consciousness is individualistic in a way that Marxist analyses are not. The Marxist view is that false consciousness and the political ignorance that it produces have much more to do with the politico-economic structure of capitalism than with the epistemic vices of individuals. This is a *structural* explanation of Sally's failings, the implication being that her false consciousness can only be dislodged by a change in the social structure. Epistemic virtues alone will not do the trick. However, as Alessandra Tanesini has pointed out, vice and structural explanations are complementary rather than competitors. People's actions are shaped by structural forces and 'the same forces, including structural power relations, shape people's psychologies including their vices and virtues' (2019: 8). There is another issue on which structural and vice explanations are in agreement: on both views, Sally can be said to suffer from a form of self-ignorance. She is either ignorant of the extent to which her thinking is shaped by structural factors or by her own epistemic vices. To put it crudely, she doesn't grasp the real basis of her political beliefs and choices.

Much depends here on how the notion of a 'basis' is understood. Constantine Sandis defines an 'agential reason' as 'any consideration upon which one actually acts or refrains from doing so' (2015: 267). When a voter reports that her reason for choosing to support a certain candidate was, say, her belief that the candidate cares about people like her, there is no need to suppose that this was not her agential reason or that she is mistaken in *this* sense about the 'basis' of her choice. Her self-ignorance pertains not to her agential reasons but to other factors, both structural and psychological, by which her thinking is likely to have been influenced. There is a sense in which people like Sally do understand the basis of their own political choices and a sense in which they do not.

These conclusions flow from the premise that Sally has a poor perception of her own in-terests but is this premise correct? In his contribution to this volume, Keith Stanovich points out that the interests that people like Sally are assumed to misperceive are their own *material* interests. However, Trump voters are not necessarily voting against their interests if these are understood more broadly to include their values and worldviews. In much the same way, it is gratuitous to assume that working-class Brexit voters only voted for Brexit for narrowly self-interested reasons. Another hypothesis is that they voted the way they did because Brexit was an expression of their values. Stanovich correctly concludes that Trump voters in 2016 were not necessarily irrational. By the same token, these voters were not necessarily suffering from false consciousness and should not be judged epistemically vicious for their political choices. In his contribution to this volume, Jeffrey Friedman criticises the propensity of psychologists to ascribe beliefs with which they disagree to the irrationality of those who hold them. By the same token, one might criticise the propensity of some vice epistemologists – myself, in the past, included – to ascribe political choices with which they disagree to the epistemic vices of those who make them. If Brexit is a stupid idea, or it is completely obvious to everyone that Trump does not care about the poor and marginalised, then how could the thinking that leads such people to vote to Trump or Brexit *not* be epistemically vicious?

This rhetorical question confirms the suspicion that vice explanations can all too easily become a way to attack one's political opponents. It also draws attention to the false consciousness of vice epistemologists who see themselves as politically impartial while only ever focusing on the deficient epistemic conduct of conservatives. The point is not that vice epistemology *has* to have a liberal bias but that it very often does. The deeper problem with the tendency to offer vice explanations of political choices with which one disagrees is that such explanations can themselves be epistemically vicious. Epistemic vices are personal qualities that get in the way of knowledge, and one such quality is what José Medina calls 'insensitivity':

> As I understand it, insensitivity involves being cognitively and affectively numbed to the lives of others: being inattentive to and unconcerned by their experiences, problems, and aspirations; and being unable to connect with them and understand their speech and action. (2013: xi)

There is no *necessary* connection between insensitivity, which might also be called lack of empathy, and the project of giving vice explanations of other people's conduct. However, when the people concerned have been marginalised by technocratic liberalism, there is a serious risk of failing to connect with them and understand their speech and action. If the action is the action of backing right-wing demagogues, then vice explanations can get in the way of knowledge, knowledge of lives that are different from one's own and that render intelligible choices that would otherwise be hard to understand. To put it another way, there is a real danger that a vice epistemological approach will be epistemically vicious in such cases by making it harder to gain a type of knowledge that is essential for a decent society: knowledge of other lives.[20]

Notes

1 See Cassam (2019a) for a defence of this view of epistemic vice.
2 For an overview of vice epistemology, see the introduction to Kidd, Battaly and Cassam (2020).
3 The practice of attributing epistemic vices to other people is closely related to what Ian James Kidd calls 'vice-charging', that is, 'the critical practice of charging other persons with epistemic vice' (2016: 181). However, 'vice-charging' sounds more heated and accusatory than merely *judging* that another person is epistemically vicious. Vice attributions are judgements. They have an evaluative dimension but needn't be accusatory, especially when the individual concerned is dead, and so not in a position to hear the charge.
4 This is not intended as an exhaustive list of the functions of vice attributions. As noted by an anonymous referee, they can also serve to diminish the epistemic standing of the target. In addition, some vice attributions attribute epistemic vices to institutions or organisations. See note 10.
5 See, for example, Wren-Lewis (2019). There are countless other examples of this style of liberal commentary.

6 Or irrational. See the papers by Stanovich and Friedman in the present volume.
7 This is the analysis of conspiracy theories given in Cassam (2019b).
8 Abiding by this principle means 'questioning one's own perspective if one cannot make rational sense out of the actions of one's fellow citizens' (Stanley 2015: 104).
9 For an exposition of the idea of false consciousness, see Meyerson (1991).
10 See Bar-Joseph and Kruglanski (2003) and chapter 2 of Cassam (2019a) for further discussion.
11 On institutional vices, see Miranda Fricker's paper 'Institutional Epistemic Vices: The case of Institutional Inertia', in Kidd, Battaly and Cassam (2021): 89–107.
12 There is more than an element of this in Cassam (2019a). Mea culpa.
13 Also relevant, and in a similar vein, is Eatwell and Goodwin (2018).
14 This involves transferring industrial production from relatively high-wage countries to ones with lower labour costs.
15 An ideology is

> an interrelated set of beliefs that provide a way for people to understand the world. Ideologies tell people what is important, who the good guys and bad guys are, what their goals are, and how those goals should be reached. Without ideologies to help categorize and interpret information, the world would be meaningless. (Uscinski & Parent 2014: 12)

16 See Galbraith (2001).
17 See https://www.theguardian.com/uk/2005/sep/27/labourconference.speeches for a transcript of Blair's speech.
18 For example, Crace (2019) repeatedly describes Conservative politicians in the United Kingdom as stupid. As a piece of political analysis this is startingly simple-minded and condescending.
19 In the terminology of Sandis (2015), such reasons are 'agential reasons'. There is more on Sandis below.
20 For a serious attempt to engage with this problem and counteract the numbness described by Medina, see Hochschild (2016). Her project is to understand what voters who cast their ballots for Trump in 2016 were thinking and feeling. For Hochschild, empathy is the key to uncovering what she calls their 'deep story' (2016: xi). What I mean by a decent society is what Avishai Margalit means by a 'civilized' society: 'one whose members do not humiliate one another' (1996: 1).

References

Bar-Joseph, Uri and Kruglanski, Arie (2003). 'Intelligence Failure and the Need for Cognitive Closure: On the Psychology of the Yom Kippur Surprise', *Political Psychology* 24: 75–99.
Cassam, Quassim (2019a). *Vices of the Mind: From the Intellectual to the Political* (Oxford: Oxford University Press).
Cassam, Quassim (2019b). *Conspiracy Theories* (Cambridge: Polity Press).
Crace, John (2019). *Decline and Fail: Read in Case of Apocalypse* (London: Faber and Faber).
Eatwell, Roger and Goodwin, Matthew (2018). *National Populism: The Revolt against Liberal Democracy* (London: Pelican Books).
Frank, Thomas (2016). *Listen, Liberal or Whatever Happened to the Party of the People?* (London & Melbourne: Scribe).
Galbraith, John Kenneth (2001). 'How the Economists Got it Wrong', *The American Prospect*, December 19, 2001.
Goodhart, David (2017). *The Road to Somewhere: The New Tribes Shaping British Politics* (London: Penguin Books).
Hannon, Michael (2019). 'Empathetic Understanding and Deliberative Democracy', *Philosophy and Phenomenological Research*: 1–24. doi:10.1111/phpr.12624.
Hochschild, Arlie Russell (2016). *Strangers in Their Own Land* (New York: New York Press).
Ignatieff, Michael (2016). 'How Globalisation Has Disempowered Elites and Fuelled Populism', *Financial Times*, September 7, 2016.
Kidd, Ian James (2016). 'Charging Others with Epistemic Vice', *Monist* 99: 181–97.
Kidd, Ian James, Battaly, Heather and Cassam, Quassim, eds. (2021). *Vice Epistemology* (Abingdon: Routledge).
Kolody, Niko and Brunero, John (2020). 'Instrumental Rationality', in *Stanford Encyclopedia of Philosophy* (Spring 2020 Edition). https://plato.stanford.edu/entries/rationality-instrumental/.

Lind, Michael (2020). *The New Class War: Saving Democracy from the Metropolitan Elite* (New York: Atlantic Books).

Margalit, Avishai (1996). *The Decent Society* (Cambridge, MA: Harvard University Press).

Medina, José (2013). *The Epistemology of Resistance: Gender and Racial Oppression, Epistemic Injustice, and Resistant Imaginations* (Oxford: Oxford University Press).

Meyerson, Denise (1991). *False Consciousness* (Oxford: Clarendon Press).

Millar, Alan (2004). *Understanding People: Normativity and Rationalizing Explanation* (Oxford: Oxford University Press).

Rovira Kaltwasser, Cristóbal, Taggart, Paul, Ochoa Espejo, Paulina and Ostiguy, Pierre. (2017). 'Populism: An Overview of the Concept and the State of the Art', in Rovira Kaltwasser, Paul Taggart, Paulina Ochoa Espejo and Pierre Ostiguy. (eds.) *The Oxford Handbook of Populism* (Oxford: Oxford University Press): 1–27.

Sandis, Constantine (2015). 'Verbal Reports and "Real" Reasons: Confabulation and Conflation', *Ethical Theory and Moral Practice* 18: 267–80.

Stanley, Jason (2015). *How Propaganda Works* (Princeton, NJ: Princeton University Press).

Tanesini, Alessandra (2019). 'Review of *Vices of the Mind*', *Mind* (online version), July 19, 2019: 1–9. https://0-academic-oup-com.pugwash.lib.warwick.ac.uk/mind/article/doi/10.1093/mind/fzz044.

Uscinski, Joseph and Parent, Joseph (2014). *American Conspiracy Theories* (Oxford: Oxford University Press).

Wren-Lewis, Simon (2019). 'Why the UK Cannot See That Brexit is Utterly, Utterly Stupid', *New Statesman*, January 28, 2019.

27

ENGAGING CLOSED-MINDEDLY WITH YOUR POLLUTED MEDIA FEED

Heather Battaly

Rewind to June 2020. Assume that most of your interactions are on-line due to the COVID-19 pandemic, and that protests against systemic racism are occurring in cities across the United States. Imagine that racist claims about crime, and fake news about COVID-19, appear in your social media feeds. You know the claims in question are false or misleading, and you care about truth. Let's call this situation 'Polluted Feed.' What should you do? Should you do nothing, or should you engage in some way? If you should engage, with what or whom should you engage? Should you engage with the posts and the people who made them, or with someone or something else? Moreover, how should you engage? Should you engage with an open mind or a closed one?

Below, I offer an argument for engaging closed-mindedly in Polluted Feed and situations like it. The argument focuses on what one should do *epistemically*, expecting this to sometimes conflict with, and be trumped by, what one should do morally or politically. Moreover, it understands claims about what one should do epistemically to be grounded in claims about what an *epistemically virtuous person* would do. In this way, it is an example of applied virtue epistemology. Its purview is restricted to epistemically virtuous persons of a particular sort— persons with *effects-virtues*, i.e., dispositions to produce a preponderance of good epistemic effects, such as true beliefs and knowledge. Virtue epistemology has focused on two main kinds of epistemic virtues—effects-virtues, which have featured in reliabilist analyses, and motives-virtues, which have featured in responsibilist analyses—with a growing consensus that there is an important role for each.[1] Taking inspiration from virtue-consequentialism, effects-virtues are dispositions that produce more good epistemic effects than bad ones. The chapter argues that persons with effects-virtues would engage closed-mindedly in the situation above, or (less technically) that engaging closed-mindedly is likely to produce better epistemic effects than engaging open-mindedly or doing nothing. This means that the action of engaging closed-mindedly need not be vicious and can be virtuous.

Section 1 analyzes the trait of closed-mindedness in a normatively neutral way, which allows the trait to be an epistemic virtue in some contexts, even if it is an epistemic vice in many. It likewise enumerates three different ways to engage closed-mindedly in situations like Polluted Feed. Section 2 makes an argument in favor of engaging closed-mindedly in Polluted Feed, building on the work of Lee McIntyre (2018, 2019, 2020), Jeremy Fantl (2018), Neil Levy (2017, 2018, 2019), and Regina Rini (2017). The conclusion indicates some likely objections and next steps. The upshot: I offer an argument for engaging closed-mindedly in Polluted Feed that is motivated by consequentialist concerns. I don't assume this argument is conclusive. That will depend on whether it can answer objections, and on ongoing empirical investigations.

1 Engaging closed-mindedly: definitions and distinctions

Is there more than one way to engage closed-mindedly in situations like Polluted Feed? And, does engaging closed-mindedly make one a closed-minded person, i.e., a person who has the general trait of closed-mindedness?[2]

1.1 Defining closed-mindedness

Let's begin with a paradigm example of closed-mindedness. Suppose Clint grew up believing that poverty is caused by laziness. He has stuck with this belief throughout his life, is unwilling to revise it, and unwilling to engage seriously with any ideas or evidence to the contrary. He dismisses competing ideas and arguments that cross his path without evaluating their merits. When the conversation turns to low wages as a cause of poverty, Clint deems it nonsense, and may even say as much, before exiting it. When he sees an article arguing that lack of opportunity contributes to poverty, he thinks it ridiculous, and may even leave a comment to that effect, before scrolling on. He recognizes that such ideas compete with his own, and rejects them privately, and even publicly, because they strike him as implausible or worse. In short, Clint is closed-minded, at least when it comes to this topic.

What does this mean? We can understand closed-mindedness to be an unwillingness (or inability) to engage seriously with relevant intellectual options—e.g., competing ideas and evidence—and/or an unwillingness to revise a belief. The features of Clint's case are sufficient for closed-mindedness, but they aren't all necessary. Clint has a specific kind of closed-mindedness: he is dogmatic. Dogmatism is an unwillingness to engage seriously with relevant alternatives to a belief one already holds, or (in cases where one is willing to engage seriously with alternatives) an unwillingness to revise a belief one already holds. Importantly, closed-mindedness includes but doesn't *require* dogmatism. This is because closed-mindedness doesn't require having extant beliefs about a topic. One can be closed-minded in arriving at an initial belief about a topic, or closed-minded in the ways one conducts inquiries more generally—in which questions one asks, methods one uses, or sources one consults.

Closed-mindedness doesn't require public speech or behavior either. It can be private—conducted inside one's own head. Clint counts as closed-minded when he privately rejects competing ideas (in the manner described above), even if he doesn't go on to publicly denounce them as 'ridiculous.' Importantly, though, public denunciation does require private rejection in order to count as closed-minded; else, the denunciation might be deceptive rather than closed-minded.

Closed-mindedness can take the form of a domain-specific disposition, or a general trait or disposition, or even an individual action. Suppose Clint's unwillingness to engage seriously with competing ideas and evidence is restricted to this one topic (the causes of poverty), and he engages seriously with respect to a wide range of other topics. If so, his closed-mindedness is domain-specific. Whereas, if he is unwilling (or unable) to engage seriously with relevant ideas, evidence, and sources across most topics and domains, his closed-mindedness will be a general trait or disposition, one that is consistent enough to count him as a closed-minded person. Compare Oscar, who is generally disposed to be *open*-minded—he usually engages seriously with ideas about this topic and others—though he falls down on this particular occasion, dismissing (privately, and even publicly) a relevant argument about the causes of poverty without weighing its merits. On this occasion, he performs a *closed-minded action*—he does what a closed-minded person would do when in this situation—but he doesn't possess a disposition (general or domain-specific) to be closed-minded. Following suit, if you occasionally dismiss posts about fake 'cures' for COVID-19, then you occasionally perform closed-minded actions. But, you can do that while still having a general disposition of open-mindedness.

It's safe to assume that Clint's and Oscar's respective manifestations of closed-mindedness are epistemically vicious in the sense that they produce a preponderance of bad epistemic effects: at a minimum, their closed-minded dispositions and actions obstruct the transmission of knowledge and/or maintain, protect, and strengthen false beliefs about the causes of poverty. In other words, Clint's closed-minded disposition is an effects-vice, and Oscar's closed-minded action is one that a person with effects-vices would perform. By comparison, Section 2 asks whether the closed-minded action of (privately and publicly) dismissing posts we know to be false could produce a preponderance of good epistemic effects, or at least minimize the production of bad epistemic effects, and in that sense be an action that a person with effects-*virtues* would perform.

1.2 Options in Polluted Feed

Return to Polluted Feed: assume that essentialist claims about race and crime have appeared in your social media feeds alongside fake 'cures.' You know these claims are false and misleading, and you care about truth. What should you do? Let's explore five of the main options. Should you:

A   Engage seriously with the posts and be willing to revise your beliefs? Or,
B   Engage seriously with the posts but be unwilling to revise your beliefs? Or,
C   Engage dismissively with the posts and be unwilling to revise your beliefs? Or,
D   Avoid engaging with the posts, and be unwilling to revise your beliefs, but engage with other aspects of the epistemic environment in an effort to counteract the posts? Or,
E   Avoid engaging with the posts, and other aspects of the epistemic environment, and do nothing?

The options above all focus on public engagement, which involves communicating with someone else, e.g., uttering/commenting 'That is false.'[3] A is a way of engaging open-mindedly. B, C, and D are different ways of engaging closed-mindedly insofar as they all entail being unwilling to revise beliefs that conflict with the posts, and all involve publicly engaging either with the posts themselves or other aspects of the epistemic environment. E amounts to doing nothing publicly, whether or not one is willing to revise beliefs that conflict with the posts. Section 2 will offer an argument for a combined strategy of pursuing D and C, and to a lesser extent B, as they are epistemically effective (and dividing our epistemic labor accordingly). To make sense of that proposal, we first need analyses of A–E.

Let's begin with C, drawing on Clint above. Clint is unwilling to revise his belief that laziness causes poverty, and dismisses competing ideas and arguments (privately, and sometimes publicly), thus failing to engage seriously with them. *Dismissing* competing ideas is one way to fail to engage seriously with them. Roughly, *engaging seriously* with an idea or argument is a matter of evaluating it on its merits. One must hear it out, make an effort to correctly understand or represent it, consider whether it is likely to be true, and evaluate whether it employs good reasoning. Serious engagement may also involve weighing the idea or argument against competing evidence, and evaluating the reliability of its source. Importantly, serious engagement does *not* require open-mindedness (open-mindedness requires both serious engagement and a willingness to revise one's beliefs—the rare conspiracy theorist who hears you out and admits your evidence has merit, but *balks* when it comes time to revise his beliefs, engages seriously but is not open-minded). Now, Clint doesn't do the things required for serious engagement. Instead, after reading or hearing just enough of a competing argument to recognize it *as* a competitor to his belief, he (i) privately rejects it as false because it seems ridiculous, and (ii) in some versions of the example, publicly says as much. Let's assume that satisfying (i) is enough for privately engaging dismissively with a competing idea. Whereas, satisfying both (i) and (ii) will be required for publicly engaging dismissively with a competing idea, which is what we are after in C. In short, one can privately dismiss without publicly dismissing, but one can't publicly dismiss without privately dismissing, if one's public dismissal is to be closed-minded rather than deceptive. The upshot: Clint fulfills all of the features of C.

In sum, pursuing C in Polluted Feed entails being unwilling to revise beliefs that conflict with the posts—being unwilling to revise your belief that there is no essential connection between race and crime, or that people shouldn't drink bleach to cure COVID-19—and being unwilling to re-open those inquiries. It also entails publicly engaging dismissively with the posts, which requires privately and publicly rejecting them as false. Public rejection can take the form of, e.g., commenting that the posts are false or ridiculous, or calling them out as racist, or commenting with a link that debunks them. Engaging dismissively precludes engaging seriously—one doesn't evaluate the specific arguments the posts make, or respond to them point-by-point, or figure out exactly where each goes wrong. Note that since I haven't delineated a precise boundary between engaging seriously and engaging dismissively, we should expect some latitude in the application of these concepts, and some tough calls at the border. If you find yourself posting not just one or two, but many, debunking links, or replying to many of the points in the posts, then you may have crossed over to engaging seriously. Finally, note that though Clint (above) is dismissing ideas that are *true*, and the agent who pursues C in Polluted Feed is dismissing ideas that are *false*, both are closed-minded. This is a strength of our analysis, which allows agents to be closed-minded whether the competing ideas they dismiss are true *or* false.

D, like C, is a way of engaging closed-mindedly, at least insofar as it entails being closed-minded about the posts (unwilling to revise beliefs that conflict with them) and involves public engagement to counteract them.[4] But, unlike C, D doesn't involve publicly engaging with the *posts themselves*—we can pursue it because we are unwilling to engage with the posts at all, even dismissively. D doesn't involve commenting on the posts, or calling them out as false, or debunking them. It involves publicly engaging with *other* people or structures in the epistemic environment in an effort to counteract the posts. To illustrate, one can pursue D by (e.g.) reporting the posts to Facebook or Twitter, or by increasing the frequency with which one posts reliable information about systemic racism and COVID-19 oneself, or by helping others learn how to identify fake news and fallacious arguments, or by publicly advocating for structural changes to social media platforms.

By comparison, those who pursue E avoid public engagement. They need not be closed-minded—they might be privately open-minded but epistemically selfish, lazy, or cowardly in public. Nor, as the above shows, is private closed-mindedness sufficient for E. Still, one likely path from private closed-mindedness to avoiding public engagement involves ignoring the posts and resigning oneself to the sad reality of a polluted epistemic environment. Note that E isn't limited to avoiding engagement with trolls. In taking E, one avoids engaging with *all* polluted posts, even the sincere ones. One also avoids engaging with any other aspects of the epistemic environment. One does nothing to try to counteract the posts.

Finally, what is the difference between A and B? Both involve serious engagement with the posts, but A is a way of engaging open-mindedly, whereas B is a way of engaging closed-mindedly. For present purposes, we can think of the trait of open-mindedness as a willingness to engage seriously with relevant alternatives to one's beliefs, and a willingness to revise one's beliefs.[5] Following suit, open-minded actions will be *instances* of engaging seriously with relevant alternatives and being willing to revise one's beliefs. Both pieces are required. If one engages seriously but isn't willing to revise one's beliefs, then one isn't performing open-minded actions. The (rare) conspiracy theorist who hears you out, correctly represents your view, and admits your evidence has merit, but still *balks* at belief revision isn't open-minded. Even though he is willing to engage seriously with your arguments, he isn't willing to re-open inquiry into whether he is right. He is closed-minded and engaging with you for some other reason—perhaps because he wants to change *your* mind. For this reason, pursuing A requires *both* serious engagement with the posts *and* a willingness to revise one's respective beliefs.

In contrast, pursuing B doesn't require a willingness to revise one's beliefs or re-open inquiry into whether one is right. Consider Daryl Davis (1958–), a black musician, who has convinced approximately two dozen KKK members to leave the Klan. Davis engages seriously with their claims and arguments: he hears them out, correctly represents their arguments, and presents counter-evidence and rebuttals. But, he does so closed-mindedly: he isn't willing to revise his belief that white supremacy is false, or re-open his inquiry into the matter. He isn't engaging with Klan members to figure out what is true—he already knows white supremacy is false; he is engaging in order to change their minds.[6]

With these distinctions in place, we can return to our main question. Which of A–E *should* you do in Polluted Feed?

2 An argument for engaging closed-mindedly in Polluted Feed

This section builds on work by McIntyre, Fantl, Levy, and Rini to argue in favor of engaging closed-mindedly in Polluted Feed. Specifically, it argues for a combined strategy of pursuing D and C, and to a lesser extent B, as they are epistemically effective. It understands claims about what one should do epistemically to be grounded in claims about what an epistemically virtuous person would do, limiting its purview to epistemically virtuous persons with effects-virtues. Roughly, effects-virtues are epistemic character traits, skills, and faculties that produce a preponderance of good epistemic effects, e.g., truths and knowledge. Importantly, effects-virtues are not restricted to reliable faculties (20/20 vision). Character traits, e.g., epistemic charity, courage, and conscientiousness are also effects-virtues insofar as they produce a preponderance of good epistemic effects. In short, the below argues that persons with effects-virtues would engage closed-mindedly in Polluted Feed, or (less technically) that engaging closed-mindedly is likely to produce better epistemic effects than engaging open-mindedly or doing nothing.

To clarify two technical points, first, the argument focuses on the *actions* of epistemically virtuous persons rather than their traits. It contends that epistemically virtuous persons will perform closed-minded actions in Polluted Feed. But, it doesn't claim that epistemically virtuous persons will have a general disposition of closed-mindedness or that the general disposition of closed-mindedness is an epistemic virtue. That would require further argument (Battaly 2018b). Second, it assumes that the action of *publicly engaging* with the posts or the environment, and doing so closed-mindedly, is simultaneously an epistemically charitable, courageous, and conscientious action, in addition to being a closed-minded action. That is to say, a person with all the epistemic effects-virtues—including charity, courage, and conscientiousness—would ultimately decide to publicly engage and do so closed-mindedly.

2.1 *McIntyre's argument*

Lee McIntyre (2018, 2019, 2020) focuses on science denial, both on-line and off. He offers a consequentialist argument against—what I have called—E and A, and for C, D, and B. I endorse his argument against E outright. With help from Fantl, Levy, and Rini, I supplement and qualify his arguments against A, and for C, D, and B.

McIntyre convincingly argues *against E*. He thinks doing nothing to counteract fake news will result in a preponderance of bad moral and epistemic effects. Epistemically, when fake news outperforms real news on social media, we can expect some of its consumers to come away with false beliefs. Some will end up believing that, e.g., climate change isn't anthropogenic, vaccines cause autism, and masks do nothing to prevent the spread of COVID-19.[7] And, even when consumers of fake news don't acquire false beliefs, doubt can erode their confidence in true beliefs, resulting in abstention and loss of knowledge (McIntyre 2018: 24). McIntyre points out that the normalization of fake news can also have bad effects on the epistemic environment as a whole, undermining the value of truth, eroding trust in testimony, and making it difficult to identify experts.[8] Compounding the problem, these bad epistemic effects can produce a preponderance of bad moral effects through their impact on behavior. False beliefs, doubt, loss of knowledge, and the erosion of trust have impacted choices about, e.g., mask-wearing, inoculations, and energy-consumption, all with devastating effects. Though McIntyre's focus is on science denial, I hope it is obvious that the effects of white silence about racism have been horrific, and have perpetuated (if not ossified) ignorance of white privilege and injustice and violence against black persons. In short, E does nothing to stem the tide of bad effects. A person with epistemic effects-virtues wouldn't do nothing. Accordingly, neither should we.

McIntyre also gets us started on an argument *against A*—engaging open-mindedly—though the worries he raises may also apply to B. He argues that A produces a preponderance of bad effects, key among them: it wastes the agent's epistemic resources, sows confusion and doubt in others, and confers credibility on ridiculous ideas. He thinks scientists who engage seriously and open-mindedly with 'crackpot theories' will amass epistemic opportunity costs, since serious engagement requires time and resources that would be better spent investigating theories for which there is some evidence (McIntyre 2019: 173). He likewise warns of the dangers of 'false equivalences' and 'platforming.' Roughly, one makes a false equivalence when one publicly engages with 'crackpot' views as if they were credible. Platforming is a variety of this, in which one provides a platform for seriously engaging with a 'crackpot' view alongside epistemically justified views, often in the form of a panel invitation (in the media or at a university). Here, McIntyre is joined by Intemann and de Melo-Martin who argue that one of the dangers of platforming climate-deniers is contributing to a "false public perception that…no scientific consensus exists" (2014: 2752). Treating deniers *as if* they were experts, and their views *as if* they were justified, contributes to public confusion and doubt. McIntyre is likewise joined by Levy (2018, 2019) who argues that platforming produces misleading higher-order evidence for the expertise of the speaker and the credibility of their view, making it difficult to identify experts.

McIntyre rightly points out some of the bad effects of A. One worry is that the bad effects he identifies may not be unique to A; i.e., serious engagement may waste time, sow confusion, and confer credibility on crackpot views, whether it is open- *or* closed-minded. This is a problem for any strategy that bars A, but allows for B. Below, we will supplement McIntyre's argument against A, with help from Fantl.

McIntyre's arguments *for C, D, and B* also point us in the right direction, though I will recommend qualification in the case of C, expansion in the case of D, and extreme caution in the case of B. McIntyre argues in favor of C—closed-mindedly dismissing the posts— because he thinks publicly calling out the posts as false (or commenting with a debunking link) will limit the overall production of bad effects. On his view, dismissing the posts is likely to prevent confusion in people who are encountering the posts for the first time (2018: 155), even though it isn't likely to change the minds of extant deniers and racists who already believed their false content.[9] In other words, McIntyre (2020) thinks dismissals of the posts work as a preventative 'pre-bunker' for people who haven't yet been exposed to them. He likewise suggests that even when pre-bunking isn't possible, it may still be helpful to dismiss and debunk the posts immediately after exposure, as this can prevent false beliefs from taking hold. In short, McIntyre argues that without "a counter-narrative from us," even more knowledge would be lost, and even worse effects would be produced (2018: 155). Given Levy's worries about debunking below, I will be recommending that we pursue C but only in conjunction with D.

Since dismissals aren't likely to change the minds of extant deniers and racists, McIntyre adds D and B to his overall strategy. With respect to D—engaging with *other* aspects of the environment to counteract the posts—he recommends flooding the environment with truths and education in critical thinking. He sees education as especially important for the yet-to-be-exposed and the recently exposed, and bombardment with truths as important for everyone, including extant deniers. On his view, bombarding deniers with truths (in non-threatening ways) will eventually help to change their minds, via 'repetition effects.'[10] While I agree that D should include these features, with Rini's help below, I suggest that they don't go far enough. Unless we also advocate for structural reform of content algorithms, our efforts at flooding the environment with truths and critical thinking aren't likely to reach their targets.

Though McIntyre (2019) argues that we shouldn't engage seriously and *open*-mindedly with extant deniers (because we shouldn't re-open our inquiries into whether our theories are true), McIntyre (2020) suggests that we should engage seriously and *closed*-mindedly with them (B) in an effort to understand why they believe what they do and help them change their minds. Specifically, he recommends building trust through face-to-face relationships. My recommendation is that we pursue B with extreme caution (a friendly amendment), since engaging seriously with extant deniers and racists and their posts can easily make matters worse. It can result in epistemic (and moral) opportunity costs for the people who seriously engage with them. It can disseminate falsehoods to others, leading to doubt and loss of knowledge, especially when efforts to debunk fail (see Levy below). It can confer credibility on deniers and racists, unwittingly helping to establish them as experts, and can normalize them and their claims and methods, further degrading the epistemic (and moral) environment. (If José Medina's arguments about the dangers of credibility excess succeed (2013: 60), it even risks facilitating epistemic vices in deniers and racists when we engage with them privately.) It is a live question as to whether Daryl Davis has ultimately made matters worse, since "by appearing with Davis, Klan leaders position themselves socially as reasonable people, people to be respected and negotiated with, not just violent racists" (Ferkany 2019: 410). Whatever conclusions we draw about Davis's case, there will be some cases in which B produces a preponderance of good effects and epistemically virtuous persons pursue it. Accordingly, B stays in the mix, with a caveat of extreme caution.

2.2 Refining the argument

Let's refine the argument for engaging closed-mindedly in Polluted Feed, with help from Fantl, Levy, and Rini. This section ultimately endorses a combined strategy of D and C, and with extreme caution B.

Against A. Fantl (2018) gives us additional reasons to reject (what I call) A, arguing that we shouldn't seriously engage open-mindedly with claims or arguments that we know to be false or misleading. His arguments against A employ a mix of non-consequentialist and consequentialist reasoning; I focus on the latter.[11] His consequentialist arguments contend that serious open-minded engagement produces a preponderance of bad epistemic effects for both the agent and the environment. He concurs with the above: A is likely to promulgate false views, confer credibility on fringe arguments, and waste the agent's epistemic resources. Importantly, he identifies two bad effects unique to A that we did not identify above and which supplement our argument against it. On his view, agents who know that p and engage *open*-mindedly with arguments for ~p are willing to reduce confidence in their belief that p in response to arguments they *know are misleading*. This saddles them with a distorted degree of confidence in belief, and puts them at risk for losing knowledge (2018: 152, 153n33)—two bad effects that do not hold for B.

Caution about B. In addition to arguing against A, Fantl argues against B, ultimately concluding that we shouldn't seriously engage open- *or* closed-mindedly with claims and arguments we know to be false or misleading. He contends that serious *closed*-minded engagement will either be (i) deceptive, if we pretend to be open-minded, in which case it is problematic, or (ii) transparent, if we come clean about being closed-minded, in which case it is ineffective. Either way, he thinks, we shouldn't pursue B. In contrast, my overall strategy exercises extreme caution in using B but still allows for B in cases where it is likely to produce a preponderance of good effects (Battaly 2020b). Accordingly, replies to Fantl's argument against B are in order.[12] First, I worry that the argument for (i) makes the conditions for pretending to be open-minded too easy to satisfy. We can satisfy them by smiling and nodding approvingly in response to an interlocutor, or by mulling over the details of her argument (Fantl 2018: 159). The problem is that smiling, nodding, and mulling over arguments (etc.) can be manifestations of virtuous epistemic humility or epistemic charity (or even empathy or understanding) and not a pretense to open-mindedness. Relatedly, and ironically, our polarized environment might be changing the conventions of political discourse such that we no longer expect behaviors like mulling over an argument to be indicative of an agent's open-mindedness. We may instead expect such behaviors to be indicative of efforts to change our minds, understand our thought-processes, or help us learn. Second, in reply to (ii), I am more optimistic about the ability of transparent closed-minded engagement to change minds. Fantl argues that coming clean about our unwillingness to revise our beliefs is off-putting to interlocutors—they see us as arrogant and get defensive. Fair enough. But, distinguishing open-minded actions from epistemically humble, charitable, and conscientious actions may help. We can (and should) perform actions of these latter sorts in engaging with interlocutors, even though we aren't willing to re-open our inquiries.

We can demonstrate that we care about truth—about maintaining it ourselves and helping others get it—and that we see our interlocutors as people, not monsters or dolts (Battaly 2020b). Granted, we need to employ this strategy with caution, and only in contexts where we are likely to change the minds of our interlocutors and unlikely to facilitate epistemic vices in them, waste our resources, propagate falsehoods, or confer credibility on dangerous views. Still, I think this strategy does sometimes work, especially when interlocutors understand where we are coming from and are willing to revise their beliefs (Ferkany 2019: 413).

For C, but not C alone. Levy (2017) marshals substantial psychological evidence to warn us off unilateral pursuit of C. He argues that dismissing the posts, in an effort to debunk them, can unwittingly produce more long-term harm than good for the yet-to-be and recently exposed, due to the dissociation of content from source, repetition and fluency effects, and priming. Consuming bits of fake news in explicit dismissals can be risky because we store content knowledge separately from source knowledge—we can remember the content of a fake news story without remembering that our source was a debunking website. Further, our familiarity with a claim—e.g., via memory—increases our fluency in processing it, which can make us more likely to believe it (Begg et al. 1992). In Levy's words: "even when repetition is explicitly in the service of debunking a claim, it may result in higher levels of acceptance by promoting processing fluency" (2017: 29). This means that even if McIntyre is correct, and pre-bunking and immediate debunking do prevent false beliefs from forming in the short term, they can still facilitate the acquisition of false beliefs over time. Adding insult to injury, even when repetition of the false claim p doesn't result in the eventual formation of a false belief that p, it can still impact cognition through fluency and priming. Repetition of the claim that race is essentially connected to crime can still slow our processing of positive claims about black persons, and prime us to remember negative true claims. The upshot: we should be wary of the long-term effects of C.

All told, McIntyre's and Levy's arguments about C show us that it should be pursued, but shouldn't be pursued alone. C should be pursued because without it, more people would believe falsehoods in the short-term. If we don't dismiss essentialist claims about race and crime, or claims about 99% of COVID-19 cases being 'totally harmless,'[13] more people, hearing them for the first time, will come to believe them (or get confused). But, C shouldn't be pursued unilaterally because it can lead to bad effects in the long-term, through the repetition of falsehoods and priming. In an effort to mitigate C's long-term bad effects, we should combine it with D. Flooding the environment with truths, and making structural changes to content algorithms, may help counteract the negative effects of C that are due to repetition, fluency, and priming, and perhaps even tip the scales toward positive effects. Unsurprisingly, that hypothesis requires empirical testing.

For D. Recall that D involves being closed-minded about the posts (being unwilling to revise beliefs that conflict with them), and engaging with *other* aspects of the environment in an effort to counteract them. In that vein, McIntyre suggested flooding the environment with truths and critical thinking: on his view, even deniers will eventually listen to truths they repeatedly hear. But, for his plan to work, the truths poured into the environment must reach deniers. The events of June 2020 confirm that increasing our efforts to flood the environment with truths (about mask-wearing and systemic racism) won't change minds if the truths aren't heard by deniers (they don't penetrate echo chambers), or if they are heard but dismissed due to motivated reasoning. To change minds (relatively quickly), truths about COVID-19 and systemic racism at least need to reach the people who deny them, reach them repeatedly,[14] and not be dismissed.[15] Accordingly, in addition to increasing our frequency of posting truths about these topics and stepping up our efforts to promote critical thinking, we should be advocating for structural reform of the content algorithms that facilitate echo chambers.

Rini (2017: 54) draws similar conclusions (albeit for different reasons) about the need for structural reform: "If we want to solve the problem of fake news, we need to look beyond individual practices—we need to look at institutions." She insightfully argues that we should use structural mechanisms to reduce bad effects. For instance, we should report suspicious posts to media platforms, so they can be fact-checked, labeled with a warning, and assigned a lower weight in content algorithms (Rini 2017: 57). At the time of writing, warning labels on Facebook and Twitter won't prevent posts from appearing in feeds (though they may appear less frequently), or from being clicked on, but will prevent their false content from being visible until clicked on (thus avoiding worries about fluency and priming).[16] Early reports show that flagging discourages clicking on the posts (Rosen 2020).

Putting all of the above together, we should engage closed-mindedly in Polluted Feed. As a group, we should divide our epistemic labor among the activities in D and C, and where effective B. We should dismiss and report false and misleading posts, while advocating for structural reform and pouring truths and critical thinking into the environment. We should also be alive to opportunities where B will be effective in changing minds. Which of these routes should *you* pursue in a given instance of Polluted Feed? That will depend on the exact features of the context and your role in the group, e.g., there may be contexts in which you should pursue B instead of D and C. No individual can solve the problem on their own, and even individuals coordinating to divide their labor won't make much progress without structural reform.[17]

3 Objections and next steps

I have offered a virtue-consequentialist argument for engaging closed-mindedly in Polluted Feed. Whether this argument is conclusive will depend on ongoing empirical investigations and on its replies to objections.

I close with six sets of objections, and briefly indicate some arguments that are worth pursuing in constructing replies. (1) Closed-mindedness pertains to *relevant* alternatives, but essentialist claims about racism, and fake cures for COVID-19, aren't true or justified. So, why would they even count as relevant? (2) Doesn't advocating closed-minded engagement in Polluted Feed encourage the development of the general trait of closed-mindedness?[18] Doesn't it make the epistemic environment worse by facilitating intellectual vices, which reinforce our own echo chambers? (3) Isn't this strategy dangerous? What happens when deniers and racists think they know that the posts in their feeds are false? Won't they lay claim to this strategy? More broadly, how can we tell when we are in Polluted Feed and when we aren't?[19] (4) How can we advocate for impeding the dissemination of falsehoods without inadvertently reinforcing our own echo chambers and without advocating for censorship? (5) Are we obligated to engage seriously with deniers and racists who are willing to revise their beliefs (or willing to engage seriously with us), even if doing so would produce a preponderance of bad effects?[20] Finally, (6) hasn't the argument above fallen short of showing that closed-mindedness produces good epistemic effects in Polluted Feed? Doesn't it only show that it minimizes bad epistemic effects?

With next steps in mind, let's indicate some arguments we can pursue in constructing replies. (1) Racist claims, and fake cures, are false and unjustified. Nevertheless and unfortunately, they are epistemically relevant insofar as they are pervasive: they are pervasive enough in our on-line environment to count as epistemically relevant even though they are false and unjustified. (2) Advocating closed-mindedness in Polluted Feed need not encourage the general trait of closed-mindedness. It need only encourage closed-mindedness that is domain-specific: specific to domains where (i) a claim is pervasive enough to count as relevant and (ii) one knows the claim is false. Note that facilitating such domain-specific closed-mindedness stands to improve the epistemic environment, as more people with knowledge will speak out. (3) Racist claims and fake cures are false, and deniers and racists do not know them. Their closed-mindedness produces a preponderance of bad epistemic effects (recall Clint), and is vicious, not virtuous. Thus, the strategy above does not apply to them. The tough question then becomes: how does one know when one is, and when one isn't, in Polluted Feed? A full reply needs to consider whether applying the strategy above requires not simply knowing that a claim is false, but also knowing that one knows that the claim is false. (4) Rini's (2017) plan for reporting false content and adjusting content algorithms avoids outright censorship. It is also worth exploring whether the domain-specificity of the recommended closed-mindedness mitigates worries about reinforcing our own echo chambers. Note that since the above strategy *isn't* recommending closed-mindedness with respect to the many claims that we don't know, the objection won't apply to them. (5) The objection that we are obligated to engage with some deniers and racists poses a serious challenge. In developing replies to it, we will need to ask: are the obligations meant to be epistemic, moral, or both? Are they meant to apply to us as group, or as individuals? If the latter, are individual persons of color obligated to engage with racists? Are there any circumstances in which prima facie obligations to engage are defeated by the harm that would be produced by engaging? If so, why aren't those circumstances satisfied in Polluted Feed?[21] Finally, (6) points out that our on-line environment may be so polluted and structurally unsound that the best our strategy can do is minimize bad effects. If so, closed-mindedness would still be a virtue, albeit a 'burdened' virtue.[22]

Notes

1 For a paradigmatic reliabilist analysis, see Sosa (2007); Zagzebski (1996) is a paradigmatic responsibilist analysis; for an overview, see Battaly (2019).
2 See Battaly (2018a, 2018b, 2020a).
3 Recall that for the public denouncement of a claim to be closed-minded, rather than deceptive, one must also privately reject it.
4 Readers who balk at this use of 'engaging closed-mindedly' are welcome to understand D as a way of 'engaging publicly while being closed-minded.'
5 This is the sub-set of open-mindedness that contrasts with dogmatism. See Battaly (2018a), cf. Baehr (2011), cf. Allen (2020).
6 Ornstein (2016); Battaly (2020b); cf. Ferkany (2019).
7 See Pulido et al. (2020), Richtel (2020), Silverman (2016), Spring (2020).
8 See Blake-Turner (2020).
9 I set aside the question of whether dismissing the posts has a "backfire effect" (which *increases* the confidence of extant believers), since this hasn't been sufficiently replicated (Nyhan and Reifler 2010). Whether or not it increases confidence, it doesn't result in belief-change.
10 See Begg et al. (1992).
11 Fantl's main argument against serious open-minded engagement is not consequentialist.
12 We should generally avoid deceiving our interlocutors. Modeling deception would contribute to facilitating it in others and further normalizing it, producing worse effects overall.
13 Rabin and Cameron (2020).
14 If you are the *only* person posting truths on a 'friend's' feed that is populated with falsehoods, the effect may be negligible.
15 Granted, repeated exposure may produce a 'sleeper effect,' whereby true beliefs are *slowly* acquired via fluency. Levy (2017: 30).

16 Conger (2020), Lerman and Timberg (2020), Roth and Pickles (2020).

17 These recommendations hold even if your own feed is not polluted.

18 Blake-Turner (2020). See also Lynch (2019: 35), but Lynch argues that political posts are functioning expressively rather than epistemically.

19 Allen (2020).

20 Ferkany (2019: 416), Gunn (Forthcoming).

21 The argument above only addresses what we should do *epistemically*; it grants that moral effects can trump epistemic effects. Sometimes we should engage because engaging is morally virtuous, even though it isn't epistemically virtuous.

22 Some additional work that may be helpful in constructing and evaluating replies includes: Nguyen (2020); Tessman (2005); and work on epistemic relevance, and on epistemic obligation. I am grateful to Michael Hannon, Jeroen de Ridder, and especially Michael Lynch, for outstanding comments on a draft.

References

Allen, T. 2020. "Engaging Others." Dissertation. University of Connecticut.

Baehr, J. 2011. *The Inquiring Mind*. Oxford: Oxford University Press.

Battaly, H. 2018a. "Closed-mindedness and dogmatism." *Episteme* 15(3): 261–82.

Battaly, H. 2018b. "Can closed-mindedness be an intellectual virtue?" *Royal Institute of Philosophy Supplements* 84: 23–45.

Battaly, H. 2019. "A third kind of intellectual virtue: Personalism." In H. Battaly (ed.) *The Routledge Handbook of Virtue Epistemology*. New York: Routledge, 115–26.

Battaly, H. 2020a. "Closed-mindedness as an Intellectual Vice." In C. Kelp and J. Greco (eds.) *Virtue Theoretic Epistemology*. Cambridge: Cambridge University Press, 15–41.

Battaly, H. 2020b. "Closed-mindedness and Arrogance." In A. Tanesini and M. P. Lynch (eds.) *Polarisation, Arrogance, and Dogmatism*. London: Routledge, 53–70.

Begg, I. M., Anas, A. and Farinacci, S. 1992. "Dissociation of processes in belief: Source recollection, statement familiarity, and the illusion of truth." *Journal of Experimental Psychology: General* 121(4): 446–58.

Blake-Turner, C. 2020. "Fake news, relevant alternatives, and the degradation of our epistemic environment." *Inquiry*. doi:10.1080/0020174X.2020.1725623.

Conger, K. 2020. "Twitter labels trump tweet about 'racist baby' as manipulated media." *New York Times*. https://www.nytimes.com/2020/06/18/technology/trump-tweet-baby-manipulated.html. Accessed: July 2, 2020.

Fantl, J. 2018. *The Limitations of the Open Mind*. Oxford: Oxford University Press.

Ferkany, M. A. 2019. "The moral limits of open-mindedness." *Educational Theory* 69(4): 403–19.

Gunn, H. K. Forthcoming. "Exclusion and epistemic community." *Revue Internationale de Philosophie*.

Intemann, K. and de Melo-Martin, I. 2014. "Are there limits to scientists' obligations to seek and engage dissenters?" *Synthese* 191: 2751–65.

Lerman, R. and Timberg, C. 2020. "Bowing to pressure, Facebook will start labeling violating posts from politicians. But critics say it's not enough." *Washington Post*. https://www.washingtonpost.com/technology/2020/06/26/facebook-hate-speech-policies/. Accessed: July 2, 2020.

Levy, N. 2017. "The bad news about fake news." *Social Epistemology Review and Reply Collective* 6(8): 20–36.

Levy, N. 2018. "Taking responsibility for health in an epistemically polluted environment." *Theoretical Medicine and Bioethics* 39: 123–41.

Levy, N. 2019. "No-platforming and higher-order evidence, or anti-anti-no-platforming." *Journal of the American Philosophical Association* 5(4): 487–502.

Lynch, M. P. 2019. *Know-It-All Society*. New York: Liveright.

McIntyre, L. 2018. *Post-Truth*. Cambridge: MIT Press.

McIntyre, L. 2019. *The Scientific Attitude*. Cambridge: MIT Press.

McIntyre, L. 2020. "Science denial, polarisation, and arrogance." In A. Tanesini and M. P. Lynch (eds.) *Polarisation, Arrogance, and Dogmatism*. London: Routledge, 193–211.

Medina, J. 2013. *The Epistemology of Resistance*. Oxford: Oxford University Press.

Nguyen, C. T. 2020. "Echo chambers and epistemic bubbles." *Episteme* 17(2): 141–61.

Nyhan, B. and Reifler J. 2010. "When corrections fail: The persistence of political misperceptions." *Political Behavior* 32: 303–30.

Ornstein, M. (Director). 2016. *Accidental Courtesy*. Sound and Vision.

Pulido, C. M., Villarego-Carballido, B., Redondo-Sama, G. and Gomez, A. 2020. "COVID-19 infodemic: More retweets for science-based information on coronavirus than for false information." *International Sociology* 35(4): 377–92.

Rabin, R. C. and Cameron, C. 2020. "Trump falsely claims '99%' of virus cases are 'totally harmless'." *New York Times*. https://www.nytimes.com/2020/07/05/us/politics/trump-coronavirus-factcheck.html. Accessed: July 9, 2020.

Richtel, M. 2020. "WHO fights a pandemic besides coronavirus: An 'infodemic'." *New York Times*. https://www.nytimes.com/2020/02/06/health/coronavirus-misinformation-social-media.html. Accessed: July 2, 2020.

Rini, R. 2017. "Fake news and partisan epistemology." *Kennedy Institute of Ethics Journal* 27(2): E43–E64.

Rosen, G. 2020. "An update on our work to keep people informed and limit misinformation about COVID-19." *Facebook Newsroom*. https://about.fb.com/news/2020/04/covid-19-misinfo-update/. Accessed: July 2, 2020.

Roth, Y. and Pickles, N. 2020. "Updating our approach to misleading information." *Twitter blog*. https://blog.twitter.com/en_us/topics/product/2020/updating-our-approach-to-misleading-information.html. Accessed: July 2, 2020.

Silverman, C. 2016. "Viral fake election news stories outperformed real news on facebook." *Buzzfeed News*. https://www.buzzfeednews.com/article/craigsilverman/viral-fake-election-news-outperformed-real-news-on-facebook. Accessed: June 25, 2020.

Sosa, E. 2007. *A Virtue Epistemology*. Oxford: Oxford University Press.

Spring, M. 2020. "Social media firms fail to act on COVID-19 fake news." *BBC News*. https://www.bbc.com/news/technology-52903680. Accessed: June 25, 2020.

Tessman, L. 2005. *Burdened Virtues*. Oxford: Oxford University Press.

Zagzebski, L. T. 1996. *Virtues of the Mind*. Cambridge: Cambridge University Press.

28
VIRTUES AND VICES IN PUBLIC AND POLITICAL DEBATES

Alessandra Tanesini

One does not need to subscribe to deliberative approaches to democracy and its institutions to grant that the exchange of ideas and arguments in debates and discussion plays a focal role in liberal democracies. For instance, politicians debate each other in televised head-to-head encounters. The press challenges elective representatives and informs the public. Ordinary citizens discuss political issues, ask questions of politicians, and try to acquire information on political matters. Hence, debates and discussions involve heterogeneous activities by diverse actors in different contexts.

These activities can be performed well or badly. Many factors contribute to success or failure. The most important are likely to be environmental. For instance, debates when people struggle to hear each other are unlikely to be fruitful. But psychological features of the individuals and groups involved are also likely to have significant impact. This chapter provides an overview of the negative effects of cognitive biases and intellectual vices on political decision-making and debate. It seeks to counter some of the widespread scepticism about people's capacity to engage fairly, rationally, and open-mindedly with viewpoints alternative to their own. Instead, it proposes that people can adopt virtuous motivations that promote individuals' ability to argue, listen, and deliberate well.

The chapter consists of three sections. In the first, after a review of some existent empirical and philosophical literature that suggests that human beings are essentially incapable of changing their mind in response to counter-evidence, I argue that motivation makes a significant difference to individuals' ability rationally to evaluate information. The second section relies on empirical work on group deliberation to argue that the motivation to learn from others, as opposed to the desire to win arguments, promotes good quality group deliberation. The third section provides an overview of some epistemic virtues and vices crucial to the politico-epistemic activities of arguing, debating, and listening to a contrary point of view.

1 Shared biases and political deliberation

Research by political and social scientists on the epistemic quality of the political reasoning, decision-making, and debates carried out by citizens and public officials alike make grim reading. First, citizens' ignorance about political matters is widespread, extending even to basic information. Second, citizens and politicians are often in denial; they are seemingly unable to evaluate fairly views that are opposed to their own. Third, when citizens come together to deliberate as a group individuals' epistemic shortcomings are amplified resulting in worse errors, polarisation, informational cascades, and common knowledge effects. In this section, I first review some of these results, before discussing whether the in-built nature of the biases that are responsible for these epistemic shortcomings entails that any effective solution must be structural. If so, one might argue that virtue epistemology has little to contribute to addressing these problems.

The evidence that citizens express views on politically relevant factual matters that are at variance with reality is robust. Citizens in the United Kingdom, for example vastly over-estimate the number of teenage pregnancies, of immigrants and unemployed individuals.[1] There is reason to believe that these shocking levels of misinformation have multiple causes. Undoubtedly, these include political propaganda and various concerted campaigns of political spin and disinformation. However, widely shared cognitive biases are also thought to be involved. Citizens, but also officials, are biased in their evaluation of politically relevant evidence. They are motivated to accept, fairly unquestioningly, information that agrees with their pre-existing opinions, while dismissing views that do not accord with them (Lodge & Taber, 2013; Taber et al., 2008).[2] Biased evaluation of the evidence, unsurprisingly, is an important source of many widespread false political beliefs. The presence of these biases is not explained by general intellectual abilities or educational attainment but by motivated reasoning that serves to protect individuals from challenges that are perceived as identity threats (Kahan, 2013). Paradoxically, individuals whose qualifications suggest a high level of general intelligence seem to exhibit higher level of bias in processing political information.[3]

Some of the political ignorance on display beggars belief to such an extent that it requires an explanation. Two related strategies prevail among those who think people's political ignorance cannot be fully explained by individuals' shockingly bad reasoning and inability to discern genuine information from false or misleading claims. Some argue that voters are rationally ignorant (Caplan, 2006; Somin, 2016). Others claim that citizen's responses do not reflect false beliefs but are expressive of one's support for one's party or political group (Hannon, forthcoming).

Since the choices of each individual voter make almost no difference to the electoral outcome, it could be argued that it would be practically irrational to invest time and energy in becoming politically informed (Somin, 2016).[4] In addition, citizens' motivated reasoning might also be seen as a case of 'rational irrationality' (Caplan, 2006). If, as some argue, citizens' engagement with political issues is not driven by a desire to figure out the truth but to get the benefits of feeling good about oneself as a member or fan of the winning group, we would expect individuals to process information defensively with the goal of protecting one's identity-defining views from the attack of criticism (Mason, 2018). If this is right, citizens treat politics as an activity where, like a sporting competition, winning is what matters while pleasure is gained through affective identification with the winning team. Hence, although motivated reasoning might be part of the explanation of political ignorance, it might also be true that people are less ignorant than political scientists have assumed. Some of the most blatant seeming endorsements of self-evident falsities might occur because people respond to survey questions not by selecting answers that they judge to be factually accurate, but by choosing those responses that best express their partisan identities (Hannon, forthcoming).

Be that as it may, these differing interpretations of how citizens arrived at their expressed political views all point to the thought that the results are from a purely epistemic point of view largely at variance with reality. Further, and perhaps, even more depressingly, these outcomes stem from features of human psychology, such as in-group favouritism, that are universal and entrenched since they might have been adaptive in early human societies where individuals lived in small closely knit communities (Van Bavel & Pereira, 2018).

Empirical research on group deliberation provides further grounds for scepticism about the epistemic quality of decision-making following group deliberation in all areas including the political domain. There is evidence that, at least under some circumstances, groups arrive at even worse decisions than individuals working in isolation. Groups would thus suffer from several epistemic shortcomings (Sunstein, 2006). First, in cases where agents rely on heuristics to reach their decisions, group judgements amplify individuals' errors. So, for example, the effects of the availability bias are more profound on deliberating groups than on lone reasoners. Second, groups are not good at sharing information that is not commonly held prior to deliberation. Thus, they do not reap the benefits of adding to their informational basis.[5] Third, groups suffer from informational cascades where members defer to the opinion of the majority, even though that opinion might have been formed in ignorance of information known only to the deferential members. Fourth, deliberating groups, especially when they primarily include like-minded individuals tend to polarise (Sunstein, 2009).

Polarisation can take many forms. It might consists in the adoption of more extreme and opposing beliefs among members of different groups or it might instead mostly consist in increased hostility and animosity directed towards an outgroup (Mason, 2018). There are also differing accounts of how polarisation in all its guises occurs. One theory holds that when deliberating with others who share one's views, one acquires novel evidence in their favour (Sunstein, 2009, ch. 2). Undoubtedly there is some truth in this account but it cannot be the whole story because it cannot explain why individuals end up holding more extreme views (rather than becoming more certain of their pre-existing opinions) and why the phenomenon occurs despite the absence of discussion. Another account holds that what drives polarisation is the desire to identify with the group. Since individuals who hold more extreme viewpoints are more vocal in debates and more prominent in the group, other members' desire to identify pushes them towards becoming more like those prominent individuals who also happen to hold the more extreme points of view. In short, polarisation occurs as a result of the need to affirm one's group identity resulting in a more entrenched commitment to a more extreme version of one's pre-existing views (for an overview, see Talisse, 2019, ch. 4).

These considerations raise grave epistemic concerns about the quality of group deliberations. While the results on which they rely are robust, they can be misleading because they hide the fact that there are equally robust results that, in other circumstances, deliberating groups outperform lone reasoners (De Dreu et al., 2008; Mercier & Sperber, 2017). I return to this topic below when I consider what it might take to deliberate well with others.

One of the lessons that can be drawn from the prevalence of biased searching, dissemination and evaluation of information resulting in epistemically bad political judgements is that human minds are naturally vicious (Olin & Doris, 2014).[6] Human cognitive processing in any domain, according to this view, is highly unreliable. Importantly, contra Samuelson and Church (2015) unreliability does not merely affect fast associative thinking but is equally prevalent when people reflect or deliberate. In short, motivated reasoning would not be limited to heuristic or automatic cognitive processes but would extend to deliberate reflection (Kahan et al., 2017).[7]

Two further pessimistic conclusions follow from this lesson. First, since these cognitive defects are in-built and arguably fixed, we cannot eradicate them. Instead, we need to look at developing structural solutions designed to minimise their impact (Anderson, 2012). Second, virtue epistemology in both its reliabilist and responsibilist incarnations has little to offer when searching for strategies to ameliorate the situation. Reflection, de-biasing, self-cultivation, and virtue habituation seem to be largely unattainable (Ahlström, 2013; Boult, forthcoming; Kornblith, 2012).

I argue below that these conclusions are premature. In what follows I begin to cast doubt on this bleak picture by drawing attention to evidence that shows that individual psychological differences can make a difference to the epistemic quality of individual and group reasoning and deliberation.

2 Motivation and group behaviour

In the previous section I have offered some empirical evidence that when people discuss matters in a group the epistemic quality of the outcome of these discussions is often poor. These bad outcomes would be attributable to features of human cognition that are so entrenched that nothing can be done to eradicate them. This evidence implies that belief in the epistemic benefits of the rational exchanges of ideas is largely misguided. In this section I explore some of the ways in which scepticism about the epistemic value of deliberation can be countered. I do not take issues with those who claim that group political debate often leads to unsatisfactory outcomes. My criticism is addressed to diagnoses of poor performance that attribute it to facts about human psychology that are so entrenched to be essentially hardwired. Instead, I show that the factors responsible for poor performance are neither universal nor unchangeable.

Deliberation is usually characterised as the exchange of views through reasoned argumentation that aims at convergence onto the truth by means of rational persuasion. The thought that the free exchange of ideas leads to the formation of, and renewed commitment to, true beliefs is due to Mill (1974) who aptly argued that discussion promotes believing the truth because it forces one to fully articulate the reasons for one's beliefs and to respond with reasons to contrary viewpoints. Mill's argument though is premised on the assumption that people would be receptive to reason. He noted that the debaters themselves might be too invested to be capable of persuasion, but he thought that even heated debates might nevertheless be of epistemic benefit to an audience capable of rational reflection. Section 1 has cast doubt on human's ability to respond to reasons and thus seemingly undermined the epistemic value of deliberation. More strongly, it might raise the suspicion that deliberation is epistemically dis-valuable since people's views are often more accurate if they avoid listening to debates and engaging in political collective deliberation.

The cognitive psychological research presented in Section 1 is designed to elide individual psychological difference to report aggregate results about statistical relations. Crudely put, it tells us that most people do not listen to reason, suffer from confirmation and my-side bias, and when discussing matters with others they polarise. Contrary to some of the lessons drawn not only by philosophers but also by the psychologists and political scientists themselves, this evidence cannot establish that these shortcomings are universal or unshakeable.

Further, as a matter of fact, the evidence on these matters is much more complex than it might appear at first. In reality, some groups polarise after deliberation and some do not. Some groups reach poor decisions, and some make excellent ones. This variety in the epistemic quality of performance is not limited to simple factual decisions but it is also present in group political deliberations (Karpowitz & Mendelberg, 2018; Myers & Mendelberg, 2013 for overviews). The variety of results is so stark to suggest that the main determinants of epistemic quality are not hardwired, or at least not near universal psychological characteristics. Rather, the most significant predictors of deliberative behaviours must be variables that are situational and/or that pertain to the psychological differences among the individuals involved. There is abundant evidence that both factors are crucial (see De Dreu et al., 2008 for an overview). My interest here, however, lies with psychological individual differences. I mention two kinds.

First, people differ from each other in their dispositional needs for closure and for cognition. Those who are high in their dispositional need for closure desire to reach quickly an unambiguous conclusion. Hence, when undecided on a topic or issue they tend to seize on information and then to become resistant to persuasion once they have frozen on their position. Everyone to some extent exhibits this need to close down issues. Further, everyone exhibits it more or less depending on situational pressures. Nevertheless, some individuals are more deeply marked by these tendencies in a broader range of circumstances. Thus, they are said to be high in dispositional need for closure (Kruglanski, 2004). Other people are high on a dispositional need for cognition. These individuals enjoy thinking through issues and finding out a lot of information that they assess carefully (Cacioppo & Petty, 1982). Research on groups' negotiation indicates that the presence of individuals who are high in the need for cognition is predictive of better joint outcomes where both parties get more of what they want (De Dreu et al., 2008). There is also evidence that enjoying cognition and being curious to learn reduce bias and polarisation when reasoning specifically on political issues (Kahan et al., 2017).

Second, individuals differ from each other in their motivations. Research shows that motivational factors are crucial in determining the epistemic quality of conclusions reached through deliberation. When deliberating or debating individuals might be highly epistemically motivated or have low motivation (De Dreu et al., 2008). When his epistemic motivation is high, the individual is prone to acquire and reflectively to evaluate information. Thus, high epistemic motivation is proportional to the need for cognition and inversely related to the need for closure. When her epistemic motivation is low, the person tends to reach a conclusion quickly often by relying on heuristics (Chen et al., 1999). Individuals' levels of epistemic motivation vary depending on the circumstances – e.g., urgency- and personal factors – e.g., dispositional need for closure. High epistemic motivation leads people to engage in reflection. But reflection can be highly biased so it should not be assumed that higher epistemic motivation is equivalent to a disposition to form more accurate beliefs.

Another set of motivations, orthogonal to epistemic motivation, are also determinant of the epistemic outcome of group deliberation. Some individuals when engaging in a group task are mostly concerned with the effects of the activity and its outcomes on themselves, while others are mostly concerned with the effects on everyone. The first family of pro-self motivations includes, for example, the desire to win an argument at all costs, or to get the most for oneself in a negotiation. The second group of motivations are pro-social. They include the desire to get along, to cooperate, to get the best joint outcome.

In the context of group deliberations or debates between dyads the interactions between individuals with differing motivations lead to outcomes of different epistemic quality. In short, when epistemic motivation is low, and individuals' motivations are pro-self, group discussions and decision-making are characterised by inaction and free-riding problems. Initial disagreements lead to vetoing and stalemates. When epistemic motivation is high groups composed by pro-self-motivated individuals are good at brainstorming, but are poor at collective decision-making and deliberation. They promote adversarial debates and thus the presentation of arguments and objections. However, highly epistemically motivated individuals whose motivations are pro-self are disposed to lie, spin, and mislead to win the argument (De Dreu et al., 2008, p. 34). They also engage in behaviour designed to shut their opponents down.

Groups composed by individuals whose motivations are pro-social also have distinctive characteristics. When epistemic motivation is low these groups tend to compromise too quickly; their members tend to mutually enhance, and to share only information that is already widely known. They tend to self-silence when they are inclined to disagree with the majority's opinion. However, when epistemic motivation is high, these groups perform well. Members of these groups pay attention to each other ideas. Discussion is information-driven with accuracy as its aim (De Dreu et al., 2008). In conclusion, the best performing groups in collective deliberation are, everything else being equal, those where members have high epistemic and pro-social motivations. Even when epistemic motivation is low, groups with socially motivated individuals outperform those whose motivation is pro-self.[8] These results strongly suggest that motivations make a difference to group performance. Individuals if they can be suitably motivated are capable of deliberating reasonably well, of listening to each other's arguments, and of evaluating these accurately.[9]

This research also chimes with recent studies of the development of children's ability to argue. Fisher and Keil (2016) have discovered that initially children have an arguing-to-learn mindset. They are cooperative, they trust other people and ask questions. At a later stage in adulthood, people start arguing to win. Fisher and Keil claim that this mindset is mostly counterproductive from an epistemic point of view. In conditions of low epistemic motivation, these individuals engage in spurious attacks of their opponents, using *ad hominem* argumentation. When epistemic motivation is high, those who are driven by the desire to win the argument engage with the opposite point of view, but are prone to evaluate it in a biased way.

Finally, they note that it is possible for adults to become less invested in the argument and to be motivated to learn. When group members are motivated to learn, they become less tribal and more able to acknowledge that there might be some truth in the viewpoint of their opponents (Fisher et al., 2018). Their collective deliberations outperform those of individuals and of groups whose members are driven by the desire to win. I think of this motivation to learn as a combination of both high epistemic and pro-social motivations since individuals who have it are keen to acquire and evaluate information but are also cooperative (as opposed to competitive) since they listen to others in order to learn from them.

One might object that although it is possible to be motivated to learn about non politicised matters, the adoption of this stance would be practically impossible in the political realm. I grant that the current political climate in many nations is a cause for concern. Nevertheless, people are able to hear the other side when they are appropriately motivated (Mutz, 2006). Importantly, there is also evidence that some people display the appropriate motivations including curiosity, the desire to learn, and a dispositional need for cognition when discussing political matters (Fisher et al., 2018; Kahan et al., 2017).

One might further object that even though some individuals are appropriately motivated, it might be impossible for others to acquire these motivations and thus improvement is beyond their reach (Ahlstrom-Vij, 2013). In response I note that there is evidence that people want to change their personalities and become, for instance, more open to experience (Hudson et al., 2019).[10] Clearly, simply wishing to change is not enough to effect change. However, research has shown that people can voluntarily bring about these changes through setting for themselves relevant goals (Hudson et al., 2019). This is a process of habituation that is akin to virtue cultivation (Snow, 2010).

3 Virtues and vices of argumentation, advocacy, and deliberation

Many debates and deliberations are pointless because the participants are only interested in point scoring. The argument so far has shown that this sorry state of affairs is not inevitable. Debates and discussions can be epistemically beneficial because it is possible for people to improve. One avenue for improvement is the development of virtues through work on motivation within contexts that offer the opportunity for such work. For simplicity sake, I sidestep debates about the nature of virtues here and merely presume that virtues are character traits and skills that promote the epistemic ends of debate and discussion including understanding, the full articulation of reasons and arguments, the dissemination of information, the reduction of epistemic injustices and convergence on the truth. These traits and skills either include good epistemic motivations or have been cultivated through habituation or repeated practice sustained by good epistemic motivations.

Argumentation virtue theorists have offered a number of distinct candidates for the virtues that would be characteristic of good arguers and deliberators. Aberdein (2010), for instance, has defended the view that the virtuous arguer is excellent at disseminating truths, as opposed to merely acquiring them for herself. Thus, partly borrowing from Cohen (2005), Aberdein identifies four broad attitudes characteristic of those who articulate, and respond to, arguments well. These are: willingness to engage in argumentation, to listen to others, to modify one's positions, to question the obvious (Aberdein, 2010, p. 175). Each of these four attitudes is associated with characteristic virtues such as intellectual courage, empathy and open-mindedness, intellectual humility, and perseverance. Opposed to these clusters of virtues lie distinctive vices of excess and deficiency. Thus, in Cohen's (2005) terminology the proper willingness to engage in argumentation is flanked by the vices of being an Argument Provocateur who is too willing to engage in argument even when the situation makes it inappropriate and a Quietist who fails to engage. Willingness to listen is opposed by deaf dogmatism and concessionism, while willingness to question is contrasted with the disposition to defend what no one questions (typical of the Unassuring Assurer) and the tendency to believe uncritically (characteristic of the Eager Believer) (cf., Aberdein, 2010, p. 174).

There are also interesting lines of convergence between work in virtue argumentative theory and psychological research on arguing to win or to learn. Discussions about the role of adversariality in debates are longstanding and unresolved (Dutilh Novaes, 2014).[11] More recently, Stevens (2016) has defended the view that it takes practical wisdom to appreciate which debates require the virtues of adversariality and which those of cooperation. She proposes that adversariality is epistemically beneficial when debaters already understand the other's point of view and their arguments are fully articulated. However, when individuals are still trying to figure out the best way of making their point or there is reason to fear that the debaters do not really understand the other's position, then the motive of cooperation and its attendant argumentative virtues are best at promoting the dissemination of true beliefs. Important among these would be the virtues attendant to treating the argument as a joint project (Cohen & Miller, 2016). At times, this joint activity would require that arguments be subjected to intense scrutiny. In other circumstances, however, the success of the joint project demands the deployment of techniques of argument repair designed to help the person with whom we disagree to develop the best version of the argument they wish to defend (Hundleby, 2019).

Good arguers also display the virtues of the good listener. Being willing to learn is essential to acquire the skills required of a good listener (Cohen, 2019). These skills include the corrective virtue of testimonial justice that consists in the ability not to let identity prejudice colour one's assessment of the credibility of subordinated individuals (Fricker, 2007).

The virtues that promote the ability to engage in debates, improve the standards of argumentation, and listen well overlap with those character traits identified by Aikin and Clanton (2010) as group deliberative virtues. These are defined as those traits and skills that promote good argumentation but that also facilitate, by different means, group synergy understood as capturing all cases where the knowledge or understanding achieved by a group outstrips what would be gained by a mere process of aggregation. Aikin and Clanton supply an extensive list that includes wit (as opposed to being a dullard or a buffoon), friendliness (as opposed to flattery and quarrelsomeness), but also collectedness (as opposed to excessive anger or excessive detachment), courage, humility, and sincerity. Several of these are not exclusively virtues of collective deliberation. Rather, they might be included in generic lists comprising ethical and intellectual virtues. Aikin and Clayton's work highlights their distinctive contribution to deliberation.

I have suggested that the willingness to learn from others is essential to good performance in debate and deliberation. It is therefore not surprising that intellectual arrogance has been singled out as an especially dangerous vice for deliberative democracy. While this vice has heterogeneous manifestations, it is best understood as a defensive attitude that leads one to be so invested in one's beliefs that any challenge to them feels like a personal attack. This defensiveness leads to a tendency to presume that one's pronouncements must be correct because they are one's own (Tanesini, 2016, 2018, 2019). This attitude is also manifested in a presumption that one's point of view cannot be improved by others (Lynch, 2018a, 2018b). In short, epistemically arrogant people are driven by the desire to win and are unwilling to learn from others. Arrogant individuals have a corrosive effect on debate and deliberation because they do not take themselves to be answerable to others for their claims and do not treat others as epistemic peers but are disrespectful of them (Lynch, 2018a, 2018b; Tanesini, 2016).

In conclusion, I have shown that pessimistic conclusions about people's ability to deliberate and debate well are premature. Spectacular ignorance, biased evaluation, point scoring are avoidable. I have argued that individuals' motivations make a difference to the epistemic quality of deliberation and debate, and that people can improve their performance by acquiring the motivation to learn from others. Finally, I have provided an overview of some of the intellectual virtues and vices of argumentation and deliberation. This list of traits is not intended to be exhaustive, but it illustrates the pivotal role of epistemic arrogance as one of the vices that is most corrosive of democratic deliberation.[12]

Notes

1 Somin (2016) offers a review of evidence of widespread political ignorance in the USA. IPSOS Mori in collaboration with Kings' College London and the Royal Statistical Society conducted surveys in 14 countries, each revealing shocking levels of political ignorance. See http://ipsos. com/ipsos-mori/en-uk/perceptions-are-not-reality-things-world-gets-wrong for a summary of the results.

2 These effects are not limited to the political domain. Human beings are motivated in every area of enquiry to seek evidence in favour of their views that they accept uncritically, while actively searching for counter-evidence for what they disagree with (Mercier & Sperber, 2017; Nickerson, 1998).

3 See, for instance, the 2008 Pew Research Centre surveys showing that among Republicans individuals with higher educational qualifications were more likely to be climate sceptics than their less educated counterparts. For a summary of findings see https://www.people-press. org/2008/05/08/a-deeper-partisan-divide-over-global-warming/.

4 There are other reasons to value the making of an informed choice that are not wholly dependent on its influence on the final outcome. I cannot address these issues here.

5 That said, at least in idealised conditions it is not always optimal for a community of enquirers motivated by the truth to share all the available information. See Zollman (2013) for a review of some of these issues applied to enquiry on purely factual matters.

6 Cognitive vice in this context is broadly equivalent to biased, in the sense of unreliable, cognition. These are vices because they systematically obstruct or block the achievement of knowledge. See Cassam (2019) for this definition of epistemic vice. As a matter of fact, these cognitive biases might not qualify as vices in Cassam's view if they do not reflect badly on their possessors.

7 Kahneman (2012) offers a good introduction to so-called dual processing accounts of cognition.

8 That said, there is a risk that in groups of mixed motivations cooperative individuals are misled by others whose motivations are pro-self.

9 I hasten to add that adopting a conciliatory stance might not always be desirable. In addition, the ability to hear the other side might also lead people to become less involved in politics (Mutz, 2006).

10 This is a personality trait positively associated with high need for cognition (Cacioppo et al., 1996).

11 Adversariality is not the same as the motivation to argue to win in so far as the latter is manifested in spinning and point scoring to prevail.

12 I would like to thank Jeroen De Ridder, Michael Hannon, and an anonymous referee for their helpful comments.

References

Aberdein, A. (2010). Virtue in Argument. *Argumentation, 24*(2), 165–79.

Ahlstrom-Vij, K. (2013). Why We Cannot Rely on Ourselves for Epistemic Improvement. *Philosophical Issues, 23*(Epistemic Agency), 276–96.

Ahlström, K. (2013). *Epistemic Paternalism: A Defence*. Basingstoke and New York: Palgrave Macmillan.

Aikin, S. F., & Clanton, C. J. (2010). Developing Group-Deliberative Virtues. *Journal of Applied Philosophy, 27*(4), 409–24. doi:10.1111/j.1468-5930.2010.00494.x.

Anderson, E. (2012). Epistemic Justice as a Virtue of Social Institutions. *Social Epistemology, 26*(2), 163–74. doi:10.1080/02691728.2011.652211.

Boult, C. (forthcoming). The (Virtue) Epistemology of Political Ignorance. *American Philosophical Quarterly*. https://philpapers.org/rec/BOUTVE

Cacioppo, J. T., & Petty, R. E. (1982). The Need for Cognition. *Journal of Personality and Social Psychology, 42*, 116–31.

Cacioppo, J. T., Petty, R. E., Feinstein, J. A., & Jarvis, W. B. G. (1996). Dispositional Differences in Cognitive Motivation: The Life and Times of Individuals Varying in Need for Cognition. *Psychological Bulletin, 119*(2), 197–253.

Caplan, B. D. (2006). *The Myth of the Rational Voter: Why Democracies Choose Bad Policies*. Princeton, NJ: Princeton University Press.

Cassam, Q. (2019). *Vices of the Mind*. Oxford: Oxford University Press.

Chen, S., Duckworth, K., & Chaiken, S. (1999). Motivated Heuristic and Systematic Processing. *Psychological Inquiry, 10*(1), 44–49. doi:10.1207/s15327965pli1001_6.

Cohen, D. H. (2005). Arguments that Backfire. In D. Hitchcock & D. Farr (Eds.), *The Uses of Argument* (pp. 58–65). Hamilton: OSSA.

Cohen, D. H. (2019). Argumentative Virtues as Conduits for Reason's Causal Efficacy: Why the Practice of Giving Reasons Requires that We Practice Hearing Reasons. *Topoi, 38*(4), 711–18. doi:10.1007/s11245-015-9364-x.

Cohen, D. H., & Miller, G. (2016). What Virtue Argumentation Theory Misses: The Case of Compathetic Argumentation. *Topoi, 35*(2), 451–60. doi:10.1007/s11245-015-9334-3.

De Dreu, C. K. W., Nijstad, B. A., & van Knippenberg, D. (2008). Motivated Information Processing in Group Judgment and Decision Making. *Personality and Social Psychology Review, 12*(1), 22–49. doi:10.1177/1088868307304092.

Dutilh Novaes, C. (2014, 19 May). Adversariality and Maximizing True Beliefs, New APPS: Art, Politics, Philosophy, Science. Retrieved from http://www.newappsblog.com/2014/05/adversariality-and-maximizing-true-beliefs.html.

Fisher, M., & Keil, F. C. (2016). The Trajectory of Argumentation and Its Multifaceted Functions. In F. Paglieri (Ed.), *The Psychology of Argument: Cognitive Approaches to Argumentation and Persuasion* (pp. 347–62). London: College Publications.

Fisher, M., Knobe, J., Strickland, B., & Keil, F. C. (2018). The Tribalism of Truth. *Scientific American, 318*(2), 50–53. doi:10.1038/scientificamerican0218-50.

Fricker, M. (2007). *Epistemic Injustice: Power & the Ethics of Knowing.* Oxford: Clarendon.

Hannon, M. (Forthcoming) Disagreement or Badmouthing? The Role of Expressive Discourse in Politics. In E. Elizabeth Edenberg & M. Hannon (Eds), *Political Epistemology.* Oxford: Oxford University Press.

Hudson, N. W., Briley, D. A., Chopik, W. J., & Derringer, J. (2019). You Have to Follow Through: Attaining Behavioral Change Goals Predicts Volitional Personality Change. *Journal of Personality and Social Psychology, 117*(4), 839–57. doi:10.1037/pspp0000221.

Hundleby, C. (2019, 3 June). Argument Repair, Open for Debate. Retrieved from https://blogs.cardiff.ac.uk/openfordebate/2019/06/03/argument-repair/.

Kahan, D. M. (2013). Ideology, Motivated Reasoning, and Cognitive Reflection. *Judgment and Decision Making, 8*(4), 407–24.

Kahan, D. M., Landrum, A., Carpenter, K., Helft, L., & Hall Jamieson, K. (2017). Science Curiosity and Political Information Processing. *Political Psychology, 38*, 179–99. doi:10.1111/pops.12396.

Kahneman, D. (2012). *Thinking, Fast and Slow.* London: Penguin.

Karpowitz, C., & Mendelberg, T. (2018). The Political Psychology of Deliberation. In A. Bächtiger, J. S. Dryzek, J. J. Mansbridge, & M. E. Warren (Eds.), *The Oxford Handbook of Deliberative Democracy* (pp. 598–621). Oxford: Oxford University Press.

Kornblith, H. (2012). *On Reflection.* Oxford: Oxford University Press.

Kruglanski, A. W. (2004). *The Psychology of Closed Mindedness.* Hove: Psychology Press.

Lodge, M., & Taber, C. S. (2013). *The Rationalizing Voter.* Cambridge and New York: Cambridge University Press.

Lynch, M. P. (2018a). Arrogance, Truth and Public Discourse. *Episteme, 15*(3 (2017 Episteme Conference)), 283–96. doi:10.1017/epi.2018.23.

Lynch, M. P. (2018b). Epistemic Arrogance and the Value of Political Dissent. In C. R. Johnson (Ed.), *Voicing Dissent: The Ethics and Epistemology of Making Disagreement Public* (pp. 129–39). New York and Abingdon: Routledge.

Mason, L. (2018). *Uncivil Agreement.* Chicago, IL: Chicago University Press.

Mercier, H., & Sperber, D. (2017). *The Enigma of Reason.* Cambridge, MA: Harvard University Press.

Mill, J. S. (1974). *On Liberty.* Edited with an introduction by Gertrude Himmelfarb. Harmondsworth: Penguin.

Mutz, D. C. (2006). *Hearing the Other Side: Deliberative versus Participatory Democracy.* Cambridge and New York: Cambridge University Press.

Myers, C. D., & Mendelberg, T. (2013). Political Deliberation. In L. Huddy, D. O. Sears, & J. S. Levy (Eds.), *The Oxford Handbook of Political Psychology* (2nd ed., pp. 699–735). Oxford: Oxford University Press.

Nickerson, R. S. (1998). Confirmation Bias: A Ubiquitous Phenomenon in Many Guises. *Review of General Psychology, 2*(2), 175–220. doi:10.1037/1089-2680.2.2.175.

Olin, L., & Doris, J. M. (2014). Vicious minds. *Philosophical Studies, 168*(3), 665–92. doi:10.1007/s11098-013-0153-3.

Samuelson, P. L., & Church, I. M. (2015). When Cognition Turns Vicious: Heuristics and Biases in Light of Virtue Epistemology. *Philosophical Psychology, 28*(8), 1095–1113. doi:10.1080/09515089.2014.904197.

Snow, N. E. (2010). *Virtue as Social Intelligence: An Empirically Grounded Theory.* New York: Routledge.

Somin, I. (2016). *Democracy and Political Ignorance: Why Smaller Government Is Smarter* (2nd ed.). Stanford, CA: Stanford Law Books, an imprint of Stanford University Press.

Stevens, K. (2016). The Virtuous Arguer: One Person, Four Roles. *Topoi, 35*(2), 375–83. doi:10.1007/s11245-015-9309-4.

Sunstein, C. R. (2006). *Infotopia: How Many Minds Produce Knowledge.* Oxford: Oxford University Press.

Sunstein, C. R. (2009). *Going to Extremes: How Like Minds Unite and Divide.* Oxford and New York: Oxford University Press.

Taber, C. S., Cann, D., & Kucsova, S. (2008). The Motivated Processing of Political Arguments. *Political Behavior, 31*(2), 137–55. doi:10.1007/s11109-008-9075-8.

Talisse, R. B. (2019). *Overdoing Democracy: Why We Must Put Politics in Its Place.* New York: Oxford University Press.

Tanesini, A. (2016). I – 'Calm Down, Dear': Intellectual Arrogance, Silencing and Ignorance. *Aristotelian Society Supplementary Volume, 90*(1), 71–92. doi:10.1093/arisup/akw011.

Tanesini, A. (2018). Arrogance, Anger and Debate. *Symposion: Theoretical and Applied Inquiries in Philosophy and Social Sciences, 5*(2 (Special Issue on Skeptical Problems in Political Epistemology, edited by Scott Aikin and Tempest Henning)), 213–27. doi:10.5840/symposion20185217.

Tanesini, A. (2019). Reducing Arrogance in Public Debate. In J. Arthur (Ed.), *Virtues in the Public Sphere* (pp. 28–38). London: Routledge.

Van Bavel, J. J., & Pereira, A. (2018). The Partisan Brain: An Identity-Based Model of Political Belief. *Trends in Cognitive Sciences, 22*(3), 213–24. doi:10.1016/j.tics.2018.01.004.

Zollman, K. J. S. (2013). Network Epistemology: Communication in Epistemic Communities. *Philosophy Compass, 8*(1), 15–27. doi:10.1111/j.1747-9991.2012.00534.x.

29

VICES OF THE PRIVILEGED AND VIRTUES OF THE OPPRESSED IN EPISTEMIC GROUP DYNAMICS[1]

José Medina

1 Introduction

In *Epistemology of Resistance* (2013) I developed a critical epistemology of the oppressed, that is, a critical epistemology that, far from indulging in ideal conditions and ideal theory, was explicitly designed to apply to actual social contexts under conditions of oppression and to provide some guidance for resisting epistemic oppression (i.e. the exclusion, marginalization, or unfair treatment in epistemic practices). In the epistemology of the oppressed I previously developed (2013) I focused too heavily on how *individual* members of oppressed groups can exhibit specific forms of epistemic virtues that are grounded in their experiences of oppression, as well as on how *individual* members of privileged groups can exhibit specific forms of epistemic vices that are grounded in their privileged life sheltered from exposure to certain realities and experiences. Although I heavily qualified my claims about the epistemic virtues often found in the standpoints of the oppressed and the epistemic vices often found in the standpoints of the privileged, the *individual* subject remained the locus to which epistemic virtues and vices were to be ascribed, and the epistemic agency involved in the cultivation and exercise of those virtues and vices was thought of as the epistemic agency of *individuals*. By contrast, in my more recent work and in this chapter, I shift the focus to collectives as the proper locus and address issues of collective epistemic agency in which individual members of the relevant groups simply partake. The individual and the collective levels of epistemic standpoint and agency are of course deeply intertwined and their separation is always somewhat artificial, so while addressing one level we are always addressing the other if only indirectly. Just like my previous work focused on the individual level but was not individualistic, my recent and ongoing analyses have a collective focus but are not collectivistic in any reductive way.

In what follows I will focus on the epistemic virtues and vices of collectives that arise and operate in contexts of oppression. More specifically, I will focus on collective epistemic vices that can be associated with privilege in contrast with collective epistemic virtues developed by oppressed or mixed groups. In Section 2 I will discuss how the epistemic vice of critical insensitivity with respect to racial bias takes different forms as an individual vice and as a group vice. In Section 3 I will further develop the distinction between individual epistemic vices and vicious epistemic group functioning by elucidating how an epistemic group vice associated with privilege can be detected in publics that function as *echo chambers*. Finally, in Section 4, I will suggest ways in which we can resist and counter epistemically vicious group agency through what I call *epistemic activism* and the *epistemic empowerment of the oppressed*.

2 The insensitivity of privilege and the epistemic lucidity of the oppressed in group dynamics

In this section my focus will be on groups or collectives. I will not talk about the epistemic virtues of the privileged or the epistemic vices of the oppressed in an individualistic way, but rather, as they can be ascribed to an entire group or collective, however these virtues and vices are distributed among the individual members of the group or collective in question. Since what I am most interested in here is particular (i.e. epistemically vicious and virtuous) forms of epistemic *agency*, my focus will be on the group's collective epistemic agency, however this agency happens to be exercised and whatever form those groups happen to take.[2] I will view *groups* or *collectives* as comprising very diverse forms of groupings and social formations ranging from highly structured and rigidly organized groups (such as the Republican party) to diffused and changing networks or publics (such as Fox News' viewership).

The significance of groups for epistemic behavior in general and for epistemic virtues and vices in particular cannot be overstated (see Tanesini's chapter in this volume). Ample evidence in cognitive science[3] has shown that individuals very often perform cognitive tasks differently by themselves and within a group; and their epistemic behavior can vary quite dramatically from one group setting to another group setting. In what follows I want to call attention to two crucial factors that prompt or inhibit epistemically virtuous or vicious behavior in group settings: (1) the composition of the group, and (2) the groups dynamics and epistemic norms of the group. Let's consider an interesting case study in social psychology that can help us distinguish between the epistemic vice of critical insensitivity to racial bias in individuals and in groups.

In "Race and the Decision Making of Juries" (2007), Samuel Sommers presents powerful evidence for how *context-specific white ignorance of racism* operates at the level of joint thinking or group cognition in jury deliberations. Sommers recorded the deliberations of 29 mock juries after being shown a video of a trial of a black defendant accused of sexual assault. Half the juries were all-white; the other half included both white and black members. Concerns about racism playing a role in the case were raised more frequently in the racially diverse juries than in the all-white juries. What is also interesting is that critical sensitivity to racism was expressed not only by black jurors but also by white jurors in the racially diverse juries. In fact, white jurors in racially diverse juries were more likely than black jurors to raise the issue of racism (Sommers 2007: 605–6). As Elizabeth Anderson puts it in her elucidations of Sommers' study, "the presence of blacks on the jury may have activated whites' knowledge of antiblack racism in the criminal justice process, while this remained latent in all-white juries" (Forthcoming: 15). Not only does the evidence strongly suggests that the presence of non-white subjects triggers white jurors' critical sensitivity with respect to racism, but it also strongly suggests that the presence of a white homogeneous composition—that is, the exclusive presence of racially privileged subjects—in the jury inhibits expressions of such critical sensitivity:

> every single time whites mentioned racism in all-white juries, other jurors called them out for raising the issue, claiming that this was irrelevant to the task at hand […]. By

contrast, in racially diverse juries, whites and blacks alike actively considered racism as a possibly relevant factor in the trial. (Ibid.)

In her elucidation of Sommers' study, Elizabeth Anderson emphasizes that the results of the study have to be understood in terms of *group belief* rather than in terms of *individual belief*:

> The jurors in all-white juries were not individually ignorant of the existence of anti-black racism. [...] Instead, jurors in all-white juries were enforcing a norm of white ignorance about racism, a group-level lack of belief—a joint determination to act, as a body of white people, in ignorance of racism. (Ibid.)

This is further supported by the evidence that in racially diverse juries white jurors had no problem in raising the issue of racism—doing so in fact more frequently than black jurors—and participated actively in deliberating about the role of racial bias in the case. As Anderson points out, in racially diverse juries the norms of white ignorance did not apply; and, we could add, a norm of critical sensitivity with respect to racism did apply and carried force for all jurors, especially white jurors. The epistemic malfunctioning of the all-white juries is to be attributed to two factors that converge in triggering the epistemic vice of critical insensitivity: the homogeneous composition of the group, and the skewed epistemic norms of the group.

First, the racial composition of the jury had a deep impact on the epistemic quality of the deliberative behavior exhibited. For Anderson, the group composition determines group belief and knowledge: "Racially diverse groups know some things that all-white groups do not" (ibid.). However, I do not think it is so much a matter of belief and knowledge, but a matter of epistemic behavior and epistemic virtue, that is, the exercise of an epistemic skill such as critical sensitivity. Indeed, if it were simply a lack of knowledge that characterized the epistemic deficiency of the all-white jury, the fitting response to raising the issue of racial bias would be simply to ask the speaker who raised the issue to explain it, but the actual response was to dismiss the issue as irrelevant out of hand. What the all-white jury seemed to lack as a group was the relevant critical sensitivity in that area and the ability to enrich the group discussion and improve the quality of the deliberations by seriously considering racial bias. What the racially diverse composition of the juries adds to those groups is not simply knowledge in the sense of more items to add in the repertoire of group beliefs (individual white jurors prove to be perfectly capable of adding those items); rather, it is a practical knowledge or sensitivity, a skill or practical ability that we can appreciate in virtuous epistemic functioning, in virtuous deliberation. This is what I call *epistemic lucidity*[4] with respect to racial bias, which, the empirical evidence suggests, is only present in racially diverse groups but not in homogeneous, racially privileged groups.

Second, what distinguishes all-white juries from racially diverse juries is the implicit epistemic norms that shape their group behavior. For Anderson, the normative backdrop of the white ignorance of the all-white jury consists in a norm that skews the assimilation of evidence: "group-level ignorance of R is instantiated by a group norm against entering evidence for R into group discussion" (ibid.). This assimilation bias filters out evidence that can enrich the deliberative process. Although I do not disagree that this assimilation bias is operating in the group dynamics of the all-white juries, it cannot be the whole story since considerations of racial bias were not fully filtered out and indeed entered the discussion even though infrequently. Besides an evidential norm, what is operating here is also a relevance norm: a group norm of relevance that deems considerations of racism irrelevant and thus inhibits the exercise of critical sensitivity in that area. This is a norm that is very hard to maintain in the presence of racially oppressed subjects whose communities have daily experiences of discrimination in the US criminal justice system and have developed epistemic lucidity in this area. But, as the evidence suggests, the epistemic and discursive norms that keep racism out of consideration are not hard to maintain in a group homogeneously composed of racially privileged subjects. The epistemic vice of critical insensitivity with respect to racism exhibited by such a group is clearly tied to having been sheltered from racial bias and having the *privilege* of being inattentive to racism, a luxury that most people of color cannot have in their daily lives. Racially diverse groups bring with them not only a richer repertoire of experiences of racial oppression, but also the possibility of cultivating critical attentiveness to racial bias and the virtuous skill of factoring in such bias in deliberations.

There are groups that have epistemically vicious normative structures, groups whose epistemic and discursive norms are set up so that normative problems such as racial biases are left unexamined. Such groups operate as *echo chambers* with respect to the issue of racism and are responsible for propagating a vicious sensibility that is resistant to learning and to the development of epistemic virtues such as criticality and open-mindedness. I follow here C. Thi Nguyen (2020) in his characterization of the phenomenon of *echo chambers* as distinct from the phenomenon of *epistemic bubbles* (see also Gunn's chapter in this volume). An epistemic bubble can be defined as a closed epistemic environment that prevents exposure to certain kinds of information, evidence, and reasons. By contrast, an echo chamber is an epistemic environment in which subjects lack the capacity for virtuous listening and for learning from certain kinds of information, evidence, and reasons. While epistemic bubbles are characterized by the exclusion of certain voices and perspectives, what characterizes echo chambers is the highly precarious inclusion of and extremely dysfunctional engagement with—indeed, typically the vilification of—certain voices and perspectives. Clearly it is echo chambers, rather than epistemic bubbles, that present the most serious epistemic challenge since it calls for more than the inclusion of voices and perspectives, more than simply expanding available forms of information, evidence, and reasons. In fact, echo chambers do contain exposure to the voices and perspectives with which it maintains a dysfunctional relation, but it is the wrong kind of exposure, a biased exposure intended exclusively to stigmatize those voices and perspectives and render them intrinsically untrustworthy in the eyes of the participants in the echo chamber. Unlike the bursting of an epistemic bubble which can be achieved through more epistemic exposure and inclusion, the overcoming of an echo chamber requires the deactivation of epistemic resistances or vices and the instilling of epistemic virtues and adequate sensibilities. As Nguyen puts it, "Mere exposure to evidence can shatter an epistemic bubble, but may actually reinforce an echo chamber. [...] Echo chambers are much harder to escape. [...] Escape from an echo chamber may require a radical rebooting of one's belief system" (2020: 141).

I will focus on the phenomenon of echo chambers to analyze how an epistemic vice that we can associate with racial privilege, such as critical insensitivity to racial bias, can be exhibited in group behavior and can be attributed to the epistemic functioning of the group. What I want to emphasize in my analysis is that the epistemic vices of groups that become echo chambers are often not reducible to the individual attitudes and habits of their members, but have to be understood as epistemic group traits that are sustained by the epistemic and discursive norms of the group, that is, by the epistemic-communicative ecosystem in which the group operates. This is often obscured by psychological models that explain the epistemic failures of such groups in terms of the epistemically deficient cognitive processing of individual minds.

3 The epistemic group vice of critical insensitivity in echo chambers

One may naively think that epistemic advocacy to promote critical sensibility with respect to racism in the criminal justice system consists simply in providing information about racism in law enforcement, as activists and community leaders often do in their media appearances. However, it is not that easy because large parts of the public may be communicatively insulated from this information even if it is widely circulated. And for some such publics, even if the information reaches them, they may assimilate it in distorted ways, so that the evidence about racial discrimination in law enforcement is discounted or reinterpreted and justified as fair treatment. This is what happens in publics in which racist stereotypes of criminality function as informational filters and norms which in some cases prevent information about racism in law enforcement from coming in (*filter bubbles*) and in other cases reinterpret, distort, and discount information as it comes in (*echo chambers*). There are different models for explaining how biased group thinking of this sort emerges and is maintained. I will briefly consider the psychological models and then focus in more detail on two additional models proposed by Elizabeth Anderson (Forthcoming): the *group cognition* model and the *discursive* model of biased group thinking. I will briefly discuss how these models shed light on epistemic bubbles and, more importantly, on echo chambers that promote critical insensitivity with respect to racial discrimination.

Two prominent psychological models of biased group thinking can be found in Cass Sunstein's *group polarization* theory and in Dan Kahan's *cultural cognition* theory. According to Sunstein's (2017) group polarization theory, individuals entrapped in epistemic bubbles assimilate information through biased processes that include a confirmation bias that leads them to seek and believe evidence that confirms their beliefs, and a disconfirmation bias that leads them to repudiate evidence that disconfirms their beliefs. As Anderson explains, "Sunstein's theory predicts group polarization entirely through ingroup processes: each relatively segregated group is separately driven to extreme beliefs on opposite sides of a particular claim" (Forthcoming: 5). By contrast, Kahan's (2012) cultural cognition theory explains the communicative insularity of polarized groups and the reluctance to learn and correct beliefs of their members in terms of hostile intergroup processes. Cultural cognition theory explains group polarization as an intergroup phenomenon produced by culturally antagonistic images and stereotypes that foster hostility between members of the groups in question: the members of one group stigmatize the members of the other group as *epistemic adversaries*[5] who are not worthy of trust and have to be excluded from epistemic cooperation and collective learning altogether.

Whether it is through assimilation biases or through antagonistic biases, the psychological models of polarized groups explain the dysfunctions of these groups in terms of the distorting cognitive attitudes of their individual members. If these psychological explanations were the whole story, it would be impossible to understand why some networks and self-segregated groups are more vulnerable to becoming polarized than others and why individuals exhibit cognitive biases and dysfunctional epistemic functioning while operating within some groups but not while operating in other groups or by themselves. So, for example, the psychological models would explain that viewers of Fox News are resistant to learning from information about racial discrimination in law enforcement whereas viewers of MSNBC are not because the former exhibit assimilation and antagonistic biases in this domain, whereas the latter do not. Although this is definitely part of the story, it does not seem to be the whole story. This individualistic explanation fails to account for how these TV networks constitute their viewership through the epistemic group functioning that they foster and the discursive norms that they use to frame and package information.

Underscoring the explanatory limitations of the psychological models that conceptualize polarization in individualistic terms, Elizabeth Anderson argues that the analysis of polarized group thinking needs to get more social and more political "by modeling cognitive biases not as operating inside individuals' heads, but as operating collectively and externally, via group epistemic and discursive norms" (Forthcoming: 1). Accordingly, Anderson proposes two additional models to supplement the psychological models: a *group cognition* model and a *discursive* model. According to the group cognition model, Anderson argues, "participation in a group that enacts biased social norms for information processing is all that is needed to explain entrapment in [epistemic] bubbles" (Forthcoming: 14), independently of whatever cognitive attitudes and habits the individuals in question happen to have outside the group. The group cognition model distinguishes norms of assertion from norms for individual belief: "To play one's role in manifesting a group belief, one need only obey the group's norms of assertion when one speaks qua group member" (Forthcoming: 17). So if, for example, a group is committed to remain ignorant with respect to racial discrimination in law enforcement, all the group needs to do is to enforce the epistemic group norm that evidence to that effect be filtered out or automatically dismissed.

Finally, Anderson also offers a discursive model that explains the communicative dysfunctions that ensue when a group follows discursive norms that arbitrarily render certain communicative contributions devoid of assertoric force and content, thus transforming, for example, an assertion that expresses a criticism or a complaint into an attack or an insult. Anderson describes this phenomenon as "discursive entrapment in an 'epistemic' bubble."

What she calls "a discursive 'epistemic' bubble" is characterized by *identity-expressive discourse*[6] that affirms and celebrates in-group members (or their creed) while rejecting and denigrating out-group members (or their discursive contributions). Discursive "epistemic" bubbles transform empirically informed and learning-oriented discourse into *ad hominem* discourse. Therefore, these bubbles are not strictly speaking *epistemic* (hence the quotation marks around the term), but their functional equivalent, since epistemic force and content disappear as a result of the discursive distortions: through manipulations of the rules of the language game being played, a game of collective learning is transformed into "a game of insults and pokes in the eye" (Forthcoming: 19). What Anderson calls "a discursive 'epistemic' bubble" is what I would call, following Nguyen (2020), *a discursive echo chamber*: a group or environment which, through distorting discursive mechanisms, instills in subjects epistemic vices (such as critical insensitivity) and resistances to listen properly and to learn.

The group cognition model and the discursive model that Anderson offers can overlap. The example of biased group thinking shaped by racist stereotypes of criminality can illustrate this. The venue of public discourse that is Fox News and the group constituted by its viewership can be characterized as an echo chamber with biased epistemic and discursive norms that create the group dysfunctions explained by Anderson's two models. When activists and community leaders give information about racial discrimination in the US criminal justice system, networks such as Fox News often depict them as the defenders of "criminals" and the attackers of the protectors of public order. They do this, for example, by associating members of Black Lives Matter with criminal life and attacking them with the opposing slogan *Blue Lives Matter*. In this discursive frame, activists are negatively stereotyped in such a way that everything they say is depicted as baseless insults and attacks on the defenders of public order or so-called "blue lives." This negative stereotyping discursively positions viewers in such a way that the only uptake that they are encouraged to give to the activists' utterances is dismissal and name-calling since their criticisms of and challenges to the criminal justice system have to be understood as concealed attacks and insults to "blue lives." What the stigmatization of activist organizations such as Black Lives Matter through racist stereotypes of criminality accomplishes is the systematic discrediting of its members and spokespersons, so that they are considered dangerous to talk to, intrinsically *untrustworthy*, and are thus excluded from epistemic transactions. And note here the convergence of discursive entrapment with epistemic entrapment: the discursive activation of stigmatizing stereotypes provides an excuse or alibi for epistemic exclusion; the discursive framing creates an epistemic environment in which the activists' evidence is filtered out or automatically rejected and presented as intrinsically flawed.

Both the discursive frames deployed by Fox News and the epistemic group functioning of its viewers cast out-group interlocutors as *adversaries* with whom no epistemic cooperation is possible. Discursive adversaries are typically also epistemic adversaries, and neither discursive adversaries nor epistemic adversaries are considered eligible for engaging in fruitful epistemic interaction, cooperation and collective learning. How are discursive and epistemic adversarial relations overcome? How do we put pressure on publics so that they become open to listen to opposed viewpoints and to critically engage with them so that there can be *epistemic friction*[7] among perspectives and collective learning? In short, how do we fight against the collective vice of critical insensitivity produced and maintained by an echo chamber?

The different dysfunctions in biased group thinking highlighted by the different models we have reviewed clue as in as to the different kinds of remedies that can be mobilized against echo chambers: in particular, psychological, discursive, and epistemic remedies.[8] At the psychological level, the goal is to eradicate the cognitive biases of individuals (overcoming assimilation biases and antagonistic biases); but at the level of group cognition and structures of public discourse, the goal is to suspend dysfunctional epistemic and discursive norms and replace them with better ones. At the discursive level, we need to unmask and denounce *ad hominem* discourse, and promote the introduction of norms against deploying discursive frames that activate stigmatizing stereotypes that turn interlocutors into adversaries with whom no fruitful discussion can be had. At the epistemic level, we need to speak against the filtering-out and automatic rejection of information and promote norms against dismissing speakers and bodies of evidence out of hand. Of course there will be discursive-epistemic environments and publics resistant to admit these changes, but the very attempt to introduce them can spark critical discussions that can facilitate the achievement of *meta-lucidity*[9] about the epistemic and discursive norms that those environments and publics are following, typically without any awareness of how these norms work or of their implications. We need collective and concerted efforts to fight against forms of epistemic marginalization and oppression such as the ones that echo chambers produce or protect. In the final section I will provide a preliminary sketch of how to think about collective epistemic resistance and what I term *epistemic activism*.

4 Resistant epistemic group agency: the epistemic empowerment of the oppressed and epistemic activism

In order to fight against epistemic group vices, we need to go to the supra-individual level and look at forms of collective agency that exert resistance against group failures in epistemic dynamics. As Lorraine Code has pointed out, addressing questions about epistemic responsibility requires engaging with epistemic subjectivities *and* epistemic communities: "It is about the ethics and politics of knowledge, and indeed about epistemic subjectivity in its multiple instantiations" (Code 2013: 90). As Code and others have emphasized, epistemic responsibility concerns the accountability and responsivity of individual knowers, but also of groups or publics and of institutions. In her discussions of "the politics of epistemic location" (2006), Code has argued that *epistemic advocacy* is required to unmask our complicity with ongoing injustices and to mobilize publics to fight against them. Code's concept of advocacy is a key component of what I have called *epistemic activism*, namely, the kind of activism that can mobilize differently situated subjects and publics in order to resist epistemic dysfunctions and pathologies of public discourse (see Medina 2019; Medina Forthcoming A and B; Medina and Whitt 2021).

As Code (2006) suggests, we need to engage in *epistemic advocacy* that denounces dysfunctional epistemic dynamics and public discourses that protect the privileged and marginalize the oppressed. But what is needed in order to overcome epistemically dysfunctional group dynamics is not simply speaking up against epistemic vices. The eradication of widespread epistemic vices requires something more than a critique. It requires epistemic resistance not only in word but indeed, that is, *epistemic resistance in action*, what I call *epistemic activism*. Epistemic activism has two principal aims and there are two kinds of activist moves and techniques associated with these aims: first, epistemic activism aims at the *epistemic empowerment* of the oppressed, that is, at gaining or augmenting epistemic agency for those who have been marginalized or disempowered in epistemic dynamics; and second, epistemic activism aims at *restructuring epistemic environments*, that is, at transforming and meliorating the structural conditions and frameworks that mediate epistemic interactions. I have discussed the structural and institutional side of epistemic activism elsewhere (Forthcoming A and B). In what follows I will briefly discuss only epistemic empowerment since this chapter has focused on the epistemic vices of groups and it is appropriate to conclude it with a brief discussion of interventions in epistemic group agency that can mitigate such vices.

As explained by Medina and Whitt (2021), we can think of *epistemic activism* as concerted efforts and interventions in epistemic practices that aim to "augment the epistemic agency of unfairly disadvantaged subjects, amplifying their voices and facilitating the development and exercise of their epistemic capacities." (309) Epistemic activism can take many different shapes and forms. Its strategies and tactics will be dictated by who engages in it, in what contexts, and against what patterns of interaction and institutional frameworks. Differently situated subjects, both oppressed and non-oppressed subjects, can become epistemic activists. "Oppressed subjects can become epistemic activists—sometimes by necessity if not by choice—when they actively fight against their epistemic marginalization and work towards forms of self-empowerment that can achieve the epistemic agency they are unjustly denied" (Medina and Whitt 2021: 312). Consider as an example the epistemic activism within the prison system examined by Medina and Whitt (2021) as a response to the phenomenon of the *epistemic neglect* experienced by inmates in carceral contexts when their complaints and grievances go unheard or are given defective uptake. Within carceral contexts, inmates themselves can (and often do) become epistemic activists by denouncing and trying to resist unfair patterns of epistemic neglect, and by expressing epistemic solidarity by backing up one another's testimonies, so that they mitigate the harmful consequences that individual acts of protest typically encounter. A good example of epistemic activism cultivated by jail inmates at the Durham County Detention Facility (DCDF) is provided by Medina and Whitt:

> At DCDF an unknown number of detainees recently organized the "First Five Grieving Committee," a "non-violent" and "non-gang affiliated" cooperative that anonymizes and amplifies the grievances of individual detainees. By working together, the members of the Committee have successfully directed their concerns to the Durham County Sheriff, whereas individual grievances are typically heard—if they are heard at all—by

subordinate staff members. This is an instance of epistemic activism, within the context of the jail, starting to ameliorate the testimonial disadvantage that detainees face."
(Medina and Whitt 2021: 312–3)

Note that the formation of the First Five Grieving Committee exemplifies the development of collective epistemic agency: inmates form a collective voice by pooling their agential resources and coordinating their epistemic actions. Inmates organize their voices and interventions in such a way that their individual epistemic acts become mutually supportive and protective of each other, thus becoming part of a collective action. This way of gaining and protecting epistemic agency through epistemic activism illustrates well how *epistemic self-empowerment* can take place even in the most adverse conditions.

Epistemic activism aimed at the epistemic empowerment of the oppressed so that their voices and perspectives are properly heard can also be exercised by groups or networks that include non-oppressed subjects. Consider here the work of epistemic resistance of the *Inside-Outside Alliance* (hereafter IOA), a local activist organization that describes itself as "a group of people trying to support the struggles of those inside (or formerly inside) Durham County jail, and their families and friends."[10] IOA members—friends and family of incarcerated subjects, formerly incarcerated subjects, and activists—engage in epistemic interventions, programs, and initiatives, which they subsume under the heading *Amplify Voices Inside*. In their coordinated actions IOA members use their collective voice and epistemic agency in order to procure epistemic standing for inmates' perspectives and some degrees of epistemic agency for their voices in the outside world. As Medina and Whitt put it,

> detainees' voices rarely reach places of political authority without being distorted, translated into other idioms or discourses, or ventriloquized by others. For this reason, it is important to have forms of epistemic activism in which outside allies lend their voices as instruments or extensions of the detainees' own, without interpreting or translating them. (Medina and Whitt 2021: 313–4)

IOA members do this "by reading detainees' letters in City Council meetings and County Commissioner meetings, disrupting 'business as usual' with the testimonies of individuals who have been excluded from the sites of official power" (314). Other ways in which IOA members seek to amplify detainee voices include publishing their letters on their website or in a print magazine. In these different ways IOA members try to ensure that the voices of inmates are heard in the outside world and their stories, problems, and concerns neglected inside the jail can reach other institutions and authorities as well as the general public. These are examples of epistemic empowerment of marginalized groups and ways of gaining epistemic agency through epistemic activism.

Through their epistemic activism, activist organizations such as IOA fight for the epistemic empowerment of oppressed groups (such as incarcerated subjects) whose voices and perspectives often encounter structural obstacles and become unable to be heard or be given due weight and consideration. Epistemic activism is used to put pressure on publics and venues of public discourse to stop following epistemic and discursive norms that stack the decks against the perspectives of oppressed subjects and trigger dysfunctional epistemic dynamics. A case in point is the phenomenon of echo chambers that keep publics actively ignorant and resistant to learn from certain marginalized perspectives such as those of subjects who experience racism in the US criminal justice system. In this sense it is not surprising that a key goal in the epistemic interventions of prison activists is to stop the circulation of stigmatizing (and often racist) stereotypes of criminality that discredit the perspectives of incarcerated subjects. For example, it is common practice among US newspapers and TV news channels to introduce the testimony of prison inmates by describing the crimes of which the testifier has been convicted even though that information is utterly irrelevant to the story, thus using a narrative frame that activates stigmatizing stereotypes of criminality and triggers dismissive attitudes and defective forms of epistemic engagement with the testimony.

We need concerted efforts to put pressure on publics—especially self-segregated and homogeneous publics—to become critically aware of (*meta-lucid* about) their epistemic group attitudes and habits and the epistemic and discursive norms underlying their group dynamics. This kind of epistemic advocacy and activism is necessary in order to hold publics accountable for the exercise of their epistemic agency and to demand epistemic melioration at the level of epistemic group dynamics (both intra- and intergroup dynamics). This kind of critical attentiveness to epistemic group dynamics and the emphasis on collective epistemic responsibility that epistemic activism tries to spur are necessary if we want to discontinue the exercise of epistemic vices associated with privilege and begin the hard work toward the cultivation of epistemic virtues under conditions of oppression.

Notes

1 I am grateful for the detailed feedback I received from the editors on prior versions of this chapter.
2 I will not get into a discussion of the composition of groups and, in particular, of whether such collectives can be viewed as summative or non-summative groups (that is, reducible or non-reducible to the attitudes of its members). For such discussion, see Lackey (2015).
3 See, for example, Palermos (2016).
4 See esp. p. 120 and pp. 186–206 of *The Epistemology of Resistance* (2013).
5 This is my own expression, which I will use and explain through an example below.
6 As Anderson puts it:

> Identity-expressive discourse expresses the speaker's group identity, and positions the speaker in relation to people with the same or other identities. It may signal whose side one is on, who is the enemy, or doesn't belong, who is illegitimate, who is superior to whom. (Forthcoming: 17)

7 For an elucidation of the notion of "epistemic friction," see Medina (2013).
8 Note that this list is far from exhaustive and focused very heavily on the cognitive side of the dysfunctions of biased group thinking. In particular, a crucial element that I am not considering here is the affective dimension of the dysfunctions in question and the emotional resistances that keep critical insensitivity in place. I have discussed elsewhere the affective side of resisting epistemic vices and dysfunctions in terms of exerting "emotional friction" that can disrupt and displace forms of antipathy and emotionally based epistemic resistances (Medina 2019).
9 See the discussions of my notion of *meta-lucidity* in *The Epistemology of Resistance* (2013), esp. pp. 186–206.
10 See www.amplifyvoices.com.

References

Anderson, Elisabeth (Forthcoming), "Epistemic Bubbles and Authoritarian Politics," in Elizabeth Edenberg and Michael Hannon (eds.), *Politics and Truth: New Perspectives in Political Epistemology*. Oxford: Oxford University Press.
Code, Lorraine (2006), *Ecological Thinking: The Politics of Epistemic Location*. New York: Oxford University Press.
Code, Lorraine (2014), "Culpable Ignorance?" *Hypatia: A Journal of Feminist Philosophy* 29(3): 670–76.
Kahan, Dan (2012), "Cultural Cognition as a Conception of the Cultural Theory of Risk," in S. Roeser (ed.), *Handbook of Risk Theory: Epistemology, Decision Theory, Ethics, and Social Implications of Risk*. New York: Springer, 725–59.

Lackey, Jennifer (2015), "A Deflationary Account of Group Testimony," in J. Lackey (ed.), *Essays in Collective Epistemology*. New York: Oxford University Press, 64–94.

Medina, José (2013), *The Epistemology of Resistance: Gender and Racial Oppression, Epistemic Injustice, and Resistant Imaginations*. New York: Oxford University Press.

Medina, José (2019), "Racial Violence, Affective Resistance, and Epistemic Activism," *Angelaki: Journal of the Theoretical Humanities* 24(4): 22–37.

Medina, José (Forthcoming A), "Capital Vices, Institutional Failures, and Epistemic Neglect in a County Jail," in Ian James Kidd, Heather Battaly, and Quassim Cassam (eds.), *Vice Epistemology: Theory and Practice*. London and New York: Routledge.

Medina, José (Forthcoming B), "Political Epistemology," in David Bordonaba, Victor Fernandez Castro, and José Ramón Torices (eds.), *The Political Turn in Analytic Philosophy*. De Gruyter.

Medina, José, and Whitt, Matt (2021), "Epistemic Activism and the Politics of Credibility: Testimonial Injustice Inside/Outside a North Carolina Jail", in Heidi Grasswick and Nancy McHugh (eds.), *Making the Case: Feminist and Critical Race Philosophers Engaging Case Studies*. Albany, NY: SUNY Press, 293–324.

Nguyen, C. Thi (2020), "Echo Chambers and Epistemic Bubbles," *Episteme* 17(2): 141–61.

Palermos, S. Orestis (2016), "The Dynamics of Group Cognition," *Minds and Machines* 26: 409–40.

Sommers, Samuel R. (2007), "Race and the Decision Making of Juries." *Legal and Criminological Psychology* 12(2): 171–87.

Sunstein, Cass R. (2017), *#Republic: Divided Democracy in the Age of Social Media*. Princeton, NJ: Princeton University Press.

30

EPISTEMIC CORRUPTION AND POLITICAL INSTITUTIONS

Ian James Kidd

1 Introduction

Institutions play an indispensable role in our political and epistemic lives. Consider political-epistemic practices, like acquiring information, criticising arguments, debating ideas, evaluating evidence, and scrutinising proposed policies. In the United Kingdom, these are institutionally realised by the Civil Service, Parliamentary Select Committees, expert advisory groups, Prime Minister's Questions and other practices, groups, and organisations. Moreover, political-epistemic institutions can also generate negative epistemic phenomena, such as groupthink, polarisation, and propaganda (see Sections 2 and 3 of this Handbook). Some have a special epistemic role within wider political systems, like the UK Office of Statistics Regulations, which ensures appropriate collection, publication and use of statistics to 'help inform decisions' by groups ranging from charities and trade unions to business and community groups (OSR 2010: 2).[1] Similarly, the second chamber of the UK Parliament, the House of Lords, 'shares the task of making and shaping laws and checking and challenging the work of the government'.

A variety of concepts and vocabularies exist for appraisal of political institutions, including 'efficiency' versus 'inefficiency', 'economical' versus 'expensive', and 'orderly' versus 'chaotic'. Some of these have epistemic dimensions. It should matter to us that our political institutions perform well epistemically – they should be *efficient,* fulfilling their mandated tasks with maximal speed and success, and *orderly,* perhaps by ensuring conscientious scrutiny of proposed legislation. In the United States, the culture of hyperpartisanship now characteristic of the Senate and Congress bakes in inefficiency and 'gridlock', to the point that 'Congress has stopped working' (Rauch 2016; Willis and Kane 2018). But there are alternative vocabularies for epistemic appraisal of political institutions, including one invoking *vices* – stable and objectionable dispositions of character, like cruelty, dogmatism, or untruthfulness (Battaly 2014: ch. 4). Some are ethical failings (like cruelty), others are epistemic failings (like dogmatism), while others are hybrid ethico-epistemic failings (such as untruthfulness).

Although *vices* are most usually attributed to individual agents, we also quite naturally attribute them to collectives and also to institutions. Certainly, attributing *vices* to institutions is a common critical practice in political discourse, arguably worth protecting for that reason (see Biddle, Kidd and Leuschner 2017; Kidd 2016). Consider the 2020 Williams Report into the UK Home Office's failings to safeguard the immigration status of the 'Windrush generation' of British-Caribbeans. It speaks of an 'institutional ignorance and thoughtlessness' in the Home Office, with its 'cultural resistance to hearing a contrary view to the department's own' and a 'defensive culture ... which often defends, deflects and dismisses criticism' (2020: 7, 14, 141). What we see here is the explicit or implicit attribution to the Home Office as an institution of a set of epistemic *vices* – thoughtlessness, dogmatism, and closed-mindedness (compare Alston 2018 on attribution of moral *vices* to contemporary British political institutions).

I want to explore the ways that a vocabulary of epistemic *vices* can be used in appraisal of political institutions. By epistemic *vices*, I mean objectionable epistemic traits or dispositions that can be attributed to *individual, collectives,* or *institutions*.[2] By vice epistemology, I refer to the philosophical study of the nature, identity, and significance of epistemic *vices* (Cassam 2019). It emerged over the last 20 years as the partner to virtue epistemology, which studies epistemic virtues, like curiosity, open-mindedness, and reflectiveness (Baehr 2011; Zagzebski 1996).

What unifies the two disciplines is a conviction that the concepts of vice and virtue can play indispensable roles in appraisal and reform of epistemic agents, institutions, and systems, a form of what is sometimes called 'regulative epistemology' (Roberts and Wood 2007: 20–23). Interestingly, various recent misadventures in British and American political history provide most of the examples in Quassim Cassam's recent book, *Vices of the Mind* – Brexit and the Second Gulf War, for instance, whose invidious realities motivate his claim that 'the project of vice reduction' gains its urgency from a painful awareness that a world of rampant, unchecked epistemically vicious behaviour is just 'too ghastly to contemplate' (Cassam 2019: 186–87). Other overtly politically engaged vice-epistemological projects include José Medina's *The Epistemology of Resistance* (2013), which involves analysis of the ways that epistemic *vices* are integral to the operations of systems of gender and racial oppression.

When urging use of a vice-epistemic vocabulary for appraisal of political institutions, there are at least two main issues that need addressing. First, why adopt that vocabulary, when there are already existing vocabularies? After all, some will protest that talk of 'vice' is archaic, moralistic, or intolerably quasi-religious. Cassam, a leading vice epistemologist, replies that we should, first, flexibly use a variety of styles of explanation for epistemic failings, and, second, acknowledge there are aspects of our epistemic failings that are uniquely captured by vice-epistemic explanations (Cassam 2019: 29 and his chapter in this Handbook).

A second issue is whether epistemic *vices* can be attributed to institutions – or, in the jargon, whether institutions are *vice-bearers*. Traditionally, accepted vice-bearers are *individual agents* ('the arrogant Minister') and, increasingly, *collective agents* ('the dogmatic committee'). Those who want to restrict the range of vice-bearers can be called *conservatives*, whereas those who wish to expand the range of bearers – to include institutions, say – are *expansionists*. The Williams Report's references to the 'thoughtless' of the *Home Office*, for instance, indicate that it is implicitly operating with an expansionist conception of epistemic vice. This matters: if institutions cannot be a genuine vice-bearer, then attributions of vice to institutions must be judged as *rhetorical* rather than *attributive*. If Williams' claim is that the Home Office *qua* institution is viciously thoughtless, then retaining that critical claim requires a defence of expansionism.

In this chapter, I begin by describing *collectivism*, focusing on a specific form recently developed by Miranda Fricker. She offers the useful concept of an *institutional ethos*, the analogue of an *individual character*. The epistemic ethos of a political institution consists of its collective motivations and its stable patterns of institutional performance. These motivations and performances can be appraised, singly or jointly, as epistemically vicious. I then discuss ways that political institutions can develop a vicious epistemic ethos, either by acquiring epistemically bad collective motivations and/or tending to evince epistemically bad patterns of performance. To help with theorising degradations of the epistemic ethos of a political institution, a useful concept is that of *epistemic corruption*.

2 Institutional ethos

Miranda Fricker argues that institutions have an *ethos*, 'the collective analogue of an individual agent's character' (2020: 90). Just as a character of an individual can be (or can become) virtuous or vicious, so, too, can the ethos of an institution. Here we should distinguish between the *vices of political agents* (civil servants, advisers, ministers) and the *vices of political institutions*. Our question is whether *vices* can be genuinely attributed to institutions, and the affirmative response Fricker develops involves her concept of institutional ethos.

Attributing *vices* to institutions mean we need to adopt some form of *collectivism*, the most general claim of which is that the epistemic behaviour and motivations of collectives cannot be reduced to those of their constituent members. Collectivists might argue that some collective or institution can have *vices* lacked by some or all of its members and, relatedly, that a group of individuals might have a vice that is not apparent in their collective behaviour (Fricker 2010; Lahroodi 2007). The rival position is summativism, according to which 'ascription of a virtue [or vice] to a group is *always* to be understood as a disguised ascription of that virtue [or vice] to individuals in the group' (Lahroodi 2019: 411). The various forms of collectivism are surveyed in Lahroodi (2019: §§33.5–6). Most rely on *divergence arguments*, a term introduced by Gilbert (1989), which appeal to divergences between individual- and collective-level behaviours and characteristics. There are at least two main types (Fricker 2010: 137–38):

- *The multiplicity of our practical identities* entail commitments to accept or to resist certain attitudes, behaviours, and goals, including specifications of the accompanying standards and procedures (e.g. a Member of Parliament accepts the reality of global heating, but is bound by loyalty and disciplinary considerations to voice and vote for the sceptical stance of their party).
- *The collective cancellation effects* occur when the attitudes and behaviours of a group of individuals tend to cancel each other out at the institutional level (e.g. the procedurally open-minded acts of a party of politicians cancel each other out at the level of the party, and the outcome of whose deliberations is therefore myopically closed-minded).

Within contemporary political institutions, instances of these divergence effects could be easily provided: think of the competing obligations and demands built into the roles of parent, member of a local community, politician, or member of the party disciplinary structure. The latter two, for instance, are subject to partisan pressures to 'show loyalty', to 'protect the party from embarrassment', to 'attack the Opposition', and so on. Moreover, such felt pressure can be amplified by institutional features, like the 'whip system' in the UK Parliament, which acts to enforce voting according to the party platform (Jones 2016). Such formal and informal structures can generate divergence between the motivations and behaviours of individual political actors and wider political institutions. Hence the introduction of *institutional ethos* as a concept apt for modelling institutional epistemic motivations and behaviours.

Since Walter Bagehot's influential 1872 essays, *The English Constitution*, the comparison of political systems has compared both the arrangements and composition of different political systems and their distinctive forms of 'corporate character' (1872: 185). A standard theme of Cold War discourses were critical reflections on the character of the rivalling systems – like the 'exploitative', 'decadent' character of capitalism, for instance, versus the 'repressive' character of socialism. The general conviction is that differences in the structure and activities of political institutions shape the irreducibly collective character of ethos of the institution as a whole. A corollary is that an institutional ethos is to a significant degree mutable, subject to contingent change and deliberate redefinition within the constraints of external influences and its internal rhythms (Clucas 2015).

Fricker characterises an institutional ethos as consisting of the 'collective motivational dispositions and evaluative attitudes within the institutional body, of which the various good or bad ends orientate the institution's activities' (2020: 91). Just as character explains the behaviour of individuals in relation to their motivations, desires, and values, so ethos explains the behaviour of an institution in relation to its constituent motivations, goals, and values – those things for which it *stands*. An ethos of justice, for instance, would consist of (i) certain values (fairmindedness, equality before the law), manifested in (ii) certain institutionalised procedures (e.g. trial by jury, right to a defence), which (iii) deliver the right sorts of results (e.g. fair sentencing). Compare, for instance, with Clucas' account of the character (or ethos) of democratic government:

> Ultimately, the question as to which institutional design is better depends on the democratic ideals one favours. It depends on what one wants out of a democracy [...] While there is no one right answer to this question, there are ideals or values that, when present in a democracy, reflect the general consent of the governed...:meaningful elections, fair representation, accountability, the balance of majority rule and minority rights, and the functionality of the state. (2020: 7–8)

Within an ethos of democratic governance, those values and ideals would be realised in appropriate political-institutional arrangements, such as the separation of powers, open and free elections, and so on. An ethos thus explains the alignment of the collective motivations of an institution and its operations and outcomes.

Fricker defines an institutional ethos as a set of interrelated dispositions and attitudes which are temporally extended and counterfactually stable and therefore a robust and enduring feature of the institution. An ethos will change over time as a result of the natural rhythms of institutional life, deliberate reformative efforts by members of the institution or external agencies, or through periodic dramatic transformative events. The interrelated character of the dispositions and attitudes is articulated using the 'joint commitment model' developed by Margaret Gilbert (1989, 2000). 'Commitment', here, is defined broadly. It ranges from explicit endorsement through to familiar modes of tacit acceptance that take the form of 'going along with' a set of institutionally mandated behaviours, whether as a result of calculated complicity, horizontal and vertical social pressures, institutional incentive structures, and so on.[3] Such joint commitments gradually create and animate an institutional ethos: a collective, intersubjectively binding set of commitments, any deviation from which entails criticism and normatively forceful interpersonal demands that offender justify their deviation. In such cases, there emerge special roles for the practices of *reneging* and *rebuking*, as is the case for some individual instances of epistemic vice (see Fricker 2010: 94f).

Fricker argues that this account explains why individuals retain trust in an institution, even when they disagree with its results (2020: 91f). Consider two epistemically charged examples:

- *Transparency*, a commitment to accurately and comprehensively record and openly report the deliberations, decisions, and composition of component groups of a political system. It can be realised by public interviews, minutes of meetings, parliamentary records, and public statements of select committees, expert advisory groups, and the cabinet.[4]
- *Truthfulness*, a normative expectation that political actors will be accurate and sincere when reporting their activities, conflicts of interest, pertinent personal contacts, and so on. It can be realised through public scrutiny of statements, fact-checking systems, a critical media, and robust regulation of statistical claims.[5]

If a political institution practically fails in some way, the public may retain trust if they recognise that the conditions of transparency and truthfulness were honoured (including in cases where there is some individual or collective culpability. The transparent disclosure of one's failings is often better than their attempted concealment and acts of truthfulness can preserve trust in one's sincerity even if trust in one's competence is dented). The 2006 Home Office strategy on immigration, for instance was titled *Fair, Effective, Transparent and Trusted: Rebuilding Confidence in our Immigration System*. An institutional ethos of accountability, transparency, and truthfulness can elicit public trust, even in the face of undesirable outcomes and practical failings, at least up to a point (O'Neill 2002: chs. 2–4).

An institutional ethos therefore consists of collective motivations (goals, values, ideals) and repeated performance (institutional systems and processes that reliably deliver certain outcomes or results). When an institution has a good ethos, the motivations are commendable and virtuous and so, too, are its consistent outcomes – accountability and representativeness find concrete express in regular meaningful elections and other appropriate activities. We might say that a virtuous ethos is one that expresses and enacts such virtues as justice and fairness. By contrast, a vicious ethos is one whose motivations and performances express and enact *vices*, including epistemic *vices*, as defined by Fricker:

> *Epistemic vices* are culpable failures of epistemic virtue either (i) in its 'inner' aspect of mediate and/or ultimate motivations to good epistemic ends, and/or (ii) in its 'outer' aspect of performance – the achievement of those ends.

Fricker builds culpability or blameworthiness into her account of *vices*. Others do not, arguing instead that *criticism* is our primary attitude to *vices*, with others being anger, blame, and so on (Cassam 2019: 21). *Mediate epistemic ends* include, for instance, assessing relevant evidence, fact-checking, soliciting criticisms, and considering alternative perspectives, while the *ultimate epistemic ends* may include epistemic responsibility or 'cognitive contact with reality' (Zagzebski 1996: 101).[6]

Coupled to the account of ethos, Fricker adds second definition:

> *Institutional epistemic vices* are displayed whenever there are culpable lapses in the collective epistemic motivations and goals of an institution and/or in their performative implementation.

Note that these two conceptions of vice – 'motivational' and 'performative' – are analogous to the two main normative models of individual epistemic vice:

> *Consequentialism* (or *reliabilism*): epistemic *vices* are dispositions or traits that are systematically productive of epistemically bad effects (eg failing to consider salient epistemic options) or that fail systematically to generate epistemically good effects (eg identifying alternative possibilities). (see Cassam 2019)
> *Responsiblism*: epistemic *vices* are dispositions or traits that express or manifest either (i) the presence of epistemically bad motives, goals, and desires (eg thwarting the epistemic agency of others) or (ii) the absence of epistemically good motives, goals, and desires (eg a respect for truth). (see Crerar 2018; Tanesini 2018)

Institutional epistemic *vices* can be understood using either the motivational or performative models. Alternatively, one can use a pluralist model (Battaly 2016; Fricker 2020).

Consider two cases:

1 A government department consistently publishes inaccurate, incomplete information about its own internal activities and the effectiveness of its policies. These failings occur due to its inadequate, outdated informational, and communicative systems. Data isn't systematically collected, fact-checking is marred by inadequate communication between staff, no clear guidelines exist describing what counts as timely or accurate reportage, etc.
2 A government department consistently publishes inaccurate, incomplete information about its own internal activities and the effectiveness of its policies. These failings occur because of a desire by the newly elected government to strategically suppress politically embarrassing information and to disguise its underfunding of the department, etc.

Case (1) involves institutional *vices* of the performative sort. By contrast, Case (2) involves institutional *vices* of the motivational sort: the failings flow from the intentional actions of the government, rather than (or perhaps as well as) any contingently inherited inadequacies in the organisation and operation of the department. Whether we should prefer pluralism over its two component positions is an open question among vice epistemologists. Consider just one point about each. First, performative accounts have a lower *attribution threshold* for institutional vice. If institution *A* reliably performs in ways that have bad epistemic effects, then *A* is institutionally epistemically vicious. Second, advocates of motivational accounts will argue that they have better *normative capture*, a richer capacity to articulate the badness of *vices* and thus given a fuller appraisal of the institution. A government that suppresses critical reports *both* impairs its citizens' epistemic activities *and* evinces a fundamental hostility to truth as an epistemic value (Cassam 2019: ch. 4). Exploring cases of institutional epistemic *vices* offers new ways to think about these foundational issues.

3 Institutional epistemic corruption

An institutional ethos can change over time for the worse. Occasional failings may be anomalies, but explicable and forgivable. Sometimes, however, they can build up and become indicative of a more systematic deterioration of the ethos. In the language I offer in this section, there could be *epistemic corruption* of the ethos – either corruption of collective motivations that guide the institution and/or the corruption of its performance, of its processes and their outcomes. Unless mitigated, the institution acquires an increasingly epistemically vicious ethos.

In its everyday sense, 'corruption' refers to a decline in the qualities of character of a person or thing and to the processes that contribute to it. Something becomes corrupted when its positive qualities are damaged or destroyed and various negative features take their place. Within political philosophy, the term is already in use. Dennis Thompson, for one, defines 'mediated corruption' as a decline in shared norms or character of a democratic system (Thompson 2005: 143–73). It has a long history within political discourse described Sparling (2019) and modern uses surveyed by Rothstein and Varraich (2017).

Within character epistemology the term was introduced to describe a specific form of damage done to the epistemic character of individual agents (Kidd 2019, 2020). It was inspired by foundational work by feminist epistemologists and ethicists interested in the ways that oppression acts on and through character, a theme developed by Claudia Card (1996), Robin Dillon (2012), and Lisa Tessman (2015). It can refer to damage done to the epistemic character of individual or collective agents and the epistemic ethos of institutions.

A working definition: epistemic corruption occurs when the character or ethos of an agent or institution is damaged by conditions, events, or processes that tend to facilitate the development and exercise of epistemic *vices*. The positive aspects of character or ethos – virtues, excellences, and integrity – all suffer deterioration or destruction; alternatively, one can say that the negative aspects – *vices*, failings – are amplified, stabilised, or otherwise boosted. What often occurs are simultaneous processes of passive and negative corruption, since the displacement of certain virtues might naturally open a way for certain *vices*.

Three comments. First, some terminology: a *corruptor* is a thing causing the corruption while a *corruptee* is a thing whose character or ethos is being damaged. In cases of institutional epistemic corruption, there will be a whole variety of corruptees – politicians, civil servants, non-governmental agencies, and so on. Second, epistemic corruption is a dynamic and diachronic process. It is a temporally extended 'back and forth' of forces, deeply textured by the structures and rhythms of institutional life. In rare cases, it might occur through a single decisive act, but is usually an assemblage of slower, subtler processes that play out in response other corrective forces.[7] Third, the term 'facilitate' is purposefully broad so as to encompass, *inter alia*, 'encourage', 'justify', 'legitimate', 'motivate', 'promote', or even 'provide receptive conditions for development and exercise of one or more *vices*'. To distinguish these, consider the major modes of epistemic corruption.

A 'mode' of epistemic corruption is a general way that an epistemic vice can be facilitated. There are at least five, the first two of which involve the acquisition or activation of new *vices* and failings, ones not previously characteristic of the ethos or operations of an institution:

1   *Acquisition*: a corruptor can enable the acquisition of new *vices*, ones not previously a feature of institutional epistemic ethos.
2   *Activation*: a corruptor can activate dormant, 'sleeping' *vices*, ones typically latent, but inactive in the institutional epistemic ethos.
    The next three modes are different, insofar as they involve enhancements to *vices* already present and active in an institution's epistemic ethos:
3   *Propagation*: a corruptor can increase the *scope* of a vice, the extent to which it spreads throughout an institution's structures, departments, and so on.
4   *Stabilisation*: a corruptor can also increase the *stability* of a vice, the extent to which it can remain active and therefore increasingly resistant to disruption.
5   *Intensification*: a corruptor can also increase the *strength* of a vice, turning relatively weaker vicious processes and collective motivations into much stronger forms

Although distinguishable, the different modes of corruption usually operate simultaneous and mutually reinforcing. Some corruptors will facilitate a specific vice, others a set of *vices* – and working out which conditions are *monocorrupting* and *polycorrupting* is a task for social and vice epistemologists to investigate.

Analysis of institutional epistemic corruption can be made easier if we point to some very general examples of corruptors – of conditions, norms, or arrangements that facilitate the development and exercise of *vices* and deterioration and destruction of virtues. Identifying this needs integration of empirical and conceptual research. These generic corruptors are a starting point:

A   *The absence of exemplars of virtue*: an institution might lack positive exemplars who model epistemic virtue – affording inspiration and practical demonstration of the virtues that may be taken up into the institutional ethos. Without exemplars of virtue, one loses an important way of encouraging and maintaining an epistemically virtuous institutional ethos (Croce and Vaccarezza 2017).

B   *The derogation of exemplars of virtue*: extant virtuous exemplars may be subject to forms of derogation – to sneering, mockery, aspersive questioning, or public or private derision. Under these conditions, the potentially transformative capacity of exemplars to maintain and promote a good institutional ethos is undermined (e.g. 'forcing out' conscientious and honest civil servants who try to maintain high epistemic standards).

C   *Suppression of critics*: institutional commitment to values like epistemic honesty and fairminded can be eroded by the suppression of those persons who attempt to initiate and take part in the critical dynamics necessary for institutional enactment of those values. Such suppressive behaviours include silencing, intimidation, demotion, expulsion, unwarranted exclusion from institutional systems and contacts, and in severe cases torture and murder. Consider cases of the orchestrated intimidation in the United States of climate scientists trying to discharge their epistemic functions by advising the public and the government of the realities of global heating (Biddle, Kidd and Leuschner 2017).

D   *The valorisation of vicious exemplars*: a corrupt institution can celebrate and reward those individuals who are exemplars of epistemic vice using formal and informal mechanisms – reward mechanisms, promotion, hierarchies of esteem, and other means of disbursing the various goods afforded by the institution (e.g. access, esteem, rank). A corrupt ethos shows itself by rewarding vicious characters (consider the various villains who have populated the Trump Administration).

E   *The rebranding of vices as virtues*: a corrupted ethos can falsely esteem *vices* as virtues in ways that aim to create corrupted collective motivations and behaviours. This can take both sincere and insincere forms, since some individuals will be aware that a rebranding is being attempted. Former British Prime Minister, Tony Blair, replied to charges of his 'arrogance' in centralising power in Downing Street by attributing to himself 'a sense of direction' (Rhoades 2011: 36) while his notorious 'spin doctor' Alasdair Campbell, famously retorted, to critics of his aggressive interpersonal style, 'I'm not a bully, I'm robust!' (Oborne 2004).

F   *Increasing the exercise costs of epistemic virtue*: this is a form of passive corruption whose aim is to discourage a virtuous epistemic ethos by increasing the practical, psychological, or social costs – to individuals or the institution – of exercises of epistemic virtue. If virtues incur a prohibitive cost, then a natural alternative is to resist their exercise, which over time can lead to the gradual diminution of the 'upwards' pressure that can sustain and protect a virtuous institutional ethos. Standard euphemisms indicative of exaggerated exercise costs includes injunctions not to 'rock the boat' and warning about 'not being a team player'.

G   *Operationalising the vices*: a corrupt ethos can manifest as procedures and policies whose enactment requires performance of epistemically vicious behaviours – such as concealing salient facts or abstaining from practices of questioning liable to lead to awkward answers. Consider the atrocious conventions of aggressive adversariality integral to interpersonal epistemic conduct in the House of Commons with its competitive ethos of political 'point-scoring', party-pleasing showboating, and jeering pantomime partisanship (Watson 2020).

Which corrupting conditions obtain will depend on the institution in question. The sheer variety of institutional arrangements and procedures offers a rich variety of options. Exploring these will require analysts of epistemic corruption to engage closely with political theorists, biographers, and anthropologists. This could yield two bonuses. First, useful *concepts*, central among which is that of a *political vice*. Civic or political virtues were features of Graeco-Roman political thought, but went out of fashion, until their revival over the last 30 years. Mark E. Button offer a useful definition in his book, *Political Vices*, whose titular subject are defined as

> acquired sensibilities and motives – embedded within social institutions and political practices – that undermine the ability of political relationships (domestic or transnational) to coordinate and conciliate diverse social parts to an ideal of the political whole in a manner of justice. (2016: 1)

A second bonus of engaging with politics researchers is insight into *corruptors* as they have existed within specific political institutors and systems:

A   *'Cultures of secrecy'*. The British government during Blair's premiership suffered from a 'combination of a genuine need for confidentiality, a siege mentality, and habitual caution'. Given these needs and entrenched mentalities, a culture of secrecy emerged that tended to 'reinforce the walls of a closed world impervious both to diverse opinions and the consequence of its own actions' (Rhoades 2011: 287). Although secrecy has important uses, a pervasive culture of secrecy progressively impairs collective epistemic functioning – such as efficient information-sharing – and scaffolds *vices* such as arrogance and dogmatism (Tanesini 2016).

B   *Performative superficiality*. Blair's premiership became synonymous with 'spin', the artful manipulation of political information to present the government in the most positive light. An ethos of performative superficiality therefore developed focused on the maintenance of a publicly presentable vision of collective epistemic competence, rather than achievement of actual patterns of epistemically effective institutional performance. If epistemic failings can be disguised or reclaimed by 'spin', the institutional focus ceases to be *doing well* and becomes fixated on *looking good* (Barnett and Gaber 2001).

Clearly, there is much scope for studies of the epistemic corruption of political institutions, a joint task for political vice epistemologists and scholars of political institutions and systems. In the future, we should ask whether putatively dysfunctional political institutions might actually be functioning perfectly well relative to their values (Klein 2020, Machiavelli 2012). We should also ask whether seemingly epistemically good procedures and policies can have bad consequences: the 'Fairness Doctrines' in the United States, for instance, led to the rise of misleading and polarising forms of populist media (Clogston 2016; Hall and Phillips 2011). We should also investigate cases where individuals challenge institutions they see as corrupted, such as whistleblowing (Ceva and Bocchiola 2019; Sontoro 2018). A final project is studying vice-corruptor pairings within political systems. Some are obvious: institutional closed-mindedness is more likely if institutions lack proper procedures for soliciting and engaging with a diversity of perspectives, using public consultations, engagement with stakeholder communities, and so on. But other pairings will be harder to spot: there are many epistemic *vices*, not all well-known, and a variety of forms of institutional arrangements. So, much to do, and, alas, many reasons for doing it.

Acknowledgements

I offer my thanks to an anonymous referee and the Editors for their helpful comments and their invitation to contribute.

Notes

1 OSR is the regulatory arm of the UK Statistics Authority, a body established by the Statistics and Registration Service Act (2007). It is independent from government Ministers and separate from producers of statistics, including the Office for National Statistics: www.statisticsauthority.gov.uk.
2 Actually, one can also arguably attribute vices to abstract objects, such as policies or doctrines (Battaly 2013), although this is currently a minority position in vice epistemology.
3 Some alternative models of collective commitment are offered by Bratman (2014) and Tuomela (2013).
4 Some epistemologists argue that transparency is not always an appropriate value in certain political contexts (John 2018).
5 Interestingly, contemporary work on politics and epistemology mainly focuses on *truth*, rather than *truthfulness* and the related vices opposed to truth – or what Crerar (2017) calls the *vices of truthlessness*. Some of those vices may include Cassam calls *epistemic insouciance* (2019, ch. 4). The classic study of the truth, truthfulness, and virtue is B. Williams (2002).
6 Abandoning the commitment to these ultimate epistemic ends is one way to think about a 'post-truth' society'.
7 Analysts of epistemic corruption should search for appropriate metaphors for describing the deterioration of epistemic systems. Some popular ones are toxicological and epidemiological metaphors of the 'poisoning', 'pollution', or 'toxification' of political cultures and discourses (Tirrell 2017).

References

Alston, P. (2018) *Statement on Visit to the United Kingdom, by Professor Philip Alston, United Nations Special Rapporteur on Extreme Poverty and Human Rights* (London: UN Office of the High Commissioner for Human Rights).
Baehr, J. (2011) *The Inquiring Mind: On Virtue Epistemology and the Intellectual Virtues* (Oxford: Oxford University Press).
Bagehot, W. (1872) *The English Constitution* (London: H. S. King & Company).
Barnett, S. and I. Gaber (2001) *Westminster Tales: The Twenty-First-Century Crisis in Political Journalism* (London: Continuum).
Battaly, H. (2013) "Detecting Epistemic Vice in Higher Education Policy: Epistemic Insensibility in the Seven Solutions and the REF," *Journal of Philosophy of Education* 47(2): 263–80.
Battaly, H. (2014) *Virtue* (Cambridge: Polity).
Battaly, H. (2016) "Epistemic Virtue and Vice: Reliabilism, Responsibilism, and Personalism," in C. Mi, M. Slote, and E. Sosa (eds.), *Moral and Intellectual Virtues in Chinese and Western Philosophy: The Turn Towards Virtue* (New York: Routledge), 99–120.

Biddle, J., I.J. Kidd, and A. Leuschner (2017) "Epistemic Corruption and Manufactured Doubt: The Case of Climate Science," *Public Affairs Quarterly* 31(3): 165–87.

Bratman, M.E. (2014) *Shared Agency: A Planning Theory of Acting Together* (Oxford: Oxford University Press).

Button, M.E. (2016) *Political Vices* (Oxford: Oxford University Press).

Card, C. (1996) *The Unnatural Lottery: Character and Moral Luck* (Philadelphia, PA: Temple University Press).

Cassam, Q. (2019) *Vices of the Mind: From the Intellectual to the Political* (Oxford: Oxford University Press).

Ceva, E. and C. Bocchiola (2019) "Personal Trust, Public Accountability, and the Justification of Whistleblowing," *Journal of Political Philosophy* 27(2): 187–206.

Clogston, J. (2016) "The Repeal of the Fairness Doctrine and the Irony of Talk Radio: A Story of Political Entrepreneurship, Risk, and Cover," *Journal of Policy History* 28(2): 375–96.

Clucas, R.A. (2015) *The Character of Democracy: How Institutions Shape Politics* (Oxford: Oxford University Press).

Crerar, C. (2017) "The Vices of Truthlessness", *Open for Debate* blog, 28 September. https://blogs.cardiff.ac.uk/openfordebate/2017/08/28/the-vices-of-truthlessness.

Crerar, C. (2018) "Motivational Approaches to Intellectual Vice," *Australasian Journal of Philosophy* 96(4): 753–66.

Croce, M. and M.S. Vaccarezza (2017) "Educating through Exemplars: Alternative Paths to Virtue," *Theory and Research in Education* 15(1): 5–19.

Dillon, R. (2012) "Critical Character Theory: Toward a Feminist Perspective on 'Vice' (and 'Virtue')," in S.L. Crasnow and A.M. Superson (eds.), *Out from the Shadows: Analytical Feminist Contributions to Traditional Philosophy* (New York: Oxford University Press), 83–114.

Fricker, M. (2010) "Can There Be Institutional Vices," in T. Gendler and J. Hawthorn (eds.), *Oxford Studies in Epistemology*, vol. 3 (Oxford: Oxford University Press), 235–52.

Fricker, M. (2020) "Institutional Epistemic Vice: The Case of Inferential Inertia," in I.J. Kidd, H. Battaly, and Q. Cassam (eds.), *Vice Epistemology* (New York: Routledge), 89–107.

Gilbert, M. (1989) *On Social Facts* (Princeton, NJ: Princeton University Press).

Gilbert, M. (2000) *Sociality and Responsibility: New Essays in Plural Subject Theory* (Lanham, MD: Rowman and Littlefield).

Hall, R.T. and J.C. Phillips (2011) "The Fairness Doctrine in Light of Hostile Media Perception," *CommLaw Conspectus* 19(2): 395–422.

John, S. (2018) "Epistemic Trust and the Ethics of Science Communication: Against Transparency, Openness, Sincerity and Honesty," *Social Epistemology* 32(2): 75–87.

Jones, H. (2016) *How to Be a Government Whip* (London: Biteback).

Kidd, I.J. (2016) "Charging Others with Epistemic Vice," *The Monist* 99(3): 181–97.

Kidd, I.J. (2019) "Epistemic Corruption and Education," *Episteme* 16(2): 220–35.

Kidd, I.J. (2020) "Epistemic Corruption and Social Oppression," in I.J. Kidd, H. Battaly, and Q. Cassam (eds.), *Vice Epistemology* (New York: Routledge), 69–85.

Klein, E. (2020) *Why We're Polarised* (New York: Simon & Schuster).

Lahroodi, R. (2007) "Collective Epistemic Virtues," *Social Epistemology* 21: 281–97.

Lahroodi, R. (2019) "Virtue Epistemology and Collective Epistemology," in H. Battaly (ed.), *Routledge Handbook to Virtue Epistemology* (New York: Routledge), 407–19.

Machiavelli (2012) in Q. Skinner and R. Price (eds.), *The Prince* [1532] (Cambridge: Cambridge University Press).

Medina, J. (2013) *The Epistemology of Resistance: Gender and Racial Oppression, Epistemic Injustice, and Resistant Imaginations* (Oxford: Oxford University Press).

O'Neill, O. (2002) *A Question of Trust* (Cambridge: Cambridge University Press).

Oborne, P. (2004) *Alasdair Campbell* (London: Aurum).

OSR (UK Office for Statistics Regulation) (2010) *Statistics that Serve the Public Good: OSR's Vision: What We Do and Why.* https://www.statisticsauthority.gov.uk/.

Rauch, J. (2016) "How American Politics Went Insane," *The Atlantic*, July/August issue.

Rhoades, R.A.W. (2011) *Everyday Life in British Government* (Oxford: Oxford University Press).

Roberts, R.C. and W.J. Wood (2007) *Intellectual Virtues: An Essay on Regulative Epistemology* (Oxford: Oxford University Press).

Rothstein, B. and A. Varraich (2017) *Making Sense of Corruption* (Cambridge: Cambridge University Press).

Sontoro, D. (2018) "Charting Dissent: Whistleblowing, Civil Disobedience, and Conscientious Objection," in D. Sontoro and M. Kumar (eds.), *Speaking Truth to Power: A Theory of Whistleblowing* (Dordrecht: Springer), 151–72.

Sparling, R.A. (2019) *Political Corruption: The Underside of Civic Morality* (Philadelphia: University of Pennsylvania Press).

Tanesini, A. (2016) "'Calm Down, Dear': Intellectual Arrogance, Silencing and Ignorance," *Aristotelian Society Supplementary Volume* 90(1): 71–92.

Tanesini, A. (2018) "Epistemic Vice and Motivation," *Metaphilosophy* 49(3): 350–67.

Tessman, L. (2005) *Burdened Virtues: Virtue Ethics for Liberatory Struggles* (New York: Oxford University Press).

Thompson, Dennis F. (2005) *Restoring Responsibility: Ethics in Government, Business, and Healthcare* (Cambridge: Cambridge University Press).

Tirrell, L. (2017) "Toxic Speech: Toward an Epidemiology of Discursive Harm," *Philosophical Topics* 45(2): 139–61.

Tuomela, R. (2013) *Social Ontology* (New York: Oxford University Press).

Watson, L. (2019) "Curiosity and Inquisitiveness," in H. Battaly (ed.), *Routledge Handbook of Virtue Epistemology* (New York: Routledge), 155–66.

Watson, L. (2020) "Vices of Questioning in Public Discourse," in I.J. Kidd, H. Battaly, and Q. Cassam (eds.), *Vice Epistemology* (New York: Routledge), in press.

Williams, B. (2002) *Truth and Truthfulness: An Essay in Genealogy* (Princeton, NJ: Princeton University Press).

Williams, W. (2020) *Windrush Lessons Learned Review* (London: Her Majesty's Stationary Office).

Willis, D. and P. Kane (2018) "How Congress Stopped Working," *ProPublia*, 5 November.

Zagzebski, L. (1996) *Virtues of the Mind: An Inquiry into the Nature of Virtue and the Ethical Foundations of Knowledge* (Cambridge: Cambridge University Press).

PART 6

Democracy and epistemology

INTRODUCTION TO PART 6

Around the world, democracy is frequently held up as the paradigmatic case of rule by and for equals. It promises a form of political authority that respects the freedom and moral equality of citizens by giving each of them an equal share of political power. The ideal of democracy is to create a free community of equals. Democracy respects this ideal by giving each person an equal say in the laws that govern our shared political lives.

But what is the *epistemic* value, if any, of democracy? Does democracy leverage the wisdom of the many? Or is it more likely to dilute the influence of the smartest and most informed citizens? Despite the moral equality of all people, we know that people have different intellectual capacities, talents, and interests. While politics captures the intellectual attention of some, many people direct their talents and curiosity toward other endeavors. As a result, the distribution of political knowledge is unequal among citizens. But in a democracy, voters are supposed to have equal political authority, regardless of the epistemic rigor of their political opinions. This is worrisome insofar as less informed voters could lead us down the wrong path, setting misguided policies based on inaccurate or incomplete information. Shouldn't we aim for policies that are both epistemically and morally robust? This conundrum has led to a long and wide-ranging debate about the epistemic values of (and threats to) democracy.

In the first chapter of this section, Hélène Landemore focuses on instrumental epistemic arguments for democracy, which justify it on the basis of the epistemic quality of the outcomes that democratic procedures generate. According to Aristotle, democracy has epistemic advantages because it maximizes the cognitive diversity it brings to bear on collective problems in the face of uncertainty. Landemore develops this epistemic argument for democracy. She claims that democracy is epistemically superior to all forms of oligarchy (including rule by the few best) because it is the regime form that, in the face of political uncertainty, best taps the collective intelligence of its people.

In stark contrast, Jason Brennan argues that democracies incentivize voters to remain ignorant, indulge biases, and vote poorly. He argues that we should therefore reject democracy (which allocates fundamental political power equally) in favor of epistocracy (which allocates political power on the basis of competence). While this may conjure up ominous images of Plato's philosopher kings, Brennan outlines a form of epistocracy—which he dubs "enlightened preference voting"—that allows all citizens to vote, but where the system also estimates what a demographically identical voting public would have wanted if it had been

361

fully informed according to some test of basic knowledge. In this way, epistocracies needn't restrict the franchise and can retain the main features of liberal, representative governments, while also reducing the dangers of incompetent democratic voting.

In the next chapter, Robert Talisse considers an epistemic argument for democracy rooted in pragmatism. He says that pragmatists are often thought to be committed to an epistemic view of democracy, but this idea is complicated by certain terminological difficulties regarding the term "pragmatism" and the concept of epistemic democracy. After distinguishing an *epistemic argument for democracy* from an *epistemic conception of it*, Talisse argues that John Dewey provides a moral argument for an epistemic conception of deliberative democracy. However, Talisse maintains that this moral argument fails to accommodate an intuitive requirement for democratic legitimacy identified by John Rawls, since Dewey's conception of human flourishing is not justifiable in terms that are insusceptible to reasonable rejection by citizens. Talisse therefore develops a Peircean epistemic argument for democracy that avoids the difficulties which beset the Deweyan position.

Fabienne Peter picks up on the question of what makes political decision-making legitimate. Like Talisse, she argues that legitimate political decisions must be underpinned by well-ordered political deliberation. This includes the decision-makers themselves, their advisory bodies, and the public at large. However, she asks: what constitutes well-ordered political deliberation? Political deliberation must be governed by the relevant norms, but it is unclear what these norms are. Peter discusses different types of norms that might govern well-ordered political deliberation, with a specific focus on epistemic norms. She considers a range of epistemic norms, such as the "truth norm," the "knowledge norm," and the "justified belief norm" of political deliberation. In doing so, this chapter sheds light on how the validity of contributions to political deliberation depends on the epistemic status of the claims made.

The topic of epistemic norms for political deliberation closely connects with the next chapter in this section, which centers on the epistemic obligations of citizens. Whereas Peter investigates the epistemic norms to which citizens must adhere for political decisions to be legitimate, Cameron Boult investigates the epistemic responsibilities of citizens in a democracy. He develops a taxonomy of views and uses this as a lens to examine some prominent approaches to epistemic democracy, epistocracy, epistemic libertarianism, and pure proceduralism. This chapter explores various options for developing an account of the epistemic responsibilities of citizens in a democracy. It also argues that several recent attacks on democracy may not adequately register the availability of a minimal approach to the epistemic responsibilities of citizens in a democracy.

In the final chapter of this section, Alex Guerrero considers the epistemic case for non-electoral forms of democracy. First, he draws attention to the epistemic shortfalls of electoral representative democracy. These shortcomings suggest that the exchange of a broader distribution of political power for the supposed epistemic benefits of using elected representatives is not worth the trade. Guerrero therefore recommends a number of non-electoral alternatives that do at least as well as electoral representative government on the democracy scorecard, and which would likely do better on the epistemic scorecard. In particular, lottocratic systems and systems of technocratic agencies coupled with extensive citizen oversight would exhibit more institutional epistemic competence than electoral representative systems. This illustrates that an emphasis on epistemic value need not push us away from democracy and toward epistocracy. Instead, there are a variety of epistemically valuable forms that democracy could take.

31

AN EPISTEMIC ARGUMENT FOR DEMOCRACY

Hélène Landemore

Traditional justifications for democracy emphasize procedural or intrinsic arguments such as those based on the ideas of freedom, equality, justice, and fairness. Democracy is supposed to be a good thing because its procedures—deliberation and voting in particular—express values we care about and treat individuals in the inclusive and egalitarian way that we have come to equate with the just way of treating people in the political sphere. There also exist, however, more instrumental arguments for democracy, which justify it on the basis of the nature of the outcomes that its inclusive and egalitarian procedures are supposed to generate, such as economic growth, the minimization of bad outcomes (e.g., famines, civil wars), or other objectively "good" outcomes (e.g., education, health, and happiness indicators).

A specific variety of instrumental argument is epistemic, namely oriented toward the knowledge generated and aggregated by democratic procedures as well as, at least in some versions of the argument, the ability of democratic outcomes informed by such knowledge to track a form of truth about the common good (generally defined in pragmatic terms, if only as the ability of the polity to thrive in the face of constantly shifting political events). The epistemic argument for democracy goes back to the old Aristotelian claim that "many heads are better than one" and that a party to which the many contribute is better than a party organized at the expense of one person only (*Politics* 3.11).[1] In recent years, works done in philosophy (e.g., Nino 1996, Anderson 2006, Estlund 1997, 2008, Misak 2000, Talisse 2009) and political sciences (e.g., Goodin 2003, 2008, Martí 2006, Ober 2010; Landemore 2013, Goodin and Spiekermann 2019) have taken up the epistemic argument in modernized forms. While they share a number of traits, epistemic arguments for democracy tend to vary along a number of dimensions:

1   The mechanism by which they explain the epistemic properties of democracies (typically deliberation versus aggregation of votes): some tend to focus on deliberation (e.g., Estlund 2008, Landemore 2013), whereas others (e.g., Goodin and Spiekermann 2019) will focus on judgment aggregation via majority rule. Others still focus on a pragmatic process of trial and errors (Talisse 2009; Knight and Johnson 2011).

2   The duration along which they examine epistemic properties: some look to the synchronic properties of democracy at time t or in the very short run (Landemore 2013); others look to the long term (e.g., Talisse 2009; Knight and Johnson 2011).

3 Whether or not they commit to the assumption of a procedure-independent standard of truth or correctness in politics, as per the seminal definition of an epistemic conception of democracy (Cohen 1986). Some explicitly posit and defend this assumption (Estlund 2009, Landemore 2013, Misak 2000, Talisse 2009, Tong 2020).[2] Others formulate a "procedural epistemic" view whereby they acknowledge the knowledge-aggregating properties of democracy but remain agnostic about, sometimes even deny, the possibility or meaningfulness of a procedure-independent standard of correct, right, or true outcomes (Habermas 1996, Peter 2013, Muirhead 2014, Schwartzberg 2015).

4 The strength of the epistemic claim for democracy, especially in relation to other regime forms. Waldron (1995) distinguishes between a weak and strong version of the argument from the wisdom of the many in Aristotle, whereby the weak version defends the superiority of democracy over the rule of the lone tyrant but not that of smart subsets of the group, and the strong version defends the superiority of democracy over all oligarchic regimes and the weak version only recognizes it over rule of one. David Estlund makes a weak epistemic claim for democracy as merely superior to a random decision-rule and as inferior to rule by the knowers, or so-called epistocrats (Estlund 2009). Landemore (2012, 2013) offers the strongest (and some would say least plausible) version of the argument to date, arguing that democracy is epistemically superior to all forms of oligarchy (including rule by the few best).

In this article I rehearse this strong epistemic case for democracy (Landemore 2012, 2013), crediting the superiority of democracy over oligarchy to its greater capacity to tap the collective intelligence of its people. The rest of the article proceeds as follows. The first section presents the argument as a whole. The second section focuses on inclusive and egalitarian deliberation as a key element of democratic decision-making and explores the theoretical reasons that can be adduced for its epistemic properties. The third section presents the epistemic argument for pure judgment aggregation via majority rule as a necessary supplement to deliberation. The conclusion briefly addresses the implications and some common objections to the argument.

1 The argument in a nutshell

The argument results from a comparison in the abstract of models of pure regime forms: the rule of one, few, and many. Democracy is here modeled as a collective decision-procedure involving the combination of two mechanisms: inclusive and egalitarian deliberation and simple majority rule.

The claim is that democracy thus defined is more likely to yield better solutions and predictions on political questions than less inclusive and less egalitarian decision-rules because it structurally maximizes the cognitive diversity brought to bear on collective problems. Cognitive diversity—here defined as the fact that people see problems in the world and make predictions based on different models of the way the world works or should be interpreted[3]—is a group property that has been shown to be a crucial factor of group performance in various contexts and indeed more important to the problem-solving abilities of a group than individual competence of the members itself (Page 2007). I argue that under the conditions of uncertainty that characterize politics (the fact that the bundle of issues to be faced by any polity over the medium to long term cannot be predicted ahead of time), political decision-making characterized by maximal inclusiveness and equality can be expected to be correlated with greater cognitive diversity, which, in turn, is correlated with better problem-solving and prediction. A central assumption of the argument is that politics is characterized by uncertainty. This uncertainty (which is an assumption about the world, not necessarily the subjective epistemic stage of the deliberators) is what renders all-inclusiveness on an equal basis epistemically attractive as a model for collective decision-making. Given this uncertainty egalitarian inclusiveness is adaptive or "ecologically rational" (Landemore 2014).

2 The epistemic properties of democratic deliberation

The central mechanism for the epistemic properties of democracy, in my model, is inclusive and egalitarian deliberation.

What reasons do we have to believe that democratic deliberation, understood as an inclusive and egalitarian way of arriving at collective decisions, has epistemic properties—that is, the ability to track a procedure-independent standard of correctness (whatever one may understand by this)? The following aims to give an account of deliberation, and more specifically democratic deliberation, as the epistemic engine of a properly conceived ("deliberative") democracy.

Deliberation means, roughly, the pondering and weighing of reasons or an exchange of arguments for or against a given view. In that sense deliberation can refer to an internal dialog in the vein of "deliberation within" (Goodin 2005), an intersubjective exercise among individuals, or a deliberation occurring among entities larger than individuals, as in system-thinking (Parkinson and Mansbridge 2012).

The idea that intersubjective deliberation (leaving aside anything about "democratic" for the moment) has epistemic properties is an old one. It can be traced back all the way to Aristotle's idea that "many heads are better than one" through to Mill's emphasis on diversity of points of view in helping the truth overcome falsities and triumph in a free competition of ideas. An underlying assumption of these views is that there is a self-revealing nature of the truth, which when made apparent by the exchange of viewpoints is supposed to convince all participants in the deliberation (if not instantaneously then over time, and if not inexorably then at least under favorable conditions). This is something best expressed, perhaps, by Habermas's idea of the "unforced force of the better argument" (Habermas 1996).

How does this "unforced force of the better argument" work in practice? Let us look at the way deliberation functions in a nicely idealized (but not *too* idealized) model: the deliberations of jurors in the film *12 Angry Men*.

One of the turning points in the deliberation comes when Juror 8 produces a copy of the murder weapon, a cheap switchblade that he said he was able to buy for a fistful of dollars around the corner of the tribunal, disproving at once the unusualness and incriminating nature of the weapon. Another argument is produced by Juror 5, who grew up in a violent slum and can explain the proper manner of using a switchblade, raising doubts in the process about the plausibility of the eyewitness's description. The eyewitness's reliability is further put in doubt when it becomes clear that she usually wears glasses (as evidenced by red marks on the side of her nose observed by the jurors when she came to testify to the bar). Ultimately a unanimous consensus emerges that the young man should be found not guilty.

The story illustrates the epistemic properties of deliberation. First, it allows participants to weed out the good arguments, interpretations, and information from the bad ones (e.g., the switchblade is not as unique a weapon as previously thought and can only be used a certain way). Second, deliberative problem-solving can also produce synergies, that is, create new solutions out of the arguments, information, and solutions brought to the table (e.g., making sense of the red marks on the eyewitness's nose in a way that proves decisive to the interpretation of her reliability). Third, hearing the perspectives of others may entirely reshape a person's view of the problem and introduce possibilities not initially considered (e.g., the eyewitness testimony cannot be trusted after all). Finally, in the ideal, deliberation produces unanimous consensus on the "right" solution ("not guilty" in this case).

The example also illustrates the specific merit of deliberation among a diverse group of people. In *12 Angry Men*, all 12 jurors mattered, in all their differences, because it is only through the interplay between their conflicting interpretations of the evidence and arguments—shaped as those are by their personal history, socio-economic background, type of intelligence, and so on—that something resembling the truth ultimately emerges. The epistemic properties of deliberation importantly manifest in spite of the fact that the protagonists are far from ideal human beings. One juror just wants to be done with the deliberation and go to a baseball game, one is a bigoted racist, another is biased by irrelevant fatherly emotions... Deliberation, in other words, can overcome a number of moral and cognitive limitations.

The logic of epistemic deliberation is well captured by a theorem by Lu Hong and Scott Page, the Diversity Trumps Ability Theorem, which states that under certain conditions[4] "a randomly selected collection of problem solvers outperforms a collection of the best individual problem solvers" (Hong and Page 2001: 16388, Page 2007: 163).[5] In other words, "diversity trumps ability" and our twelve angry men are better than twelve clones of, say, Juror 8 (arguably the smartest of the lot) would have been. Diversity here refers to *cognitive* diversity, which, as defined earlier, is roughly the difference in the ways different people will think about a problem in the world.[6]

While the arguments above may account for the epistemic properties of deliberation among cognitively diverse people, they do not quite justify democratic deliberation in the sense of deliberation that (1) involves all and (2) involves all on an equal standing. Democratic deliberation can indeed be specified as intersubjective deliberation that takes place specifically in a "public" manner "among free and equal individuals" (adapted from Cohen 1989) and is also inclusive of the entirety of the relevant group, though this condition is generally left implicit in a lot of the literature in deliberative democracy.

Democratic deliberation, in order to count as plausibly democratic, thus requires publicity of its exchanges, full inclusiveness, and equal standing and equal opportunities for participation among participants ("free and equal"). Theorists appreciative of the epistemic value of deliberation may not necessarily see the epistemic value of *democratic* deliberation thus understood. Mill, after all, though a deliberative democrat on most readings, was also an advocate of a plural voting scheme that gave more voice (in the form of votes) to the learned. Clearly one can believe in the value of deliberation and not think that all involved should have an absolutely equal right to be heard.

In my book (Landemore 2013) I have provided the missing link between the epistemic properties of deliberation and democracy per se, at least when it comes to the inclusive and egalitarian features of democratic deliberation (the publicity element has yet to be shown to have epistemic properties of its own). I argue that more inclusive assemblies are simply more likely to be cognitively diverse. To the extent that cognitive diversity is a key ingredient of collective intelligence, and specifically one that matters more than average individual ability, the more inclusive the deliberation process is, the smarter the solutions resulting from it should be, overall. Numbers, in other words, function as a proxy for diversity. In the end, my argument for democracy hinges not just on the Diversity Trumps Ability Theorem, as Brennan, for example, mistakenly argues (Brennan 2016: 185) but *on my own generalization of it, under conditions of uncertainty, as the "Numbers Trump Ability Theorem"* (Landemore 2013: 104; further clarified in Landemore 2014b: 188). To quote from Landemore 2014b:

> The second step of my argument—my addendum to Page and Hong—proposes that the "cheapest" (i.e., easiest and most economical) way to achieve cognitive diversity in the absence of knowledge about the nature of complex and ever-changing political problems is to include everyone in the group. My argument here is that including everyone is the only way to get all the perspectives, heuristics, interpretations, predictive models, and information that may matter at some point (although you do not know in advance when). […] This "Numbers Trump Ability Theorem" thus supports a strong epistemic case for democracy, in which my key innovation is to support inclusiveness for its instrumental, specifically epistemic properties: Under the right conditions, including everyone in the decision-making process simply makes the group more likely to get the right (or, at least better) answers.

In other words, under conditions of uncertainty, which are argue are central to politics, the best proxy for cognitive diversity is full inclusiveness (i.e., "numbers") or, where unfeasible (for practical reasons having to do with the unfeasibility of proper, legitimacy-granting deliberation at scale), random selection.

3 Majority rule with universal suffrage

Deliberation is far from being a perfect or complete decision-mechanism, in part because it is time-consuming and rarely produces unanimity. In most cases, it needs to be supplemented by another decision-procedure: majority rule. While majority rule is more efficient time-wise, it does not permit problem-solving. It allows for, however, choosing between pre-determined options, ideally defined in the deliberation period. Far from just being a fair way to settle disagreement about the choice of an option, majority rule is also a reliable way to improve the chances of the group picking the right option (where "right" is simply the better one compared to the other options). Majority rule aggregates individuals' judgments about the best course of action to take or the right candidate to elect. In other words, majority rule is not only a fair way to settle on a decision when time is running out for deliberation, but a way to turn imperfect individual predictions into accurate collective ones. Again, since majority rule is available to the lone tyrant, who is the majority by himself, and a group of oligarchs, we need to consider whether majority rule under universal suffrage is superior to majority rule used by a minority within the larger group (it is not). There exist at least three related but distinct theoretical arguments for the epistemic properties of majority rule: the Condorcet Jury Theorem, the "Miracle of Aggregation," and Scott Page's "The Crowd Beats the Average Law." Together, they add up to an argument for the epistemic properties of majority rule, that is, decision made by the larger rather than the smaller group, on the basis of one person, one vote.

Both the Condorcet Jury Theorem[7] and the Miracle of Aggregation[8] are a version of the Law of Large Numbers, meaning that the epistemic properties of judgment aggregation only manifest with certainty at the limit for an infinity of voters (provided the relevant conditions are met). For example, the CJT demonstrates that among large electorates voting on some yes or no question, majoritarian outcomes are virtually certain to track the "truth," as long as three conditions hold: (1) voters are better than random at choosing true propositions; (2) they vote independently of each other; and (3) they vote sincerely or truthfully. The most established version of the "miracle of aggregation" explains it as the statistical phenomenon by which a few informed people in a group are enough to guide the group to the right average answer, as long as the mean of uninformed people's answers is zero.[9] Here collective intelligence actually depends on extracting the information held by an informed elite from the mass of noise represented by other people's opinions. As long as a sizeable minority in the crowd (the minority needs to be pivotal) knows the right answer and everyone else makes mistakes that cancel each other out, the right answer is still going to rise to the surface, so to speak. The typical example illustrating the Miracle of Aggregation is the weight guessing game observed by the nineteenth-century statistician Francis Galton at a country fair, in which the average answer of 800 participants' guesses regarding the weight of an ox once slaughtered and dressed turned out to fall within one pound of the right answer the right answer.[10] Galton is said to have been prompted by this result to compare the gambling situation with democratic voting and to conclude that: "The result seems more creditable to the trustworthiness of democratic judgment than might have been expected" (Galton 1907: 451).

The account I want to focus on here, however, is that of Lu Hong and Scott Page, which is based not on the law of large numbers but on models of cognitive diversity. In a book (Page 2007) and a series of articles with Lu Hong (Hong and Page 2001, 2004, 2009), Scott Page proposes a model of how large groups of people can make good judgments and, in particular, accurate predictions. Although Page's model generally applies to numerical predictions that are not of a binary form (e.g., predicting sales figures), it can be applied to scenarios where judgments are binary as well (e.g., predicting whether a candidate is competent or incompetent). In my view, Page's model can thus be used as a nicely tailored account of majority rule's epistemic properties that presents several advantages over more "statistical" accounts building on the law of large numbers.

The logic of cognitive diversity in group judgment aggregation is formalized in two mathematical results: the Diversity Prediction Theorem and the Crowd Beats Average Law. The first theorem states that when we average people's predictions, a group's collective error equals the average individual error minus their predictive diversity (Page 2007: 208). In other words, when it comes to predicting outcomes, cognitive differences among voters matter just as much as individual ability. Increasing prediction diversity by one unit results in the same reduction in collective error as does increasing average ability by one unit.

The second theorem—the Crowd Beats Average Law—states that the accuracy of the group's prediction cannot be worse than the average accuracy of its members. In other words, the group necessarily predicts more accurately than its average member. Further, the amount by which the group outpredicts its average member increases as the group becomes more diverse (Page 2007: 197). This law follows directly from the Diversity Prediction Theorem.

What does all of this mean? It means that in order to maximize our chances of picking the better of two options, we are better off, as a group, taking the average (or potentially median) answer of a sufficiently cognitively diverse group of people than letting a randomly selected individual in that group make the choice for the group. This is so because, for a given group of people using different predictive models, the predictions will be negatively correlated and mistakes will cancel each other out not randomly but systematically. As a result, the average error of the group will be less than the average error of a randomly selected voter. This is true to a greater degree as the difference between the predictive models used by the voters increases (i.e., as there is more cognitive diversity in the group).

It might not be immediately obvious how this account of the properties of the average (or median) judgment of a group applies to majority rule, which generally involves yes or no questions where no average is available. Yet, as in the case of the Miracle of Aggregation, the logic of the cognitive diversity account can be extended to such binary answers by turning each option into a quantifiable value (with yes corresponding to the value 1 and no corresponding to the value 0, for example) and seeing the majoritarian result as the closest rounding of the average result. Note that this suggests the superiority of a rating system (like so-called majority judgment) over majority rule per se.

The superiority of Page's account over the CJT or the Miracle of Aggregation, in my view, is at least twofold. First, their account circumvents the problematic assumption of judgment independence, which rendered both the CJT and the Miracle of Aggregation somewhat unrealistic. The independence assumption is now applied, more plausibly, not to people's actual judgments (their outputs) but to the cognitive processes leading to those judgments (i.e., the predictive models people use to generate judgments and predictions about the world). By internalizing the independence constraint, so to speak, that is, focusing on the independence of cognitive processes inside people's brains, rather than the independence of their resulting judgments and opinions, Page's model opens up the black box of voters' decision-making process. It also makes it possible for citizens to share information, premises, and even conclusions, while remaining "independent" in terms of the cognitive processes that treated the shared information and generated the shared conclusions.[11]

The second advantage is that Hong and Page's model supports the epistemic reliability of majority rule used among small groups.[12] The emphasis in Page's account is not so much on the existence of a large number of votes as it is on the existence of sufficient cognitive diversity in the group, no matter its size (since cognitive diversity is what ensures that votes (or predictions) are not independent but, on the contrary, negatively correlated so as to ensure systematic cancellations of individual mistakes). Unlike what happens with the CJT or the Miracle of Aggregation, we do not need to have an infinity of voters for majority rule to guarantee 100% predictive accuracy. Because cognitive diversity can exist as soon as there is more than one person making the prediction, the magic can work for as small a group as three people and is substantially increased for any addition of a person with a sufficiently diverse predictive model to the group. (In the CJT, by contrast, the major payoff of majority rule is only with large numbers, and adding one person to the group does not make much of a difference.)

The flip side of this, however, is that in Page's model there is a theoretical limitation to how much including more and more people improves collective judgment. Cognitive diversity in judgment aggregation is not a linear function of numbers and there are in fact diminishing returns to adding more people past a certain point. What the cognitive model suggests here is that it is probably better to aggregate the views of a limited number of representatives than those of millions of voters. At the scale of an assembly of representatives, aggregating more judgments can be expected to have increasing returns in terms of cognitive diversity, which may be lost when we aggregate the views of millions of citizens.

Whichever account of the epistemic properties of majority rule is favored—CJT, Miracle of Aggregation, or Cognitive Diversity Models—the conclusion is the same: the group's prediction, using majority rule, will be epistemically superior to that of the average citizen in the group. We thus have an argument why the rule of the many is superior to the rule of one (when the one is randomly chosen). This, however, does not give us a maximal argument for majority rule since majority rule among the many does not systematically beat majority rule used among a few smart people. It is therefore the superiority of democratic deliberation over oligarchic deliberation that allows us to derive the more ambitious claim for democracy as a combination of deliberation and majority rule.

4 Conclusion

The argument presented here is based on a simple model of democracy and is entirely deductive. It essentially credits the epistemic superiority of democracy to inclusive deliberation, that is, deliberation involving all the members of the community (whether directly or, where unfeasible, through their democratic representatives). The assumptions of this model can be judged too unrealistic, too ideal, or too optimistic. The applicability of the epistemic argument to real-world democracies has been questioned (e.g., Brennan 2014). In reply I have pointed out the merits of model-thinking and the fact that my deductive approach is hypothesis-generating and, ultimately, falsifiable. By contrast, the "abductive" process that consists in inducing that democracies can't possibly work on the basis of a collection of "facts" about American voters' incompetence has problems of its own (see Landemore 2014 and Landemore in Brennan and Landemore Forthcoming). The advantage of my deductive epistemic argument, ultimately, is that even if it fails to explain the way actual democracies work, it can serve as a useful normative benchmark to diagnose the way in which existing democracies epistemically dysfunction and imagine alternative institutional arrangements. One implication of the epistemic argument is indeed that in order to obtain the theoretically promised epistemic benefits of democracy, we would need to make the decision-procedures used in actual democracies a lot more inclusive and a lot more egalitarian than they are at present. Institutional reforms that the argument points toward include the replacement of elected representatives with randomly selected ones and a greater use of simple majoritarian decision-making (see Landemore 2012, 2020).

Pure proceduralist democrats, who reject outcome-oriented justifications of democracy, have also criticized the epistemic argument as a depoliticization of politics because, in their view, epistemic democrats flatten the question of value conflicts into the mundane question of disagreements about facts. In my reply to Muirhead (Landemore 2014) and my criticism of Linda Zerilli (Landemore 2018), I emphasize that politics is not strictly just about "world-building" but also, in a world of natural laws, finite resources, and mortal bodies, about "world-tracking." This latter task should not be trivialized as mere administration and is at least as political as figuring out answers to fundamental value conflicts about the proper trade-offs between inequality and freedom or the legality of abortion. Coming to the rescue of epistemic democracy from a realist position in international relations, Zhichao Tong (2020) has recently made the case that if anything it is pure procedural democrats, not epistemic democrats, who de-politicize politics by ignoring the constraints put on governments by what he calls "the circumstances of international politics," namely the fact that states operate in a competitive international ecology in which they need to display superior epistemic abilities to outcompete other states.

Other pure proceduralists have called epistemic democracy a "disfiguration" of democracy because epistemic concerns about democracy seemingly subordinate the value of political equality to instrumental or efficiency concerns (Urbinati and Saffon 2013, Urbinati 2014). The epistemic turn has even been decried as a "democratic U-turn" (Palumbo 2012), counterproductively placing the emphasis on the instrumental value of political participation as opposed to its intrinsic value. I have replied to this by arguing that epistemic democracy is not meant to be an all-encompassing, or reductionist theory of democracy and is compatible with pure procedural arguments for it. The advantage of an epistemic argument for democracy is to offer a functionalist account of why we should care about equality and inclusion, which are taken as faith tenets in pure procedural accounts.

Other critics (e.g., Ingham 2013, Schwartzberg 2015) recognize the relevance of the category of "knowledge" and "truth" for democracy but question the plausibility of the assumption of a procedure-independent standard of correctness by which we could assess democratic performance because (1) many citizens may disagree with it and (2) we can never be sure whether we have achieved it or not. To this I reply that most societies sufficiently agree on enough criteria of success for them to add up to some kind of standard (avoidance of famines, happiness index, etc.) and that the performance of democracies along such standards can be measured at least on the long term and in the aggregate. The Covid-19 pandemic has recently provided us with another clear-cut and, to a degree (assuming confounding factors can be controlled for), internationally commensurable example of procedure-independent standard of correctness: number of Covid-19 deaths (in absolute value or per capita).

Participatory deliberative democrats, finally, see the epistemic argument for democracy as an epistemocratic claim in democratic disguise seeking to short-circuit mass participation in political decision-making (Lafont 2020). My recent book on "open democracy," where I rethink democratic representation to make it as inclusive and equally accessible as possible, even as I'm skeptical that we have yet figured out how to realize proper, policy-legitimizing "mass deliberation," hopefully demonstrates that this accusation is also unfounded.

Notes

1   The epistemic argument can arguably be traced further back to the Sophist Protagoras's claim that political wisdom is widely distributed among men and that a polity is viable only when we are equally allowed to share that divine sparkle in the public form. The long history of the argument goes through authors like Spinoza, Machiavelli, Rousseau, Condorcet, Mill, and John Dewey (see Landemore 2013, Chapter 3).

2   The epistemic democrats committed to the existence of a procedure-independent standard of correctness usually understand it in a non-Platonic, minimal, and generally pragmatic way (as the context-dependent horizon of political inquiry so to speak).

3   Cognitive diversity is distinct from both its symptoms (a different set of viewpoints or opinions) and its possible root causes (gender or ethnic diversity) as well as a diversity that is actually epistemically harmful, namely a diversity of goals or values. In an epistemic framework, all the members of the group are supposed to pursue the same goal and want the same thing, namely find the right answer or make an accurate prediction.

4   There are four distinct conditions for the Diversity Trumps Ability Theorem to apply (Page 2007: 163). Whether or not they all translate neatly to the real world of politics and democratic citizens is a contested issue. See Anderson (2006) and Landemore (2013) for application to the democratic context.

5   For critics of the theorem, see Thompson 2014 and for a reply, see Kuehn (2017), Page (2015), and Singer (2018).

6   Please note that the epistemic logic at work in problem-solving among cognitively diverse groups is distinct from the statistical logic behind the Condorcet Jury Theorem, the Miracle of Aggregation, or Hong and Page's other results, the Diversity Prediction Theorem and the Crowd Beats Average Law, more on which in Section 3) in that *the deliberative logic has nothing to do with the law of large numbers*. The point here is not that a clear signal will emerge out of the noise of random errors that cancel out, even though the good and bad input alike get aggregated. It is that deliberation will weed out the bad information and arguments from the outcome entirely.

7   First formulated by the Marquis de Condorcet at the end of the eighteenth century (Condorcet 1785), the CJT was rediscovered by Duncan Black in the 1950s. It has since then spawned many formal analyses (e.g., to name a very few, Grofman, Owen and Feld 1983, Ladha 1992, List and Goodin 2001, and Bovens and Rabinowicz 2006) and been the object of a book-length study (Goodin and Spiekerman 2019). I refer the reader to these sources for an in-depth exploration.

8   See Converse (1990), Page and Shapiro (1992), Wittman (1995), Caplan (2007), and Landemore (2013) for relevant analyses.

9   This version probably goes back to Berelson, Lazarsfeld and McPhee (1954).

10   Many other anecdotes, recounted in both Surowiecki (2004) and Sunstein (2006), vividly illustrate the same "miracle" of group intelligence.

11   See also Lackey (2013) for a related defense of the presumed independence of other people's judgments as a reason to agree with the judgment of the majority.

12 In fact, their account is more optimistic for small groups than very large ones. I do not have the space to address this concern here. It seems to be the case though that majority rule used in representative assemblies is more likely to have epistemic properties than majority rule used in referendums.

References

Anderson, Elizabeth. 2006. "The Epistemology of Democracy." *Episteme: A Journal of Social Epistemology* 3(1): 8–22.

Berelson, Bernard R., Paul F. Lazarsfeld, and William N. McPhee. *1954. Voting: A Study of Opinion Formation in a Presidential Campaign*. Chicago, IL: University of Chicago Press.

Brennan, Jason. 2014. "How Smart is Democracy? You Can't Answer that Question a Priori." *Critical Review* 26(1–2): 33–58.

Brennan, Jason. 2016. *Against Democracy*. Princeton, NJ: Princeton University Press.

Bovens, Luc, and Wlodek Rabinowicz. 2006. "Democratic Answers to Complex Questions—An Epistemic Perspective." *Synthese* 150(1): 131–53.

Caplan, Bryan. 2007. *The Myth of the Rational Voter: Why Democracies Choose Bad Policies*. Princeton, NJ: Princeton University Press.

Cohen, Joshua. 1986. "An Epistemic Conception of Democracy." *Ethics* 97(1): 26–38.

Cohen, Joshua. 1989. "Deliberation and democratic legitimacy." In *The Good Polity*, edited by A. Hamlin and P. Pettit, 17–34. New York: Basil Blackwell.

Condorcet, M. 1785. *Essai sur l'Application de l'Analyse à la Probabilité des Décisions Rendues à la Pluralité des Voix*. Paris: Imprimerie Royale.

Converse, Philip. 1990. "Popular Representation and the Distribution of Information." In *Information and Democratic Processes*, edited by J. A. Ferejohn and J. H. Kuklinski, 369–89. Chicago: University of Illinois Press.

Estlund, David. 1997. "Beyond Fairness and Deliberation: The Epistemic Dimension of Democratic Authority." In *Deliberative Democracy: Essays on Reason and Politics*, edited by J. Bohman and W. Rehg, 173–204. Cambridge: MIT Press.

Estlund, David. 2009. *Democratic Authority: A Philosophical Framework*. Princeton, NJ: Princeton University Press.

Galton, Francis. 1907. "Vox Populi." *Nature* 75 (March 7): 450–51.

Goodin, Robert E., and Christian List. 2001. "Epistemic Democracy: Generalizing the Condorcet Jury Theorem." *Journal of Political Philosophy* 9(3): 277–306.

Goodin, Robert. 2003. *Reflective Democracy*. Oxford: Oxford University Press.

Goodin, Robert. 2008. *Innovating Democracy: Democratic Theory and Practice after the Deliberative Turn*. Oxford: Oxford University Press.

Goodin, Robert and Kai Spiekermann. 2019. *An Epistemic Theory of Democracy*. Oxford: Oxford University Press.

Grofman, Bernard, and Scott L. Feld. 1988. "Rousseau's General Will: A Condorcetian Perspective." *American Political Science Review* 82: 567–76.

Grofman, Bernard, Guillermo Owen, and Scott L. Feld. 1983. "Thirteen Theorems in Search of Truth." *Theory and Decision* 15: 261–78.

Habermas, Jürgen. 1996. *Between Facts and Norms: Contributions to a Discourse Theory of Law and Democracy*. Cambridge: Polity Press.

Hong, Lu, and Scott E. Page. 2001. "Problem Solving by Heterogeneous Agents." *Journal of Economic Theory* 97(1): 123–63.

Hong, Lu and Scott E. Page. 2004. "Groups of Diverse Problem Solvers Can Outperform Groups of High-Ability Problem Solvers." *Proceedings of the National Academy of Sciences of the United States* 101(46): 16385–89.

Hong, Lu and Scott E. Page. 2009. "Interpreted and Generated Signals." *Journal of Economic Theory* 144(5): 2174–96.

Ingham, Sean. 2013. "Disagreement and Epistemic Arguments for Democracy." *Politics, Philosophy & Economics* 12(2): xxx.

Knight, Jack, and James Johnson. 2011. *The Priority of Democracy: Political Consequences of Pragmatism*. Princeton: Princeton University Press.

Kuehn, Daniel. 2017. "Diversity, Ability, and Democracy: A Note on Thompson's Challenge to Hong and Page." *Critical Review: A Journal of Politics and Society* 29(1): 72–87.

Lackey, Jennifer. 2013. "Disagreement and Belief Dependence: Why Numbers Matter." In *The Epistemology of Disagreement: New Essays*, edited by David Christensen and Jennifer Lackey, *243–68*. Oxford: Oxford University Press.

Lafont, Cristina. 2020. *Democracy without Shortcuts*. Oxford: Oxford University Press.

Landemore, Hélène. 2012. "Deliberation, Cognitive Diversity, and Democratic Inclusiveness: An Epistemic Argument for the Random Selection of Representatives." *Synthese* 190(7): 1209–31.

Landemore, Hélène. 2013. *Democratic Reason: Politics, Collective Intelligence, and the Rule of the Many*. Princeton, NJ: Princeton University Press.

Landemore, Hélène. 2014a. "Democracy as Heuristic: The Ecological Rationality of Political Equality." *The Good Society* 23(2): 160–78.

Landemore, Hélène. 2014b. "Yes We Can (Make It Up on Volume): Reply to Critics." *Critical Review* 6(1–2): 184–237.

Landemore, Hélène. 2018. "Political Epistemology in the Age of Alternative Facts: On World-Building, Truth-Tracking, and Arendtian Vacillations in Linda Zerilli's A Democratic Theory of Judgment." *Political Theory* 46(4): 611–23.

Landemore, Hélène. 2020. *Open Democracy: Reinventing Popular Rule for the 21st Century*. Princeton, NJ: Princeton University Press.

Landemore, Hélène. 2021. "Let's Try Real Democracy." In *Debating Democracy*, edited by J. Brennan and H. Landemore. Oxford: Oxford University Press.

Ladha, Krishna. 1992. "The Condorcet Jury Theorem, Free Speech, and Correlated Votes." *American Journal of Political Science* 36(3): 617–34.

List and Goodin. 2001. "Epistemic Democracy: Generalizing the Condorcet Jury Theorem." *The Journal of Political Philosophy* 9(3): 277–306.

Martí, José Luis. 2006. "The Epistemic Conception of Deliberative Democracy Defended." In *Democracy and Its Discontents: National and Post-national Challenges*, edited by S. Besson and J. L. Mart., 27–56. Burlington, VT: Ashgate.

Misak, Cheryl. 2000. *Truth, Politics, Morality: Pragmatism and Deliberation*. London: Routledge.

Muirhead, Russel. 2014. "The Politics of Getting It Right." *Critical Review* 26(1–2): 115–128.

Nino, C. S. 1996. *The Constitution of Deliberative Democracy*. New Haven, CT: Yale University Press.

Ober, Josiah. 2010. *Democracy and Knowledge: Innovation and Learning in Classical Athens*. Princeton, NJ: Princeton University Press.

Page, Benjamin I., and Robert Y. Shapiro. 1992. *The Rational Public: Fifty Years of Trends in Americans' Policy Preferences*. Chicago, IL: University of Chicago Press.

Page, Scott E. 2007. *The Difference: How the Power of Diversity Creates Better Groups, Firms, Schools, and Societies*. Princeton, NJ: Princeton University Press.

Parkinson and Mansbridge. 2012. *Deliberative Systems: Deliberative Democracy at the Large Scale*. Cambridge: Cambridge University Press.

Peter, Fabienne. 2013. "The Procedural Epistemic Value of Deliberation." *Synthese* 190: 1253–66.

Schwartzberg, Melissa. 2015. "Epistemic Democracy and Its Challenges." *Annual Review of Political Science* 18: 187–203.

Singer, Daniel J. 2018. "Diversity, Not Randomness, Trumps Ability." *Philosophy of Science* 86(1): 178–91.

Sunstein, Cass. 2006. *Infotopia: How Many Minds Produce Knowledge*. London: Oxford University Press.

Surowiecki, James. 2004. *The Wisdom of Crowds: Why the Many Are Smarter than the Few and How Collective Wisdom Shapes Business, Economies, Societies, and Nations*. New York: Doubleday.

Talisse, Robert. 2009. *Democracy and Moral Conflict*. Cambridge: Cambridge University Press.

Thompson, Abigail. 2014. "Does Diversity Trump Ability? An Example of the Misuse of Mathematics in the Social Sciences." *Notices of the American Mathematical Society* 61(9): 1024–30.

Tong, Zhichao. 2020. "Political Realism and Epistemic Democracy: An International Perspective." *European Journal of Political Theory* 19(2): 184–205.

Urbinati, Nadia and Maria Paul Saffon. 2013. "Procedural Democracy, the Bulwark of Equal Liberty." *Political Theory* 41(3): 441–481.

Urbinati, Nadia. 2014. *Democracy Disfigured: Opinion, Truth, and the People*. Cambridge, MA: Harvard University Press.

Waldron, Jeremy. 1995. "The Wisdom of the Multitude: Some Reflections on Book 3, Chapter 11 of Aristotle's Politics." *Political Theory* 23(4): 563–84.

Wittman, Donald. 1995. *The Myth of Democratic Failure: Why Political Institutions Are Efficient*. Chicago: The University of Chicago Press.

32

IN DEFENSE OF EPISTOCRACY

Enlightened preference voting

Jason Brennan

In June 2016, a slight majority of British voters voted to leave the EU. Economists widely believed—and still believe—this will harm the very citizens who voted to leave. Should they have gotten their way?

Maybe not. The polling form Ipsos Mori discovered that the British public was systematically misinformed about the basic facts relevant to the decision. Leave voters believed that EU immigrants constituted 20% of the UK's population; Remain voters estimated 10%. The correct figure is about 5%. On average, both Leave and Remain voters overestimated by a factor of 40–100 what the UK pays in Child Benefits to members of other EU countries. Both vastly underestimated the amount of foreign investment from the EU and vastly overestimated the amount from China.[1] Both Leave and Remain voters got the basic facts wrong, but the more wrong a person was, the more likely they were to vote Leave. It is plausible that if the populace were better informed, Remain would have won.

In general, in most democratic elections and referenda, citizens are ignorant and misinformed about the basic facts. Their mistakes are systematic and their worldviews unsophisticated. They process information in deeply irrational ways. Only a minority have stable political beliefs or opinions. We ask them to choose leaders and, in some cases, choose laws, but they rarely have any clue what they are doing.

Democracies generally outperform other forms of government we have tried. Just why that is so is disputed (Acemoglu and Robinson 2013; Jones 2020). However, most other historical forms of government—from monarchies to oligarchies to one-party states—primarily existed to enable government elites to exploit the masses. In the same way, a bungling, inept mother who means well is better than an abusive mother. The bar is low.

This chapter outlines an alternative political system called *epistocracy*. Epistocracies retain most of the features of modern social democracies, including liberal constitutions limiting government power, the separation and devolution of powers, frequent contested elections, contestatory forums, and the like. But epistocracies apportion political power on the basis of knowledge and political competence, in order to reduce the harm caused by the ignorant, misinformed, and irrational electorate.

Voter behavior 101

In primary school, many of us learn a particular theory of how democracy functions. Let's call it the "popular sovereignty model." The theory goes as follows: first, it posits that citizens have various concerns and goals, some selfish, and some not. Second, they learn how the world, politics, and economy work. They form political beliefs and being to advocate various political policies, because they believe those policies will realize their goals. Third, they examine the candidates and parties on offer, and tend vote for the best match with a real chance of winning. Fourth, since everybody does that, the winning candidates or parties will tend to match what the majority wants. Thus, the policies and laws that are implemented after the election tend to reflect the ideological preferences of the winning coalition of voters. Finally, and fifth, if leaders do a bad job, voters punish them by voting them out in the next election.

Unfortunately, the popular sovereignty model is wrong. Or, more precisely, it describes a tiny minority of citizens, perhaps as few as 1 in 10 (Achen and Bartels 2016; Kinder and Kalmoe 2017). Political scientists, psychologists, and economists have studied voter behavior for over 60 years. They've conducted thousands of studies and amassed a huge amount of data. Their findings are largely uniform and depressing. In general, voters are ignorant, misinformed, and biased. However, there is tremendous variance. Some people know a lot, most people know nothing, and many people know *less* than nothing, because they are systematically mistaken (Campbell et al. 1960; Converse 1964; Delli-Carpini and Keeter 1996; Friedman 2006; Caplan 2007; Somin 2013).

For instance, during election years, most citizens cannot identify any congressional candidates in their district (Hardin 2009, 60). Citizens generally don't know which party controls Congress (Somin 2013, 17–21). During the 2000 US Presidential Election, while slightly more than half of all Americans knew Gore was more liberal than Bush, significantly less than half knew that Gore was more supportive of abortion rights, more supportive of welfare-state programs, favored a higher degree of aid to blacks, or was more supportive of environmental regulation (Somin 2013, 31). They do understand what political labels such as "liberal" or "conservative" signify (Kinder and Kalmoe 2017).

Voters are not merely ignorant, but many are misinformed. They make systematic mistakes about basic economic theory (Caplan 2007) and about how political power functions (Caplan et al. 2013). The American National Election Studies, conducted every other year, often test basic political knowledge. The bottom 25% of voters often perform worse than chance (Althaus 2003).

Citizens are also epistemically irrational. They suffer from cognitive biases which prevent them from processing information in a reasonable or truth-tracking way. Strong emotions cause them to reason poorly. They tend to look for and accept evidence that confirms their pre-existing beliefs, but dismiss or ignore evidence which contradicts what they believe. They quickly rationalize and dismiss bad behavior on their side but interpret even good behavior from the other side in a negative way. They tend to assume those they disagree with are stupid and evil. They try to twist evidence to claim it supports whatever they want it to (Tversky and Kahneman 1973; Tajfel and Turner 1979; Tajfel 1981; Tajfel 1982; Kahneman et al. 1982; Rasinki 1989; Bartels 2003; Arceneaux and Stein 2006; Taber and Lodge 2006; Westen et al. 2006; Westen, 2008; Haidt 2012; Kelly 2012; Chong 2013; Lodge and Taber 2013; Taber and Young 2013; Erison et al. 2014).

Information matters. The policies people prefer depends in part on how informed they are. When controlling for the influence of sex, race, and income, highly informed citizens have systematically different policy preferences from ignorant or misinformed voters (Althaus 2003).

However, most citizens lack stable political beliefs or ideologies. While many citizens label themselves conservative or liberal, or attach themselves to political parties, only a small minority, fewer than 1 in 5, have stable beliefs over time, or have real political opinions. A large segment of the population is politically agnostic (Converse 1964; Barnes 1971; Inglehart and Klingemann 1976; Arian and Shamir 1983; Converse and Pierce 1986; Zaller 1992; McCann 1997; Goren 2005; Zachmeister 2006; Lewis-Beck et al. 2008; Achen and Bartels 2016; Kinder and Kalmoe 2017; Mason 2018).

Political affiliation is largely not about belief or policy. As Anthony Appiah (2018) says, "People don't vote for what they want. They vote for who they are." Citizens vote largely on the basis of partisan loyalties grounded in their identities, which do not track ideology, sincere policy preferences, or their interests. Rather, partisan attachments usually result from accidental, historical connections between certain identity groups and certain political movements and parties. In the same way that people from Boston root for the Patriots to demonstrate their fidelity to their group, Boston Irish people vote Democrat, Southern Evangelicals vote Republican, and so on. Citizens often change their expressed "beliefs" to fit their party; they rarely choose a party on the basis of shared beliefs (Cohen 2003; Mutz 2006; Iyengar et al. 2012; Kahan et al. 2013; Somin 2013; Iyengar and Westwood 2015; Achen and Bartels 2016).

Citizens are bad at retrospective voting (Healy and Malholtra 2010). Retrospective voting demands a great deal of voters. They must know who was in power, what they did, what they could have done, how to evaluate what they did versus what they could have done, and finally whether the challengers are likely to be any better. In fact, it appears that voters at best tend to punish or reward incumbents for the last sixth months or so of economic performance. However, as Achen and Bartels say, if the incumbents were not responsible for those outcomes, this is little better than kicking the dog because one had a bad day at work (Achen and Bartels 2016).

In political science and economics, the dominant explanation for *why* citizens behave so poorly is that democracy incentivizes them to do so. Because individual votes count for so little, citizens generally have no incentive to be informed, no incentive to correct their errors, and every incentive to indulge their worst biases. They are ignorant, misinformed, and biased because the expected costs of acquiring information and overcoming their biases exceed the expected benefits. They are *rationally ignorant* and *rationally irrational*.

We don't make it up in bulk

Most voters are ignorant, misinformed, irrational, tribalistic followers. Still, in some cases, large groups of people can be wise as a collective even though the individuals within those crowds are not wise. For instance, when we ask people to guess the number of jellybeans in a jar, most individual's answers are mistaken. But their mean guess is quite accurate. Indeed, the more people we add, the more accurate the mean becomes.

Perhaps democratic voting has the same features, in which the group is wise even though the individuals within the group are not. Three popular mathematical models are often invoked to defend democracy in just this way:

1   *The Miracle of Aggregation*: Ignorant voters will vote randomly. Accordingly, they will cancel each other out, leaving the well-informed minority to decide the election. A large electorate composed mostly of ignorant voters performs like an informed electorate.
2   *Condorcet's Jury Theorem*: If the average reliability of individuals in a collective decision is greater than 0.5, then as the number of individuals gets higher, the probability that the group will select the right answer approaches 1. (However, if their mean reliability is <0.5, then the probability the group will select the *wrong* answer approaches 1.)
3   *Hong-Page Theorem*: Under certain conditions, when groups are making a collective decision, increasing the cognitive diversity of members of the group better enhances the reliability of the group as a whole than increasing the reliability of individual members of that group.

Each of these theorems relies upon a mathematical model. The important question is whether the models correspond to what happens in real-life democratic decision-making.

It's worth noting that while the mathematics of the third theorem is highly controversial. Mathematician Abigail Thompson claims that the proof of the Hong-Page Theorem rests on several identifiable mathematical errors. She further claims that the mathematical stand in for "diversity" in the theorem does not correspond to anything that we might call "cognitive diversity" in the real world. She also argues the proof is not generalizable (Thompson 2014). Similarly, Paul Quirk, among others, claims that the "proof" depends upon a series of computer experiments "strongly biased toward that result [that diversity trumps ability] and argues that it tells us nothing about decision-making in real-world political settings" (Quirk 2014). Further, as many have noted, one reason why "diversity trumps ability" in the Hong-Page Theorem, as groups become larger, is that the theorem in effect models large groups as including the most elite performers and deferring to them when they are right. Philosopher David Wallace notes that theorem simply assumes that whenever smart agents get stuck, there is always another person who can and will improve the group's decision. The theorem is supposed to prove this, he says, but in fact Hong and Page bake these assumptions in as *premises*. Thus, their result is trivial.[2]

Let's put these worries aside. Instead, consider what Hélène Landemore (2012, 195) says:

> The main problem with the optimistic conclusions about group intelligence…is that in some way or another they rely on the assumption that there is a symmetrical distribution (random or otherwise) of errors around the right answer (Miracle of Aggregation) or that errors are negatively correlated (Hong and Page).

If citizens' errors are not randomly or symmetrically distributed, or if citizens tend to make systematic mistakes, tend to follow one another's opinions, or tend to be systematically misinformed and unreliable, then these mathematical theorems cannot be used in support of democracy. (Landemore herself nevertheless supports highly optimistic conclusions about how well democracy performs.)

As discussed in previous section, the empirical literature supports the following claims:

1   Citizens do not form their ideas or decide how to vote independently and separately. They follow one another, and in particular, tend to parrot whatever their party happens to say.
2   Citizens vote for largely non-cognitive and non-ideological problems. They are cheering for their team, not trying to discover the right answer.

3   Most citizens have very unsophisticated mental models of politics and very low levels of information.
4   Citizens make systematic errors and are systematically mistaken about a wide range of basic political facts and more advanced social scientific knowledge.

These points are fatal to "wisdom of the crowd" defenses of democracy. Voters' errors compound rather than cancel. They lack the kind of cognitive diversity and basic sophistication the Hong-Page Theorem. Condorcet's Jury Theorem, rather than being used to defend democracy, might be used to critique it.

Incompetent rule is unjust

Imagine a capital murder case. Suppose that the trial proceeds as normal, with both the prosecution and defense presenting their arguments, evidence, and so on. However, suppose the jury has any or all of the following features:

1   They are *ignorant*. They pay no attention to the facts of the case. They refuse to read the transcript. They flip a coin and find the defendant guilty.
2   They are *misinformed*. The jury deeply misunderstands the facts of the case. For instance, they have clearly false beliefs about where the defendant was during the murder, what the defendant's relationship to the victim was, and so on. Their false beliefs explain why they found him guilty.
3   They are *irrational*. They pay attention to the facts of the case, which indicate rather clearly that the defendant is innocent. However, the jurors process information in deeply irrational way, and so conclude he is guilty.
4   They are *malicious, selfish, or acting in bad faith*. They find the defendant guilty because he is a member of disliked religious group, or because he owns a rival restaurant, or because they took a bribe.
5   They are *tribalistic*. They find the defendant guilty because they are just the kind of people who vote guilty every time, regardless of the facts.

In these cases, if we knew the jury decided in any of these ways, it would be wrong and unjust to enforce their decision. Their decision would lack authority. Indeed, in some US states, if a defendant who demonstrated the jury made a decision on any such grounds would be entitled to a retrial.

What seems to explain these intuitions are the following: the jury is charged with administrating justice. They act as representatives of society as a whole. They will impose their will upon a possibly innocent person. Their decision is high stakes, and can deprive a person of property, freedom, and even life. In situations like this, a *minimal condition* for the decision to be legitimate and authoritative is that they decide competently and in good faith. If they are incompetent as a body in general, or if they make this particular decision incompetently and in bad faith, then it would be wrong to enforce their decision.

This point generalizes to other political decision. Many political decisions are high stakes, can greatly affect other people's welfare, alter their life prospects, and deprive them of life, liberty, property, and happiness. The people making these decisions are usually charged with acting on behalf of the common good and are supposed to aim for just outcomes. Thus, I think juries, judges, police officers, presidents, legislators, bureaucrats, governors, and even *the voting public* is constrained by what I call the *Competence Principle*:

The competence principle

It is presumed to be unjust and to violate a citizen's rights to forcibly deprive them of life, liberty, or property, or significantly harm their life prospects, as a result of decisions made by an incompetent deliberative body, or as a result of decisions made in an incompetent way or in bad faith. Political decisions are presumed legitimate and authoritative only when produced by competent political bodies in a competent way and in good faith.

In short, the idea is that a minimal condition of a political decision being authoritative and legitimate is that it must be made by a reliable/competent body or decision-making process, in a competent way, and in good faith.

To make my argument work, I do not need to defend some precise theory of political competence. Any plausible theory of competence and good faith would agree that the jurors are incompetent or acting in bad faith in 1–5 above. If one is ignorant or misinformed despite salient information being available, if one sticks to the same beliefs come what may, or if one forms beliefs almost entirely on the basis of non-evidentiary factors, then one acts incompetently.

Notice that the electorate's decisions have the same morally salient features as the jury decisions:

1   Electorates are charged with making morally momentous decisions, as they must decide how to apply principles of justice, and how to shape many of the basic institutions of society. They are one of the main vehicles through which justice is to be established.
2   Electoral decisions tend to be of major significance. They can significantly alter the life prospects of citizens, and deprive them of life, liberty, and property.
3   The electorate claims sole jurisdiction for making certain kinds of decisions over certain people within a geographic area. The electorate expects people to accept and abide by their decisions.
4   The outcomes of decisions are imposed involuntarily through violence and threats of violence.

This is strong presumptive reason to hold that the Competence Principle applies not merely to juries, judges, presidents, and the like, but even to the voting electorate as a whole.

How the group votes matters. Voters sometimes directly choose policy. Other times, they choose representatives who, in turn, create policy. If voters choose badly, they can cause serious injustices. They can choose leaders who will implement destructive tariffs, run up the debt, leave the poor behind, start unnecessary and unjust wars, ignore or exacerbate existential threats, or mismanage criminal justice, among other things.

When democracies make bad choices, this is not the moral equivalent of a single person making poor choices for herself. When the democratic majority or winning plurality makes bad choices, they impose their will upon the losing minorities, residents unable to vote, future generations, and foreigners who must live with the consequences.

Enlightened preference voting

There are many possible ways to mitigate the harmfulness of bad voting. Here, I'll discuss one possibility.

Ample work in political science and economics shows that low-information and high-information voters have different policy preferences. Martin Gilens notes that even within a single party, the high-information and low-information members disagree. For instance, high-information Democrats are more pro-free-trade and less militaristic than low-information Democrats (Gilens 2012, 106–11).

However, we also know that information is correlated with various demographic factors. A persistent finding over the past 60 years in the US is that, when it comes to basic political knowledge, the rich know more than the poor, men know more than women, whites know more than blacks, and so on. In short, the more privileged tend also to be better informed (Delli-Carpini and Keeter 1996, 135–77). Thus, one might worry that if informed people disagree with the uninformed, these demographic factors rather than information might confound or even drive the results. Since high-information voters also tend to be rich, perhaps it's their income rather than the information that makes them pro-free-trade.

Fortunately, researchers are already aware of this and have developed research methods which allow us to test the effect of information, while controlling for demographics, and vice versa. The basic method goes as follows:

1 Give everyone a test of some aspect of political knowledge. Find out what they know.
2 Collect information about their demographics. Find out who they are.
3 Survey them on their opinions, beliefs, etc. Find out what they want.

Once we have all three sets of data, we can assess the independent effect of knowledge or the independent effect of demographics, all while controlling for confounds. Further, we can statistically estimate what the public *would* have wanted if things changed. This method allows to estimate, for instance, what an otherwise identical but all-female or all-male public would want. Most importantly for our purposes here, it allows us to estimate what a demographically identical public would want if it had gotten a perfect score on the knowledge test. Call this the publics' *enlightened preferences* (Althaus 2003; Caplan 2007).

I suggest we use this method to produce better political outcomes. The procedure goes as follows. On election day, everyone is allowed to vote, including children. When they vote, though, they must do three things:

1 Take a 40-question, closed-book quiz on basic political knowledge.
2 Tell us their demographic factors. (Perhaps this can be set ahead of time on a voter ID card.)
3 Tell us their opinion on whatever the election is about, for instance, which candidate or party they support, or which position they take on a referendum.

Afterward, all the voting data is anonymized and made public. The government then calculates—using methods that can be checked by any major newspaper and many statistically savvy researchers—what a demographically identical public would have wanted if it had gotten a perfect score on the quiz. In short, we calculate the electorates' enlightened preferences and implement those instead of their actual, unenlightened preferences. Call this *enlightened preference voting.*

Keep in mind that the quality of the candidates on the ballot, the quality of the policies they espouse, and the ways parties are organized are not exogenous factors. They depend significantly on the kind of voting system used and on the quality of the voters themselves.

Parties want to win, and so the positions they push and candidates they forward depend on what they believe will help them win. Enlightened preference voting will not merely tend to ensure we select the better choices on the ballot; it will tend to ensure that all the choices that make it on the ballot are already better.

Now, one might argue this counts as a form of democracy rather than epistocracy. After all, no one is excluded. Citizens are not required to pass the quiz to earn the right to vote. It's not exactly true that the more knowledgeable receive more votes than the less knowledgeable. Rather, everyone has equal input, and we use these inputs to estimate what an informed but otherwise identical public would have wanted. We can mathematically estimate afterwards that different citizens had different *average* or *marginal* effects, but even this is somewhat artificial. For this reason, a committed democrat who likes this idea might insist that enlightened preference voting is a form of democracy. Rather than excluding some people or elevating some above others, it is simply a better method for extracting the hidden wisdom of the crowd. On the other hand, in enlightened preference voting, the "people" do not get their way; rather, the ruling group is a hypothetical electorate statistically derived from the actual electorate. This counts against calling the system democracy. Still, rather than resolve this definitional debate here, I will simply note the issue.

One virtue of this system is that it allows us to test to what degree various political outcomes results from demographic bias. We can simulate whether, for instance, an all-black or all-female polity would have chosen differently. With such information, we could in principle correct for problems which arise when small minorities have their (enlightened) preferences thwarted time and time again.

There are good questions about how to design this system. Who decides which questions go on the quiz? Who decides what the demographic categories will be?

This might matter less than one would suspect. After all, as of now, various political scientists and economists have employed the enlightened preference on different data sets, using different groups of people, different demographic categories, and different tests of competence and knowledge. So far, they tend to generate similar results despite that: the enlightened public is more free trade, more in favor of interactions with foreigners, more civil libertarian, and more in favor of tax increases to offset the deficit (Althaus 2003; Caplan 2007; Gilens 2012).

Regardless, I recommend that in order to reduce the amount of political gaming and rent seeking that might corrupt the system, we let the people design it. Allow elections to proceed as normal. However, three weeks or so before the election, we randomly select 500 citizens. They are paid to spend a weekend together deliberating to choose the questions which go on the quiz. They also can revise the demographic indicators.

This may seem paradoxical. I have argued citizens are largely incompetent to choose policy or leaders. They lack basic political information. Why then would they be competent to design the quiz? They know an informed citizen needs to know who is in power, what they did, how to assess what they did, whether people are getting richer or poorer, healthier or less healthy, or whether crime is up or down. Here, the problem is not that citizens lack a good grasp of what the right questions are. Rather, the problem is that they lack the answers. The question "what counts as an informed citizen" is an easy one where the crowd can produce a good answer, even if though most in the crowd are not informed. Further, the citizens who design the poll can piggy-back off of things like the American National Election Studies or the US citizenship exam. Further, one advantage of this system is that, with only 500 citizens choosing what appears on the test, they will have stronger incentives to do their jobs well.

In the real world, I expect this system to be flawed, just as in the real world, any democratic voting system is flawed. The question is not whether it will be perfect. The question is whether it will be *better*. Democracy has many virtues compared to the systems we have tried. It also has a systematic flaw: it spreads power out widely, and in virtue of doing so, incentivizes those who hold that power to use it unwisely. We have a moral obligation to fix this problem as best we can.

Notes

1 https://www.ipsos-mori.com/researchpublications/researcharchive/3742/The-Perils-of-Perception-and-the-EU.aspx.
2 https://leiterreports.typepad.com/blog/2019/11/a-mathematical-proof-that-diversity-trumps-ability-turns-out-to-be-just-more-diversity-blather.html.

Works cited

Acemoglu, Daron, and Robinson, James. 2013. *Why Nations Fail*. New York: Currency.
Achen, Christopher, and Bartels, Larry. 2016. *Democratic Theory for Realists*. New York: Princeton University Press.
Althaus, Scott. 2003. *Collective Preferences in Democratic Politics*. New York: Cambridge University Press.
Appiah, Anthony. 2018. "People Don't Vote for What They Want. They Vote for Who They Are," *Washington Post*, August 30. https://www.washingtonpost.com/outlook/people-dont-vote-for-want-they-want-they-vote-for-who-they-are/2018/08/30/fb5b7e44-abd7-11e8-8a0c-70b618c98d3c_story.html.
Arceneaux, Kevin, and Stein, Robert M. 2006. "Who Is Held Responsible When Disaster Strikes? The Attribution of Responsibility for a Natural Disaster in an Urban Election," *Journal of Urban Affairs* 28: 43–53.
Arian, Asher, and Schamir, Michal. 1983. "The Primarily Political Functions of the Left-Right Continuum," *Comparative Politics* 15: 139–58.
Barnes, Samuel H. 1971. "Left, Right, and the Italian Voter," *Comparative Political Studies* 4: 157–75.
Bartels, Larry. 2003. "Democracy with Attitudes," in *Electoral Democracy*, ed. George Rabinowitz and Michael B. MacKeun, pp. 48–82. New York: Oxford University Press.
Campbell, Angus, Converse, Philip E., Miller, Warren E., and Stokes, Donald E. 1960. *The American Voter*. New York: John Wiley.
Caplan, Bryan. 2007. *The Myth of the Rational Voter*. Princeton, NJ: Princeton University Press.
Caplan, Bryan, Crampton, Eric, Grove, Wayne A., and Somin, Ilya. 2013. "Systematically Biased Beliefs about Political Influence: Evidence from the Perceptions of Political Influence on Policy Outcomes Survey," *PS: Political Science and Politics* 46: 760–7.
Chong, Dennis. 2013. "Degrees of Rationality in Politics," in *The Oxford Handbook of Political Psychology*, ed. David O. Sears and Jack S. Levy, pp. 96–129. New York: Oxford University Press.
Cohen, Geoffrey. 2003. "Party over Policy: The Dominating Impact of Group Influence on Political Beliefs," *Journal of Personality and Social Psychology* 85: 808–22.
Converse, Philip. 1964. "The Nature of Belief Systems in Mass Publics," in *Ideology and Discontent*, ed. D. E. Apter, pp. 206–61. London: Free Press of Glencoe.
Converse, Philip, and Pierce, Richard. 1986. *Political Representation in France*. Cambridge, MA: Harvard University Press.
Delli-Carpini, Michael X., and Keeter, Scott. 1996. *What Americans Know about Politics and Why It Matters*. New Haven, CT: Yale University Press.
Erison, Cengiz, Lodge, Milton, and Taber, Charles S. 2014. "Affective Contagion in Effortful Political Thinking," *Political Psychology* 35(2014): 187–206.
Friedman, Jeffrey. 2006. "Democratic Competence in Normative and Positive Theory: Neglected Implications of 'The Nature of Belief Systems in Mass Publics'," *Critical Review* 18: i–xliii.
Gilens, Martin. 2012. *Affluence and Influence*. Princeton, NJ: Princeton University Press.
Goren, Paul. "Party identification and core political values." *American Journal of Political Science* 49.4(2005): 881–896.

Guerrero, Alexander. 2010. "The Paradox of Voting and the Ethics of Political Representation," *Philosophy and Public Affairs* 38: 272–306.

Haidt, Jonathan. 2012. *The Righteous Mind.* New York: Pantheon.

Hardin, Russell. 2009. *The Economics of Ordinary Knowledge.* Princeton, NJ: Princeton University Press.

Healy, Andrew, and Malholtra, Neil. 2010. ""Random Events, Economic Losses, and Retrospective Voting: Implications for Democratic Competence," *Quarterly Journal of Political Science* 5: 193–208.

Inglehart, Ronald, and Klingemann, Hans. 1976. "Party Identification, Ideological Preference, and the Left-Right Dimension among Western Mass Publics," in *Party Identification and Beyond*, ed. Ian Budge, Ivor Crewe, and Dennis Fairlie, pp. 243–73. London: Wiley.

Iyengar, Shanto, Sood, Guarav, and Lelkes, Yphtach. 2012. "Affect, Not Ideology: A Social Identity Perspective on Polarization," *Public Opinion Quarterly* 76: 405–31.

Iyengar, Shanto, and Westwood, Sean J. 2015. "Fear and Loathing Across Party Lines: New Evidence on Group Polarization," *American Journal of Political Science* 59: 690–707.

Jones, Garrett. 2020. *10% Less Democracy.* Stanford, CA: Stanford University Press.

Kahan, Dan, Peters, Ellen, Cantrell Dawson, Erica, and Slovic, Paul. 2013. "Motivated Numeracy and Enlightened Self-Government," *Behavioral Public Policy* 1: 54–86.

Kahneman, Daniel, Slovic, Paul, and Tversky, Amos, eds. 1982. *Judgment under Uncertainty: Heuristics and Biases.* New York: Cambridge University Press.

Kelly, James Terence. 2012. *Framing Democracy.* Princeton, NJ: Princeton University Press.

Kinder, Donald and Kalmoe, Nathan. 2017. *Neither Liberal nor Conservative: Ideological Innocence in the American Public.* Chicago, IL: University of Chicago Press.

Landemore, Hélène. 2012. *Democratic Reason.* Princeton: Princeton University Press.

Lewis-Beck, Michael, Jacoby, William, Norpoth, Helmut, and Weisberg, Herbert. 2008. *The American Voter Revisited.* Ann Arbor: University of Michigan Press.

Lodge, Milton, and Taber, Charles. 2013. *The Rationalizing Voter.* New York: Cambridge University Press.

Mason, Lilliana. 2018. "Ideologues without Issues: The Polarizing Consequences of Ideological Identities," *Public Opinion Quarterly* 82: 280–301.

McCann, James A. 1997. "Electoral Choices and Core Value Change: The 1992 Presidential Campaign," *American Journal of Political Science* 41: 564–83.

Mutz, Diana. 2006. *Hearing the Other Side.* Cambridge: Cambridge University Press.

Quirk, Paul. 2014. "Making It Up on Volume: Are Large Groups Really Smarter?," *Critical Review* 26: 129–50.

Rasinki, Kenneth A. 1989. "The Effect on Question Wording on Public Support for Government Spending," *Public Opinion Quarterly* 53: 388–94.

Somin, Ilya. 2013. *Democracy and Political Ignorance.* Stanford, CA: Stanford University Press.

Taber, Charles, and Lodge, Milton R. 2006. "Motivated Skepticism in the Evaluation of Political Beliefs," *American Journal of Political Science* 50: 755–69.

Taber, Charles, and Young, Everett. 2013. "Political Information Processing," in ed. Leonie Huddy, David Sears, and Jack Levy 2013, pp. 525–58.

Tajfel, Henri. 1982. *Social Identity and Intergroup Relations.* Cambridge: Cambridge University Press.

Tajfel, Henry. 1981. *Human Groups and Social Categories.* New York: Cambridge University Press.

Tajfel, Henry, and Turner, J.C. 1979. "An Integrative Theory of Intergroup Conflict," in *The Social Psychology of Intergroup Relations*, ed. W. G. Austin and S. Worchel. pp. 33–37. Monterey, CA: Brooks-Cole.

Thompson, Abigail. 2014. "Does Diversity Trump Ability?," *Notices of the American Mathematical Society* 61: 1–24.

Tversky, Andrew, and Kahneman, Daniel. 1973. "Availability: A Heuristic for Judging Frequency and Probability," *Cognitive Psychology* 5: 207–33.

Westen, Drew. 2008. *The Political Brain.* New York: Perseus Books.

Westen, Drew, Blagov, Pavel S., Harenski, Keith, Kilts, Clint, and Hamann, Stephan. 2006. "The Neural Basis of Motivated Reasoning: An fMRI Study of Emotional Constraints on Political Judgment during the U.S. Presidential Election of 2004." *The Journal of Cognitive Neuroscience* 18: 1947–58.

Zachmeister, Elizabeth. 2006. "What's Left and Who's Right? A Q-method Study of Individual and Contextual Influences on the Meaning of Ideological Labels," *Political Behavior* 28: 151–73.

Zaller, John. 1992. *The Nature and Origins of Mass Opinion.* New York: Cambridge University Press.

33

A PRAGMATIST EPISTEMIC ARGUMENT FOR DEMOCRACY

Robert B. Talisse

It is commonly thought that pragmatists must be committed to an epistemic view of democracy.[1] That strikes me as correct, though the matter is complicated by ambiguities concerning both pragmatism and epistemic democracy. Hence it will be helpful to begin with some taxonomizing remarks. With the requisite clarifications in place, I'll examine the most influential pragmatist approach to democracy, which derives from John Dewey. After arguing that the Deweyan view is flawed on pragmatist grounds, a superior pragmatist approach rooted in a Peircean social epistemology will be sketched.

Terminological preliminaries

Call a conception of democracy *epistemic* if it contends that democracy's value, legitimacy, or justification lies centrally in some epistemological capacity or property it manifests. According to some such conceptions, democracy's value lies in its ability to produce wise or correct outcomes (Nino 1998; Estlund 2007; Landemore 2012). Other epistemic views look inward, holding that democracy's value lies in the epistemic benefits it confers on its citizens; some views of this kind claim that democracy creates a better-informed and more rational citizenry (Cohen 1986; Benhabib 1994). There are several additional variants.

It is commonly argued by epistemic democrats that democracy's epistemic potential is the *reason why* we should be democrats. In some cases, the epistemic capacity of democracy is presented as a sufficient reason to favor democracy over alternatives. Others constrain the warranting power of the epistemic considerations within some broader moral requirement; for example, David Estlund (2007) argues that we should favor democracy because it is epistemically best among the morally permissible political orders. This view appeals to moral considerations in rejecting political arrangements that are epistemically superior to democracy.

Naturally, there are many different ways of coupling an epistemic conception of democracy with an epistemic argument in its favor. But we need not linger on these complexities. The point thus far is simply that we can distinguish between epistemic conceptions of democracy and different kinds of epistemic arguments for them.

Epistemic conceptions of democracy are to be contrasted with non-epistemic conceptions, the most prevalent of which are those that cast democracy's value, legitimacy, or justification in fundamentally *moral* terms. On these views, democratic arrangements need not realize some epistemic good, but instead satisfy some moral requirement, such as that governments must treat persons as equals (Dworkin 2000; Christiano 2008). Other moral views contend that democracy is that political order that performs the moral function of constraining power and avoiding domination (Pettit 2012; Shaipro 2016) or achieving a properly inclusive (Young 2000) or free (Gould 1988) society. Importantly, moral conceptions of democracy need not deny that democracy is epistemically beneficial. They must claim only that the epistemic merits of democracy, whatever they may be, are not central to democracy's value or legitimacy.

A different variety of non-epistemic conception, often called "realist," holds that democracy's central virtue is neither moral nor epistemic, but prudential, such as that democracy reliably produces political stability and efficiency (Riker 1982; Posner 2003; Somin 2020). These views tend to reject claims regarding the epistemic power of democracy, and many of them are skeptical of the very idea that our political arrangements answer to any normative standards – be they epistemic or moral – at all.

In addition, there are some views in currency that adopt the epistemic democrats' basic stance about what justifies democratic arrangements, and then argue that actually existing democracies are irredeemably defective from the epistemic point of view. Some theorists of this stripe argue that a suitably designed *epistocracy* (rule of the wise) is preferable to democracy (Brennan 2016); others propose to introduce elements of *epistemic paternalism* into politics (Ahlstrom-Vij 2013).

Turn next to pragmatism. Although it is common to talk about pragmatism as if it were a unified school or perspective, its three originators – Charles Peirce, William James, and John Dewey – differed over fundamental questions concerning meaning, truth, knowledge, and value. These differences produced at least two distinct strands in "classical" pragmatism: a Pericean view that upheld an objectivist conception of meaning and truth, and the more subjectivist or instrumentalist versions of James and Dewey.[2] Contemporary pragmatism remains varied along similar lines, as Susan Haack's (1997) "dialogue" between Peirce and Richard Rorty demonstrates.[3] Consequently, one looks in vain for a more accurate encapsulation of pragmatism than this: pragmatism is a variety of naturalist empiricism that places human activity at the heart of philosophical theorizing.

Though correct as far it goes, this summation of pragmatism doesn't go far. Observe that many non-pragmatist varieties of empiricism satisfy the description. More importantly, philosophical disputes over what is meant by "naturalism," "empiricism," "human activity," and "philosophical theorizing" run deep. Such disputes thrive among pragmatists, accounting for the divergent varieties of pragmatism. For example, those who, like Nelson Goodman (1978), see human activity as paradigmatically *creative* tend to embrace the Jamesian strand, while those who, with Cheryl Misak (1999), instead see human activity as marked by the struggle to *find things out* lean toward the Peircean pole.

Many additional positions lie within that spectrum. As early as 1908, A. O. Lovejoy was able to discern 13 distinct varieties of pragmatism (1908). Today the number is far higher. It is tempting to join W. V. O. Quine in simply dropping the term "pragmatism" for the impeccably pragmatist reason that it "draws a pragmatic blank" (1981: 23). For what it's worth, my own inclination is to abandon the term as a characterization of philosophers and their overall systems of thinking; there are arguments, intuitions, and considerations that are appropriately regarded as "pragmatist," but there is no "pragmatism" *uberhaupt*, and there's no pragmatically clear sense in calling any philosopher a pragmatist, except as a shorthand for picking out a relatively nebulous subpopulation within the community of academic philosophy (Talisse 2018).

That pragmatism itself should admit of a characterization only at such a high degree of abstraction is an irony that can't be explored here.[4] Still, in turning to the topic of pragmatism and democracy, a different irony confronts us. One might expect that an idiom that tethers theorizing to human activity would be centrally focused on topics in political philosophy. Alas, Peirce wrote nothing in political philosophy and James devoted very little attention to political topics. John Dewey is the first among the pragmatists to place political philosophy – in particular, democracy – at the center of the pragmatist idiom. In this, he was followed by his most faithful, though sadly now neglected, student, Sidney Hook.[5] Among most contemporary pragmatists who work in political philosophy, Dewey's writings on democracy remain the lodestar.

For this reason, our substantive discussion must begin with Dewey. Yet, as I mentioned, it cannot end there because Deweyan democracy is ultimately nonviable. Laying out the limitations of Deweyan democracy will set the stage for a more promising approach rooted in Peirce's pragmatist epistemology.

Deweyan democracy and its limitations

In order to get a handle on Deweyan democracy, it helps to begin with the larger picture of Dewey's philosophy. Dewey advanced an empiricism rooted in the idea that experience is fundamentally an experimental *problem-solving* circuit of successive doing and undergoing (MW10: 9).[6] According to Dewey, when the phases of this circuit are made explicit within experience, the resulting activity is called *inquiry* (LW12: 108). Whereas all experience is a transaction between an active organism and various obstacles within its environment, inquiry ensues when this process is directed by the agent in a deliberate way (LW12: 105).

As the appeal to organisms and environments suggests, Dewey saw his empiricism as rooted in a philosophical extrapolation of Darwinism (MW4: 3). On this view, experience is not a mental affair of being "appeared to" or of "receiving" impressions, but rather a naturalized process of an organism interacting with its environment (MW10: 6). This conception of experience enables Dewey to embrace a broad *holism* of individuals, communities, and their physical and social environs. On his view, then, experience, and thus all inquiry, is ineliminably social. It is not too far off the mark to say that Dewey's philosophy is, broadly speaking, a *social epistemology*.

Given this, we can see why Dewey would have proposed an epistemic conception of democracy. He held that democracy is the mode of social living that releases human experience from artificial constraints and thus most effectively facilitates free inquiry across all domains of experience. His idea here is that a properly ordered democratic society would function much like a model scientific community: individual inquirers work together in groups on relatively local problems, information and results are distributed across increasingly broader social formations of inquirers, the pool of shared knowledge continually expands, and the experimental methods of piecemeal problem-solving are applied across the board.

Accordingly, Dewey prefigures contemporary deliberative conceptions of democracy. When democracy is understood as the application of collective intelligence to common social problems (LW11: 37; LW11: 25), the fundamental political activity is the "give and take" of free and open discussion (LW2: 332) where citizens can "convince and be convinced by reason" (MW10: 404). Hence the "heart and guarantee of democracy is in free gatherings of neighbors on the street corner to discuss back and forth what is read in uncensored news of the day" (LW14: 227).

As with other deliberativist views, Dewey's picture stands in contrast with views that locate democracy within the familiar institutional devices of equal voting, majority rule, and accountable representation. According to Dewey, "there is no sanctity" (LW2: 326) in these institutional norms; they are merely "devices" for "securing" democracy (LW2: 325–26). For he ultimately understands democracy not as a kind of state or a mode of politics, but as a "way of life" (LW2: 325), a "truly human way of living" (LW11: 218) that must govern "all areas" of society (LW11: 25) and "must affect all modes of human association, the family, the school, industry, religion" (LW2: 325). Indeed, Dewey contends that "democracy is a form of government only because it is a form of moral and spiritual association" (EW1: 240).

Return now to our preliminary remarks about democratic theory. Although Dewey's conception of democracy is centrally epistemic, his view of democracy's *value* is largely moral, as is his argument for democracy. That is, Dewey understands that his vision of democratic society rests upon an *ethos*, the "possession and continual use of certain attitudes, forming personal character and determining desire and purpose in all the relations of life" (LW14: 226). He describes this ethos as the "scientific attitude" (LW13: 168). But that is not all. Dewey also identifies democracy's value with the cultivation of that ethos. Rejecting the "old-time separation between politics and morals" (MW12: 192), Dewey contends that democracy is not a "means for obtaining something for individuals... but for *creating* individuals" (MW12: 191). Accordingly, he claims that success at cultivating the proper kind of individual is the "criterion" (MW5: 431), "standard" (MW9: 89), and "supreme test" (MW12: 186) of whether a society is democratic. Thus his striking claim that "Democracy and the one, ultimate, ethical ideal of humanity are... synonyms" (EW1: 248).

Dewey underwrites his epistemic conception of democracy by way of his theory of human flourishing. This theory then supplies Dewey's account of democracy's value. On his view, we should embrace democracy because it nurtures the scientific ethos across all social associations, and humans thrive when embodying that ethos. Although Dewey's conception of democracy is epistemic, his argument for democracy is of the familiar moral kind. In fact, it is of the same form as Aristotle's argument for aristocracy. The difference rests in each philosopher's conception of human flourishing.

Therein lies the trouble. John Rawls (2005) established that the task of formulating a justification for democracy is internally fraught. On the one hand, it is a constitutive norm of such an order that it stands *in need of* justification; among free and equal citizens, a political order is legitimate only when it can be justified in terms that each can embrace (Waldron 1993: 37). However, an intrinsic byproduct of the freedom that democracy secures is the "fact of reasonable pluralism," the fact that under democratic conditions a plurality of "comprehensive doctrines" will thrive among citizens that are inconsistent with each other, but compatible with the fundamental tenets of a democratic society (2005: 36–37).

This Rawlsian insight sets an intuitive test for political legitimacy (2005: 136). A democratic order can be legitimate only if it is justifiable in terms that are insusceptible to reasonable rejection by its citizens. Crucially, *reasonable* functions here as a technical term; a justification is reasonably rejectable when its rejection is consistent with embracing the ideal of a constitutional democracy as a fair system of social cooperation among free and equal moral persons. From this emerges the corollary that a person is reasonable to the extent she seeks a political order whose basis is beyond reasonable rejection. The challenge for democratic theory is to articulate a vision of democracy that does not exclusively rely upon – or presuppose the correctness of – any of the moral doctrines that reasonable citizens may embrace, given the fact of reasonable pluralism.

Deweyan democracy finds its justification in an appeal to Dewey's unique conception of human flourishing. That conception identifies flourishing with the cultivation of the scientific ethos. Consequently, Dewey's conception of flourishing is overtly naturalist. It thus stands in opposition to standard versions of deontology and Natural Law. It is also consequentialist, which places it in opposition to contractualism. However, it additionally rejects the hedonist theory of value; thus, it opposes utilitarianism. Surely there are reasonable versions of these competing doctrines. Therefore, Dewey's conception of flourishing is reasonably rejectable. As it presupposes Dewey's conception of flourishing, Deweyan democracy fails the intuitive Rawlsian test of legitimacy, and thus is unfit as a political ideal for democratic citizens.

Although this argument relies on vocabulary introduced by Rawls, it is not beholden to his broader political philosophy. The Rawlsian idiom is pragmatically apt because it helps in formulating a problem that confronts modern democracies. To wit, a political order among free and equal persons must be *acceptable* to them. It is obvious that where citizens disagree over fundamental matters of value, a democratic order that presupposes the correctness of a subset of the commitments over which they are divided will fail to be acceptable to all. When a democracy is organized around a moral ideal that can be reasonably rejected, many of its citizens will see the social and political world in which they are embedded as an alien imposition, an affront to their equality and dignity. That's a *pragmatic* failure.[7]

In short, a normative conception of democracy must confront the *Rawlsian problematic*. It must formulate a view that does not rely exclusively on any particular reasonable comprehensive doctrine. Dewey's otherwise attractive epistemic conception of democracy is undone by his account of democracy's value, which relies too heavily on a reasonably rejectable conception of human flourishing.

It remains open to enthusiasts of Deweyan democracy to either detach the appealing elements of Dewey's democratic theory from its wider Deweyan setting or else downplay the reasonably rejectable content of that setting.[8] One difficulty with such efforts is that, when they are successful, the result typically has no distinctively *Deweyan* identity.

A Peircean alternative

The most promising non-Deweyan pragmatist and epistemic approach to democracy draws centrally from Peirce.[9] As I suggested earlier, the very idea of a Peircean approach to democracy is strained. Peirce seems to have thought that politics is not a proper subject of philosophical thinking.[10] Additionally, it appears that he held odious political opinions.[11] It should be emphasized, then, that the alternative pragmatist approach is not meant to capture anything that Peirce endorsed about democracy. Still, one of the founding documents of pragmatism, Peirce's "The Fixation of Belief," contains the root of a powerful epistemic argument for democracy.

The argument of "The Fixation of Belief" is disputed. On its face, the essay defends what Peirce identifies as the "method of science" by way of an elimination argument: he identifies three other purported methods of inquiry, finds them all lacking for various reasons, and then, without subjecting it to the same level of scrutiny, touts the virtues of the method of science. By nearly all accounts, on the most straightforward reading, the argument is a failure.[12] I have argued elsewhere (Talisse 2004) that there is way to read Peirce's essay that makes the argument clear and compelling. But this exegetical issue can be set aside; we are concerned only with a point about belief from which Peirce begins.

"The Fixation of Belief" begins with an important conceptual truth. It is a "mere tautology" to assert of a belief that one holds that it is true (CP5.375).[13] To hold a belief *simply is* to take it to be true. This is why, as Bernard Williams put it, falsity is a "fatal objection" to a belief (2002: 670). This conceptual tie between belief and truth-aspiration provides the basis for a *constitutive norm* governing our beliefs (Misak 2004b: 12). The alternative pragmatist epistemic argument for democracy extrapolates from this norm to more broadly social norms of the kind that underwrite democracy.

Start with an observation regarding what we might call the *phenomenology* of belief. To assess a given belief we hold as false tends to be sufficient to dissolve the belief. To put the point in a helpful way that owes to G. E. Moore (1993), any assessment of the form "I believe that *p*, and *p* is false" is paradoxical, even though the second-personal belief "he believes that *p*, and *p* is false" is not.[14] Thus, when one's belief that p does not recede in light of what one assesses as decisive evidence against p, one no longer is able to regard one's state with respect to p as properly a *belief*. Here we deploy the diagnostic idiom of obsession, delusion, compulsion, and confabulation.

This shows that one must be able to assess one's beliefs as true in order to regard them *as beliefs*. Talk about persistent false beliefs, irrational believing, delusion, and obsession is almost always talk about *others'* beliefs. Truth-aspiration hence is a *constitutive norm* of belief. That is, in order for a state to count as a belief, one must assess it as true from the first-personal point of view.

The truth-aspiring nature of belief helps to explain the incoherence of instantaneous "deciding to believe."[15] As beliefs are constitutively truth-aspiring, one cannot produce the belief that p except by way of activity that one regards as sensitive to truth-indicators with respect to p, namely, reasons, arguments, and evidence. Similarly, when one assesses one's evidence for one's belief that p as insufficient or defeated, one typically feels the need to take epistemic action. One must reflect, revise, reconsider, or (as is sadly more common) dismiss, confabulate, fabricate, rationalize, and self-deceive. When maneuvers of these kinds fail, either the belief recedes or else it becomes unrecognizable as a belief – again, it begins to look like a symptom, something requiring diagnosis.

Returning to the Moorean style of articulating the point, one could say that a first-personal assessment of the form, "I believe that *p*, but all of my evidence shows that *p* is false" is paradoxical in roughly the same way as "I believe that *p*, but *p* is false" is. When we believe, we take our belief not only to be true but also to be in line with the best evidence. Of course, people frequently hold beliefs for insufficient reasons; indeed, they often hold beliefs for objectively bad and fabricated evidence. Nothing in the present view denies that; recall that we are thus far only examining the first-personal phenomenology of belief, how we must *regard our beliefs* if we are to sustain them as beliefs. One can *take* one's belief that p to be in line with the best evidence even in cases where p is wholly lacking evidential support. The claim thus far is only that one cannot *assess* one's belief that p in that way without causing it to thereby look distorted and improperly formed.

To repeat, people commonly believe on the basis of no real reasons at all. Note that the view on offer explains the prevalence of self-deception, confabulation, rationalization, and the like. Were belief not governed by a norm of reason-responsiveness, there would be no need for such measures. Self-deception, confabulation, and the like are measures by which one manufactures the *appearance* of evidence where there is none. If there were no norm tying belief to reasons and evidence, we simply wouldn't bother. Yet we do.

Thus, Peircean pragmatism sets out from an analysis that conceptually ties belief to truth and evidence in the following way: when one believes, one takes the belief to be true, and one takes oneself to be responding appropriately to the relevant reasons. We thus can identify two constitutive norms of belief: truth-aspiration and reason-responsiveness (Misak 2004b: 12; Talisse 2007: 62). To be sure, the claim at present is not that this view of belief is *exclusive* to pragmatism or available only to the pragmatist. My point is rather that Peirce's pragmatism begins from this insight and derives it from the first-personal phenomenology of belief itself.

We can further capture the pragmatist pedigree of this view by observing how these constitutive norms come together in a proper rendering of Peirce's infamous "end of inquiry" remarks about truth. In his "How to Make Our Ideas Clear," Peirce appears to define truth as "the opinion which is fated to be ultimately agreed to by all who investigate" (CP5.407). However, as Misak has argued (2004a, 2013), Peirce's remarks are best understood not as an attempt to *define* truth, but to provide a *pragmatist elucidation* of the function of the truth predicate in discourse that employs it.[16] Peirce's point is that we (implicitly) employ the truth predicate whenever we adopt a belief or assert a proposition, and in doing so, we affirm that the proposition believed or asserted could withstand scrutiny. Thus, to call a belief true is to affirm that it will remain undefeated no matter how much further investigation we conduct.

We have identified two constitutive norms of belief. As they set standards that we must take a belief to have passed in order to sustain it, we can call these *first-personal doxastic norms*. Still, what has been established seems strikingly distant from any concern with democracy. The task now is to argue that we can take our beliefs to have satisfied the first-personal doxastic norms only under certain social conditions, that the first-personal doxastic norms implicate a series of social-epistemic norms.

Consider another first-personal truism about belief. Our beliefs have their source in our interactions with others. With a little reflection, we recognize that, given the limitations of our individual cognitive resources, we *must* depend on others for information, including reasons and evidence. Crucially, in the course of gathering and evaluating our evidence, we inevitably come to realize that others hold beliefs that differ from our own. At least sometimes we come into contact with others who take the reasons we have for our beliefs to be insufficient or corrupt; we find that they can offer us evidence that countervails our beliefs and favors different ones.

We can say, then, that there are certain *dialectical* or *discursive* norms associated with believing. Insofar as we aim to believe in a reason-responsive way, we aim to believe in accordance not only with whatever evidence we happen to have acquired, but with *all the relevant evidence there is*. Now, it is clear that when forming a belief, we cannot consult *all* possible sources of evidence; we aim instead *not to overlook* or *discount* possible sites of disconfirming or confounding evidence. This requires us to take seriously the reasons, objections, and arguments of those with whom we disagree (Misak 2000: 94). Accordingly, when we find ourselves unable to respond to objections or account for countervailing evidence, we assess our belief as deficient; and unless we are able to successfully revise, reformulate, rationalize, or dismiss, our belief is jeopardized.[17] In general, some degree of dialectical success is necessary for a positive evaluation of our beliefs from the perspective of the first-personal doxastic norms.

Return to the Moorean style of elucidating the point: the first-personal assessment "I believe that *p*, but I always lose arguments with *p*'s critics" indicates a deficiency in one's belief – one has an inadequate *command* of the relevant reasons. In this sense, we do not only depend on others in forming our beliefs, we rely on them in helping us to evaluate the reasons that bear on our beliefs. Consequently, our first-personal doxastic norms entail dialectical social-epistemic norms.

Similar considerations identify social-epistemic norms that are *institutional* rather than dialectical. In order to assess ourselves as having formed our beliefs properly, we have to be able to assess ourselves as functioning within a cognitive environment that is not systematically and severely distorted. Again, the Moorean assessment "I believe that *p*, but all evidence has been rigged to favor *p*" signals an epistemic defect. In order to assess our beliefs positively, we must be able to reasonably assess our cognitive environment as one in which crucial or especially weighty evidence with respect to important matters would emerge and be widely disseminated, were it to exist.[18]

Relatedly, consider Moorean assessments like "I believe that *p*, but all critics of *p* have been silenced" and "I believe that *p*, but those who question *p* are imprisoned." These indicate respects in which p falls short of satisfying the first-personal doxastic norms. Accordingly, the first-personal doxastic norms suggest institutional norms of free expression, open inquiry, freedom of information, and protected dissent. With a little more work, we can build similar social-epistemic cases for further institutional norms, including freedom of the press, compulsory public education, and government provisions for the protection of public space. There may also be social-epistemic arguments for government support for the arts and progressive taxation, though I am not able to explore this here.

The Peircean epistemic argument for democracy now can be summarized. First-personal doxastic norms that are constitutive of belief can be reliably satisfied only within the kind of social-epistemic environment that is secured under democratic conditions. One can take oneself to satisfy the norms proper to belief only if one can take oneself to be adequately reason responsive. And one can take oneself to be adequately reason responsive only if one can take oneself to be functioning within a social context, which reliably allows access to reasons. In this way, the epistemic norms governing belief give rise to social-epistemic norms concerning the exchanging, sharing, and evaluating of reasons. This, in turn, means that the processes by which we can reason together must be formally secured – there must be free speech, free association, freedom of conscience, as well as various kinds of protections for dissent, disagreement, and protest. The social-epistemic environment requisite for proper believing is best secured under democratic political conditions. Consequently, each of us has compelling epistemic reasons to embrace democracy.

An epistemic argument and an epistemic conception

The foregoing section showed that a few distinctively Peircean-pragmatist insights about belief yield an epistemic argument for democracy. However, it remains to be shown that the underlying conception of democracy is itself epistemic. The Peircean argument also proposes a novel kind of epistemic conception of democracy that avoids the problems besetting Deweyan democracy.

Recall that contemporary epistemic conceptions of democracy tend to divide over the *site* of democracy's epistemic value. Some locate the epistemic value of democracy in its ability to produce *outcomes* that are epistemically superior to non-democratic alternatives. Others look to *inputs*, arguing that the epistemic value of democracy lies in its ability to improve citizens' contributions to democratic decision-making.

The Peircean view fixes on a different site. With Dewey, the Peircean locates democracy's epistemic power in its ability to pool cognitive resources in ways that could facilitate their application to social problems. To be sure, this way of construing the connection between democracy and epistemology is *consistent* with the broader claims that democracy improves both inputs and outputs, but the core insight is distinct from these proposals. To claim that democracy's epistemic value lies in its capacity to pool cognitive resources is to invite the thought that democracy is fundamentally a *social epistemic enterprise*, an ongoing collective endeavor aimed at applying proper epistemic norms in the processes by which we direct our shared social and political life.

The Peircean view nevertheless avoids the controversial moral commitments of Deweyan democracy. Note that the Peircean argument draws strictly from first-personal constitutive norms of belief and our doxastic practices. So whereas the Deweyan holds that democracy is the social order that extends to our political life the kinds of epistemic practices that we *ought* to adopt in our individual lives, the Peircean view claims that democracy is the political manifestation of the social-epistemic norms that we in fact cannot but adopt in our individual lives. In drawing only on the constitutive norms of belief and their social-epistemic correlates, the Peircean view eschews dependence on a conception of human flourishing. It provides an epistemic argument for an epistemic conception of democracy that does not run afoul of the fact of reasonable pluralism. Unlike the Deweyan view, Peircean democracy successfully navigates the Rawlsian problematic.

Notes

1   See, for example, Putnam (1992). Richard Rorty is an outlier in holding that pragmatism has no particular political implications, and so is consistent with fascism (1999: 23).
2   See Misak (2013) and Burke (2013).
3   Using only quotations from their work, Haack crafts a discussion between Peirce and Rorty that demonstrates how deep their divisions run.
4   See Aikin and Talisse (2018: Ch. 1).
5   See especially Hook (1940). See also Talisse (2007: Ch. 6).
6   References to Dewey's work refer to the *Collected Works*. Citations employ the standard formula: (Volume: page number).
7   For the initial formulations of this argument, see Talisse (2003, 2007). The latest version of the argument, as well as a survey of the intervening debate, can be found in Aikin and Talisse (2018: Ch. 6).
8   For the former strategy, see Anderson (2006); for the latter, see Forstenzer (2019).
9   For the main statements of this view, see Misak (1999, 2004b) and Talisse (2007, 2009, 2013).
10   None of Peirce's many projections for his systematic *magnum opus* proposes a treatment of politics.
11   Peirce was opposed both to the abolition of slavery and to women's suffrage.
12   For a review of the literature about Peirce's "Fixation," see Aikin and Talisse (2018: Ch. 3).
13   Citations to Peirce's writing will refer to the *Collected Papers* and follow the standard formula (volume number, paragraph number).
14   Moore's Paradox is actually an umbrella for a range of closely related phenomena concerning our first-personal perspective on our beliefs. For example, any belief of the form "*p* is true, but I do not believe that *p*" is similarly paradoxical. Questions concerning differences between the so-called "omissive" and "commissive" instantiations of the paradox lie beyond the scope of this discussion.
15   See Williams (1970). Williams' point, which I accept on Peircean grounds, is that it is a *conceptual* fact deriving from the nature of belief that one cannot come to believe by the direct exercise of one's will.
16   See also Price (2003). It is worth noting in this connection that the infamous quotation just cited ends with Peirce claiming that he has offered an account of "what we mean by the truth" (CP5.407).
17   The matter is complicated by the fact of epistemic deference. After all, we often believe on the basis of expert testimony. In such cases, my belief that p is based on what an expert has said, and I cannot address criticisms of p. However, when beliefs of this kind are proper, also I believe that a suitably informed expert about *p* would be able to meet criticisms of *p*; and *that's* my defense of

my belief that *p*. If I believed in this case that p could not be defended adequately by the relevant expert, my belief would indeed be improper.

18 Compare Goldberg's illuminating analysis of thoughts of the kind "if that were true, I would have heard about it by now" (2010: Ch. 6).

Works cited

Ahlstrom-Vij, Kristoffer. 2013. *Epistemic Paternalism: A Defence*. New York: Palgrave Macmillan.

Aikin, Scott F. and Robert B. Talisse. 2018. *Pragmatism, Pluralism, and the Nature of Philosophy*. New York: Routledge.

Anderson, Elizabeth. 2006. "The Epistemology of Democracy." *Episteme* 3: 8–22.

Benhabib, Seyla. 1994. "Deliberative Rationality and Models of Democratic Legitimacy." *Constellations* 1.1: 26–52.

Brennan, Jason. 2016. *Against Democracy*. Princeton, NJ: Princeton University Press.

Burke, Thomas F. 2013. *What Pragmatism Was*. Bloomington: University of Indiana Press.

Christiano, Thomas. 2008. *The Constitution of Equality*. New York: Oxford University Press.

Cohen, Joshua. 1986. "An Epistemic Conception of Democracy." *Ethics* 97.1: 26–38.

Dewey, John. 1969–1991. In *The Collected Works of John Dewey: The Early Works, The Middle Works, The Later Works*, 37 vols., ed. Jo Ann Boydston. Carbondale: Southern Illinois University Press.

Dworkin, Ronald. 2000. *Sovereign Virtue*. Cambridge, MA: Harvard University Press.

Estlund, David. 2007. *Democratic Authority*. Princeton, NJ: Princeton University Press.

Forstenzer, Joshua. 2019. *Deweyan Experimentalism and the Problem of Method in Political Philosophy*. New York: Routledge.

Goldberg, Sanford. 2010. *Relying on Others*. New York: Oxford University Press.

Goodman, Nelson. 1978. *Ways of Worldmaking*. Indianapolis, IN: Hackett Publishing.

Gould, Carol. 1988. *Rethinking Democracy*. Cambridge: Cambridge University Press.

Haack, Susan. 1997. "We pragmatists… Peirce and Rorty in Conversation." *The Partisan Review* LXIV.1: 91–107.

Hook, Sidney. 1940. "The Democratic Way of Life." In *Reason, Social Myths, and Democracy*. New York: Humanities Press, 283–97.

Landemore, Helene. 2012. *Democratic Reason*. New York: Oxford University Press.

Lovejoy, A. O. 1908. *The Thirteen Pragmatisms*. Baltimore, MD: Johns Hopkins University Press.

Misak, Cheryl. 2000. *Truth, Politics, Morality*. New York: Routledge.

Misak, Cheryl. 2004a. *Truth and the End of Inquiry*. New York: Oxford University Press.

Misak, Cheryl. 2004b. "Making Disagreement Matter." *The Journal of Speculative Philosophy* 18.1: 9–22

Misak, Cheryl. 2013. *The American Pragmatists*. New York: Oxford University Press.

Moore, G. E. 1993. "Moore's Paradox." In *G. E. Moore: Selected Writings*, ed. Thomas Baldwin. London: Routledge, 207–12.

Nino, Carlos. 1998. *The Constitution of Deliberative Democracy*. New Haven, CT: Yale University Press.

Peirce, Charles Sanders. 1931–1958. *The Collected Works of Charles Sanders Peirce*, 8 vols. Cambridge: Harvard University Press.

Pettit, Philip. 2012. *On the People's Terms*. New York: Oxford University Press.

Posner, Richard. 2003. *Law, Pragmatism, and Democracy*. Cambridge, MA: Harvard University Press.

Price, Huw. 2003. "Truth as Convenient Friction." *Journal of Philosophy* 100.4: 167–90.

Putnam, Hilary. 1992. "A Reconsideration of Deweyan Democracy." In *Renewing Philosophy*. Cambridge: Harvard University Press, 180–202.

Quine, Willard V. O. 1981. "The *Pragmatists' Place in Empiricism*." In *Pragmatism: Its Sources and Prospects*, ed. R. J. Mulvaney and P. M. Zeltner. Columbia: University of South Carolina Press, 21–40.

Rawls, John. 2005. *Political Liberalism*. New York: Columbia University Press.

Riker, Walter. 1982. *Liberalism against Populism*. Long Grove, IL: Waveland Press.

Rorty, Richard. 1999. *Philosophy and Social Hope*. New York: Penguin.

Shaipro, Ian. 2016. *Politics against Domination*. Cambridge, MA: Harvard University Press.

Somin, Ilya. 2020. *Free to Move*. New York: Oxford University Press.

Talisse, Robert B. 2003. "Can Democracy be a Way of Life?" *Transactions of the Charles S. Peirce Society* 39.1: 1–21.

Talisse, Robert B. 2004. "Towards a Peircean Politics of Inquiry." *Transactions of the Charles S. Peirce Society* 40.1: 21–38.

Talisse, Robert B. 2007. *A Pragmatist Philosophy of Democracy.* New York: Routledge.

Talisse, Robert B. 2009. *Democracy and Moral Conflict.* Cambridge: Cambridge University Press.

Talisse, Robert B. 2013. "Sustaining Democracy." *Critical Review of International Social and Political Philosophy* 16.4: 500–19.

Talisse, Robert B. 2018. "Pragmatism Deflated." *Transactions of the Charles S. Peirce Society* 54.3: 409–16.

Waldron, Jeremy. 1993. *Liberal Rights.* Cambridge: Cambridge University Press.

Williams, Bernard. 1970. "Deciding to Believe." In *Problems of the Self.* Cambridge: Cambridge University Press, 136–51.

Williams, Bernard. 2002. *Truth and Truthfulness.* Princeton, NJ: Princeton University Press.

Young, Iris M. 2000. *Inclusion and Democracy.* New York: Oxford University Press.

34

EPISTEMIC NORMS OF POLITICAL DELIBERATION

Fabienne Peter

1 Introduction

Political deliberation is the broad, multi-stranded process in which political proposals get considered and critically scrutinised.[1] There are many forums in which political deliberation takes place. Some of them are formal institutions of government such as the cabinet and parliament. Other forums of political deliberation include advisory bodies, government agencies, political parties and interest groups, the press and other broadcasters, and, increasingly, social media platforms. The latter are not directly associated with political decision-making but still play an important role in the generation of new political proposals and the critical assessment of actual or proposed political decisions (see Parkinson and Mansbridge 2012). Political deliberation, in practice, includes parliamentary debate as much as it includes a Twitter tread by a political journalist, a Sunday op-ed, pamphlets from Extinction Rebellion or a TV interview with a cabinet minister.

On many theories of democracy, political deliberation underpins political legitimacy. Political deliberation influences whether citizens accept or reject certain political decisions and, as such, plays an important role in the *de facto* legitimacy of those decisions. But political deliberation also has a role to play in settling whether citizens should accept or reject certain political decisions as it assesses the reasons for and against certain political decisions. As such, political deliberation matters for the normative legitimacy of political decisions.

My focus in this chapter is on the normative role of political deliberation. To facilitate legitimate political decision-making, political deliberation must be well-ordered. Well-ordered political deliberation is pushed forward by and adequately responds to all valid contributions. This raises a question of what counts as a valid contribution to political deliberation, and this is the main question I will be discussing in this chapter.

I shall interpret valid contributions as those that satisfy appropriate norms of deliberation. The norms of political deliberation specify which contributions should and should not be allowed to influence the course of political deliberation. There are different types of norms that potentially apply to political deliberation. The most obvious candidates are participation norms, on the one hand, and epistemic norms, on the other. Participation norms focus on standing to contribute to political deliberation. A good example is a norm that aims to secure the equal freedom to contribute for all citizens, such as a free speech norm. Epistemic norms focus on what can be validly asserted in political deliberation. These are less frequently discussed, but recent political developments suggest that we need a better understanding of this type of constraint on political deliberation.[2]

I will discuss a range of different epistemic norms. First, I consider truth norms. The appeal of a truth norm is captured in the well-weathered slogan of "speaking truth to power". And in response to more recent discussions about the dangers of post-truth politics, it might be tempting to think that political deliberation should be subject to a truth norm. There are serious objections against subjecting political deliberation to a truth norm, however, and I will explain what they are.

I then turn my attention to epistemic norms that link what can be validly asserted in political deliberation to what we know or justifiably believe, and to how we respond to what others have asserted. There has been a lot of political focus recently on the question of how much political deliberation should respond to expertise. A good example is Michael Gove's infamous proclamation, in the context of the Brexit debate, that the British public has had enough of experts. Another example is the discussions of how different governments responded to scientific advice on how to manage the Covid-19 outbreak. While the issue is thus clearly important, the epistemic norms that govern well-ordered political deliberation are currently not well-understood.

The chapter is organised as follows. I'll start by saying a bit more on the role of political deliberation in legitimate political decision-making (Section 2). In Section 3, I introduce epistemic norms of political deliberation, in general, before moving on to discuss different types of epistemic norms. In Section 4 I focus on a truth norm of political deliberation and discuss why it's problematic. In Sections 5 and 6 I discuss further candidate epistemic norms, distinguishing between substantive epistemic norms (Section 5) and procedural epistemic norms (Section 6). Section 7 concludes.

2 Political deliberation and political legitimacy

Why think that political deliberation is subject to certain norms? The reason is that well-ordered political deliberation is necessary for the justification of political decisions and, as such, for their legitimacy. Before discussing candidate norms of political deliberation, it is helpful to first shed some more light on this relationship between political deliberation and political legitimacy.

I take the mainstream view of political legitimacy to be, following Rawls (1993) and Habermas (1996), that political legitimacy derives from the justification of political decisions.[3] Call this the justificationist view of political legitimacy.

Taking the justificationist view of political legitimacy as our starting-point, we can explain the significance of well-ordered political deliberation for political legitimacy. If the aim of political decision-making is a justified political decision, it becomes clear why political deliberation is an essential feature of politically legitimate decision-making. In political deliberation, possible decisions and their pro tanto justifications are critically examined. If all goes well, then political deliberation supports legitimate political decisions, i.e. decisions that are overall justified. To support legitimate political decision-making in this way, political deliberation must be well-ordered. It should consider all valid contributions and not get side-tracked by contributions that are not valid, where valid contributions are those that satisfy the norms that govern political deliberation.

Note that political deliberation might not be sufficient for political legitimacy, as even well-ordered political deliberation often fails to reach a consensus on what should be done

(Bohman and Richardson 2009). Politically legitimate decision-making might then require some additional decision-making mechanism – voting, for example. But well-ordered political deliberation is still essential for the legitimacy of the political decision, even in this scenario, because it helps with the agenda-setting process and ensures that voting is informed by all valid contributions.

In sum, on a justificationist view of political legitimacy, well-ordered political deliberation is necessary for legitimate political decision-making as it is through political deliberation, in its many forums, that alternative political decisions and their pro tanto justifications can be considered, with a view to facilitate reaching a political decision that is overall justified, i.e. legitimate.

3 Epistemic norms of political deliberation

What are the norms that determine the validity of contributions to political deliberation? As I mentioned in the introduction, most of the literature on deliberative democracy, in particular, has focussed on participation norms of political deliberation.[4] Participation norms are important for democratic political deliberation as they secure inclusion. If there is one lesson that recent political developments have taught us, however, it's that democratic participation norms are not sufficient for legitimacy-conferring political deliberation. What matters, in addition to democratic inclusivity, is that contributions to political deliberation are well anchored in reality and that political decision-making aims to make the right decisions (Peter 2020a).

One way in which political philosophers and political theorists have thought about supplementing participation norms is through some norms of practical rationality or good reasoning. It has been argued that well-ordered political deliberation, in addition to being inclusive, should be governed by "the force of the better argument" (Habermas 1996), or respond only to contributions that respect constraints of reasonableness (Rawls 1993), e.g. in the form of a norm of equal respect (Larmore 2008), or to contributions that are the result of a respectable amount of good reasoning (Gaus 2011: 250).

These considerations are all important. But well-ordered political deliberation also depends on what is asserted in deliberation. So in addition to norms of participation and norms of rationality or good reasoning, we need to consider epistemic norms that determine what can be validly asserted in political deliberation. Political deliberation and legitimate political decision-making suffer if the public sphere is flooded with false claims such as that injecting bleach could treat Covid-19, for example, or that Brexit would generate a massive cash boost for the UK's National Health Service. Because epistemic norms of political deliberation are less well-understood than the other norms, I will focus on those norms in the rest of this chapter.

Epistemic norms of political deliberation can be generally, if somewhat vacuously, described as follows:

> Epistemic Norm of Political Deliberation: Everything else equal, your contribution to political deliberation involving a politically relevant proposition p as a premise is valid iff p can be validly asserted in this context.

To illustrate the idea, the norm states that the validity of your contribution that we shouldn't further enhance airport capacity when we need to limit carbon emissions to tackle the climate crisis because enhancing airport capacity leads to higher carbon emissions depends on whether you can validly assert (i) that we need to tackle the climate crisis (a normative claim) and (ii) that enhancing airport capacity leads to higher carbon emissions (an empirical claim).

The task in the rest of this chapter will be to clarify what can be validly asserted in political contexts and discuss different interpretations of the general norm. But before I get to this, it will be helpful to comment on the scope of this type of norm.

A first clarificatory comment concerns the importance of context. I stipulate here, without further argument, that what can be validly asserted might differ from one context to another. For example, I take it as a given that certain speculative claims can be validly asserted in a scientific context, but not necessarily in other contexts, e.g. in a context of policy-planning. The general form of epistemic norms of political deliberation factors in such differences by relativising validity to context. In what follows, I will not discuss norms of assertion, in general. My focus will be exclusively on the epistemic norms that could apply in the context of political deliberation.[5]

A related comment concerns the heterogeneity of the public sphere. As I mentioned in the introduction, political deliberation comprises a wide variety of contributions – from parliamentary debates to Twitter threads and everything in between. Not all contributions are equally influential in shaping political decision-making and for some contributions the stakes are higher than they are for others. A political representative's contribution to parliamentary debate typically is more influential than the pamphlet of a small political interest group. And an incendiary Tweet spiked with false claims by President Trump is far more detrimental for well-ordered political deliberation than a similar Tweet by an anonymous contributor with no followers. It is likely that different epistemic norms apply in high-stakes and low-stakes contexts.[6] While I lack the space to do this here, when it comes to developing a theory of the epistemic norms that should govern political deliberation, it will be important to spell out which norms apply in which political contexts.

A further clarificatory comment concerns the relation between participation norms and epistemic norms of political deliberation. By stating the general form of epistemic norms as including necessary and sufficient conditions, I do not mean to imply that this type of norm determines the validity of contributions to political deliberation on its own. I prefaced the main part of the norm by an everything-else-equal clause to allow for room for other conditions of validity, including conditions that might have normative priority. Different conceptions of political legitimacy will understand the role of political deliberation in different ways and, and as a result, prioritise different norms of political deliberation. For example, a strongly democratic conception of political legitimacy might give much more weight to inclusive political participation than to epistemic norms (e.g. Christiano 2008). By contrast, conceptions of political legitimacy that place more emphasis on getting to the right decisions, such as those drawing on Raz's normal justification thesis of political authority (Raz 1986), for example, might give more weight to epistemic norms instead.

The question of what conception of political legitimacy should inform our understanding of well-ordered political deliberation has to be settled elsewhere, and, with that, the question of what much weight epistemic norms should have in our account of well-ordered political deliberation.[7] In this chapter, our main question, then is this. What can be validly asserted in political contexts, that is to say, what are plausible candidate epistemic norms for political deliberation?

4 A truth norm of political deliberation?

A first candidate is a Truth Norm, which might look as follows:

> Truth Norm of Political Deliberation: Everything else equal, your contribution to political deliberation involving a politically relevant proposition p as a premise is valid iff p is true.[8]

This norm specifies that the validity of contributions to political deliberation is determined by the truth of the premises on which the contribution rests. In response to worries about post-truth politics and fake news, it might be tempting to think that political deliberation should be subject to a Truth Norm. The norm also gains support from ideas such as the importance of speaking truth to power. For example, the Truth Norm could lend validity to claims that struggle to get heard in political deliberation even though, and perhaps because, they report grave social injustices. Some claims about racist or sexist discrimination, for example, might gain validity independently of the hard evidence for such discrimination and of the entrenched disagreements about their seriousness that might surround them (see Srinivasan 2020, for example).

However tempting a Truth Norm might be, such a norm is not a plausible constraint on political deliberation. There are several problems with it. First, the norm is too demanding. The norm would rule out too many perfectly adequate contributions to political deliberation. Consider this contribution, for example: our best epidemiological models show that lockdown is required to minimise unnecessary deaths from Covid-19, therefore we should adopt a lockdown policy. I take it everyone will agree that there is nothing wrong with a contribution of this kind. But as the contribution itself highlights, while we have reason to believe the politically relevant premise p on which it rests – lockdown being necessary to minimise deaths – it's not asserting a truth. And indeed, the premise may well be false. Scientific models tend to simplify and only focus on certain considerations. They give us good reasons for believing that something is the case, but they rarely give us truth (e.g. Cartwright 1983). If that's the right account of how scientific models explain, we have to conclude that what renders contributions to political deliberation that draw on scientific expertise valid isn't the truth of the premises on which the contribution rests. Instead, their validity derives from how scientific studies respond to the evidence. In general, as much political deliberation takes place in the realm of uncertainty about the circumstances of political decision-making and often involves assumptions that turn out to be false in hindsight, the Truth Norm would rule out too many contributions as not valid.

To be fair, the Truth Norm as I've stated it is quite strong. Weaker versions of this Truth Norm include either the necessity or the sufficiency condition, but not both.

> Truth Norm of Political Deliberation$_N$: Everything else equal, your contribution to political deliberation involving a politically relevant proposition p as a premise is valid only if p is true.
>
> Truth Norm of Political Deliberation$_S$: Everything else equal, your contribution to political deliberation involving a politically relevant proposition p as a premise is valid if p is true.

Can these weaker versions of the Truth Norm escape the demandingness objection? The necessity version can't as it says that only contributions that rest on true premises are valid. The sufficiency version of the Truth Norm can, however. As it only says that truth is sufficient for the validity of a contribution, not that truth is required, contributions that involve false premises might still be valid.

However, a further, related, problem with the Truth Norm also affects the sufficiency condition. The problem arises because truth is often inaccessible and the Truth Norm fails to effectively govern deliberation in circumstances where it is not self-evident which premises are true. The Truth Norm is silent on how political deliberation ought to respond to the scarcity of epistemic resources, so to speak. If the political context was characterised by an abundance of epistemic resources, such that true claims could easily be identified and distinguished from false claims, the Truth Norm would be appropriate. It would guide political deliberation towards the right political decisions. But the political context is very messy and complex, and political deliberation typically proceeds in conditions where it is unclear, to say the least, what the right political decisions are. An effective norm of political deliberation should thus not be silent on how to respond to available evidence, to disagreement, and to demands for reasoned justification for conflicting claims.

Because of its inability to guide political deliberation in circumstances of epistemic scarcity, a Truth Norm, and the sufficiency version, in particular, could end up supporting problematic recklessness in political deliberation and political decision-making.[9] If contributions to political deliberation were valid as long as they are true, this would de-emphasise the need to provide evidential support for one's claims and to demonstrate that they constitute an adequate response to the inevitable uncertainty that surrounds much political deliberation and decision-making. Given epistemic scarcity, the possibility of making wrong, even very wrong, political decisions always looms large. And plausible norms of political deliberation should thus guide us in identifying better and worse responses to this epistemic predicament – something that the Truth Norm cannot do.

In this section, I have argued that political deliberation should not be subject to a Truth Norm because of the demandingness problem and the recklessness problem. To help stir political deliberation towards the right decisions and prevent it from supporting the wrong decisions, epistemic norms shouldn't just focus on the content of assertions, independently of whether it is accessible. Instead, they should focus on our political beliefs and anchor political deliberation in what we should believe about politically relevant normative and empirical facts.

The Truth Norm is an example of a substantive epistemic norm. Substantive epistemic norms relate the validity of contributions to political deliberation involving a politically relevant premise p to first-order considerations bearing on assertions involving p. Procedural epistemic norms, by contrast, relate it to higher-order considerations. In the next section, I will discuss substantive epistemic norms that are alternatives to the Truth Norm. In the following section, I will discuss procedural epistemic norms.

5 Other substantive epistemic norms

My focus in this section is on substantive epistemic norms that relate the validity of contributions to political deliberation to the epistemic status, or value, of political beliefs. A first norm of this kind is a Knowledge Norm:

> Knowledge Norm of Political Deliberation: Everything else equal, your contribution to political deliberation involving a politically relevant proposition p as a premise is valid if(f) you know that p.[10]

What should we say about the Knowledge Norm? I've already argued against the Truth Norm on the basis of it being too demanding. The necessity version of the Knowledge Norm, which, on a standard account of knowledge, requires that a premise is both true and believed (with some justification), is even more demanding and that suggests that we should not expect political deliberation to conform to the Knowledge Norm. There are too many uncertainties in the political context to allow for a meaningful restriction of well-ordered political deliberation to what is known. Even the best scientific advice – the kind of advice we would want political decisions to be based on – tends not to consist of what is known but reflects a temporary broad consensus among scientists about what is justifiably believed in this regard. More generally, we typically neither know all relevant details of the situation we're in nor what the future holds, but political decisions need to be made and assessed anyway. As the Dutch prime minister Mark Rutte put the problem after the Covid-19 crisis broke out: "In crises like this, you have to make 100 percent of the decisions with 50 percent of the knowledge".[11]

To clarify, I'm not arguing against the sufficiency version of the Knowledge Norm, which says that contributions that are based on premises that are known are valid. That version of the Knowledge Norm will be unproblematic in most contexts of political deliberation. I will argue below, however, that contributions that satisfy weaker norms might also be valid in many contexts.

In addition, let me also point out that while the necessity version of the Knowledge Norm is too demanding, compared to the Truth Norm, it has the advantage of not running into the recklessness problem. If valid contributions to political deliberation are restricted to claims that are based on what is known, then problematic political risk-taking is ruled out. For example, suppose it is known that a recently introduced social benefits scheme is causing involuntary homelessness, and it is also known that there is an alternative scheme that is less harmful in this regard. A contribution to political deliberation, then, that argues for the reform of the current scheme based on the known fact of the alternative scheme's lesser harmfulness is not running a risk.

The example should also make clear, however, that much of political deliberation takes place in very different epistemic circumstances. We normally do not have knowledge of all the politically relevant premises. This suggests that plausible norms of political deliberation should be weaker than the Knowledge Norm.

A second substantive epistemic norm is a norm that requires that political deliberation is based on what is justifiably, or reasonably (Lackey 2007: 596), believed:

> Justified Belief Norm of Political Deliberation: Everything else equal, your contribution to political deliberation involving a politically relevant proposition p as a premise is valid if(f) you are justified to believe that p.

This norm is distinctive as long as knowledge and/or truth are not required for a justified belief. A Justified Belief Norm, thus understood, is a much more plausible constraint on political deliberation than knowledge or truth norms.[12] It is less demanding than either of those norms because it accommodates the need for making assumptions in political deliberation that may, in hindsight, turn out to have been false. Under this norm, contributions that are based on recognised scientific expertise – as in the lockdown example – qualify as valid.

The Justified Belief Norm also helps to keep political recklessness in check. To be sure, it doesn't save us from grave political mistakes. What is justifiably, or reasonably, believed may well turn out to be very far off the mark. But it blocks contributions based on groundless beliefs and unwarranted confidence. In addition, the Justified Belief Norm helps to keep recklessness in check because it invites the interrogation of all contributions to political deliberation. If the validity of your contribution depends on whether you are justified to believe a politically relevant premise p, it is meaningful to ask you about that justification.[13]

While I take this feature of political deliberation subject to a Justified Belief Norm to be appealing, some might worry that it would go too far and subject political deliberation to too much unwarranted interrogation and even censorship. Who is well-placed to examine the justification of our beliefs? The problem will be particularly tricky for some of our moral beliefs.

In light of the censorship worry, it might seem advisable to retreat to an even weaker epistemic norm of political justification. The Justified Belief Norm, like the Knowledge Norm and the Truth Norm, are positive epistemic norms: they focus on what counts as a valid contribution to political deliberation. But epistemic norms can also be negative and focus on what is invalid. Consider the following norm, which rules out contributions to political deliberation based on obvious falsehoods:

> Avoiding Obvious Falsehoods Norm of Political Deliberation: Everything else equal, your contribution to political deliberation involving a politically relevant proposition p as a premise is not valid if p is obviously and demonstrably false.

A good example for a contribution to political deliberation that violates this norm is the obviously and demonstrably false claim that more people attended Trump's inauguration event in January 2017 than Obama's inauguration in 2009.

Because it only rules out contributions that involve obviously and demonstrably false premises, the falsity of which anyone can detect at very low cost to themselves, the Avoiding Obvious Falsehoods Norm avoids the censorship worry. It is also most certainly not demanding. There is a concern that it might be demanding too little, of course, and whether that's a price worth paying for avoiding excessive censorship.

How does the Avoiding Obvious Falsehoods Norm fare in relation to the recklessness worry? Because it rules out as invalid contributions to political deliberation that wilfully ignore well-known threats and dangers, it does provide some shield against this worry. But it doesn't shield us as much from the recklessness worry as the Justified Belief Norm. The reason is that there is less pressure to ensure that a contribution to political deliberation is a best response to the available evidence.

Still, how much of a shield is this? Even the Truth Norm would rule out as invalid contributions to political deliberation that will-fully ignore well-known threats and dangers, so the Avoiding Falsehoods Norm isn't much help here. It might even fare worse than the Truth Norm in this regard because the Avoiding Falsehood Norm is negative and doesn't commit political deliberation to the aim of truth in the way that the Truth Norm does. So the recklessness worry looms large for the Avoiding Obvious Falsehoods Norm.

6 Procedural epistemic norms

In this section, I discuss procedural epistemic norms, which are concerned with how political beliefs respond to higher-order evidence available in the form of contributions from other participants in political deliberation. Procedural epistemic norms are important, above and beyond substantive norms, because they govern the process through which well-ordered political deliberation transforms political beliefs. The capacity of political deliberation to change political beliefs has been highlighted by John Stuart Mill, for example, captured in the somewhat unfortunate metaphor of the marketplace for ideas (Mill 1991 [1859]). In the more recent literature, many deliberative democrats have argued that the capacity of political deliberation to transform political beliefs through reasoned argument is a key feature of the legitimacy of democracy (e.g. Manin 1987: 352).

Well-ordered political deliberation ensures that all contributions are given the consideration they deserve. There are two concerns here. One is that valid contributions to political deliberation receive some uptake from other participants. The second is that the uptake they receive is not arbitrarily distorted by non-epistemic considerations such as membership in particular social groups.

We can capture the first concern in a responsiveness norm:

> Responsiveness Norm of Political Deliberation: Everything else equal, your contribution to political deliberation involving a politically relevant proposition p as a premise is valid if you have appropriately adjusted your original confidence in p in response to political disagreements concerning p.

This norm captures a core idea of the epistemology of disagreements (Christensen 2007; Kelly 2010; Lackey 2010), which is that some of your disagreements with others have the capacity to change the justification you originally had for your belief and to put you under a normative expectation to adjust your belief. If this norm applies, the validity of contributions to political deliberation thus doesn't just depend on deliberation-independent evidence for one's beliefs, it also depends on how participants respond to each other's contributions in political deliberation.[14]

In the general form in which I have stated it, the Responsiveness Norm is compatible with different ways of spelling out what counts as an appropriate response and it can thus be fleshed out in different ways. As such, this norm is not vulnerable to most of the objections that have been raised against particular positions in the epistemology of disagreement. The reason for having such a norm is to secure some level of uptake and to rule out extreme forms of dogmatism, which would lead you to ignore the contributions of others, no matter how well-founded. But the norm doesn't imply that well-ordered deliberation always requires keeping an open mind. It leaves open, for example, whether only disagreements with people you regard as your epistemic peers have this capacity, or whether other disagreements have this capacity as well.[15] It also leaves open whether disagreements with epistemic peers always require that you reduce confidence in your original belief or whether this is not so. In matters of public controversy, it is often difficult to separate out what one should believe about a particular political issue, whether it is Brexit, or climate change, or health care reform, and what one should believe about different contributors' abilities to assess the issue. This difficulty can remove pressures to conciliate and means that the Responsiveness is compatible with deep political disagreements.[16]

The second concern I mentioned above points to an epistemic justice norm. There are different forms of epistemic injustice, a key distinction being between distributive and discriminatory forms of epistemic injustice (Fricker 2013). The former highlights problems in the distribution of epistemic goods such as education. The latter highlights problems with "identity prejudice" (Fricker 2007) in assessing the contributions of different epistemic agents. Epistemic agents are wronged if non-epistemic considerations such as someone's social identify – their gender, race, or class, for example – are having an effect on their standing as epistemic agents.

Distributive epistemic justice is of instrumental value for well-ordered political deliberation and will also be an important aspect of properly fleshed out participation norms. Avoiding epistemic discrimination injustice, by contrast, is integral to the epistemic well-orderedness of political deliberation. Political deliberation is epistemically skewed if only the contributions of some groups of citizens are perceived as valid, on grounds of their social identify, and if those of others are discounted for non-epistemic reasons.

Here's an attempt to capture the basic idea in a negative epistemic norm, i.e. a norm that focusses on how epistemic injustice undermines the validity of contributions to political deliberation:

> Epistemic Justice Norm of Political Deliberation: Everything else equal, your contribution to political deliberation involving a politically relevant proposition p as a premise is not valid if your confidence in p is the result of discounting p-related testimony or disagreements because of identity prejudice.

The Epistemic Justice Norm says that well-ordered political deliberation refrains from denying some groups of citizens standing in relation to p on grounds to do with their social identity, not the epistemic status of their p-related belief. Epistemically well-ordered political deliberation doesn't silence some social groups on non-epistemic grounds. It factors in all p-related contributions as long as belief in p has a certain epistemic status or value.

The Responsiveness Norm and the Epistemic Justice Norm are two procedural epistemic norms that complement each other. Together they ensure that what counts as an appropriate response to political disagreements isn't biased by identity prejudice. For example, they rule out that judgements of who counts as an epistemic peer favour members of some social groups and discriminate against others. Whatever we might want to say about the substantive norms that should govern political deliberation, and there is room for controversy there, it seems to me that there is less room for controversy about these procedural epistemic norms, especially in the generic form in which I have presented them. Political deliberation that is riddled by discriminatory epistemic injustice and by a failure to respond adequately to political disagreements is not well-ordered. How exactly these norms should be fleshed out requires further research, however.

7 Concluding remarks

This chapter has discussed candidate epistemic norms of well-ordered political deliberation. Well-ordered political deliberation is conducive to legitimate political decision-making. Epistemic norms help ensure, minimally, that political deliberation isn't side-tracked by claims that have no epistemic justification and, more ambitiously, that it responds appropriately to all epistemically justified claims.

As I have also explained, epistemic norms, although important, aren't the only norms to which political deliberation is subject to. In addition, there are participation norms, which regulate the inclusivity of political deliberation, as well as norms of good reasoning. An important task for a more comprehensive account of the norms of political deliberation, which has to be developed elsewhere, is to clarify how the different types of norms can fit together into a coherent normative framework for legitimacy-supporting political deliberation.

Notes

1 I have received helpful comments on an earlier version of this paper from Jeroen de Ridder, Michael Hannon, and an external referee. I also benefitted from conversations with Nathalie Ashton, Rowan Cruft, and Jonathan Heawood in the context of our ARHC project on Norms for the New Public Sphere and from discussions at the NYU Political Economy and Political theory workshop, especially with Dimitri Landa, Ryan Pevnick, and Melissa Schwartzberg.
2 But see Cohen (1986), Bohman (1998), Estlund (2008), Peter (2009), Talisse (2009), Landemore (2012), and Chambers (2017), among others, for discussions of the epistemic dimension of the theory of deliberative democracy.
3 Relevant justifications can be based on substantive or on procedural considerations, or on a combination of the two (see Cohen 1997). Simmons is a prominent critic of this justificationist view (see Simmons 2001); he advocates a view that bases political legitimacy on the actual consent of the citizens.
4 See, for example, Habermas (1996), Rawls (1993), and Mansbridge et al. (2006).
5 My discussion is informed by the literature on the epistemology of practical reasoning – Brown (2008) has a helpful overview of the broader debate.
6 See Gerken (2011) on the general question of how norms of practical reasoning vary with what is at stake.
7 In Peter (2020a) I develop a hybrid conception of political legitimacy that accommodates both the importance of well-informed political decision-making and of heeding normatively significant disagreements.
8 This norm draws its inspiration from the truth norm of assertions defended by Weiner (2005) and Whiting (2013).
9 See Peter (2020b) for a longer discussion of this point. The recklessness worry, in a context of moral truths, also echoes Rawls' well-known worry that truth-driven political deliberation is divisive (Rawls 1993).
10 The Knowledge Norm draws (loosely) on Williamson (2000) and Stanley and Hawthorne (2008).
11 See https://nltimes.nl/2020/03/12/everyone-stay-home-sick-many-events-banned-dutch-government-tightens-coronavirus-rules. I thank Jeroen de Ridder for the example.
12 See Peter (2019) for a longer discussion of this norm of political deliberation and its significance for legitimate political decision-making.
13 I'll come back to this below when I consider whether political deliberation itself can have an effect on the justification for belief.
14 In Peter (2013) I captured this idea in a mutual accountability norm of deliberation.
15 An epistemic peer is someone that you regard as equally likely to form a correct belief regarding p.
16 See Christensen (2014) on this, as well as several contributions in Johnson (2018).

References

Bohman, James. 1998. "Survey Article: The Coming of Age of Deliberative Democracy". *The Journal of Political Philosophy* 6(4): 400–25.
Bohman, James and Richardson, Henry S. 2009. "Liberalism, Deliberative Democracy, and 'Reasons that All Can Accept'." *Journal of Political Philosophy* 17(3): 253–74.
Brown, Jessica. 2008. "Knowledge and Practical Reason." *Philosophy Compass* 3(6): 1135–52.
Cartwright, Nancy. 1983. *How the Laws of Physics Lie*. Oxford: Oxford University Press.
Chambers, Simone. 2017. "The Epistemic Ideal of Reason-Giving in Deliberative Democracy." *Social Epistemology Review and Reply Collective* 6(10): 59–64.
Christensen, David. 2007. "Epistemology of Disagreement: The Good News." *Philosophical Review* 116: 187–217.
Christensen, David. 2014. "Disagreement and Public Controversy." In Jennifer Lackey (ed.), *Essays in Collective Epistemology*. Oxford: Oxford University Press, pp. 142–64.
Christiano, Thomas. 2008. *The Constitution of Equality*. Oxford: Oxford University Press.
Cohen, Joshua. 1986. "An Epistemic Conception of Democracy." *Ethics* 97(1): 26–38.
Cohen, Joshua. 1997. "Procedure and Substance in Deliberative Democracy." In James Bohman and William Rehg (eds.), *Deliberative Democracy*. Cambridge: MIT Press, 407–37.

Estlund, David. 2008. *Democratic Authority*. Princeton, NJ: Princeton University Press.

Fricker, Miranda. 2007. *Epistemic Injustice: Power and the Ethics of Knowing*. Oxford: Oxford University Press.

Fricker, Miranda. 2013. "Epistemic Injustice as a Condition of Political Freedom?" *Synthese* 190(7): 1317–32.

Gaus, Gerald. 2011. *The Order of Public Reason*. Cambridge: Cambridge University Press.

Habermas, Jürgen. 1996. *Between Facts and Norms*. Transl. by William Rehg. Cambridge: MIT Press.

Gerken, Mikkel. 2011. "Warrant and Action," *Synthese* 178(3): 529–47.

Johnson, Casey Rebecca (ed.). 2018. *Voicing Dissent: The Ethics and Epistemology of Making Disagreement Public*. New York: Routledge.

Kelly Thomas. 2010. "Peer Disagreement and Higher-Order Evidence." In Richard Feldman and T. A. Warfield (eds.), *Disagreement*. Oxford: Oxford University Press, pp. 111–74.

Lackey, Jennifer. 2007. "Norms of Assertion." *Noûs* 41(4): 594–626.

Lackey, Jennifer. 2010. "A Justificationist View of Disagreement's Epistemic Significance." In Adrian Haddock, Alan Millar, and Duncan Pritchard (eds.), *Social Epistemology*. Oxford: Oxford University Press, pp. 298–325.

Landemore, Helene. 2012. *Democratic Reason*. Princeton: Princeton University Press.

Larmore, Charles. 2008. *The Autonomy of Morality*. Cambridge: Cambridge University Press.

Manin, Bernard 1987. "On Legitimacy and Political Deliberation." *Political Theory* 15: 338–68.

Mansbridge, Jane, Hartz-Karp, Janette, Amengual, Matthew, and Gastil, John. 2006. "Norms of Deliberation: An Inductive Study." *Journal of Public Deliberation* 2(1): Article 7.

Mill, John Stuart. 1991 [1859]. In John Gray (ed.), *On Liberty and Other Essays*. Oxford: Oxford University Press.

Parkinson, James and Mansbridge, Jane (eds.). 2012. *Deliberative Systems*. Cambridge: Cambridge University Press.

Peter, Fabienne. 2009. *Democratic Legitimacy*. New York: Routledge.

Peter, Fabienne. 2013. "The Procedural Epistemic Value of Deliberation." *Synthese* 190(7): 1253–66.

Peter, Fabienne. 2019. "Political Legitimacy under Epistemic Constraints: Why Public Reasons Matter." In Jack Knight and Melissa Schwartzberg (eds.), *Political Legitimacy*. Nomos, Nomos Volume LX (61). New York: NYU Press, pp. 147–73.

Peter, Fabienne. 2020a. "The Grounds of Political Legitimacy." *Journal of the American Philosophical Association*, online first. doi:10.1017/apa.2020.6.

Peter, Fabienne. 2020b. "Truth and Uncertainty in Political Justification." In Elizabeth Edenberg and Michael Hannon (eds.), *Politics and Truth: New Perspectives in Political Epistemology*. Oxford: Oxford University Press, forthcoming.

Rawls, John. 1993. *Political Liberalism*. New York: Columbia University Press.

Raz, Joseph. 1986. *The Morality of Freedom*. Oxford: Oxford University Press.

Simmons, A. John. 2001. *Justification and Legitimacy*. Cambridge: Cambridge University Press.

Srinivasan, Amia. 2020. "Radical Externalism." *Philosophical Review* 29(3): 395–431.

Stanley, Jason and Hawthorne, John. 2008. "Knowledge and Action." *Journal of Philosophy* 105(10): 571–90.

Talisse, Robert B. 2009. *Democracy and Moral Conflict*. Cambridge: Cambridge University Press.

Weiner, Matthew. 2005. "Must We Know What We Say?" *Philosophical Review* 114: 227–51.

Whiting, Daniel. 2013. "Stick to the Facts: On the Norms of Assertion." *Erkenntnis* 78: 847–67.

Williamson, Timothy. 2000. *Knowledge and its Limits*. Oxford: Oxford University Press.

35

THE EPISTEMIC RESPONSIBILITIES OF CITIZENS IN A DEMOCRACY

Cameron Boult

1 Introduction

Does democratic participation come with a responsibility to be informed about politics? What about a responsibility to think rationally, or be open-minded and intellectually virtuous in other ways when engaging in political deliberation? To what extent are ordinary citizens informed, rational, and intellectually virtuous when engaging in politics?

Questions at the intersection of democratic theory and epistemology go back at least as far as Plato, and have remained a central focus of political philosophy throughout history. More recently, they have been taken up in empirically informed ways by political theorists, economists, and cognitive psychologists. For example, a vast empirical literature probes the extent to which citizens of large representative democracies tend to be ignorant[1] or uninformed about political matters. Numerous other studies examine the cognitive behaviour of individual citizens when deliberating about politics (Brennan 2021; Somin 2021).

This chapter seeks to provide a roadmap through some of this complex terrain. It does so by developing a taxonomy, dividing the terrain into three broad stances on the "epistemic responsibilities" of citizens in a democracy. I call these stances *non-epistemicism*, *optimism*, and *pessimism*. Each stance represents a kind of extreme in a matrix of possible views about the relationship between the epistemic responsibilities, if any, that democratic participation generates for citizens, and the epistemic competences that those citizens have. I examine how recent approaches to epistemic democracy, epistocracy, epistemic libertarianism, and pure proceduralism fit within this three-pronged taxonomy. My main aim is to explore the options for developing an account of the epistemic responsibilities of citizens in a democracy. I also aim to shed light on how there is considerable room for a fairly minimal approach to epistemic responsibilities of citizens in a democracy—one that, in my view, a number of theorists have not adequately registered in their recent attacks on democracy.

2 The taxonomy

John is a citizen of a large representative democracy electing a new federal government. One of the key policy differences between parties in the election concerns action on climate change. As part of his voting deliberations, John has done some careful research on what climate change is and what's causing it. He's also done some research on what each of the parties proposes to do about climate change. He's thought and discussed open-mindedly and critically with others about how effective each of those proposals would be if adopted. He's done something similar regarding other platform differences on issues he's inclined to find important. As a result of all this research and discussion, John prefers party A over party B, and his vote will reflect this.

In at least some respects, John is a relatively rare citizen. Not very many of us have the time or energy to be as epistemically diligent in deciding who to vote for. Many of us simply vote for a particular party out of habit, or because of some deep commitment that tends to override specifics on issues of the day (Lenz 2012; Mason 2018). Yet there is something intuitive about the idea that John is, at least with respect to these features of his voting behaviour, an example of responsible democratic participation. We can couch the idea that John is an example of responsible democratic participation in terms of the notion of a "political epistemic responsibility" (PER):

> **PER**: a defeasible responsibility to meet certain epistemic criteria in contributing to the democratic decision-making process.

The idea is that John is an example of responsible democratic participation at least partly because he lives up to his PERs, whatever those are exactly.

This definition of a PER is very open-ended. Many of the important details in the discussion to follow concern what these epistemic criteria are, and what the nature of this putative responsibility is, among other things. For example, here is one distinction to draw between two senses of "responsibility" that may be at play when talking about PERs:

> **R(functional):** X is an R(functional) responsibility of S's only if X is a necessary condition S must meet in order to successfully play S's role in contributing to the goal(s), aim(s), or function(s) of practice Y.
>
> **R(normative):** X is an R(normative) responsibility of S's only if X is a necessary condition S must meet in order to successfully play S's role in contributing to the goals(s), aim(s), or function(s) of practice Y, and Y ought to be practiced.

Assume for the sake of argument that at least one central aim or goal of democratic decision-making is to represent the interests of the majority of citizens (we might have this aim for many reasons—including epistemic ones). If a necessary condition on achieving this aim is that each citizen (or some percentage of citizens) is informed about P in coming to believe that party A, and not B, will best promote their interests (and voting on that basis), then we might say that being informed about P is an R(functional) of those citizens, vis-à-vis this putative aim of democracy. If it turns out this process of democratic decision-making is a practice that genuinely *ought* to be practised, perhaps meeting those epistemic conditions is an R(normative) for those citizens. For the most part, I wish to remain neutral on whether democracy is something that *ought* to be practised. So, I leave it an open question whether the responsibilities at play when I speak of PERs are R(functional) or R(normative).

My primary concern is to categorize possible views about the epistemic responsibilities of citizens in a democracy along two broad axes. The first axis is about *demands*: does the practice of democratic participation in some way generate PERs? If so, what kind, and for whom? The second axis is about *competences*: what sorts of epistemic competences *do* citizens

Table 35.1 On the epistemic responsibilities of citizens in a democracy

		Competences	
		Citizens tend to be epistemically competent	*Citizens do not tend to be epistemically competent*
Demands	Democratic participation generates PERs for citizens	Optimism • aggregative epistemic democrats • deliberative epistemic democrats	Pessimism • epistemic libertarians • epistocrats
	Democratic participation does not generate PERs for citizens	Non-epistemicism • pure proceduralists • classical deliberative democrats	

in a democracy actually tend to have? Do they tend to be informed about politics, and/or to deliberate rationally in forming political beliefs? Under what conditions?

If we divide views along each axis into two opposing extremes, we generate three broadly different camps of interest (differences on the epistemic abilities axis between proponents of non-epistemicism (those who hold that democratic participation does not generate PERs for citizens) do not really matter for our purposes). Actual views held by political theorists and philosophers about the nature and value[2] of democracy tend to fall somewhere in a matrix between the extremes represented in the above Table 35.1.

In the next few sections, I examine forms of non-epistemicism, pessimism, and optimism, highlighting some of the main commitments and motivations of thinkers who've defended views in democratic theory that fit within one or another of these categories.

3 Non-epistemicism

Much recent literature at the intersection of political theory and epistemology focusses on the amount of political ignorance and irrationality we seem to find among citizens in large representative democracies. Many of us are familiar with references to survey data detailing a supposedly staggering degree of ignorance about even the most basic "politically relevant" facts among a large percentage of the American electorate. Ilya Somin offers the following claims as paradigm examples:

> Much of the time, only a bare majority [of Americans] know which party has control of the Senate, some 70 percent cannot name both of their state's senators, and the majority cannot name any congressional candidate in their district at the height of a campaign. (Somin 2013: 19)
> A 2006 Zogby poll found that only 42 percent of Americans could even name the three branches of the federal government: executive, legislative, and judicial. (Somin 2013: 19)

We might take these results to suggest, prima facie, that if citizens have PERs, whatever they are exactly, then citizens must surely fall seriously short of meeting them. We might also wonder what, if anything, should be done about that. I will get to an assessment of the relevance of such survey data to questions about PERs shortly. For now, a natural alternative reaction might be to shrug one's shoulders. Why think citizens have PERs in the first place? From the point of view of the value of democracy, perhaps it's neither here nor there how informed and rational people are about politics (or anything else).

A longstanding tradition in democratic theory defends the value of democracy in terms of the intrinsic value of things like fairness, liberty, and equality. What matters, according to this tradition, is that democratic procedures—authorizing laws by voting, or electing representative legislators—are fair, or respect individual liberty, or have other intrinsically valuable properties. This approach to democratic theory—often referred to as "pure proceduralism"—would seem to entail, or at least leave open, the view about the PERs of citizens in a democracy that I call non-epistemicism.

One form of pure proceduralism is *fair* proceduralism. The basic idea is that voting is a fair procedure for making collective decisions among people who disagree. As long as everyone has an equal role to play in determining the outcome, the outcome has value (and may even have the power to render laws legitimate and authoritative), regardless of how we assess it by other, procedure-independent standards.

An advantage of this approach is that it renders unnecessary the potentially messy business of determining what procedure-independent criteria to use in assessing the value of democratically produced outcomes. It also seems immune to worries about voter ignorance. As David Estlund points out: "A procedure can be fair to participants whether or not they are smart, or well informed, or virtuous" (Estlund 2008: 66). For my purposes, this is the main point. The fact that a procedure can be fair, irrespective of facts about epistemic competences of citizens, and the fact that fair proceduralism grounds the value of democratically determined outcomes on the idea that those outcomes are the result of a fair procedure, seems to imply that democratic participation does not, in its own right, generate PERs for citizens. In other words, pure proceduralism—at least of this paradigmatic variety—seems at odds with the idea that there are PERs. Hence it is a kind of non-epistemicism.[3]

4 Pessimism

Much recent democratic theory has taken a more instrumentalist turn. There are well-known *critiques* as well as *defences* of democracy that hinge, in part, on an instrumentalist turn. By instrumentalist, I mean the idea that the value of democracy should be judged according to procedure-*independent* criteria, perhaps in addition to procedural criteria. For example, an instrumentalist might maintain that a democratic decision-making procedure has value only if it is more likely (under certain conditions) to lead to a "correct" outcome than a non-democratic decision-making procedure, such as oligarchy, or dictatorship. Recall John and the difference between party A and party B on climate change. The idea of a correct outcome is that one of these parties has the correct view about what to do about climate change.[4] Instrumentalists may also focus on the tendency of democracy to produce morally good laws, or other practical benefits. In the remainder of this chapter, I focus on epistemic forms of instrumentalism.

Starting with critiques of democracy, one form of pessimism is embodied in a view we can call "epistemic libertarianism". Epistemic libertarians, such as Ilya Somin (2013) and Bryan Caplan (2007), have argued that we should abandon centralized governments in favour of highly decentralized federal states; we should minimize and localize government, and leave more decision-making to the free-market. As Somin puts it, we should minimize centralized governments to make more room for "foot voting", the process by which citizens who dislike the policies they live under pursue improvement by literally moving to a jurisdiction with more favourable policies (Somin 2013: 119–55). The primary *basis* for their proposals is an epistemic one.

These theorists take the survey data mentioned above very much to heart (Caplan 2007: 50–94; Somin 2013: 17–61). According to epistemic libertarians, if the electorate resembles—even remotely—the picture we get from political knowledge survey data, then that electorate should not be guiding the political decision-making process, at least not in the way it does in a representative democracy. In addition to relying on such survey results, Somin and Caplan defend the idea that, in societies with large populations and fairly centralized governments, we should *expect* citizens to be massively politically ignorant and irrational. Epistemic libertarians take a cue from Anthony Downs (1957), arguing that political ignorance is *instrumentally* rational. According to Downs (and others), the rationality of political ignorance is an upshot of the nature of voting in a representative democracy with millions of voters; it's an upshot of the fact that the chances of an individual citizen's vote being a deciding factor in an election or referendum are near zero. The idea is that this has a significant impact on citizens' incentive to be informed about whatever it is they are voting on. Caplan takes the claim further, arguing it is instrumentally rational for voters to be (epistemically) *irrational* in forming political beliefs (Caplan 2007: 114–42). The idea is that it makes more sense, from the point of view of practical rationality, to succumb to biases and prejudices that protect one's sense of self and identity, when forming political beliefs, than it does to try to form beliefs that are carefully proportioned to the evidence. According to epistemic libertarians, citizens in smaller, federalized, and free-market-driven societies would have greater incentive to remain informed and rational in their political deliberations.[5]

Another form of pessimism is embodied in "epistocracy". Like epistemic libertarians, the most prominent contemporary advocate of epistocracy, Jason Brennan, tends to place a lot of store in survey data about political ignorance, as well as worries about the rationality of citizens in forming political beliefs (often for similar reasons) (Brennan 2016: 23–74; cf. Lopez-Guerra 2014: Ch. 2). Brennan differs, however, in the conclusions he draws from these worries. Rather than recommending shrinking government and leaving more decisions to the free-market, epistocracy recommends adopting legal restrictions on who can vote, how votes are counted, or how individual votes ultimately contribute to democratic decision-making processes. Epistocratic approaches to restricting the franchise range from J.S. Mill's epistocracy of the educated (plural votes for the "educated"), to voter competence exams, to universal suffrage with "epistemic veto", whereby a "cognitively elite" body has the opportunity to veto decisions it deems unjustified or bad ("malicious, incompetent, or unreasonable") (Brennan 2016: 204–31; see Brennan 2021 for a defence of "enlightened preference voting").

Setting the details of these positive proposals aside, both epistemic libertarians and epistocrats suggest a picture according to which it is *democracy*, or more specifically, the kind of democratic participation involved in large representative democracies, that generates the sorts of PERs that citizens are supposedly not to be able to meet. By advocating for epistocracy, Brennan effectively advocates for a political system in which low-competence citizens no longer have PERs, because they are no longer voters. By advocating for "foot voting", Caplan and Somin effectively advocate for a political system in which low-competence citizens have a lot less to think about (and a lot more incentive to try harder), because they are voting on much more local issues. We can draw out claims about PERs implied by these approaches by thinking about the following question: what sorts of demands would citizens need to meet in order for these pessimists to stop being worried about democracy? Both epistemic libertarians and epistocrats tend to have a fairly *stringent* view of what constitutes epistemic competence of voters in a democracy. They regard detailed information about government structures, political processes, and economics as relevant (perhaps even central) to our understanding of voter competency. As we'll see below, optimists tend to reject these assumptions about the nature of PERs.

5 Optimism

In stark opposition to both epistemic libertarians and epistocrats, "epistemic democrats" *defend* democracy in part on the basis of claims about its tendency to produce (epistemically) good decisions.[6] Epistemic democrats tend to focus on the epistemic benefits of vote aggregation, the epistemic benefits of "deliberation", or some combination of both. Aggregative and deliberative approaches may have different upshots for our understanding of the nature of citizens' PERs.

Starting with aggregative approaches, theorists tend to rely on versions of the Condorcet Jury Theorem (CJT), the "miracle of aggregation", or ways in which the benefits of cognitive diversity can be reaped through aggregation processes. See Heléne Landemore's excellent overview of CJT and the miracle of aggregation in her chapter in this volume.[7]

Here I will focus on the implications for PERs of the CJT approach, particularly as they arise from the so-called "competence" and "independence" conditions (Landemore 2021). We can draw these out by thinking about the following question: what sorts of demands would citizens need to meet in order for these conditions to be satisfied? Minimally, to satisfy the competence condition, it seems voters must be *better than random* at "getting things right". The independence condition requires that the probability of one person being right on any binary question must be the same regardless of the probability of another person being right for that same question (Landemore 2013: 73). So, to satisfy the independence condition, it seems citizens must avoid being systematically influenced by others in casting their votes. There are any number of things we might take this to imply about the PERs of individuals—perhaps it corresponds with a demand of intellectual autonomy, or intellectual courage (Grasswick 2019).

Despite the fact that according to these approaches much of the epistemic work is done by aggregation itself, citizens have a role to play at the individual level. To make this more vivid, note that the competence condition is cast in terms of probabilities of being right. There are at least two dimensions relevant to that probability: the individual's abilities, and the *environment* in which they find themselves. When it comes to the latter dimension, note how hostile the epistemic environment is for citizens gathering political information: news outlets often put a great deal of spin on their reporting, personalization algorithms influence access to social media, politicians have agendas that can affect their presentation of information, and so on (Battaly 2021). Even if citizens tend to have a high degree of epistemic competence, the probability of choosing the correct option may nevertheless be quite low, given this hostile environment. In this regard, perhaps the competence condition places a more stringent epistemic demand on individuals than it at first seems (cf. Worsnip 2018).

Let's turn to deliberative forms of epistemic democracy. "Deliberation" refers to the process of exchanging reasons and argumentation with the aim of reaching a decision. Deliberation takes place in many contexts—from within one's own mind, to between citizens, to between elected legislators, and so on. In reality, decisions in a democracy are never reached through deliberation alone. At some point, a non-deliberative decision procedure, such as voting, must be used to settle residual disagreement. But the idea that deliberative epistemic democrats typically embrace is that deliberation:

i   Enlarges the pools of ideas and information.
ii Weeds out good arguments from the bad.
iii Leads to a consensus on the "better" or "more reasonable" solution.

(Landemore 2013: 97)

Epistemic democrats such as Landemore (2013, 2021) and James Bohman (2006) emphasize that we shouldn't expect deliberation, all by itself, to do these things; rather, deliberation must take place under constraints, which defenders of deliberative epistemic democracy argue democratic institutions can provide. In particular, it's widely thought that *diversity* and *inclusiveness* are necessary conditions on the epistemic benefits of deliberation. Typically, not much is said in terms of specifics about what sorts of epistemic competences individuals must have for a deliberative process to achieve anything like (i)–(iii). There is also much controversy over the question of whether deliberation really is likely to do (i), (ii), or (iii), or whether any of (i)–(iii) is necessary or sufficient for deliberation to reap the epistemic benefits claimed by epistemic democrats.

One strategy for teasing out implications of deliberative epistemic democracy for our understanding of PERs is to look at some of the most compelling arguments *against* the epistemic benefits of deliberation, and ask: what sorts of demands would citizens need to meet in order for these arguments to fail? Hannon (2020) has recently summarized a number of well-known arguments against the epistemic benefits of deliberation, highlighting empirical arguments for the pervasiveness of phenomena such as group polarization (Sunstein 2002), cultural cognition (Kahan et al. 2011), and motivated reasoning in a political deliberative context (Haidt 2012). If these really are a threat to the epistemic benefits of deliberation, then, minimally, it would seem an epistemic demand on citizens, according to deliberative epistemic democracy, is that citizens have the epistemic competences needed (perhaps only after certain kinds of training) to render these threats unproblematic. However stringent PERs would have to be in this regard seems difficult to precisely specify. But this gives us at least a basic sense of the interaction between deliberative epistemic democracy and our understanding of PERs.

Some proponents of the epistemic benefits of deliberation may be prepared to grant that individual citizens tend to fit the profile ascribed to them by those who advance these objections, but maintain that deliberation has epistemic benefits nonetheless. The idea is to argue that the epistemic benefits of deliberation are the result of *collective* or *distributed* features of deliberation, as opposed to facts about individuals involved. Landemore (2013) focusses on "models of cognitive diversity" (drawing on work by Lu Hong and Scott Page) to argue that, in both a deliberative and aggregative context, the epistemic value of democracy is not so much a function of individual epistemic ability, as it is "cognitive diversity" (understood as a plurality of modes of thinking and interpretations of the world) (Landemore 2021).

On this latter picture, the main (epistemic) lesson of deliberative epistemic democracy for individuals is something like: be yourself! This is an upshot of the idea that the more diverse the deliberating group is, the better. There is a limit to the value of diversity—not *all* views should be taken into account—but this far from imagining that being a good citizen requires citizens to be up to date on the latest political issues, to have encyclopaedic knowledge of the mechanisms and structure of government, and a firm grasp of economics. The epistemic benefits of deliberation are such that, when large groups of people, with many different perspectives on an issue, contribute to the process of exchange of reasons, that group is likely to produce a better outcome than any subset of the group would produce (at least over time, over a long chain of decisions).

6 Hybrid views

Some prominent defences and critiques of democracy may not fit neatly within my taxonomy. To illustrate with just one example, start with the observation that the optimists and pessimists we've discussed so far have presupposed a "veritistic" conception of the epistemic benefits and drawbacks of democracy. Veritistic epistemic goods are epistemic goods that derive their value from the value of *truth*.

Michael Hannon (2020) has recently argued for a shift in focus towards non-veritistic goods, such as "empathetic understanding". Empathetic understanding is the ability to take up another person's viewpoint, to be able to see *why* another person believes what they do (2020: 9). Hannon's view is motivated by a worry shared by many of the pessimists discussed above, namely, that there are serious grounds for concern about citizens' ability to be *informed* and *rational* in their political decision-making. But perhaps we shouldn't see such goods as the aim of deliberative structures and processes in the first place. Another way of thinking about the epistemic goods that democratic participation both *requires* and *tends to promote* is in terms of empathetic understanding.[8] To understand others, we need to empathize with their thinking, and this minimally requires:

* Being willing to listen.
* Having the ability to take up another person's perspective.

Hannon argues that, provided citizens meet these conditions, democratic deliberation will promote empathetic understanding among the citizenry (which may, in turn, promote other good things). And that might be one reason to think deliberative democracy is a good idea, in comparison with other democratic models, such as pure aggregation models. According to this picture, we might say that the PERs of citizens in a democracy include a responsibility towards empathetically understanding other citizens. As Hannon acknowledges, there is room for debate about whether empathetic understanding is a genuinely *epistemic* good (2020: 20). If one were to disagree about that, then, given his scepticism about veritistic forms of deliberative epistemic democracy, we might be tempted to place him somewhere on a hazy line between pessimism and non-epistemicism.[9]

7 What counts as competence, and how it's determined

As we've seen, pessimists tend to rely on survey data about political ignorance in challenging democracy, in addition to a priori arguments about the incentives of voters. There are a number of interconnected issues we can raise about this sort of reliance on survey data, as well as these a priori arguments.

Arthur Lupia (2016) has argued that a good deal of work needs to be done by pessimists to articulate a clear logic getting them from claims about survey data, to claims about voter competence (see esp. Chs. 15 and 16). A closely related issue surrounds the use of "political knowledge scales" to arrive at conclusions about citizens' political knowledge. Surveys such as the American National Elections Studies (ANES) simply aggregate the scores of individuals' answers to a small set of questions about politics. While these questions are chosen for specific reasons—presumably with the aim of making them representative of "political knowledge"—Lupia argues that there is simply no evidence that political knowledge scales like those of the ANES are representative of anything we can fairly label "political knowledge". Rather, they may well be representative of much more specific kinds of knowledge (and ignorance), which, as Lupia also argues, may or may not be a necessary or sufficient condition on having a high-value competence relevant to democratic participation (Lupia 2016: Ch. 16). The basic issue here is about how the term "political knowledge" tends to be operationalized in various studies (cf. Landemore 2013: 199–200).[10]

Optimists have much to say about how citizens who don't know much about the sorts of things asked on political knowledge surveys can contribute valuably to the democratic process. Often, (as seen with Landemore) authors focus on how informational and cognitive processes in a democracy are *distributed*. Others rely more heavily on claims about citizen use of "information shortcuts", heuristics enabling people to make the same decisions with respect to some set of options that they would if they were "fully informed" about the options. Examples of information shortcuts frequently discussed in the literature include: party identification, retrospective evaluations of the economy, and relying on opinion leaders (for influential work on this topic, see Popkin 1994; Lupia and McCubbins 1998; Robertson 1976).

Thomas Christiano, a prominent defender of democracy against empirically based worries about voter ignorance and irrationality, focusses on the division of intellectual labour and the use of information shortcuts in democratic societies; he's developed an expansive account of the resources available to citizens in contributing to the democratic process (2001, 2015). Christiano points to the fact that real-world political deliberation happens across numerous levels, from citizens, to experts, to opinion leaders, and politicians. Each level plays a different role in deliberation, requiring different kinds of intellectual capacities. Real-world polities rely on a stratification of deliberative tasks. Even within levels—at the level of ordinary conversations among citizens about politics, for example—people can rely on one another (along with other information shortcuts) in a division of intellectual labour. For example, John might happen to know a good deal about climate change, but not much about foreign policy. John's friend Linda might be in the opposite position. Christiano suggests that, as long as certain conditions are met—such as each person having relevant background knowledge about the other—John and Linda can reasonably trust one another's say-so when it comes to politically relevant factual information on these topics. As externalists in epistemology are well aware, lacking the ability to positively justify one's beliefs on a given topic need not undermine the possibility that one's beliefs are warranted (Christiano 2015: 261).

We can also push back on Downsian claims about incentives of voters to be informed and rational when voting in large representative democracies. Mackie (2012) has argued that Downs' idea presupposes a mistaken model of why people vote in the first place. Mackie argues for a "contributory model", according to which the aim of voting isn't *merely* to get someone to win, but also to show that whoever you're voting for, even if they lose, has a certain *mandate* behind them.

There is of course much room for debate about the efficacy of mechanisms for the division of cognitive labour, as well as voter incentives to be informed.[11] But this section has canvassed some ways one might challenge the degree of stringency assumed in many pessimistic views about PERs. Moreover, it has explained why, even if pessimists are right about stringency, it's far from clear that we have an accurate picture of whether or to what extent citizens really do tend to fall short of their PERs.

8 Conclusion

We have identified a number of important choice points for our understanding of PERs of citizens in a democracy.

- Views may differ on the question of whether PERs are R(normative) or merely R(functional) responsibilities.
- They may also differ on the question of stringency—for instance, on the extent to which technical, detailed information about government structures, political processes, and economics are relevant to voter competence.
- There may also be room for debate about whether PERs should be understood in veritistic or non-veritistic terms.

By placing some prominent views in democratic theory within the three-pronged distinction between non-epistemicism, pessimism, and optimism, we have been able to draw out these possibilities, while keeping their broader implications for our understanding of democracy in view. I have also suggested that there is room for a fairly minimal approach to PERs—one that, in my view, many pessimists do not always seem to pay adequate attention to in their attacks on democracy.

Notes

1 I use the term "ignorant" to cover both the *false* belief sense of ignorant and the *lack* of belief sense. I use the term "irrational" to denote a further epistemic lack, one having to do with lack of evidential support.
2 Theorists are often interested in more specific issues, such as the *legitimacy, authority*, or *justification* of democracy. I wish to remain neutral on those issues, so I simply discuss views insofar as they defend or challenge the claim that democracy is in some broad sense a good idea.
3 Early forms of deliberative democracy emphasize the intrinsic value of a "reasonable exchange" of viewpoints and ideas, where "reasonable exchange" is not intended to be understood with reference to procedure-independent criteria. These approaches might best be classified under non-epistemicism.
4 We can distinguish between claims about the proper *aims* of democratic decision-making (e.g. should we reduce human impact on climate change?) and claims about the *means* to those aims (e.g. how to reduce human impact on climate change?). Many, though by no means all, instrumentalists are wary of talking about correct answers to ends-type (value-laden) questions. For sake of space I bracket this issue.
5 Some have argued that we should not expect voters to become significantly more informed of about political issues and their governments even if these become downsized and de-centralized (Christiano 2015).
6 Not all epistemic democrats presuppose instrumentalism (Peter 2008).
7 Prominent objections to CJT target the competence and independence conditions, along with other requirements such as that voters must be sincere, and that political decisions have correct outcomes. Robert Goodin and Kai Spiekermann (2018) build on classical versions of CJT, largely in response to these sorts of worries, resulting in a complex version of aggregative democracy (see also Landemore 2013: pp. 149–56, for an accessible, qualified defence).
8 Hannon couches his epistemic defence of democracy in terms of epistemic benefits to *individuals*, as opposed to epistemic benefits democracy has for society's *decision-making* as a whole. See Hannon (2020: 21) for discussion of whether empathetic understanding really is a non-veritistic epistemic good.
9 Anne Jeffreys' "limited epistocracy" (2018) and David Estlund's (2008) "epistemic proceduralism" strike me as other potential hybrid views.
10 Additional issues in this area include *how* survey questions are posed, and the context in which questions are asked. For example, significant differences arise when participants are offered a dollar

for each correct answer to a survey question, or given 24 hours to respond (Prior and Lupia 2008: 169). Also, the way *accuracy* of participant answers is measured is crucial. What counts as a "correct" answer or "nearly correct" answer to certain questions can sometimes be fuzzy to interpret (Lupia 2016: 209).

11 For a helpful summary of some compelling pessimistic responses, see Somin (2015: 386–89).

References

Battaly, H. (2021). "Engaging Closed-mindedly with your Polluted Media Feed," in *The Routledge Handbook of Political Epistemology*, London: Routledge.

Brennan, J. (2016) *Against Democracy*, Princeton, NJ: Princeton University Press.

———. (2021) "In Defense of Epistocracy: Enlightened Preference Voting," in M. Hannon & J. de Ridder (eds.), *The Routledge Handbook of Political Epistemology*, London: Routledge.

Bohman, J. (2006) "Deliberative Democracy and the Epistemic Benefits of Diversity," *Episteme*, 3(3): 175–91.

Caplan, B. (2007) *The Myth of the Rational Voter*, Princeton, NJ: Princeton University Press.

Christiano, T. (2001) "Democracy and Social Epistemology," *Philosophical Topics*, 29(2): 67–90.

———. (2015) "Voter Ignorance Is Not Necessarily a Problem," *Critical Review*, 27(4): 253–69.

Downs, A. (1957) *An Economic Theory of Democracy*, New York: Harper.

Estlund, D. (2008) *Democratic Authority: A Philosophical Framework*, Princeton, NJ: Princeton University Press.

Goodin, R. & Spiekermann, K. (2018) *An Epistemic Theory of Democracy*, Oxford: Oxford University Press.

Grasswick, H. (2019). "Epistemic Autonomy in a Social World of Knowing," in H. Battaly (ed.), *The Routledge Handbook of Virtue Epistemology*, London: Routledge, 196–208.

Haidt, J. (2012). *The Righteous Mind: Why Good People are Divided by Politics and Religion*, New York: Vintage.

Hannon, M. (2020) "Empathetic Understanding and Deliberative Democracy," *Philosophy and Phenomenological Research*, 101(3): 591–611.

Jeffrey, A. (2018) "Limited Epistocracy and Political Inclusion," *Episteme*, 15(4): 412–32.

Kahan, D.M., Jenkins-Smith, H. & Braman, D. (2011) "Cultural Cognition of Scientific Consensus," *Journal of Risk Research*, 14(2): 147–74.

Landemore, H. (2013) *Democratic Reason: Politics, Collective Intelligence, and the Rule of the Many*, Princeton, NJ: Princeton University Press.

———. (2021) "An Epistemic Argument for Democracy," in M. Hannon & J. de Ridder (eds.), *The Routledge Handbook of Political Epistemology*, London: Routledge.

Lenz, G. (2012). *Follow the Leader? How Voters Respond to Politicians' Policies and Performance*, Chicago, IL: University of Chicago Press.

Lopez-Guerra, C. (2014). *Democracy and Disenfranchisement: The Morality of Electoral Exclusions*. Oxford: Oxford University Press.

Lupia, A. (2016) *Uninformed: Why People Know so Little about Politics and What We Can do about It*, Oxford: Oxford University Press.

Lupia, R. & McCubbins, M. (1998) *The Democratic Dilemma: Can Citizens Learn What They Need to Know?* Cambridge: Cambridge University Press.

Mackie, G. (2012) "Rational Ignorance and Beyond," in J. Elster & H. Landemore (eds.), *Collective Wisdom: Principles and Mechanisms*, Cambridge: Cambridge University Press, 290–318.

Mason, L. (2018). *Uncivil Agreement: How Politics Became Our Identity*. Chicago, IL: Chicago University Press.

Peter, F. (2008) "Pure Epistemic Proceduralism," *Episteme*, 5(1): 33–55.

Popkin, S. (1994) *The Reasoning Voter*, Chicago, IL: University of Chicago Press.

Prior, M. & Lupia, A. (2008) "Money, Time, and Political Knowledge: Distinguishing Quick Recall and Political Learning Skills," *American Journal of Political Science*, 52(1): 169–83.

Robertson, D. (1976) "Surrogates for Party Identification in the Rational Choice Framework," in I. Budge (ed.), *Party Identification and Beyond: Representations of Voting and Party Competition*, London: Wiley, 365–382.

Somin, I. (2013) *Democracy and Political Ignorance*, Stanford, CA: Stanford University Press.

———. (2015) "The Ongoing Debate over Political Ignorance: Reply to My Critics," *Critical Review*, 27(3–4): 380–414.

———. (2021) "Is Political Ignorance Rational?" in M. Hannon & J. de Ridder, *The Routledge Handbook of Political Epistemology*, London: Routledge.

Sunstein, C. (2002) "The Law of Group Polarization," *Journal of Political Philosophy*, 10(2): 175–95.

Worsnip, A. (2018) "The Obligation to Diversify One's Sources: Against Epistemic Partisanship in the Consumption of News Media," in C. Fox & J. Saunders (eds.), *Media Ethics: Free Speech and the Requirements of Democracy*, Abingdon: Routledge, 240–264.

36

THE EPISTEMIC CASE FOR NON-ELECTORAL FORMS OF DEMOCRACY

Alexander Guerrero

Electoral representative government embodies a compromise, exchanging political equality and broad distribution of political power for supposed epistemic benefit from the use of elected representatives. Direct democracy would do better by considerations of political equality, inclusivity, self-government, and other aspects of political morality commonly brought under the heading of "democracy," but it also would almost certainly result in epistemically poorer decision-making. In this chapter, I draw attention to the significant epistemic shortfalls of electoral representative democracy and suggest that this is a compromise that is not working out. Perhaps more surprisingly, I will suggest that there are non-electoral alternatives that do at least as well as electoral representative government on the democracy scorecard, and which would likely to better than electoral representative government on the epistemic scorecard.

1 Against electoral representative democracy: the epistemic case

As suggested above, the use of elected representatives embodies a compromise that is supposed to yield epistemic benefits. Here and elsewhere (Guerrero, 2021a, 2021b), I argue that under the conditions present in many modern political communities, electoral representative government is failing to do well—even and perhaps especially in epistemic terms—and that this is in significant part *because* of elections.

In the background is a view that presupposes that political institutions are tools that can be used to help us solve problems of moral significance that arise in our political community. These problems differ depending on the particulars of the sociopolitical context, but, crucially, there are still some general claims we can make about what institutional capacities will be required for political institutions to do well at solving problems, regardless of the details of those problems. To consistently solve problems requires capacities of at least two distinct kinds: (1) appreciating (or understanding or knowing) the world as it is, and (2) responding to the world in light of this appreciation. The first of these concerns epistemic, diagnostic capacities of institutions. The second concerns agential capacities (responsiveness, morality, steadfastness) of institutions. Epistemic capacities, which will be our focus, include the ability and propensity of the institutions to gather and generate relevant evidence (evidence relevant to the decisions that need to be made); to engage with and draw from diverse sources of knowledge, including extant technical, esoteric, and expert knowledge; to accurately and appropriately assess, weigh, and evaluate evidence; and to organize and disseminate evidence and knowledge so that it is readily available and appropriately salient for decision-making purposes. In this part of the chapter, I will highlight some of the central epistemic concerns about the use of elections in modern political contexts.

1.1 *The conditions of modern politics*

Let me begin my drawing attention to those conditions that make trouble for the epistemic capacities of electoral representative government and which strike me as indelible features of the modern political world. These conditions are not necessary features of the world, nor are they constitutive features of human existence or social organization. Instead, these are features of the specific sociopolitical communities that we often find ourselves in today, but we should treat them as fixed for the purposes of comparison with non-electoral systems.

The first condition is the *sheer size and scale* of modern political systems. Most modern country-level political systems operate over large political jurisdictions in terms of both geographic size and population. This size makes it so that the overwhelming majority of citizens do not know each other personally, and it creates problems in terms of mass communication, control of media and technological infrastructure, and economic and environmental regulation. Additionally, governing territories of this size that include this many people creates the need for multiple layers of government. Most political systems have a central federal government as well as (still large) sub-units—states, provinces, counties, cantons, townships, municipalities—that have their own distinctive political organization and political actors.

The second condition follows from this size and scale: the problems confronted by political institutions are *highly complex*. There are people, institutions, and other actors, with distinct kinds of beliefs, motivations, and preferences, engaging in conduct that has many different possible, hard to disentangle effects. The correct diagnosis of political problems is complicated. The institutions, laws, and policies that might be proposed to address the problems themselves will be complicated (with many moving parts and interrelated components), and it will be difficult to discern whether the proposed solution will actually work—or even whether it is working or has worked after having been implemented.

The third condition follows from the fact of complexity: to do well at identifying and solving the problems that actually exist, political systems will be significantly epistemically *dependent on expert input*. Complexity results in the need for division of labor—epistemic and otherwise—which results in the development of subsets of people who are experts, technocrats, and policy wonks. Even basic problem-solving presents technical problems that require expert input.

The fourth condition might be seen as a corollary of these others (bolstered by a familiar story about rational incentives): we should expect high levels of *citizen ignorance* regarding almost all aspects of politics and political problems. The size, scale, complexity, and technical nature of political problems confronted in modern politics means that ordinary knowledge or common sense will be insufficient for policymaking and understanding and addressing most political problems.

A fifth condition, not present to the same extent everywhere but significantly present in most modern political communities, is a *significant level of inequality* in terms of wealth, income, and socioeconomic power. Income and wealth inequality often generate further inequalities in education, employment opportunities, media influence and control, and social capital and influence, particularly as the effects compound over time and across generations.

A final common condition is that of *significant social division* along lines of race, ethnicity, linguistic background, political ideology, and/or religion, often resulting in entrenched majority/minority political dynamics. Given the worldwide history of colonialism and the common problem in many political communities of historical racial injustice, many political communities have not just social division but a particular kind of social division as a background condition, giving rise to a similar set of political problems.

1.2 Epistemic challenges for electoral representative institutions

Competent problem-solving under these political conditions will require institutions and mechanisms that can function well despite the size and scale, complexity, dependence on expertise, extensive citizen ignorance, high levels of inequality, and significant social division that characterize these political communities. Electoral representative systems encounter a number of significant epistemic challenges.

As noted above, making good political decisions requires a wide variety of specific, esoteric knowledge. One must know facts about the world that relate to politics; one must know political facts of various kinds about how various political institutions work and about their history and past actions; one must know about the political problems that exist or are on the horizon, as well as about various proposals to address those problems; and one must know what members of the political community think about those problems and purported solutions, including which they see as most important, most threatening, and so on. This motivates the use of elected representatives, who will have political decision-making as their full-time job, as well as funding and support to engage in the relevant investigation. The theory is that elected representatives will have incentives to acquire and to act on the relevant knowledge, as they face electoral consequences if they do not.

But there's a hole in the theory. Selecting political officials and monitoring and holding them accountable requires that voters know enough to provide an effective political check through elections: disciplining elected officials who are not working to address the extant problems, alerting candidates as to what the issues that matter most to them are, and having a well-enough informed view about the world so that their judgment about what problems matter corresponds tolerably well to the problems that actually exist. This requires knowing about what elected representatives are doing, knowing about the extant problems, knowing whether what is being done is working, and knowing enough to be able to spot and alert others to new problems on the horizon, or the need to reprioritize problems, and so on. Citizens don't need to know everything that representatives need to know for the system to work well. But they do need to know something pretty substantial, and they don't currently know what they need to know.

This is not surprising. Members of the political community do not have enough time or incentive to become adequately well informed about the problems that exist, nor about the possible solutions to those problems, resulting in systemic, widespread ignorance. This voter ignorance may result in direct uninformed influence on policymaking and problem-solving, which would be bad, epistemically. Alternatively, voter ignorance might lead to an erosion of meaningful electoral accountability, resulting in powerful special interests capturing political representatives.

Efforts to address the citizen ignorance problem might focus either on general education or on news media and news media consumption choices. But although improving mass public education (and things like statistical literacy) might be a necessary condition of addressing the ignorance problem, it is not a sufficient condition of doing so. Mass public education is not sufficient because the information needed to serve the necessary electoral accountability function is too small scale, micro level, of the moment—concerning particular people, their actions, and present problems—for it to be supplied by general mass public education. An additional reason for this: in most countries, people under 18 cannot vote. So, for many people, they have left formal educational settings behind by the time they become politically active. We need the news.

The Pew Research Center for the People & the Press reports that the average American spends 70 minutes per day taking in the news through TV, radio, newspapers, or through other online (non-social media) content.[1] That is a lot of time. And yet we remain almost entirely ignorant of everything about politics and economics that we might need to know. Why? The short answer is that we choose what news we consume for the same reason most of us watch or read anything: it's fun, enraging, entertaining, exciting. It makes us feel connected or like a part of something bigger than ourselves. We have a side, a team, and we watch our heroes and their opponents every night on TV. That, by itself, might not be bad. But it shapes our search function—what news we seek out and how we seek it out—and that, through the market, affects what news exists. The news media is supported by the for-profit market and so its form and content are driven by entertainment incentives, not informational or educational ones (Postman, 1985).

In a world of even higher levels of media choice—cable news and internet sources, in particular—these entertainment incentives have led us into echo chambers, highly partisan pathways, and the dissipation of common epistemic sources. This, in turn, has resulted in re-inforced prejudices and biases, false views about the problems we face, heightened attention on issues that divide us and enrage us, and a generally impoverished level of political knowledge and discussion. Higher quality news and relatively non-partisan local news has struggled to survive, and many cities and counties now exist in news deserts (Abernathy, 2018).

The picture of the world that we get through these lenses is deeply distorted, highly partisan, rarely challenged, and makes it very difficult to pay attention to the problems that actually exist, let alone to devise solutions to them, and it makes it nearly impossible to imagine working together, all of us, toward implementing those solutions. When we add regular elections on top of this, particularly given the use of single-member districts and plurality voting rules that ensure two dominant political parties as described in what has come to be known as Duverger's Law (Duverger, 1954), we get a deeply divided, us vs. them dynamic in ordinary political life. Elections both create and exacerbate these conditions, as we don't know enough to pay attention to the issues, but it is easy to have opinions about individuals, particularly once we know what team's uniform they wear. And elections tap into familiar ingroup/outgroup psychological dynamics—dynamics whose strength increase as we become convinced that more and more is at stake in each election (as we become convinced by the news we consume that the other side is even more threatening than before).

A number of powerful epistemic pathologies result from our political teams regularly squaring off over and over again through elections with this mass information environment as our epistemic background. Distrust in citizens who are on the other side, segregation by party affiliation in all realms of life, vilification of those who disagree with us politically—all are now commonplace. We have divided our political communities in deep ways that affect who we listen to, who we trust, how we try to find out about the world, what we believe, who we care about, and what we value. Liliana Mason, a political scientist who documents these trends, says that our partisan identities have become "mega-identities" and paints "a picture of a nation whose partisan teams are raring to fight, despite an almost total lack of any substantive policy reasons to do so" (Mason, 2018, p. 88). That makes it very hard for any kind of political institution to work effectively to address the problems that afflict our communities. For-profit, entertainment-focused news media and regular elections together drive this pretty hate machine. It serves to distract us. It makes it hard to work together. And it dramatically distorts the background epistemic landscape in which we attempt to do so.

Even leaving aside hyper-partisanship, elections introduce yet further problems. As noted earlier, general ignorance and complexity makes it hard for members of the political community to know whether an elected representative has actually acted or tried to act to address a political problem—particularly in the short term, such as the time between election cycles. For problems with a long-time horizon, such as climate change, things are even worse. It is comparatively easy to deny the existence of the problem, even when the best evidence suggests otherwise. The evidence may be technical and complex, and—as bearing on a somewhat distant projection—far from certain in its implications. If there are salient costs to actually addressing the problem, then elected officials will have electoral incentives to compete by avoiding incurring these costs, even if this will make everyone worse off. One effective way to compete on this front is through disinformation and epistemic pollution: spreading false information, undermining reliance on actual experts, propping up pseudo-experts and junk science, manufacturing controversy where none should exist, and so on. And, of course, all of this is easier when there is a background context of broad ignorance and intense political division.

Finally, elections select the socioeconomic elite as our political representatives. In 2015, for example, 130 of the 535 members of Congress had a net worth of over $2 million; 80% were male; 84% were white, and more than half were lawyers or businesspeople. The epistemic implications of this distorted selection are significant. Members of the elite will have little personal interest in or experience with many of the urgent problems faced by the non-elite. They may also be overconfident in thinking that they do understand these issues, even when they do not. Diversity in terms of life experience—including occupational experience, religious experience, cultural experience, experience occupying different social positions, educational experience—is important for epistemic reasons. By using elections, we are losing out on much of the available knowledge about the world, and we are choosing people with their own sense of what is most urgent and important to address. This affects the ability of elected representative political institutions to identify and effectively respond to the actual problems the political community faces.

★ ★ ★

Some of these problems are caused by the use of elections—the hyper-partisanship, short-term bias, focus on individuals rather than issues, and selection of unrepresentative representatives all stem from the central role that elections play in our system. Other problems are not endemic to electoral representation, but result instead from the poor fit of elections on top of the background conditions that have come to characterize modern political life: extensive size and scale of the political community, issue complexity, dependence on expertise, extensive citizen ignorance, and high levels of inequality. All should make us concerned about the viability of electoral representative democracy on epistemic grounds.

2 Considering non-electoral democracy: the epistemic case

The idea of "non-electoral democracy" might sound like an oxymoron. Of course, we are already familiar with something that would count as "democracy" but which does not involve elections: direct democracy, in which all adult citizens are allowed to vote or otherwise directly decide on policy matters, without electing anyone to govern in their stead. Here, I want to offer two more alternatives to electoral representative government that do not employ elections but which arguably do satisfy the extant constraints of political morality and which might be comparatively attractive in terms of their epistemic performance under conditions like those that exist in the modern political world.

2.1 Constraints of political morality

There are important values—apart from epistemic and instrumental values—that limit which kinds of political institutions are morally permissible (politically legitimate, all things considered normatively attractive, and so on). Although the purpose of political institutions may be to help us solve various problems we encounter, there are constraints on how those solutions can be pursued. Here are three such constraints: the right to popular sovereignty, the right of individuals to be treated as morally equal under the law, and respect for individual rights of freedom of body and mind (rights of life, bodily integrity, physical liberty and movement, speech, thought, and association). Political institutions must respect these rights, which are rights of individuals in their capacities as members of political communities. It is plausible that "democracy" has come to be reserved for political systems that observe and respect these constraints. The last two constraints are intuitive and familiar, and I won't say more about them here. But let me say something about the first, as it is in need of elaboration.

Some have a view on which democracy requires popular sovereignty, in that "the people" have political control; it is government "by the people." On a certain understanding of that requirement, electoral representative democracy would be straightforwardly incompatible with it. Let us assume that electoral representative democracy is compatible with this right to popular sovereignty, so that the right must be able to be respected by something far less than equal distribution of political power. Consider a different conception of popular sovereignty:

> **Consistent Responsiveness**: There is popular sovereignty in some political jurisdiction only if and only because there is consistently responsive government in that political jurisdiction, government that generates responsive outcomes. Political outcomes are responsive to the extent that they track what the people living in the political jurisdiction believe, prefer, or value, so that if those beliefs, preferences, or values were different, the political outcomes would also be different, would be different in a similar direction, and would be different because the beliefs, preferences, and values were different. Government is consistently responsive if and only if there are institutional mechanisms in place to ensure that, over the long run, political outcomes will be responsive.

Responsiveness is a multifaceted, complicated idea. For example, the people living in a jurisdiction will not have uniform beliefs, preferences, or values—so there is a question of whether and how these are to be aggregated or measured in order to assess responsiveness. For the purposes of this discussion, these complexities need not detain us. I will assume that this is a constraint on political systems, and that it is a construal of a right to popular sovereignty. Note that this is a "tracking" conception of popular sovereignty, rather than a "power" conception. I take it some conception of popular sovereignty of this kind is required if electoral representative government is to satisfy a popular sovereignty requirement.

2.2 The epistemic promise of non-electoral democratic institutions

In thinking about institutional alternatives, we should start by thinking about what institutional mechanisms are needed to ensure or at least make it likely that political institutions will be up to the task of identify, diagnosing, and responding to the problems that political communities are facing. Let's start with some basic questions that should be at the forefront of our minds when thinking about the epistemic issues modern political systems face. We can see these as raising questions about requirements or conditions of epistemic success. Call these *core questions of institutional epistemic competence*:

> Citizen Knowledge: Does high quality epistemic performance depend on a highly informed citizenry? Does it require broad citizen education in order to function? How is this to be accomplished?
>
> Broad Input: Are there mechanisms by which the entirety of the broadly dispersed local knowledge and evidence possessed in the political community can be used and drawn on to identify problems and inform responses to them?
>
> Community Trust: Are there mechanisms to enhance community cooperation, collaboration, and trust? Does the system do anything to exacerbate political division and distrust, resulting in echo chambers, discrediting significant portions of the community as testifiers, and the dissolution of common sources of evidence?
>
> Managing Expertise: Are there mechanisms by which expertise can be drawn on in an epistemically responsible way to address the complex, technically sophisticated problems we face? Are there mechanisms that enable the use of expertise but in a way that is ultimately monitored and regulated by the broader political community and filtered through the community's values and expert-informed preferences?
>
> Appropriate Attention: Are there mechanisms that ensure or incentivize focus on the most pressing actual political problems and issues, rather than those issues that are most divisive or most entertaining or otherwise interesting? Are there mechanisms that improve the system's ability to focus in a long-term way, looking out for big but perhaps more temporally distant problems?
>
> Countering Disinformation: Are there mechanisms to counter broad popular attempts at disinformation through highly partisan "infotainment" news media, bots, manipulation of social media, and so on, so that these don't substantially influence political decisionmaking and problem-solving efforts?
>
> Issue Coverage: What mechanisms are in place to ensure that issues and problems in all politically relevant domains are attended to, so as to avoid distorted or captured policymaking and policymaking done in darkness?

This list is intended as a starting point for thinking about how political systems might be designed to do well epistemically under modern political conditions. As suggested in the first section, electoral representative democracy does poorly by many of these. One thing to notice is that simply by moving away from elections, one eliminates some of the sources of epistemic difficulty, including the drive toward hyper-partisan conflict and distrust, the easy distraction away from issues to focus on individuals and personalities and sites of disagreement, the focus on the short-term, and the epistemic demand for something close to a pristine mass information environment.

2.3 Lottocratic institutions

In other work, I introduce and defend a non-electoral form of democracy that I call "lottocracy" (Guerrero, 2014, 2021b), and which I argue does well by these considerations. The basics of that system are these:

1   Single Issue: rather than a single generalist legislature, in a lottocratic system there would be, say, 20 standing, single-issue legislative bodies, with each legislative institution focusing on one policy area or sub-area (e.g. agriculture, immigration, health care, trade, education, energy, etc.).
2   Lottery Selection: the 300 members of each single-issue legislature are chosen by lottery from the relevant political jurisdiction, selected to serve three-year terms, with the terms staggered so that 100 new people start every year.
3   Learning Phases: the members of the single-issue legislatures hear from a variety of experts, advocates, and stakeholders on the relevant topic at the beginning of and at various stages throughout each decision-making session.
4   Community Consultation: beyond the learning phases, the members of the single-issue legislature spend some structured time talking to, interacting with, and hearing from members of the public, including activists and stakeholders affected by proposed action.
5   Direct Enactment: the members of the single-issue legislature either have the capacity to directly enact policy or, in some cases, to do so jointly with other single-issue legislatures.

I don't want to defend the full merits of this system here. Instead, let me briefly draw attention to some of the institutional mechanisms it uses and how they address the questions above.

First, lottocratic institutions don't require an antecedently highly informed citizenry. Instead, citizens who are selected come to learn about the particular issue over a period of time post-selection. This learning phase is also a means by which expertise can be managed and integrated into the decision-making process, and a way in which to counter broad popular attempts at disinformation. Randomly chosen citizens might have encountered some disinformation prior to being selected, but there will be an extended period of time during which that can be addressed and engaged—albeit perhaps imperfectly. There are important issues about how experts would be identified as qualified and selected to speak, something which I discuss at length in the book and in other work (Guerrero, 2017, 2021b). Using random selection to pick representatives ensures broad input along many dimensions, as people from all backgrounds will be brought into the decision-making process and given an opportunity to share their knowledge and perspectives. Bringing a group of people together—from all different backgrounds—and having them work in a focused way on one set of issues helps to build a collaborative, cooperative spirit and a sense of trust in each other, even in the face of disagreement.[2] The single-issue focus creates a more manageable epistemic burden for those selected, but more importantly it also makes appropriate attention to all politically important issues, rather than just a few, much more likely. By eliminating electoral incentives, those who are randomly chosen can focus on the long-term when it seems appropriate to do so.

There are, of course, concerns about whether randomly chosen individuals will be up to the task, whether the experts and stakeholders they hear from can be adequately vetted and appropriately selected so that they represent the actual best state of information on the topic (rather than the views of those who have been captured or cherry-picked by industry), whether deliberations among randomly chosen citizens will problematically replicate background social dynamics and hierarchies, and whether single-issue focus in policymaking will lead to problematically inconsistent results—to name just a few concerns. I spend chapters on each of these issues in the book; I only mention them here. Furthermore, if embedded in the right kind of constitutional framework, alongside a constitutional court, it could certainly respect the rights to popular sovereignty, the right of individuals to be treated as morally equal under the law, and individual rights of freedom of body and mind. Indeed, one might see much more responsive lawmaking with a lottocratic system, as the representatives would be a genuine microcosm of the political community, rather than an elite subset of that community.

2.4 Technocratic agencies with citizen oversight and incentive alignment

In most modern political systems, administrative agencies and other technocratic bodies already play a significant role in terms of creating regulations and addressing problems that arise in the political community. These are often created by the legislature or the executive and are often overseen (at some remove) by courts and/or the legislative and executive institutions that created them. In some cases, they are relatively political, with their leadership appointed by elected politicians. In other cases, the aim is for them to be above (or at least outside of) the normal political fray, so that they are insulated from political pressures. They are not comprised of elected officials, the people who serve in them are appointed to these roles for their expertise or are selected through at least nominally competitive, meritocratic processes for their qualifications and expertise. They typically have a topical, single-issue focus, addressing, say, environmental protection, regulation of markets in financial instruments, the setting of interest rates and monetary policy more broadly, food and drug safety, and so on.

There are two frequently voiced sources of concerns with these institutions. The first is that they are easily captured by the industries that they are supposed to be regulating. The second is that they are inadequately "democratic" as they make decisions of great consequence, often with little real political oversight. This second concern might connect to concerns about popular sovereignty and political legitimacy. One of the largest problems—related to both of these—is that most voters are ignorant of what these agencies do (except those who are trying to avoid their regulation), and elected officials who are themselves captured by industry have straightforward incentives to allow industries to effectively capture these administrative agencies. It might thus seem a bad idea to expand their role. There are many responses one might have to these worries.

A response I want to urge is worth considering is to use citizens' assemblies—randomly chosen citizens—to serve as oversight bodies, so that each technocratic agency would have an accompanying citizens' oversight assembly. Doing this might combine the epistemic merits of technocratic decision-making while having general public oversight to ensure these bodies were acting in a responsive, public-regarding way, rather than as agents of industry. Imagine that there were a large number of standing administrative agencies with oversight assemblies, and that these replaced the elected representative legislature as the engine of lawmaking and regulatory policy. The suggestion here is that these technocratic bodies could be expanded to take on the bulk of the political problem-solving role, if combined with the right kinds of additional mechanisms.

Combining administrative agencies with citizens' assembly oversight could take a number of distinct forms. The structure of citizens' assemblies is fairly consistent across the 120-plus examples around the world since 2000.[3] Those who participate spend some time learning about an issue, usually through a combination of educational reading and discussion, as well as in-person presentations from various experts and policy advocates. In this context, one possibility would be to involve the randomly chosen citizens as both the group who would oversee a meritocratic hiring process of high-level bureaucrats to run the technocratic agencies and serve a final check on regulatory and policy decisions of a particular agency. This oversight process would have the administrative agency officials explain the proposed regulation or policy and the problem it addresses, and the randomly chosen citizens would also hear from experts and stakeholders from outside of the agency about the claims made by the agency. This could replace or supplement "notice and comment" rulemaking that already requires broad public consultation regarding proposed regulations.

If randomly chosen citizens served for terms of three years (for example), focused on a particular agency, they would have time to develop competence so as to be able to follow the discussion and gauge the plausibility of what was being suggested. Voting power within the oversight assembly could even be staggered so those with more seniority would have more voting power. This basic combination of expert policymaking and broad public oversight seems worth considering, at least in the comparative assessment with electoral representative decision-making on these issues that are often relegated to the shadows. Technocratic decision-making often seems to run afoul of popular sovereignty, but if the vetting process by the citizens' oversight assemblies were effective, this might be a way of addressing that concern so as to result in highly responsive, epistemically effective political problem-solving over time.

A central issue is the issue of attention: which issues would get a devoted agency, what issues should be given attention, how much money should be spent to address which problems, and so on. One possibility here would be to give the citizens' oversight assemblies a partial agenda-setting role. An alternative would be to use mechanisms of popular budgeting and priority-setting, as in the well-known case of "participatory budgeting" in Porto Alegre, where broad community input influences the general distribution of public resources and attention toward political problems.[4] The details of these mechanisms vary, but typically have some large group of unelected citizens who come together to express their views about what proportion of the budget should be spent on which political problems. Similar mechanisms could be used to determine which particular issues the standing agencies should focus on.

This kind of largely technocratic system would do well by integration of expertise, perhaps, but there are concerns about whether ordinary citizens would be able to hold the technocrats adequately accountable over time. An additional mechanism here would be to implement various kinds of incentive alignment strategies to condition the technocrats' compensation and promotion and so forth on successfully addressing various problems. For example, if the issue is how to remove dangerously high levels of lead from drinking water, payment could be conditioned on the extent to which that aim is actually achieved over a five-year period.

As with the lottocratic system, the technocratic agencies + citizen oversight system would avoid extensive political division, the need to have all citizens become well informed about all issues, and would draw on available relevant expertise. One source of concerns—that value questions are not properly settled by issue-specific technocrats—could be ameliorated by the combination of randomly chosen citizens in an oversight role, along with a broad participatory agenda-setting mechanism. This might help expand coverage of issues, and disinformation at early stages in the process might be effectively countered by expertise and the learning of the oversight bodies over time. With a strong veto held by randomly chosen citizens and a significant and widespread use of broad participatory agenda-setting mechanisms, this kind of system would also count as a kind of democracy—at least if electoral representative systems do.

3 Conclusion

In this chapter, I hope to have highlighted some core questions of institutional epistemic competence that we should be asking when thinking about political systems. More tentatively and speculatively, I hope to have piqued interest in actual institutional alternatives to electoral representative democracy, and to have suggested ways in which they might be both epistemically attractive and capable of satisfying relevant demands of political morality.

Notes

1 See https://transition.fcc.gov/osp/inc-report/INoC-20-News-Consumption.pdf.
2 For examples of how this has worked in practice, see Warren and Pearse (2008); Chalmers (2018).
3 For a detailed spreadsheet of all of these, see "Sortition in the world, 2000-present" https://docs.google.com/spreadsheets/d/1kwgOpxMX4pwR3Myu4pXku4gjcnOS53bPOKwOGjZNxyI/edit#gid=0.
4 For discussion of the more than 1,000 municipalities in Latin America and the 100 municipalities in Europe that have used participatory budgeting mechanisms, and regarding participatory budgeting more generally, see Sintomer, Herzberg and Rocke (2008).

References

Abernathy, P. M. (2018) *The Expanding News Desert.* Chapel Hill: The University of North Carolina Press.

Chalmers, P. (2018) 'How 99 Strangers in a Dublin Hotel Broke Ireland's Abortion Deadlock.' *The Guardian*, March 8, 2018.

Duverger, M. (1954) *Political Parties: Their Organization and Activity in the Modern State.* London: Methuen & Co.

Guerrero, A. (2014) 'Against Elections: The Lottocratic Alternative.' *Philosophy and Public Affairs*, 42, pp. 135–78.

Guerrero, A. (2017) 'Living with Ignorance in a World of Experts.' in Peels, R. (ed.), *Perspectives on Ignorance Moral and Social Philosophy.* London: Routledge, pp. 156–85.

Guerrero, A. (2021a) 'The Epistemic Pathologies of Elections and the Epistemic Promise of Lottocracy.' in Edenberg, E. and Hannon, M. (eds.), *Political Epistemology.* Oxford: Oxford University Press, Forthcoming.

Guerrero, A. (2021b) *The Lottocratic Alternative.* Oxford: Oxford University Press, Forthcoming.

Mason, L. (2018) *Uncivil Agreement: How Politics Became Our Identity.* Chicago, IL: University of Chicago Press.

Postman, N. (1985) *Amusing Ourselves to Death: Public Discourse in the Age of Show Business.* London: Penguin Books.

Sintomer, Y., Herzberg, C. and Rocke, A. (2008) 'Participatory Budgeting in Europe: Potentials and Challenges.' *International Journal of Urban and Regional Research*, 32(1), pp. 164–78.

Warren, M. and Pearse, H. (2008) *Designing Deliberative Democracy: The British Columbia Citizens' Assembly.* Cambridge: Cambridge University Press.

PART 7

Trust, expertise, and doubt

INTRODUCTION TO PART 7

The tension between expertise and democracy is a familiar one and was already noted in the introduction to the previous section. On most interpretations, democracy is wedded to giving equal political power to all citizens. But, plausibly, some people have a much deeper understanding of political problems and their solutions than others and are therefore in a much better position to make decisions that will ultimately be better for everyone. Isn't it entirely sensible to give them more political power? Doing so, however, pulls one in the direction of epistocracy or technocracy and away from democratic ideals of robust equality. How do we reconcile justified trust in expertise—scientific or other—with democratic ideals?

An approach that shies away from awarding more political power to experts but still recognizes the added value of the epistemic input they can provide to political decision-making is to have citizens and politicians take advice from experts where needed and defer to expert judgment when appropriate. But this raises thorny questions: who are the experts, how can we know, and how can we agree on answers to these questions in a polarized and fragmentation information environment where expertise is often contested and politicized? And, in view of recent developments, is there any hope of restoring justified trust in experts when, as conservative MP Michael Gove put it before the 2016 Brexit referendum, "the people … have had enough of experts"? The question is all the more pressing since Gove was not entirely wrong when he motivated his claim by adding that experts have been "saying that they know what is best and getting it consistently wrong."

The chapters in this section look at trust, expertise, and doubt from a variety of angles. They try to shed new light on topical controversies by bringing traditional philosophical theorizing to bear on the current political landscape, but also revisit familiar philosophical concepts to see whether recent developments prompt changes to these concepts.

Heather Douglas describes the development of ideas on the role of scientific expertise in democracies, from the Lippmann–Dewey debates of the 1920s, through the independent science advisor model of the Cold War, to the tensions that arose because of the untenability of that model starting in the late 1960s. A historical case study demonstrates that current controversies about science advice are not new. Douglas proposes an alternative to the independence model for understanding scientific expertise in democracy, arguing for three lines of accountability—to the scientific community, to the advisee, and to the broader public—that science advisors must respect in order to do their job properly. Integrity in science advice, she argues, is found not through independence from politics but from joint accountability along these three lines.

Maria Baghramian and Michel Croce tackle fundamental questions about the nature of expertise and trust. They consider four main questions. How should experts and their expertise be characterized? How can non-experts recognize a reliable expert? What does it take for non-experts to trust experts? What problems impede trust in experts? After outlining a variety of accounts of expertise and a number of ways for novices to identify experts, they provide a survey of three broad accounts of trust: predictive accounts, normative accounts, and combined accounts. The chapter concludes by examining some of the reasons for a breakdown of trust toward experts, such as epistemic bubbles, cognitive bias, and populism.

Hallvard Lillehammer's chapter also addresses when we ought to defer to expert judgment in politics. It defends a qualified endorsement of epistemic deference in politics on the basis of an epistemic division of labor. Deference in politics is consistent with the values of authenticity, virtue, knowledge, understanding, responsibility, mutual justifiability, equal opportunity for influence, and a rational attitude toward risk and trust, Lillehammer argues.

Alex Worsnip asks what, if anything, climate change skepticism has to do with philosophical radical skepticism and whether ongoing debates about both kinds of skepticism have anything to learn from each other. The external world skeptic raises deep questions that are important for our everyday deliberation about what to believe, and there are significant structural parallels between the arguments for external world skepticism and those for at least a form of climate change skepticism that is idealized—but not too idealized!—from the views of flesh-and-blood climate change skeptics. Hence there are strong reasons to think in parallel about how to reply to both skeptics' challenges. Worsnip considers how different widespread responses to the external world skeptic might or might not generalize to the climate change skeptic's challenge.

Our mechanisms for deciding whom to trust evolved in physical environments with primarily face-to-face interactions. Mark Alfano and Emily Sullivan point out that the usefulness of these evolved mechanisms is severely limited in an environment where much social interaction happens at a distance and online. The institutions that might help us decide whom to trust need to have their own trustworthiness verified. Currently, they are mostly corporations such as Facebook and Twitter, which have checkered track records at best. To make matters worse, the social media sector is a natural monopoly, and Big Tech has shown that it is willing to use its market power unscrupulously. For these reasons, Alfano and Sullivan propose that social media should be treated like other natural monopolies: it should either be nationalized, highly regulated, or broken up through antitrust legal actions.

37

THE ROLE OF SCIENTIFIC EXPERTISE IN DEMOCRACY

Heather Douglas

Scientific expertise has become increasingly central to democratic governance over the past century. The scientific expert has gone from an occasionally consulted figure to a permanent fixture of government, through science advisory bodies and government scientists embedded within bureaucratic agencies (Douglas 2009: chap. 2, Jasanoff 1990). Yet this growth in the importance of the scientific advisor for democracies has not been accompanied by a clearer normative positioning of that expertise within democratic governance. Even 100 years ago, when the science advisor was not yet a central figure of government, Walter Lippmann and John Dewey debated the place of the expert in democracies. The underlying issues of their debate remain with us. The issues were papered over during the Cold War period, when science advising grew dramatically, but they have persisted and more frequently erupted, with the result that expertise seems to have never been so influential and yet so disregarded in democratic policy-making (Gluckman and Wilsdon 2016).

This chapter will first describe the debate between Lippmann and Dewey to explore the underlying difficulties of relying upon scientific expertise in democratic governance. Such reliance is crucial to good governance, but not normatively straightforward because of the demands of democratic accountability. Lippmann argued, and many have followed in this line of thought, that the expert needs to be as independent as possible from the political sphere in order to do their work properly. Dewey disagreed, arguing for more accountability for the expert to the public. This tension, between independence and accountability (to the political or public sphere), has been central to debates over the role of the science advisor.

I will then describe the embrace of the independence model for science advising in the Cold War and why that model began to fail by the late 1960s. I will examine one particular dispute over science advice, the dispute over supersonic transport (SST) in the Nixon administration that had important consequences for the US science advising system. This example shows that current disputes over scientific expertise in governance are not new, that the tensions over science advice have deep historical and theoretical roots.

I will suggest in the final section that instead of the independence model, a more apt understanding of the role of scientific expertise in democracy places the expert in the middle of a set of obligations, to the scientific community, to the advisee, and to the public. This replaces struggles over independence with multiple lines of accountability that maintain the science advisor's integrity.

I The normative issues: Lippmann vs. Dewey

In the 1920s, a debate between Walter Lippmann and John Dewey mapped out the contours of the problem of scientific expertise in democratic societies. Walter Lippmann, a respected and prominent public intellectual of the era, published *Public Opinion* in 1922. In this opening volley of their exchange, Lippmann argued that the complexities of governance, and the needed expertise for that governance, were now beyond the epistemic capacities and attention span of the contemporary public. Lippmann noted the technical expertise that was needed to govern large, complex democracies, from the Census Bureau to the Geological Survey to intelligence reports from offices overseas (Lippmann 1922: chap. XXVI). This work was crucial to making good governance decisions and running democratic societies, including setting the conditions for fair elections (e.g., through the work of the census bureau). Yet the public in general had (and has) neither the capacity nor the inclination to follow the work of these bodies carefully, especially given the numerous issues the public would need to follow closely. There is simply too much information being produced by this "intelligence work" (as Lippmann called it) for the public to keep track of it, and the details of this work involve intricacies that often require specialized expertise.

For Lippmann, the public was largely an emotional and disjointed mass of people, easily manipulated by the media and politicians. Good governance was best pursued behind the scenes, out of the public eye. Further, Lippmann argued that the intelligence work was best done separated as much as possible from the policy decisions to be made, so that the desires of the politicians would not distort the knowledge produced, and so that the expert would not wield undue power (ibid.). For Lippmann, the power wielded by the expert was to be constrained by separation of expert investigation (or inquiry) from decision-making on policy. Independent expertise embedded in government, but separated from democratically accountable decision-makers, was how Lippmann thought modern democratic systems should be structured. There was no need for the public to follow such expertise closely. The experts would speak to the decision-makers, informing their decisions, and the public would vote those decision-makers in and out of office.

John Dewey wrote *The Public and Its Problems* (1927) in direct response to Lippmann. Dewey agreed that the mass public was precisely as Lippmann diagnosed—volatile, easily manipulated, unfocused. Yet Dewey did not think that this led to Lippmann's required separation of the experts from the public. Instead, Dewey noted necessary connections between expertise and the public. First, expertise was often needed for the very formation of the public. For Dewey, a public was formed, brought into existence, when there was a detection of substantial impacts of private actions on those not involved in decision-making about those actions. Those so impacted became a public. This allowed Dewey to define the public realm in a way that was flexible to changing knowledge about what broader impacts of private choices were, without reifying public vs. private realms, and allowing for the shifting of boundaries between the public and the private (Dewey 1927: 66–69). Historically, the realm of the public has expanded or contracted, depending upon the issue at stake. For example, the issue of faith-based belief has gone from a public issue to a private one, whereas the handling of sewage has gone from a private matter to a public one. The detection of impacts on a broader set of people often depended upon specialized expertise.

Second, Dewey argued that the public had an important role in evaluating specialized expertise. This was in part because "[a] class of experts is inevitably so removed from common interests as to become a class with private interests and private knowledge, which in social matters is not knowledge at all" (Dewey 1927: 224). It was essential, for Dewey, that expert knowledge be part of the public discourse justifying governance decisions, and that the public have the freedom and capacity to evaluate the expertise. As he wrote:

> It is not necessary that the many should have the knowledge and skill to carry on the needed investigations; what is required is that they have the ability to judge the bearing of the knowledge supplied by others upon common concerns. (Ibid.: 225)

Further, Dewey argued that the many often do have this capacity, just as the wearer of a shoe may not be able to make a shoe, but can tell where it pinches and thus what needs to be remedied (ibid.: 224).

Dewey thus did not argue for the most separation possible between experts and policy-makers or experts and the public, or for independent expertise. Instead, he argued that communication and interchange was needed for both the public assessment and utilization of expertise and for the proper formation of public interests. Dewey's arguments are bolstered by the recognition that social values are an essential and ineliminable part of the direction of expert attention and the decision to conclude inquiry (assessments of evidential sufficiency) (Kitcher 2011, Douglas 2016). Scientific experts are not just neutral inquirers who then impart packets of truth to government or the public. Because value judgments are a necessary part of scientific inquiry, experts should not be independent from public understandings of those values (Douglas 2008). For Dewey, experts needed to remain in the public eye, accountable to both the public and to the decision-makers whom they advised. The insulation of experts from the broader public would make their expertise less valuable rather than more, as Lippmann had argued.

Despite the potency of Dewey's concerns about experts in democratic systems, Lippmann's vision of independent experts separated from the public and the political sphere took hold after World War II. The crucial complexities of scientific expertise in democracies were papered over in the post-World War II context.

II Papering over the issues: the Cold War social contract with science

World War II changed the discourse about scientific experts and democratic governance. Merton's (1942) essay on the ethos of science presaged this shift when he argued that democratic societies were more congenial to scientific investigation than authoritarian or fascist ones, and thus that democratic societies (i.e., the Allies) were more likely to win the devastating war that beset the world (Merton 1942). Merton was right, and scientific expertise did prove crucial, from war-winning proximity fuses and penicillin to war-ending nuclear weapons (Kevles 1995: chap. XX). By 1945, it was clear to all the important role science had played. The question was, what role should science play going forward, into peacetime?

In debates about science policy in the mid-1940s, several lines of argument intersected. The first was about the freedom vs. accountability of scientists to the public and the public purse. Legislators like Harvey Kilgore in the United States and authors like J.D. Bernal in the United Kingdom thought scientists' efforts should be directed at public problems and scientific funding from the public should be distributed accordingly (Kleinman 1995). For scientists involved in the Society for Freedom in Science (SFS), such direction of scientific effort was an anathema that would hamper the pursuit of basic research. Leaders of the SFS like Michael Polanyi and Percy Bridgman argued that public funds should be distributed to the best scientists (as determined by the scientists themselves) and that scientists should be left free to pursue those projects they thought were most interesting (McGucken 1978). Vannevar Bush solidified this approach in his 1945 report, *Science: The Endless Frontier*, which argued that public good would come inevitably from public funding of basic science, which was also the science that private industry could not afford to pursue (it being too far removed from application) (Bush 1945). Public money was thus needed to enable the pursuit of this precursor of all applications, and it was in the application of science that public good, and public value, would arise.

This model of scientific funding, which became known as the linear model, presumed a uni-directional pipeline for science. Public funds were put into the pipeline at one end, scientists themselves decided (through funding agencies and peer review) how to best direct those funds, basic scientific knowledge would then flow out to applied scientists and engineers working in commercial labs, which then would produce the public goods (often commercial goods) that would justify public expenditure.

A similar pipeline model arose for science advising. Scientists in advisory positions were construed as value-neutral and apolitical purveyors of scientific facts to decision-makers. Scientific expertise would be provided to decision-makers (e.g., politicians or political appointees), who would then use that knowledge to make better decisions. The knowledge provided would have been created by scientists independent of the governments that used it. The more such scientists were insulated from the political forces and from messy social values, the better that system would work—and the more reliable the scientific knowledge would be.

Finally, a similar model was also developed for issues of scientific literacy and public engagement with science. The more the public was properly educated about science (i.e., knew scientific facts produced by the pipeline), the more the public would agree with the advice of scientists and scientific statements generally. Disagreements between the public and scientists were simply the result of public ignorance. All of these models presumed science should be a value-free, politically neutral endeavor, insulated and isolated from broader political and societal concerns.

The idea that science could be so value-free was easier to believe when a relative uniformity about values was held across society. At the height of the Cold War, with Soviet Communism held up as the key enemy of free democratic societies, differences in central value commitments were harder to see and articulate. If all (or most) scientists, and most of society, agreed upon the most important value commitments, such commitments become relatively invisible. It was during this period that the science advisor held the most sway in the halls of government. For example in the US, the "golden age" of science advice is often thought to be when the Chief Science Advisor and the Presidential Science Advisory Commission had the most influence, from 1957–1963 (Wang 2008: 312). The goal of defending the country from Soviet Communism created a general unified value commitment that made the linear models of advising and science policy appear plausible.

Yet that overarching value uniformity was not to be long-lived. By the late 1960s, serious disputes about value commitments (e.g., which was more important, ecological health or commercial development? human health protection or economic efficiency? ecological protection or military advantage?) had erupted, and created genuine conflicts among not just politicians and the public but also among scientists involved in advisory systems. The next section looks in detail at such a dispute.

III Science advice in action: the SST dispute in the United States (1969–1972)

Amidst other science policy disputes of the late 1960s, such as whether to pursue anti-ballistic missile systems, the role of science in the Vietnam War, and the growing concern about persistent environmental contaminants like DDT, President Richard Nixon's first term in office also witnessed a crucial dispute about the public funding for and support for civilian supersonic transport (SST). This potent public and technical controversy led President Nixon to disband his Presidential Science Advisory Committee (PSAC), which had been a mainstay of science advising in the US government since the Eisenhower administration, and led the US Congress to pass the Federal Advisory Committee Act (FACA). It displays clearly the challenges that can arise with scientific expertise in democracy.

The effort to create civilian supersonic transport began while the military was pursuing supersonic bombers in the 1950s. The US Federal Aviation Administration thought that if the military pursued a supersonic bomber, then that technological development could help civilian SST and lead to economically viable civilian SST in a way similar to the development of jet engine technology (which revolutionized civilian aviation). But the military scrapped the supersonic bomber idea by 1962. Despite the military's rejection of SST for heavy payloads, SST for civilian use got a boost from the Kennedy administration, when in 1963, President Kennedy declared his support for a government-industry joint effort to build a prototype, to compete with the British and French efforts (Carter 1970, Herken 1992: 177). Technical and financial hurdles arose quickly. A study of the effects and acceptability of sonic booms (the inevitable accompaniment of supersonic travel) done over Oklahoma City in 1964 was not reassuring, with small booms producing thousands of claims for property damage (Shurcliff 1970: 111–12). While there were potential technical solutions to reduce sonic booms, they increased the weight of the aircraft to the point where it would likely not be economically feasible for commercial purposes. In addition, by the late 1960s, with $1 billion of public funds already sunk into the program, some began to wonder whether the government should be subsidizing what should be a private industrial effort (Carter 1970).

Thus, when President Nixon won the election in 1968, the SST issue was already on the docket. In early 1969, Nixon asked for a review of the project from five different sources: (1) a review by the airlines, (2) a review by government aeronautical experts, (3) a review by three external aeronautical experts, (4) a review by Nixon's Presidential Science Advisory Committee (PSAC), and (5) a review by an interagency group (Carter 1970: 354). For the PSAC review, then PSAC-chair Lee DuBridge created an ad hoc committee, headed by Richard Garwin (Herken 1992: 178). While the first three reports (largely focused on aeronautical issues) supported SST, the other two reports were not favorable to the project. Of the two, the Garwin Report (as it became known) from PSAC was far more critical and blunt. There were serious environmental and financial problems that looked insurmountable, and the Garwin Report recommended the project be scrapped (ibid.). Nixon did not like the conclusions. In a September 1969 press conference, he announced that he supported the SST program, and refused to release either report critical of the project (ibid.).

Nevertheless, public debate on SST heated up. Citizens in League Against the Sonic Boom joined forces with Friends of the Earth to use a Freedom of Information Act request to get the Garwin Report. Nixon claimed executive privilege over the report, refusing to release it. Congress did approve new appropriations for SST in 1969, but in the spring of 1970, the controversy got particularly pointed. A joint committee of the House and Senate had been unable to get a copy of the Garwin Report from Nixon, and so had asked Garwin to testify at hearing scheduled for May 1970, shortly after the first Earth Day (Conway 2005: 141, US Congress 1970). Garwin's decision to testify was fraught. The standard view of PSAC's advice at the time was that it was private, solely for the president. But as Garwin recalled in 1981:

> I looked at the government testimony [from the Department of Transportation Officials] and decided it was really dishonest and misleading. Really just awful. The government was concealing information and giving false information. So I said, "Yes, I'll testify, but you can't ask me about the report." (quoted in Marshall 1981: 765)

Garwin had consulted with PSAC Chair DuBridge about what he should do, and DuBridge had suggested that as long as he left out of his testimony information gleaned as part of his PSAC activities, and used only publicly available documents, he could ethically testify in front of Congress on the SST (Conway 2005: 141—see also fn. 99). The transcripts empha-sized that despite Garwin's long history of science advising, he was testifying "only in his capacity as a concerned citizen" (US Congress 1970: 890).

Garwin's public testimony proved devastating. He criticized not only the SST program, but the way in which the Nixon administration was handling the technical advice and decision-making process. He stated that it was his "belief that there has been less than ad-equate, and in many cases distorted information available for this decision process, both within the administration and in the presentations to the Congress" (US Congress 1970: 904). He painted a picture of a deceptive bait and switch, where the aircraft actually under consideration was not the same one on which technical details had been discussed, and that the deception was covering up the fact that the technically acceptable aircraft would not be economically viable, and vice versa. He also argued that billions more in public money would be needed to complete the project, that private financing would not be forthcoming (ibid.: 905). Perhaps most pointedly, Garwin suggested that the noise from one SST aircraft would amount to "50 747's taking off simultaneously," an assessment that reverberated in the press (ibid.: 907). By the following year, the SST program was dead (Herken 1992: 179).

The scientific community was divided over Garwin's decision to go public. Some thought he should have resigned from PSAC before testifying publicly (Herken 1992: 179). Others thought he did the right thing, arguing that being on PSAC did not mean that "the pres-ident owns your opinion before all possible fora" (quoted in Herken, ibid.). In a National Academy of Science poll of scientists, respondents roughly split between deeming his actions appropriate or inappropriate (ibid.: fn. 98, 322). The Nixon administration, in contrast, was uniformly furious. As quoted in Herken, one staffer exclaimed: "Who in the hell do those science bastards think they are?" Another queried: "Who needs this bunch of vipers in our nest?" (ibid.: 180).

When Nixon succeeded in getting re-elected in the fall of 1972, he disbanded the PSAC as one of his first acts of his second term and got rid of his presidential science advisor (mov-ing the science advisory function to the far remove of the National Science Foundation) (Herken 1992: 180). PSAC members were shocked and had no idea the demise of PSAC was on the horizon. Nixon responded to the perceived disloyalty of his science advisory system by removing them from the White House and from close contact with the President.

While Garwin's decision to provide such public and devastating testimony, going against PSAC tradition, led to the demise of PSAC, it also demonstrated the importance of scientific advice being made public. This case of science advice raised serious questions about what kind of loyalty was owed to politicians for whom science advisors worked, how science advisors should be selected for their positions, and what kinds of information should be made public or kept confidential. The US Congress was not happy with their inability to access the advice the Nixon administration was both generating and using to justify their decisions. Congress responded by passing the Federal Advisory Committee Act (FACA) in 1972.

FACA addressed many of the most serious problems encountered by science advisors under Nixon. No longer were advisory meetings to be held behind closed doors and results withheld from the public (unless national security demanded it). Advisory committee meetings had to be announced publicly ahead of time, be generally open to the public, and perhaps most crucially, meeting minutes and results (such as advising reports) had to be made public. One did not need to go through the trouble of a Freedom of Information Act request to access to such reports, and executive privilege could not (generally) be asserted. This provision also prevented agencies from being simply uncooperative with public requests for information (Levine 1973: 231). The public, and the public's representatives in Congress, were thought to have a right to know the technical advice the government was receiving.[1] The scientists did not owe loyalty just to their advisees—they also owed loyalty to other political bodies and to the public generally. FACA ensures that politicians cannot claim a particular piece of science advice supports their position when it does not, and it ensures that both other elected officials and the public have the information they need to assess whether or not a policy is supported by the available expertise.

This example (and others like it) shows the inadequacy of the Lippmann model for expertise in democratic societies. The generation of science advice is not just for the use of decision-makers; it is also crucial that advice be shared with other political actors and with the broader public, so that a proper assessment of the actions of the decision-maker can be made. It is true that most of the public and probably most elected officials do not closely follow technical advising reports most of the time, lacking the inclination, time, energy, and expertise to do so, but then neither do experts outside their areas of expertise. However, when civil society groups and elected officials do weigh in on an issue, it is crucial that they have access to the relevant science advising reports, both to assess whether those reports address the issues of concern to them and to assess whether the decision-makers at whose request the reports were generated are responding properly to the advice.

The SST controversy also shows the importance of social and ethical values in science advising. Technical advice is never purely just technical. There are crucial issues of framing a technical scientific issue—what is part of the assessment, and what is not—which in the SST case produced different assessments of the technology. Yes, SST planes were technically feasible. The questions most relevant to the public were whether they were socially acceptable (because of sonic boom issues) and whether possible technical fixes to the sonic boom issues made the project infeasible economically. This revealed value disputes: what was more important, the pursuit of a project that would project US economic and technological power and that is technically feasible (as the aeronautic reports suggested), or the impact of that technology on citizens who would likely not have access to its benefits (because of the high costs)? The viability of SST was not a purely technical issue but also about the cost and benefits, and the distribution of costs and benefits, in the broader society. Consideration of these factors was by no means value-free. And the public needed to hear what experts had to say about such issues, and to see how their elected officials responded to the experts' assessments.

IV Beyond independence: integrity through accountability in science advice

The SST dispute described above illustrates the challenges of science advice in democratic societies. Science advisors serve at the pleasure of those they advise, but they do not (and should not) have loyalties just to those at whose pleasure they serve. In particular, science advisors should never accept the abuse of the authority of science by politicians to say the opposite of what the scientific assessment reveals. To allow this would be to fail in their obligations to the public. If, as Garwin thought, some scientific or technical advice is misleading or just flat out inaccurate, scientists have an obligation to speak publicly about that.[2]

A further complication is that science advice is rarely univocal. Different experts will see the same issue differently, either because of how they frame the issue or because of different assessments of whether the available evidence is strong enough to make a particular claim. This means that science advice is not and cannot be value-free, because social and ethical values are central to how problems are framed (which aspects are included or excluded) and because social and ethical values are crucial to assessments of evidential sufficiency (Douglas 2008, 2016). While broad societal agreement over values can make this aspect of science advice invisible, when values diverge, this aspect of advice becomes visible and important. The issue then centers on the nature of integrity in science advice.

I argue here that because of the importance of science advice to good decision-making in democratic governance, the lines of accountability that structure obligations of science advisors are at least three-fold: to the science, to the advisee, and to the public. Maintaining all three lines of accountability is crucial to the maintenance of integrity in science advice.

The first line of accountability for scientific expert advisors is to the scientific evidence and the scientific community that produces, interprets, and debates the evidence. The scientific evidence does not show up and speak for itself; scientists are required for the production and interpretation of the evidence.[3] The scientific community engages in an ongoing discussion and debate over what the evidence means, which evidence is the most reliable, and when the evidence is sufficiently supportive that a particular empirical claim is "proven." It is essential that science advisors be part of this discussion (in their areas of expertise) and that their advice (as much as possible) be open to the assessment of scientific community which produced the evidence on which the advice is presumably based. There may be exceptions when science advice is confidential, because of national security concerns or because it is informal advice given to a particular politician. (That such informal advice be allowed to be confidential assists with the ability of politicians to discuss ideas, even hare-brained schemes, with science advisors and receive candid feedback.) But in the vast majority of cases, and particularly when science advice is wielded by a politician in a public dispute, the science advice should be made public. It is through the response of the expert scientific community to the content of science advice that the science advisors remain accountable to the science.

The second line of accountability is to the decision-makers (politicians, appointed policy-makers) for whom the advice is intended. The obligation here is to make the advice relevant to the concerns of the advisee, taking into account their social and ethical values, at the same time that the advice is scientifically accurate (and would thus pass muster with the scientific community, as discussed above). When the advice is geared toward a specific person, the advisor can ensure that the advice takes into consideration the framing of interest to the advisee and the values relevant to the assessment of evidential strength (including what kinds of errors the advisee would find tolerable). However, much advice is directed toward decision-making bodies, rather than particular individuals. In these cases, especially with formal advisory committees that produce lengthy advising reports, advice should make clear the framing decisions for the advice, any debates over evidential sufficiency that remain, and the value judgments that are part of the science advice (Douglas 2008, Havstad and Brown 2017). Only with such clarifications can the advice be properly deployed by the decision-makers.

The third line of accountability is to the general public. This is necessary because the public needs both to use science advice to inform whether a concern is a public matter and to evaluate the response of their elected officials (or their appointees) to science advice. For both these reasons, science advice should generally be made available to the public, with the exceptions noted above. (This also assists with the accountability of the advice to the scientific community.) Not every member of the public will read carefully, and evaluate the response to, every piece of science advice. But when an issue of import arises for a member of the public, it is crucial that they have access to the advice so that they can read the advice, and evaluate the response to the advice by the decision-maker. This was one of the key aspects of US FACA law, and is central to the use of scientific expertise in democracies. The public can hold scientific experts accountable by granting or withholding trust in their expertise.

With this understanding of accountability, it should be clear that integrity in science advice is not manifested by a simple independence of science from politics or from values. Values, including social and political values, are deeply relevant to the advising process, and properly so. Integrity instead consists of maintaining *all* the lines of accountability, in the process of generating and providing science advice. It means scientific experts should be concerned about their obligations to the scientific community, to their advisees, and to the public, all at the same time.

In practice, this means being open about the debates that hone scientific results and about the value judgments that are used to frame scientific issues and to assess the whether the available evidence is strong enough to come to a particular conclusion. Scientists should not use their authority to hide complexity because they are concerned the public, or policy-makers, cannot handle the complexity. Messages should not be oversimplified or dumbed-down in order to produce a particular response in the receivers of the advice; doing so would fail to meet the accountability concerns to the public and the politician. Nor should politicians lean on advisors to produce a desired result because it would be politically preferable. Demanding that science advisors produce a particular result would undo their accountability to the scientific community and the evidence it produces. Integrity requires respecting all the lines of accountability, that they all be held in mind, when giving and utilizing expertise in democratic decision-making.

As I write this, in the midst of global pandemic and against the backdrop of the ongoing climate crisis, both the importance of science advice and the contentiousness that comes with it remain apparent. Experts debate what the rate of infection of COVID-19 actually is, which treatments may be effective, and what we should be doing to reduce the harmful impacts of the pandemic. Much remains disputed. But the centrality of scientific expertise in detecting the virus that is sweeping the world and in working to reduce its damage is undisputed. It is a good thing that many of the debates that experts are having are taking place in the public eye. The public has proven adept at understanding aspects of expert thought quickly (e.g., the way in which the public has grasped the idea of "flattening the curve," a concept few in 2019 would have understood). We do not all need to be experts to be able to assess expertise, our elected officials' response to expertise, and expertise's impact on policy. We do need access to that expertise, to see the advice the experts give, and to assess the values at stake. Such assessments will be crucial to how we hold our elected officials accountable in future elections.

Scientific expertise will remain central for good democratic governance. Science has become too important, too powerful a force in society, and too many crucial public issues hang on the technical details of scientific assessment. Understanding the lines of accountability that structure science advice, and attending to the process of providing scientific expertise for governance to bolster those lines of accountability, will help us make the most of it.

Notes

1 FACA also has provisions calling for fair balance "in terms of points of view represented and functions to be performed" (FACA Statute). This provision forestalls an advisory committee made up solely of a particular advocacy position. What constitutes an acceptable balance for any given committee remains contentious.
2 Some see this as a crucial failing of the scientists who were providing earthquake risk assessment to L'Aquila, Italy. They failed to correct grossly inaccurate statements by the elected official (Hall 2011).
3 It is crucial that politicians not try to suppress the generation of evidence they would find embarrassing or unwelcome. Such an abuse of power would greatly hamper the ability of the public to assess the impacts of policies, and of the politicians who push for them.

References

Bush, V. (1945). *Science: The Endless Frontier.* Washington, DC: U.S. Government Printing Office.
Carter, L. (1970). SST: Commercial Race or Technology Experiment? *Science, 169*(3943), pp. 352–55.
Conway, E. (2005). *High Speed Dreams: NASA and the Technopolitics of Supersonic Transportation, 1945–1999.* Baltimore, MA: The John Hopkins University Press.
Dewey, J. (1927/2016). In: M. Rogers, ed., *The Public and Its Problems: An Essay in Political Inquiry.* Athens, OH: Swallow Press.
Douglas, H. (2008). The Role of Values in Expert Reasoning. *Public Affairs Quarterly, 22*(1), pp. 1–18.
Douglas, H. (2009). *Science, Policy, and the Value-Free Ideal.* University of Pittsburgh Press.
Douglas, H. (2016). Values in Science. In: P. Humphreys, ed., *The Oxford Handbook of Philosophy of Science*, 1st ed. New York: Oxford University Press, pp. 609–32.
Gluckman, P. and Wilsdon, J. (2016). From Paradox to Principles: Where Next for Scientific Advice to Governments? *Palgrave Communications, 2*, p. 16077 [online]. Available at: https://doi.org/10.1057/palcomms.2016.77 [Accessed September 15, 2020].
Hall, S. (2011). At Fault? In 2009, an Earthquake Devastated the Italian City of L'Aquila and Killed More than 300 People. Now, Scientists Are on Trial for Manslaughter. *Nature, 477*(7364), pp. 264–70.
Havstad, J. and Brown, M. (2017). Inductive Risk, Deferred Decisions, and Climate Science Advising. In: K. Elliott and T. Richards, eds., *Exploring Inductive Risk: Case Studies in Values in Science*, 1st ed. New York: Oxford University Press, pp. 101–23.
Herken, G. (1992). *Cardinal Choices: Presidential Science Advising from the Atomic Bomb to SDI.* Stanford, CA: Stanford University Press.
Jasanoff, S. (1990). *The Fifth Branch: Science Advisers as Policymakers.* Cambridge, MA: Harvard University Press.
Kevles, D. (1995). *The Physicists: The History of a Scientific Community in Modern America.* Cambridge, MA: Harvard University Press.
Kitcher, P. (2011). *Science in a Democratic Society.* New York: Prometheus Press.
Kleinman, D. (1995). *Politics on the Endless Frontier.* Durham, NC: Duke University Press.
Levine, R. (1973). Federal Advisory Committee Act. *Harvard Journal on Legislation, 10*, pp. 217–35.
Lippmann, W. (1922). *Public Opinion.* New York: MacMillan Company.
Marshall, E. (1981). Richard Garwin: Defense Adviser and Critic. *Science, 212*(4496), pp. 763–66.
Merton, R. (1942). A Note on Science and Democracy. *Journal of Legal and Political Sociology, 1*, pp. 115–26.
McGucken, W. (1978). On Freedom and Planning in Science: The Society for Freedom in Science, 1940–46. *Minerva, 16*(1), pp. 42–72.

Shurcliff, W. (1970). *S/S/T and Sonic Boom Handbook*. New York: Ballantine Books.

US Congress. (1970). *Economic Analysis and the Efficiency of Government. Hearings before the Subcommittee on Economy and Government of the Joint Economic Committee, 91st Congress of the United States. Part 4-Supersonic Transport Development. May 7, 11, and 12, 1970*. Washington, DC: U.S. Government Printing Office.

Wang, Z., (2008). *In Sputnik's Shadow: The President's Science Advisory Committee and Cold War America*. New Brunswick, NJ: Rutgers University Press.

38

EXPERTS, PUBLIC POLICY, AND THE QUESTION OF TRUST

Maria Baghramian and Michel Croce

1 Introduction: experts and their political function[1]

In our daily lives we routinely depend on experts of various kinds, their skills and their advice. From matters of health to technology, weather forecasts to air-travel, even in mundane matters of dealing with blocked drainpipes or broken washing machines, experts have a ubiquitous role in our lives and guide our choices. Experts and our reliance on them become a political matter when they are involved in policy formation and implementation. Cognitive experts (Goldman 2001: 91) in different fields, experts who have epistemic competences in some domain of inquiry, rather than *practical* or performative expertise (Watson 2018: 40), are increasingly called upon to provide data and evidence in the service of governmental policy goals. We review and briefly address four questions on experts and their role from the perspective of political epistemology: (§2) How should we characterize experts and their expertise? (§3) How can non-experts recognize a reliable expert? (§4) What does it take for non-experts to trust experts? (§5) What problems impede trust in experts?

Recent years have seen a sharp turn towards populist politics with leaders claiming to represent the univocal "will of the people" and to stand against "liberal elite" enemies and the privileged cosmopolitan educated classes (e.g. Canovan 1999). This anti-elitist rhetoric has put the scientific advisory process under serious stress (OECD 2015). Policy advice on health and environmental issues has proven particularly controversial and led to partisan political debates and confrontations, not just in the United States, but across the world. While headline figures in recent surveys on trust in scientific expertise do not indicate a drop in trust levels—unlike trust in politicians and the media—the public discourse around expertise has noticeably changed and there is evidence of a breakdown of trust in specific policy areas such as vaccination and climate change (Facciolà et al., 2019).

2 What is expertise?

The term "expert" is defined in various ways. At first blush, and very roughly, an expert is a person with a high level of knowledge in a particular domain. Predictably, though, the question of how to understand the notion has generated lively and timely discussions among social epistemologists.

Alvin Goldman's (2001) paper has become a classic of the field and almost all subsequent debates on the topic define their position in relation to it. His theory of expertise is grounded in a conceptual analysis approach and has two main features: it is a veritistic and realist theory of expertise, where *veritistic* means that expertise is measured by the amount of true beliefs one possesses in a given domain—more precisely, by the ratio of true to false beliefs in the domain—and where *realist* means that one's possession of expertise does not depend on social recognition within one's community or attribution by one's clients (Collins and Evans 2007: 2–3). Briefly put, on Goldman's view, experts are those who get things right in a domain of inquiry more often than most members of a community.

Over the last decade, an upsurge of alternative views of expertise has challenged the main features of Goldman's theory. One influential approach—embraced by Goldman in more recent work—identifies experts in terms of their socio-epistemic functions, or the service they provide within an epistemic community. Functionalist accounts cash out the notion of expertise "by reference to what experts can do for laypersons by means of their special knowledge or skill" (Goldman 2018: 3) and (only) then assess the "categorical states" that underpin the functional requirements of expertise (4). The question about the function of an expert may be seen as complementary to the definitional question about what an expert is—Goldman does not seem to take a clear stand on the issue, though others tend to favour a functionalist approach over a realist one (e.g. Quast 2018).

Novice-oriented accounts (Goldman 2018; Quast 2018) capture the idea that a community relies on experts to ensure that laypeople receive the help required to acquire reliable information in domains in which they are incompetent. If we stick to John Greco's characterization of social epistemology (2020: §2), it could be argued that experts have a prominent role in *knowledge distribution*, in that they make available information accessible to lay members of the community.

In contrast, research-oriented accounts (Croce 2019) capture the idea that a community relies on experts to ensure "epistemic progress" by, among other things, addressing extant problems and answering new questions in various disciplines. Experts, seen in this light, perform a "*gatekeeping* function" (Greco 2020; Henderson 2009) insofar as they take care of the business of acquiring, selecting and introducing new information within an epistemic community. Grundmann (forthcoming) has recently argued against functionalist views of expertise, instead defining experts as those who possess better evidence in a given domain as well as more reliable reasoning skills compared to other members of an epistemic community (ibid.).[2] Other attempts to broaden Goldman's veritistic approach have been offered by proponents of what Grundmann calls "the gnostic account", where the epistemic superiority of experts is cashed out in terms of their superior knowledge and understanding in a given domain (Croce 2019; Jäger 2016). There are also those who argue that expertise does not simply reduce to epistemic superiority within a community, but that part of experts' competence has to do with their epistemic—if not moral—character, that is, with how they conduct their inquiries, their impartiality, intellectual honesty, epistemic autonomy, open-mindedness, etc. (Collins 2014; Croce 2018; Grundmann 2017; Shapin 2008).

Sociological discussions of expertise are an important source of critiques of the realist views. Sociologists and social theorists tend to endorse a *relational* view of expertise, according to which expertise is not a status one possesses in virtue of one's epistemic achievements in a domain, but one conferred or attributed by others—typically by experts' clients rather than their peers (Grundmann 2017). Expertise on this view comes down to a specific form of social recognition that individuals receive as a result of their services within the community.

This view of expertise is important not only because it departs from the realist approach, but because it shows that analysis of experts should not be reduced to that of "pure scientists"—those who care only about acquiring and sharing knowledge and show no interest in how their information addresses concrete issues (Douglas 2009; Pielke 2007). A key limitation of the traditional model is that the role expert knowledge plays in collective and personal decision-making processes is inadequately considered. While questions about the nature of expertise may be separate from those about the social roles of experts, in discussing expertise in the context of policy decisions, a characterization of what experts are that does not account for their specific role in the epistemic landscape of their society is bound to be incomplete. Relational accounts attempt to address this particular deficit.

This dimension of expertise, we believe, is key to placing the notion in a social and political context. While it may be plausible to contend that an epistemic community expects its competent members to fulfil functions such as maximizing its overall epistemic welfare, teaching or conducting research, and that it recognizes members as experts in virtue of such roles, experts in policy-making contexts are given more limited and tightly delineated roles. Expert advice at the political level takes a variety of forms: experts are frequently part of statutory national and international science advisory committees, academic bodies or think tanks that produce policy reports and advise governments (Holst and Molander 2019), with their advice elicited on an ongoing basis or on specific occasions. Individual experts are also invited to act as advisors in a formal or informal capacity for specific purposes. Their advice is used to design and implement policy but also to boost policy credibility. Occasionally, they are used as scapegoats for policy failures.[3] The engagement of experts with policy matters often gives them an advisory or consultative role, which does not require first-hand research on their part, even if their advice is expected to be informed by the most up to date research. Jasanoff (2011: 21) characterizes the role of experts, in this context, as translators or mediators between knowledge and decision-making professionals, bridges between science and policy.

On those occasions when experts involved in policy advice are required to undertake new research, they are often expected to produce what Salter et al. (1988) have called "mandated science", that is, the type of research that is commissioned or supported by governmental or other public bodies for specific purposes. Mandated science, more so than pure or autonomous research should, it is argued, work for the benefit of the society and its members (Powys et al. 2010; Scheman 2011). This expectation introduces a normative dimension to the politics of expertise.

This line has been strongly pursued by political scientists investigating the political functions of expert knowledge. Christina Boswell (2009), for instance, has argued that in addition to a standard *instrumental* function of improving the quality of political decision-making by grounding policies in sound reasoning and empirical data, institutional appeal to expert knowledge in public policy decision-making helps to enhance the credibility of organizations and their policies. This symbolic role boils down to two specific socio-epistemic functions: a *legitimizing* function, in that relying on expert knowledge endows institutions with epistemic authority; and a *substantiating* function, in that relying on expert knowledge gives credibility to an organization's policy preferences and contributes to undermining the policies of rival organizations (2009: 7). A substantiating function is particularly helpful in cases of contested policies and widespread professional disagreement, because it allows the organization to move the discussion from the level of values, interests, and public opinion to the level of scientific evidence and well-founded reasoning (81).

Importantly, however, despite recent attempts to bridge the disciplinary gaps (Baghramian and Martini 2018), not enough has been done to develop a unified—or, at least, multi-faceted—account of experts and expertise that captures both the epistemic and political dimensions of their work and role. Certainly, the proposed considerations about the understanding of expert knowledge in politics, especially in highly contested domains, call for further inquiry into the rational criteria for identifying experts. As we shall show in the next section, several problems complicate the matter, but none completely undermines the possibility of recognizing whose expertise should be trusted.

3 Expertise and the credentials problem

All societies' knowledge economies operate on the basis of division of epistemic labour—that we do not all know the same things and are not equally knowledgeable about the same issues (Goldberg 2011). The division of labour will operate smoothly only on the assumption of epistemic trust, that is, our willingness to accept others, under appropriate conditions, as sources of authority on matters where we presume they are more knowledgeable. The ever-increasing scope and depth of cognitive specialization makes us epistemically dependent on others, and this dependence highlights the need for trust.

Considering the role experts play in policy decisions, the key debates or disagreements are not normally about what class of people count as experts. Policy-makers frequently seek expert advice by choosing from the top tiers of Elizabeth Anderson's (2011) hierarchy of expertise:

a   Scientists whose current research is widely recognized by other experts. This can be determined by considering factors such as citation counts, impact factors of the journals in which they publish, and record in winning major grants.
b   Scientists who are leaders in the field—who have taken leading roles in advancing theories that have won scientific consensus or opened up major new lines of research, or in developing instruments and methods that have become standard practice. In addition [...], leadership is indicated by election to prestigious positions in the field's professional societies, election to honorary scientific societies, such as the National Academy of Science, and receipt of major prizes in the field, such as the Nobel Prize (146–47).

The disagreements come at later stages, over whether a particular person meets these qualifications, and more significantly, over how to choose between experts with similar qualifications who provide contradictory advice, and relatedly, over when and how much should the general public and policy-makers trust experts and their advice.

This recognition problem for expertise (Watson forthcoming) boils down to at least two questions. The first, typically called the credentials problem (Cholbi 2007) or the novice/expert problem (Goldman 2001), asks how a novice can come to recognize an expert. The second question, typically called the problem of conflicting expert testimony (Ballantyne 2019: 222) or the novice/2-experts problem (Goldman 2001), asks how a novice can decide what to believe when the experts disagree on the matter at issue.[4]

Both questions are extremely complex and discussions around them show no signs of attenuation. However, while expert disagreement might justify a prudent suspension of judgement in laypeople and force them to cope with some level of uncertainty, a list of criteria to work around the credentials problem—even if imperfect—is needed by epistemically dependent beings like us. For this reason—and given constraints of space—we shall focus on the credentials problem and postpone discussion of conflicting expert testimony to another occasion.[5]

Let us set aside situations in which novices have direct or first-order evidence in favour of an expert opinion and can verify the reliability of expert opinion by checking how things are in the world, for instance by following an expert's directions and seeing where they lead or by figuring out whether a practical expert succeeds in repairing a defective mechanism (Goldman 1999: 269). The relevant cases are those in which novices can only rely on indirect or second-order evidence of an expert's trustworthiness. In such circumstances, assessing one's expertise requires more cognitive effort on the novice's part. Elizabeth Anderson has identified four main dimensions of an expert's trustworthiness—namely, expertise, honesty, epistemic responsibility, and consensus—which we can consider as criteria laypeople should rely on to decide whom to trust (2011).[6]

Indirect evidence concerning someone's *expertise* in a given domain D is provided at least by the following factors (Goldman 2001; Grundmann forthcoming; Martini 2019; Watson forthcoming): (i) a track record of accurate predictions or other kinds of success depending on the specifics of D (see also Collins and Evans 2007); (ii) one's qualifications and reputation within D, which can be derived from one's CV and professional position, and one's status within a community of peers, such as citations, impact factor, grants and awards, and reputation in general (e.g. Origgi 2019); (iii) one's argumentative skills, including the ability to present evidence supporting one's judgements, the ability to distinguish between similar but not equivalent cases, and the ability to offer consistent judgements; and (iv) one's dialectical skills, including the behavioural reaction—in terms of smoothness, quickness, and confidence—one is able to offer to such challenges.

The proposed list of markers is far short of necessary and/or sufficient conditions for identifying experts. Though most scholars agree on track record as a key requirement, they have different takes on the other markers. For example, Grundmann suggests *the selection by the procedural standards of science*—including conditions about the required talent, training, critical thinking and character traits of its members, but also about science's openness to diversity, free competition, independent peer review—as the only consideration that makes it sufficiently likely that a member of the scientific community is a genuine expert. Collins and Evans (2007: 67) dispute the reliability of (ii), in that it unduly restricts the notion of expertise to professional roles, but include (v) experience, which they define as the familiarity one has with the questions arising in D and the methods deployed to address them. Origgi and colleagues seem to agree with the aforementioned markers but would include one's *popularity*, intended as one's capacity to generate actions in other people (Branch et al. 2020).

As regards *honesty*, novices can at least be sensitive to negative markers or cues of misbehaviour, such as conflicts of interests, plagiarism, cherry-picking data or misrepresenting views of other experts (Anderson 2011: 147). Anderson proposes a similar approach to the evaluation of the *epistemic responsibility* of experts: novices should be on the lookout for cues of blunt irrationality (e.g. sticking to views proven false), evasion of peer-review standards, and *epistemic trespassing*—the practice of passing along judgements in areas outside of expertise (Ballantyne 2019). Finally, *consensus*, where the opinions of a putative expert are backed by a notable proportion of peers, gives lay people a good reason to consider this person an expert. Cues of a consensus among experts in a domain D include surveys of trustworthy sources within D, reviews of the available literature, and official reports by leaders and well-established institutions in D.[7]

To conclude our analysis of the credentials problem, none of these factors, taken individually, ensures that a novice is in a position to individuate experts reliably; rather, at best a combination of these criteria—depending on the specifics of context under consideration—increases the likelihood that a layperson would successfully identify someone as a genuine expert. Our analysis has moved from the (esoteric) contents of expert testimony and the mode of communication of such contents to the trustworthiness of experts and the manifestation of character traits such as honesty. As noted above, the moral dimension of scientific expertise becomes particularly important where experts take part in informing policy decisions and take on a wider range of socio-epistemic responsibilities (Hardwig 1991; Rolin 2020). We will return to this point in the next section, when discussing the question of trust in experts.

4 A question of trust

As we saw, epistemic dependence on experts is bound up with the question of trust. The peculiar form of trust at stake in discussing the relationship between experts and non-experts is epistemic trust or trust that applies to agents' beliefs and the reasons provided for their beliefs, rather than their actions (Hardwig 1991: 697). Epistemic trust in general, and trust in experts in particular, often take the form of testimonial trust, i.e. trusting what the experts tell the non-experts as well as the policies that are based on these recommendations. The considerations offered in the previous section illustrated what kinds of indicators non-experts should look for to individuate whom is worthy of their trust. However, recognizing a trustworthy source is one thing, while trusting a trustworthy source is another. In this section, we inquire into the nature of the trust-attitude that non-experts should have towards experts.

Three main families of views—predictive accounts, normative accounts, and combined accounts (Dormandy 2020)—dominate current discussions of the philosophy of trust. Predictive accounts argue that to trust someone amounts to forming a positive expectation—if not a belief—that they will behave as agreed or required by the situation (Hardin 1993). Normative accounts, by contrast, argue that to trust someone involves expectations about how the trustee ought to behave (Darwall 2017; Faulkner 2007; Holton 1994; Jones 1996). In other words, trust presupposes a normative demand that the trustee will behave as expected because the trustor is not just predicting but also counting on the trustee to do so. A weak version of this view concedes that one can trust another while suspending judgement about the likelihood that they will behave as expected, but, does not concede that one can have negative expectations towards the trustee (e.g. Holton 1994). In contrast, the strong version of the normative account is compatible with negative predictive expectations, in that all it takes for one to trust another is to place normative expectations on their behaviour and to be optimistic about their fulfilment (Jones 2004).

When it comes to trust in experts in the policy domain, it looks as though a purely normative view is a non-starter, in that such accounts concede that one can trust another even when one believes that the trustee will not act as agreed or expected. We can make sense of this view in the context of a relationship, say, between parents and children, but surely it cannot apply to the domain of policy expertise, where no institution would request consultation from someone they consider unable or unwilling to deliver the requested outputs. To put it differently, there seems to be little room for *therapeutic trust* in the context of expert advice and policy-making (Faulkner 2007; Nickel 2007).

The predictive account of trust fares better because it accommodates the intuitive idea that non-experts and institutions select experts to provide policy advice based on the aforementioned credentials, that is, based on a considered—and likely reliable—esteem that such experts are able and willing to fulfil their function. Crucially, this view predicts that the experts will deliver the expected results. Predictive expectations take numerous forms, ranging from placing a high degree of confidence in the information provided, relying on the information provided, ascribing credibility to sources of information (including the person testifying) and having justified expectation of accuracy, usually cashed out in terms of truth. What these kinds of predictive expectations have in common is their epistemic goal—namely, the production of epistemic goods such as knowledge, justified beliefs, understanding, and inquiry (Grasswick 2020).

One reason we might want to go beyond a purely predictive view of trust, even in the policy domain, is that this view reduces trust to mere reliance (e.g. Goldberg 2020), where the latter—unlike the former—requires no commitment on the part of the trustee to display an appropriate reaction to the trustor's attitude. Yet, it could be argued that when non-experts and institutions put their trust in a policy advisor, they expect both that the trustee will act as predicted and that the trustee will do so because of a normative stance that the trust-relationship creates.

This normative stance can be cashed out in various ways. Some regard it as an expectation of the trustee's goodwill (Almassi 2012; Baier 1986; Cogley 2012; Frost-Arnold 2013; Wilholt 2013); others as a participant stance according to which the trustor treats the trustee as a person who bears responsibility for their actions (Holton 1994); others, finally, as a mere responsiveness of the trustee to the fact that the trustor is counting on them to act as expected (Faulkner 2017). Normative and affective expectations, unlike predictive ones, lead to feelings of betrayal and not just disappointment when the trust is broken (Baier 1986: 285). A plausible way to account for this normative dimension of a trust-relationship in the context of expert advice involves requiring that experts at least comply with the ethical and epistemic norms of scientific practice, or, that they display honesty, integrity, and the other moral-epistemic virtues we require from scientists.[8] A willingness to act in the interest of the recipients of their advice is also seen as a feature of the integrity expected of the experts and such willingness is taken as an indicator of their benevolence (see Hawley 2017 for contrary view). These normative and affective expectations are the reassurances that we need in the face of the risks we take in trusting and justify the hope and confidence we place on those we trust. As we will see in the next section, not fulfilling such expectations is one of the reasons for the breakdown of trust in experts.

5 The breakdown of trust

Mistrust of experts is a source of socio-political concern and a topic of philosophical interest. This section briefly examines some of the reasons for withdrawals of trust from experts.

Mistrust of experts, like trust, has many sources and explanations. Trust can justifiably be withdrawn from experts who are judged to have made serious mistakes or have been dishonest, untruthful or biased. The legitimacy of these concerns, at least in principle, is acknowledged by experts and non-experts alike. But it is easy to imagine that adequate training, professional vigilance and public monitoring of the markers of intellectual *integrity*, as well as vigilance around the institutional norms governing the work of expert bodies—e.g. rigorous review mechanisms, political independence, etc. *could address* such concerns. Serious disagreement among experts is thought to have an impact on the perceptions of the trustworthiness of their advice, but the exact scope of this concern is in question (Dellsén 2020).

The question remains why large numbers of people reject scientific consensus on crucial issues like climate change (in the United States) and vaccination (the United Kingdom and the United States). Scepticism about expert advice in such cases rarely comes down to the details of the scientific evidence or the methodology scientists employ, but is linked to social, psychological and broadly normative considerations (Levy 2019).

Let us consider the psychological aspects first. At an individual level, traditional cognitive biases such as confirmation bias, desirability bias and motivated reasoning obstruct trust-relationships whenever there is a clash of opinions between the expert and the lay person (e.g. Nichols 2017). At a collective level, the opportunity to establish immediate connections with people who share one's own worldview—typically online, via social media—makes novices prone to group polarization, that is, the tendency to take one's beliefs to extremes when participating in a group of individuals who share one's views (Sunstein 2017). Combining these factors, we can easily make sense of Kahan and colleagues' *cultural cognition thesis*, namely, that people tend to form beliefs about societal risks and factual information that sustain their personal values, and *political motivated reasoning*, that is, the idea that people trust those experts who appear to share their values and distrust those who seem to hold diverging views (2010). The icing on the cake is offered by the *Dunning-Kruger effect* (Kruger and Dunning 1999), that is, the tendency of novices to overestimate their ability in a given domain; as Ballantyne (2019) and Brennan (2020) point out, this psychological phenomenon is particularly relevant in cases where laypeople seem unable to acknowledge who is epistemically superior in a given domain.

Socio-epistemic structures such as epistemic bubbles and echo chambers, which reinforce ideological exclusion in different ways (Nguyen 2020), strengthen psychological support for mistrust (see also Hanna Kiri Gunn's chapter 17 in this volume). Their combination leads us to increase in in-group trust and higher levels of distrust of outsiders regardless of their expertise.

A further, but no less threatening, aspect has to do with the suspicion, if not outright disdain, shown towards experts and their advice by populist politicians. The negative attitude of populist leaders towards experts is unsurprising. Populists wish to govern directly, establishing an unmediated, emotionally replete bond with the "real people". Experts, with their evidence-based policy recommendations, aspirations of cool-headed objectivity, high educational achievements and unabashed desire to be among the elite in their field, stand in stark contrast to the populist vision of politics and become ready targets of their ire.

Finally, there is the broader worry concerning the role of experts in democratic governance and the extent of their influence (Landemore 2017; Moore 2017). Briefly put, the question is not whether we should trust expert advice in particular domains, but whether we should accept the prominent role given to experts in policy decisions. The worry is around a possible tension between the ideals of autonomy and freedom, embedded in the liberal democratic tradition, and the deference that lay persons are expected to afford experts. The point is not new—the problem was discussed by John Dewey (1927) in countering the journalist Walter Lippmann's enthusiasm for the technocracy of a "bureau of experts" (see Heather Douglas's chapter 37 in this handbook) and was reiterated by Hannah Arendt who warned against the steadily increasing prestige of "scientifically minded brain-trusters" in the government councils (Arendt 1972: 108). The worry is that by trusting experts to guide our policies, in an important sense, we are not only relinquishing autonomy but also, contrary to democratic principles, we are accepting the authority of unelected persons and bodies.

Concern around the democratic deficit in experts' roles has a strong ethical dimension. Naomi Scheman (2011) has argued that epistemic trust in scientists involves reliance on scientific institutions' ability to take responsibility, not merely for epistemic justice, but more broadly for social justice. When the trustworthiness of scientists is understood to require goodwill towards those who are epistemically dependent on the scientists, scientists may lack trustworthiness in the eyes of marginal social groups even when they are honest and competent. The lack of trustworthiness may be due to historical connections between science and social injustices (e.g. past uses of science against the interests of particular social groups, the unjust underrepresentation of particular social groups within professional science, and the abuse of members of particular social groups in scientific research). As Scheman (2001: 43) argues: "It is, in short, irrational to expect people to place their trust in the results of practices about which they know little and that emerge from institutions—universities, corporations, government agencies—which they know to be inequitable". We also know that invocation of experts has not always been benevolent and included unwelcome examples such as the US administration's reliance on expert psychological advice on enhanced interrogation tactics in the years 2002–2006 (Washington Post, October 13, 2017).

6 Conclusion

Despite these concerns, it remains unquestionable that we need experts to advise our institutions, provide novices with manageable information, and facilitate epistemic progress. Proposed remedies to local or global breakdown of trust in experts, on the novice side, range from steps to enhance laypeople's intellectual character—e.g. increasing their sensitivity to cognitive biases (Cassam 2019)—to suggesting changes in the infrastructures of social networks and other epistemic landscapes that obstruct trust-relationship between novices and experts (e.g. De Cruz 2020; Rini 2017). What is required of the experts, on the other hand, is greater transparency, intellectual humility and openness to direct public scrutiny—in other words, genuine efforts to prove their trustworthiness.

Acknowledgement

Work on this paper has been made possible by funding from the European Union's Horizon 2020 research and innovation programme for the project Policy, Expertise and Trust in Action (PEriTiA) under grant agreement No 870883.

Notes

1 We would like to thank Catherine Holst, Carlo Martini, Clare Moriarty and the editors of this collection for their helpful and generous comments on earlier drafts of this chapter.
2 Grundmann deploys the tools of network analysis, which starts by providing a list of common platitudes about experts and then involves checking whether standard accounts of experts match those platitudes (forthcoming).
3 For a detailed study of use of experts in specific policy contexts, see Owens (2015).
4 For an alternative presentation of the two problems, see Martini (2019: 119–20).
5 For a discussion of the latter problem see, among others, Lane (2014); Dellsén and Baghramian (2020, forthcoming).
6 See Johnston et al. (2015) for empirical evidence partly supporting Anderson's diagnosis.
7 Critical discussions of Anderson's criteria for identifying experts are offered in Brennan (2020), Brown (2014), Guerrero (2017), and Lane (2014).
8 Those who do not buy into the combined account of trust may locate trust in the prudential, rather than moral, domain. There are distinct social, financial, and personal advantages in being judged reliable and trustworthy (Frost-Arnold 2013: 302; Rolin 2020). "A self-interest account of trust shifts the focus away from an individual scientist's moral and epistemic character to the social practices of scientific communities and the institutions of science. When the social practices and institutions of science are well-designed, there are incentives for scientists to behave in a trustworthy way, and prudential considerations are likely to ensure that they will actually do so" (Rolin 2020).

References

Almassi, B. (2012) 'Climate Change, Epistemic Trust, and Expert Trustworthiness'. *Ethics & The Environment*, 17(2), 29–49.

Anderson, E. (2011) 'Democracy, Public Policy, and Lay Assessments of Scientific Testimony'. *Episteme*, 8(2), 144–64.

Arendt, H. (1972) *The Crises of the Republic: Lying in Politics; Civil Disobedience; On Violence; Thoughts on Politics and Revolution*. New York: Harcourt Brace & Co.

Baghramian, M. and Martini, C. (2018) 'Expertise and Expert Knowledge'. Special issue of *Social Epistemology*, 32(6), 351–419.

Baier, A. (1986) 'Trust and Antitrust'. *Ethics*, 96(2), 231–60.

Ballantyne, N. (2019) *Knowing Our Limits*. Oxford: Oxford University Press.

Boswell, C. (2009) *The Political Uses of Expert Knowledge*. Cambridge: Cambridge University Press.

Branch, T., Morisseau, T., and Origgi, G. (2020) 'Trust, Expertise, and the Controversy over Hydroxychloroquine'. Unpublished manuscript.

Brennan, J. (2020) 'Can Novices Trust Themselves to Choose Trustworthy Experts? Reasons for (Reserved) Optimism'. *Social Epistemology*, 34(3), 227–40.

Brown, M. B. (2014) 'Expertise and Deliberative Democracy'. In Elstub, S. and McLaverty, P. (eds.), *Deliberative Democracy: Issues and Cases*. Edinburgh: Edinburgh University Press, pp. 50–68.

Canovan, M. (1999) 'Trust the People! Populism and the Two Faces of Democracy'. *Political Studies*, 47, 2–16.

Cassam, Q. (2019) *Vices of the Mind: From the Intellectual to the Political*. Oxford: Oxford University Press.

Cogley, Z. (2012) 'Trust and the Trickster Problem'. *Analytic Philosophy*, 53(1), 30–47.

Cholbi, M. (2007) 'Moral Expertise and the Credentials Problem'. *Ethical Theory and Moral Practice*, 10, 323–34.

Collins, H. (2014) *Are We All Scientific Experts Now?* Cambridge: Polity Press.

Collins, H. and Evans, R. (2007) *Rethinking Expertise*. Chicago, IL: University of Chicago Press.

Croce, M. (2018) 'Expert-Oriented Abilities vs. Novice-Oriented Abilities: An Alternative Account of Epistemic Authority'. *Episteme*, 15(4), 476–98.

Croce, M. (2019) 'On What It Takes to Be an Expert'. *The Philosophical Quarterly*, 69, 1–21.

Darwall, S. (2017) 'Trust as a Second-Personal Attitude of the Hearth'. In Faulkner, P. and Simpson, T. (eds.), *The Philosophy of Trust*. Oxford: Oxford University Press, pp. 35–50.

De Cruz, H. (2020) 'Believing to Belong: Addressing the Novice-Expert Problem in Polarized Scientific Communication'. *Social Epistemology*, 34(5), 440–52.

Dellsén, F. (2020) The epistemic value of expert autonomy. *Philosophy and Phenomenological Research*, 100(2), 344–61.

Dellsén, F. and Baghramian, M. (2020) Disagreement in science: introduction to the special issue. *Synthese*, doi:10.1007/s11229-020-02767-0.

Dewey, J. (1927) *The Public and Its Problems*. New York: Henry Holt & Co.

Dormandy, K. (2020) 'Introduction: An Overview of Trust and Some Key Epistemological Applications'. In Dormandy, K. (ed.), *Trust in Epistemology*. London: Routledge, pp. 1–40.

Douglas, H. (2009). *Science, Policy, and the Value-free Ideal*. Pittsburgh, PA: University of Pittsburgh Press.

Facciolà, A., Visalli, G., Orlando, A., Bertuccio, M. P., Spataro, P., Squeri, R., Picerno, I., and Di Pietro, A. (2019) 'Vaccine Hesitancy: An Overview on Parents' Opinions about Vaccination and Possible Reasons of Vaccine Refusal'. *Journal of Public Health Research*, 8(1), 1436.

Faulkner, P. (2007) 'On Telling and Trusting'. *Mind*, 116(464), 875–902.

Faulkner, P. (2017) 'The Problem of Trust'. In Faulkner, P. and Simpson, T. (eds.), *The Philosophy of Trust*. Oxford: Oxford University Press, pp. 110–29.

Frost-Arnold, K. (2013) 'Moral Trust and Scientific Collaboration'. *Studies in History and Philosophy of Science Part A*, 44(3), 301–10.

Goldberg, S. (2011) 'The Division of Epistemic Labor'. *Episteme*, 8(1), 112–25.

Goldberg, S. (2020) 'Trust and Reliance'. In Simon, J. (ed.), *The Routledge Handbook of Trust and Philosophy*, New York: Routledge, pp. 97–108.

Goldman, A. (1999) *Knowledge in a Social World*. Oxford: Oxford University Press.

Goldman, A. (2001) 'Experts: Which Ones Should You Trust?'. *Philosophy and Phenomenological Research*, 63, 85–110.

Goldman, A. (2018) 'Expertise'. *Topoi*, 37(1), 3–10.

Grasswick, H. (2020) 'Reconciling Epistemic Trust and Responsibility'. In Dormandy, K. (ed.), *Trust in Epistemology*. London: Routledge, pp. 161–88.

Greco, J. (2020) *The Transmission of Knowledge*. Cambridge: Cambridge University Press.

Grundmann, R. (2017) 'The Problem of Expertise in Knowledge Societies'. *Minerva*, 55, 25–48.

Grundmann, T. (forthcoming) 'Experts: What Are They and How Can Laypeople Identify Them?'. In Lackey, J. and McGlynn, A. (eds.), *Oxford Handbook of Social Epistemology*. Oxford: Oxford University Press.

Guerrero, A. (2017) 'Living with Ignorance in a World of Experts'. In Peels, R. (ed.), *Perspectives on Ignorance from Moral and Social Philosophy*. New York: Routledge, pp. 135–77.

Hardin, R. (1993) 'The Street-Level Epistemology of Trust'. *Politics and Society*, 21(4), 505–29.

Hardwig, J. (1991) 'The Role of Trust in Knowledge'. *Journal of Philosophy*, 88(12), 693–708.

Hawley, K. J. (2017) "Trustworthy Groups and Organisations". In Faulkner, P. & Simpson, T. (eds.), *The Philosophy of Trust*. Oxford: Oxford University Press, pp. 230–50.

Henderson, D. (2009) 'Motivated Contextualism'. *Philosophical Studies*, 142(1), 119–31.

Holst, C. and Molander, A. (2019) 'Epistemic Democracy and the Role of Experts'. *Contemporary Political Theory*, 18(4), 541–61.

Holton, R. (1994) 'Deciding to Trust, Coming to Believe'. *Australasian Journal of Philosophy*, 72(1), 63–76.

Jäger, C. (2016) 'Epistemic Authority, Preemptive Reasons, and Understanding'. *Episteme*, 13(2), 167–85.

Jasanoff, S. (2011) 'Quality Control and Peer Review in Advisory Science'. In Weingart, P. and Lentsch, J. (eds.), *The Politics of Scientific Advice. Institutional Design for Quality Assurance*. Cambridge: Cambridge University Press, pp. 19–35.

Johnston, A. M., Mills, C. M., and Landrum, A. R. (2015). How Do Children Weigh Competence and Benevolence when deciding whom to trust? *Cognition*, 144, 76–90.

Jones, K. (1996) 'Trust as an Affective Attitude'. *Ethics*, 107(1), 4–25.

Jones, K. (2004) 'Trust and Terror'. In DesAutels, P. and Urban Walker, M. (eds.), *Moral Psychology: Feminist Ethics and Social Theory*. Lanham, MD: Rowman and Littlefield, pp. 3–18.

Kahan, D., Jenkins-Smith, H., and Braman, D. (2010) 'Cultural Cognition of Scientific Consensus'. *Journal of Risk Research*, 14(2), 147–74.

Kruger, J. and Dunning, D. (1999) 'Unskilled and Unaware of It: How Difficulties in Recognizing One's Own Incompetence Lead to Inflated Self-Assessments'. *Journal of Personality and Social Psychology*, 77(6), 1121–34.

Landemore, H. (2017) 'Beyond the Fact of Disagreement: The Epistemic Turn in Deliberative Democracy'. *Social Epistemology*, 31(3), 277–95.

Lane, M. (2014) 'When the Experts are Uncertain: Scientific Knowledge and the Ethics of Democratic Judgment'. *Episteme*, 11(1), 97–118.

Levy, N. (2019) 'Due Deference to Denialism: Explaining Ordinary People's Rejection of Established Scientific Findings'. *Synthese*, 196(1), 313–27.

Martini, C. (2019) 'The Epistemology of Expertise'. In: Graham, P., Fricker, M., Henderson, D., and Pedersen, N. (eds.), *Routledge Handbook of Social Epistemology*. London: Routledge, pp. 115–22.

Moore, A. (2017) *Critical Elitism: Deliberation, Democracy, and the Problem of Expertise*. Cambridge: Cambridge University Press.

Nichols, T. (2017) *The Death of Expertise: The Campaign against Established Knowledge and Why It Matters*. New York: Oxford University Press.

Nickel, P. J. (2007), 'Trust and Obligation-Ascription'. *Ethical Theory and Moral Practice*, 10(3), 309–19.

Nguyen, T. (2020) 'Echo Chambers and Epistemic Bubbles'. *Episteme*, 17(2), 141–61.

OECD (2015) "Scientific Advice for Policy Making: The Role and Responsibility of Expert Bodies and Individual Scientists", *OECD Science, Technology and Industry Policy Papers*, No. 21, OECD Publishing, Paris, doi:10.1787/5js33l1jcpwb-en

O'Neill, O. (2019) 'Linking Trust to Trustworthiness'. *International Journal of Philosophical Studies*, 26(2), 293–300.

Owens, S. (2015) *Knowledge, Policy, and Expertise*. The UK Royal Commission on Environmental Pollution 1970–2011. Oxford: Oxford University Press.

Origgi, G. (2019) *Reputation: What It Is and Why It Matters*. Princeton, NJ: Princeton University Press.

Pielke Jr., R. (2007) *The Honest Broker: Making Sense of Science in Policy and Politics.* Cambridge: Cambridge University Press.

Powys Whyte, K. and Crease, R. P. (2010) 'Trust, Expertise, and the Philosophy of Science'. *Synthese*, 177, 411–25.

Rini, R. (2017) 'Fake News and Partisan Epistemology'. *Kennedy Institute of Ethics Journal*, 27(S2), E43–E64.

Rolin, K. (2020) 'Trust in Science'. In: Simon, J. (ed.), *Routledge Handbook of Trust and Philosophy.* New York: Routledge, pp. 354–66.

Quast, C. (2018) 'Expertise: A Practical Explanation'. *Topoi*, 37(1), 11–27.

Salter, L., Levy, E., and Leiss, W. (1988) *Mandated Science: Science and Scientists in the Making of Standards.* Berlin: Springer.

Scheman, N. (2001) 'Epistemology Resuscitated: Objectivity as Trustworthiness'. In Tuana, N., and Morgen, S. (eds.), *Engendering Rationalities*, Albany: State University of New York Press, 23–52.

Scheman, N. (2011) *Shifting Ground: Knowledge and Reality, Transgression and Trustworthiness.* Oxford: Oxford University Press.

Shapin, S. (2008) *The Scientific Life: A Moral History of a Late Modern Vocation.* Chicago, IL: University of Chicago Press.

Sunstein, C. (2017) *#Republic: Divided Democracy in the Age of Social Media.* Princeton, NJ: Princeton University Press.

Watson, J. C. (2018) 'The Shoulders of Giants: A Case for Non-veritism about Expert Authority'. *Topoi*, 37(1), 39–53.

Watson, J. C. (forthcoming) *A History and Philosophy of Expertise.* London: Bloomsbury.

Wilholt, T. (2013) 'Epistemic Trust in Science'. *British Journal for Philosophy of Science*, 64, 233–53.

39

TESTIMONY, DEFERENCE, AND VALUE

Hallvard Lillehammer

The problem

As I understand it in what follows, the *general* problem of deference in *politics* is that of work-ing out the extent to which some people should defer to others when decisions are made about institutional arrangements within a social domain, such as the modern nation state. The *specific* problem of deference in *political epistemology* is that of working out whether, and if so how, some people should defer to others when *making up their mind* about what decisions should be made regarding institutional arrangements within such domains. These forms of deference are logically distinct. On the one hand, a member of a political organization can defer politically to its executive committee as a matter of collective responsibility even if they believe that executive's decision is wrongheaded. (This can happen when some members of said executive are out-voted by others.) On the other hand, a member of a political orga-nization can defer epistemically to a panel of experts even if the final decision on what to do is up to that member alone. (This can happen when the leader of a political party makes an executive decision based on expert advice.) If politics is about the justified exercise of power, political epistemology is about the justification of the beliefs with which that power is exercised and distributed. Yet even though the specific problem of deference in political epistemology is not the same as the general problem of deference in politics, it is an import-ant part of that problem insofar as it matters that political power is exercised and distributed with epistemic justification.

All else being equal, it makes sense to defer to someone else's judgment if the following conditions are met. First, their judgment is better than ours in terms of accuracy, reliability or understanding of the subject at hand. In other words, when deferring to the judgment of others we may hope to defer to someone whose judgment is epistemically better than our own. Let's call this the *insight condition* on reasonable deference. Second, what someone communicates to us when we defer to their judgment is an accurate or fair representation of the content of that judgment. In other words, when deferring to the judgment of others we hope they will not mislead us about or incorrectly report what their judgment is. Let's call this the *transfer condition* on reasonable deference. From the perspective of a neutral observer it might seem that only the first of these conditions is an *epistemic* condition on reasonable deference, the second being partly an *ethical* condition on good communication. Yet even if it is possible to consider the epistemic and ethical aspects of deference independently this way, the epistemic relevance of the transfer condition is evident once we consider the first person perspective of someone deferring. From their perspective, both the insight condition and the transfer condition are relevant to the question of whether it is epistemically reasonable to defer. In order for this to be the case, there needs to be evidence not only that the persons deferred to possess the relevant insights, but also that they will pass over those insights in an honest or transparent way. Thus, it is a common trope in contemporary politics that politicians, pundits and other people in positions of authority cannot be trusted (O'Neill 2002). What is at stake for those who make this complaint is just as often that the persons in question are lying or otherwise dishonest as that they don't know what they are talking about. To this extent, the problem of deference in political epistemology has both a narrowly epistemic and a wider ethical dimension. And although it is primarily the narrowly epistemic dimension that is at issue in what follows, it is incumbent on any plausible political epistemology to bear in mind the ubiquitous relevance of broader ethical issues in the philosophy of communication.

The epistemic dimension on deference in politics has two interacting and overlapping targets. The first of these consists of broadly 'descriptive' claims about what the social world is like and how it can be made to work. This is the aspect of epistemic deference that is commonly associated with the idea of professional expertise that political representatives solicit and receive, and that media outlets often put on display. It is also the aspect of epistemic deference that is least controversial. Although there is plenty of expert disagreement on descriptive as well as normative issues, the idea that there is *nothing whatsoever* to the idea of an expert in such areas as climate science, historical demography, applied economics or epidemiology does not withstand serious scrutiny. (The fact that experts are fallible, exaggerate and represent the vested interests of their paymasters is a different matter.) Having said that, claims to expert authority in these fields are sometimes presented as though they are purely descriptive when they are not. This is not only because normative judgments are sometimes made implicitly by way of using what looks like purely descriptive language (e.g. 'The equity markets will never comply with that'). It is also because the theories employed by experts to make sense of politics embody idealizing assumptions that 'model' the social world without accurately describing it (e.g. by assuming that political actors are consistent, rational, or acting in light of more information than they have). To this extent, the case for epistemic deference to experts along the descriptive dimension must be qualified to the extent that the expertise in question either relies on, or implies, commitments that go beyond strict descriptive accuracy.

The second target of the epistemic aspect of deference in politics consists of normative claims about how the social world should (or should not) be. To that extent, this component is both aspirational and to some extent possible to grasp independently of how things actually are. It is with respect to this component that the case for epistemic deference to experts and other sources of epistemic authority is most controversial, not only in politics but also in the normative domain more generally (see e.g. Williams 1985; Jones 1999; Hopkins 2007; Hills 2009, 2013; McShane 2018; McGrath 2019). Reflecting on the sources of this controversy, a simple argument against epistemic deference in politics can be formulated as follows. Our political aspirations are a function of how we think the world should be. Questions of how the world should be can be formulated by means of basic evaluative and normative concepts (e.g. just/unjust; good/bad; right/wrong) that any competent citizen is able to grasp, in some cases as 'self-evident'. For example, an average competent citizen is capable of grasping that a world without extreme poverty, ecological destruction and coercive behavior toward vulnerable others is better than a world that displays these features, and is therefore better than the actual world. No experts are required to inform the average citizen of this, and similarly basic, normative facts. Therefore, there is no case for epistemic deference in politics with respect to its basic normative aspects. At best, epistemic deference in politics is reasonable with respect to its descriptive aspect, where experts may offer specialized factual insights on how what we independently know to be a better world can actually be brought about, or disaster effectively prevented.

This argument is too quick. Assume that the average competent citizen is in a position to grasp a set of basic truths about which worlds would be better or worse with respect to a wide range of basic values, such as life, well-being or justice. It does not follow that this grasp would make epistemic deference in politics redundant. First, although what it makes sense to aspire to in politics is not narrowly constrained by how the world actually works, it is constrained by how it could actually be made to work. To the extent that expertise with respect to the descriptive target of epistemic deference is relevant in order to answer the latter question, it is therefore also relevant to the formation of reasonable political aspirations. Second, even if it is possible to formulate some political aspirations in abstraction from expertise about how the social world should *ideally* work (e.g. by way of some negative critique of a 'whatever, so long as it is not *this*' variety (see e.g. Finlayson 2015)), factual assumptions about how the world actually works will inevitably form a part of any interesting judgment that registers the *sources* of those aspirations (such as the negative effects of current economic arrangements.) It follows that there is room for epistemic deference with respect to judgments about what options *not* to favor (e.g. in the form of political programs). Finally, it is not clear that the assumption that the average competent citizen is capable of grasping a set of basic truths about which worlds would be better or worse with respect to a range of basic values will get us very far. As historically embodied at any given time and place the values of life, well-being and justice have been variously interpreted and instantiated, and have been realized in ways that give rise to deep and enduring conflicts that would challenge the comprehension of even the most knowledgeable expert. Consider: is the European Union a progressive alliance working toward peace, prosperity and global justice; an aggressive 'neo-liberal' trading block; or both; or neither? The claim that the average competent citizen is in a position to see through the conceptual and empirical thickets of questions like this unaided is no more plausible than the claim that there are people to whom they can reasonably defer (c.f. Enoch 2014).

An argument for epistemic deference

Perhaps the most straightforward argument *in favor* of epistemic deference in politics takes a broadly teleological form and appeals to the idea of an *epistemic division of labor* (c.f. Christiano 2012). This is a relatively modest argument, in that it requires us to make few controversial assumptions either about the persons advised to defer, or about those whom they are advised to defer to. Thus, it is not assumed that either part in the relationship enjoys a privileged status or authority that legitimates their epistemic privilege. Nor is it assumed that the persons deferring are in principle less able to form a sound judgment on the issues in question than the persons to whom they defer (although the argument is consistent with both possibilities). Instead, the argument is based on the effectiveness of epistemic deference in producing good political outcomes. According to this argument, better political outcomes are sometimes produced by people 'outsourcing' their political judgment to others because of the epistemically advantageous position of those others in a given deliberative context. The central claim of the argument is that if better political outcomes can be produced by such distribution of deliberative 'load', then epistemic deference is justified, or even required (c.f. Ahlstrom-Vij 2015).

The idea of distributing deliberative 'load' in this way is not especially esoteric. Nor is it specific to politics. A representative democratic system where elected politicians are free to vote on matters of state according to their own best judgment is a *de facto* mechanism for dividing the labor of political judgment along these lines. Second, and insofar as members of political parties 'adhere' to political programs, their adherence to those programs will sometimes involve an element of epistemic deference with respect to the soundness of certain aspects of the policies proposed (e.g. aspects they have not considered at length themselves). Third, the epistemic division of labor extends across institutional practice beyond the realm of politics. For example, norms of confidentiality regarding personal information (such as employee health records) frequently put certain colleagues in positions of epistemic privilege in ways that don't permit all stakeholders to fully access the grounds of their decisions. This fact on its own does not make it unreasonable for said stakeholders to defer to said colleagues, even if they consider themselves perfectly able to judge the matter if presented with the information in question.

This argument for epistemic deference raises two important questions about the nature of politics. The first question is what politics fundamentally *is*, or *is for* (c.f. Geuss 2008). Thus, it might be objected that the argument relies on a conception of political thought as purely *instrumental*, whereby the role of individual deliberation is essentially conceived as an input to a collective mechanism designed to produce desirable outputs. On this conception of politics, it is hardly a big surprise if the efficiency in question will sometimes benefit from divisions of labor, some of which could be epistemic. Yet to conceive of politics this way is not politically neutral, insofar as it implies the basic legitimacy of a set of deliberative mechanisms conceived of as *means* to social *ends*, where both the means and ends in question are frequently very controversial. If one of the basic questions of politics is (in words attributed to Lenin): '*Who can do what to whom?*' (a question that alerts us to the possibility that a political arrangements can be deemed unacceptable whatever it is said to 'deliver'), then one of the things one might want deliberative mechanisms to reflect is the refusal, rejection or resistance of those to whom political power is applied. To take just one example: in the context of social arrangements in which some demographic groups are consistently excluded (whether intentionally or as a side effect) from the social position of being 'in the know', the question of *how knowledge is distributed* might well be perceived as being just as important as the question of *what knowledge is said to 'deliver'*. In these circumstances, the epistemic privilege enjoyed by those in power might be regarded by those excluded from power as part of the problem, not the solution.

A second question about the division of labor-based argument in favor of epistemic deference in politics arises not from the question what *politics* is (or is for), but from the question what *episteme* (or deliberation) is for *in politics*. Thus, it might be objected that the argument above implicitly relies on a conception of political epistemology that is primarily instrumental, and according to which the role of epistemic efforts in politics is to produce desirable epistemic outputs (such as political knowledge, or expertise). On such an instrumentalist conception of political epistemology it is hardly a big surprise if the efficiency in question is found to benefit from epistemic divisions of labor. Yet to conceive of epistemology this way is not politically neutral either, insofar as it can be said to presuppose a division of epistemic values in politics into the *intrinsic* and the merely *instrumental* that is itself politically controversial. To take one example: in the context of public education there is a potential tension between the value of being able to 'deliver' true answers to historical questions and the value of being able to give a narrative account that manifests a broader understanding of the historical events in question, where the ability to score maximally on one of these measures does not inevitably bring with it the ability to score maximally on the other (c.f. Elgin 2017). If one of the things one values epistemically is the ability to 'give an account', then one of the things one might want epistemic subjects to achieve in politics is a kind of deliberative ability that epistemic deference may stand in the way of acquiring. Thus, it might be argued that just as individual citizens have a duty to make themselves informed enough to participate in the political process in an epistemically competent way, the state (or whichever political agency one might prefer to substitute for it) has a duty to enable or facilitate citizens in their efforts to exercise those duties. Indeed, it might be argued that placing others in a situation of dependency in which they systematically have to rely on epistemic deference is to impose a regime of 'epistemic injustice' in politics (c.f. Fricker 2007).

In light of these considerations, it might be tempting to conclude that the above case for epistemic deference in politics turns on the plausibility of *Consequentialism*, in the sense that the rightness of actions, policies or practices is a function of the value of their outcomes, or effects (c.f. Ahlstrom-Vij & Dunn 2014). Yet this is also too quick. The ability of Consequentialists to (re-) model pre-theoretical thought is almost indefinitely flexible, and consists in re-interpreting what non-Consequentialist objectors construe as *constraints* on the promotion of the good as *a proper part of the good* itself. This strategy is applicable to the present case by means of a case-by-case 'transfer' of whatever value the Consequentialist is alleged to have missed (such as 'the ability to give an account') from the purely 'instrumental' to the 'intrinsic' values of political thought. (The remaining question is then to weigh, rank or otherwise compare the intrinsic values in question.) In any case, the idea that the problems just raised for epistemic deference in politics turn primarily on the formal structure of Consequentialism is arguably too esoteric to do justice to the substantial issues at stake in these debates.

Against deference: testimony and value

Attitudes to epistemic deference in politics are partly a function of attitudes to the relation between politics and morality. One way of mapping problems about epistemic deference in politics is therefore to locate them with respect to a pair of potentially overlapping spheres, where one sphere represents problems that are paradigmatically moral in content and the other problems that are paradigmatically political. What to say about a given problem involving epistemic deference is then partly determined by whether or not what is at stake in that problem can be located at a point where the two spheres overlap. For example, those who argue that questions of politics are generally best thought of as independent of questions of personal morality might argue that even if there are problems about epistemic deference on narrowly moral issues, these are not necessarily relevant in the sphere of politics (c.f. Quinton 1993). On the other hand, both those who think of political conviction as a deeply personal matter (c.f. Sartre 1946/2007) and those who think of morality and politics as contextually specific applications of the same set of basic normative principles (see e.g. Dworkin 2011) are likely to consider the problem of epistemic deference on moral and political issues as complimentary aspects of a single sphere. (On the complex interplay of moral and political considerations in the context of a feminist critique of contemporary epistemology, see e.g. Fricker 2007.)

The downstream effects of this question about the relationship between politics and morality can be illustrated by considering a number of values that have recently been said to conflict with reliance on *moral testimony* (where for present purposes we can understand reliance on moral testimony as *deferring to someone else's moral judgment by accepting that judgment on the basis of their 'say-so'*). It has recently been suggested, for example, that the practice of relying on moral testimony is incompatible with the requirements of *virtue*; a fully virtuous person not only being a person who acts in the right way but also someone who acts in the right way for the right reasons (and who knows the 'why'; the 'why of the why', and so on (see e.g. Hills 2009)). Assume for the sake of argument that a fully virtuous person would never rely on *moral* testimony (but see Lillehammer 2014). It does not follow that reliance on *political* testimony is incompatible with the better exercise of one's civic responsibilities as a political subject. First, in modern liberal democracies, at least, the state does not demand of its citizens that they are morally virtuous across all aspects of their lives, including the moment when they anonymously exercise their voting rights at the ballot box, potentially voting on favor of what they take to be their personal, or their social group's, best interest. Indeed, it is one of the cornerstones of the more palatable versions of modern liberalism that they do not, and that a state that demanded moral perfection of its citizens would be a form of tyranny (c.f. Rawls 1993). (This is not to deny that political authorities have a legitimate interest in the moral virtues of their citizens, e.g. in terms of encouraging their development by means of education, or by excluding certain criminals from the census) Second, the manifestation of virtue in *politics* requires the disposition to behave in ways that display some understanding of how *political*, as opposed to familial, filial, or other personal relationships work. If political relationships are such as to invite or require certain forms of epistemic deference, it is no good objecting that such forms of epistemic difference conflict with the virtuous cultivation of different social relationships.

A closely related claim has been made about an alleged conflict between reliance on moral testimony and the achievement of moral *knowledge* and/or *understanding* (see e.g. Hills 2009, whose argument is focused on understanding). Assume that genuine moral knowledge and/or understanding of a moral issue requires not having deferentially formed one's judgment on the basis of someone else's say-so (but see Lillehammer 2014). This is obviously a more palatable hypothesis on the assumption that for a significant number of normal human adults the knowledge and/or understanding of the relevant moral issues are in principle within reach. Yet when extended to the case of politics the tension alleged to exist in the moral case is much less plausible and fails to present a good argument against reliance on political testimony. The alleged tension is less plausible in the political case because one way to display knowledge and/or understanding of political reality is to appreciate that there are some issues (including *both* complex decisions requiring technical expertise *and* substantially normative matters requiring personal sensitivity or insight) on which *one* responsible way to exercise knowledge and/or understanding *of politics* is to epistemically defer (e.g. in the case of the leader of a political organization who makes an executive decision based on expert and/or confidential advice). If legitimate political practice depends on political subjects exercising their general knowledge and/or understanding of politics in the absence of topic-specific knowledge and/or understanding of some political questions, there is no case for the claim that reliance on political testimony is incompatible with epistemic excellence in politics.

The fact that general knowledge and/or understanding of politics can be displayed by a political subject deciding to epistemically defer helps to address another potential obstacle to reliance on political testimony, namely, one that has historically been formulated in the language of *autonomy* and/or *responsibility* (see e.g. Dworkin 1988; Driver 2006). In the moral case, the claim is that since it is in our nature as responsible moral subjects to be autonomous legislators of our own lives, no moral subject could rationally 'outsource' that legislation to an external source, such as another person's will. Assume that there is a serious moral objection to abdicating responsibility for one's own life to the will of another agent. It is far from obvious what, if anything, follows from this about one's particular responsibilities as a political subject. First, and building on a point made in the previous paragraph, to show epistemic deference in light of knowledge and/or understanding that on the issue in question there are other people better placed to judge could in principle be one way of responsibly exercising one's capacity for autonomous choice. Second, for a politically active person their reliance on political testimony could be a matter of deferring to the judgment of others on a set of institutionally mediated questions that arise with respect to *some* aspects of their life, but *not all*. Third, although an act of epistemic deference *could* be premised on a belief that the persons or institutions to which one defers have some normatively privileged status from which one is in principle excluded, this need not be so. As we have already seen, some acts of epistemic deference are premised on no more than the contingent social position of the people involved with respect to the information in question.

Similar observations can be made about the application to politics of the suggestion that reliance on moral testimony is incompatible with the value of *authenticity* (see e.g. Mogensen 2015). Assume that being authentic (in the sense of being 'true to oneself') is an important moral value (but see Adorno 1973). In response to this suggestion, we should first note that it is not obvious that being true to oneself has any necessary connection to what most people would recognize as politics. (For better or worse, quite a few people claim to have 'no interest in politics'.) Second, we should note that given the potentially different 'selves' to which different authentic subjects could be 'true', there is more than one way for the value of authenticity to be manifested even within politics. True, Aristotle famously thought that the human being (whoever exactly he intended to include in that category) is an essentially political animal (Aristotle 1981). Yet what, exactly, does that imply with respect to the question of epistemic deference? As we know, political arrangements come in many varieties (including the politics of Aristotle's Athens, which went through more and less democratic phases, and which was generally favorable toward a division of adult humans into citizens, barbarians and slaves). Exactly which, if any, of these different kinds of politics, is it my identification with which would qualify me as truly 'authentic'? Far from a refusal to epistemically defer in politics being a *condition* of authenticity, therefore, it is more charitably interpreted as one potential way, among others, for a selective group of people to think about their own personal relationship to politics in highly specific circumstances.

A further concern is that epistemic deference in the form of *political* testimony conflicts with the democratic values of *mutual justifiability* and *equal opportunity for political influence* (van Wietmarschen 2018). Yet the values that motivate this concern are arguably consistent with the practice of epistemic deference in democratic politics, whether by way of relying on political testimony or otherwise. First, epistemic deference in the form of political testimony is in principle consistent with mutual justifiability, albeit in ways that are often institutionally mediated and therefore indirect (e.g. by way of publicity constraints such as data protection; freedom of information; judicial review, or other democratically enforced mechanisms). Second, epistemic deference in the form of political testimony is consistent with equal opportunity for political influence insofar as political 'positions' of epistemic privilege are not reserved for some non-democratically specified subset of the population, and are open to change over time (e.g. by way of individual citizens being effectively empowered to defer or not; to stand for office in regular elections; or be elected by lot). The extent to which any actual political arrangements approximate to these conditions of justifiability and opportunity is a good, but different, question.

Qualifying deference: risk and trust

There are other sources of skepticism toward epistemic deference in politics that make less problematic assumptions about the relationship between morality and politics. Two such sources are the problems of *risk* and *trust*. The problem of *risk* arises for the obvious reasons that not only are the facts of politics highly complex and subject to deep disagreement, there is good evidence that much political disagreement is a result of systematic ignorance, entrenched bias and deliberate manipulation (including 'spin' or suppressed evidence; hostile depictions of out-groups; 'fake news'; fraudulent 'fact-checking' services or 'personalized' and self-reinforcing internet search algorithms). Short of being able to purchase a reliable 'bullshit detector' to separate sound from unsound opinion, it might be thought that the best epistemic strategy is to think things through for oneself on the merits of the individual case.

The problem of *trust* arises for closely related reasons. Politics is a web of vested interests in which conflicting parties have a stake in keeping the voting citizen confident enough to stay on their side; getting them 'hooked' on ideas that bring them into the fold if they are undecided; or undermining their confidence in case they belong to 'the other side'. Hence the way that emotive political issues are differentially depicted by different media outlets (e.g. to trigger anxiety or hostility by means of repetition; tendentious labeling or alarmist news items). Once more, short of being able to purchase a reliable 'bullshit detector' to separate sound from unsound opinion, it might be thought that the best epistemic strategy is to think things through for oneself on the merits of the individual case.

No plausible political epistemology would advocate the universal lowering of our epistemic guard in these respects. There are excellent reasons for this, quite apart from any naive optimism about the democratic distribution of sound political judgment. After all, whichever way we actually arrive at our political judgments, those judgments often involve decisions that – short of cultural or self-induced amnesia – have to be *lived with by us*. Given that events often turn out rather differently that we hope (e.g. in the case of controversial policies proposed in response to a national emergency or global pandemic), it might be a source of spiritual comfort that at least we came to our judgment (whatever it was) by ourselves, and by exercising such socio-political knowledge and/or understanding as we had. Yet we have already seen that the responsible exercise of political judgment is consistent with epistemic deference in some cases, and further reflection on the problems of risk and trust only serve to reinforce this claim, for the following three reasons.

First, no person ever exercised political judgment in a *psychological vacuum*. For example, there seems to be an unfortunate tendency for people to underestimate the extent to which we ourselves are the 'victims' of the kinds of self-deception and self-reinforcing biases that during the course of political discussion we are often quick to attribute to our adversaries. Hence, someone on the political 'left' might be stubbornly convinced that people on the 'right' are selfishly reluctant to contribute to the collective purse, while someone of the political 'right' might be equally stubbornly convinced that people on the 'left' are selfishly feeding on it. The difficulty of 'thinking oneself' out of this predicament on one's own is not one that should be underestimated.

Second, no person ever exercised political judgment in a *social vacuum*. For example, there seems to be an unfortunate tendency for members of different social groups to collectively engage in self-reinforcing interpretations of social facts to the extent of becoming the social vehicles for precisely the kinds of 'demonizing' narratives and confirmation biases we are often quick to attribute to our adversaries. Hence, people on either side of a political 'spectrum' being ever so quick to find examples of their political opponents behaving 'hypocritically', as opposed to having had to moderate their lofty political ideals in the face of complex socio-political realities. Once more, the difficulty of 'thinking oneself' out of this predicament on one's own is not one that should be underestimated.

Third, some degree of perspectival 'bias' is inescapable in all political thought, insofar as none of us have autonomously chosen or created the concepts by means of which we are constrained to interpret the social world in the first place. The very idea of 'making up one's own mind' or 'relying on one's own best judgment' is necessarily infused with the influence of others, if not by explicit deference then by implicit or pre-reflective 'osmosis'. No individual is ever in possession of purely context-independent first-personal epistemic privilege about how, and to what extent, this is the case. A certain degree of modesty is therefore in order when contemplating the idea of transcending epistemic deference in politics in favor of our own individual judgment.

Conclusions

Epistemic deference in politics is in principle consistent with authenticity, virtue, knowledge, understanding, responsibility, mutual justifiability, equal opportunity for influence, and a rational attitude toward risk and trust. It is also arguably inevitable. This does not mean that people should never think 'for themselves'. If I trust someone else's judgment, I am not thereby abandoning my own judgment altogether, insofar as I could be making a judgment about who to trust. Furthermore, we all know that unless we are either very privileged or extremely lucky, it is not always the best strategy to trust oneself. We also know that it is not always an option merely to 'suspend judgment', if only because the reluctance to judge which 'side' is right is often *de facto* equivalent to choosing the wrong side. The result is that we often have no realistic option but to place our trust in people or institutions the political judgments of which transcend our epistemic reach. And although there is much the average citizen of the contemporary information society can do in order to place that trust responsibly (such as 'calibrating' the incoming bombardment of information by consulting a broad range of different sources), there is no prospect of infallibility in this respect. Yet to think the solution is therefore only to rely on one's own 'individual' judgment is at best simplistic and at worst a fantasy.

Related topics

Chapter 4, 'Mill, Liberalism, and Epistemic Diversity'; Chapter 6, 'Politics, Truth, Posttruth, and Postmodernism'; Chapter 12, 'Epistemic Networks and Polarization'; Chapter 13, 'Affective Polarization, Evidence, and Evidentialism?'; Chapter 17, 'Filter Bubbles, Echo Chambers, Online Communities'; Chapter 21, 'Is Political Ignorance Rational?' Chapter 25, 'Asymmetrical Irrationality: Are Only Other People Stupid?'; Chapter 28, 'Virtues and Vices in Public and Political Debate'; Chapter 29, 'Vices of the Privileged and Virtues of the Oppressed in Epistemic Group Dynamics'; Chapter 32, 'In Defense of Epistocracy'; Chapter 33, 'A Pragmatist's Epistemic Argument for Democracy'; Chapter 34, 'Epistemic Norms of Political Deliberation'; Chapter 35, 'The Epistemic Responsibilities of Citizens in a Democracy'; Chapter 40, 'The Skeptic and the Climate Change Skeptic'; Chapter 41, 'Online Trust and Distrust'.

References

Adorno, Theodor (1973), *The Jargon of Authenticity*, London: Routledge & Kegan Paul.

Ahlstrom-Vij, Kristoffer (2015), 'The Social Virtue of Blind Deference', *Philosophy and Phenomenological Research* 91, 545–82.

Ahlstrom-Vij, Kristoffer & Dunn, Jeffrey (2014), 'A Defence of Epistemic Consequentialism', *The Philosophical Quarterly* 64, 541–51.

Aristotle (1981), *Politics*, Transl. T. Sinclair, Harmondsworth: Penguin Classics.

Christiano, Tom (2012), 'Rational Deliberation among Experts and Citizens', in John Parkinson & Jane Mansbridge (eds.), *Deliberative Systems*, Cambridge: Cambridge University Press, 27–51.

Driver, Julia (2006), 'Autonomy and the Asymmetry Problem for Moral Expertise', *Philosophical Studies* 128, 619–44.

Dworkin, Gerald (1988), *The Theory and Practice of Autonomy*, Cambridge: Cambridge University Press.

Dworkin, Ronald (2011), *Justice for Hedgehogs*, Cambridge, MA: Harvard University Press.

Enoch, David (2014), 'A Defense of Moral Deference', *The Journal of Philosophy* 111, 229–58.

Finlayson, Lorna (2015), *The Political Is Political*, London: Rowman & Littlefield.

Fricker, Miranda (2007), *Epistemic Injustice: Power and the Ethics of Knowing*, Oxford: Oxford University Press.

Geuss, Raymond (2008), *Philosophy and Real Politics*, Princeton, NJ: Princeton University of Press.

Hills, Alison (2009), 'Moral Testimony and Moral Epistemology', *Ethics* 120, 94–127.

Hills, Alison (2013), 'Moral Testimony', *Philosophy Compass* 8, 552–59.

Hopkins, Robert (2007), 'What Is Wrong with Moral Testimony?', *Philosophy and Phenomenological Research* 74, 611–34.

Jones, Karen (1999), 'Second-hand Moral Knowledge', *The Journal of Philosophy* 96, 55–78.

Lillehammer, Hallvard (2014), 'Moral Testimony, Moral Virtue and the Value of Autonomy', *Proceedings of the Aristotelian Society*, Supplementary Volume LXXXVIII, 111–27.

McGrath, Sarah (2019), *Moral Knowledge*, Oxford: Oxford University Press.

McShane, Paddy Jane (2018), 'The Non-remedial Value of Dependence on Moral Testimony', *Philosophical Studies* 175, 629–47.

Mogensen, Andreas (2015), 'Moral Testimony Skepticism and the Uncertain Value of Authenticity', *Philosophy and Phenomenological Research* 95, 261–84.

O'Neill, Onora (2002), *A Question of Trust*, Cambridge: Cambridge University Press.

Quinton, Anthony (1993), 'Morals and Politics', *Royal Institute of Philosophy Supplements* 35, 95–106.

Rawls, John (1993), *Political Liberalism*, Cambridge, MA: Cambridge University Press.

Sartre, Jean-Paul (1946/2007), *Existentialism & Humanism*, London: Methuen.

Van Wietmarschen, Han (2019), 'Political Testimony', *Politics, Philosophy & Economics* 18, 23–45.

Further reading

Anscombe, Elizabeth (1962), 'Authority in Morals', in Todd, J. M. ed. *Problems of Authority*, London: Darton, Longman, A. Todd, 179–188.

Berker, Selim (2013), 'The Rejection of Epistemic Consequentialism', *Philosophical Issues* 23, 363–87.

Brennan, Jason (2016), *Against Democracy*, Princeton, NJ: Princeton University Press.

Crisp, R. (2014), 'Moral Testimony Skepticism: A Defense', *Proceedings of the Aristotelian Society*, Supplementary Volume 88, 129–43.

Elgin, Catherine (2017), *True Enough*, Cambridge, MA: MIT Press.

Estlund, David M. (2008), *Democratic Authority: A Philosophical Framework*, Princeton, NJ: Princeton University Press.

Geuss, Raymond (2014), *A World without Why*, Princeton, NJ: Princeton University Press.

Grice, H. P. (1989), *Studies in the Way of Words*, Cambridge, MA: Harvard University Press.

Howell, Robert J. (2014), 'Google Morals, Virtue and the Asymmetry of Deference', *Nous* 48, 380–415.

Kant, Immanuel (1998), *Groundwork of the Metaphysics of Morals*, Mary Gregor (ed.), Intro. Christine M. Korsgaard, Cambridge: Cambridge University Press.

Korsgaard, C. (2009), *Self-Constitution*, Oxford: Oxford University Press.

Plato (2007), *The Republic*, Transl. D. Lee, Intro. M. Lane, Harmondsworth: Penguin Classics.

Raz, Joseph (1986), *The Morality of Freedom*, Oxford: Oxford University Press.

Sen, Amartya (2004), *Rationality and Freedom*, Cambridge, MA: Harvard University Press.

Sen, Amartya (2009), *The Idea of Justice*, Cambridge, MA: Harvard University Press.

Sliwa, Paulina (2015), 'Understanding and Knowing', *Proceedings of the Aristotelian Society* 115, 57–74.

Taylor, Charles (1992), *The Ethics of Authenticity*, Cambridge, MA: Harvard University Press.

Williams, Bernard (1985), *Ethics and the Limits of Philosophy*, London: Fontana.

Wolff, Robert Paul (1970), *In Defense of Anarchism*, London: Harper & Row.

Zabzebski, Linda Trinkaus (2012), *Epistemic Authority: A Theory of Trust, Authority and Autonomy in Belief*, Oxford: Oxford University Press.

Zuboff, Soshana (2018), *The Age of Surveillance Capitalism*, London: Profile Books.

40

THE SKEPTIC AND THE CLIMATE CHANGE SKEPTIC

Alex Worsnip

1 Introduction

The problem of skepticism, it hardly needs to be said, is widely regarded as one of the deepest and most important problems in philosophy. Skepticism is often personified in the shadowy figure of "the skeptic," who denies, of some large swathe of what we take to be our ordinary knowledge, that we know it after all. The philosophical challenge – as it's sometimes framed, though this way of setting the problem up has its critics – is to say whether there's anything we can say to the skeptic that rationally ought to change her mind.

Outside the philosophy classroom, global skeptics – skeptics about all purported knowledge, or at least all purported empirical knowledge about the external world – are rare. But there are people who describe themselves as "skeptics" about various more specific domains. Among these are self-professed "climate change skeptics" – skeptics about the reality of anthropogenic climate change.

There is little philosophical literature that juxtaposes the climate change skeptic with the external world skeptic, or that explores the parallels between the problems that these two figures pose.[1] Of the philosophical literature that there is on climate change *skepticism* specifically, most of it focuses on the quasi-sociological project of explaining why climate change skepticism abounds, despite the strong expert consensus that anthropogenic climate change is real.[2]

Part of the explanation of this state of affairs is that, while both the external world skeptic and the climate change skeptic are typically cast as nefarious figures, many "traditional" epistemologists likely take it for granted that the former poses a serious philosophical challenge in a way that the latter doesn't. Addressing the external world skeptic is taken to be a highly ambitious philosophical project, one that has stalked millennia of philosophical tradition. The climate change skeptic, by contrast, seems to just be obviously and demonstrably failing to respond correctly to her evidence.[3] Put in a picturesque way, the thought is that philosophical analysis of the climate change skeptic must operate in the space of causes rather than the space of reasons – for the reasons are clearly settled.

At the same time, many of those who are interested in applied epistemology and climate change may think that there is not much to be learned from debates about the external world skeptic. They may find the external world skeptic's challenge to *all* our knowledge to be distant from both common sense and real-world concerns,[4] and the attention to it symptomatic of what's wrong with "traditional" or "individual" epistemology. And they may not see much of a parallel between the climate change skeptic's arguments and those of the external world skeptic.

Here, I'll try to show that both of these views are mistaken. I think that the external world skeptic raises deep questions that *are* important for our everyday deliberation about what to believe. And I also think that there are significant parallels between the arguments for external world skepticism and those for a form of climate change skepticism that is idealized – but not *too* idealized! – from the views of real-world, flesh-and-blood climate change skeptics. As such, the idealized climate change skeptic poses a challenge quite analogous to that of the external world skeptic.

In drawing this parallel, I do not intend to honor the climate change skeptic. I agree with the mainstream consensus that the climate change skeptic is irrational. That said, as I'll try to show, some of the same difficulties with creating a persuasive reply to the external world skeptic carry over to the case of the climate change skeptic.

2 The external world skeptic

Obviously, it's beyond the scope of this chapter to provide a comprehensive survey of different arguments for external world skepticism. I'll make do with a brief review of one common, famous skeptical strategy.

This strategy begins by describing some *skeptical scenario*. A skeptical scenario is a hypothetical situation in which one is radically deceived about how the external world is: where there is a giant difference between appearances and reality. One of the most famous skeptical scenarios is the brain-in-a-vat scenario. In this scenario, you have no human body as we would ordinarily think of it; you are just a brain in a vat of jelly. Scientists have hooked wires up to the brain, and stimulate it to make things appear a certain way. But none of the appearances match reality. So, when it seems to you as if you are seated in a room, reading a philosophy book, really the scientists are just making things appear that way: in fact, you are just a brain-in-a-vat being made to think that you are seated in a room, reading a philosophy book. And similarly for all your other empirical beliefs about how the external world is.

The skeptic does not, of course, affirmatively claim that you *are* a brain-in-a-vat, or the victim of a skeptical scenario more generally. Rather, the skeptic's claim is that you don't know that you aren't a brain-in-a-vat. This claim, together with an application of the "closure" principle for knowledge, forms the basis for what Keith DeRose (1995) calls the Argument from Ignorance:

1   You don't know that you're not a brain-in-a-vat.
2   If you don't know that you're not a brain-in-a-vat, then you don't know that you're seated in a room, reading a philosophy book.
     Therefore,
3   You don't know that you're seated in a room, reading a philosophy book.

If successful, the argument generalizes to show that you don't know *any* ordinary proposition about how the external world is – provided it is something the scientists could be deceiving you about, just substitute the relevant proposition into the consequent of premise (2), and the conclusion.

Some have said that the Argument from Ignorance is not a particularly compelling skeptical argument as it stands, because its first premise can't just be taken for granted.[5] But there are ancillary arguments to be made for the first premise. Here is one. You could only know that you're not a brain-in-a-vat by possessing some evidence that you're not a brain-in-a-vat. But it's unclear what this evidence could be. You might try saying that it doesn't *look* like you're a brain-in-a-vat. But it's built into the brain-in-a-vat scenario that if you were in this scenario, it wouldn't look to you like you are, since it's part of the scenario that the scientists are making it appear that you have an ordinary human body. Since it would appear that you're not a brain-in-a-vat whether you were a brain-in-a-vat or not, this appearance isn't evidence that you aren't a brain-in-a-vat. The brain-in-a-vat scenario is capable of explaining away any apparent evidence against itself, so that nothing can count as evidence against it. (Indeed, this is what makes it such an effective skeptical scenario.[6]) Thus, the skeptic claims, you cannot know that it doesn't obtain.

Additionally, some have thought that the Argument from Ignorance should not worry us because it only targets our *knowledge* of ordinary propositions, and not the claim that we *justifiably believe* such propositions.[7] Perhaps we shouldn't be too worried about whether we have knowledge; (highly) justified belief may be all we need. However, the ancillary argument for the first premise of the argument points the way to an answer to this objection too. For, if that ancillary argument is right, then we have *no* evidence that we are not brains-in-vats – nothing that favors the hypothesis that we aren't brains-in-vats over the hypothesis that we are. If this is so, it seems we're not even justified in believing that we're not brains-in-vats. And then – assuming a "closure" principle for justification – it seems that we're not justified in holding ordinary beliefs, like your belief that you're seated in a room, reading a philosophy book.

3 The idealized climate change skeptic

Different people who call themselves "climate change skeptics" hold different views, and some of these views are more analogous to the external world skeptic than others. To make the climate change skeptic somewhat analogous to the external world skeptic, we'll have to stipulate a number of things about him. This is, of course, to idealize somewhat from the messy and indeterminate states of mind that many real world "climate change skeptics" have. So let me sketch an "idealized" climate change skeptic. By calling this skeptic "idealized," I don't mean to say that he meets some important normative ideal, but simply that he has been imagined so as to be as analogous to the external world skeptic as possible.

First, and most importantly, the idealized climate change skeptic will genuinely be a climate change *skeptic*. Some self-described climate change "skeptics" positively affirm that anthropogenic climate change is not occurring – that it is a "hoax." Such people aren't really skeptics in the sense that is operative in epistemology. A skeptic about some domain is someone who affirms that knowledge about that domain is not possible. Thus, a climate change skeptic is someone who affirms that we cannot know whether anthropogenic climate change is occurring. By contrast, someone who positively asserts that anthropogenic climate change is *not* occurring is better called a climate change *denier*. The analog of the climate change denier is not the external world skeptic, but the idealist, who affirms that there is no (material) external world.

It's very hard to see what could possibly justify an ordinary person in engaging in outright climate change denial. Since an ordinary person lacks the competence to responsibly evaluate the first-order scientific evidence about climate change for himself, it does not seem that he could be justified on the basis of a direct examination of that evidence. Nor does it seem that he could be justified on the basis of the testimony from the very small percentage of experts who deny the existence of anthropogenic climate change – at least not if he is aware of the many experts who hold the opposite view. One can't (justifiably) just arbitrarily pick and choose the experts one heeds in this way.[8] If denial can't be justified either on the basis of direct examination of the first-order evidence, or on the basis of testimony, then plausibly, it cannot be justified at all.

But although no doubt many professed climate change "skeptics" are in fact deniers rather than skeptics, this is not true of all such people. In their book *Merchants of Doubt*, which details the attempts of corporately funded renegade scientists to sow confusion about the reality of (among other things) anthropogenic climate change, Naomi Oreskes and Erik Conway stress that the narratives advanced in this cause are often ones of doubt, uncertainty, and a multiplicity of competing explanations of the data, rather than of certainty that anthropogenic climate change is *not* occurring.[9] The aim, essentially, is to get people to be skeptics about climate change.

A second feature of the idealized climate change skeptic is that his skepticism is not due to straightforwardly false factual beliefs about what the expert consensus about climate change is. According to survey data from the PEW Research Center as of 2016, 35% of Americans say that the percentage of climate scientists who say that human behavior is mostly responsible for climate change is "about half," "fewer than half," or "almost none."[10] Since these answers are straightforwardly factually inaccurate – surveys of climate scientists show that the vast majority say that human behavior is mostly responsible for climate change[11] – skepticism that is founded on them is not especially philosophically interesting. Rather, the more philosophically interesting climate change skeptic is one who is aware of the expert consensus on climate change, but distrusts or is uncertain of the reliability of these experts. This too is common: the same PEW survey shows that only 32% of Americans think that the research findings of climate scientists are influenced by "the best available evidence" most of the time, and that respondents are about as likely to attribute scientists' findings to "scientists' own political leanings" (27%) or their "desire to advance their careers" (36%).[12]

This leads directly into the third feature of the idealized climate change skeptic: he has a skeptical scenario that, if it obtained, would explain away the apparent evidence for climate change (namely, the expert consensus). The skeptical scenario is likely to be something like this:

> **Conspiracy**. There is no anthropogenic climate change, but there is an elaborate scientific conspiracy to suggest that there is, motivated by factors like scientists' political leanings and desire to advance their careers. Some scientists knowingly lie to sustain the conspiracy, while others are more unwitting participants, genuinely convincing themselves of the reality of anthropogenic climate change through wishful thinking, motivated reasoning, selective or biased processing of the evidence, or groupthink. Scientists are consciously and subconsciously disincentivized from uncovering the conspiracy or revealing the truth that it hides, since if they do so, they will be denied publications, grants and jobs. Those who do speak out against the conspiracy are marginalized, forced out of the profession, or hushed up.

Conspiracy-type scenarios play the same sort of role for the idealized climate change skeptic that brain-in-a-vat-type scenarios play for the external world skeptic. (Indeed, both scenarios involve nefarious scientists deceiving us!) To maintain the parallel between the cases, our idealized climate change skeptic won't positively affirm that the Conspiracy scenario obtains. Rather, he will hold only that we don't have evidence that enables us to rule the Conspiracy scenario out. The expert consensus on climate change, he'll concede, *could* be explained by the reality of anthropogenic climate change (much as the appearance as of sitting in a room could be explained by actually sitting in a room). But it could also be explained by a Conspiracy-type scenario (much as the appearance as of sitting in a room could be explained by being a brain-in-a-vat deceived to think you're sitting in a room). The existence of the consensus, he claims, doesn't tell between these two hypotheses (just as the appearance of sitting in a room doesn't tell between the actually sitting-in-a-room hypothesis and the brain-in-a-vat hypothesis).

As with the external world skeptic, this position is made harder to argue against by the fact that the Conspiracy scenario, suitably developed, conveniently explains away any potential piece of (apparent) evidence against itself. All the appearances of non-conspiracy – like the lack of scientific results uncovering the conspiracy – can themselves be hypothesized to be a part of, or explained by, the conspiracy.

An objection may be raised here.[13] The "Conspiracy" scenario as I imagined it involves some elements that are not in themselves conspiratorial in a narrow sense, such as motivated reasoning, bias, and groupthink.[14] But to the extent that the climate change skeptic stresses these factors more than he stresses deliberate, conscious conspiracy, perhaps this opens up an important disanalogy between him and the external world skeptic. In particular, these charges of motivated reasoning, bias, and groupthink seem open to empirical refutation in a way that both brain-in-a-vat and (narrowly) conspiracy-theoretic hypotheses are not. In my view, however, there is not as big a difference here as the objector makes out. From the point of view of a layperson it seems close to impossible – in practice if not in principle – to definitively rule out the possibility that the scientific consensus is due to motivated reasoning or groupthink, rather than a convergence on the truth. The best way of determining this would be to directly evaluate whether the scientific data actually supports the consensus, but the layperson lacks the scientific competence to do this. Moreover, responses to the charge that a particular conclusion is due to bias, motivated reasoning and groupthink can themselves be charged with being a product of bias or groupthink. So I don't think that whether the climate change skeptic stresses conscious conspiracy or these more subconscious elements makes a huge difference to the structure of the dialectic between the skeptic and the non-skeptic.[15]

To make the parallel with external world skepticism crisper and clearer, we can imagine our idealized climate change skeptic advancing an adapted version of the Argument from Ignorance:

1   You don't know that the Conspiracy scenario doesn't obtain.
2   If you don't know that the Conspiracy scenario doesn't obtain, then you don't know that anthropogenic climate change is occurring.
    Therefore,
3   You don't know that anthropogenic climate change is occurring.

As with the original argument for ignorance, the argument can be generalized from knowledge to justification. If the Conspiracy scenario explains away any potential piece of (apparent) evidence against itself – such that you would have this (apparent) evidence even if the Conspiracy scenario obtained – then it seems that none of this evidence really is evidence against the Conspiracy scenario. But if you don't have any evidence against the Conspiracy scenario, you can't be justified in believing that the Conspiracy scenario doesn't obtain. And if that's so, then (it seems), you can't be justified in believing that anthropogenic climate change is occurring.

Lest it seem fanciful to imagine a real-world climate change skeptic developing a Conspiracy scenario of the sort that this argument employs, it is worth summarizing a real-world instance detailed by Oreskes and Conway (2010: 207–8). In 1996, the Intergovernmental Panel on Climate Change (IPCC) published a working group report on climate change, which included a chapter on "Detection of Climate Change and Attribution of Causes." The chapter, prepared by 36 of the world's leading climate scientists before being reviewed by representatives of governments participated in the IPCC, was a landmark in making the claim that "the balance of evidence suggests that there is a discernible human influence on global climate." In response, two prominent representatives of the oil industry accused two of the lead scientists behind the chapter of "secretly altering the IPCC report, suppressing dissent by other scientists, and eliminating references to scientific uncertainties." And the physicist and climate change skeptic Fred Seitz proclaimed that he had "never witnessed a more disturbing corruption of the peer-review process than the events that led to the IPCC report" and that "nearly all [of the revisions] worked to remove hints of the skepticism with which many scientists regard claims that human activities are having a major impact on climate."

These are positive allegations of conspiracy and cover-up, rather than merely floatings of such a possibility. But we can imagine some non-expert who hears the IPCC report on the one hand, and the accusations of conspiracy on the other, and does not know which to believe. For such an individual, the Conspiracy-type scenario is salient, and even if she does not affirmatively believe that this scenario obtains, she may find herself unsure how to rule it out. Her position may be made even harder by the fact that there are accusations of conspiracy on *both* sides of the debate.[16] Seitz and others accused the IPCC authors of being engaged in a politically motivated conspiracy to distort the scientific consensus on climate change to make it seem more weighted in *favor* of anthropogenic hypotheses than it was. The IPCC authors and their allies responded by emphatically denying this, and by, in turn, alleging that it was in fact Seitz who was engaged in a politically (and financially) motivated conspiracy to distort the scientific consensus on climate change to make it seem more weighted *against* anthropogenic hypotheses than it was – which Seitz, in turn, strongly denied. Each side thus strongly denied being engaged in a conspiracy, and accused the other side of being engaged in one. To the non-expert, these allegations of conspiracy might seem on a par with one another, especially if she doesn't antecedently trust one side more than the other. And this might leave her tempted by the adapted Argument from Ignorance.

4 Summing up the idealized climate change skeptic's challenge

The idealized climate change skeptic, I think, poses two problems to the defender of beliefs based on mainstream climate science. The first is a practical problem: the idealized climate change skeptic is dialectically very hard to convince. The problem is that anything that we can try to marshal to support our beliefs in anthropogenic climate change is itself called into question by the skeptic's Conspiracy scenario. This is an instance of a more general problem emphasized by Michael Lynch (2012, 2020): it is very hard to mount a defense of our views about which sources to trust from first principles, without relying on (some of) the very sources under dispute. Thus, we often won't be able to say anything persuasive in defense of these sources to someone who doubts them.[17]

In addition to this practical problem, the idealized climate change skeptic also poses us a more philosophical challenge, very similar to that of the external world skeptic. The challenge is to explain on what grounds we can justifiably dismiss the Conspiracy scenario – or to explain how, even though we can't dismiss it, we're still justified in continuing to believe in anthropogenic climate change, rather than suspending judgment. Though I am not a climate change skeptic, I am bothered by the question of how to respond to the climate change skeptic's challenge (just as I am bothered by the question of how to respond to the external world skeptic's challenge). Though I can't settle this definitively here, the next and final section surveys some possible answers.

5 Responding to the idealized climate change skeptic

One strategy is to try to give some specific response to the idealized climate change skeptic that isn't intended to generalize to address the external world skeptic. We might try to directly examine the scientific data to confirm that they *do* support belief in anthropogenic climate change, and thus that the scientific consensus is not merely a result of conspiracy. But a layperson, who lacks scientific competence, can't responsibly or accurately evaluate the scientific data and its implications without deferring to experts – so I take it this option is unavailable for her.

Somewhat more promisingly, we might say that our evidence against the Conspiracy scenario is that scientific conspiracies are rare, and there haven't been many in the past. However, if the idealized climate change skeptic is deft enough, she can explain away these facts as part of her skeptical hypotheses, alleging a broader conspiracy. Moreover, while deliberate scientific conspiracies may be rare, the literature on pessimistic (meta-)induction arguments in philosophy of science reminds us that scientific views that were once orthodox and enjoyed great consensus have very often turned out to be false.[18]

So I think we should look at responses to the idealized climate change skeptic that draw on the parallel with the external world skeptic. One prominent anti-skeptical idea is that we enjoy a "default justification" or "unearned entitlement," to accept, without evidence, certain propositions that play a role as "cornerstones" or "foundational assumptions" in our thought.[19] However, while the proposition that we're not brains-in-vats – or, at least the proposition that the world is roughly as it appears to be – plausibly occupies this kind of role in our thought, the proposition that there is no elaborate scientific conspiracy to fake anthropogenic global warming does not seem to be such a cornerstone. It's easy to imagine us going on with our cognitive lives without it, without a fundamental restructuring of our cognitive architecture or any change in our way of using appearances as a guide to reality. It's thus hard to see why we would have an "unearned" entitlement to accept it without evidence.

A different prominent anti-skeptical view is "dogmatism" of the sort defended by Pryor (2000). According to the dogmatist, perceptual experiences as of *p* (defeasibly) justify you in believing *p*, in a way that doesn't presuppose or rest on any antecedent justification for believing anything else. So, for example, a perceptual experience as of being seated in a room, reading a philosophy book defeasibly justifies you in believing that you are seated in a room, reading a philosophy book – regardless of whether you have any antecedent justification for believing that you are not a brain-in-a-vat. In itself, this view does not say anything about what, if anything, does ultimately justify you in believing that you are not a brain-in-a-vat.

But it's commonly assumed that the dogmatist will go on to say that your experience (e.g.) as of being seated in a room, reading a philosophy book, justifies you not only in believing that you are seated in a room, reading a philosophy book, but also in believing that you are not a brain-in-a-vat being deceived to think that you're seated in a room reading a philosophy book.

Again, however, it's not clear how this dogmatist position generalizes to deal with the idealized climate change skeptic. The evidence that ordinary people have in favor of anthropogenic climate change – namely, the testimony of scientists to that effect – is not perceptual in the standard sense. One might try to extend the dogmatist position to testimony. But an analogous principle for testimony would say that when someone tells you that p, this (defeasibly) justifies you in believing p, regardless of whether you have any antecedent justification for believing the testifier to be reliable, or for believing that she is not trying to deceive you. This does not seem all that plausible.

However, even if the dogmatist position cannot be worked out to give a reply to the climate change skeptic, there may be an insight to be mined from it. The insight is this: just because two hypotheses are equally consistent with, or well-predicted by, your evidence, it need not be that they are both equally credible. Indeed, if this were so, it wouldn't just be that you'd need to give equal credence to the hypothesis that things are roughly as they appear to be and the hypothesis that you're a brain-in-a-vat being fed misleading appearances. There are a vast multitude, perhaps an infinitude, of *other* imaginable skeptical scenarios that are also equally well-predicted by the evidence (ones involving dreaming, or evil demons, etc.). The principle under consideration would thus say that you'd need to divide your credence equally across *all* of these hypotheses, where the hypothesis that things are roughly as they seem to be is just one of them, such that your credence that things are roughly as they seem to be becomes extremely, perhaps infinitesimally, small. This seems a lot to stomach even for the external world skeptic.

This still leaves us with the question of why we should positively think the hypothesis that things are roughly as they appear to be is more credible than the hypothesis that you're a brain-in-a-vat being fed misleading appearances. One view here is that, all other things equal, the *simpler* hypothesis is more credible.[20] The hypothesis that things are roughly as they appear to be is simpler than the hypothesis that there's an elaborate plot involving scientists and vats to make them seem as they appear to be. And the hypothesis that anthropogenic climate change is really occurring is simpler than the hypothesis that there's an elaborate scientific plot to make it seem like it's occurring.

Relatedly, one might wonder whether there is something non-credible about hypotheses that have been designed specifically to explain away all of the potential counterevidence against them. As we saw earlier, whenever there's some putative piece of evidence that seems to indicate that you're not a brain-in-a-vat, the external world skeptic just explains it away by building it into the story about the vatmasters' deception. Similarly, whenever there's some putative piece of evidence that seems to indicate that anthropogenic climate change is occurring, the climate change skeptic just explains it away by building it into the story about the climate scientists' conspiracy. These moves made the skeptic frustratingly hard to refute, but they also may be vulnerable to a charge of *ad hockery*. The skeptic's whole strategy is to make their own hypothesis impossible to falsify by building whatever complications she needs to in order to refute the counterevidence into her hypothesis, on an *ad hoc* basis as and when that counterevidence needs refuting. Perhaps the fact that a hypothesis has been developed in this fashion diminishes its credibility. Or perhaps a hypothesis is more credible when we know what evidence *would* count against it, and still, we haven't received that evidence.[21] That is so with the hypothesis that you're currently sitting in a room reading a philosophy book, but not with the hypothesis that you're a brain-in-a-vat. And it is so with the hypothesis that anthropogenic climate change is occurring, but not with the hypothesis that there's an elaborate scientific plot to make it seem like it's occurring.

The comparison between the two kinds of skepticism also creates a problem for the climate change skeptic that is independent of any particular response to her view. The problem is this: the climate change skeptic, presumably, does *not* want to be an external world skeptic. She wants to bring down our beliefs about anthropogenic climate change, not our beliefs about everything! But if the climate change skeptic's argument trades on the same skeptical strategy that the external world skeptic employs – if, for example, it relies on the principle that two hypotheses that predict the evidence equally well must be equally credible – then it is very hard to see how the climate change skeptic avoids a slide into a more general skepticism. Thus, the challenge for the climate change skeptic is to explain how her reasoning doesn't generalize. Without a response to this challenge, her *local* climate change skepticism looks unprincipled, and likely, politically motivated.

6 Conclusion

Thus, if the most philosophically respectable version of climate change skepticism relies on reasoning that leads us into such wholesale external world skepticism, the climate change skeptic is in trouble. But equally, this parallel may also cast the external world skeptic in a negative light. The skeptical hypothesis that she employs seems to have the same *ad hoc*, deliberately unfalsifiable nature as the conspiracy hypothesis that the climate change skeptic employs, and her style of argument works in the same way as the idealized climate change skeptic's. Perhaps, then, the external world skeptic herself is just another conspiracy theorist.

If the external world skeptic's challenge and the (idealized) climate change skeptic's challenge are effectively instances of the same central problem – namely, how we are to justifiably dismiss seemingly far-fetched hypotheses that are designed to explain away all of our apparent evidence against them – then a good response to the external world skeptic will be able to generalize to the climate change skeptic. But as we have seen, some of the most prominent responses to the external world skeptic seem not to happily generalize in this way. This is a mark against these responses.

To some, the debate about skepticism is philosophy at its silliest: the project of asking ourselves whether we really know that there are chairs and trees and hands and so on is supposed to be an amusing example of philosophy's excesses and deviation from common sense. But the way in which the external world skeptic's reasoning shows up so analogously in the real-life case of the climate change skeptic illustrates why the debate about skepticism matters. It matters because it raises deep and fundamental questions about what evidential support is, and about how to choose between competing hypotheses that purport to explain the evidence. These questions are imminent in real-world deliberation about what to believe. When we are facing the climate change skeptic down, we need some account of why it is OK to dismiss her skeptical conspiracy hypothesis. And without such an account, we cannot legitimately expect her to change her mind. Thus, developing such an account is a task of immense importance.[22]

Notes

1 An exception is an op-ed in the *New York Times* by the philosopher N. Ángel Pinillos (2018).
2 See, e.g., Anderson (2011), Gelfert (2013), Almassi (2017), Levy (2019), Kovaka (forthcoming), and Greco (forthcoming).
3 John Broome (2017), for example, writes that someone who believes that climate change is a hoax must "not [have] taken even a moment to consider the evidence."
4 See, e.g., Coady and Corry (2013: 12).
5 See, e.g., Pryor (2000: 522); Conee and Feldman (2004: 300).
6 Cf. Cross (2010).
7 See, e.g., Pryor (2000: 523).
8 Although, no doubt, many climate change deniers do pick and choose their experts in this way. Such biased handling of evidence is a classic hallmark of motivated reasoning (Kunda 1990), where one (perhaps subconsciously) has a conclusion one wants to reach in advance, and then sets up one's reasoning and inquiry to reach that conclusion, albeit through what *seems* or *feels* like a rational procedure. For further discussion of motivated reasoning in the context of beliefs about climate change see, e.g., Kahan et al. (2011), Gerken (2020), and Greco (forthcoming).
9 Oreskes and Conway (2010: see esp. 178, 186–90, 192, 213).
10 Funk and Kennedy (2016: 26).
11 Ibid.
12 Ibid.: 29.
13 Thanks to an anonymous referee for pressing it.
14 See Miller (2013) for more on these as explanations of consensus.
15 Another possibility is that the skeptic proceeds by advancing a less "global" skeptical hypothesis, focusing instead on "local" skeptical hypotheses that attempt to explain various pieces of climate data without appeal to anthropogenic factors. (Thanks to Mikkel Gerken for pressing this possibility on me.) However, in making the judgment that these explanations are as good as the explanations that do invoke anthropogenic factors, the skeptic is straying into making her own first-order assessments of scientific data and its upshots. As I've already said, an ordinary non-scientist is not justified in doing this. The global hypothesis offers the skeptic her best shot of making a skeptical argument without having to stray into fist-order assessments of the scientific data. Moreover, if the scientific consensus *were* mistaken in the way that the local skeptical hypotheses suggest, it's not clear what would explain the widespread mistake if not *something* in the ballpark of the factors I've collected under the "conspiracy" hypothesis.
16 Indeed, if a conspiracy theory is just a theory that explains something in terms of the presence of a conspiracy, there are surely true and justified conspiracy theories, since some things *are* down to conspiracies (cf. Pigden 1995, 2007; Coady 2012: ch. 5).
17 Consider Oreskes and Conway's responses to the conspiracy theories detailed at the end of the previous section (Oreskes and Conway 2010: 208–9). Their response is essentially to quote the emphatic denials of the subjects of the conspiracy theory (i.e. the IPCC authors). But for obvious reasons, this won't move someone in the grips of the conspiracy theory.
18 See, e.g., Laudan (1981).
19 Cf., e.g., Wright (2004) and Coliva (2015).
20 Cf. Vogel (1990).
21 Cf. Popper (1959).
22 For helpful comments, I'm grateful to Mikkel Gerken, Michael Hannon, Jeroen de Ridder, and an anonymous referee.

References

Almassi, B. (2017). "Experts in the Climate Change Debate," in K. Lippert-Rasmussen, K. Brownlee & D. Coady (eds.), *A Companion to Applied Philosophy*, pp. 133–47. Chichester: Wiley.
Anderson, E. (2011). "Democracy, Public Policy, and Lay Assessments of Scientific Testimony," *Episteme*, 8/2: 144–64.
Broome, J. (2017). "Trump and Climate Change," *The Philosophers' Magazine*, 76: 22.
Coady, D. (2012). *What to Believe Now: Applying Epistemology to Contemporary Issues*. Chichester: Wiley-Blackwell.

Coady, D. & Corry, R. (2013). *The Climate Change Debate: An Epistemic and Ethical Enquiry.* London: Palgrave Macmillan.

Coliva, A. (2015). *Extended Rationality: A Hinge Epistemology.* London: Palgrave.

Conee, E. & Feldman, R. (2004). *Evidentialism.* Oxford: Oxford University Press.

Cross, T. (2010). "Skeptical Success," *Oxford Studies in Epistemology*, 3: 35–62.

DeRose, K. (1995). "Solving the Skeptical Problem," *Philosophical Review*, 104/1: 1–52.

Funk, C. & Kennedy, B. (2016). "The Politics of Climate." Pew Research Center report available at https://www.pewresearch.org/internet/wp-content/uploads/sites/9/2016/10/PS_2016.10.04_Politics-of-Climate_FINAL.pdf.

Gelfert, A. (2013). "Climate Scepticism, Epistemic Dissonance, and the Ethics of Uncertainty," *Philosophy and Public Issues*, 3/1: 167–208.

Gerken, M. (2020). "Public Scientific Testimony in the Scientific Image," *Studies in History and Philosophy of Science Part A*, 80: 90–101.

Greco, D. (forthcoming). "Climate Change and Cultural Cognition," in M. Budolfson, T. McPherson & D. Plunkett (eds.), *Philosophy and Climate Change.* Oxford: Oxford University Press.

Kahan, D., Jenkins-Smith, H. & Braman, D. (2011). "Cultural Cognition of Scientific Consensus," *Journal of Risk Research*, 14/2: 147–74.

Kovaka, K. (forthcoming). "Climate Change Denial and Beliefs about Science," *Synthese*, Online Early Access. doi: 10.1007/s11229-019-02210-z.

Kunda, Z. (1990) "The Case for Motivated Reasoning," *Psychological Bulletin*, 108/3: 480–98.

Laudan, L. (1981). "A Confutation of Convergent Realism," *Philosophy of Science*, 48/1: 19–49.

Levy, N. (2019). "Due Deference to Denialism: Explaining Ordinary People's Rejection of Established Scientific Findings," *Synthese*, 196/1: 313–27.

Lynch, M. P. (2012). *In Praise of Reason: Why Rationality Matters for Democracy.* Cambridge, MA: MIT Press.

———. (2020). "Polarization and the Problem of Spreading Arrogance," in A. Tanesini & M. P. Lynch (eds.), *Polarisation, Arrogance, and Dogmatism: Philosophical Perspectives*, pp. 141–57. Abingdon: Routledge.

Miller, B. (2013). "When Is Shared Consensus Knowledge Based? Distinguishing Shared Knowledge from Mere Agreement," *Synthese*, 190/7: 1293–316.

Oreskes, N. & Conway, E. (2010). *Merchants of Doubt: How a Handful of Scientists Obscured the Truth on Issues from Tobacco Smoke to Climate Change.* New York: Bloomsbury.

Pigden, C. (1995). "Popper Revisited, or What Is Wrong with Conspiracy Theories?," *Philosophy of the Social Sciences*, 25/1: 3–34.

———. (2007). "Conspiracy Theories and the Conventional Wisdom," *Episteme*, 4/2: 219–32.

Pinillos, N. Ángel (2018). "Knowledge, Ignorance and Climate Change," *The New York Times*, Nov. 26, 2018.

Popper, K. (1959). *The Logic of Scientific Discovery.* London: Hutchinson.

Pryor, J. (2000). "The Skeptic and the Dogmatist," *Noûs*, 34/4: 517–49.

Vogel, J. (1990). "Cartesian Skepticism and Inference to the Best Explanation," *Journal of Philosophy*, 87/11: 658–66.

Wright, C. (2004). 'Warrant for Nothing (and Foundations for Free)?,' *Proceedings of the Aristotelian Society Supplementary Volume*, 78: 167–212.

41

ONLINE TRUST AND DISTRUST

Mark Alfano and Emily Sullivan

Introduction

Trust makes cooperation possible.[1] It enables us to learn from others and at a distance. It is a prerequisite for democratic deliberation and decision-making (Lynch 2018). But it also makes us vulnerable: when we place our trust in another's word, we are liable to be deceived—sometimes intentionally, sometimes unintentionally. Many of our evolved mechanisms for deciding whom to trust and whom to distrust rely on face-to-face interactions with people whose reputation we can both access and influence. Online, these mechanisms are largely useless, and the institutions that might supplant them need to have their own trustworthiness verified. Currently, many of those institutions are social media corporations such as Facebook and Twitter, which have checkered track records at best. To make matters worse, the social media sector exhibits natural monopoly characteristics, and companies like Facebook have shown that they are willing to use their market power unscrupulously. For these reasons, we argue that social media should be treated like other natural monopolies: it should be nationalized, highly regulated, or broken up through antitrust legal actions.

What is (dis)trust?

There are many definitions of trust in the philosophical literature. According to one attractive definition, a person puts trust in another person or institution when they allow or volunteer themselves to be dependent on the other's competence and motivation to act as counted upon (Jones 2012). In the case of trust in testimony, this comes down to being willing to take someone's word for it, or to allowing their testimony to influence one's credences. The trusted person is trustworthy just in case they actually have and are willing to exercise the relevant competence should they be trusted. In addition, Jones points out that an agent's being trustworthy without anyone being able to tell that she is trustworthy is inefficient. Such a person may end up being trusted haphazardly, but her dependency-responsiveness will go largely unnoticed, unappreciated, and unused. For this reason, Jones suggests that it is also important to be able to signal reliably whether a potential partner can reasonably trust you, a power that she calls "rich trustworthiness." Alfano & Huijts (2020) generalize the notion of rich trustworthiness from a single partner to all of one's social relations.

By contrast, Nguyen (forthcoming) sees trust not as a conscious attitude directed at another person but as an *unquestioning* attitude. On this view, to trust someone or something (e.g. your newsfeed) is to rely on it unquestioningly. For instance, someone might be disposed to automatically accept the claims made in their newsfeed, a problem addressed by Levy (2017) and Alfano et al. (2020). As Alfano & Klein (2019; see also Alfano & Skorburg 2018) have emphasized, this sort of unquestioning reliance boosts efficiency at the price of epistemic vulnerability. In a similar vein, D'Cruz (2019) elaborates on the vulnerabilities and harms that can result from unwarranted *dis*trust, including biased interpretation, self-perpetuation of bias, and self-confirmation of prejudiced attitudes.

As work on the psychological and neurological limits of direct sociality shows (Dunbar 1992), there are interesting and distinctive phenomena associated with trust at different social scales. One source of the needed motivation on the part of the trustee is *goodwill*, as Baier (1986) points out. Goodwill is established and maintained through activities like social grooming (Dunbar 1993), laughing together (Dezecache & Dunbar 2012), singing and dancing together (Dunbar 2012), and enduring traumatic loss together (Elder & Clipp 1988). Jones (2012) persuasively argues, however, that there can be motivational sources other than goodwill. One important additional motivator is concern for *reputation*, which is especially pertinent when one is embedded in a social structure that makes it likely that others will acquire mutual knowledge of what one has done and for what reasons one has acted (Dunbar 2005; Origgi 2017). One-off defection or betrayal in an interaction (e.g. lying or misleading someone) exposes one to loss of reputation and thereby to exclusion from the benefits of further cooperation and coordination. In a community with short epistemic geodesics, reputation-relevant information is likely to travel quickly and reliably. Dunbar (1993) estimates that at least 60% of human conversational time comprises gossip about relationships and personal experiences.

Unfortunately, the mechanisms that work well in small groups of up to 150 break down in larger groups. There just isn't enough time in the day to groom thousands of others. It's hard to sing and dance with more than a few dozen other people. Moreover, mechanisms that work well in groups where reputation can be reliably tracked and updated cease to function effectively in pseudonymous and (even more so) anonymous groups (Veliz 2018). In the next section, we address these breakdowns in the context of online communication with special attention to social media.

What makes online (dis)trust special?

A substantial proportion of people's trust and distrust when it comes to important political, economic, and medical issues is steered by social media. Recent studies indicate that half or more of people in North America, South America, Australia, and Europe use social media as a source of news.[2] Some of them use it as their primary or only source. Beyond more stereotypical platforms such as Facebook and Twitter, which have well-documented problems in allowing and even promoting the spread of fake news and disinformation,[3] there are other platforms such as Reddit, which has whole communities devoted to conspiracy theorizing (Klein et al. 2018, 2019), and YouTube, whose recommender system sometimes ends up promoting conspiracy theories and radicalizing content (Alfano et al. 2018, 2020). It is difficult to ascertain whether consumers of social media trust their sources versus treating them simply as entertainment. However, this distinction may be moot if people tend to start out consuming news on social media as entertainment and then subsequently end up accepting it as authoritative and true. Indeed, the line between entertainment and reportage has become so blurred in recent decades (think Rush Limbaugh to The Apprentice to the Trump presidency) that the distinction may no longer be viable. In any event, the epistemic power of a few celebrities to set the agenda, direct people's attention, and influence what they do and don't believe can be deeply problematic (Archer et al. 2020). For instance, as of the writing of this chapter, Donald Trump has made at least 20,055 false or misleading claims during his presidency of the United States, many of them via his Twitter account.[4] In the spring of 2020, he has started to claim that the coronavirus pandemic is a "hoax" perpetrated by the Democratic Party and the mainstream media to undermine his chances of reelection.[5] To the extent that a large number of people place their trust in Trump's pronouncements on his Twitter feed, this is an extremely dangerous state of affairs.

Compared to traditional epistemic networks, the internet—and social media in particular—has catalyzed both quantitative and qualitative shifts in the information ecology along multiple dimensions (Alfano & Klein 2019):

Volume: we have access to more information.
Velocity: we have access to information more quickly and fluently.
Veracity: we have access to more accurate information.
Variety: we have access to more diverse information sources.
Voice: we have more power to make ourselves and others heard.

Because of these developments, it's arguably the case that the capacity for information (and disinformation) to be spread on social media is greater than for any other medium in human history (Lu et al. 2014). In our quest to believe the truth and avoid error (James 1896/1979), these might seem like welcome developments. In the halcyon early days of the internet, it seemed to some that we were on our way to an epistemic utopia in which we spend less time and effort on basic cognitive tasks, freeing up attention for complex and collaborative inquiry. In this utopia, the vices arising from cognitive miserliness (Fiske & Taylor 1984) would be rebaptized as the virtues of thrift.

The actual outcome has been more mixed. The internet has made available an unprecedented number of accurate sources. However, they must be sifted from the spammers, trolls, sealions, practical jokers, conspiracy theorists, counterintelligence sock-puppets, liars, and ordinary uninformed and misinformed citizens who also proliferate online. This problem relates to Jones's (2012) conception of rich trustworthiness: not only are there many more voices insisting without much evidence that they are trustworthy, but also those same voices tend to cast aspersions on the trustworthiness of others, making it difficult for reliable signals of trustworthiness to be broadcast. Political operatives like Steve Bannon deliberately make use of the increased volume and velocity of information online to "flood the zone with shit," knowing that it takes too much time and effort to refute all of their lies and misleading statements.[6] Following up on sociological work by Conway & Oreskes (2010), network simulations have shown that a determined propagandist in a testimonial network is often capable of shifting the opinions of many other nodes (Weatherall et al. 2019).

Furthermore, information now comes at us so quickly and in such volume that we may neglect to exercise critical scrutiny, which means that we cannot properly update the epistemic track records of our sources and hence cannot rely on their reputations. And the promise of diverse information sources is easily quashed as we construct "filter bubbles" and "echo chambers" around ourselves (Pariser 2011; Lynch 2016; Sunstein 2017; Nguyen 2018; Sullivan et al. 2019) and choose experts who confirm our pre-existing biases (Goldman 2001).

While worries about filter bubbles, echo chambers, and other epistemically problematic structures online are at this point no longer new, a slew of recent studies suggest that we were right to be worried. For example, Vosoughi et al. (2018) found, in a large dataset of tweets dating from 2006 to 2017, that falsehoods spread significantly farther, faster, deeper, and more broadly than truths. This was especially so for false political news. What seems to have driven this effect is the novelty of false news, which tends to inspire fear, disgust, and surprise. Moreover, Vosoughi and colleagues found no evidence that the dissemination of false news was driven by automated accounts ("bots"): instead, it seems that human cognitive dispositions related to capturing and keeping attention, along with the urge to spread novel information, drove the effect (see also Brady et al. 2020). The blurring of the line between entertainment and news mentioned above may contribute to this problem. Furthermore, this result is consistent with a recent paper by Guess et al. (2019), who show that, in the run-up to the 2016 US presidential election, individual differences explain a lot of the variance in sharing of fake political news on Facebook. In particular, conservatives were more likely to share fake news, and users aged 65 or older were *seven times* as likely to share fake news as younger users. In a similar vein, Meyer and Alfano (under review; see also Meyer 2019) found that individuals who score high in intellectual vice (especially closed-mindedness and incorrigibility) are especially liable to place their epistemic trust in online fake news.

While individual dispositions no doubt influence the spread of false information, the design of social media platforms also plays a role. According to Brady et al. (2020), "people are motivated to share moral-emotional content; that such content is especially likely to capture attention; and that the design of social media platforms further facilitates its spread." One design feature that Brady and colleagues find especially troubling is "the ability to provide immediate and quantifiable social feedback in response to other people's content (e.g. likes, shares, retweets)," especially when such feedback tends to be delivered on an irregular reinforcement schedule (which is known to be addictive). They suggest that this kind of feedback "may amplify our propensity to express moral emotions in response to morally-relevant content," which, in turn, may lead outrage over false claims to go viral. In a nutshell, the gamification of news-sharing transforms it into a quest for social feedback rather than an epistemically oriented interaction. Changing the incentive structure in this way contributes to the spread of misinformation and disinformation.

Yet another problematic yet common design feature relates to the high fidelity of sharing, retweeting, and screenshotting. In older forms of communication, messages decay as they spread, but on social media "sharing fully reproduces the original content, allowing anyone who perceives the shared content to glean identical information as the original perceiver's representation."[7] Brady and colleagues go on to point out that

> this feature makes it more likely for someone to understand a moral violation that is the object of an emotion expression [.... But] the content that is shared is only high fidelity in the sense that it copies the way the original poster described the experience. In other words, social media allows for high fidelity sharing of emotion expression, but the original emotion expression could be an incomplete representation of the poster's experience.

An article from a satirical website like *The Onion* might go viral among people who think that it is real news, essentially shifting the kind of speech act it is understood to represent (Sullivan 2019).[8]

Other researchers have also criticized the design features of prominent social media platforms on epistemic grounds. For instance, Arfini et al. (2018) argue that the way that online communities tend to be built up emphasizes establishing as many connections as possible (cf. Facebook's supposed mantra to "connect the world"[9]), which makes them ill-suited to spreading true information. Hahn et al. (2018) use network simulations to show that connectivity (average node degree) and clustering (ratio of closed to open triangles) strongly predict failures of collective epistemic competence. Essentially, networks that are too interconnected or too clustered tend to engage in bandwagoning, which can take them toward the truth but can just as easily take them toward errors that are then very difficult to dislodge.[10] This problem is exacerbated by another common feature of social media platforms: displaying the number of times an article has already been shared by others. Research suggests that people are up to seven times more likely to share content online when they see others are already doing so (Bakshy et al. 2012). This problem relates to another common cue of trustworthiness in offline communities: if a large number of people independently come to the same conclusion, it's reasonable to place some trust in that consensus. However, in tight-knit online communities, the independence criterion is massively violated, leading people to place their trust in the madness of masses rather than the wisdom of crowds.[11]

An additional reason why highly interconnected networks tend to spread false information relates to fact-checking and content moderation. The proliferation of connections and the volume and velocity of posts on social media mean that false, poor, and unvalidated information and opinions can spread despite efforts to fact-check them. Fact-checking has traditionally been a centralized process in newsrooms. Now that people are getting their news not directly from the *New York Times* but via newsfeeds on Facebook and Twitter that may link to reputable sources such as the *Times* but may instead link to sources that perform no serious fact-checking or that intentionally promote misinformation, that fact-checking process is no longer efficient or effective. Moreover, a recent report found that content moderators for Facebook often end up believing the very conspiracy theories they are meant to screen (Newton 2019). Lewandowsky (forthcoming) argues that the current predicament is problematic in part because of the sheer volume and velocity of falsehoods (especially political falsehoods) being disseminated by accounts with immense reach, such as @realdonaldtrump on Twitter. Some of the actors on these platforms exhibit epistemic insouciance—blatant disregard for the truth (Cassam 2019; see also Benkler et al. 2018 for an analysis of systemic epistemic insouciance in the right-wing news sector in the United States). When such insouciance comes with no costs, the reputation mechanism that supports trust breaks down. Moreover, the platforms themselves are currently directed by their profit motives, which are orthogonal to or even inimical to epistemic values such as truth. Lewandowsky despairs of post-hoc fact-checking, in part because of the mere-exposure effect, which leads people to trust and believe claims they've encountered even when those claims are subsequently debunked.[12] Instead, he recommends "inoculating" people against misinformation before they encounter it by warning them that the claims they are about to encounter are untrue, exaggerated, or from an unreliable source.

A final design feature that makes the placement of trust online especially problematic also relates to reputation. As we mentioned above, when someone's reputation can suffer for spreading false information, that creates an incentive to engage in critical scrutiny before sharing. However, if someone can maintain multiple anonymous or pseudonymous accounts (as is the case on many popular platforms), this reputational concern evaporates. This is why Veliz (2018) suggests that it is important to have "sticky" pseudonyms (everyone has exactly one pseudonym that they cannot easily switch out for another pseudonym to reset their reputational score) that ensure that reputation still does its essential work.

No doubt there are other elements of human psychology and technological design that contribute to the spread of misinformation online. However, it should be clear at this point that a lot of the problems relate to the business model of these platforms: in order to make money by selling advertisements, they endeavor to promote content that captures and keeps people's attention. And as it turns out, the kind of thing that captures and keeps human attention is novel information that arouses emotional and moral reactions. Whether information is novel and arousing, however, is orthogonal to its truth value. Thus, as a side effect of their business models, these platforms end up promoting falsehoods and misinformation. What's needed, it would seem, is a change to the business model. But these companies are unlikely to voluntarily reduce their own profits. In the next section, we discuss why competitors to the current social media giants are unlikely to emerge. Then, in the final section, we make a proposal to address this problem.

The underlying problem: social media is a natural monopoly

In allegedly democratic societies in which citizens are expected to be informed enough to vote in referenda or for parliamentary representatives, the news infrastructure is clearly critical infrastructure, in much the same way that energy, water, sewage, firefighting, and so on are critical infrastructures.[13] If these are not secure, the whole society is imperiled. Unfortunately, social media platforms are now governed almost entirely by their profit motives, with little regulatory oversight. This laxity in regulation has enabled the problems documented in the previous section to run amok. For instance, social media companies are incentivized by their business models to promote engagement, which undermines the effectiveness of reputation. Similarly, these companies have an incentive to disguise dependencies among people's sources, which undermines the reliability of apparent consensus. We would (rightly) not put up with such monopolistic abuse in the case of our energy infrastructure; for instance, we require energy utilities to charge all customers the price, and to serve even those in difficult-to-reach areas. We should not put up with unregulated monopolies to run our trust infrastructure.

Unfortunately, social media is a monopoly, and the big platforms are unlikely to change their business models unless they are forced to—a problem that, to our knowledge, has not been addressed by philosophers or other normative thinkers.[14] As of the writing of this chapter, just three companies account for nearly 90% of global market share.[15] Facebook alone enjoys 64.22%, plus another 7.05% from Instagram (which Facebook owns). Twitter enjoys 13.96%, and YouTube 3.79%. This ecosystem is already an oligopoly flirting with monopoly.

In what follows, we will use Joskow's (2007) magisterial analysis and evaluation of natural monopolies to make the case that Facebook and other large platforms should either be heavily regulated, broken up through antitrust legal action, or nationalized. According to Joskow, markets dominated by natural monopolies "lead to a variety of economic performance problems: excessive prices, production inefficiencies, costly duplication of facilities, poor service quality, and to have potentially undesirable distributional impacts." He offers two definitions of natural monopoly, one for single-product markets and the other for multi-product markets. First, "a firm producing a single homogeneous product is a natural monopoly when it is less costly to produce any level of output of this product within a single firm than with two or more firms." This definition is framed in terms of efficiency: all else being equal, if it is less costly for a single firm to produce than for multiple firms to produce, markets will tend toward monopoly or oligopoly. This tends to happen when the marginal cost of producing the n + 1th product is lower than the cost of producing the nth item, for all n for which there is or might be demand, i.e. when the sector is characterized by economies of scale.[16] It should be obvious that it is nearly costless for Facebook to add one more user at this point, while it would be rather costly for a competitor firm to add their first user.

Economies of scale are sufficient but not necessary for natural monopoly. Another mechanism is *network effects* (Posner 1969). Network effects relate more to the demand side than the supply side: customers are often more inclined to join a large, existing network than to be among the first to join a smaller, newer network. As far back as 1890, De Viti de Marco pointed to network effects as causes of natural monopolies. He remarked of the telephone sector, "The consumers enjoy a utility that is greater, the greater the number of subscribers with whom they can communicate when necessary" (de Viti de Marco 1890/2001). Once again, it should be fairly obvious that there are network effects in the social media sector. Most people would rather join a network where many of their friends and acquaintances are already members than join a newer, smaller network where very few people they would like to interact with are members. An additional network effect operating in this sector is the high cost of exit for users who want to leave one platform and join another; in many cases, they would end up abandoning both the connections they had made on the incumbent platform and the content they had created there. While it is *technically* possible to export these, most users presumably lack the wherewithal to accomplish it, making them essentially prisoners of the incumbent platform.

According to Joskow's second definition, "multiproduct firms are firms that have technologies that make it more economical to produce two or more products within the same firm than in two or more firms. Production technologies with this attribute are characterized by *economies of scope*." Economies of scale are more characteristic of horizontal monopolies, whereas economies of scope are more characteristic of vertically integrated monopolies (e.g. where the firm produces intermediate goods that it then uses). To put this in context, Facebook has recently gotten into the health care sector, arguing that its existing trove of personal information could be usefully integrated with health records.[17]

Joskow argues that, whether a natural monopoly emerges due to economies of scale, network effects, or economies of scope, in general, for a natural monopoly to exist, "the proportion of fixed to variable costs must be high and [...] the products produced from competing firms must be close substitutes." One especially important type of fixed costs is sunk costs, which are not just accounting gimmicks but investments and expenditures that cannot easily be undone, such as building a road, digging a canal, constructing a telephone network, or building a social network. According to Jaskow, sunk costs "create potential opportunities for strategic behavior by the incumbent designed both to sustain prices [above] the break-even level while simultaneously discouraging entry." For instance, an incumbent can buy up their upstart competitors to ensure that none of them achieves sufficient scale to challenge the incumbent's economies of scale and scape, as well as their network advantages. Evidently, this is what Facebook did by acquiring Instagram and WhatsApp.[18]

Joskow goes on to point out that monopolies "are valuable to their owners because they produce monopoly profits. These potential profits create incentives for firms to expend resources to attain or maintain a monopoly position," including "expenditures to curry political favor to obtain a legal monopoly." Just such expenditures were made by Facebook (among other firms) to curry favor with the Trump 2016 election campaign (Kreiss & McGregor 2017). And, as we mentioned above, Facebook (though not Twitter) has committed to not fact-checking political advertising during the 2020 American Presidential race. Moreover, it was recently reported that Mark Zuckerberg, the CEO and majority shareholder of Facebook, had an undisclosed dinner with Trump in October 2019, though the content of their discussion has remained confidential.[19] In light of the theory of natural monopoly canvassed above, these developments should be extremely worrisome. They indicate that Facebook in particular, which commands the lion's share of the social media market, is in no way constrained to ensure that the content spread on its platform is trustworthy, or that peddlers of misinformation are punished reputationally. Indeed, it seems likely that some peddlers of misinformation are outright rewarded by Facebook, making reputation and the other mechanisms that support trust in large-scale interactions useless on this platform.

A proposal

If the situation is as dire as the previous section suggests, legislative or policy solutions to the problem of natural monopoly in our trust infrastructure are desperately needed. In this concluding section, we articulate three potential solutions that could be pursued either independently or in parallel: regulation, antitrust, and nationalization.

The most common and successful way to regulate a natural monopoly is to place it under an independent regulatory commission. Joskow (2007) articulates what this would look like in practice:

> This approach creates a separate board or commission, typically with a staff of engineers, accountants, finance specialists and economists, and gives it the responsibility to regulate prices and other terms and conditions of services provided by the companies that have been given charters, franchises, licenses or other permissions to provide a specific service "in the public interest." The responsibilities typically extend to the corporate forms of the regulated firms, their finances, the lines of business they may enter and their relationships with affiliates. Regulatory agencies are also given various authorities to establish accounting standards and access to the books, records and other information relevant for fulfilling their regulatory responsibilities, to approve investment plans and financings, and to establish service quality standards.

Had such a commission been in place before Facebook acquired Instagram and WhatsApp, the deals might have been prevented because they so clearly consolidated market share in a single firm. In addition, opening up the books of a secretive, privately held (indeed, *individually* held) firm like Facebook would enable regulators to examine and counteract other potential abuses of market power.

Beyond these simplistic interventions, regulation could require monopolists to allow entry by competitor firms and to better-enable current users to export their data to alternative platforms. As Joskow says, "The introduction and success of competition in one or more of these vertical segments often involves providing access to network facilities that continue to be controlled by the incumbent and subject to price regulation."

Perhaps an even more ambitious way to foster competition would be to develop an open, decentralized standard for social media similar to Standard Mail Transfer Protocol (SMTP). In fact, Twitter recently announced a new project to help build such a protocol.[20] Such a standard would make it possible for platforms to compete for market share based not just on engagement but also on accuracy, reliability, and other epistemic criteria for which their newsfeed algorithms could be optimized.

Additional regulation could help to address the problems in the economy of trust discussed above, for instance by classifying social media companies as news agencies and holding them to the standards other news agencies face, or by forcing them to move away from the current attention-economy business model toward one that is more consistent with epistemic norms. For instance, they could be required to devote a percentage of revenue to fact-checking, and people and firms that systematically share fake news and conspiracy theories could be penalized (proportionately, and in most cases temporarily) under the new regulatory regime.

Beyond regulating existing firms, it may be necessary to break up horizontally and vertically integrated monopolies in the social media sector. As we mentioned above, Facebook currently has over 70% of global market share, which should make even dyed-in-the-wool capitalists nervous. On top of that, Facebook and other social media giants are entering other sectors (e.g. health care) where their troves of data and expertise in artificial intelligence mean that they are poised to further distort markets. Antitrust law could be used to break up monopolies and ensure that no single firm dominates many markets. As Joskow says,

> To the extent that the economies of vertical integration led to the integration of a production segment with natural monopoly characteristics with a production segment without natural monopoly characteristics, the effect of vertical integration is to extend the natural monopoly to the potentially competitive segments as well.

In such cases, there is an urgent need to break the company up. The competitive component could then be allowed to continue operating in the market, while the non-competitive component could be regulated as above or nationalized as below. Breaking companies up would also make it possible to introduce tariffs on over-posting, essentially creating some friction to address the problems of velocity and volume discussed above.

Finally, the most extreme solution to the problem of natural monopoly in social media is nationalization (or some form of broader international ownership, e.g. by the European Union). As Joskow (2007; see also Andrejevic 2013) says,

> A final approach to "the natural monopoly problem" has been to rely on public ownership. Under a public ownership model, the government owns the entity providing the services, is responsible for its governance, including the choice of senior management, and sets prices and other terms and conditions. Public ownership may be effected through the creation of a bureau or department of the municipal or state government that provides the services by creating a separate corporate entity organized as a public benefit corporation with the government as its sole owner.

As the regulatory infrastructure surrounding nationalized platforms grows, democratically chosen representatives with technical expertise could experiment with tweaks to various algorithms for recommending followership and promoting content, audit the results with an eye to ensuring that trust and distrust are being managed in a reasonable way, and make suitably anonymized data and results open to researchers and the public for inspection, analysis, and deliberation. In so doing, we would be able to decide how best to place our trust, rather than allowing patterns of trust and distrust to emerge purely as a side-effect of social media platforms' business models.

Notes

1 By this, we do not mean that cooperation is impossible without trust, but that cooperation is greatly enhanced when people trust each other. In this chapter, we focus only on epistemic trust rather than practical trust.
2 See, among others, https://www.journalism.org/2018/09/10/news-use-across-social-media-platforms-2018/.
3 See, among others, https://www.theguardian.com/media/commentisfree/2020/jan/12/facebook-us-election-2020-news-lies-campaigns-fact-check.

4 See https://www.washingtonpost.com/graphics/politics/trump-claims-database/ for an updated tally.
5 See https://www.nytimes.com/2020/02/28/us/politics/trump-accuses-media-democrats-coro-navirus.html and https://www.nbcnews.com/health/health-news/man-dies-after-ingesting-chloroquine-attempt-prevent-coronavirus-n1167166.
6 See https://www.vox.com/policy-and-politics/2020/1/16/20991816/impeachment-trial-trump-ban-non-misinformation. This is related to what is sometimes called "Brandolini's Law," according to which "the amount of energy needed to refute bullshit is an order of magnitude [greater] than to produce it." See: https://twitter.com/ziobrando/status/289635060758507521.
7 This observation is distinct from the further problem that screenshots can be photoshopped and videos can be deep-faked.
8 The following website collects examples: https://literallyunbelievable.tumblr.com/.
9 See https://www.facebook.com/notes/mark-zuckerberg/bringing-the-world-closer-together/10154944663901634/.
10 For more on this, see Zollman (2007) and O'Connor & Weatherall (2018).
11 For more on this problem, see Sullivan et al. (2019) and Mercier (2020).
12 For more on the relationship between mere exposure and the spread of false information and fake news, see Levy (2017) and Alfano et al. (2020).
13 For more on critical infrastructures, see Lauge et al. (2015) and Alcaraz & Zeadally (2015).
14 As of March 4, 2020, a search searching philpapers.org for "natural monopoly" and "social media" turned up zero hits, and searching Google scholar turned up just two that seem to be relevant. For an intellectual history of the phrase and concept of natural monopoly, see Mosca (2008). For a recent monograph on this problem from the perspective of political science see Hindman (2018).
15 For up-to-date statistics, see https://gs.statcounter.com/social-media-stats.
16 This problem was already recognized by John Stuart Mill (1848).
17 See https://www.cnbc.com/2018/10/10/facebooks-dr-freddy-abnousi-wants-doctors-to-have-more-patient-data.html.
18 See https://nypost.com/2019/02/26/facebook-boasted-of-buying-instagram-to-kill-the-compe-tition-sources/.
19 See https://www.nbcnews.com/tech/tech-news/trump-hosted-zuckerberg-undisclosed-dinner-white-house-october-n1087986.
20 See https://twitter.com/jack/status/1204766078468911106.

References

Alcaraz, C. & Zeadally, S. (2015). Critical infrastructure protection: Requirements and challenges for the 21ˢᵗ century. *International Journal of Critical Infrastructure Protection*, 8: 53–66.
Alfano, M., Carter, J. A., & Cheong, M. (2018). Technological seduction and self-radicalization. *Journal of the American Philosophical Association*, 4(3): 298–322.
Alfano, M., Fard, A. E., Carter, J. A., Clutton, P., & Klein, C. (2020). Technologically scaffolded atypical cognition: The case of YouTube's recommender system. *Synthese*. https://doi.org/10.1007/s11229-020-02724-x
Alfano, M. & Huijts, N. (2020). Trust and distrust in institutions and governance. In J. Simon (ed.), *Handbook of Trust and Philosophy*. New York: Routledge, 256–71.
Alfano, M. & Klein, C. (2019). Trust in a social and digital world. *Social Epistemology Review and Reply Collective*, 8(10): 1–8.
Alfano, M. & Skorburg, J. A. (2018). Extended knowledge, the recognition heuristic, and epistemic injustice. In D. Pritchard, J. Kallestrup, O. Palermos, & J. A. Carter (eds.), *Extended Knowledge*. Oxford: Oxford University Press, 239–65.
Andrejevic, M. (2013). Public service media utilities: Rethinking search engines and social networking as public goods. *Media International Australia*, 146(1): 123–32.
Archer, A., Cawston, A., Matheson, B., & Geuskens, M. P. (2020). Celebrity, democracy, and epistemic power. *Perspectives on Politics*, 1: 27–42.
Arfini, S., Bertolotti, T., & Magnani, L. (2018). The diffusion of ignorance in on-line communities. *International Journal of Technoethics*, 9(1): 37–50.
Baier, A. (1986). Trust and antitrust. *Ethics*, 96: 231–60.

Bakshy, E., Rosenn, I., Marlow, C., & Adamic, L. (2012). The role of social networks in information diffusion. *WWW 2012 – Session: Information Diffusion in Social Networks*, April 16–20, 2012, Lyon, France, 519–28.

Benkler, Y., Faris, R., & Roberts, H. (2018). *Network Propaganda: Manipulation, Disinformation, and Radicalization in American Politics*. Princeton, NJ: Princeton University Press.

Brady, W., Crocket, M., & Van Bavel, J. (2020). The MAD model of moral contagion. The role of motivation, attention and design in the spread of moralized content online. *Perspectives on Psychological Science*, 15(4): 978–1010.

Cassam, Q. (2019). *Vices of the Mind: From the Intellectual to the Political*. Oxford: Oxford University Press.

Conway, E. & Oreskes, N. (2010). *Merchants of Doubt*. London: Bloomsbury.

D'Cruz, J. (2019). Humble trust. *Philosophical Studies*, 176(4): 933–53.

De Viti de Marco, A. (1890). L'industria dei telefoni e l'esercizio di Stato. *Giornale degli economisti*, September, 279–306.

Dezecache, G. & Dunbar, R. (2012). Sharing the joke: The size of natural language groups. *Evolution & Human Behavior*, 33(6): 775–79.

Dunbar, R. (1992). Neocortex size as a constraint on group size in primates. *Journal of Human Evolution*, 22(6): 469–93.

Dunbar, R. (1993). Coevolution of neocortical size, group size and language in humans. *Behavioral and Brain Sciences*, 16(4): 681–735.

Dunbar, R. (2005). Gossip in evolutionary perspective. *Review of General Psychology*, 8: 100–10.

Dunbar, R. (2012). On the evolutionary function of song and dance. In N. Bannan (ed.), *Music, Language and Human Evolution*, pp. 201–14. Oxford: Oxford University Press.

Elder, G. & Clipp, E. (1988). Wartime losses and social bonding: Influences across 40 years in men's lives. *Psychiatry*, 51(2): 177–98.

Fiske, S. & Taylor, S. (1984). *Social Cognition*. Boston, MA: Addison-Wesley.

Goldman, A. (2001). Experts: Which ones should you trust? *Philosophy and Phenomenological Research*, 63(1): 85–110.

Guess, A., Nagler, J., & Tucker, J. (2019). Less than you think: Prevalence and predictors of fake news dissemination on Facebook. *Science Advances*, 5: eaau4586.

Hahn, U., Hansen, J. U., & Olsson, E. (2018). Truth tracking performance of social networks: How connectivity and clustering can make groups less competent. *Synthese*, 197: 1511–41.

Hindman, M. (2018). *The Internet Trap: How the Digital Economy Builds Monopolies and Undermines Democracy*. Princeton, NJ: Princeton University Press.

James, W. (1896/1979). The will to believe. In Burkhardt, F., Bowers, F., & Skrupskelis, I. (eds.), *The Will to Believe and Other Essays in Popular Philosophy*, pp. 291–341. Cambridge, MA: Harvard University Press.

Jones, K. (2012). Trustworthiness. *Ethics*, 123(1): 61–85.

Joskow, P. (2007). Regulation of natural monopoly. In A. Polinsky & S. Shavell (eds.), *Handbook of Law and Economics*, vol. 2, pp. 1227–348. Amsterdam: Elsevier.

Klein, C., Clutton, P., & Dunn, A. (2019). Pathways to conspiracy: The social and linguistic precursors of involvement in Reddit's conspiracy theory forum. *PLOS ONE*, 14(11): 1–23.

Klein, C., Clutton, P., & Polito, V. (2018). Topic modeling reveals distinct interests within an online conspiracy forum. *Frontiers in Psychology*, 9: 189.

Kreiss, D. & McGregor, S. (2017). Technology firms shape political communication: The work of Microsoft, Facebook, Twitter, and Google with Campaigns during the 2016 U.S. presidential cycle. *Political Communication*, 35(2): 155–77.

Lauge, A., Hernantes, J., & Sarriegi, J. (2015). Critical infrastructure dependencies: A holistic, dynamic and quantitative approach. *International Journal of Critical Infrastructure Protection*, 8: 15–23.

Levy, N. (2017). The bad news about fake news. *Social Epistemology Review and Reply Collective*, 6(8): 20–36.

Lewandowsky, S. (forthcoming). The 'post-truth' world, misinformation, and information literacy: A perspective from cognitive science. In S. Goldstein (ed.), *Informed Societies – Why Information Literacy Matters for Citizenship, Participation and Democracy*. Facet Publishing.

Lu, Z., Wen, Y., & Cao, G. (2014). Information diffusion in mobile social networks: The speed perspective. In *Proceedings – IEEE INFOCOM*, 1932–1940.

Lynch, M. (2016). *The Internet of Us: Knowing More and Understanding Less in the Age of Big Data*. New York: Liveright.

Lynch, M. P. (2018). Arrogance, truth and public discourse. *Episteme*, 15(3): 283–96.

Mercier, H. (2020). *Not Born Yesterday: The Science of Who We Trust and What We Believe*. Princeton, NJ: Princeton University Press.

Meyer, M. (2019). Fake news, conspiracy, and intellectual vice. *Social Epistemology Review and Reply Collective*, 8(10): 9–19.

Mill, J. S. (1848). *The Principles of Political Economy: With Some of their Applications to Social Philosophy*. London: John W. Parker.

Mosca, M. (2008). On the origins of the concept of natural monopoly: Economies of scale and competition. *The European Journal of the History of Economic Thought*, 15(2): 317–53.

Meyer, M. & Alfano, M. (under review). Fake news, conspiracy theories, and intellectual virtue.

Newton, C. (2019). The trauma floor: The secret lives of Facebook moderators in America. *The Verge*. https://www.theverge.com/2019/2/25/18229714/cognizant-facebook-content-moderator-interviews-trauma-working-conditions-arizona, accessed 20 December 2020.

Nguyen, C. T. (2018). Echo chambers and epistemic bubbles. *Episteme*: 17(2): 141–61.

Nguyen, C. T. (forthcoming). Trust as an unquestioning attitude. *Oxford Studies in Epistemology*.

O'Connor, C. & Weatherall, J. (2018). *The Misinformation Age*. New Haven, NJ: Yale University Press.

Origgi, G. (2017). *Reputation: What It Is and Why It Matters*. Princeton, NJ: Princeton University Press.

Pariser, E. (2011). *The Filter Bubble: What the Internet is Hiding from You*. New York: Penguin Press.

Posner, R. (1969). Natural monopoly and regulation. *Stanford Law Review*, 21: 548–643.

Sullivan, E. (2019). Beyond testimony: When online information sharing is not testifying. *Social Epistemology Review and Reply Collective*, 8(10): 20–24.

Sullivan, E., Sondag, M., Rutter, I., Meulemans, W., Cunningham, S., Speckmann, B., & Alfano, M. (2019). Can real social epistemic networks deliver the wisdom of crowds? In T. Lombrozo, J. Knobe, & S. Nichols (eds.), *Oxford Studies in Experimental Philosophy*, 29–63. Oxford: Oxford University Press.

Sunstein, C. (2017). *#Republic: Divided Democracy in the Age of Social Media*. Princeton, NJ: Princeton University Press.

Sutton, J. (1991). *Sunk Costs and Market Structure*. Boston, MA: MIT Press.

Veliz, C. (2018). Online masquerade: Redesigning the Internet for free speech through the use of pseudonyms. *Journal of Applied Philosophy*, 36(4): 643–58.

Vosoughi, S., Roy, D., & Aral, S. (2018). The spread of true and false news online. *Science*, 359: 1146–51.

Weatherall, J., O'Connor, C., & Bruner, J. (2019). How to beat science and influence people: Policymakers and propaganda in epistemic networks. *British Journal for the Philosophy of Science*, 71(3): 1157–86.

Zollman, K. (2007). The communication structure of epistemic communities. *Philosophy of Science*, 74(5): 574–87.

INDEX

Note: *Italic* page numbers refer to figures and page numbers followed by "n" denote endnotes.

Abduh, M. 39, 40
Aberdein, A. 331
accountability 15, 434, 435, 442, 443
Achen, C. 156, 160
acquisition 353; epistemic corruption 353; of
    false beliefs 320; of knowledge and virtue 47;
    of political information 248
adaptive beliefs 157, 158
ad hominem argumentation 330
administrative agencies 427, 428
adversariality 331, 333n11
affective polarization 87, 163, 199; behavioral
    evidence 94–95; implicit measures 92–93;
    social distance indicators 93–94; survey
    measures, partisan affect *91*, 91–92
Affordable Care Act 97
al-Afghani, Jamal al-Din 39
Aikin, S. F. 177, 332
Alfano, M. 199, 434, 480, 481
Al-Qaeda 40
'alternative facts' 1, 79, 80, 195, 305
American National Elections Studies (ANES)
    375, 381, 414, 415
American politics 87; affective 91–95; definition
    90; in-group *vs.* out-group distinction 90,
    92; partisan identity 90–91; partisans and co-
    partisans 95; social homophily 96
Amplify Voices Inside 344
Anarcho-Socialism 42–43
Anderson, C. 260, 345n6
Anderson, E. 337, 338, 341, 449, 450
anthropogenic climate change 471, 475, 477
anti-ballistic missile systems 439
anti-drug program 278
anti-elitist rhetoric 446

anti-EU ideology 307
anti-fake news legislation 171
anti-labor management 230
'anti-Perfectionist' Liberals 41
anti-Semitic conspiracy theories 302
anti-tyranny 80, 82
Appiah, A. 376
Aquinas, T. St. 37
arbitrariness-based objections 114
Arendt, H. 1, 3, 11, 12, 55–63, 170, 231, 232,
    453; culture and politics 56; factual truths
    (*see* factual truths); judgment and decision 56;
    opinion- formation 62; plurality and equality
    62; politico-philosophical perspective 55;
    press, "branch of government" 55; truth and
    knowledge 56; truth *vs.* politics 55
Arfini, S. 484
argumentation virtue theorists 331
Argument from Ignorance 470, 471, 473
Aristotle 17–18
A System of Logic (1843) 45, 46
Athenian democracy 11; *boulē* (council) 14;
    dikastai (jurors) 14; *ekklēsia* (assembly) 14;
    evidence 15; political participation 13
The Atlantic (Serwer) 274
Austin, J. L. 103
authenticity, value of 464
Avoiding Obvious Falsehoods Norm 402

backfire effect 179, 186
Bacon, F. 67, 70
bad political judgements 327
Baehr, J. 148, 153
Bagehot, W. 350
Baghramian, M. 434

Baier, A. 481
Ballantyne, N. 219, 453
Bannon, S. 482
Barberá, P. 197
Bar-Joseph, U. 302
Bartels, L. 156, 160
"base-rate neglect" 270
Battaly, H. 299
behavioral economics 269, 270
belief-first model 156, 163
belief-forming process 106
beliefs 88, 115, 116, 117, 120; arbitrariness 116;
    attitudes and beliefs 182; constitutive norm
    of 389; COVID-19 pandemic 208; epistemic
    circularity 105–106; fake news 184–187; false
    (*see* false beliefs); misinformation 215–216;
    phenomenology of 389; polarisation 198–199;
    propaganda 226–230; public 210; rationality
    128; religious 123; social shaping 76–77 (*see
    also* truth); true 183; truth 163; truth-aspiring
    nature of 389
Bellarmine, C. 102–104
Benkler, Y. 197
Bentham, J. 45, 46, 50
Berinsky, A. 183
Berkeley, G. 45, 46, 65
Bernal, J.D. 437
bias blind spot 219, 240, 274, 279–281
biased group thinking 340–342, 345n8
big data 93
Bin Laden, O. 40
Blackburn, S. 12
Black Lives Matter 341, 342
Blair, T. 243, 354
blame, notion of 290
Bloom, P. 158
Blue Lives Matter (slogan) 341
Boghossian, P. 103, 104, 106
Bohman, J. 413
Boomgaarden, H. 255
Booth, A. 3, 11–12
Boswell, C. 448
Boudreau, C. 254
Boult, C. 6, 254, 362
Boutyline, A. 197
Boxell, L. 97
Boyd, K. 240
Brady, W. 483
Bramson, A. 139, 140, 198
Brennan, J. 361, 453
Brexit:identity 101, 102; referendum 433; voters
    274, 302–304
Bridgman, P. 438
British voters 374
Brown, É. 5, 170
Bruner, J. 209, 210
Bullock, J.G. 159, 183, 184
Bush, G. W. 172

Bush, V. 438
Buss, S. 218
Buturovic, Z. 277

Caliph concept 35
Campbell, A. 354
Capella, J. N. 197
capitalism 350; politico-economic structure
    of 308
Caplan, B. 410, 411
Card, C. 353
Cardenal, A. S. 194, 197
Carlyle, T. 45, 46
Carothers, T. 137
Carter, J.A. 87
Cassam, Q. 299, 348
Catriona, conservative narrative 290
Chamberlain, J. 67
Chinese political theory: communitarian
    consequentialism 24; conformity 29;
    epistemic authority 27–28; epistemic
    consensus 32; epistemic unity 30; legitimacy
    30–33; origin of, Mohists 25–27; rewards and
    punishments 29, 32; social order 29, 30
Choi, D. 195
Christiano, T. 415
Church, I. M. 327
Cicero 19
citizens 299, 326, 381; administrative agencies
    428; considering non-electoral democracy
    427–429; epistemic responsibilities of 409;
    knowledge 425
civic friendship 216–217
civic peers 125–127
Civil Service 347
Clanton, C. J. 332
"classical" pragmatism 385
Clegg, N. 307
Clifford, S. 184
climate change 285–287, 289, 317
climate change skepticism 7, 434, 469, 470,
    471–473, 477
climate science 276, 459
Clinton, H. 96, 176, 216, 302
Clinton voters 159, 182, 277, 279; *vs.* Trump
    voters 275
Clint's case 313, 314
closed-mindedness 5–6, 299, 301, 303, 312–314,
    312–317, 318, 321–323, 348, 356
Code, L. 195, 200, 342, 343
coercive power 3, 41, 127
cognitive asymmetries 286
cognitive bias 2, 4, 5, 124, 196, 219, 228, 239,
    240, 242, 248, 280, 325, 326, 340, 341, 342,
    375, 434, 453, 454
cognitive diversity 6, 259–260, 361, 364–365,
    366–369, 368, 369, 371n3, 377, 412, 413
Cognitive Reflection Test (CRT) 185

cognitive science 181; attitudes and beliefs 182; "Birther" theory 182; Obamacare 182
cognitive symmetry 286; between liberals and conservatives 286, 287
Cohen, G. 161
Cohen, J. 161
Cohen, J. 330
Colbert Report 172
Cold War 304, 350, 433, 437
Coleridge, S. T. 45
collective agents 348; collective epistemic agency 344
collective cancellation effects 349
collectivism 348, 349
Collingwood, R. G. 72
Collins, H. 450
communal identity 75
communicative dysfunctions 341
community trust 425
comparative advantage theory 244
"competence" conditions 412
competence principle 377–378
compromise policy 118
Comte, A. 45
Condorcet Jury Theorem (CJT) 367, 371n6, 377, 412
de Condorcet, M. 371n7
Conee, E. 148, 149
confirmation bias 196
consequentialism (reliabilism) 352, 462
conservatism 45, 162, 279
conservative narrative, law and order 290
conservative pundit 265
Considerations on Representative Government (1861) 45, 50
considering non-electoral democracy: citizen, technocratic agencies with 427–429; epistemic promise of 425; incentive alignment 427–429; lottocratic institutions 426–427; political morality, constraints of 424
conspiracy: scenario 472–473, 475; theory 268
contemporary pragmatism 385
contextualism 108
Converse, P. 162–163
Conway, E. M. 209, 472, 474, 482
Conway, K. 79–80
'corporate character' 350
cosmopolitanism 12
cost of voting 242, 257
COVID-19 pandemic 312, 314, 315, 320, 443
Craig, E. 66
Cratylus 69
credentials problem 449
"crime," definition of 289
criminality, racist stereotypes of 341–342, 345
criminal justice system 341

critical insensitivity: collective vice of 342; in echo chambers 340; epistemic group vice of 340; epistemic vice of 330, 336–338
critical sensibility 340
Croce, M. 434
Crowd Beats Average Law 368
cultural cognition theory 340
culture and politics 56
'cultures of secrecy' 354
cyberbalkanization 193, 196

Davis, D. 316, 318
D'Cruz, J. 481
decision-making process 327, 369, 378
deep disagreement 103; 'non-Archimedean' deep disagreement 103
de facto mechanism 461
DeGroot, M. H. 139
deliberation 11, 412; co-deliberation 79; collective 13; democratic context 18; liberal democracy 50–52; postures 80; rational 14; voting 163
democracy: in ancient Greece 13–20; citizenship 216, 239; conception of 384, 387; conformity 49–50; critiques of 410, 414; decision-making 408; democratic government 299; epistemic capacity of 384; epistemic view of 362; independent effect of 380; liberalism 69; normative conception of 388; "pure proceduralist" theories 249; scientific expertise 435; threaten 97
democratic culture 302
democratic deliberation: "disfiguration" of 370; epistemic benefits of 412; epistemic properties of 365; epistemic value of 366; implications of 413
Democratic Party 276
democratic theory 5, 6, 12, 89, 163, 240, 248–249, 387, 388, 407, 409, 410; and epistemology 407; implications for 248–249; rational ignorance 245
DeRose, K. 470
Derrida, J. 73
desire-dependence 69; epistemic rationality 115; practical rationality 115
despotic power 3
De Viti de Marco, A. 486
De Vreese, C.H. 255
Deweyan democracy 386, 388
Dewey, J. 65, 362, 384, 385–387, 435–437, 453
Dillon, R. 353
Dinges, A. 254
disagreement 11, 123, 171; causes 124–125; circularity question 102, 105–106; civic peers 125–127; depth question 102–104; epistemic 114, 129; epistemic peers 125, 126, 129; evidence 124; experiences and circumstances 125; factual truth 59; healthy democracy 87;

idealized conception 126, 130; ideal theory/
non-ideal theory 88, 126, 131; inheritance
tax 118; interpretation 124; legitimate
government 127; rational resolution 128;
relativism 107–109; social epistemology 127;
types 125; values 125
discriminatory epistemic injustice 259
discursive model 340, 341
Disraeli, B. 67
Ditto, P.H. 278, 280
diversity 377; epistemic diversity 18, 45, 47;
imperialism 12
Diversity Prediction Theorem 368
Diversity Trumps Ability Theorem 366,
371n4, 377
Divine Authority 41, 42
dogmatism 269, 307, 313, 331, 347, 348, 355,
403, 475
Dotson, K. 195
doubt 7, 106
doubt liberalism 81
Douglas, H. 433
Downs, A. 411
doxastic attitudes 120
'drain the swamp,' attractions of 306
DuBridge, L. 439
Dunbar, R. 481
Dunning-Kruger effect 453
Durham County Detention Facility
(DCDF) 343

echo chambers 192, 194–195, 198–200;
characterization of 339; critical insensitivity
in 340
economic inequality 304, 306;
exclusionary-type echo chamber 195;
rumour echo chambers 195
Edenberg, E. 88
Edlin, A. 258
education 277, 279, 280
effects-virtues 312
egalitarianism 13
Eisenhower administration 439
electoral representative democracy 419;
epistemic challenges for 421–423; modern
politics, conditions of 420–421
empathetic understanding 414
empathy, lack of 309
empirical political epistemology 264
empiricism 45
endoxic method 17
engaging closed-mindedly: definitions and
distinctions 313; objections of 321; in Polluted
Feed 316, 319; virtue-consequentialist
argument 321
The English Constitution (Bagehot) 350
enlightened preference voting
379–381

epistemic: activism 342–344; advocacy 343;
agency 337; argument 391; attitudes 4;
behavior 337; commitment 119; conception
391; condition 458; empowerment 342,
343; environment 316, 317, 339; externalist
106; justification 4; liberalism 45–46;
responsibility 199–200; segregation 195–196;
self-empowerment 344; subjectivity 342
epistemically virtuous persons 312, 316
epistemic asymmetry thesis 285; climate change
286; cognitive asymmetries 286; ideologically
motivated reasoning 287; in intellectual
virtue 291; internalist and externalist
approaches 290; Kahan's argument
against 288
epistemic authority: knowledge and expertise
46; political authority 27–28; substantiating
function 48
epistemic bubbles 194, 339–341; discursive
"epistemic" bubbles 341
epistemic corruption 352–353; analysts of 356n7;
characterization of 300, 353; collective
motivations 352; definition of 353; mode of
353; of political institutions 355
epistemic deference: argument for 460;
downstream effects of 462; epistemic and
ethical aspects of 459; labor-based argument
461; political epistemology 458; political
testimony conflicts 464; risk and trust 465;
testimony and value 462
epistemic democracy 362, 370, 384, 407,
412–414
epistemic elites 48, 50
Epistemic Justice Norm 404
epistemic libertarianism 45–46, 410–412
epistemic lucidity 338
epistemic motivation 329, 330
epistemic paternalism 285
epistemic peers 125, 126, 129
epistemic value 328, 361
epistemic vices 5–6, 17, 267, 300, 301–309, 312,
320, 325, 336–341, 343, 348, 351–354
epistemic virtues 5–6, 17, 300, 301, 308, 312,
325, 336–339, 348, 351, 354; group dynamics
337; privilege, insensitivity of 337
epistocracy 6, 15, 361–362, 374–382, 385, 407,
411, 433
Estlund, D. 284, 364, 384, 410
Evans, R. 450
evidence 173, 206, 210; desire-dependence
115–116; political beliefs 161–163; political
disagreements 104
evidence-based political decisions 299
evidentialism 35–36, 35–37; evidentialist
analysis 146–151; evidentialist theory 4, 88,
145; proof of prophecy 36–37
*An Examination of Sir William Hamilton's
Philosophy* (Mill) 45

"expert," definition of 446
expertise theory 7, 46, 50, 447; dimension
    of 448; epistemic responsibility of 450;
    Goldman's theory 447; knowledge 46; realist
    approach 448; and realist theory of 447;
    recognition problem for 449
expressive rationality 278–279
"externalism" 291

Facebook 220–221, 321, 481, 486, 487
factual evidence 58
factual truths: characteristics 57; normativity
    58–60; *vs.* rational 56–58; validity 60–62
"faculty virtues" 292
'Fairness Doctrines' in United States 355
faith-based belief 436
fake news 4–5, 169, 170; anti-fake news
    legislation 171; beliefs 184–187; borderline
    cases 177–178; 'bullshit' 175, 176; cognitive
    science 181–187; Covid-19 pandemic 171;
    dimensions 173–174; epistemic dimension
    173, 175; epistemic routines 179; exploratory
    concept 172; Facebook 172; functional
    role 173; intentional dimension 173, 175;
    journalistic mistakes 173; media literacy 172;
    medium dimension 173, 175; post-truth 174;
    proposals types 179; SARS-CoV 2 virus 171;
    Twitter 172
fallibility 265, 267
Fallis, D. 176, 177
Falsafa 36, 39
false beliefs 157, 159, 227; decision-making 203;
    domain-specific knowledge 203; models
    205–208; social epistemology 203–205
false consciousness 307
false news 173, 220–221
false testimony 58
Fantl, J. 312, 316, 319
al-Farabi 37, 38, 39, 42, 43n13
faultless 88
Federal Advisory Committee Act
    (FACA) 439, 441
Feldman, R. 148, 149
Fershtman, C. 94
filter bubbles 192–195, 198–200
First Five Grieving Committee 344
first-order belief 267
first-personal doxastic norms 391
Fisher, M. 330
Flaxman, S. 197
Fleck, L. 71
Foreign Policy magazine 274
Fox News 341, 342
Frank, T. 275, 304
Fraser, C. 3, 11
Freedom of Information Act 441
Frege, G. 69
French Jr. J. 139

Fricker, M. 300, 349, 350
Friedman, J. 240, 243, 246, 309; rationally
    ignorant voter 247

Galbraith, J. K. 304
Galileo 102–104
Galton, F. 368
Ganzach, Y. 275
Garwin, R. 439
Gelfert, A. 4, 169, 177
Gelman, A. 242
Gentzkow, M. 97
geocentrism 103
George W. Bush 186
Gerken, M. 259
German culture 266, 267
Geschke, D. 196
Gettier, E. 65, 66
Gift, K. 95
Gift, T. 95
Gilbert, M. 349, 350
Gilens, M. 380
globalisation 305
Gneezy, U. 94
"gnostic account" 447
Goldman, A. 38, 447
Golub, B. 206
Goodhart, D. 304
Goodman, N. 385
Gorgias (Plato) 239
Gove, M. 396, 433
governance, complexities of 436
Granovetter, M. 206
Greco, J. 447
Greek democracy 13–20
Greene, A. 3, 12
Grim, P. 135, 136, 137, 140
Grote, G. 51
group-addressing speech 231
group-agency landscape 230, 234
group behaviour 328
group cognition model 340, 341
group-forming speech 231
group polarization theory 340
Grundmann, R. 447, 450
Grundmann, T. 176
Guerrero, A. 6, 362
Guess, A. M. 179, 187, 214, 219, 483
gullibility 302, 306, 308
Gunn, H. K. 170

Haack, S. 385
Habermas, J. 82, 364, 365, 396, 397, 405n4
Hahn, U. 484
Haidt, J. 79, 83n9, 280, 375, 413
Halberstam, Y. 197
Hales, S. D. 105
Hannon, M. 88, 405n1, 413, 414

Hare, T. 51
Hartley 46
Hatemi, R. K. 96
Hawthorne, J. 260
Hayek, F. A. 52
Hegselmann, R. 133, 138, 139
Hellenistic philosophy 18–20
Henderson, J. 246
Hobbes, T. 65
Holman, B. 209, 210
homophily 196
Hong, L. 366, 368, 370
Hong-Page Theorem 377
Huber, G. A. 93, 94
Huijts, N. 480
human flourishing theory 387
Hume, D. 45, 46, 65, 68
Hussein, S. 178
Hyska, M. 4, 170

Ibn Rushd 37
Ibn Sina 37
ideal conditions 336
idealized climate change skeptic 474–475
ideal theory 336
"identifying upward" process *see* Chinese
    political theory
identity-expressive discourse 341
"identity prejudice" 403
identity protective cognition 184, 278
ideological innocence 163
ideologically motivated reasoning (IMR) 287
ideological polarization 96, 97, 163
ideological variability 280
Ignatieff, M. 307
ignorance 57; extensive citizen ignorance 421;
    and feminist epistemology 195; inadvertent
    ignorance 242; individual-level ignorance
    259; irrational ignorance 239, 242; original
    argument for 473; political ignorance
    239–250, 253–261, 308, 326, 409, 411, 414;
    and politics, irrationality in 5
immigration 348
impartiality 12, 60, 75, 78
inadvertent ignorance theory 239, 242, 245–247
'in-between' beliefs 160–161
incentive alignment 427–429
Independence Thesis 207
independent expertise 436–437
individual agents 348
indulgent pluralism 113, 115, 116, 120
industrial selection 210, 211
information cascades 195
information shortcuts 248
information technology revolution 247
'inherently undemocratic' ideology 304
insensitivity 309

Inside-Outside Alliance (IOA) 344
insight condition 458
Instagram 486, 487
institutional epistemic corruption 352–356
institutional epistemic vices 303, 351
institutional ethos 348–352; of accountability
    351; definition of 350
intellectual charity 266, 267
intellectual humility 219
intelligence 276
Intemann, K. 317
Intergovernmental Panel on Climate Change
    (IPCC) 474
internalist and externalist approaches 290
interpretive charity 266
invariantism 108, 109
irrational "emotion and ideology" 270
irrational ignorance 239, 242, 247–248
Irrationality Condition (IC) 5, 228
Islamic democracy 42
Islamic Moderate Evidentialism 12, 35–38, 41,
    42, 43
Islamic modernism 39–41
Islamic Modernist Reform movement 39, 40
Islamic Philosophy: Anarcho-Socialism 42–43;
    Caliph concept 35; 'classical' period 35;
    Divine Authority 41, 42; Evidentialism
    35–37; Islamic democracy 42; Liberalism
    35, 40; 'Modernist' Movement 35; Muslim
    Brotherhood 40; neo-Marxism 39–41;
    'Perfectionist' Liberalism 41, 42; political
    legitimacy 41; prophet law-maker 38–39;
    Qutb 41–42; Western Capitalism 40; Western
    democracy 42
Iyengar, S. 87, 92, 94, 97, 183

Jackson, M. O. 205, 206
James, W. 70, 385, 386
Jamieson, K. H. 197
Jasanoff, S. 448
Jaster, R. 176
Johnson, B. 266
'joint commitment model' 350
Jones, K. 481, 482
Joskow, P. 485–487
Jost, J. T. 279
journalism 79
Justified Belief Norm 401, 402

Kahan, D.M. 184–185, 270, 278, 285, 287, 291,
    333n7, 340
Kalmoe, N. 162
Kant, I. 45, 218
Keil, F. C. 330
Kelly, P. 12
Kelly, T. 153
Khalidi, R. 42

Kidd, I. J. 2–3, 6, 300, 309n3
Kinder, D. 162
al-Kindi 36, 37
Kippur, Y. 304
Klein, D. B. 277, 481
Klofstad, C. 96
Knight, B. 197
knowledge 65, 277; acquisition 46, 47, 49, 50; and action relationship 254; Anarcho-Socialism 42–43; in ancient Greece 13–20; esoteric 37; expertise 46; scientific belief 46; and truth 56
Knowledge Norm 400–402
Kornblith, H. 147–148
Krause, U. 133, 138, 139
Kruglanski, A. 302
Kuhnian paradigm shift 117
Kuhn, T. 71
Kuklinski, J. 162

labor-based argument 461
labor, epistemic division of 460
labor market 95
Lahroodi, R. 349
Landemore, H. 361, 367, 377, 412, 413
Langer, G. 160
Lanius, D. 176
legitimation 81
legitimizing function 448
Lelkes, Y. 97
Lenin, V. 40
Lerman, R. 182
Levy, N. 169–170, 175, 288–291, 312, 316, 319, 320, 481
Lewandowsky, S. 286
liberal democracies 214
Liberal Democrat party 307
liberalism 35, 40, 52–54, 69; internal economy 80
liberal multiculturalism 53–54
liberal narrative 290
liberal political cognition 288
Lillehammer, H. 434
Lind, M. 304
Lippmann, W. 216, 435, 436, 453
literature curiosity 292
Locke, J. 45
Lodge, M. 269, 271
Lord, C.G. 141
lottocracy 426, 428; lottocratic institutions 426–427
Lovejoy, A. O. 385
Luks, S. 182
Lupia, A. 254, 281, 414
Lutzke, L. 186
Lynch, M. 474

McCain, K. 148, 149, 150, 275
McConnell, C. 95
McDermott, R. 96
MacFarlane, J. 107–109
McGrath, S. 182
McIntyre, L. 312, 316, 317, 320
McKenna, R. 240
Mackie, G. 415
McWilliam, E. C. 88
Madison, J. 239
Malhotra, N. 93, 94
marginalized groups 258, 259
Marxist view 308
Mason, L. 95
Mathiesen, K. 176, 177
Maududi, Abul A'la 12, 42
Mayo-Wilson, C. 207
media literacy 172
'mediated corruption' 353
medieval Islamic philosophy 12
Medina, J. 2–3, 5–6, 195, 300, 309, 343, 344, 348
Meiklejohn, A. 216
de Melo-Martin, I. 317
Merkel, A. 266
Merkley, E. 186
Merton, R. 437
Meyerson, D. 308
Michaelson, E. 172–173
Michael Williams 102
Millar, A. 302, 328, 365
Miller, B. 194
Mill, J. S. 1, 3, 11, 12, 45–53, 70, 76, 77, 80, 82, 245, 249, 328, 365, 366, 403, 411; British East India Company 52, 53; censorship 47; education 48; epistemic elites 48, 50; epistemic liberalism 45–46; expertise 46, 50; knowledge acquisition 46, 47, 49, 50; knowledge growth 53; liberal multiculturalism 53–54; libertarian approach 47; liberty *vs.* authority 49; moral elites 50; non-propositional speech 47; populism 50; religious beliefs 48; representative government 49, 51; truths 48
Mills, C. 195
minority group 258, 259, 276
minority voter 258
"miracle of aggregation" theory 248, 367, 368, 369, 371n6, 377, 412
Misak, C. 385
misinformation 4–5, 169, 187; alarmist 214; beliefs 215–216; civic friendship 216–217; deflationary 214; democratic citizens 216; governmental action 221–223; individual self-regulation 218–220; intentional 215; liberal democracies 214; personal autonomy 217–218; physical harm 217; platform-based

innovations 220–221; political judgements 216; spread of 215
Mò Dí 24
Mohseni, A. 208
Mooney, C. 276
Moorean assessments 391
Moore, G. E. 389, 392n14
moral elites 50
Moss, S. 147
"motivated ignorance" 242
"motivated-reasoning" framework 269
"motivated skepticism" 242
Muhammad (Prophet) 35, 36
Mukerji, N. 175
Munton, J. 152
Muslim Brotherhood 40
myside bias 278–279

naïve realism 265, 268–271; methodological consequence of 266
Nawar, T. 3, 11
neo-Marxism 39–41
network effects 486
The New Republic 274
The New York Times 55, 267, 484
Nguyen, C. T. 194, 339, 481
Nixon, R. 439; administration 435
"noble lie," social harmony 11
"non-electoral democracy" 423
non-electoral systems 420
non-epistemic conceptions 384, 385
non-epistemicism 409, 410
non-liberal societies 81
Nyhan, B. 214, 219

Obama, B. 98, 156, 182
Oberauer, K. 286
Ober, J. 14, 15
O'Connor, C. 5, 133, 141, 142, 170, 207, 208
O'Donohue, A. 137
Olbermann, K. 98
The Onion 483
On Liberty (1859) 45, 47, 48
online communities 195
online misinformation *see* misinformation
open-mindedness 315, 316, 318, 319
optimism 412
Ordinary Science Intelligence scale 184
Oreskes, N. 209, 472, 474, 482
The Origins of Totalitarianism (1994) 231
Osmundsen, M. 216
Ottoman Empire 39

Page, S. 366–368
pandemic examples 263–264
Parfit, D. 255
Pariser, E. 193, 194
Parliamentary Select Committees 347

"participatory budgeting" 428
partisan asymmetries 285, 291
partisan epistemology 288–291
partisanship agreement 93, 96
Party Implicit Association Test 92
"party of science" 276, 277
Paul, L. A. 117
Peircean approach 388
Peircean-pragmatist insights 391
Peirce, C. S. 65, 69, 285, 385, 388
Pennycook, G. 185, 187, 221
Pentagon Papers 55
Pepp, J. 172–173
Perfectionism 42
'Perfectionist' Liberalism 41, 42
permissivism 113, 114, 118
personalisation algorithm 193, 194
Peter, F. 6, 362
Peterson, E. 183
Pinillos, N. Ángel 254
Plato 1, 3, 11, 13, 15–17, 19, 20, 20n5, 39, 50, 65, 67, 169, 239, 264, 361, 407; democracy 239; *Gorgias* 239; 'master argument' against democracy 15–17, 19
pluralism 88; arbitrariness 113–114; indulgent 113, 115, 116, 118; practical 115, 116; reasonable 113, 114
Pohlhaus, G. Jr. 2–3
Polanyi, M. 438
polarisation 3–4, 87, 327; affective 91–95; beliefs 198–199; communities 198–199; definition 90; in-group *vs.* out-group distinction 90, 92; partisan identity 90–91; partisans and co-partisans 95; politics 198–199; self-categorization theory 104; social homophily 96; Western democracies 101
political action, practical rationality of 257
political and "hot" scientific issues 287, 291
political authority 11; epistemic authority 27–28; legitimacy 25, 32; origin of 25–27
political belief-formation 4, 5
political decision-making process 395, 411, 433
political deliberation 75; citizens' ignorance 325; epistemic norms of 397; epistemic value of 328; ideas and arguments 325; normative role of 395; political decisions 395; political legitimacy 396; and shared biases 325; truth norm of 399
political disagreement 3–4; *see also* disagreement
political equality 58
"political fans" 244, 245
political ignorance 239; in challenging democracy 414; definition of 254; epistemic injustice 258–259; *vs.* pragmatic encroachment 240; rational ignorance idea 241; voter ignorance 421
political irrationality: false attributions of 271; naïve realism 268–271; pandemic examples 263;

political ignorance to 240; political psychologism 264

'Political Islam' 35, 40

political knowledge 240; concept of 258; definition of 254; and political ignorance 254–256; pragmatic encroachment 259–260; representative of 415

"political knowledge scales" 414

Political legitimacy 6, 12, 30–32, 396; Islamic Philosophy 41; truth 80–81

Politico 268

Polluted Feed 312, 314–316; engaging closed-mindedly 316–317; McIntyre's argument 317–319

Polybius 19

Popper, K. 52

"popular sovereignty model" 375

popular sovereignty, "tracking" conception of 424

populism 49–50

post-Hellenistic philosophy 18–20

postmodernism 65, 71–73

post-truth 12, 67–71; accuracy 74; dynamics 74; dystopia 78; environment 65; fake news 174; heartlanders 75, 76; metropolitans 75; political climate 74; politics 3, 80, 81, 82, 396; sincerity 74

practical identities, multiplicity of 349

pragmatic encroachment 240, 253–254; acquiring political knowledge 258; critics of 258; epistemic injustice 258–259; general consequence of 256; political action, practical rationality of 257; political ignorance 258–259; political knowledge value 259–260; rationalizing political ignorance 257–258

"pragmatism" 362, 385, 386

Pratchett, T. 193

Presidential Science Advisory Committee (PSAC) 439

Principle of Charity 302, 303, 306

The Principles of Political Economy (1848) 45

Prior, M. 183

privilege, insensitivity of 337

procedural epistemic norms 402

proceduralism 410

'professionalism' 304

Pronin, E. 279

propaganda 4–5, 169, 170; belief 226–230; epistemic communities 208–211; Negative Ideology 40; positive account 231–233; Positive Ideology 40

public ignorance 244

"pure proceduralist" theories 249

Putnam, H. 46

Quine, W.V.O. 46

Quirk, P. 377

Qutb, S. 40

racism 317, 338

radical skepticism 7

Ramsey 65

rational choice theory 244

rational decision-maker 242

rational deliberation 14

rational ignorance: formal social science analysis 244; framework of 247; idea of 241, 242; inadvertent ignorance 242, 245–247; irrational ignorance 242, 247–248; theory of 239, 243, 244

'rational irrationality' 326

rationalism 36–37

rationality: belief states 123–124, 128; desire-dependence 115–116; doxastic attitudes 119; epistemic 114, 115, 290; indulgent practical pluralism 115; instrumental 5; moral commitments 116; practical 114; resoluteness *vs.* readiness to revise 116–118

rationally ignorant voter 247

rational political ignorance 255

rational truth-seeking 265

Rawlsian idiom 388

Rawls, J. 1, 2, 113, 123, 124, 136, 140, 362, 387, 388, 396

Reasonable Pluralism 113, 114, 118

Record, I. 194

'regulative epistemology' 348

Reifler, J. 214, 219

relativism 102, 103, 107–109

relativist semantics 107–108

religious beliefs 48, 123

Republican Party 276

"responsibilist virtue epistemology" (RVE) 292

responsibility 408

responsiblism 352

Responsiveness Norm 403

"retrospective voting" 248

"rich trustworthiness" 480

de Ridder, J. 88, 405n1

Rini, R. 174, 220, 288–291, 312, 316, 319, 321, 322

Rodrigo, C. M. 221

Rogers, B. W. 205

Roman liberty 19

Romney voters 275

Rorty, R. 103, 385

Rosenstock, S. 207

Ross, L. 269

Ross, R. 169–170

Rothstein, B. 353

Rowland, R. 88

Rozenbeek, J. 219

Rutte, M. 401

Ru Ye 117

Sally's false consciousness 307–308

Salter, L. 448

Samuelson, P. L. 327
Sandis, C. 308
Sankey, H. 12, 105
Sari, Y. 12
"satisficing" decision 242
scepticism 45, 68, 72, 105, 219
Schaffner, B.F. 182
Schelling 45
Scheman, N. 453, 454
Schwitzgebel, E. 160
science curiosity 291–292
"science denialism" 286
scientific expertise: independence model for 435;
    normative issues 436
scientific funding model 438
secret Internet technologies 194
selective sharing 210
self-deception 78
Sellars, W. S. 71
Shapiro, J. M. 97
sheer aggregation procedure 18
Shermer, M. 279
shortcut literature, critics of 248
Simon, H. 242
Simpson, R. 4, 88
Singer, D. J. 4, 88, 133, 136, 137–142, 140, 141
skeptical scenario 470
skepticism: anti-skeptical view 475; external
    world skeptic 470; problem of 469
social bonding 158
social identity 4, 5
socially adaptive beliefs 157–159
social media 169, 485
Society for Freedom in Science (SFS) 437
Somin, I. 255, 332n1, 410, 411
Sommers, S. 337, 338
Son of Heaven policy 25–30
Sood, G. 97
Sosa, E. 105, 106
Soviet Communism 438
Sparling, R.A. 353
Standard Mail Transfer Protocol (SMTP) 487
Stanley, J. 228, 233, 302
Stanovich, K. 240
Starbird, K. 215
Stephenson, N. 192
Sterken, R. 172–173
Stevens, K. 331
Strong, T. B. 61
substantive epistemic norms 400
Sullivan, E. 434
Sunstein, C. 193, 194, 195, 340
system democracy 381
systemic racism 320

Taber, C. 269, 271
'take back control,' attractions of 306

Talisse, R. B. 6, 177, 199, 362 6, 177, 199, 362
Tanesini, A. 5–6, 300, 308
technocratic liberalism 304
Tessman, L. 353
therapeutic trust 451
Thompson, A. 377
Thompson, D. 353
Tong, Z. 370
Toplak, M. 274
transfer condition 458
transformative experience 117
transparency 15, 351
Traub, J. 274
"tribal" allegiances 5
tribalism 77–79
truism 80–81
Trump, D. 1, 67, 79, 90, 96–98, 103, 104, 106,
    159–161, 172, 176, 178, 181, 182, 185, 203,
    268, 274–279, 302–309, 398, 402, 482, 486;
    reelection 268; Sally, voting for 307–308;
    United States election 302; vice
    epistemology 308
Trump voters 307; *vs.* Clinton voters 275;
    epistemic domain 276; instrumental
    and epistemic critiques of 275–278;
    misinformation 277
trust 7, 19; breakdown of 452–454; definitions
    of 480; dictator games 94; epistemic 451;
    goodwill 481; question of 451–452
truth-conducive 292
truthfulness 77–81, 351
Truth Norm 399, 400, 401
truth–relativist semantics 107–108
truths 3, 11, 38, 48, 70–71; assessment-sensitive
    109; and empire 52–54; facts *vs.* values
    79–80; factual (*see* factual truths); falsity 68;
    guarantee 173; and knowledge 56; political
    legitimacy 80–81; *vs.* politics 55; post-truth
    67–71 (*see also* post-truth); rational 63; role of
    12; sincerity and accuracy 75, 82; tribalism
    77–79; value of 317
Tuck, R. 244
Tversky, A. 270
Twitter 321, 398, 481, 482, 487
two-party partisan system 197
tyranny 80, 81

"unforced force of the better argument" 365
United Kingdom 274
US Congress 243, 441
US criminal justice system 339, 341, 344
US FACA law 443
US Federal Aviation Administration 439
US presidential election 279, 305; in 2008 239;
    in 2016 274, 483; in 2000 375
US science advising system 435
utilitarianism 52

Utilitarianism (1863) 45, 46
utilitarian liberalism 45
utilitarian libertarianism 49
utility calculation 255–256, 261n10

van der Linden, S. 219
Varraich, A. 353
"veritistic" conception 414
vice epistemology 300, 301, 348; *see also*
    epistemic vices
vice explanations 299, 302; explanatory role for
    306; false consciousness 307; limits of 302;
    philosophical doubts 307; of political agents
    349; of political institutions 349; political
    judgement 304; political vices 354; vice
    attribution 301, 307
Vietnam War 439
virtue-consequentialism 312, 321–322
virtue cultivation 330
virtue epistemology 292, 300, 308, 312, 348;
    intellectual/epistemic virtues 291, 301; *see also*
    epistemic virtues
voluntary exposure 194
Vosoughi, S. 483
voters: decision-making process 369; educational
    attainment 243; political knowledge
    242; psychological characteristics of 280;
    rationality of 270; US, knowledge levels 243

Wallace, D. 377
The Wall Street Journal 274
Warner, M. R. 222
"warrant" 290
Weatherall, J. O. 5, 133, 141, 142, 170, 207, 208
Weber, M. 79
Wedeen, L. 228

Weinstock, D. 119, 120
welfare 257, 258
Western democracy 3, 42
Western liberal democracies 101
Western Moderate Evidentialism 37
Westlund, A. 218
West, R. 274
Westwood, S. J. 92, 94
WhatsApp 486, 487
Whitt, M. 343, 344
Willer, R. 197
Williams, B. 12, 74, 77, 78, 80, 82,
    115, 389
Williams, C. R. 208
Williams, H. T. 197
2020 Williams Report 348
Williams, W. 158
willingness 330, 452
Wimberly, C. 227, 231
Wittgenstein 65
working-class Brexit voters 308
working-class Republican voters 275
worldview-based commitments 117
World War II 437
Worsnip, A 7, 434

yellow journalism 4
YouTube 481

Zakkou, J. 254
Zaller, J. 162
al-Zawahiri, A. 40
Zeno of Citium 19
Zollman effect 207
Zollman, K. J. S. 133, 136, 207
Zuckerberg, M. 217, 486

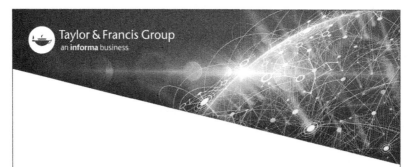

Made in the USA
Monee, IL
27 August 2024

64742092R00286